WARFARE IN ANCIENT INDIA

WARFARE IN ANCIENT INDIA

Organizational and Operational Dimensions

UMA PRASAD THAPLIYAL

MANOHAR
2024

First published 2010
Reprinted 2024

ISBN 978-81-7304-842-5 (hardbound)
ISBN 978-93-6080-401-5 (ebook)

Published by
Ajay Kumar Jain *for*
Manohar Publishers & Distributors
4753/23 Ansari Road, Daryaganj
New Delhi 110 002

Printed and bound by CPI Group (UK) Ltd, Croydon, CRo 4YY

Dedicated to

JADAVPUR UNIVERSITY

with gratitude

Contents

Plates

Figures

Preface

In 1994, I happened to be in Jadavpur University, Calcutta, in connection with a meeting of the Indian Historical Records Commission. After the inaugural session when the members gathered for lunch, a tall young boy, perhaps a M.Phil. student, approached me and said that he had studied my book *Foreign Elements in Ancient Indian Society* and that he found it to be most useful.

During further conversation he requested me to write a book on military history of Ancient India as there was need for it in the University. After this chance meeting I completely lost the track of this young man and even forgot his name. But his request I could not forget. It is a matter of great satisfaction to me that I have lived to comply with the request made by a student in 1994. I wish my effort measures up to his expectations. This book, which took me about ten years to complete, is dedicated as a token of gratitude to Jadavpur University.

In writing this book I have mainly depended on the information culled from the Vedas, Brāhmaṇas, epics, Dharmaśāstras, Purāṇas and Niti works, archeological reports and inscriptional and numismatic sources. I am particularly indebted to the pioneering works of A.C. Das (*Ṛgvedic Culture*), E.W. Hopkins (*The Social and Military Position of the Ruling Caste in Ancient India*), V.R.R. Dikshitar (*War in Ancient India*), P.C. Chakravorty (*Art of War in Ancient India*), G.N. Pant (*Studies in Indian Weapons and Warfare*), S.D. Singh (*Ancient Indian Warfare with Special Reference to the Vedic Period*), and many others whose works have been mentioned in the bibliography.

In the context of this study it is notable that India suffered many foreign invasions during the long course of her history. These invasions, besides influencing the social and cultural life of the people, may have profoundly influenced the military system and the art of warfare. This aspect has been touched upon in this volume to some extent but for a subtle assessment of foreign influence, a more comprehensive effort would be required. I wish somebody makes it a subject of research study.

The subject has been divided into nine chapters with a view to examine it comprehensively. The introduction deals with the basics of warfare relevant in Indian context. The first chapter portrays the general scenario of wars in India from proto-historic times and is fundamental to the contents of the following chapters which include Military Organization, Conduct of War, Strategical and Tactical Concepts, Weapons and Armour, Fortification and Siege craft, Education and Training and Military Symbols and Ceremonials.

A word may be added here on the chronological aspect of the source material as there are serious differences among scholars on dating archeological and literary data. To illustrate the point, the Harappan civilization is dated anywhere between 3000 BC and 1500 BC. The compilation of Vedas or Vedic corpus is dated between 1500 BC and 500 BC. The *Mahābhārata* is said to have been compiled anywhere between 3000 BC and AD 400. The *Arthaśāstra* was supposedly compiled between fourth century BC and third century AD. Interpolations are rampant in all works.

However, this monograph is based on the assumption that *Ṛgveda* was finally compiled around tenth century BC, Buddhist *Nikāyas* and *Vinaya* texts in fourth century BC, *Rāmāyaṇa* around second century AD, the *Mahābhārata* around fourth century AD and the *Arthaśāstra* around second century AD. Each of these compilations, however, contains data pertaining to earlier periods as well. To illustrate the point the references to the predominance of chariot in the battlefield and the coronation of *senāpati* before assuming the command of troops suggest definite Vedic association.

In most of these works fantasies and myths are inextricably mixed with historical facts making it really difficult to separate the two. In this study the material culled from the Vedas, epics, Purāṇas, Dharmaśāstras and Nīti works has been assessed and utilized in historical perspective. Myths and legends unsupported by historical evidence have been summarily ignored.

I would like to express by gratitude to my teachers Dr. Romila Thapar of Jawaharlal Nehru University, Dr. Devahuti of University of Delhi, Prof. J.S. Negi of Allahabad University, and Dr. S.N. Prasad of the Ministry of Defence who taught me the lessons of history. I also bow my head to the sacred memory of my parents, Pt. Suresha Nand Thapliyal and Smt. Sarasvati Devi, persons of great wisdom, who always reminded me of the value of education.

I also express my thanks to my friends Sarvashri Dr. G.P. Bhatt, G.B. Singh, R.S. Bisht, D.D. Nautiyal, H.N. Nautiyal, Bijai Singh Rawat, Smt. Reva Dhanedhar, Smt. Karuna Srivastava and Shri Umesh Chand Nailwal for the help rendered in various measures. My brother Shri S.P. Suman, wife Sarojini and brother-in-law Shri J.P. Ghildiyal have always been a source of inspiration to me.

I have no words to express my gratitude to my brothers late Shri Dwarika Prasad Thapliyal and Bhagwati Prasad Thapliyal who gave me the vision to see the world of letters.

Finally, I record my thanks to Shri Ramesh Jain of Manohar Publishers & Distributors, for his effort to publish this volume.

UMA PRASAD THAPLIYAL

Transliteration

अ	a
आ	ā
इ	i
ई	ī
उ	u
ऊ	ū
ऋ	ṛ
लृ	lṛ
ए	e
ऐ	ei
ओ	o
औ	au
अं	m/ṅ
अः	h
क्	k
ख्	kh
ग्	g
घ्	gh
ङ्	ṅ
च्	c
छ्	ch
ज	j
झ्	jh
ञ्	ñ
ट्	ṭ
ठ्	ṭh
ड्	ḍ
ढ्	ḍh
ण्	ṇ
त्	t
थ्	th
द्	d
ध्	dh
न्	n
प्	p
फ्	ph
ब्	b
भ्	bh
म्	m
य्	y
र्	r
ल्	l
व्	v
श्	ś
ष	ṣ
स्	s
ह्	h
क्ष्	kṣ
त्र्	tr
ज्ञ	jñ

Introduction

Indian Warfare: Some Determinants

CONCEPTUAL FRAMEWORK

Indian political thinkers considered war as an extension of politics, a fallout of interstate relations. They held that *upāyacatuṣṭaya* (four means), viz., *sāma* (conciliation), *dāna* (gift), *daṇḍa* (punishment) and *bheda* (discord) should be applied to serve the interest of a state. Of these *daṇḍa*, which means resort to war, was to be applied to only when the other three have failed to achieve the desired objective, for war was a risky proposition.

The *Manusmṛti* says that a ruler should try to achieve his political objective by influencing or alluring the rival king, his ministers and commander-in-chief. Alternatively, he should sow seeds of discord among his ministers and officials and then taking advantage of the situation pressurize him to accept his demands.[1] Evidently, Manu was in favour of avoiding war as far as possible.

This concept of war is reiterated in the *Mahābhārata* also. While deliberating upon the future course of action by the Pāṇḍavas, Kṛṣṇa pleaded for reconciliation. When he went to Kaurava court as an emissary of Pāṇḍavas he strongly pleaded against war. It was only after Duryodhana refused to return even five villages to Pāṇḍavas that Kṛṣṇa consented to the application of *daṇḍa*.[2] The epic, therefore, considered the victory earned by tact (*sāma* and *dāna*) as the best, the victory earned by discord (*bheda*) as the next best and the victory earned by war (*yuddha*) to be the last in terms of preference.[3] At another place the epic says that a king who has the welfare of the state in his heart should avoid war and should remain satisfied by the gains made by the measures of *sāma*, *dāna* and *bheda*.[4] Kauṭilya also refers to these four means of state policy and their application in inter-state relations and personal relations.[5]

The *Yājñavalkya Smṛti* says that the option of war should be exercised only after all other options have been exhausted.[6] The *Śukranīti* elaborates that each of the four means should be applied by the ruler in such a manner that friends, neutrals and foes alike remain in his grip. It says that first the policy of *sāma* should be applied. In the event it fails, the principle of *dāna* should be applied. If it also fails, as a third option, *bheda* should be resorted to. The policy of *daṇḍa* or war should be applied only when the existence of the state is threatened.[7]

Related to these four means of state policy there were the six measures (*ṣāḍaguṇya*), viz., *sandhi* (treaty), *vigraha* (conflict), *āsana* (staying quiet), *yāna* (marching), *saṁśraya* (seeking shelter) and *dvaidhībhāva* (dual policy).[8] Kauṭilya advises that when a ruler is weak as compared to enemy he should conclude treaty with him. When he thinks that neither he nor the enemy is capable of harming each other he should stay quiet. When possessed of invincible might he should march against the enemy but when weak in strength he should seek shelter with a more powerful ruler. If the objective could be achieved with the help of an associate king, a dual policy of war and peace should be followed. A resort to war was to be made only when a ruler was prospering and militarily strong.[9]

The *Manusmṛti* advises that these six measures should be applied after deep thought and hard deliberations. It elaborates, that each of these measures could be applied in two ways though the ultimate objective remained the same.[10] Purāṇas also hold similar views.[11] Thus in ancient India the option of *daṇḍa* (war) or *vigraha* (conflict) as a means of state policy was chosen after great care and that also when all other measures have failed in realizing the political objective.

WAR GALORE

Despite this much espoused aversion to war, the history of India is crowded with wars as detailed in Chapter 1. Behind this unending story of wars in India two factors stand out as important. Firstly, it was the large size of the country which encouraged the growth of tiny kingdoms and their unending conflicts. In this context it is notable that whenever a mighty ruler imposed his hegemony over the country the frequency of wars slowed down. To illustrate the point, after Candragupta Maurya had succeeded in unifying the country politically, not many wars were fought during the rule of his successors, Bindusāra and Aśoka. Similarly, after Samudragupta, his successors Candragupta and Kumāragupta hardly faced any challenge to their authority. On the other hand, the decline of Maurya, Kuṣāṇa and Gupta empires was followed by political upheavals and wars.

MOTIVATION

From the earliest times the Indian rulers harboured the ambition of wielding unfettered authority. A hymn in the *Atharvaveda* demonstrates this:

> Increase, O Indra, this kṣatriya for me: make thou this man sole chief of the clan: unman all his enemies: make them subject to him in the contests for pre-eminence.

This concept later manifested in rulers assuming titles like *samrāṭ*, *ekarāṭ*, *sārvabhauma*, *cakravartin*, etc. Some even aspired to achieve *indratva* (the status of Indra).

Ambitious kings went about performing sacrifices like *aśvamedha*, *rājasūya*, etc., to demonstrate their superior status in the community of rulers. In the epics Rāma and Yudhiṣṭhira are described as having performed these sacrifices. Ancient Indian history is replete with references to kings who performed *aśvamedha* sacrifice. Since conquest of all kingdoms was a necessary precondition for undertaking these sacrifices many wars might have been fought on this account only. In fact, war in itself was considered a *yajña* or sacred ritual in the Brāhmaṇic pantheon.

JUST WARS

The warfare in ancient India generally remained immune from savagery. The battles were fought between the contending armies, and civilian population was left undisturbed to go about its vocations. This is amply borne out by the references in the epics. Megasthenese, the Greek ambassador in the court of Candragupta Maurya attests to this:

> Whereas among other nations it is usual in the contests of war to ravage the soil and thus reduce it to an uncultivated waste, among the Indians, on the contrary, by whom husbandmen are regarded as a class that is sacred and inviolable, the tillers of the soil, even when battle is raging in their neighbourhood are undisturbed by any sense of danger.

This practice continued even afterwards.

PRE-STATE WAR

War is prior to state in the sense that it precedes the evolution of the state. The overriding necessity of a leader among the ancient tribal hordes, who were perpetually at war, may have led to the elevation of the most powerful member of the tribe as commander or king. Indra, the Vedic god of war, has been addressed as a commander and not as a king in the *Ṛgveda*. In the *Aitareya Brāhmaṇa* a story goes that at one time a war erupted between Devas and Asuras in which the former suffered a crushing defeat. Pondering over the cause of their defeat the Devas concluded that Asuras owed their victory to their leader. They also elected a leader who led them to victory in war.

This story may be referring to some real historical content, picked up from an earlier period. The Āryan hordes during their military adventures may have suffered reverses at the hands of their opponents who were perhaps better led by a capable commander. Following them the Āryans also elected the bravest among them as leader, and defeated the Asuras.

LARGE ARMIES

In ancient India the evolution of large armies was intimately related to the emergence of kingdoms. Earlier to this the tribal states organized small armies or say militia for the defence of their territory. But in the new political setup the kings needed large armies both for defensive and offensive needs as they were generally in a state of war. Conquests earned them the status of a *samrāṭ*, *virāṭ*, etc.

The ambitious rulers went about performing *aśvamedha*, *rājasūya* and *vājapeya* sacrifices to bring as much territory as possible under their sphere of influence. No doubt any such effort required the backup of a powerful army. Thus the institution of monarchy encouraged the growth of large armies in ancient India.

THE AFFLUENCE

Foreign invasions also contributed to this war galore, substantially. What attracted the foreign invaders to India was the fertility of the land and the prosperity of the people. In respect of the Āryans it could be said with greater certainty. That the Āryans believed in seeking wealth through war is abundantly clear from Vedic literature. A Ṛgvedic hymn (1.4.76) addresed to Aśvins says: 'O mighty ones, ye gave Sudāsa abundant food, brought on your treasure-laden car; so now vouchsafe to us the wealth which many crave, either from heaven or from the sea.' Another hymn (9.67.6) prays to Indra: 'Hither, O Indra, bring us wealth in steeds and cattle hundredfold; bring wealth, O Soma, thousandfold.' The story of cattle lifting by Kauravas as narrated in the epic may as well be a reminder of the pristine society where kine was the chief motivating factor behind war.

The Persian monarch Darius may have turned towards India for economic reasons as he might have learnt about the affluence of Sindh and Punjab. This is proved by the fact that these Indian Kṣatrapies (provinces) contributed the highest tribute to the imperial treasury.

TRADE FACTOR

The march of the Bactrian Greeks may have been inspired to an extent by the need to open a trade route from Taxilā to Gangetic plains. The Śakas and Kuṣāṇas once settled in the north-west conquered territories in the south and east to share the wealth of the country, generated by flourishing trade with Rome. The long drawn war between the Śakas and Sātavāhanas may have been inspired by conflicting trade interests, particularly on the western coast.

Indian trade with the countries of South-East Asia may have been backed up by military might. Samudragupta exercised political authority over some island kingdoms. It is believed, and perhaps rightly so, that the Cola invasion of South-East Asian kingdoms was an extension of plunder dynamic of military conquests and that the Cola warfare should be viewed as an economic activity. The Arab conquest of Sindh was also prompted by trade interests.

NEGLECTED NORTH-WEST

In ancient period the country witnessed major political developments in the eastern region. Consequently, the great Indian empires had their capital located in the east at Pāṭaliputra. Generally, the north-western part of the country which was away from the seat of imperial power was ruled by some petty subordinates or independent rulers and therefore, suffered neglect. If the centre of political power had been located at Peshawar or Lahore, perhaps the invaders may not have had a free run into India.

GEOGRAPHICAL SYNDROME

Related to this phenomenon of foreign invasions is the geographical setting of what may be called strategical topography of the Indian subcontinent. Himālayas in the north, sea in the south, desert in the west and the dense forests and inhospitable lands in the east made any ingress from these directions difficult. The only direction which was left open to invaders lay in the north-west, the Khyber and Bolan passes, allowing passage through the Kabul valley or the Sulaiman range.

There was also a route through the northern mountains—the one that follows the Karakoram highway through Gilgit, Chitral and the Hunza valley. This route might have been used more frequently during the time of Kaniṣka, who ruled over Kashmir as well as the adjoining Central Asian territories of Kashgar, Khotan and Yarkand. Though the route might have been used by travellers through the ages there is no evidence to suggest that invading armies marched into India through the Karakoram highway.

The sea routes were known to Indians from proto-historic times, but these were often used for carrying peaceful trade with the countries of South-East Asia and the Roman empire. Surprisingly, no invasion was launched against India through the sea route in ancient times. However, some south Indian kingdoms did carry arms across the seas, perhaps to secure their trading interests.

The geography again determined the mode of Indian warfare. The geographical setting of India was such that most of the battles were fought in the plains of Punjab and Uttar Pradesh, which fell on the route of the invaders. This was perhaps the reason why Indian military thinkers like Kauṭilya, Kāmandaka or Śukrācārya do not speak of battles in jungles and hills. The system of *vyūhas* (battle arrays) propounded in the epics also suggests this.

THE TERRAIN

The terrain also determined the use of various arms in the battlefield. The chariot was used in Indian warfare from the Vedic times because the battles were generally fought in level terrain. This also explains the wide use of elephants. The cavalry and foot soldiers did not command a high respect among the arms in ancient India because of their limited utility in a war, which was dominated by chariots and elephants.

Alexander's invasion and subsequent Śaka-Kuṣāṇa invasions changed the Indian perception about the utility of chariot in war and gradually it faded out of the Indian battlefield. But the elephant continued to maintain its supremacy through the centuries despite many obstacles. The disadvantage in the use of chariots and elephants in the battle was that they did not allow the full use of the tactics of surprise, mobility and deception in warfare. The Śaka-Kuṣāṇa invaders, with mounted archer as their principal arm, introduced these elements but the traditional Indian system generally remained unimpressed.

FORTIFICATION

Indians had developed a good fortification system as early as the chalcolithic times is evident from the excavations of the Indus sites such as Mohenjo-daro, Harappa, Kalibangan, Lothal and Dholavira. During their territorial expansion in India, Āryans encountered a number of forts, built by the Asuras, who were perhaps the original inhabitants of India. The epics, the *Arthaśāstra* and the accounts left behind by the Greek historians give details of the Indian forts. The Greeks and the Śaka-Kuṣāṇas also built forts around their habitations. But the most significant fact is that despite abundance of forts Indians never succeeded in checking the advance of the invaders. Obviously, these forts failed to stand before the assault of the invading armies. In fact, these forts were generally built to give protection to the cities and were not built at strategic points of military importance. In ancient Indian literature there is not a single reference where an invading army was repulsed by the forces stationed at a fort. An elaborate system of mobile and immobile weapons mentioned in the epics and the *Arthaśāstra*, which was meant to provide protection to the fort, simply did not work.

REFUSAL TO LEARN

Indians had developed a sound military system but they never updated it in the light of experience gained in the battlefield and do not seem to have learnt much from their unsuccessful encounters with Achaemenids, Macedonians and the Śaka-Kuṣāṇas. They clung to their traditional mode of warfare unmindful of the ground realities. Though chariot had been discredited in the battle of Jhelum and elsewhere it took Indians centuries to discard it as an instrument of war. On the other hand, despite the established superiority of mounted archer of the Śaka-Kuṣāṇa army, Indians did not adopt this novelty in their system of warfare. Ironiclly, soon after settling in India, the invaders also became enamoured of Indian elephant and discarded the advantage of mobility in war, associated with the use of horse. This was surprisingly true in the case of Mihirakula, the Hūṇa invader. He is said to have maintained a large force of 2000 elephants. Each elephant carried ten men armed with sword and spear on its back. To fight at close quarters, swords were also tied to the trunks of elephants.[12]

In conclusion, it appears that the system of warfare in ancient India, though conceptually sound, proved a failure when it came to application, as it could not adjust to the changing times and situations.

NOTES

1. साम्ना दानेन भेदेन समस्तैरथवा पृथक्।
   विजेतुं प्रयतेतारीन्न युद्धेन कदाचन।। *Manusmṛti*, 7.198
2. सर्वं भवतु ते राज्यं पञ्च ग्रामान्विसर्जय।
   अवश्यं भरणीया हि पितुस्ते राजसत्तम।।
   एवमुक्तस्तु दुष्टात्मा नैव भावं व्यमुञ्चत।
   दण्डं चतुर्थं पश्यामि तेषु पापेषु नान्यथा।। *MB*, Udyoga, 148.16-17
3. उपायविजयं श्रेष्ठमाहुर्भेदेन मध्यमम्।
   जघन्य एष विजयो यो युद्धेन विशाम्पते।। Ibid., Bhīṣma, 4.32.

4. वर्जनीयं सदा युद्धं राज्यकामेन धीमता।
उपयैस्त्रिभिरादानमर्थस्याह बृहस्पतिः।। Ibid., Śānti, 69.23; Similar views are expressed in the *Rāmāyaṇa* also. Yuddha, 41.58-61.
5. *Arthaśāstra*, 9.7.72-5.
6. उपायाः साम दानं च भेदो दण्डस्तथैव च।
सम्यकप्रयुक्ताः सिद्धयेयुर्दण्ड स्त्वगतिका गतिः। *Yājñavalkya Smṛti*, 1.346.
7. सामेव प्रथमं श्रेष्ठं दानं तु तदनन्तरम्।
सर्वदा भेदनं शत्रोर्दण्डनं प्राणसंशये।। *Śukranīti*, 4.1.38; Also
उपायान् षड्गुणान् वीक्ष्य शत्रेः स्वस्यापि सर्वदा।
युद्धं प्राणत्यपे कुर्यात् सर्वस्वहरणे सति।। Ibid., 4.7.299.
8. संधिविग्रहासनयानसंश्रयद्वैधीभावाः षाड्गुण्यम् इत्याचार्याः। *Arthaśāstra*, 7.1.2; These attributes have been stated in the *MB;* also:
षाड्गुण्यमिति यत् प्रोक्तं तन्निवोध युधिष्ठिर।
संधानासनमित्येव यात्रासंधानमेव च।
विगृह्यासनमित्येव यात्रां सम्परिगृह्य च।
द्वैधीभावस्तथान्येषां संश्रयोऽथ परस्य च। *MB*, Śānti, 69.65-6; also *Manusmṛti*, 7.160-61; *Matsya Pu.*, 215.16; *Śukranīti*, 4.7.285-92; *Agni Pu.*, 234
9. परस्माद्धीयमानः संदधीत। अभ्युच्चीयमानो विगृह्णीयात्। 'न मां परो नाहं परमुपहन्तुं शक्तः' इत्यासीत। गुणातिशययुक्तो यायात्। शक्तिहीनः संश्रयेत। सहायसाध्ये कार्ये द्वैधीभावं गच्छेत्। *Arthaśāstra*, 7.1.13-18
10. संधिं तु द्विविधं विद्याद्राजा विग्रहमेव च।
उभे यानासने चैव द्विविधः संश्रयः स्मृतः।। *Manusmṛti*, 7.162; Also *Yājñavalkya Smṛti*, 1.347
11. षाड्गुण्यविधितत्त्वज्ञो देशभाषाविशारदः।
सन्धिविग्रहिकः कार्य्यो राज्ञा नयविशारदः।। *Matsya Pu.*, 215.16.
12. Atreyi Biswas, *The Political History of the Hūṇas in India*, p. 74.

Chapter 1

Warfare in Ancient India: A Survey

CHALCOLITHIC AGE

The history of warfare in India is traceable to chalcolithic age, as represented by the Indus Valley Civilization. That the authors of this civilization, though considered to be a people of peaceful demeanour, maintained armies and fought wars is borne out by archaeological discoveries. Excavations at many Harappan sites have revealed the existence of well laid out citadels or protective walls. At some Harappan sites small rooms adjacent to bigger structures look like guard-rooms. Barrack like structures have been identified at Lothal, Mohenjo-daro and Harappa. Moreover, if the Harappans were imperialists, who colonized the peripheral area outside the Indus valley proper, they must have maintained a series of garrisoned and fortified outposts to hold the colonies under control. J.P. Joshi holds that Surkotada in Kachchh was a defence complex guarding a vital route of communication between Saurashtra and Sind.[1] Incidentally, some male head types found at Harappa and Mohenjo-daro have been identified as warrior type.[2]

VEDIC AGE

The Indus valley people met a violent end, perhaps at the hands of Āryan immigrants, who entered India from the direction of central Asia. According to Marshall 'nothing has yet been found either at Mohenjo-daro or Harappa that conflicts with the orthodox theory that the Indo-Āryans entered the Punjab about the middle of the second millennium BC'.[3]

The Āryans, during their expansion towards east, fought innumerable battles. In the *Ṛgveda* there are numerous references to Maruts, the Āryan soldiers.[4] A long drawn war was fought by King Suśravā against a confederation of twenty kings, who had fielded an army of more than 60,000 men (*RV*, 1.53.9-10). There are also references to wars between the Āryan tribes Anu, Yadu, Puru, Turvasu and Druhyu (*pañcajanāh*). Bharata, Tṛtṣu, Śṛñjaya, Pañcāla, Matsya and Uśīnara rose to prominence by virtue of their military might. Divodāsa of the Tṛtṣu tribe fought many sanguine battles with Turvasus, Yadus and Purus. He also fought successfully against the Paṇis, Parvatas and Bṛsayas. In the battle of Paruṣṇī (Rāvī), Sudās, the leader of Bharata tribe, inflicted a crushing defeat on the confedaration of ten kings and in the process three confederate kings perished.[5] Sudās also defeated the confederation of Aja, Śigru and Yakṣu tribes, led by King Bheda, on the banks of river Yamunā.[6]

The Āryans during their eastward march, fought many battles with the natives called Dāsa or Dasyu in the Vedas. Indra is said to have joined Kutsa in his battle against the Dasyus and killed 50,000 of them in an encounter. He also destroyed many of their forts.[7] Indra also killed 1,05,000 followers of Varcin, a Dāsa king.[8] In an effort to protect his favourite hermit Dabhīti, he killed another 30,000 Dāsas.[9] King Divodāsa of the Bharata tribe defeated the Dāsa chief Śambara. Bharatas also led an expedition against Kīkaṭas, a native tribe, inhabiting Magadha region. A Puru king assumed the title *Trasadasyu*, chastiser of Dasyus, perhaps after defeating many native kings.[10]

LATER VEDIC AGE

The conflict between the Āryans and the natives continued in the later Vedic age.[11] The *Śatapatha Brāhmaṇa* refers to a fierce battle between Bharata Dauṣyanti and Satvantas, in which the latter were routed.[12] Another battle was fought between Satrājit and Dhṛtarāṣṭra, the ruler of Kāśī, in which the former emerged victorious.[13] The native tribes who were defeated by the Āryans may also have waged wars against each other.

As the Āryans pushed towards the east, some old Vedic tribes vanished and some new ones came into prominence. The Bharatas of Ṛgvedic fame were replaced by Kuru-Pañcālas and the tribes like

Anu, Druhyu and Turvaśa lost their identity. Many wars may have preceded these political upheavals. The tribal chieftains of the Vedic age now appear with appellations like *Adhirāja*, *Rājādhirāja*, *Samrāṭ*, *Virāṭ*, *Ekarāṭ* and *Sārvabhauma.*[14] They took pride in exhibiting their military might by performing military ceremonials.[15] The powerful kingdoms of the age included Videha, Kāśī, Kośala, Aṅga, Magadha, Gandhāra, Kaikeya, Madra, Uśīnara, etc.

EPIC REFERENCES

In the epics there are references to many wars. At the time of *Rājasūya* sacrifice Pāṇḍava brothers earned victories in all the four quarters.[16] In the great war of Kurukṣetra, all rulers of India, barring a few exceptions, participated either on the side of the Pāṇḍavas or the Kauravas. Not many survived to see the end of the eighteen days war. Ābhīras wiped out the whole Vṛṣṇi clan in a surprise attack on Dvārakā. Śrīkṛṣṇa perished and even Arjuna could not stem the rot.[17] In the battle of Laṅkā the whole family of Rāvaṇa perished. Though the epics are late compositions, their contents are said to represent India of the later Vedic period.

AGE OF *MAHĀJANAPADAS*

In the sixth century BC sixteen *Mahājanapadas* were ruling over northern India.[18] About the same time ten autonomous clans, formed in some kind of republics, ruled eastern India.[19] In course of time the kingdoms of Magadha, Vatsa, Avantī and Kośala emerged powerful. Bimbisāra the ruler of Magadha, defeated the kingdom of Aṅga and annexed it. His son Ajātaśatru fought a long war with the Licchavis of Vaiśālī and destroyed them. He built a fort at the confluence of Śona and Gaṅgā (Patna) to ward off an attack by Pradyota, the ruler of Avantī.[20] His successors, proved to be weak rulers and finally one *amātya* Śiśunāga seized the throne of Magadha.[21] He defeated Pradyotas, and annexed the whole of Madhyadeśa, Mālava, etc., to his kingdom.[22]

PERSIAN INVASIONS

By sixth century BC the centre of political gravity in India had shifted to Magadha. Consequently, western and north-western India came to suffer neglect and many petty principalities mushroomed all over the region. Taking advantage of the situation Achaemenid ruler Cyrus (558-30 BC) conquered Gandhāra. Subsequently, Darius I (522-486 BC) also invaded India some time after 518 BC and annexed some territory in the Indus region. The Indian territory thus annexed by Darius I constituted the twentieth *kṣatrapī* of Persian empire and yielded a tribute of 360 Euboic talents of gold dust, equal to about one million sterling, to their treasury.[23] Persians continued to maintain their authority over north-west India and Indian mercenaries 'clad in cotton' and bearing 'cane bows and arrows tipped with iron' joined the expeditionary force of Xerxes (486-465 BC) against Hellas and performed well in the battle of Thermopilae. It is said that Indians also fought against Alexander as a part of the army of Darius III.[24]

INVASION OF ALEXANDER

Then came the invasion of Alexander. After defeating the Persians in 331 BC his army advanced towards India and reached her borders in 327 BC. His first major encounter took place with Aśpasioi (Aśvakas), a people inhabiting Alisang-Kunar valley. He subdued them and captured 40,000 men and 2,30,000 oxen. It is reported that the choicest of these oxen were transported to Macedonia for use in agriculture.[25]

Another battle was fought with Assakenoi (Asmakas), who opposed him with an army of 20,000 cavalry, 30,000 infantry and 30 elephants. It is said that in a fierce battle outside the fort of Massaga, when men lay dead, women picked up the weapons of the slain and continued the fight to the tragic end.[26]

After subjugating the frontier region Alexander crossed the river Sindhu, befriended the rulers of Taxilā and Abhisāra and marched against Porus. Porus took the field with an army of 30,000 foot, 4,000 horses, 300 chariots and 200 elephants on the bank of Jhelum. In a hard fought encounter Porus suffered defeat and chose to submit.[27] Alexander then defeated Glaukanikai (Glaucukāyanakas) and captured thirty-seven cities.[28] In August 326 BC, he crossed Rāvī and defeated Adraistai (Ariṣṭas).[29]

Alexander then proceeded to invade Sangala, the stronghold of Kaṭhaians (Kaṭhas), a people who enjoyed the highest reputation for courage and skill in the art of war. The Kaṭhaians fought courageously and Alexander could defeat them only when Porus joined him with a force of 5,000 Indians. In the end when the fort fell 17,000 Kaṭhaian defenders lay dead. More than 70,000 men, 300 wagons and 500 horses were captured by the Macedonians. The fort of Sangala was razed to the ground.[30]

Alexander had a desire to conquer more Indian territories to the east of Beas, but his troops refused to cooperate. It is reported that the mighty empire of Agrammes (Nanda king), which lay ahead frightened them. Alexander was left with no option other than to return.

During his return journey Alexander again fought many battles. First, he received the surrender of the king of Sophytes (Saubhūti), the ruler of the Salt Range. This country was famous for dogs of astonishing courage, who could fight even a lion.[31] It may be mentioned here that dogs were used for military purpose in India even in the Vedic times.[32]

Sailing down the river, Alexander defeated Siboi (Śivis), who opposed him with a force of 40,000 foot. But the Agalassians (Agalassoi) who joined the battle with a force of 40,000 foot and 3,000 horses, repulsed the first attack. Subsequently, when the defenders lost all hope of victory they set fire to their houses and cast themselves along with their wives and children into the flames.[33] A precursor of Rajput *jauhar* indeed.

However, Malloi (Mālavas) and Oxydrakai (Kṣudrakas), the most warlike of the Indian tribes, posed a more serious challenge before Alexander. They jointly fielded an army of 90,000 foot, 10,000 horses and 9,000 elephants. In the ensuing battle Alexander was wounded. His revengeful troops then carried out the massacre of Malloi, sparing neither men, women or children.[34] Perdiccas, a general of Alexander, on his way defeated Abastanoi (Ambaṣṭhas) who challenged him with a force of 60,000 foot, 6,000 horses and 500 chariots.[35] The other tribes which were subjugated by Alexander in the lower Indus valley included Xathroi (Kṣatri), Ossadioi (Vasāti), Sodrai (Śūdras), Brahmanoi (Brāhmaṇas) and the Massanoi (Muṣikas). He also defeated a number of kings, viz., Mousikanos, Oxykanos and Sambos.[36] Thus during his 19-months stay in India Alexander fought scores of battles. Many more may have been fought by the Indian rulers among themselves. We know for certain that Āmbhi and Porus were arch enemies and so were the Malloi and Oxydrakai people.

NANDA-MAURYA PERIOD

All wars fought on the Indian soil during the later half of fourth century BC were not of Alexander's making. Farther east, the Nandas with a powerful army, which according to Greek writers numbered 2,00,000 foot, 20,000 cavalry, 2,000 chariots and 3,000 elephants, were busy in waging wars. Mahāpadma Nanda is said to have subverted many royal houses including the Ikṣvākus, Kurus, Pañcālas, Kāśīs, Śūrasenas, Maithilas, Kaliṅgas, Aśmakas, Haihayas, etc., as also a host of *kṣatriya* rulers (*akhilakṣatrāntakārī*). This was also the time when Candragupta Maurya entered the Indian political stage. He engineered revolts in the Greek held territory of western India and soon brought it under his control. After building a strong army he crossed sword with the Nandas of Magadha and destroyed them.

The empire of Candragupta Maurya covered almost the whole of India. Saurāṣṭra formed a part of his empire. His invasion of the south included Podiyil Hill in the Tinnevalley district. His might was also felt in Karnāṭaka. Perhaps he also earned a victory against Seleukos, a general of Alexander, who was ruling over Western Asia in 305 BC. The Greek ruler was compelled to cede the *kṣatrapīs* of Aria (Herat), Arachosia (Kandahar), Paropanisadae (Kabul) and Gedrosia (Baluchistan) to the Indian victor.[37] Candragupta owed these victories to his large army which according to Greek sources included 6,00,000 infantry, 30,000 horses, 36,000 elephants and 24,000 chariots.[38]

Not much is known about the military exploits of Bindusāra, but his son Aśoka did undertake military operations against Taxilā, Nepal and Kaliṅga. It is said that during his war against Kaliṅga 1,50,000 men were captured, 1,00,000 men were slain and many more died for other reasons. This blood-bath so much hurt him that he abandoned the pursuit of war forever.

The reign of Aśoka ended in 232 BC, but the Maurya dynasty lasted till 187 BC, when Senāpati Puṣyamitra Śuṅga eliminated the last Maurya king and occupied the throne of Magadha. Puṣyamitra also defeated Yajñasena, the ruler of Vidarbha. He also beat back a Yavana invader, who had advanced up to Sāketa.[39]

SĀTAVĀHANAS

Devahūti, the last ruler of Śuṅga line, was defeated and killed by one Vāsudeva Kaṇva.[40] His dynasty ruled for 45 years and was in turn destroyed by Simuka, the founder of Sātavāhana dynasty. His son Śātakarṇi was a powerful ruler who conquered many territories and performed two horse sacrifices. This was also the time when Śaka invaders emerged in western India. They defeated Sātavāhanas and wrested some of their territories. But Gautamīputra Śātakarṇi, recaptured the lost territories after defeating the Śakas. He also defeated Yavanas, Pallavas and a host of Kṣatriya rulers.[41] Sātavāhanas again suffered some reverses at the hands of Śaka Kṣatrapa Rudradāman, during the rule of Pulamāvi, in early second century AD.[42] It appears that fortune again favoured Sātavāhanas as Yajña Śrī Śātakarṇi (AD 165-95) ruled from the Bay of Bengal to Arabian Sea, of course after recapturing the territories lost to the Śakas by his father.[43] But the Sātavāhanas could not keep hold on their empire for long. The Ābhīras rose to power in Mahārāṣṭra and the Ikṣvākus and the Pallavas carved out kingdoms in their eastern provinces. Many wars may have been fought in the process.

When a fierce battle was raging between the Sātavāhanas and Śakas for domination in western India, Khāravela of the Cedi dynasty was going strong in Orissa in the third quarter of first century BC. He defied powerful Śātakarṇi, humbled the city of Muśikas, forced the Rathikas and Bhojakas to submit and invaded the Magadhan kingdom twice. He also defeated a Yavana king and subdued a Pāṇḍyan ruler.[44]

FOREIGN INVASIONS

When the Seleucid empire disintegrated in third century BC, its Bactrian and Parthian governors became independent rulers. Demetrius, the ruler of Bactria, crossed Hindukush in about 183 BC and conquered Punjab. He made inroads deep into India as far east as Sāketa, Pañcāla, Mathurā and Pāṭaliputra.[45] Subsequently, Eucratides (165-160 BC), another ruler of Bactria, conquered India and became the ruler of 1,000 cities. Menander, another ruler of Eukratides house is reported to have conquered more nations than Alexander. That many princes of Greek lineage ruled over western India around the beginning of the Christian era is amply borne out by palaeographic and numismatic evidence. Conquests alone could have enabled them to occupy western India.[46]

Then came the Śaka invasion. The political turmoil in Central Asia in second century BC forced the Śakas to seek safety elsewhere. Defeating the Parthian and Greek opposition en route, they reached India in early first century BC. Maues, the first Śaka ruler of India, supplanted the Greek rulers of Gandhāra and Punjab. His successors Azes I and Azileses also won victories against the Greeks in western India. About the beginning of the Christian era many Śaka families established their rule in various parts of India including Taxilā, Mathurā and Ujjain. Śakas of Ujjain fought a long drawn war for supremacy with the Sātavāhanas.

Meanwhile, Pahlavas also marched in from eastern Iran. Venones, a Parthian prince, captured Arachosia (Kandahar) and Seistan (Śakastan) and made some gains in north-west India at the cost of the Śakas. He also adopted the title the 'great king of kings'. However, Gondopharnes was the most powerful Indo-Parthian ruler in north-west India in early first century AD. After his death, the Parthian kingdom disintegrated into tiny principalities, and these were soon eliminated by the advancing Kuṣāṇas.

In mid first century AD the Kuṣāṇa leader Vima Kadphises, son of Kujula Kadphises, invaded India and established his rule over Sind, Punjab and parts of Gaṅgā-Yamunā basin. His successor Kaniṣka conquered Magadha and Sāketa and beat back a Parthian invasion. He also led an expedition against the Chinese Turkistan and captured some territories. Subsequently, general Pan-Chao of China defeated Kaniṣka and retrieved the lost territories. But soon after the death of Pan-Chao, Kaniṣka led another expedition across the Pamirs.[47] Though the gains made by Kaniṣka were short-lived, he taught Indians the lesson that conquests could be made from the Indian side as well.

Beyond the boundaries of India Kaniṣka conquered Afghanistan, Bactria, Kashgar, Yarkand and Khotan. Within the country he conquered the territories of Punjab, Kashmir, Sind, Gaṅgā-Yamunā basin, and perhaps also parts of Bengal and Bihar. His successors could not sustain the empire and soon many principalities rose on its ruins. The Sassanian invasion in early third century AD struck a death blow to the Kuṣāṇa power in India.

GUPTA PERIOD

A period of wars and upheavals followed the decline of Kuṣāṇas. It appears that out of this political confusion Nāgas emerged victorious in northern India. They performed as many as ten sacrifices to celebrate their conquests.[48] But it were the Guptas who finally cleared the mist of political uncertainly in early fourth century AD.

Śrīgupta and Ghaṭotkacagupta, the two early rulers of the dynasty, were perhaps feudatories who bore the title of *mahārāja*. Candragupta (AD 320-35), the third ruler of the dynasty, however, laid the foundation of an empire. He may have fought many battles in the process of extending his kingdom over south Bihar, Prayāga, Sāketa and the adjoining regions before assuming the title of *mahārājādhirāja*.

His son Samudragupta (AD 335-75) was a great warrior and his victories are graphically described in Allahabad pillar inscription.[49] First, he led a campaign in Āryāvarta and exterminated the nine rulers who challenged his authority. The victory in the north was followed by a military expedition to the south. Twelve rulers were defeated, captured, released and finally restored to their kingdoms as a magnanimous gesture. Awed by his might the five frontier states submitted to him.[50] Nine tribal states which included Mālavas, Ārjunāyanas, Yaudheyas, etc., also accepted his suzerainty. The inscription also says that the *Daivaputra-Śāhī-Śāhānuśāhī*, the *Śaka-Muruṇḍa* as also the people of Siṁhala and other islands purchased peace by surrender and presentation of maidens.[51] After completing his victory campaign (*digvijaya*) Samudragupta performed *aśvamedha* sacrifice.

Candragupta II (AD 375-414), son of Samudragupta, further expanded the empire by subjugating the Śakas of western India. This brought the regions of Mālava, Gujarāt and Saurāṣṭra under his rule. Incidentally, this also opened up great opportunities of overseas commerce for Indians. It appears that Vākāṭakas and Kadambas had also accepted the hegemony of the Guptas. Kumāragupta I (AD 414-55), the son of Candragupta II, maintained an empire which extended from Bengal to Saurāṣṭra and from Himālaya to Narmadā. He also performed a horse sacrifice, perhaps at the end of a sucessful military campaign. He fought a sanguine war with the Puṣyamitras, in which his son Skandagupta distinguished himself.[52] Skandagupta (AD 455-

67), soon after his enthronement, faced the grave challenge posed by the Hūṇa invaders. He kept them at bay for some time but their repeated attacks weakened the empire gradually. His successors somehow sustained the empire but finally during the rule of Bhānugupta (AD 495-510) the Hūṇas earned a convincing victory. However, the empire dragged on till AD 550.

VĀKĀṬAKAS

Vākāṭakas rose to power in Bundelkhand region in the last quarter of third century AD under Vindhyaśakti, the founder-ruler. His son Pravarasena I was a powerful ruler who assumed the title *samrāṭ* and performed four horse sacrifices. His grandson Rudrasena I suffered defeat at the hands of Samudragupta and lost central India to him. Subsequently, Rudrasena II of this dynasty married Gupta princess Prabhāvatī. However, the most powerful Vākāṭaka king was Hariṣeṇa, who ruled at the close of the fifth century AD and made extensive conquests. He is reported to have invaded Kuntala, Avanti, Kaliṅga, Kośala, Trikūṭa (Konkan), Lāṭa and Andhra (region between rivers Godāvarī and Kṛṣṇā). The Vākāṭaka power was supplanted by the Kalacuris in the second quarter of sixth century AD.

HŪṆAS

Hūṇas were a Central Asian tribe, which invaded India in fifth century AD. In AD 458, they had an encounter with Skandagupta and suffered defeat. But the gradual weakening of Gupta power encouraged them to strike again and again. The Gupta ruler Bhānugupta suffered a humiliating defeat at the hands of Toramāṇa in AD 510. His son Mihirakula also waged wars against Bālāditya of Magadha and Yaśodharman of Mālwā, though not successfully. It is said that the Hūṇas accelerated the downfall of the Gupta empire, and the older dominant tribes of Rajasthan and other part of western India almost completely disappeared as a result of their attacks.[53] Yaśodharman is credited to have conquered more territories than the Guptas.[54]

POST-GUPTA PERIOD

The disintegration of Gupta empire led to the growth of many independent kingdoms. Hūṇas rose to power in central India and western India. Yośodharman ruled over Mālwā. Maitrakas founded a kingdom in Valabhī at the end of fifth century AD. Dhruvasena II, his son Dharasena and grandson Dharasena IV were powerful rulers who earned many victories and assumed imperial titles. The dynasty lasted till the eighth century, when it fell to Arab invaders.

The later Gupta dynasty founded by one Kṛṣṇagupta also rose on the ruins of imperial Guptas. Kumāragupta III was a powerful ruler of this house. He earned some victories and extended his rule as far as Prayāga. His son Dāmodaragupta was defeated and killed by a Maukhari ruler. Mahāsenagupta, the son of Dāmodaragupta, was forced to seek shelter in eastern Mālwā where he consolidated his position and carried his arms as far as Lauhitya. His son Devagupta conspired with Śaśāṅka, the ruler of Gauḍa, to defeat and kill Maukhari king Gṛhavarman. The murder was, however, avenged by Rājyavardhana of Thānesar soon after. The last important ruler of this dynasty was Ādityasena, who became independent after the death of Harṣavardhana. He performed a horse sacrifice, adopted imperial titles and claimed to have ruled the earth up to the shores of ocean.[55]

The Maukharis rose to power in Kanauj on the ruins of the Gupta empire. Īśānavarman was the most powerful ruler of this dynasty. He conquered the Āndhras, vanquished the Śulikas and reined the Gauḍas.[56] His son Sarvavarman defeated the Hūṇas and also Dāmodaragupta. Gṛhavarman, the last Maukhari king, was defeated and killed by Devagupta of Mālwā, and thereafter Kanauj became a part of the Vardhana kingdom of Thānesar.[57]

VARDHANAS

The Vardhanas of Thānesar also emerged out of the ruins of Gupta empire. The dynasty grew strong under Prabhākaravardhana, who defeated Hūṇas, Sindhurāja, Gurjaras, Gandhāras, Lāṭas and Mālavas.[58] His son Rājyavardhana defeated the later Gupta king Devagupta but was in turn killed treacherously by Śaśāṅkadeva, the Gauḍa king. His brother Harṣavardhana (AD 606-47) was a great warrior who conquered many kingdoms from east to west and carried his arms to remote areas.[59] He achieved military success against the ruler of Valabhī but suffered defeat at the hands of Cālukya ruler Pulakeśin II. He defeated Śaśāṅka and drove him out from Kanauj. The king of Sindh suffered a humiliating defeat at his hands. In the east, he conquered Bihar, Bengal and Orissa including the Ganjam region.

The ruler of Assam accepted his overlordship. Broadly speaking, the empire of Harṣa included parts of eastern Punjab and major portions of present day UP, Bihar, Bengal and Orissa. For the security of his vast empire Harṣa maintained a big army comprising 60,000 elephants, 1,00,000 horses and a large infantry.[60]

POST-HARṢA PERIOD

The death of Harṣa in AD 647 led to the disintegration of Vardhana empire. Arjuna, a minister of Harṣa, usurped the throne after his death. But his wayward behaviour invited the wrath of a Tibetan prince, who invaded his kingdom and carried him to China for punishment. Bhāṣkaravarman of Assam, an ally of Harṣa, annexed Karṇasuvarṇa. Ādityasena of Magadha, a feudatory, also declared his independence and performed a horse sacrifice.

Sindh also became independent under a Buddhist ruler. But a Brāhmaṇa minister Chacha, soon usurped the throne and extended his sway up to the borders of Kashmir. His son Dāhir suffered defeat at the hands of Muhammad bin Kāsim, the leader of Arab invasion, in AD 712. The Arabs conducted many raids in the Sindh region and captured some territory also, but they avoided deep penetration inside the country for the fear of Pratihāras.

Kanauj continued to enjoy its primacy in the politics of the country for some more time. Yaśovarman (AD 725-52) is credited to have defeated many rulers including the king of Magadha. The Āyudha dynasty which followed him, however, suffered many invasions during the last quarter of eighth century AD. During the reign of Indrāyudha (AD 779-94) the tripartite struggle among the Rāṣṭrakūṭas, Pālas and Āyudhas intensified and in consequence the last two suffered defeat. Rāṣṭrakūṭa ruler Govinda III inflicted a crippling blow on the Āyudhas and taking advantage of the situation one Nāgabhaṭṭa of Pratihāra family annexed Kanauj and founded a new dynasty there.

PRATIHĀRAS

Pratihāra rulers of Kanauj also fought many battles. The dynasty, to begin with, was a small chieftaincy in Mandor (Jodhpur) region. It soon subjugated Ujjain and Kanauj. Nāgabhaṭa II (AD 805-33) defeated Dharmapāla of Bengal and won victories over Ānartta (north Kathiawad), Mālwā (central India), Matsya (east Rajputana), Kirātas

(Himalayan region), Turuṣkas (Arab settlers of western India) and Vatsas (Kośāmbī). Mihira Bhoja (AD 836-85), who followed him, established supremacy over Bundelkhand and Marwar regions and exercised authority as far north as the foothills of Himālayas. He crossed swords with the Pālas in the east and Gurjaras in the west. He also captured southern Rajputana and Ujjain region up to Narmadā River. Mihira Bhoja also suffered a defeat at the hands of Rāṣṭrakūṭa rulers.

The reign of Mahendrapāla I (AD 885-910) was marked by many wars. He conquered Magadha and north Bengal and exercised authority over Saurāṣṭra. But he seems to have lost some territory to Śaṅkaravarman, the ruler of Kashmir. Following his death there was some internal strife out of which Mahipāla (AD 912-44) emerged successful. Taking advantage of the situation the Rāṣṭrakūṭas and Pālas waged war against him and made some territorial gains. But Mahipāla soon went on offensive and the people called Muralas, Mekhalas, Kaliṅgas, Keralas, Kulūtas, Kuntalas and Ramaṭhas acknowledged his authority. Near the end of his reign he suffered a defeat at the hands of Rāṣṭrakūṭa ruler Kṛṣṇa III.

Bad days soon befell the dynasty. During the reign of Devapāla, who ascended the throne around AD 948, Candelas of Jajakabhukti carved out a kingdom. Soon after on the ruins of Pratihāras rose the Cālukyas of Anhilwāṣa, Kacchapaghātas of Gwalior, Cedis of Dāhala, Paramāras of Mālwā, Guhilas of southern Rajputana and Cāhamānas of Śākaṁbharī. Some other kingdoms which rose to power during this period included Gāhaḍavālas of Kanauj, Hindū Śāhī of Afghanistan and Punjab, Karakoṭakas of Kashmir, Varmans of Kāmarūpa, Pālas and Senas of Bengal, Kalacuris of Tripuri, etc. Pratihāra empire, thus reduced to a tiny kingdom, fell to the lot of Rājyapāla in the last decade of tenth century AD. His help to the Śāhīs of Udbhāṇḍpur (Bhatinda) proved inadequate to fight back the Turk invaders. The establishment of Turk rule in India was now a near certainty.

PENINSULAR WARS

Indian peninsula did not lag behind in the frequency of wars. The Āryan penetration towards the south may have necessitated conflict with the natives. The expansion of Mauryan empire to the borders of south Indian kingdoms of Coḍas, Pāṇḍyas, Satiyaputras and Keralaputras may not have been possible without resort to arms.

PALLAVAS

The Pallavas rose to power on the ruins of Sātavāhanas in Amarāvatī and Kāñcī region in mid-third century AD under one Bappadeva. His son Śivaskandavarman was a great warrior and conqueror who performed *Aśvamedha*, *Vājapeya* and *Agniṣṭoma* sacrifices. One of his successors named Viṣṇugopa suffered defeat at the hands of Samudragupta. Pallavas attained political eminence in sixth century AD under the leadership of Siṁhaviṣṇu, who is said to have defeated Pāṇḍyas, Kalabharas and Mālavas and extended his sway up to Kāverī, defeating the Colas.

His son Mahendravarman I, who ascended the throne in early seventh century AD, fought a long war with Cālukya Pulakeśin II, and suffered some reverses and loss of territory. But his son Narasiṁhavarman inflicted a crushing defeat on Pulakeśin II near Kāñcī. He stormed Vātāpi in AD 642 and assumed the title *vātāpikoṇḍa.* He also despatched two naval expeditions to Ceylon in support of his protege there. His successors Nandivarman, etc., waged a long war with Cālukyas for supremacy in the south but no decisive victory could be won by either side. Pallavas also crossed swords with Pāṇḍyas, Rāṣṭrakūṭas and Colas in ninth century. Aparājitavarman (AD 876-95), the last ruler of the Pallava dynasty, was defeated by Cola ruler Āditya I in AD 890.

CĀLUKYAS

Cālukyas rose to power in early sixth century AD in Vātāpi (Bādāmī) region. Cālukya king, Kīrtivarman, defeated the Mauryas of north Konkarn, Kadambas of Banavāsī and Nalas of southern Kośala. He is also said to have invaded Bihar and Bengal in the east and Cola and Pāṇḍya territories in the south.

Pulakeśin II was the most powerful ruler of this dynasty. He led successful campaigns against Vanavāsī (north Kanara), Gaṅgavāḍi (modern Mysore), Malabar, north Konkan and Puri. The Lāṭas of southern Gujarat, the Mālavas and the Gurjaras submitted to him. He also inflicted a defeat on Harṣavardhana of Kanauj. He even threatened Kāñcīpuram, the capital of Pallavas. The adjacent kingdoms of

Kośala and Kaliṅga in the east and Cola, Pāṇḍya and Kerala in the south were always scared of him. Pulakeśin met a heroic death when Pallavas stormed Bādāmī in AD 643.

His son Vikramāditya I avenged the defeat and death of his father by storming Kāñcī in AD 654. Perhaps, he also crossed swords with Colas, Pāṇḍyas and Keralas in the south. The weight of his arms was also felt in north India. The old feud with the Pallavas was continued by his successors. Kīrtivarman was the last known ruler of this dynasty.

Rāṣṭrakūṭas

Rāṣṭrakūṭas rose to greatness in eighth century AD during the rule of Dantidurga. He conquered Cālukyas in mid-eighth century and defeated the rulers of Kāñcī, Kaliṅga, Kośala, Mālwā, Lāṭa, Taṅka and Śrīśaila. His paternal uncle Kṛṣṇa I, who succeeded him, completed the overthrow of Cālukyas. His arms also reached Konkan, Gaṅgavāḍi and Veṅgī.

Dhruva Nirūpam, who ascended the throne in AD 779, conquered the Gaṅga king and annexed his territory. The Pallava king submitted before his might. He drove away the Pratihāra king, invaded Gangetic plain and defeated the Gauḍa ruler. His son Govinda III was also a great conqueror. To begin with, he defeated his recalcitrant brother and his allies. Thereafter, he conquered Gaṅgas, Pallavas and eastern Cālukyas. He also led a victorious campaign against the northern kingdoms and the rulers of Kanauj and Gauḍa submitted to his power. His greatest achievement was the victory over the confederacy of five southern kingdoms, viz., Colas, Pāṇḍyas, Pallavas, Gaṅgas and Keralas.

Amoghavarṣa I ascended the throne in AD 814. His rule was marked by internal strife and external aggression. His successors also fought wars with their neighbours, especially the Pratihāras, but without much success.

Kṛṣṇa III, the last great ruler of the dynasty, ascended the throne in AD 840. First he dethroned the recalcitrant Gaṅga ruler and then marched against the Gurjara ruler, depriving him of Kālañjara and Citrakūṭa.[61] In the south he humbled Colas and Pallavas and occupied their capitals. During his reign Pāṇḍyas and Keralas remained subdued and the ruler of Ceylon paid homage to him. He placed his ally on the throne of Veṅgi. The Arabs considered him as one of the four greatest rulers of the world.

The Colas of Tañjāvur, Pāṇḍyas of Madurā, Ceras of Kerala, Cālukyas of Kalyāṇī, Yādavas of Devagiri, Kadambas of Vanavāsī, Gaṅgas of Talkad, Hoysalas of Dvārsamudra were the other known royal houses of Deccan, who were always ready to shed blood.

Colas

The antiquity of Colas is traceable to third century BC, as they find mention in Aśokan inscriptions. In second century BC, a Cola ruler is said to have invaded Ceylon. The Colas gained in power and territory under Kalikāla after the beginning of the Christian Era. One of his successors even performed a *Rājasūya* sacrifice. Colas suffered a setback in fourth century AD owing to the rise of Pallava power and the growing military might of Pāṇḍyas and Ceras.

Ancient Colas came into prominence again in ninth century AD in Tanjore area under King Vijayālaya, who was perhaps a feudatory of Pallavas. His successors Āditya I and Parāntaka I (AD 907-53) put the dynasty on the road to greatness despite the fact that the latter was defeated by Rāṣṭrakūṭa Govinda III. They remained quiet for some time but Rājarāja I (AD 985-1014) again put them on the path of glory. He earned many victories and his empire covered present Madras presidency, Coorg, parts of Mysore, Ceylon and some other islands. Rājendra I (AD 1014-44) and Rājādhirāja I (AD 1044-52) were the other two great kings of the dynasty, who waged many successful wars. Rājendra I subdued Kerala and Pāṇḍya kings, crossed swords with Cālukya ruler Jayasiṁha I, invaded north up to river Gaṅgā and marched eastwards up to Gauḍa kingdom. With a powerful navy he captured the whole of Ceylon as also Kaṭāha and Kadāram beyond the seas. His son Rājādhirāja I also defeated Pāṇḍya and Kerala kings and also subjugated some Ceylon rulers. To celebrate his victories he performed horse sacrifice. He lost his life in a battle against Someśvara I, the western Cālukya king, in AD 1052. War against the western Cālukyas was continued by his successors, who fought many more battles in the neighbourhood.

Kulotuṅga (AD 1070-1122) was the last great ruler of this dynasty. He defeated the Cera and Pāṇḍya rulers and some other feudatories, and crossed swords with western Cālukyas and eastern Gaṅgas. He also fought wars with the rulers of Mālwā and Kaliṅga. By the end of his reign he appears to have suffered some loss of territory in southern Mysore to the Hoysalas. His successors continued to wage wars with the same incessancy but these earned no additional territory to the kingdom. Rājendra III (AD 1252-69) could not prevent the disintegration of the empire in the face of the mighty challenge posed by the Pāṇḍya king and some feudatories. Hoysalas and Kākatīyas also prospered at the cost of the Colas.

Pāṇḍyas

The Pāṇḍya kingdom existed in third century BC on the southern frontiers of Aśokan empire. Khāravela of Kaliṅga defeated them in first century BC. In Saṅgam literature there are references to Pāṇḍyan conquests but the dynasty as such came into prominence only in seventh century AD. In eighth century Neḍunjaḍayan (Varaguṇa I), the Pāṇḍya king, made some gains at the cost of Colas, Keralas and other neighbouring kingdoms. His successor Śrī-Māra-Śrī-Vallabha (AD 815-62) was the greatest ruler of this dynasty, who not only defeated the strong confederacy of Pallavas, Gaṅgas and Colas at Kumbhakoṇam but even carried his arms to Ceylon. But finally the combination defeated the Pāṇḍyas in AD 880 and their empire passed on to the Colas.

The Pāṇḍyas again emerged powerful in the thirteenth century, under the leadership of Sundara Pāṇḍya (AD 1216-38), who repeatedly defeated the Colas. His successors not only crushed the Colas but also subdued the Cera country, Koṅgudeśa and Ceylon and occupied Kāñcī. They also defeated Hoysalas, Kākatīyas and Pallavas of Śendamaṅgalam and earned some victories in Kerala and Ceylon. The invasion of Malik Kafur in AD 1310 finished the decaying Pāṇḍya empire.

Ceras

The earliest reference to Ceras is met in the Aśokan inscriptions. Their kingdom seems to have comprised parts of modern Kerala and Tamil Nadu. Senaguttuvan, a powerful Cera ruler, defeated many neighbouring kingdoms in second century AD. His successors also waged wars against Colas and Pāṇḍyas. In eighth century Ceras reappear on the political map of India as waging war against the Pallavas.

In the later half of the century they suffered aggression of the Pāṇḍyas. About the end of tenth century the Cola ruler Rājarāja I brought them under subjugation. After the decline of the Colas, Pāṇḍyas subjugated them in thirteenth century. Later, after the sack of Madurā by Malik Kafur in AD 1310, Ravivarman Kulaśekhara, the Cera ruler, freed himself from the Pāṇḍyan yoke. But the Ceras soon faded out from the political stage of India.

PURĀṆIC WARS

Before ending with this long story of wars it may be mentioned that Indian Purāṇic literature is also replete with references to wars, fought between the Devas (gods) and Dasyus or Dānavas (devils). In the *Matsya Purāṇa*[62] alone there are references to twelve such battles:

1. Battle between Narasiṁha and Hiraṇyakaśyapa, in which the latter was killed.
2. Battle between Vāmana and Bali in which Bali was made captive.
3. Battle between Varāha and Hiraṇyākṣa in which the latter was vanquished.
4. Battle between Indra and Prahlāda in which the latter was vanquished.
5. Tāraka-Maya war fought between Indra and Vairocana in which the latter was killed.
6. Āḍibaka war fought between Śiva and Tripura in which the latter was killed.
7. Tripura war fought between Śiva and Daityas in which the latter were killed.
8. Andhaka war fought between Śiva and Daityas in which the latter were killed.
9. Vṛtranāśaka war fought between Indra and Vṛtrāsura in which the latter perished.
10. Dhātri war fought between Indra and the Dānavas, in which the latter were killed.
11. Halāhala war fought between Indra and Dānavas in which the latter were killed.
12. Kolāhala war fought between Indra and Vipracita in which the latter was killed.

Purāṇas are replete with references to wars suggesting that Indian gods were as big warmongers as their devotees.

POINTS TO PONDER

The incidence of war and conflict thus pervaded the land of Bhāratavarṣa from the earliest times. Many of these wars were thrust by the invaders who discovered an easy passage in the north-west. Achaemenids, Macedonians, Bactrian Greeks, Pahlavas, Śakas, Kuṣāṇas, Sassanians and Hūṇas invaded India, one after another. Indian rulers also fought innumerable wars among themselves. The ambition to become a *cakravartin* and performer of *Aśvamedha* fuelled their zeal for war. This review throws up some interesting points with a bearing on Indian military history:

Firstly, it was the large size of the country which encouraged the growth of small kingdoms and their unending conflicts. But, in the event a mighty ruler imposed his hegemony over the country the tide of wars abated. The successors of Candragupta Maurya and Samudragupta enjoyed comparatively peaceful times.

Secondly, India was subjected to foreign invasions frequently. Geographical setting or what may be called the strategical topography of the country perhaps contributed to this immensely. The absence of a Himālayan barrier in the north-west made it easy for the Central Asian nomads to invade India, whenever there was a turmoil in the steppes.

Thirdly, Indians hardly put any resistance to the invaders, who swept from west to east. It is astonishing that in second century BC a Greek king of Bactria marched from Peshawar to Pāṭaliputra unchallenged. The Śakas and Kuṣāṇas also earned easy victories in India.

Fourthly, all invaders who came to India settled here. Perhaps the affluence of the conquered land encouraged them to settle down. Further, the Assam jungles may have discouraged them to look eastward.

Fifthly, Indians always exhibited a defensive mentality. The abundance of forts in India amply proves this. But these forts, despite the huge stocks of arms stored in them, failed to stand the assault of the invading armies. The defenders of the forts seldom thought of coming out and chasing away the enemy.

Sixthly, Indian military thinkers had a myopic vision of warfare. They modelled their strategies of war keeping in view the plain battlefields of Punjab and did not visualize wars in jungles and mountains. Their concept of *caturaṅgiṇī* (fourfold army) and *vyūha* (battle array) seems to confirm this.

The following aspects of war need perhaps more extensive analysis in the Indian perspective to arrive at a meaningful conclusion:

1. Despite repeated invasions from the north-west, Indians never took measures to defend their borders effectively.
2. Despite overwhelming superiority in numbers, Indian armies always suffered defeat at the hands of invaders, barring a few exceptions.
3. Indian rulers never invaded lands beyond their frontiers, with the sole exception of Kaniṣka who conquered some parts of central Asia from the Chinese in first century AD.
4. The never ending drama of warfare did not generally disturb the peace of the people, who went about their vocations undisturbed. This perhaps explains for the great progress made by the Indians in various arts and sciences.

NOTES

1. Y.M. Citalwala, *Frontiers of the Indus Civilization* (ed. B.B. Lal and S.P. Gupta), pp. 212-13.
2. Ibid.
3. J. Marshall, *Mohenjo-daro and the Indus Civilization*, p. 112, also see p. 432.
4. Priyavrata, *Prācīna Bhārat Men Pratirakṣā Vyavasthā*, pp. 11-51.
5. *Ṛgveda*, 7.33.3.
6. Ibid., 7.18.
7. Ibid., 4.16.
8. Ibid., 4.30.
9. Ibid.
10. Ibid. 1.112.14, etc.
11. *Aitareya Brāhmaṇa*, I.14.
12. *Śatapatha Brāhmaṇa*, 13.5.4.11.
13. Ibid., 13.5.4.19-23.
14. R.S. Tripathi, *History of Ancient India*, p. 43.
15. *Śatapatha Brāhmaṇa*, 13.5.4.19-23.
16. *MB*, Sabhā, 47, 48.

17. Ibid., Mausala, 8
18. Kāśī, Kośala, Aṅga, Magadha, Vajji, Malla, Cedi, Vaṁsa, Kuru, Pañcāla, Matsya, Śurasena, Assaka, Avanti, Gandhāra and Kamboja. *Aṅguttara Nikāya*, vol. 1, p. 192; vol. 4, p. 172.
19. These included Bhaggas, Bulis, Kālamas, Koliyas, Mallas, Morias, Videhas, Licchavis and Śākyas. Rhys Davids, *Buddhist India*, pp. 23-9.
20. R.S. Tripathi, op. cit., p. 108.
21. Ibid., p. 109.
22. Ibid.
23. E.J. Rapson, *Cambridge History of India*, vol. 1, p. 300.
24. Ibid., pp. 304-05.
25. J.W. M'crindle, *The Invasion of India*, p. 65.
26. Ibid., pp. 66, 269-70.
27. Ibid., pp. 102, 211.
28. Ibid., pp. 111-12.
29. Ibid., p. 116.
30. Ibid., p. 119.
31. Ibid., pp. 219-20.
32. नमः श्वभ्यः श्वपतिम्यश्च वो नमः। *Yajurveda*, 16.28; also *Atharvaveda*, 11.2.30.
33. J.W. M'crindle, op. cit., pp. 232, 285.
34. Ibid., pp. 144-54, 248-9.
35. Ibid., p. 292, also 155-6.
36. Ibid., pp. 155-9.
37. K.A. Nilkanta Sastri, *Age of the Nandas and Mauryas*, p. 153, V.A. Smith, *The Early History of India* (4th edn.), pp. 158-60.
38. V.A. Smith, op. cit., p. 132.
39. *Gārgī Saṁhitā*, *Indian Historical Quarterly*, 1925, pp. 214ff; also *Mālavikāgnimitram*, Act 5, after sloka 14.
40. *Harṣacarita*, p. 193.
41. खतियदपमानमदनस सकयवनपल्हवनिसूदनस. . . खखरातवसनिरवसेसकरस सातवाहनकुलयस-पतिथापनकरस. . .। *Epigraphia Indica*, vol. VIII, p. 60.
42. दक्षिणापथपतेस्सातकर्णेर्द्विरपि नीर्व्याजमवजित्या वजीत्य सम्बन्धाविदूरयानुत्सादनात्प्राप्तयशसा। *Epigraphia Indica*, vol. VIII, pp. 44, 47.
43. This is borne out by numismatic evidence.
44. *Epigraphia Indica*, vol. XX, pp. 80-1.
45. ततः साकेतमाक्राम्य पांचाला मथुरास्तथा।
    यवनाश्च सुविक्रान्ताः प्राप्स्यन्ति कुसुमध्वजम्।। *Yuga Pu.*, *JUPHS*, vol. XX, 94-5.
46. For details see W.T. Tarn, *Greeks in Bactria and India.*
47. V.A. Smith, op. cit., p. 278.

48. पराक्रमाधिगतभागीरथ्यमलजलमूर्द्धाभिषिक्तानां दशाश्वमेधावभृथस्नानां भारशिवानाम्। R.S. Tripathi, op. cit., p. 235; for details on Bhāraśiva Nāgas see K.P. Jayaswal, *JBORS*, 1933.
49. J.F. Fleet, *Corpus Inscriptionum Indicarum*, vol. III, pp. 211-15.
50. सर्वकरदानाज्ञाकरणप्रणामागमनपरितोषित प्रचण्डशासनस्य। Ibid., p. 213.
51. दैवपुत्रषाहिषाहानुषाहिशकमुरुण्डै: सैंहलकादिभिश्च सर्व्वद्वीपवासिभि:। Ibid.
52. विचलितकुललक्ष्मीस्तम्भनायोद्यतेन क्षितितलशयनीये येन नीता त्रियामा। Ibid., p. 315.
53. A.L. Basham, *The Political History of Hūṇas in India* by Atreyi Biswas, Preface, p. xiii.
54. Ibid., pp. 88-9.
55. R.S. Tripathi, op. cit., p. 287.
56. *Epigraphia Indica*, vol. XIV, p. 117.
57. R.S. Tripathi, op. cit., p. 295.
58. *Harṣacarita*, p. 101.
59. T. Watters, *On Yuan Chwang's Travels in India*, vol. II, p. 239.
60. Ibid., vol. I, p. 343.
61. दक्षिणदिग्दुर्गविजयमाकर्ण्य गलिता गूर्जरहृदयात्कालंजर चित्रकूटाशा। *Epigraphia Indica*, vol. V, p. 194.
62. प्रथमो नारसिंहस्तु द्वितीयश्चापि वामन:।।
    तृतीयस्तु वराहश्च चतुर्थोऽमृतमन्थन:।
    संग्राम: पञ्चमश्चैव सञ्जातस्तारकामय:।।
    षष्टोह्याडीबकारव्यस्तु सप्तमस्त्रैपुरस्तथा।
    अन्धकाख्योऽष्टमस्तेषां नवमो वृत्रघातक:।।
    धात्रश्च दशामश्चैव ततो हलाहल: स्मृत:।
    प्रथितो द्वादशस्तेषां घोरं कोलाहलस्तथा।। *Matsya Pu*, 47.42-5; *Agni Pu*, 276.10-12; also see *Viṣṇu Pu*, *Bhāgavata Pu*, *Śiva Pu*, *Brahmāṇḍa Pu*, etc.

Chapter 2

Military Organization

Ancient Indian literature generally refers to seven constituents (*saptāṅga*) of the state, viz., *svāmin* (king), *amātya* (minister), *suhṛt* (friend), *kośa* (treasury), *rāṣṭra* (country), *durga* (fort) and *bala* (army).[1] The *bala* or *senā*, the seventh constituent,[2] has been defined by Śukrācārya as an organized group of men well provided with offensive and defensive weapons.[3] For the proper conduct of war armies were organized in various classes, arms and units. Commanders were appointed to lead the armies in the battlefield. An efficient logistics system backed up the army effort. The military organization was thus oriented to cater for the operational needs.

CLASSIFICATION OF ARMIES

In the Vedic age probably the king did not maintain a regular army and some kind of guards may have taken care of his personal safety and his property. In times of war the king may have raised a volunteer force and may also have called in the village contingents led by *grāmaṇīs*. Thus the army in the Vedic times included the personal guards of the king, the volunteer force and the village contingents.

In the *Rāmāyaṇa* the armies (*balas*) have been classified into five categories, viz., *mitra* (friendly), *āṭavī* (forest), *maula* (hereditary), *bhṛtya* (hired) and *dviṣad* (enemy).[4] The *Mahābhārata* adds *śreṇī* (guild) to these types.[5] The *Arthaśāstra*,[6] *Kāmandakīya Nītisāra*,[7] *Agni Purāṇa*,[8] *Mānasollāsa*,[9] and the early epigraphs also follow this lead.[10]

According to the *Mahābhārata*, *maula* and *mitra* are the best armies while *bhṛtya* and *śreṇī*, though equally important, are the second best.[11] It seems that for recruitment in the state army (*maula-bala*) the aspirants had to undergo some kind of selection process.[12] This was perhaps done at the village level by village headmen who were entrusted with some military duties (*saṅgrāmakṛtyam*) and in this they were assisted by an official called *saciva.*[13] In terms of importance the *Arthaśāstra* rates the armies as *maula*, *bhṛtya*, *śreṇī*, *mitra* and *āṭavī* respectively.[14] The *Kāmandakīya Nītisāra* and the *Agni Purāṇa* also follow this rating of the armies. A brief description of these armies may be useful in understanding their functions.

Maula-Bala (Hereditary Army)

Maula-bala was like a regular army which was maintained at the state expense.[15] The selection to the force was based on merit, but the son of an ex-soldier could join the force on the death or retirement of his father.[16] Megasthenese refers to army as the fifth segment of the Indian society. When the soldiers of this elite force were not engaged in war, they spent their time in idleness or drinking. They only carried their own self as all their needs were taken care of by the state.[17] Elaborating on this Arrian says:

> The fifth caste among the Indians consists of the warriors who are second in point of numbers to the husbandmen, but lead a life of supreme freedom and enjoyment. They have only military duties to perform. Others make their arms, and others supply them the horses, and they have others to attend on them in the camp, who take care of their horses, clean their arms, drive their elephants, prepare their chariots and act as their charioteers. As long as they are required to fight they fight, and when peace returns they abandon themselves to enjoyment,—the pay which they receive from the state being so liberal that they can with ease maintain themselves and others besides.[18]

The soldiers of the *maula-bala*, rated as the best,[19] were emotionally attached to the king and he in turn was reverential to them.[20] Describing the hereditary army of Harṣavardhana, Hiuen-tsang says that 'the National Guard (lit. warriors) are heroes of choice valour, and, as the profession is hereditary, they become adepts in military tactics. In peace they guard the sovereign's residence, and in war they become the intrepid vanguard.'[21]

Bhṛtya-Bala (Mercenary Force)

Bhṛtya-bala or mercenary force was considered the second best in the order of precedence.[22] Being close to the ruler, *bhṛtyas* were ever prepared for war. Pāṇini refers to a class of people, inhabiting western India, who depended on arms for their living and fought as mercenaries.[23] The *Arthaśāstra* also refers to ancient Kambojas, Surāṣṭras, Kṣatriyas and *Śreṇīs* who earned their living by commercial activity and also by fighting as mercenaries.[24] Hiuen-tsang who visited India in seventh century AD also refers to *bhṛtyabala*.[25]

It seems that some small rulers depended on mercenaries (*āyudhajīvins*) for the protection of their state. During his stay at Taxilā Appolonius of Tyana was told by the ruler that 'he paid blackmail to a tribe of barbarians on his borders for the protection of his dominions against the attack of other barbarous tribes'.[26]

Śreṇī-Bala (Guild Force)

In the order of precedence *śreṇī-bala* occupied the third place.[27] As this force was composed of the natives its interests were identical to that of the ruler.[28] In ancient Indian economic system *śreṇīs* (trade guilds) occupied an important place.[29] They maintained armies, which could perhaps be called on state service in times of need. A Gupta inscription refers to an army maintained by a guild of weavers. It comprised excellent bow-men, capable of annihilating their adversaries in a sharp encounter.[30] Thus *śreṇī-bala* was an important component of the armies in ancient India.[31]

Mitra-Bala (Friendly Force)

Mitra-bala was ranked fourth in importance.[32] It comprised the troops contributed by friendly rulers to fight against a common adversary. As *mitra-bala* had a common objective with the ruler they were siding with, it was considered dependable.[33]

Dviṣad-Bala (Enemy Force)

It was placed fifth in the order of precedence.[34] This force included the soldiers who had either been recruited inside the enemy territory or had been enticed to join in after deserting their master. As the main objective of this force in a war was arson and loot, it was considered dangerous like a serpent.[35] But as this force was led by Āryan commanders, it was considered better than *āṭavī-bala*.[36]

ĀṬAVĪ-BALA (FOREST ARMY)

This army comprising the forest-dwellers and led by non-Āryan commanders was rated as inferior.[37] It is stated to have comprised Niṣādas, Mlecchas and the inhabitants of mountainous regions.[38] As these people generally lived on loot the rulers were advised to use them carefully.[39] In this connection it is notable that the repeated mention of *aṭavikas* in the *Arthaśāstra*, etc., suggests that they played a crucial role in ancient Indian warfare. Since large areas of northern plain were still forested no ruler could afford to ignore their presence in the neighbourhood.

OTHER CLASSIFICATIONS

Another classification of armies, based on the quality of the troops, is met in the *Mahābhārata*. The best troops from all arms were categorized as *sāra*, the second best as *madhyama* and the weakest as *phalgu*.[40] While deploying various arms for a battle this categorization was kept in view by the commanders.[41] This classification with minor variations is also met in the *Arthaśāstra* as it mentions *sāra*, *anusāra*, *tṛtīyasāra* and *phalgu*.[42] *Anusāra* and *tṛtīyasāra* were indeed inferior to *sāra* and could be categorized as second and third grade *sāra balas* respectively.

The *Śukranīti* classifies the armies into two categories—*anyagam* and *svagam*. The *svagam* army included infantry which moved on its own without the help of any mount, whereas *anyagam* army marched mounted on elephants, horses and chariots.[43] *Śukranīti* has given some more classifications of armies such as *svīya* and *maitra*, *maula* and *sādyaska*, *sāra* and *asāra*, *aśīkṣita* and *śīkṣita*, *gulmībhūta* and *agulmaka*, *dattāstra* and *svaśastrāstra* and *svavāhi* and *dattavāhana*.[44] *Svīya* army has been explained as salaried army, *maitra* as friendly, *maula* as traditional, *sādyaska* as emergency army, *sāra* as ready to fight, *asāra* as reluctant to fight, *śīkṣita* as tranied in battle arrays, *aśīkṣita* as untrained in battle arrays, *gulmībhūta* as organized under a commander, *agulmaka* as unorganized, *dattāstra* as equipped by the state, *svaśastrāstra* as carrying own weapons, *svavāhī* as user of private mount and *dattavāhana* as provided with mount.[45]

In the south Indian *Saṅgam* literature three types of armies, viz., *kṣatriya*, *paradavar* and *maravar* are referred to. These are comparable to *maula*, *bhṛtya* and *āṭavī balas* described above. *Paradavar*, the natives of far south, were famous for their bravery and were in great demand in the southern states. *Maravar* lived on loot.[46]

Mantra-Bala

Before ending with the *balas* a word may be said about the *mantra-bala* (power of charms), which was considered to be an effective medium for winning wars by ancient Indians. In fact, it was considered superior to the power of courage (*utsāha*) and influence (*prabhāva*). In the *Agni Purāṇa* it is said that Śukrācārya, the perceptor of Rākṣasas, was vanquished by Bṛhaspati, the perceptor of Devas, by his power of incantation.[47] It also refers to some charms like *garuḍa-cakra, bhaṅga-vidyā, mṛtyuñjaya-yantra, trilokya-vijaya-vidyā, saṅgrāma-vijaya-vidyā*, etc., which could defeat the enemy and force him to run away from the battlefield.[48] Such references to charms are abounding in Purāṇic literature.

In this context it is notable that faith in the efficacy of *mantras* (charms) as a means of victory in war, had come into vogue in India in the Vedic times. In the Vedas, particularly in the *Atharvaveda*, there are numerous hymns which invoke charms to vanquish or destroy the enemy. Such *mantras* are also met with in the ancillary Brāhmaṇas. By seventh-century AD tantrism had completely caught hold of the psyche of the people. The rulers now sought to defeat their foes more with charms than with arms. This no doubt resulted in the neglect of the armies.

CASTE SYSTEM AND MILITARY SERVICE

The Vedic society comprised three classes, viz., Brāhmaṇa, Rājanya (Kṣatriya) and Viśa. Brāhmaṇas attended to the religious duties, Rājanyas to the governance and military duties and Viśa to agriculture, etc. Though warfare was mainly a concern of the Rājanyas, the Viśa also contributed to it. *Grāmaṇī*, the commander of the village army, was generally a Vaiśya.[49] In this context the observations made in *Vedic Index* are significant:

> At the head of the village was the *Grāmaṇī*, or 'leader of the village', who is referred to in the *Rigveda*, and often in the later Saṁhitās and in the Brāhmaṇas. The exact meaning of the title is not certain. By Zimmer the *Grāmaṇī* is regarded as having had military functions only, and he

is certainly often connected with the *Senānī*, or 'leader of an army'. But there is no reason so to restrict the sense : presumably the *Grāmaṇi* was the head of the village both for civil purposes and for military operations.[50]

It seams that to begin with Vaiśyas as peasants or landholders were also a class of soldiers. In fact, the two occupations may have been inextricably mixed during the Vedic times.

In the Epic age the predominance of Kṣatriya class in military matters was recognized,[51] but other caste people were no less involved.[52] The greatest military thinkers of the age, viz., Bṛhaspati, Śukra and Paraśurāma were all Brāhmaṇas. Kṛpācārya and Droṇācārya, two well-known military experts of the age, were also Brāhmaṇas. But strangely the profession of *yuddhācārya* (teacher of military science) has not been considered respectable for the Brāhmaṇas in the *Manusmṛti*.[53] Karṇa and Ekalavya, two famous bow-men belonged to lower castes. Further, the soldiers who gathered to fight in the battlefield of Kurukṣetra belonged to all castes (*varṇas*).[54] A 60,000 strong select army of Yudhiṣṭhira included men of all castes, who lived together.[55] Karṇa was consecrated as *senāpati* by Duryodhana and representatives from all castes including Śūdras, in the battlefield of Kurukṣetra.[56]

Kauṭilya believed in the superiority of Kṣatriyas as a fighter class. Earlier to him some thinkers believed that Brāhmaṇas, Kṣatriyas, Vaiśyas and Śūdras were superior soldiers in the same order. Kauṭilya, disagreeing with this view said that Brāhmaṇa soldiers, who could be lured by the enemy by prostrating before them, were not dependable. In his view a Kṣatriya army which is well trained in weaponry or a Vaiśya army which is large in strength is superior.[57] *Agni Purāṇa*[58] and *Kāmandaka Nītisāra*[59] also admit the role of other castes in war though they concede the superiority of Brāhmaṇas and Kṣatriyas. The *Śukranīti*, however, says that a person who is disciplined, knows Nītiśāstras and is expert in the science of weapons and the *vyūhas* alone should be made commander or a soldier without considering that he is a Śūdra, Vaiśya or Mleccha.[60] In *Mṛcchakaṭika* there is a reference to a tanner and a barber serving as army commanders.[61] Epigraphic evidence is also abounding on this point. In fact, the diminance of Kṣatriyas in the profession of arms could never have been total for the following reasons:

1. In six types of armies referred to above, dominance of Kṣatriyas, if any, could have been restricted to *maula-bala* only. In other five types of armies it was just not possible.
2. According to Hiuen-tsang 'the soldiers are levied according to the recruitments of service; they are promised certain payments and are publicly enrolled'.[62]
3. In the recruitment of soldiers, the nativity was considered a determining factor. In the *Mahābhārata* the natives of Magadha are stated to be good at using elephants in war, Yavanas, Kambojas and the natives of Mathurā as good cavalry soldiers and the natives of south India as good swordsmen.[63] The *Manusmṛti* says that the natives of Kurukṣetra, Pañcāla, Śūrasena and Matsyadeśa made good soldiers.[64] The aspect of nativity is also emphasized in the Purāṇas.[65] Thus the factor of nativity may have influenced the process of recruitment in the armies of India considerably.
4. Men who were physically fit alone could be selected for the army. The *Agni Purāṇa* says that the men of tall stature with acquiline nose, big eyes, well-blended eyebrows, irascible, fond of quarrels, contented, happy and lustful made bold soldiers.[66] Thus for recruitment in the army the caste factor had a limited role.
5. *Dharmaśāstras* permit Brāhmaṇas to wield weapons in evil times when the religion and the country are threatened.[67]

EVOLUTION OF ARMS

The Indians, inhabiting the Indus Valley region in the chalcolithic age, fought on foot. The horse-drawn chariot entered the Indian battlefield with the Āryans. The use of horse for military purpose also started simultaneously. In the Vedic age the armies comprised three divisions, viz., infantry, cavalry and chariot corps.[68]

In the *Yajurveda* (chap. 16) there are many terms of military connotation which are a sure guide to the evolution of military organization in the Vedic age. These terms are generally used in relation to Rudra, a powerful deity, who was feared and respected both. In this context reference is made to army and army commander,[69] horse and commander of the horse,[70] chariot warrior and non-chariot warrior,[71] *gaṇa* and commander of *gaṇa*,[72] producer of weapons and equipment like bow, arrows, quiver, chariot, etc.,[73] fast moving chariots and armies.[74] All this goes to suggest that in the Vedic times elephant corps was little known and armies comprised only infantry, cavalry and chariot corps.

The earliest reference to fourfold division of the army (*caturaṅgiṇī*) is met in the later Vedic period.[75] The *Aṣṭādhyāyī* of Pāṇini, a composition of sixth century BC, also refers to it.[76] In the *Mahābhārata*[77] and the *Rāmāyaṇa*[78] the terms *caturaṅgabala* and *caturaṅgiṇī* which included infantry, cavalry, chariot corps and elephant corps are repeatedly used. The early Buddhist literature[79] and the *Arthaśāstra*[80] also refer to this fourfold division of the army, but the latter adds *viṣṭikarmāṇi* (supporting services) to this classification.[81] The earliest representation of fourfold army is met in the Sāñcī art, dated around the beginning of the Christian era.[82]

Megasthenese, the Greek ambassador in the Mauryan court, says that the military affairs of Candragupta were monitored by a committee which had six sub-committees with five members each. The first sub-committee was in-charge of navy, second of bullock trains (supply system), third of infantry, fourth of cavalry, fifth of chariot corps, and sixth of elephant corps.[83] Subsequently, the addition of *kośa* and *mantra* made the army *ṣaḍāṅgiṇī* (sixfold).[84] The *Kāmandakīya Nīti*, a work of Gupta age, also follows the epics.[85]

In the epics there are occasional references to eightfold division (*aṣṭāṅgiṇī*) of the army. Perhaps, in course of time two additional elements called *cara* (spy) and *deśika* (road-finders) were added to the six divisions.[86] In the *Mahābhārata* these eight divisions of the army have been called as known (*prakāśa*) elements. The secret elements comprised *jaṅgama* (liquid) and *ajaṅgama* (solid) poisons. Perhaps, liquid poison was used to destroy the enemy by applying it to his clothings or by mixing it to his food.[87] The available evidence generally indicates the following stages in the evolution of army organisation in ancient India:

1. *Ekāṅgiṇī* - Proto-historic age
2. *Tri-aṅgiṇī* - Vedic age
3. *Caturaṅgiṇī* - Later Vedic age
4. *Ṣaḍāṅgiṇī* - Maurya age
5. *Aṣṭāṅgiṇī* - Gupta age

FUNCTIONS OF ARMS

Over the centuries Indians also learnt about the efficacy of different arms in the battlefield. The *Agni Purāṇa* has described these functions in some detail.[68] The main task of the infantry (*pattikarma*) at the battlefield was to remove the dead and wounded soldiers, give water to the elephants and supply weapons to the soldiers. The sword and shield-bearers protected own army from enemy attack and also sought to pierce the enemy array. The function of the archers was to chase away the enemy.

The function of the chariot corps (*rathakarma*) was to create terror in the enemy ranks. Chariots also removed seriously wounded soldiers from the battlefield. The elephant corps was used to break the enemy arrays and to destroy his forts. Cavalry conducted the survey of the battle zone, protected the supply line and chased the fleeing enemy.[89]

DEVELOPMENT OF VARIOUS ARMS

INFANTRY (*PADĀTI-BALA*)

To begin with, man fought on foot. The inhabitants of Indus Valley perhaps knew no other arm as the archaeological discoveries at Harappa and Mohenjo-daro do not suggest the use of horse, horse-chariot or elephant in war. The Ṛgvedic references to large armies of ten kings allude to Infantry only.[90]

Among the Āryans infantry occupied an important place in the army.[91] Men from various tribes joined to form the infantry and the elite class led them mounted on chariots.[92] In the Epic age an army with large infantry component was considered powerful.[93] Still, in comparison to chariot or elephant it was considered inferior.

In fourth century BC infantry was considered the most important arm. During his invasion of India Alexander generally encountered infantry.[94] Porus, the Indian adversary of Alexander maintained a strong infantry, which fought with long bow and carried a buckler made of undressed ox-hide.[95] Some fought with javelins but all soldiers carried a broad-bladed sword, which was slightly shorter than three cubits. In a straight fight it was wielded with both hands to add force to it.[96]

Candragupta maintained a strong infantry which according to Greek sources comprised 6,00,000 men.[97] Infantry continued to enjoy importance in the Indian battlefield till about the beginning of the Christian era as the armed men represented in the art of Bhārhut and Sāñcī are mostly foot soldiers. The *Arthaśāstra* also acknowledges the importance of infantry as it could be used to attack the enemy at all places and at all times. It could fight in deserts, forests and inside the trenches, during the day or the night.[98]

The infantry suffered a setback around the beginning of the Christian era, when it failed to withstand the mounted archer of Scytho-Kuṣāṇa invaders.[99] Still, it survived as a useful arm[100] and in south India it maintained an edge over other arms for a much longer period. Foot soldiers equipped with swords, circular shields and bandages wound round their stomachs, led the attack while the cavalry and elephant corps on the wings and the archers from behind supported them.[101]

Chariot Corps (*Ratha-Bala*)

The ox-drawn cart was known to Indians in the chalcolithic age and they might have used it in the battlefield as well. 'A precursor of the horse-drawn chariot, it could give mobility and a charge of ox-chariots could disperse resisting infantry.'[102] A chariot yoked to a pair of bullocks and driven by a nude human figure, all in bronze, has been discovered at Daimabad and identified as Harappan.[103]

The horse chariot introduced an element of mobility in the warfare. The chariot-warrior could move much faster than the foot-soldier, carry more weapons and was advantageously placed to fight from a height. The mount saved him from the fatigue of carrying the load of weapons and also of the long march to the battlefield.

It is said that the introduction of the horse as a draft animal in about 2000 BC was the final step in the development of chariot into a military arm which revolutionized warfare in the ancient world by providing armies with unprecedented mobility. Chariotry contributed to the victories of the Hyksos in Egypt, the Hittites in Anatolia, the Āryans in northern India and the Mycenaeans in Greece in the second millennium BC.[104] The horse-chariot was introduced in the Indian battlefield by the Vedic Āryans. It was revered as a divinity and hymns were composed in its honour.

Lord of the wood, be firm and strong in body: be, bearing us, a brave victorious hero. Show forth thy strength, compact with straps of leather, and let thy rider win all spoils of battle. . . . Thou bolt of Indra, vanguard of the Maruts, close knit to Varuṇa and child of Mitra. As such accepting gifts which here we offer, receive, O Godlike chariot, these oblations.[105]

In the Vedic age the chariot warrior performed the dual task of fighter and charioteer. He could have, therefore, joined the battle only after bringing the chariot to a halt and this might have greatly compromised its effectiveness in respect of mobility and manoeuvrability. Subsequently, the appointment of charioteer removed this handicap. Perhaps, this change was introduced in the later Vedic age, as the term *sārathi* is mentioned for the first time in the Brāhmaṇas.[106] The charioteer occupied the seat on the right side of the vehicle whereas the warrior took position on the left.

In the *Sāṅkhyāyana Śrautasūtra* there is a reference to war-chariot: 'The sacrificial fee is a horse chariot, coated with rhinoceros hide, covered with tiger-felt, with a quiver of boar-hide, with a bow-case of panther-hide, drawn by brown horses.'[107]

In Vedic times the person who specialized in making chariots was known as *rathakāra*. In two Ṛgvedic verses Bhṛgus, a celebrated priestly family, is said to be engaged in the manufacture of cariots.[108] Perhaps, chariot-making was not considered an undignified profession in Vedic times.

In the Epics chariot corps is described as the most important arm. The chariot was protected with armour made of the skin of lion or tiger and was richly decorated.[109] The chariot-warriors came to be classifed as *ardharathī*, *atirathī*, etc.,[110] depending on their skill to fight. The charioteer (*sārathi*) was considered an integral part of chariot ensemble and commanded great respect. Śrīkṛṣṇa and Śalya were the two best known charioteers of the Epic age.

It seems that, to begin with, chariot was a two-wheeled vehicle drawn by two horses and driven by the warrior himself. Subsequently, two outside horses were fastened to the axle end, driven by one driver apiece. Some chariots were drawn by as many as eight horses.[111] However, the two-wheeled chariot was the most popular vehicle of war in ancient India.[112]

In fourth century BC the Greeks witnessed Indian chariots being drawn to the battlefield by bullocks. The horses were taken separately tied to a rope so that they did not get wounded, provoked, tired or weakened by drawing the chariot. It was on the battlefield that they were yoked to the vehicle. Generally, a charioteer and two warriors occupied the chariot[113] but large-sized chariots could carry as many as six men.[114] In the battle of Jhelum Porus was accompanied by 300 chariots.[115] The vehicle could also be drawn by bullocks, camels and asses.[116]

The importance of chariot is also highlighted in the *Arthaśāstra*. The superintendent of chariot corps (*rathādhyakṣa*) besides leading his men into war, also established factories to manufacture chariots of various sizes. The large-sized one was 10 *puruṣas* (7.6 feet) in height and 12 *puruṣas* (9 feet) in length. The small-sized ones were made one *puruṣa* (9 inches) short in length in successive order, the smallest one being 6 *puruṣas* (4.6 feet).[117]

The chariots were classified as temple chariot (*devaratha*), festive chariot (*puṣyaratha*), war chariot (*saṅgrāmika*), travelling chariot (*pāriyāṇika*), marching chariot (*parapurābhiyānika*) and training chariot (*vainayikā*). Of these the last four were put to military use.[118] According to the *Amarakośa*, *śatāṅga*, *syandana* and *ratha* were the three chariot types which were put to military use.[119] The *Arthaśāstra* says that the main functions of the chariot corps included guarding own troops, repelling enemy attack, breaking enemy formations, grouping own formations, causing terror in enemy ranks, etc.[120]

Chariot corps continued to maintain its superiority over other arms till fourth century BC. Megasthenese says that an eastern kingdom of India maintained a chariot corps of 8,000 vehicles.[121] Diodotus and Curtius put the number of chariots in the army of Candragupta Maurya at 2,000 while Plutarch puts the number at 8,000.[122]

Decline of Chariot

It seems that by fourth century BC, the chariot had lost some of its aura. In Buddhist *Nikāyas* it does not figure as the most important arm. Porus, the famous adversary of Alexander, did not go to war in a chariot but on an elephant. Further, in the battle of Jhelum the chariot failed miserably. In the army of Candragupta Maurya chariot does not appear to command the traditional superiority. In the armies of foreign invaders like Greeks, Scythians, and Kuṣāṇas, who ruled over large Indian territories around the beginning of the Christian era, chariot did not find a place. Evidently, they were not impressed by the efficacy of chariot in the battlefield. But the Indians continued to use it for some more time is evident from the art and literary sources.

In the art of Sāñcī a few chariots have been represented. These are either two-wheeled or four-wheeled and seem to be war vehicles. The chariot portrayed in the 'War of Relics' scene bears two wheels with spokes designed in a petal shape. On either side and on the front side it is provided with curved projections, perhaps intended to serve as a protective guard to the occupants. The upper rims of these guards are decorated with chevron band. A pole joins the body of the car to the yoke placed on the neck of the steeds, with fastenings, perhaps made of leather (Pl. 1).

It appears that the Gupta rulers, following the lead of the foreign invaders, ignored chariot as it is neither portrayed on their coins nor mentioned in their inscriptions. Harṣavardhana, who ruled over north India in seventh century AD maintained a chariot corps,[123] but it does not seem to have enjoyed much importance. The Banskhera and Madhuban grants of Harṣavardhana which were issued from a victory camp refer to boats, elephants and horses but not to chariots.[124] The *Harṣacarita* and *Bṛhatsaṁhitā* also do not refer to chariot. Most importantly, Muhammad bin Kāsim, who invaded Sindh in early eighth century AD, did not encounter any chariot on the Indian side.

However, chariot did not fade out from the Indian battlefield after Harṣavardhana. There are references to its use in some copper plates dated after the seventh century AD. The Daulatpur plate of Bhāgadeva I (AD 706) says that his camp was marked by the presence of chariots, besides boats, elephants and foot soldiers.[125] The Nālandā copper plate of King Dharmapāla refers to fivefold division of the army, which included chariot corps and navy.[126] In a copper-plate grant Rāṣṭrakūṭa king Dantidurga (AD 753) claims to have defeated his adversary with an army of chariots and horses.[127]

The war-chariots were mounted with skin or cloth for protection and decoration. A chariot if covered with skin was called *dvaipa* or *vaiyāghra*, if covered with yellow blanket, *pāṇḍukambala* and if covered with cloth, *vastra* or *dukūla*.[128] The iron or metal coverings which provided protection to the chariot were called *rathagupti* or *varūtha*.[129]

Plate 1: Chariot, Sāñcī

It is surprising that, despite the near eclipse of chariot from the Indian battlefield, the *Nīti* works continued to describe chariot corps as an important arm,[130] oblivious of the change in the Indian warfare. But the reasons behind the exit of chariot from the Indian battlefield have not been satisfactorily explained so far. Perhaps, there were two important reasons for this. The military reason was that the elements of surprise, deception and mobility introduced by Scytho-Kuṣāṇa cavalry, particularly its archers, rendered chariot vulnerable and compromised its utility as a dependable arm. The political reason was the decline of imperial Guptas and the rise of petty states on its ruins. These petty states sought security in their forts than in their armies. In reducing these forts to submission elephant proved far more useful than chariot or even horse. But Macdonell has explained it differently. 'The use of chariot both for war and for racing gradually died out in Hindustan partly perhaps owing to the enervating influence of the climate and partly to the scarcity of the horses which had to be brought from the region of Indus.'[131]

Elephant Corps (*Hasti-Bala*)

The Harappans[132] and the Vedic Āryans[133] were acquainted with the elephant, but its use in battlefield seems to have started in the age of Brāhmaṇas.[134] In the Epic times the elephant corps had fully evolved as some warriors are reported fighting mounted on elephants,[135] but in terms of reputation it was still far behind the chariot. Significantly, an Indian ruler of north-west India had sent a contingent of elephants to the Iranian king Darius III during his war against the Greeks.[136] In the battle of Jhelum the presence of elephants on the battlefield frightened the Greek soldiers.[137] Porus, the Indian ruler, faced Alexander mounted on an elephant.[138] The army of Candragupta Maurya included a large number of elephants, which the Greek sources put at 8,000.[139]

According to Megasthenese:

> The war elephant either in what is called the tower, or on his bare back in sooth, carries three fighting men, of whom two shoot from the side while one shoots from behind. There is also a fourth man who carries in his hand the goad wherewith he guides this animal, much in the same way as the pilot and captain of a ship direct the course with the helm.[140]

But the epic puts the number of men carried by an elephant at seven: two goad holders, two archers, two swordsmen and one trident or spear holder.[141] Interestingly, in Sāñcī sculptures the number of elephant riders is generally three.[142] In Ajantā art the elephants are generally shown as mounted by archers.

The *Arthaśāstra* says that the focal point in the formation of a battle array was an elephant or a chariot and the other arms were adjusted in it appropriately.[143] It also highlights the reliability of the elephant in war. These could be used for marching in the front, for protecting the flanks, for breaking the enemy ranks, for trampling the enemy army, for causing terror in the enemy ranks, and for destroying forts, etc.[144] Therefore, the importance of elephant suffered only marginally during the foreign invasions.

In the art of Bhārhut and Sāñcī the elephants are widely represented (Pl. 2). Again, the war scenes represented in the art of Ajantā are full of combating elephants (Pl. 3). By this time, a belief had gained ground that an army powerful in elephants wins the war.[145] Elephant enjoyed superiority over other arms in southern India, where the commander generally led his army mounted on an elephant.[146] Harṣavardhana, the ruler of Thānesar, maintained an elephant corps of 60,000.[147] This importance of elephant on the Indian battlefield continued in the medieval period.[148]

It seems that in the post-Gupta period the elephant corps developed into the most important arm after the Chariot had faded out from the Indian battlefield. This is evident from the fact that the army of Harṣavardhana comprised 60,000 elephants. Harṣa had to witness 'his rows of lordly elephants fallen in battle' during the war with Pulkeśin II. In the *Viṣṇudharmottara Purāṇa* the tasks assigned to elephant corps included breaking through the enemy lines, destruction of enemy troops and dismantling of hurdles like fort walls.[149] To fulfil these tasks some improvements were introduced in the equipment of elephant:

1. Further tightening of the girth to keep the housing firm.
2. Providing the tusk of the elephant with a barbed cover.[150]
3. A band of cloth to cover the eyes (वक्त्रछद: or चक्षुवारणम्).[151]

Now the elephant was expected to serve as a vehicle of war and also as a machine of war. Consequently, his equipment was tightened.

Plate 2: Caparisoned Elephant, Sāñcī

Plate 3: Caparisoned Elephant, Ajantā

The covering for the tusk served as an armour and also as a weapon to break hurdles like the fort walls and gates. Covering for the eyes kept him immune from the tumult of the battle till the actual fighting commenced.

Cavalry (*Aśva-Bala*)

The use of cavalry was not known to the Harappans.[152] The Āryans, however, used it in war is clearly borne out by the following hymn: 'The whip is laid upon the flank. The heroes stretch their thighs apart, like women when the babe is born.'[153] At another place devotees solicit Indra for a thousand well-trained swift-going horses.[154] Yet another hymn refers to the horse with saddle on the back and bridle in the nostrils.[155] By the later Vedic age cavalry had grown into an important arm.[156] The *Atharvaveda* contains even some hymns in the honour of the horse.[157] In early Buddhist literature also there are references to fourfold army, including cavalry.[158]

In view of the above the observation that 'horse appears to have gained in importance on the Indian battlefield perhaps due to contact with Medians and Persians, who relied more on cavalry and infantry than on chariotry in war'[159] does not sound convincing. In Vedic times cavalry formed an important component of the armies in India and this could certainly not have been an influence of the Medians and Persians.

The army of Porus included 4,000 horses.[160] Assakenians and Kṣudrakas fought Alexander fielding 20,000 and 10,000 strong cavalry respectively.[161] Candragupta Maurya maintained a 30,000 strong cavalry.[162] Perhaps the horses were not then provided with saddle, bit and stirrup. A cavalry soldier carried two spears and a shield.[163] The *Arthaśāstra* considered cavalry as an important arm which was put to various uses such as to rush forward, around, beyond and back, hold the enemy forces, outflank them by pincer movement, retreat and renew attack, protect the broken ranks and pursue the enemy when routed.[164] This seems to explain for the large presence of horse in Sāñcī sculptures (Pl. 4).

The *Arthaśastra* also says that the quality war horses of India 'came from Kāmboja, Sindhu, Āraṭṭa and Vanāyu, the middling from Bāhlīka, Pāpeya, Sauvīra and Titala, the rest are inferior'.[165] Among these places if Vanāyu and Bāhlīka have been rightly identified with Persia or Arabia and Bactria respectively it would follow

Plate 4: Caparisoned Horse, Sāñcī

that India did import horses from areas beyond their borders. In any case many breeds of horses entered India from Central Asia and Persia from time to time with the invaders.

It seems that the cavalry gained in importance after the foreign invasions. Among the Śaka invaders horse was a favourite mount and bow a favourite weapon.[166] The Junagadh inscription of Rudradāman describes cavalry as superior to all other arms.[167] The invaders also brought in the cavalry accoutrement like saddle, bit and stirrup.[168] The wide representation of horse in the contemporary Indian art suggests Śaka-Kuṣāṇa influence.[169] It is also attested to by the wide issue of horseman type coins by Indo-Parthian, Śaka and Gupta kings.[170] The army of King Harṣavardhana included 1,00,000 cavalry.[171] The art of Ajantā represents many horses, fully equipped for war[172] (Pl. 5). In the *Nīti* works cavalry is rated as an important arm.[173] The protective armour of horse was called *uraśchada.*

As for the equipment of horse Daṇḍin has referred to many items such as *khalīna* (bridle), *kharakhalīna* (thorny bridle), *urovadhra* (stirrup), *parayāṇa* (saddle), *graiveya* (collar), *kakṣya* (girth for tying on the sides of the trail), *pakṣacarman* (leather coverings for eyes) and *maṇḍūka* (iron-scale). The ornaments of the horse included *ratakas* (rings on forefeet), *camaramālā* (chowrie string), *pulakapaṅkti* (necklace), *ghurghuramālikā* (string of bells) and *aṣṭamaṅgalā* (string of eight auspicious devices).[174] In the *Amarakośa* the words *kavikā* and *khalīna* have been used for bridle.[175]

It is not known whether ancient Indians put brandmarks on the body of their horses for easy identification. In large cavalry forces the brandings may have been followed universally, as a necessity. The Scythians, Sassanians and Hūṇas, who were closely associated with India followed this practice.[176]

It is not known that the Indians castrated their horses to make them more useful for war purpose. The Scythians and Sarmatians of south Russia are said to have followed the practice to make their horses manageable. It is likely that Scythians introduced this practice in India.[177]

Treasury and Counsel (*Kośa and Mantra*)

Kośa (treasury) and *mantra* (counsel), were also two important components of military machine in ancient India. The *Kāmandaka Nīti*

Plate 5: Caparisoned Horse, Ajantā

even suggests that it is better to leave aside the fourfold army and fight with the help of solvent treasury and good counsel. It was, therefore, advisable for a wise king to conquer his enemies with *mantra* and *kośa*.[178] It further says that in a battle fought with the power of counsel, victory can be secured with little effort. Otherwise, in a battle where the time (*kāla*) and terrain (*deśa*) factors are not favourable, the loss suffered could be immense.[179] The *Arthaśāstra* has described in detail the application of the power of counsel.[180]

Navy (*Nau-Bala*)

The Harappans were maintaining trade relations with West Asian countries[181] and this could have been possible only with a fleet of ships. In the Vedic literature also there are references to sea voyages, sea faring ships and sea trade. To make the sea voyage danger-free, ships with three masts (*tribandhura*) and ten oars (*daśaritra*) and even a hundred oars (*śataritra*) were commissioned.[182] This generated wealth is evident from the following Ṛgvedic hymn: 'From every side, O Soma, for our profit, pour thou forth four seas. Filled full of riches thousandfold.'[183] There is also a reference to four ships sent by Aśvins to the oceans to save Bhujyu, the son of Tugra.[184] The great victory of Nakula over many islands as described in the *Mahābhārata* also implies the existence of a good fleet.[185] By fourth century BC, the Indians had definitely gained expertise in the production of ships.[186] Maurya administration provided for a separate department to look after the naval affairs.[187] According to Arrian, the naval fleet of Candragupta comprised 800 ships. But Curtius and Diodotus raise this figure to 1,000 ships. Ptolemy, however, puts the total number of Mauryan fleet around 2,000 ships. In the *Manusmṛti* there are indications of oceanic warfare and ships.[188] The *Arthaśāstra* says that the naval affairs of the state were supervised by the controller of shipping.[189]

Samudragupta conquered many island kingdoms with a powerful fleet.[190] His successors also maintained a good fleet.[191] In Ajantā art there are many scenes depicting the launching of naval expeditions.[192]

The naval arm received better attention among the south Indian states. According to Smith 'the Tamil states maintained powerful navies and were visited freely by ships from both east and west, which brought merchants of various races.'[193] These navies may have been put to military use as well to protect trade and territory. Proximity to sea coast, growing trade relations with South-East Asian and Mediterranean countries and ambition to conquer island kingdoms prompted them to maintain a strong fleet. On some Sātavāhana coins, ships with two sails are represented, suggesting that they maintained a navy.[194] In the south Indian *Saṅgam* literature, composed during the early centuries of Christian era, the naval activities are described in detail.[195] The south Indian inscriptions are replete with the references to the naval might of Pāṇḍyas, Pallavas and Cālukyas. Subsequently, the Colas earned glory by dint of their naval might.[196]

Air Arm (*Vimāna-Bala*)

The references to *vimānas* in the epics and the Purāṇas suggest that Indians had visualized the concept of air travel or air war around the beginning of the Christian era. Though the concept of air-arm as met in the epics and Purāṇas find little credence among historians still if it were a fantasy of Indian sages, no one can ignore the ever present thread of logic behind it. *Vimāna* is a combination of the words *vi* and *māna*—*vi* meaning bird or sky and *māna* meaning likeness. *Vimāna* could, therefore, be explained as something which appeared and functioned like a bird. In the *Bṛhadvimānaśāstra*, which was certainly composed much before anyone had conceptualized aircraft in Europe. Bhāradvāja has quoted the definitions of *vimāna* as given by ancient *ācāryas* of India. According to Nārāyaṇa, a *vimāna* can travel through the water, the land, and the air on its own power, like a bird.[197] Ācārya Viśvambhara says that a *vimāna* can travel from one island to another, from one land to another and from one world to another through the sky.[198] Ācārya Halla has given a more simple definition stating that in moving through the sky which could be compared with the birds was a *vimāna*.[199]

In the epics and the Purāṇas *vimāna* appears as a means of transport and also as a vehicle of war. *Saubha vimāna*,[200] *Hiraṇyapura vimāna* and *Puṣpaka vimāna*[201] were used for both purposes. In the *Harivaṁśa Purāṇa* there is a reference to Kubera, the god of riches, fighting mounted on *Puṣpaka vimāna*.[202] Lord Mahādeva fought Andhaka mounted on a *vimāna*.[203] The *Harivaṁśa Purāṇa* is replete with references to *vimānas* in the context of the war between Devas and Asuras.[204] During Tāraka-Maya *saṁgrāma*, Mayāsura fought mounted on a *vimāna* which thundered like clouds.[205] On occasions, even ordinary soldiers fought mounted on speedy *vimānas*.[206] Some *vimānas*, nose dived and flew back again.[207] The *vimānas* which were destroyed during the war fell down and lay scattered on earth in pieces.[208] Interestingly, in epics and Purāṇas the *vimānas* are spoken of in relation to gods and demons but not humans.

Vimāna was also used as a means of transport and there are many references to it in the epics.

1. When Gaṅgā descended on earth gods, sages, Gandharvas, Yakṣas and Siddhas witnessed the great event mounted on *vimānas*, elephants and horses.[209]
2. Kabandha, a ferocious Rākṣasa, after his release from *Rākṣasa yoni* ascended to heaven in a shining *vimāna* drawn by swans.[210]
3. The chariot of Rāvaṇa, which was carried by asses could fly in the sky. He carried Sītā to Laṅkā mounted on this chariot.[211]
4. On his arrival in Laṅkā Hanumān saw the *Puṣpaka vimāna* of Rāvaṇa, which compared with the *vimāna* carried by swans in the sky.[212]
5. After defeating Rāvaṇa, Rāma returned to Ayodhyā along with Sītā, Sugrīva, Vibhīṣaṇa, etc., mounted on the *Puṣpaka vimāna*.[213]
6. King Śveta of Vidarbha travelled in a *vimāna*.[214]
7. Many gods, led by Indra, came down to see the fierce battle between Arjuna and Kṛpācārya, mounted on *vimānas*.[215]
8. Varuṇadeva came to see Arjuna mounted on his *vimāna* of very bright texture.[216]
9. People, rich or poor, who observe fast, ascend to heaven mounted on a *vimāna* with nymphs in attendance.[217]

In the *Harṣacarita* there is a very interesting reference to *nabhayāna*. Kākavarṇa, a scion of Śiśunāga family, was very fond of wonders (*āścarya*). Once out of curiosity he mounted a *nabhayāna* (aircraft) invented by a Yavana (perhaps a person of Greek origin). The Yavana took him up in the sky and killed him near the city.[218]

In the *Samarāṅgaṇasūtradhāra* of Bhojarāja again there is reference to a *vimāna*, which flew in the sky powered by mercury.[219] In the *Yuktikalpataru* also there is a reference to *vimāna*.[220]

The most exhaustive treatment of the *vimānas* in ancient India is met in the *Bṛhadvimānaśāstra*, which formed a part of *Yantrasarvasva*, a compilation of sage Bhāradvāja. It is astonishing that the subject of *vimāna* had attracted the attention of Indian scholars in great measure even before Bhāradvāja. In this context *Vimānacandrikā* of Nārāyaṇamuni, *Vyomayānatantra* of Śaunaka, *Yantrakalpa* of Garga, *Yānabindu* of Vācaspati, *Kheṭayānapradīpikā* of Cakrayāni and *Vyomayānakaprakāśa* of Ghuṇḍinātha may be mentioned.[221] Bhāradvāja has mentioned as many as 36 scholars who contributed towards the furtherance of *Vimānaśāstra*. These included Lalla, Viśvambhara, Saṁkha, Gautama, Govila, Gālava, etc.[222] Viśvakarmā, Chāyāpuruṣa, Manu and Maya are stated to be the inventors of *vimāna*.[223]

In *Bṛhadvimānaśāstra* three classes of aircraft have been mentioned, viz., *mantrika*, *tantrika* and *kṛtaka* (*yantrika*). Of these *tantrika* had 56 types and *yantrika* 25 types. *Tripura vimāna* was a class by itself as it could move on earth, water and sky.

This mass of evidence on *vimāna* has been brushed aside by many noted historians like Louis Renou.

> Certain Indian authors have believed or claim to believe in 'aviation' in ancient India, on the ground of the mention of *vimāna* or ariel chariots . . . in the epics. Simple poetical fantasies are given a trifle more solidity by the pseudo technical description of 'flying machines' found in *Samarāṅgaṇasūtra*, a treatise on architecture attributed to King Bhoja (11th century). In any case there is nowhere any clear mention of the use of such machines in war.[224]

In the present state of our knowledge it is difficult to explain the syndrome of *vimāna* in relation to war in ancient India. But even if references to air warfare in the epics and Purāṇas are considered imaginary, it is an undeniable fact that ancient Indians had visualized air warfare as early as the beginning of the Christian era, some two thousand years before the world could think of it.

THE LOGISTICS (*VIṢṬIKARMA*)

Maintenance of troops during a military expedition has always been an important aspect of warfare. Kāmandaka believed that an army which was not backed up by proper supply or support system (*vividha*) was incapable of fighting.[225] According to him the repair of wells, bathing places (*tīrtha*), roads and tents and the provision of food and fodders form a part of logistics (*viṣṭikarma*).[226]

In the beginning when the duration of war was short and number of fighting troops small, perhaps soldiers carried their weapons and food on their back or used dogs and oxen to ferry them. But the emergence of bigger armies in the Vedic age may have necessitated an organized system to maintain troops.[227] In this connection the observations made by Das are significant.

> When engaged in active service, the army had to be fed and supplied with regular daily rations, which we can suppose, were supplied by the state, or collected from the voluntary contributions of the people themselves. It is also possible that supplies were often 'Commandeered' from the inhabitants of the villages through which the royal army marched, which must have given rise to the description of the king as the 'devourer of the people' (*RV* 1.65.4; *AV* 4.22.7). Of course, there were also raids and forays for the supply of provisions when the soldiers in active service were in need of them.[228]

Epic Descriptions

The epics suggest that *viṣṭikarma* was organized on a larger scale. The bullock-cart was widely used for carrying military supplies, though occasionally chariots were also used. When the Pāṇḍava army proceeded to the battlefield of Kurukṣetra it was accompanied by bullock-carts, chariots, various kinds of vehicles, etc., carrying treasury, machines, weapons, physicians, surgeons, etc., in the rear.[229] Aśvatthāman, a great warrior, carried eight cart loads of arrows for a day's battle.[230] Karṇa proceeded to the battlefield with carts and chariots laden with arrows and other weapons.[231] Atikāya, a son of Rāvaṇa, joined the battle of Laṅkā, after stocking his chariot with twenty quivers, ten bows, eight bow-strings and two shining swords.[232] The military camps were provided with store-houses.[233] All kinds of weapons, food articles, water, fodder for animals, honey, butter, etc., were stocked in them.[234] These camps were connected by good roads so that food supplies could be brought there conveniently. The roads were well protected so that the enemy could not damage them.[235] The general needs of the army were, however, met by the professionals, such as tailors, weavers, builders, weapon-makers, washermen, etc., who accompanied it to the battlefield.[236]

Maurya System

During the Maurya period a committee of five members supervised the logistics of the army. It worked in coordination with the officer-in-charge of the carts, who transported food, fodder and other necessities of war. Megasthenese has touched upon this aspect of military administration in some detail:

> There is a third governing body which directs military affairs. This also consists of six divisions with five members in each. One of these divisions cooperates with the superintendent of the bullock trains which are used for transporting engines of war, food for the soldiers, provender for the cattle, and other military requisites. They supply servants who beat the drum and others who carry gongs; grooms also for the horses and mechanists and their assistants. To the sound of the gong they send out foragers to bring in grass, and by a system of rewards and punishments ensure the work being done with dispatch and safety. . . . There are royal stables for the horses and elephants and also a royal magazine for the arms, because the soldier has to return his arms to the magazine and his horse and elephant to the stables.[237]

The *Arthaśāstra* emphasizes the need for an efficient supply system.[238] The matter was thoroughly considered even before the army marched out for a war.

> After calculating the halts on the way in villages and in forests, in accordance with the supply of fodder, fuel and water and (calculating) the time for camping, halting and marching, he (ruler) should start on the expedition. He should cause food and equipment to be transported in double the quantity required to meet the case. Or, if unable to do so, he should assign it to the troops, or should store them at intervals on the route.[239]

In a waterless region, he should make carts and animals carry water according to their capacity, in conformity with the length of the route.[240] Labourers were employed to carry military supplies. 'The work of clearing camps, roads, water works, wells and fords, carrying machines, weapons, armours, implements and food, and removing from the battlefield weapons, armours and wounded men are the functions of labourers.'[241] They were provided space to live in at the army camp.[242] The system of logistics is also referred to in the Junagadh inscription of Rudradāman.[243]

The *Arthaśāstra* has referred to three kinds of supplies—gathered from forest; collected from own country and sent by allies.[244] Since the strength of an army could be assessed by watching its supplies of food, fodder, bed-spreads, etc., it was advisable to keep them concealed from the enemy.[245] Further, it was considered easy to defeat an enemy by choking his supply system. It could also be done by poisoning the foodstuffs and fodder stored in the enemy camp.[246] It was advisable for a ruler to ensure that troops are supplied with abundant and excellent grains, forest produce, machines, weapons, armours, etc., before mounting an attack or laying a siege.[247] The ideal situation was to launch an attack on the enemy when his old stocks had been exhausted and new ones had not arrived.[248]

As the roads are the means by which the supplies are despatched, Kauṭilya advises their proper protection.[249] In fourth century BC, elephant was the best means of transport, followed by four-horsed chariot, camel and horse. Among the slow moving carriers, donkey, mare and bullock-cart were important.[250]

Gupta Age and After

The transportation of supplies engaged the maximum attention during the army's march. This is vividly described in the *Harṣacarita*:

> Leathern bags bursting with fullness, were extended upon the dusty backs of elephants, which had been rubbed down by strokes from wisps of hay. Servants of house-builders (*gṛhacintaka*) rolled up awnings and cloth screens belonging to tents and marquees. Leathern sacks were filled to roundness with bundles of pegs. Store-room stewards collected stores of platters. Many elephant attendants were pressed to convey the stores. . . . Wicked elephants were loaded with cargo of utensils hurriedly tossed upon them by travel-practised domestics. . . . Camels, as sacks were set on their backs, bellowed at the outrage. . . . Donkeys ridden by throngs of bags accompanied the march. Crowds of carts with creaking wheels occupied the trampled roads.[251]

The task of bringing supplies to the camp was also entrusted to the contractors, who collected them from the villages on the road sides. This was indeed a difficult task specially when the cooperation was not easily coming from the villagers.[252] It appears that some military hardware was deposited in improvized stores in villages and towns on the way, even before the army marched out.[253] An official called *nāyaka*, who marched in the forefront, was responsible for arranging food and other necessities of the army during the march.[254] It was advisable to attack the enemy in a territory where the supplies could be despatched conveniently,[255] for an army which was cut-off from the supply of food and clothing (*vividha*) was incapable of fighting.[256]

It seems that around seventh century AD the military supply system underwent a change. The responsibility of carrying supplies for the army now fell on the traders, who accompanied the army to the field. When the army halted at the camp for the night the traders also pitched up tents and displayed their wares.[257]

The *Śukranīti* has emphasized that a good supply system ensures victory for the army.[258] It advises that a wise ruler should weaken the enemy by cutting off his supply of food, fodder, water, etc.[259] Among the means of transport the *Śukranīti* considers elephant as the best followed by camel, bullock and horse. The cart was, however, considered the best carriage for all times, except the rainy season.[260]

Though the military setup in ancient India was generally based on *Caturaṅgiṇī*, the number of arms may have increased or decreased depending on the size, power, geography, economy and threat perception of the state concerned. Candragupta Maurya created a commissariat to provide logistical support to his large army during military campaigns.[261] He also built up a navy[262] when his empire came to incorporate large coastal areas. The southern kingdoms of Colas, Ceras, Pāṇḍyas and Sātavāhanas being coastal states also maintained sizeable naval arm. The successors of the Mauryas did away with the naval arms because they had no coast to defend. It seems that some kingdoms which spread over desert areas maintained a camel corps. The army of one Jīvitagupta II is said to have included a camel corps.[263] The *Śukranīti* also refers to camel corps as an arm.[264]

On the other hand the kingdoms ruling over mountainous and densely forested area may not have maintained chariot corps. Some tiny kingdoms may have maintained only cavalry and infantry because elephant corps and chariot corps involved considerable financial burden.

ARMY FORMATIONS: VEDIC AND EPIC TIMES

For proper administration, discipline and deployment, the army was organized in units. In the Vedic age the terms *śardha*, *vrāta* and *gaṇa* perhaps denoted army units.[265] Zimmer has said that *viśa* and *grāma* represented army formations in the Vedic age[266] and this appears true because in the Vedic literature there are references to training of *viśa* in warfare.[267] The terms *senā*, *anīka* and *varūtha*, widely used in the sense of military formations in later literature, had also come into vogue in the Vedic age.[268] In the *Ṛgveda* there are many references to large armies:

1. Indra killed 10,000 Vṛtras (1.53.6), obviously a reference to enemy soldiers.
2. Indra overthrew twenty kings and their 60,099 followers (1.53.9).
3. Indra killed 66,660 soldiers of Anus and Druhyus while siding with Sudās (7.18.14).
4. Indra eliminated 50,000 enemy soldiers (4.16.13).

These armies could have been taken to the battlefield only after organizing them in proper formations.

It seems that for the purpose of war the Vedic field formations were organized in numbers of 10s, 100s and 1000s. In the *Ṛgveda* Maruts have been described as *daśagvāh* , i.e. moving in a profile of 10s.[269] At another place they have been called *śatino*,[270] i.e. moving in a profile of 100 and still at another place *sahasriyāsah*,[271] i.e. moving in a profile of 1,000. Evidently, these numbers were related to army formations.

In the *Mahābhārata* nine types of army formations, viz., *patti*, *senāmukha*, *gulma*, *gaṇa*, *vāhinī*, *pṛtanā*, *camū*, *anīkanī* and *akṣauhiṇī* are mentioned.[272] *Patti* was the smallest unit and *akṣauhiṇī* the biggest. The composition of army formations in the Epic is given in the following table:

Unit	Chariot	Elephant	Horse	Foot	Total
Patti	1	1	3	5	10
Senāmukha	3	3	9	15	30
Gulma	9	9	27	45	90
Gaṇa	27	27	81	135	270
Vāhinī	81	81	243	405	810
Pṛtanā	243	243	729	1,215	2,430
Camū	729	729	2,187	3,645	7,290
Anīkanī	2,187	2,187	6,561	10,935	21,870
Akṣauhiṇī	21,870	21,870	65,610	1,09,350	2,18,700

It would be seen that except *akṣauhiṇī*, which was considered ten times bigger to *anīkanī*, all other units were three times bigger to the unit preceding it. If the same rule of triplication is applied to *anīkanī* then the strength of *akṣauhiṇī* would stand at 65,610, a more reasonable figure. This sequence of military formations is also spoken of by Alberuni, a foreign traveller, who visited India in tenth century AD.[273] Significantly, among these formations *patti* is comparable to the present-day section, *senāmukha* to platoon, *gulma* to company, *vāhinī* to battalion, *pṛtanā* to brigade, *camū* to division, *anīkanī* to corps and *akṣauhiṇī* to army.

STRENGTH OF FORMATIONS

In a particular context in the *Mahābhārata*, the total strength of Kaurava army is stated to be 22 *anīkanīs*.[274] This implies that the 11 *akṣauhiṇīs* of the Kaurava army comprised 2 *anīkanīs* each. As the strength of an *anīkanī* was 21,870, the strength of an *akṣauhiṇī* would amount to 43,740. This would place the strength of the Kaurava army at 4,81,140 men.

Elsewhere, in the *Mahābhārata*, the composition of *akṣauhiṇī* is described differently.[275] It is said that 500 elephants, 500 chariots, 1,500 cavalry and 2,500 foot-soldiers formed the military unit called *senā*, 10 *senās* formed a *pṛtanā*, 10 *pṛtanās* a *vāhinī*, 10 *vāhinīs* a *dhvajinī*, 10 *dhvajinīs* a *camū* and 10 *camūs* an *akṣauhiṇī*.[276] These figures if added would make *akṣauhiṇī* 50 crore strong. The army of king Daśaratha, the ruler of Ayodhyā, is stated to have numbered an *akṣauhiṇī*.[277] When prince Bharata went to forest to meet Rāma he was accompanied by an army which included 9,000 elephants, 60,000 chariots, 1,00,000 horses and a large infantry.[278] The *Rāmāyaṇa* thus puts the strength of *akṣauhiṇī* between 3,00,000 to 5,00,000.

The *Amarakośa* adds one more formation called *dasānīkanī* to this list. *Dasānīkanī* is said to be three times bigger than *anīkanī* and *akṣauhiṇī* three times bigger than *dasānīkanī*. The *Amarakośa* thus puts the strength of *akṣauhiṇī* at 1,96,830.[279] But literally speaking *dasānīkanī* should have been ten times bigger then *anīkanī*.

In the *Garga Saṁhitā* a typical sequence of formations comprising *senā*, *caturaṅgiṇī*, *vāhinī*, *dhvajinī*, *pṛtanā*, and *akṣauhiṇī* is given. It puts the strength of *vāhinī* at 400 elephants, 10,000 chariots, 4,00,000 horses and 1,00,00,000 infantry. *Dhvajinī* was double the strength of *vāhinī*, *pṛtanā* double the strength of *dhvajinī*, *anīkanī* double the strength of *pṛtanā* and *akṣauhiṇī* double the strength of *anīkanī*. The figures given in this text are just unbelievable.[280] In the *Dhanurveda* the highest military formation is called *Mahākṣauhiṇī*.[281]

The battle of Kurukṣetra was fought by 11 *akṣauhiṇīs* on the Kaurava side and 7 *akṣauhiṇīs* on the Pāṇḍava side, making a total of 18 *akṣauhiṇīs*.[282] On the last day of war this force was reduced to 3 *akṣauhiṇīs* on the Kaurava side and 1 *akṣauhiṇī* on the Pāṇḍava side.[283] This implies that fourteen *akṣauhiṇīs* or 30,61,800 (2,18,700x14) men perished in the great war. In reply to a question from Dhṛtarāṣṭra Yudhiṣṭhira said that as many as 1,66,00,20,006 men were killed and 24,165 went missing in the war.[284] In the *Rāmāyaṇa*, Rāvaṇa's army is stated to have comprised 10,000 elephants, 10,000 chariots, 20,000 horses, and 1,00,00,000 Rākṣasas.[285] The army of Rāma is said to have comprised 10,00,00,000 monkeys.[286] The strength of the armies and army units as stated in the epics and the Purāṇas is highly exaggerated and therefore, totally unbelievable.

Greek Accounts

The Greek historians have furnished the following figures regarding the strength of the armies of some Indian states in fourth century BC.

1. Army of Porus: 50,000 infantry, 3,000 cavalry, 1,000 chariots and 130 elephants.
2. Army of Kṣudraka and Mālava: 30,000 infantry, 10,000 cavalry and 700 chariots.
3. Army of Agalasseis: 40,000 infantry and 3,000 cavalry.
4. Army of Sobarcae: 60,000 infantry, 6,000 cavalry and 500 chariots.
5. Army of Agrammes (Nanda king): 2,00,000 infantry, 20,000 cavalry, 4,000 elephants and 2,000 chariots.
6. Army of Candragupta Maurya: 6,00,000 infantry, 30,000 horses, 36,000 elephants and 24,000 chariots.

These figures also appear highly exaggerated like the figures met in the epics and the Purāṇas. In this connection the observations made by Romila Thapar are notable.

The reliability of these figures can be doubted for various reasons: they are from sources which are later than the events which they describe; the locations of the cities are not always correct; the figures are said to be approximations, but the approximations could have been exaggerated in order to demonstrate the mighty armies with which Alexander had to do battle. It is curious that in many cases these are mentioned, but Alexander does not face the armies and is instead involved either in negotiations or in laying siege to the cities. The autonomous cities were small city-states and could not have maintained such large armies as listed in these sources. The figures mentioned were probably larger than even the population of the autonomous cities. If what Greek writers call autonomous cities were organized as *gaṇa-saṅghas* as Indian sources suggest, then it is unlikely that they would have maintained armies.

Commenting on the large army of Candragupta, Thapar says that 'there is an evident juggling with figures, and these need not therefore be taken literally'. Further, 'the main question is whether the Mauryan state would have had the finances to maintain armies as enormous as is represented in these figures'.[287] This could be said about the armies of other states as well.

In this context the observations made by Creveld are also significant. 'Given the roads, transport, and food storage technologies, the physical impossibility of feeding, let alone controlling, a field army much larger than 20,000 makes these ancient Indian battlefield troop strengths and casualty reports difficult to believe.'[288]

Evidence of *Arthaśāstra*

According to the *Arthaśāstra* the composition of army formations was based on the basic unit comprising a chariot or elephant, 5 horses, 15 soldiers and 15 guards.[289] A 1-chariot formation, when deployed in one row (1 centre, 2 flanks, 2 wings), included 5 chariots, 25 horses, 75 soldiers and 75 guards. A 3-chariot formation organized in three rows thus included 45 chariots, 225 horses, 675 soldiers and 675 guards.[290] The strength of 3-chariot formation could be raised up by adding 2-chariot formations to 5, 7, 9, 11, 13, 15, 17, 19 or 21.[291] In this manner the largest army formation of the *Arthaśāstra* included 315 chariots, 1,925 horses, 4,725 foot and 4,725 guards. Interestingly, 1-chariot unit, 3-chariot unit and 21-chariot unit of the *Arthaśāstra* compare well with the present-day company, battalion and divisional set up in respect of numbers.

Views of *Śukranīti*

According to *Śukranīti* an army should comprise infantry, cavalry, elephant corps, chariot corps, bullocks, camels and *bṛhannālika* (machine). The number of infantry soldiers was to be four times the cavalry soldiers, whereas bullocks were to number one-fifth and camels one-eighth of them. Elephants were to number one-fourth of the camel corps whereas the chariots were to be half of the elephants. The machines were to number double the chariots.[292] To illustrate, an army comprising 20,000 cavalry would include 80,000 infantry, 4,000 bullocks, 2,500 camels, 625 elephants, 312 chariots and 625 machines according to the dispensation of Śukrācārya. Bṛhannālikā is certainly a later interpolation, if it is interpreted to mean a machine gun.

COMMAND STRUCTURE

As the ruler was the highest authority of the state he was also the prime mover of the military machine. To begin with, king himself served as *senāpati* and the effusiveness of the Vedas about the fighting qualities of the king confirms this. Indra was the king and the commander of the Devas. Subsequently, with the growing size of the state and manifold increase in the responsibilities of the ruler, warfare became the primary concern of the *senāpati.* Still important decisions on military matters were taken with the approval of an advisory council which generally comprised the king, the minister and the commander-in-chief. The *Mahābhārata* speaks of a council which was presided over by the ruler and included three members who were patriotic, scholarly and adept in military matters.[293] The aspect of military consultations has been repeatedly emphasized in the epics.

The *Arthaśāstra* says that all undertakings of military nature should be preceded by consultations.

> He (King) should hold consulations with three or four councillors. For holding the consultation with one (only), he may not (be able to) reach a decision in difficult matters. And a single councillor behaves as he pleases without restraint. Holding consultation with two, he is controlled by the two if united and ruined by them if at war (with each other). With three or four, that becomes possible (only) with difficulty.[294]

It was advisable to hold consultations at a secluded place, which could not be peeped in even by birds, so that talks are not heard from outside.[295] The *Manusmṛti* also emphasizes the need for secret deliberations.[296]

In the *Rāmāyaṇa* there is an interesting reference to the importance of consultations. When in Laṅkā, Hanumān angered by the behaviour of the palace guards, ravaged many gardens and killed many Rākṣasas. Rāvaṇa to counter this threat sought the advice of his ministers stating that wise (*uttama*) people are guided by the considered advice tendered by the learned and well-wishers. He also stated that the advice tendered by ministers (*mantrī*) was of three types—best (*uttama*), medium (*madhyama*), and poor (*adhama*).[297] Before mounting the attack on Laṅkā, Rāma also held consultations with Sugrīva, Hanumān, Jāmavanta, Aṅgada, etc., for *mantra* was considered the root of all victories.[298] The *Manusmṛti* says that a ruler should appoint seven or eight advisers (*saciva*) after giving due thought to their bravery and ability to shoot the target and use arms.[299] It also states that military consultations should be made by the ruler at late hours of the night.[300] The *Śukranīti* also says that the king should consult his ministers on future undertakings at a secret place.[301] The *Agni Purāṇa* includes the following five subjects under the purview of consultations (*mantra*):[302]

1. Knowledge of the known
2. Confirmation of the known
3. Removal of doubts, when in two minds
4. Division of time and space
5. Safety against dangers

SENĀPATI

In the Vedic Age the office of *senāpati* did not exist and the king himself led the army to the battlefield.[303] In fact, the very creation of the institution of king was prompted by the need for a commander, who could vanquish the enemy.[304] In many Vedic hymns Indra is repeatedly described as king and commander.[305] In a particular hymn he is said to be surrounded by the powerful armies intent on repulsing the enemy forces.[306] Subsequently, the emergence of big states and consequent increase in the responsibilities of the ruler necessitated the office of *senānī*. Presumably, he was appointed by the king, not by the people, to command in war when the king became too important to lead every little fray in person.[307] Soon he came to enjoy the status of a *ratnin*.[308]

Importance

The appointment of *senāpati* was considered necessary for the proper conduct of war. This is borne out by an anecdote in the *Mahābhārata*: At one time a war took place between the Brāhmaṇa, Vaiśya and Śūdra coalition and the Kṣatriyas in which the latter emerged victorious. When asked about the secret of their victory the Kṣatriyas said that they owed it to their *senāpati*. Brāhmaṇas, knowing the secret of success appointed a *senāpati* and defeated the Kṣatriyas.[309] The moral of the story is that an army led by a sincere and brave *senāpati* conquers the enemy.[310] A Purāṇic story also confirms this. When the Devas suffered defeat after defeat at the hands of Asuras led by Tāraka, they went to god Viṣṇu for help. Viṣṇu advised them to appoint Kumāra, the son of god Śiva, as their *senāpati* to fight Asuras. Kumāra defeated many Asura leaders including Tāraka.[311]

In a war every effort was made to kill the enemy *senāpati*. A warrior who killed him was entitled to an award of 50,000 *paṇas* according to the *Arthaśāstra*.[312] The *Mahābhārata* says that a warrior who killed an enemy commander and mounted his chariot was equal to Viṣṇu in strength and Bṛhaspati in intelligence.[313] The commander on the other hand preferred death to the ignominy of falling into enemy hand.[314]

Consecration

The person appointed as *senāpati* was duly consecrated. This is reminiscent of the times when king functioned as *senāpati* as well. Hopkins says that 'the early king was his own Commander; the later Commander-in-Chief represented the dying military function of the now effeminate monarch'.[315] It was also a reminder of the older times when king was chosen by the people for his exceptional military qualities and invariably shouldered the burden of command.[316]

In the Epic war Duryodhana made Bhīṣma the commander-in-chief of the Kaurava army. This was done after performing the ritual of consecration.[317] Duryodhana also consecrated the eleven warriors, who led his 11 *akṣauhiṇīs* in war as *senāpatis*, before marching to the battlefield.[318] Yudhiṣṭhira also consecrated his seven *senāpatis* including Dhṛṣṭadyumna before joining the battle.[319] After the death of Bhīṣma, Droṇācārya was consecrated as the *senāpati* of Kaurava army by Duryodhana and other kings.[320] After the death of Droṇa, Karṇa was appointed as the *senāpati* of Kauravas. He was consecrated by the people of all castes with sanctified waters mixed with perfumes and medicines.[321] Subsequently, Śalya and Aśvatthāman were also consecrated as *senāpatis* of Kaurava army.[322] The *Rāmāyaṇa* also refers to this custom.[323]

Selection

The selection of a *senāpati* involved long deliberations. Pāṇḍavas appointed Dhṛṣṭadyumna as their *sarva-senāpati* (commander-in-chief) after a long debate.[324] After his appointment as *senāpati*, Bhīṣma addressed the Kaurava war council as follows:

> I dedicate my prayers to Śubrahmaṇya the generalissimo of gods and happily accept the responsibility of chief *senāpati* put on my shoulders. Being well-versed in the art and science of war, I know the way of conducting the regular and irregular (*bhṛtya* and *abhṛtya*) soldiers of different grades. Consider me Bṛhaspati in both strategy and tactics of war. I am expert in *deva, gandharva* and *mānuṣa* type of battle arrays. I will apply them against the Pāṇḍavas. Therefore, O king, discard all fears. I will fight with the enemy and protect your army. May the sorrow of your heart vanish.[325]

After the death of Droṇācārya, Aśvatthāman proposed the appointment of Karṇa as *senāpati.*[326] Duryodhana seconded the proposal and all allies agreed to it.[327]

In the battle of Kurukṣetra each of the 18 *akṣauhiṇīs*, which fought on the Kaurava and Pāṇḍava sides was led by a *senāpati.* The 11 *akṣauhiṇīs* of Kauravas were led by warriors like Kṛpācārya, Droṇācārya, Aśvatthāman, Śalya, Jayadratha, Sudakṣiṇa, Kṛtavarmā, Karṇa, Bhūriśravas, Śakuni and Bāhlīka.[328] On the Pāṇḍava side Yudhiṣṭhira appointed Drupada, Virāṭa, Sātyaki, Dhṛṣṭadyumna, Dhṛṣṭaketu, Śikhaṇḍin and Magadha king Sahadeva to lead his 7 *akṣauhiṇīs* as *senāpatis.* Dhṛṣṭadyumna was made *sarva-senāpati* in addition.[329] In another context the names of Dhṛṣṭaketu and Sahadeva are omitted and Bhīmsena and Cekitāna are said to be the commanders.[330]

In the selection of *senāpati*, caste was not considered a determining factor. Among the Kaurava *senāpatis* Bhīṣma was a Kṣatriya, Droṇa, Kṛpācārya and Aśvatthāman were Brāhmaṇas and Karṇa was a *Sūta*. Despite the fact that there were many senior commanders on both Kaurava and Pāṇḍava sides, it was for their exceptional knowledge of warfare, that Dhṛṣṭadyumna and Karṇa were selected *senāpatis*. According to the *Śukranīti* any person who was capable and brave could be appointed *senāpati* or *sainika* irrespective of his caste.[331] However, the Purāṇas and the *Nīti* works generally favour the appointment of a Brāhmaṇa or a Kṣatriya to the office of *senāpati*.[332]

The commander of the army was called *senānī* in Vedic Age.[333] In the later Vedic age the words *senānī*, *senāpati* and *pattīnām-pati* came to denote the office.[334] In the *Rāmāyaṇa*, the terms *senāpati*, *vāhinīpati*, *camūpati* and *sainyapāla* are used for the commander-in-chief.[335] The terms *senāpati* also finds mention in Pāli literature[336] and the *Arthaśāstra*.[337] During the Scytho-Kuṣāṇa rule the terms *kṣatrapa* and *mahākṣatrapa* have also been used in the sense of *senāpati*.[338] In the Gupta inscriptions the terms *mahābalādhikṛta*,[339] *mahābalādhyakṣa*[340] and *mahāsenāpati*[341] have been widely used in the sense of *senāpati*. Subsequently, the term *senādhyakṣa* and *senādhipati* also came into currency.[342]

The terms *mahābalādhyakṣa* and *mahābalādhikṛta*, widely met in the Gupta inscriptions, are generally interpreted to mean *senāpati*.[343] But a more closer look suggests that, *mahābalādhyakṣa* was the real synonym of *senāpati*. As the chiefs of the four arms of the army were called *adhyakṣas* such as *hastyādhyakṣa*, *rathādhyakṣa*, etc., the chief of all arms would have been appropriately designated as *mahābalādhyakṣa*. *Mahābalādhikṛta* was perhaps the minister, who looked after the military affairs of the state. In the Gupta period *senāpatis* were appointed in the provinces and perhaps the more powerful of them was designated *mahāsenāpati*,[344] a term which is used in inscriptions alongside the titles of *mahāsāmanta*, *mahārāja*, etc. Occasionally, the terms like *balamukhya*, *balanāyaka*, and *camūnātha* were also used for *senāpati*.[345]

Powers, Qualities and Privileges

The *senāpati* wielded great influence in the affairs of the state. The ruler discussed military matters with him for one and a half hour everyday.[346] Great rulers looked small in the presence of *senāpatis* like Bhīṣma and Droṇa. Prahasta, the *senāpati* of Rāvaṇa, enjoyed full control over the military machine of the state.[347] Siṁhanāda, the *senāpati* of Harṣavardhana, was again an influential person.[348] Inscriptions of the Gupta age and after bear witness to the importance of the office.

As stated earlier a serious debate preceded the selection of Dhṛṣṭadyumna as Pāṇḍava *senāpati.*[349] In this debate Nakula, Arjuna and Bhīma recommended the names of King Virāṭa, Dhṛṣṭadyumna and Śikhaṇḍin respectively, describing their exceptional qualities. Briefly, these qualities included knowledge, bravery, good character, morality, specialization in warfare, humanity, strength, truthfulness, reputation, etc.

The *Harṣacarita* says that a *senāpati* was expected to be an expert in warfare, courageous, modest, well-behaved, clever and well-versed in the *śāstras.*[350] Siṁhanāda, the *senāpati* of Thānesar is described as:

> a man foremost in every fight, in person yellow as a hill of orpiment, stately as a great full-grown sāl tree's stem, and tall as if ripened by valour's exceeding heat. . . . Of fury's fire he was the rubbing stick, of valour the lordliness, of arrogance the arrogant quality, of pride the erysipelas, of violence the heart, of martial ardour the life, of enterprise the panting gasp: to the infuriate a hook, of noxious kings an elephant's goad, the colophon of chivalry, the family priest of martial companies, the scale-beam of the brave . . . the sustainer of the routed, the executor of pledges, the authority on openings in great wars, the reveille-drum of battle devotees. His very voice, deep as the booming of a drum, inspired the warriors with lust for battle.[351]

These qualities of *senāpati* are also mentioned in the *Matsya Purāṇa,*[352] the *Kāmandaka Nīti* [353] and the *Śukranīti.*[354]

Senāpati enjoyed certain privileges. He lived in a palace and displayed a parasol like that of the queen and the prince.[355] He also wore a crown.[356] It appear that rulers occasionally conferred the titles like *sāmanta* or *mahāsāmanta* on him. This seems to explain the numerous references to the presence of *sāmantas* in the battlefield in the Gupta inscriptions.[357] Perhaps, the custom of granting fiefs to *senāpatis* in lieu of cash salary may also have turned many of them into *sāmantas.*

In the political system of ancient India *senāpati* occupied a crucial position. If not handled carefully a *senāpati* could cause the loss of throne and even life to the king. The founders of Śuṅga, Ābhīra and Maitraka dynasties were *senāpatis*.

OTHER RANKS

In the Vedic age there were military officers like *grāmaṇī* and *vrājapati* who perhaps led the troops under the overall command of *senānī*.[358] A foot soldier was called *patti*.[359] In sixth century BC *senāpati*, *aśvapati* and *sainika* or *yodhā* were important military ranks. The wielders of sword, spear and bow were known as *asika*, *prāsaka* and *dhanuṣka* respectively.[360]

In the Epic senior military officers are called *yūthapa*, *akṣauhiṇīpati*, *senāpati* and *vāhinīpati*.[361] *Daśādhipati*, *śatādhipati* and *sahasrādhipati* were the commanders of 10, 100 and 1000 soldiers respectively.[362] A common soldier was known as *sainika* or *yodha*.[363] The warriors who fought mounted on chariots were called *rathodara*, *rathī*, *ardharathī*, *mahārathī*, *atirathī* and *rathayūthapa-yūthapa*. Among the warriors Droṇa, Arjuna, Sātyaki and Abhimanyu held the rank of *rathayūthapa-yūthapa*, the highest military rank. Bhīṣma held the rank of *atirathī*, the second highest rank. Virāṭa, Drupada, Aśvatthāman, Kṛpācārya and Śalya were also *atirathīs*. In the *Rāmāyaṇa*, Rāma is called an *atirathī*. Yudhiṣṭhira, Nakula, Sahadeva, etc., were *rathīs*.[364]

Some other ranks mentioned in relation to chariot warriors included *śreṣṭharathī*, *dviguṇarathī*, *aṣṭaguṇarathī*, *rathamukhya*, etc. In another context the grading of commandant is mentioned as *adhipati*, *daśādhipati* and *śatādhipati*.[365]

In the Epic age, the commanders were very conscious of their might and rank. Karṇa, who was considered more powerful than two *rathīs*, was once called an *ardharathī* by Bhīṣma in an assembly of noted warriors. This so much hurt Karṇa that he refused to fight as long as Bhīṣma led the Kaurava army.[366]

RANKS IN *ARTHAŚĀSTRA*

The *Arthaśāstra* gives a clearer picture of rank structure of the army. The commander-in-chief or *senāpati* was the highest ranking military officer. Then followed the commanders of arms, viz., commander of elephant corps (*hastyadhyakṣa*), commander of chariot corps (*rathādhyakṣa*), commander of cavalry (*aśvādhyakṣa*), commander of infantry (*pattyadhyakṣa*) and also commander of ordnance (*āyudhā-gārādhyakṣa*) and commander of navy (*navādhyakṣa*).[367] Under these commanders there was a chain of deputy commanders. There were also officers who were assigned miscellaneous duties. To illustrate, the camp superintendent was responsible for proper arrangements during the stay of the army in a camp. But it appears that most of these appointments were administrative in nature. The officers responsible for conducting the troops in war are named *pattika* (or *padika*), *senāpati* and *nāyaka*.[368] In the later literature and epigraphic records the following military ranks are mentioned:[369]

1. *Mahāsenāpati, sarvadaṇḍanāyaka, kampanādhipati, mahā-balādhyakṣa:* Chiefs of the army.
2. *Senāpati, balādhyakṣa:* Senior military officers.
3. *Mahāvyūhapati:* Principal officer who arrayed the troops.
4. *Vyūhapati:* Officer who arrayed the troops.
5. *Mahāpilupati:* Principal officer of elephant corps.
6. *Pīlupati or Gajapati:* Officer of elephant corps.
7. *Mahāśvasādhanika:* Principal officer of cavalry.
8. *Aśvasādhanika, Aśvapati:* Officer of cavalry.
9. *Nāyaka:* A military officer.
10. *Dikpāla, avantapāla* and *prāntapāla:* Defender of the borders.
11. *Gulmapati:* Officer who led a *gulma* (an army unit).
12. *Durgapāla, koṭapāla:* Defender of fort.
13. *Kaṭakeśa, kaṭakādhīśa:* Officer who looked after the military camps.
14. *Khaṇḍarakṣa:* Defender of a *khaṇḍa* (territory).
15. *Bhaṭa, yodhā, yodhṛ:* Regular soldier.
16. *Cāṭa:* Irregular soldier.

Śukranīti

The *Śukranīti* gives an entirely different list of military ranks as follows:[370]

1. *Pattipāla* : Commander of 5 or 6 foot-soldiers
2. *Gaulmika* : Commander of 30 foot-soldiers
3. *Śatānīka* : Commander of 100 foot-soldiers
4. *Sāhaśrika* : Commander of 1,000 foot-soldiers
5. *Ayutika* : Commander of 10,000 foot-soldiers
6. *Nāyaka* : Commander of 20 elephants or 20 horses

7. *Senādhipa* : Commander of an army unit
8. *Senānī* : Commander of the troops

Śatānīka was a crucial rank as he was responsible for training the troops in the formation of battle arrays and also for managing provisions. In this he was assisted by an officer called *anuśātika*.[371]

Nītiprakāśikā

The *Nītiprakāśikā* also refers to the rank structure of the army, but in this it largely follows the Epic.[372] On top of the structure stood the commander-in-chief (*sarvasenādhipa*). Under him came *akṣauhiṇīpatis*. Then followed the commanders of *anīkanī, camū, pṛtanā, vāhinī, gaṇa, gulma, senāmukha* and *patti*. Each of these commanders led two or three formations, e.g. the commander of *senāmukha* led two or three *pattis*, commander of *gulma* two or three *senāmukhas*, and so on.

There were definite rules regarding the seniority of commanders and soldiers. It was laid down that whoever in whatever branch (of the service) has been first appointed to a command, should be secured in his seniority, and that his juniors should be under his orders. The king appointed eight commanders (beginning with *patti*) who were made subject to the orders of the commander of an *akṣauhiṇī*. The soldiers were thus ranked according to seniority.[373]

Strangely, in the above rank structure the *Nitīprakāśikā* does not mention any of the officers like *yuvarāja, atiratha, mahāratha*, etc., who have been referred to in connection with the salaries of army personnel.[374] Perhaps *yuvarāja, atiratha*, etc., indicated the status or rank of the person in the military hierarchy, whereas *akṣauhiṇīpati, vāhinīpati*, etc., referred to the office held by him.

SALARIES OF SOLDIERS

Vedic System

The institution of salaried soldier did not exist in the Vedic period as there were no regular armies. In times of war men enlisted as soldiers voluntarily. They carried weapon, mounted a horse or chariot and fought under their own commander. The village contingents also joined in with their own weapons. The people generally fought for their own safety, and did not expect much from the state in return.

The love for adventure as also loot, plunder and share in booty may also have encouraged men to take up arms.[375] The assumption of Hopkins that in the pre-epic period the soldier's pay was a part of the booty thus seems to be nearer to the truth.[376] In fact, rules had been framed about the distribution of spoils among various arms and the chariot corps was entitled to a larger share, accounting for one-fourth of the total booty.[377] The term *vetana* (salary) figures in the *Aṣṭādhyāyī*[378] indicating that soldiers were paid salary for the service rendered by them in the sixth century BC.

EPIC TIMES

The Epic says that an enlisted soldier 'belonged wholly to the king and drew his pay from his valour, or, later still, from a regular stipend plus what (with certain exceptions) his individual bravery enabled him to seize as private booty on the field of war. . . . He receives a regular wage which ought to be paid in advance.'[379] Andhaka-Vṛṣṇi soldiers of Dvārakā received a fixed salary, as also uniform and weapons from the state.[380] In the army of Yudhiṣṭhira all soldiers were paid good salaries.[381] An expert archer could earn a salary of 1,00,000 coins per annum.[382] In exceptional circumstances an archer could be given a high salary of 1,000 coins per diem.[383]

In the Epic times judicious distribution of salary was considered necessary to keep the army contented. In the *Mahābhārata* sage Nārada asks King Yudhiṣṭhira: 'Do you give to your troops the sanctioned rations and wages at the appointed time or do you cause resentment by withholding them? Do you know that irritation caused by arrears of pay and irregularity in the distribution of rations goads the troops to rebellion.'[384] During his meeting with Bharata, Rāma also emphasized the need for timely payment of salary to the soldiers.[385] Dhṛtarāṣṭra felt sad when his soldiers were repeatedly defeated by Arjuna, despite the fact that they were treated well and offered good salaries.[386] When Yudhiṣṭhira ascended the throne he appointed Nakula to supervise the matters related to food (*bhakta*) and salary (*vetana*) of the army.[387]

Nothing definite is known about the pay structure of the soldiers of the Mauryan army. But the Greek accounts attest to the fact that the soldiers were paid handsome salaries to enable them to live frugally. According to Arrian 'the pay which they receive from the state being so liberal that they can with ease maintain themselves and others besides'.[388]

Arthaśāstra on Salaries

The *Arthaśāstra* says that the salaries of state employees were based on certain principles. These could exhaust one quarter of the state revenue, while conforming with the principles of *dharma* and *artha*.[389] Grain could be substituted for cash wages on the basis of the formula that an annual salary of 60 *paṇas* is equal to 1 *āḍhaka* of grain per day. One *āḍhaka* sufficed for four meals for one Āryan male.[390] Important military functionaries were entitled to the following pay per annum.[391]

1.	Commander-in-Chief (सेनापति):	48,000 *paṇas*
2.	Chief of Palace Guards (दैवारिक):	24,000 *paṇas*
3.	City Commandant/Director of Factories (पौरनायक/कर्मान्तिक):	12,000 *paṇas*
4.	Chief Commanders of Infantry, Cavalry, Elephent Corps & Chariot Corps (हस्त्यश्वरथमुख्याः):	8,000 *paṇas*
5.	Deputy Commander of Infantry, etc. (पत्त्यश्वरथहस्त्यध्यक्षः):	4,000 *paṇas*
6.	Camp Superintendent, Chariot Rider and Physician (रथिकानीकस्थचिकित्सकः) :	2,000 *paṇas*
7.	King's Charioteer (सूत):	1,000 *paṇas*
8.	Specialist Soldiers (शिल्पवन्तः पादताः):	500 *paṇas*

The salaries were fixed in accordance with the nature and responsibilities of the office held by a person. The chiefs of various arms and other senior commanders were paid handsomely so that they were not tempted by bribe and thought of revolt.[392] The sons and wives of those who died on duty were entitled to food and wages and their old and sick dependants also received help from the state. The king was obliged to grant them money and do them honour on occasions.[393]

In the Gupta age regular salaries were paid to the state employees like bodyguards and soldiers. The Chinese traveller Fa-hien has reported that in the country of Mathurā the 'King's bodyguards and attendants all have salaries'.[394] The imperial Guptas thus followed the wise policy of the Mauryans in paying fixed salaries to their troops.[395]

VIEWS OF *ŚUKRANĪTI*

The *Śukranīti* refers to the salaries of the soldiers but does not specify them. It states that full pay should be granted to those who are trained soldiers and half pay to those who are under training.[396] The rulers are advised to enhance the salary of their officers by about a quarter at the beginning of an expedition.[397] The *Śukranīti* does not specify the salaries given to various ranks of the army but it mentions the status enjoyed by them *vis-à-vis* the civilian administrators as follows:[398]

1. *Sādin* (horseman):	Head of a village.
2. *Śatānīka* (Commander of 100 troops):	Head of the ten villages (*nāyaka*). He could travel on horseback with attendants.
3. *Sāhaśrika* (Commander of 1,000 troops):	Head of 100 villages (*sāmanta*). He could travel in chariot or on horse with 10 attendants.
4. *Ayutika* (Commander of 10,000 troops):	Head of 1,000 villages (*māṇḍalika*). He could travel by a vehicle drawn by two horses with 10 attendants.
5. Commander of 50,000 troops:	Head of 10,000 villages (*svarāṭ*). He could use vehicle drawn by 4 horses with 10 attendants.

As the annual income of *sāmanta*, *māṇḍalika* and *svarāṭ* was rated over 1,00,000, 10,00,000 and 1,00,00,000 rupees (*karṣa*) respectively, the pay of military officers of equivalent status could be calculated accordingly.[399] The salary of *senādhipa* may have been much more than that of the commander of 50,000 troops, indeed.

NĪTIPRAKĀŚIKĀ

The *Nītiprakāśikā* also deals with the salaries of army personnel in some detail. They were entitled to following salaries per mensum.[400]

1. Crown Prince (*Yuvarāja*)	5,000 *varvas*
2. Commander-in-Chief (*Sarvasenāpranetra*)	4,000 "
3. *Atiratha* (Supreme Chariot-commander)	3,000 "

4. *Mahāratha* (Great Chariot-commander)	2,000 *varvas*
5. *Rathika/Gajayodhi* (Chariot or Elephant-commander)	1,000 "
6. *Ardharatha* (Deputy Chariot-commander)	500 "
7. *Ekaratha/Gajasādin* (Chariot-or Elephant-Warrior)	300 *niṣkas*
8. *Sarvāśvādhipati* (Commander of Cavalry)	3,000 "
9. *Padātādhipati* (Commander of Infantry)	2,000 "
10. Commander of 1,000 Infantry	500 "
11. Commander of 1,000 Cavalry	1,000 "
12. Cavalry Soldier, Charioteer, Standard-bearer, etc.	7 *varvas*
13. Foot-Soldier	3 *suvarṇas*

In this connection the *Nītiprakāśikā* refers to coins of three denominations, viz., *varvas, niṣkas* and *suvarṇas.* After examining the salary structure it appears that those coin types enjoyed the same value. The salary of *atiratha* as 3,000 *varvas* and that of *sarvāśvādhipati* as 3,000 *niṣkas* appears matching. But the reference to different coin types in giving salaries to different army personnel is difficult to explain.

PENSION

In ancient India there also existed the system of granting pension to retired soldiers and the dependents of the soldiers killed in battle.[401] The *Arthaśāstra* says that

> of those dying while on duty, the sons and wives shall receive the food and wages. And their minor children, old and sick persons should be helped. And he should grant them money and do honour on occasions of death, illness and birth ceremonies. If he has a small treasury, he should give forest produce, cattle and fields and a little money.[402]

In this connection, the *Nītiprakāśikā* has the following details:

> To the relations of those who have for his sake been killed in battle by the enemy, and also to those who are worn out (*sevayā jīritā*) in his service, he should give pensions (*jīvanam*).

> To the families of those who are dead and to those who are living, but have in the past served the king very faithfully, he should give half of their former pay (*ardhijīvanam*).

To the young soldiers, who while facing the enemy in battle become cripples and unfit for service of the king he should give half of their former pay.[403]

DEFENCE PRODUCTION

In early days man fought with stones and sticks. Gradually, he started shaping these objects to make them more effective. Subsequently, the invention of metal enabled him to produce more powerful weapons. The evolution of large states necessitated large armies and also the mechanism to provide them with weapons.

EARLY SYSTEM

The organized defence production in India perhaps started with the Harappan people. The archaeological findings from the Harappan sites include copper and bronze weapons like, arrow, mace, javelin, etc.[404] According to Piggot the uniformity in the make and shape suggests that some trade guilds working under state supervision and control manufactured these weapons.[405]

In the Vedic age professionals were engaged in the production of weapons and equipment for war purposes.[406] These professionals were divided in various castes such as *rathakāra* (maker of chariots), *iṣukāra* (maker of shafts), *jyākāra* (maker of bow-strings) and *dhanuṣkāra* (maker of bows).[407] It would thus appear that production of various types of weapons required specialization. The department engaged in the production of nooses manufactured *jyā-pāśa*,[408] *kavaca-pāśa*[409] and *apva-pāśa.*[410] In the Vedas there are many references to *varuṇa-pāśa.*[411] In the Vedic age the craftsmen engaged in the production of bows and arrows, called *karmāra-takṣa*, commanded great respect in the society.[412] Perhaps, the craftsmen were given raw material and monetary assistance by the state for producing weapons and equipment. In the *Aṣṭādhyāyī* of Pāṇini such craftsmen are referred to as *rājya-śilpin* (state-artisans).[413]

The epics refer to the participation of the state in defence production. King Daśaratha settled expert artisans in his kingdom to manufacture weapons.[414] The *Mahābhārata* says that the weapon makers were settled, aided and at times honoured by the state, suggesting that the industry of defence production functioned under the state control. The state supplied raw material and tools (*dravyopakaraṇam*) to all artisans (*sarvaśilpīnām*) for four months at a time. They were also given four months wages in advance.[415] A ruler was expected to maintain large stocks of military ware such as armour made of the skin of cow, ox and python for elephants, nails of iron, armour of skin for soldiers, quality weapons, flags and banners of various colours and many types of weapons for ready use.[416] The *Manusmṛti* refers to arm dealers (*śastra vikrayiṇo*)[417] and producers (*śilpibhiḥ*).[418] The craftsmen were allotted space within the fort to undertake arms production. The king made regular inspection of weapons and stores.[419] The Brāhmaṇas engaged in the production of weapons like bows and arrows did not command respect in the society.[420]

System in *Arthaśāstra*

According to the *Arthaśāstra*,

> the superintendent of armoury *Āyudhāgārādhyakṣa* should cause to be made machines for use in battles, for the defence of the forts and for assault on enemies' cities, also weapons, armours and accoutrements by artisans and artists expert in those lines, producing goods with an agreement as to the amount of work, time allowed and wages, and should store them in places suitable for each. He should frequently change their places and expose them to sun and wind. He should store in a different way what is being damaged by heat, moisture or insects. And he should know them by their class, appearance, characteristics, quantity, source, price and place of storing.[421]

The space for the workshops to the workers engaged in defence production, including items like shields, armours, leather, etc., was provided in the north-west part of the fort whereas residential space was allotted to them in western quarter of the fort.[422] The defence goods thus produced such as stones, spades, axes, arrows, choppers, etc., were to be stored carefully inside the fort.[423] In short, he ensured the production of all kinds of fixed machines (*sthitayantrāṇi*), mobile machines (*calayantrāṇi*), weapons (*āyudhāni*), armour (*varmāni*), shields (*āvaraṇāni*) and accoutrements (*upakaraṇāṇi*).[424]

In times of war an *āyudhāgāra* was established at the army camp,[425] perhaps to meet the immediate needs of the army. The *Agni Purāṇa* says that *āyudhāgārādhyakṣa* should be intelligent and well conversant with various types of weapons.[426] His functions included the following:

1. To employ experienced workmen to manufacture arms and armour.
2. To stock weapons in the armoury after their approval by examiner.
3. To issue weapons to soldiers and collect them back after training.
4. To maintain accounts of expenditure.
5. To supervise the work of his subordinates.

Greek Accounts

There is some interesting evidence of state control on defence production in India in Greek accounts. Referring to the artisans engaged in defence production, Megasthenese says that they were exempted from paying taxes and even received maintenance from royal exchequer.[427] They constituted the fourth class of Indian society and were engaged in many trades.

> Some of them pay tributes and render to the state certain prescribed services. But the armour makers and ship builders receive wages and their victuals from the king, for whom alone they work. The general in command of the army, supplies the soldiers with weapons, and the admiral of the fleet jets out ships on hire for the transport of both passengers and merchandize.[428]

Arrian puts it slightly differently

> The fourth class consists of handicraftsmen and retail dealers. They have to perform gratuitously certain public services and to pay tribute from the products of their labour. An exception is, however, made in favour of those who fabricate weapons of war and not only so, but they even draw pay from the state. In the class are included the ship builders and the sailors employed in the navigation of the rivers.[429]

State control over the military machine was near complete as reported by Strabo: 'There are royal stables for the horses and elephants, and also a royal magazine for the arms, because the soldier has to return his arms to the magazine and his horse and his elephant to the stables.'[430]

Foreign invaders like the Greeks, the Śakas and the Kuṣāṇas introduced Indians to a new system of weapons and warfare. The *Milindapañho*, refers to three industries engaged in the manufacture of bows, arrows and other weapon types.[431] The emergence of mounted bowman led to far-reaching changes in the military costume and weapon system. A heavy javelin, heavy straight long sword, double-curved bow and the defensive armour were new innovations in weaponry. In this context the following observation of R.S. Sharma is notable:

> Six types of lances, six types of swords, various types of sheaths, three types of shields and five types of daggers are known from the sculptures of the period. These sculptures obviously belong to the second century BC-second century AD. . . . These sculptures suggest that weapon making was a thriving industry and inscriptions indicate that blacksmiths and traders in iron objects were an important group, and their activities may have something to do with the steel goods that were sent to Rome.[432]

The Gupta rulers, perhaps enriched traditional weapon system with this new-found knowledge. The *Viṣṇudharmottara Purāṇa* also furnishes some useful information on defence production. By the time it was composed some regions of the country had specialized in the production of certain weapon types like bows,[433] arrows,[434] and swords.[435]

SALUTATION

In the *Rāmāyaṇa* many types of salutations are mentioned, viz., *praṇāma*,[436] *prāñjali*,[437] *añjalipuṭa*[438] and *praṇipāta*.[439] The hand-shake was also in vogue.[440] But which of these types was followed by the soldiers is not mentioned. In seventh century AD the military salute was made by bowing and touching the sword with the forehead.[441]

WOMEN IN ARMS

In Vedic India women did not generally participate in war but quite a few of them knew the art of wielding weapons. Viśpalā, the wife of King Khela, accompanied her husband in war and in the process lost one of her legs. Aśvins treated her and provided her with an iron leg. She finally won the battle.[442] Indrasenā, the wife of sage Mudgala, fought a gang of dacoits with her husband. When the sage became tired she picked up his bow and chased away the dacoits.[443] The non-Āryan (*dāsa*) women, who were more enthusiastic soldiers, perhaps underwent some kind of military training. They commanded respect as warriors and brave men of the times did not consider it ungallant to cross-sword with them.[444]

Greek accounts report that in fourth century BC women actively participated in war in some states of north-west India. Alexander treacherously attacked a military camp of Massaga and caused heavy casualties among the soldiers.

> When many were thus wounded and not a few killed, the women, picking the arms of the fallen, fought side by side with the men, for the imminence of the danger and the great interest at stake forced them to do violence to their nature, and to take an active part in the defence. Accordingly, some of them who had supplied themselves with arms, did their best to cover their husbands with their shields, while others who were without arms did much to impede the enemy by bringing themselves upon them and catching hold of their shields. The defenders, however, after fighting desperately along with their wives were at last overpowered by superior numbers.[445]

Incidentally, Kaikeyī, the wife of Daśaratha, the ruler of Ayodhyā, hailed from this region.

When the Mauryan king went out on hunting he was accompanied by a crowd of women—'some on the chariots, some on horses and some even on elephants, and they are equipped with weapons of every kind, as if they were going on a campaign'.[446] The *Arthaśāstra* says that 'when risen from the bed, he (king) should be surrounded by female guards bearing bows'.[447] In later literature the women appear performing the duty of bodyguard, standard-bearer and arms-bearer of the king. This implies that these women underwent some sort of military training.

This is also borne out by the art evidence. In Sāñcī reliefs (northern gate) some female pairs have been depicted with drawn swords and bucklers in their hands.[448] This surely proves that occasionally women also picked up sword. Significantly, the Ranigumpha cave at Udayagiri depicts a violent combat between a man and a woman, both equipped with drawn swords and shields.[449]

In the *Mahābhārata* there is a reference to a large number of *mātrikās* (female warriors), who assisted Skanda in his war with demons like Tārakāsura and Mahiṣāsura.[450] Purāṇas also furnish some interesting evidence on this point. Durgā, the mother goddess, battled with many demons and Purāṇas are full of her heroic exploits. In the

Brahmāṇḍa Purāṇa the bravery of Lalitā and her *śaktis* (troops), who fought with Asura Vāsukī, is vividly described.[451] This proves beyond doubt that Indian women were not totally ignorant of the art of war.

During the march of the army the wives (*kalatra*) were positioned in the centre along with the king and the treasury.[452] But it was generally believed that an army without women could perform better in the battlefield.[453]

The military organization in ancient India, theoritically speaking, provided for all the necessary ingredients to meet the challenges of war. The army was organized in various categories and arms and the role of each category and arm was specified. The social system did not deprive any class of people from military service. An effective supply system maintained the army in the field. Troops were organized in units and sub-units for proper command and control. Strong command structure framed the policy of war. *Senāpati* led the army into war. All men under arms were paid respectable salaries. State looked after a well oiled defence production apparatus. How the Indians applied this system for conducting wars would be seen in the following chapter.

NOTES

1. स्वाम्यमात्यश्च राष्ट्रं च दुर्गं कोषो बलं सुहृत्।
   परस्परोपकारीदं सप्तांङ्ग राज्यमुच्यते।। *Kāmandaka Nīti*, 4.1;
   स्वाम्यमात्यसुहृत्कोशराष्ट्रदुर्गबलानि च।
   सप्तांगमुच्यते राज्यं तत्र मूर्द्धा नृपः स्मृतः।। *Śukranīti*, 1.61.
2. *Śukranīti*, Ibid.
3. सेना शस्त्रास्त्रसंयुक्तमनुष्यादिगणात्मिका। Ibid., 4.7.1.
4. मित्राटविबलं चैव मौलभृत्यबलं तथा।
   सर्वमेतद् बलं ग्राह्यं वर्जयित्वा द्विषद्बलम्।। *Ram*, Yuddha, 17.24.
5. आददीत बलं राजा मौलं मित्रबलं तथा।
   अटवीबलं भृतं चैव तथा श्रेणीबलं च यत्।। *Mahābhārata* (*MB*), Āśrama, 12.7;
   In this connection it is remarkable that in Sabhā Parvan (5.53) the *śreṇī* and *amitra balas* are not mentioned. However, in Āśramavāsika Parvan only *amitra-bala* is omitted.
6. स मौलभृतश्रेणिमित्रामित्राटवीबलानां सारफल्गुतां विद्यात्। *AS*, 2.33.8; also 7.8.27, 9.2.1.

7. *Kāmandaka Nīti*, 18.3-23.
8. मौलं भृतं श्रेणिसुहृद्द्विषदाटविकं बलम्। *Agni Pu.*, 242.1-2.
9. मौल भृत्यं तथा मैत्रं श्रैणमाटविकं बलम्।
अमित्रमपरं षष्टं सप्तमं नोपलभ्यते।। *Mānasollāsa*, 2.6.556.
10. मौलभृतमित्रश्रेणी बलावाप्त राज्यश्रीः J.F. Fleet, *Corpus Inscriptionum Indicarum*, vol. III, p. 165.
11. तत्र मित्रबलं राजन् मौलेन च विशिष्यते।
श्रेणीबलं भृतं चैव तुल्य एवेति मे मतिः।। *MB*, Āśrama, 12.7-8.
12. भृताश्च बहवो योधाः परीक्ष्यैव महारथाः।
वेतनेन यथायोग्यं प्रियवादेन चापरे।। *MB*, Droṇa, 89.21.
13. तथा यद् ग्रामकृत्यं स्याद् ग्रामिकृत्यं च ते स्वयम्।।
धर्मज्ञः सचिवः कश्चित्तत्प्रपश्येदतन्द्रितः।
Ibid., Śānti, 88.9.
14. मौलभृतकश्रेणीमित्रामित्राटवीबलानां समुद्दानकालाः। *AS*, 9.2.1; also T. Watters, *Travels*, vol. I, p. 171.
15. तद्भावभावित्वान्नित्यसत्कारानुगमाच्च मौलबलं भृतबलाच्छ्रेयः। Ibid., 9.2.14; also T. Watters, op. cit., p. 171.
16. पितृपुत्रभ्रातृकाणामायुधीयानामध्वजं मुण्डानीकं राजस्थानम्। *AS*, 10.3.39; *MB*, Ādi, 40; P.V. Kane, *History of Dharmaśāstra*, vol. III, p. 200.
17. J.W. M'crindle, *Ancient India*, p. 85.
18. Ibid., p. 211.
19. *AS*, 9.2.14.
20. तद्भावभावित्वान्नित्यसत्कारानुगमाच्च मौलबलं भृतबलाच्छ्रेयः। Ibid., 9.2.14; *Śukranīti*, 4.7.182-3.
21. T. Watters, op. cit., p. 171.
22. नित्यानन्तरं क्षिप्रोत्थायि वश्यं च भृतबलं श्रेणीबलाच्छ्रेयः। *AS*, 9.2.15.
23. आयुधाच्छ च। *Aṣṭādhyāyī*, 4.4.14.
24. कम्बोजसुराष्ट्रक्षत्रियश्रेण्यादयो वार्त्ताशस्त्रोपजीविनः। *AS*, 11.1.4.
25. T. Watters, op. cit., p. 171.
26. J.W. M'crindle, *Ancient India*, p. 193.
27. *AS*, 9.2.16.
28. जनपदमेकार्थोपगतं तुल्यसंघर्षामर्षसिद्धिलाभं च श्रेणीबलं मित्रबलाच्छ्रेयः। Ibid., 9.2.16; also 9.2.4, 7.16.16.
29. Moti Chandra, *Sārthavāha*, pp. 64-5, 178.
30. J.F. Fleet, op. cit., vol. III, p. 85.
31. *Kāmandaka Nīti*, 19.5-6.
32. *AS*, 9.2.1, 5.
33. अपरिमितदेशकालमेकार्थोपगमाच्च मित्रबलममित्रबलाच्छ्रेयः। Ibid., 9.2.17.
34. Ibid., 9.2.1, 6.

35. अविलोपे व्यसने च ताभ्यामहिभयं स्यात्। Ibid., 9.2.20.
36. आर्याधिष्ठितममित्रबलमटवीबलाच्छ्रेयः। Ibid., 9.2.18.
37. Ibid.
38. पर्वतोपान्तसंवासिनिषादम्लेच्छजातिकम्। अधमंतत्समाख्यातं बलमाटविकंबुधैः।। *Mānasollāsa*, 2.6.559.
39. Ibid.,
40. नरहस्तिरथाश्वानां सारं मध्यं च फल्गु च।
    सर्वेष्वेतेष्वनीकेषु संदिदेश महीपतिः।। *MB*, Udyoga, 152.2.
41. Ibid.
42. *AS*, 10.5, 44-5.
43. स्वगमान्यगमा चेति द्विधा सैव प्रथक् त्रिधा।
    दैव्यासुरी मानवी च पूर्वपूर्वा बलाधिका।।
    स्वगमा या स्वयं गन्त्री यानगार्न्यिगमा स्मृता।
    पादातं स्वगमं चान्यद् रथाश्वगजगं त्रिधा।। *Śukranīti*, 4.7.2-3.
44. सेनाबलंतु द्विविधं स्वीयं मैत्रं च तद् द्विधा।
    मौलसाद्यस्कभेदाभ्यां सारासारं पुनर्द्विधा।।
    आशिक्षितं शिक्षितं च गुल्मीभूतमगुल्मकम्।
    दत्तास्त्रादि स्वशस्त्रास्त्रं स्ववाहि दत्तवाहनम्।। Ibid., 4.7.9-10.
45. Ibid., 4.7.11-14.
46. N. Subrahmanian, *Saṅgam Polity*, p. 142.
47. प्रभावोत्साहशक्तिभ्यां मंत्रशक्तिः प्रशस्यते।
    प्रभावोत्साहवान्काव्यो जितो देवपुरोधसा।। *Agni Pu.*, 241.1.
48. Ibid., 133-5, 148, etc.
49. Macdonell and Keith, *Vedic Index*, vol. II, p. 334.
50. Ibid., vol. I, p. 247.
51. धर्म्याद्धि युद्धाच्छ्रेयोऽन्यत्क्षत्रियस्य न विद्यते। *MB*, Bhīṣma, 24.31.
52. अस्ति कश्चिद्विशिष्टो वा मद्विधो वा भवेद्युधि।
    शूद्रो वैश्यः क्षत्रियो वा ब्राह्मणो वापि शस्त्रभृत्।। *MB*, Udyoga, 94.7.
53. *Manusmṛti*, 3.163.
54. एकस्थाः सर्ववर्णास्ते। *MB*, Bhīṣma, 1.9.
55. एवं वर्णस्य वर्णस्य समुच्चीय सहस्रशः। *MB*, Sabhā, 54.25.
56. ब्राह्मणाः क्षत्रिया वैश्यास्तथा शूद्राश्च सम्मताः।
    तुष्टुवुस्तं महात्मानमभिषिक्तं वरासने।। Ibid., Karṇa, 10.47, Bombay Edition (BE).
57. 'ब्राह्मणक्षत्रियवैश्यशूद्रसैन्यानां तेजः प्राधान्यात्पूर्वं पूर्वं श्रेयः संनाहयितुम्' इत्याचार्यः। नेति कौटिल्यः। प्रणिपातेन ब्राह्मणबलं परोऽभिहारयेत्। प्रहरणविद्याविनीतं तु क्षत्रियबलं श्रेयः, बहुलसारं वा वैश्यशूद्रबलमिति। *AS*, 9.2.21-4; also 12.1.3-5.
58. युद्धाधिकारः शूद्रस्य स्वयं चाऽर्पिदि शिक्षया। *Agni Pu.*, 249.8.

59. प्रवासायासदु:खेषु युद्धेषु च कृतश्रम:।
अद्वैध्य: क्षत्रियप्रायो दण्डो दण्डविदां मत:।। *Kāmandaka Nīti*, 4.65.
60. शूद्रा वा क्षत्रिया वैश्या म्लेच्छा संकरसम्भवा:।
सेनाधिपा: सैनिकाश्च कार्या राज्ञा जयार्थिना।। *Śukranīti*, 2.140.
61. *Mṛcchakaṭika*, 6.22-23.
62. S. Beal, *Life of Hiuen Tsang*, vol. I, p. 77.
63. यथाचरितमेवात्र शस्त्रपत्रं विधीयते।
आचारादेव पुरुषस्तथा कर्मसु वर्तते।।
गान्धारा: सिन्धुसौवीरा नखरप्रासयोधिन:।
आभीरा: सुबलिनस्तद्बलं सर्वपारगम्।।
सर्वशस्त्रेषु कुशला: सत्त्ववन्तो ह्युशीनरा:।
प्राच्या मातंगयुद्धेषु कुशला: शठयोधिन:।।
तथा यवनकाम्बोजा मथुरामभितश्च ये।
एते नियुद्धकुशला दाक्षिणात्यासिचर्मिण:।। *MB*, Śānti, 102.2-5.
64. कुरुक्षेत्रांश्च मत्स्यांश्च पञ्चालाञ्शूरसेनजान्।
दीर्घांल्लघूंश्चैव नरानग्रानीकेषु योजयेत्।। *Manusmṛti*, 7.193.
65. दक्षिणात्याश्च विज्ञेया: कुशला: खड्गवर्मिण:।।
वंङ्कला धान्विनो ज्ञेया: पर्वतीयास्तथैव च।।
पाषाणयुद्धकुशलास्तथा पर्वतवासिन:।
पांचाला: शूरसेनाश्च रथेषु कुशला नरा:।।
कम्बोजा ये च गान्धारा: कुशलास्ते हयेषु च।।
प्रायशश्च तथा म्लेच्छा विज्ञेया पाशयोधिन:।।
अंगा वंगा कलिंगाश्च ज्ञेया मातंगयोधिन:। *Vis. Dh. Purāṇa*, 2.177.40-3.
66. प्रांशव: शुकनासाश्च ये चाजिप्रेक्षणा नरा:।
संहतभ्रूयुगाश्चैव क्रोधिन: कलहप्रिया:।।
नित्यहृष्टा: प्रहृष्टाश्च शूरा ज्ञेयाश्च कामिन:। *Agni Pu.*, 236.43-4.
67. शस्त्रं द्विजातिभिर्ग्राह्यं धर्मो यत्रोपरुध्यते।
द्विजातीनां च वर्णानां विप्लवे कालकारिते।। *Manusmṛti*, 8.348.
68. The elephant entered the Indian battlefield much later.
69. पत्तीनां पतये नम:। *Yajurveda*, 16.19.
नम: सेनाभ्य: सेनानिभ्यश्च वो नमो। Ibid., 16.26.
70. नमो अश्वेभ्यो अश्वपतिभ्यश्च वो नमो। Ibid., 16.24.
71. नमो रथिभ्यो अरथेभ्यश्च वो नमो। Ibid., 16.26.
72. नमो गणेभ्यो गणपतिभ्यश्च वो नमो। Ibid., 16.25.
73. नमस्तक्षभ्यो रथकारेभ्यश्च वो नमो। Ibid., 16.27.
74. नमो आशुशेणाय चाशुरथाय च। Ibid., 16.34.
75. हस्त्यश्वरथपदातीनाम्। *Sāmavidhāna Brāhmaṇa*, 3.6.11.
76. सेना-अङ्गानाम्। *Aṣṭādhyāyī*, 2.4.2.

77. पदात्यश्वरथद्विपैः। *MB*, Droṇa, 19.15; also Udyoga, 19.1, 30.25; चतुरङ्गबलोपेताः। Vana, 17.2; Karṇa, 15.11; वाहिनीं चतुरङ्गिगिणीम्। Virāṭa, 63.13; Śalya, 8.2, 22.84.
78. चतुरङ्गेण सैन्येन। *Rām*, Yuddha, 3.25.
79. *Aṅguttara Nikāya*, vol. III, pp. 116, 282; in *Saṁyukta Nikāya*, *Jātakas* and *Milindapraśna* there are many references to fourfold army.
80. *AS*, 10.4.
81. शिविरमार्गसेतुकूपतीर्थशोधनकर्म यंत्रायुधावरणोपकरणग्रासवहन-मायोधनाच्चप्रहरणावरण-प्रतिविद्धापनयनमिति विष्टिकर्माणि। *AS*, 10.4.17.
82. A. Foucher and J. Marshall, *Monuments of Sāñcī*, pl. 15.
83. J.W. M'crindle, *Ancient India*, p. 88.
84. स राजा महतीं सेनां योजयित्वा षडङ्गिनीम्। *MB*, Udyoga, 94.16;
यदा स्यान्महती सेना हयनागरथाकुला।
पदातियंत्र बहुला स्वनुरक्ता षडङ्गिनी।। *Śānti*, 104.37; *Manusmṛti*, 7.185.
85. षडगं मंत्रकोशाभ्यां पदात्यश्वरथद्विपैः।। *Kāmandakīya Nīti*, 19.24; also *Agni Pu*, 242.2; *Raghuvaṁśa*, 4.26.
86. रथा नागा हयाश्चैव पादाताश्चैव पाण्डव।
विष्टिर्नावश्चराश्चैव देशिकाः पथि चाष्टकम्।। *MB*, Śānti, 59.41;also 121.43-4.
87. अङ्गान्येतानि कौरव्य प्रकाशानि बलस्य तु।
जङ्गमाजङ्गमाश्चोक्ताश्चूर्णयोगा विषादयः।। Ibid., Śānti, 59.42.
88. *Agni Pu.*, 236.44-9; For details see *Agni Pu.*, 242.23-31.
89. *Agni Pu.*, 242.26-7.
90. The army of the confederacy of ten kings was more than 60,000. *Ṛgveda*, 1.53.9; Elsewhere, 1,00,000 troops are mentioned. Also 4.16.13, 30.21.
91. Indra captured large wealth with the help of his infantry and chariot corps. *Ṛgveda*, 1.100.10.
92. S.D. Singh, *Ancient Indian Warfare*, p. 9.
93. पदातिबहुला सेना दृढा भवति भारत। *MB*, Śānti, 101.21.
94. This is evident from the Greek records, see J.W. M'crindle, *The Invasion of India.*
95. J.W. M'crindle, *Ancient India*, pp. 220-1.
96. Ibid., p. 221.
97. Ibid., p. 139.
98. *AS*, 10.4.16; also 10.4.2; 7.10.34-5.
99. U.P. Thapliyal, *Indo-Iranica*, 1975, p. 10.
100. *Kāmandaka Nīti*, 19.36-39; The *Agni Purāṇa* describes the infantry as the winning factor.
सेना पदातिबहुला शत्रुं जयति सर्वदा। *Agni Pu.*, 228.7.

101. K.A. Nilakanta Sastri, *A History of South India*, p. 97.
102. Irfan Habib, *The Indus Civilization*, p. 61.
103. Joshi and Bisht, *India and the Indus Civilization*, pl. 20, p. 42.
104. *The New Encyclopaedia Britannica*, vol. III, p. 102 (2002).
105. इन्द्रस्य वज्रो मरुतामनीकं मित्रस्य गर्भो वरुणस्य नाभिः।
सेमां नो हव्यदातिं जुषाणो देव रथ प्रति हव्या गृभाय।। *Ṛgveda*, 6.47.28; Toy chariots have been found in the Harappan excavations. M.S. Vats, *Excavations at Harappa*, pp. 99, 452; but there is little to suggest that the chariot was actually used in war at that time.
106. *Aitareya Brāhmaṇa*, 2.25.
107. *Sāṅkhyāyana Śrautasūtra*, 14.33.20.
108. *Ṛgveda*, 4.16.20; 10.39.14; also *Atharvaveda*, 3.5.6.
109. सिंहव्याघ्रतनुत्राणैर्दन्तिकाञ्चनराजतीः। *Rām*, Sundara, 6.6.
The war chariots are generally described as richly decorated in the epics:
तं मेरुशिखराकारं तप्तकाञ्चनभूषणम्। *Rām*, Araṇya, 22.13.
प्रतप्तजाम्बूनदजालचित्रितम्। Ibid., Sundara, 47.4.
स रथं भूषयित्वाथ रुचिरं हेमभूषितम्। Ibid., Yuddha, 90.9.
ततः काञ्चनचित्राङ्गः किङ्किणीशतभूषितः। Ibid., Yuddha, 102.10.
110. *MB*, Karṇa, 51.68.
111. *Rām*, Yuddha, 95.33; in the *Mahabhārata* there are many references to three charioteers—one central charioteer and two side charioteers (पार्ष्णिसारथी). Udyoga, 152.11; Bhīṣma, 80.22; Droṇa, 47.14, 28, 32, etc.
112. E.W. Hopkins, *The Social and Military Position of the Ruling Caste in Ancient India*, pp. 194-5.
113. J.W. M'crindle, *Ancient India*, pp. 88-9.
114. J.W. M'crindle, *The Invasion of India*, p. 207.
115. Ibid., pp. 101-2.
116. रथान् मण्डलचक्रांश्च योजयित्वा परः शतम्।
उष्ट्रगोर्श्विखरैर्भृत्या भरतं यान्तमन्वयुः।। *Rām*, Ayodhyā, 70.29; The chariot of Aśvins was also pulled by ass. *Ṛgveda*, 8.74.7.
117. तस्मादेकान्तरावरा आ षडन्तरादिति सप्त रथाः। *AS*, 2.33.4; also *Agni Pu*., 242.25.
118. देवरथपुष्यरथसांग्रामिकपारियाणिकपरपुराभियानिकवैनयिकांश्च रथान् कारयेत्। Ibid., 2.33.5; in the *Rāmāyaṇa saṅgrāmika ratha* is mentioned. Araṇya, 65.6.
119. याने चक्रिणि युद्धार्थे शताङ्गः स्यन्दनो रथः। *Amarakośa*, 2.8.51.
120. *AS*, 10.4.15.
121. J.W. M'crindle, *Invasion of India*, p. 310.

122. K.A. Nilakanta Sastri, *The Age of the Nandas and Mauryas*, p. 188.
123. 'The chariot in which an officer sits is drawn by four horses, whilst infantry guarded it on both sides.' T. Watters, op. cit., p. 171.
124. K.K. Thapliyal, *Inscriptions of the Maukharis, Later Guptas, Puṣpabhūtis and Yaśovarman of Kannauj*, p. 104.
Prior to this, there is a reference to chariots in *Saṅgam* literature. N. Subrahmanian, *Saṅgam Polity*, p. 147 Note 130; in *Śilāpaḍikāram* there is a reference to 100 chariots in the army of a Tamil king. Ibid., p. 157.
125. G.N. Sinha, *Post-Gupta Polity*, p. 144.
126. R.C. Majumdar, *History of Bengal*, vol. I, p. 179.
127. *IA*, vol. XIII, p. 140.
128. *Amarakośa*, 2.8.53-54.
Significantly, Pāṇini has also used the terms *Pāṇḍukambala*, *dvaipa* and *vaiyāghra* in the context of a chariot, *Aṣṭādhyāyī*, 4.2.
129. Ibid., 2.8.57.
130. *Kāmandaka Nīti*, 20.36-39; *Śukranīti*, 4.7.41.
131. A.A. Macdonell, *A History of Sanskrit Literature*, p. 168.
132. J. Marshall, *Mohenjo-daro and the Indus Civilization*, pp. 72, 653; M.S. Vats, *Excavations at Harappa*, pp. 308, 322; *Indian Archaeology*, 1960-61, p. 488.
133. *Ṛgveda*, 1.64.7; 8.33.8;8.45.5; *Atharvaveda*, 9.3.17.
134. In *Sāmavidhāna Brāhmaṇa* (3.6.11) there is a reference to *caturaṅgiṇī senā*.
135. *MB*, Virāṭa, 60.8; Bhīṣma, 91.25-6.
136. E.J. Rapson, *Cambridge History of India*, vol. I, pp. 305-6.
137. J.W. M'crindle, *The Invasion of India*, p. 103.
138. Ibid., p. 108.
139. J.W. M'crindle, *Ancient India*, p. 156; also p. 139.
140. Ibid., p. 90.
141. यथा रथास्तथा नागा बद्धकक्ष्याः स्वलंकृताः।
बभूवुः सप्त पुरुषा रत्नवन्त इवाद्रयः।।
द्वावङ्कुशधरौ तेषु द्वावुत्तमधनुर्धरौ।
द्वौ वरासिधरौ राजन्नेकः शक्तिपताकधृक्।। *MB*, *Udyoga*, 152.13-14.
142. J. Marshall and A. Foucher, *The Monuments of Sāñchī*, Pls.
143. रथव्यूहेन हस्तिव्यूहो व्याख्यातः। *AS*, 10.5.30.
144. Ibid., 10.4.14; 10.5.53-4; *Kāmandaka Nīti*, 20.3; *Agni Pu.*, 242.21-4.
145. नागेषु हि क्षितिभृतां विजयो निबद्धस्तस्माद् गजाधिकबलो नृपतिः सदा स्यात्। *Kāmandaka Nīti*, 20.61; also see P.V. Kane, *History of Dharmaśāstra*, vol. III, pp. 203-4.

146. N. Subrahmanian, *Saṅgam, Polity*, p. 146.
147. T. Watters, op. cit., p. 343.
148. The *Agni Purāṇa* (252.31) says that six warriors could sit on the back of an elephant—two hook-bearers, two bowmen and two swordsmen. It adds that there should be four soldiers to guard each foot of an elephant. Ibid., 236.38, *Kāmandaka Nīti*, 19.1-3, 60-2; The *Śukranīti* (4.7.45-6) accepts the importance of elephant but says that their number should be restricted.
149. *Viṣṇudharmottara Pu.*, 2.177.48.
150. T. Watters, op. cit., p. 171.
151. *Śiśupālavadha*, 18.28-30.
152. J. Marshall, *Mohenjo-daro and the Indus Civilization*, pp. 28, 653-4; B.B. Lal believes in the presence of horse in Indus civilization, *The Earliest Civilization of South Asia*, pp. 285-6.
153. *Ṛgveda*, 5.61.3.
154. सहस्रं व्यतीनां युक्तानामिन्द्रमीमहे। *Ṛgveda*, 4.32.17.
155. पृष्ठे सदो नसोर्यमः। Ibid., 5.61.2.
156. *Sāmavidhāna Brāhmaṇa*, 3.6.11.
157. *Atharvaveda*, 6.92; The horse was called *haya* when used by Devas, *vaji* when used by Gandharvas, *arvā* when used by Asuras and *aśva* when used by Mānavas *Bṛhadāraṇyaka Up.* I.1.2.
158. *Saṁyukta Nikāya*, vol. I, p. 110.
159. B.P. Sinha, 'Cavalry in Ancient Indian Army 600 BC-AD 300', in *Studies in Cultural Development of India*, ed. N.R. Ray, Calcutta, 1991.
160. J.W. M'crindle, *The Invasion of India*, p. 102.
161. Ibid., pp. 194, 234.
162. J.W. M'crindle, *Ancient India*, pp. 139, 156.
163. Ibid. p. 221.
164. *AS*, 2.30; also 10.3.13; *Kāmandaka Nīti*, 20.5-6.
165. *AS*, 2.30.29.
166. U.P. Thapliyal, *Indo-Iranica*, 1975, p. 10; according to the *Agni Purāṇa* (249.37) the bow could be used by warriors mounted on elephants, chariots or horses.
167. D.C. Sircar, *Select Inscriptions,* vol. II, p. 173, Surprisingly, Rudradaman also maintained a fourfold army like the native rulers.
168. For details see P.C. Chakravarty *The Art of War in Ancient India*, pp. 38-49.
169. J. Marshall and A. Foucher, *The Monuments of Sāñchī*, Pls.
170. A.S. Altekar, *Catalogue of the Gupta Gold Coins in the Bayana Hoard*, pls. IV, XIII, XIV.

171. T. Watters, *Travels*, vol. I, p. 343.
172. G. Yajdani, *Ajantā*, pt. 2, pl. 37, pt. 4, pls. 43A, 55, 57.
173. *Kāmandaka Nīti*, 20.5-6, 36-9; *Śukranīti*, 4.7.85-212; *Agni Pu.*, 242.25-7.
174. D.K. Gupta, *Society and Culture in the Time of Daṇḍin*, pp. 180-1.
175. कविका तु खलीनोऽस्त्री। *Amarakośa*, 2.8.49. Also 3.5.35; 3.3.237.
176. Maenchen-Helfen, *The World of the Huns*, pp. 210-13.
177. Ibid., pp. 213-14.
178. चतुरङ्ग बलं मुत्त्वा कोशो मंत्रस्य युध्यते।
    तत् साधुमंत्रो मंत्रेण कोशेन च जयेदरीन्।। *Kāmandaka Nīti*, 18.2.
179. प्रायो मन्त्रेण योद्धव्यमल्पायासेन चैव हि।
    अल्पः कालस्तु देशो वाप्रभूतौ च क्षयव्ययौ।। Ibid., 19.16.
180. *AS*, 1.15.
181. J. Marshall, *Mohenjo-daro and the Indus Civilization*, p. 76.
182. B.B. Lal, *The Earliest Civililzation of South Asia*, p. 285.
183. *Ṛgveda*, 9.33.6.
184. चतस्रो नावो। *Ṛgveda*, 1.182.6.
185. *MB*, Sabhā, 28.44, 29.15-16; also Śānti, 59.41; There is also a reference to navy in the *Rāmāyaṇa*. *Rām*, Yuddha, 8.8.
186. J.W. M'crindle, *The Invasion of India*, p. 156.
187. Ibid., *Ancient India*, p. 88.
188. *Manusmṛti*, 7.192.
189. *AS*, 2.28.1.
190. सिंहलकादिभिश्च सर्वद्वीपवासिभिः आत्मनिवेदन कन्योपायनदान
    गरुत्मदंक स्वविषयभुक्ति शासन याचन। J.F. Fleet, op. cit., p. 8.
191. Ibid., p. 217.
192. G. Yajdani, *Ajantā*, pt. 1, pl. 19; pt. 2, pl. 42.
193. V.A. Smith, *The Early History of India*, p. 462.
194. P.C. Chakravarty, 'Naval Warfare in Ancient India', *Indian Historical Quarterly*, vol. VI, p. 650.
195. S.K. Aiyangar, *Some Contributions of South India to Indian Culture*, pp. 318-49, N. Subrahmanian, *Saṅgam Polity*, p. 147; K.A. Nilakanta Sastri, *A History of South India*, p. 118.
196. K.A. Nilakanta Sastri, *The Colas*, pp. 458-60.
197. पृथिव्यपस्वन्तरिक्षेषु खगवद्वेगतः स्वयम्।
    यस्समर्थो भवेदगंतुम् स विमान इति स्मृतः।। *Bṛhadvimānaśāstra*, 1.1.5.
198. देशाद्देशान्तरं तद्वद्द्वीपान्तरं तथा।
    लोकाल्लोकान्तरं चापि योहम्बरे गन्तुमर्हति
    स विमान इति प्रोक्तो खेटशास्त्रविदां वरैः Viśvambhara, *Bṛhadvimānaśāstra*, 1.1.7.

199. विसोपमानं गमने येषामस्ति खमण्डले।
ते विमाना इति प्रोक्तो यानशास्त्रविशारदैः।। Lalla, *Bṛhadvimānaśāstra*, 1.1.4
200. *Harivaṁśa Pu.*, *Harivaṁśa*, 12; *MB*, Vana, 23.3-6.
201. *Rām*, Yuddha, 124; Uttara, 18.1, 22.50.
202. विमानयोधी धनदो विमाने पुष्पके स्थितः। *Harivaṁśa Pu.*, *Harivaṁśa*, 34.17.
203. *Kūrma Pu.*, Pūrvabhāga, 16.181.
204. *Harivaṁśa Pu.*, *Harivaṁśa*, 36.20, 37.29.
205. दीप्तमाकाशगं दिव्यं रथं पररथारुजम्।
अतिष्ठत्समराकाङ्क्षी मेरुं दीप्त इवांशुमान्।। *Harivaṁśa Pu.*, *Harivaṁśa*, 33.8
206. Ibid., 37.29.
207. पेतुरुल्कासहस्राणि पेतुराकाशगान्यपि।
न्युब्जानि च विमानानि प्रपतन्त्युत्पतन्ति च।। Ibid., 32.16.
208. विमानानि विचित्राणि प्रपतन्त्युत्पतन्ति च। Ibid., 36.20.
209. विमानैर्नगराकारैर्हयैर्गजवरैस्तदा *Rām*, Bāla, 43.18.
210. विमाने भास्वरे तिष्ठन् हंसयुक्ते यशस्करे, *Rām*, Araṇya, 72.6.
211. यस्य तत् पुष्पकं नाम विमानं कामगं शुभम्।
वीर्यादावर्जितं भद्रे येन यामि विहायसम्।। *Rām*, Araṇya, 48.6; also 49.23.
212. हंसप्रवेकैरिव वाप्रमानं।
श्रिया युतं खे सुकृतं विमानम्।। *Rām*, Sundara, 7.7; also 7.11.
213. खगतेन विमानेन हंसयुक्तेन भास्वता। *Rām*, Yuddha, 122.26.
214. विमानं परमोदारं हंसयुक्तं मनोजवम्। *Rām*, Uttara, 77.11.
215. सर्वदेवनिकायाश्च सिद्धाश्च परमर्षयः।
अर्जुनस्य कुरूणां च द्रष्टुं युद्धमुपागताः।। *MB*, Virāṭa, 51.13.
216. विमानानि चकाशिरे। *MB*, Virāṭa, 51.12; There are many more references to *vimānas* in the *Mahābhārata*; It is said that *vimāna* is referred to in the *Mahābhārata* at 41 places. D.K. Kanjilal, *Vimāna in Ancient India*, p. 17.
217. *MB*, Anuśāsana, 106.
218. *Harṣacarita*, p. 353.
219. लघु दारुमयं महाविहङ्गं दृढसुश्लिष्टतनुं विधाय तस्य।
उदरे रसयंत्रमादधीत ज्वलनाधारमधोऽस्य चति(ग्नि)पूर्णम्।। *Samarāṅgaṇasūtradhāra*, yantravidhānam, 31.95.
220. व्योमयानं विमानं वा पूर्वमासीन्महीभुजाम्। *Yuktikalpataru*, Yāna, 50.
221. नारायणः शौनकश्च गर्गो वाचस्पतिस्तथा।
चक्रायणिर्घुण्डिनाथश्चेति शास्त्रकृतस्स्वयम्।।
विमानचन्द्रिका व्योमयानतन्त्रस्तथैव च।
यन्त्रकल्पो यानबिन्दुः खेटयानप्रदीपिका।। *Bṛhadvimānaśāstra*, Vaimānika-prakarṇam, 34-6.

222. Ibid., 1.1.6-7, etc.
223. Ibid., 1.2-3, p. 10.
224. Louis Renou (tr), *The Civilization in Ancient India*, pp. 120-1; Recently, I chanced to see a book entitled *Vimāna in Ancient India* by D.K. Kanjilal. In his thorough study he has said that till now *Vaimānika Śāstra* apart, *Samarāṅgaṇasūtradhāra, Yuktikalpataru* and *Mayamatam* are known to have dealt with the topic of *vimāna* in a scientific perspective. In addition to these works about 150 verses of the *Ṛgveda, Yajurveda* and the *Atharvaveda*, a lot of passages in the *Ramāyaṇa, Mahāhbhārata, Purāṇas, Raghuvaṁśa, Śākuntalam, Jātakas, Avadānas* and *Kathāsaritasāgara* and a number of other literary works contain references to aerial flights or mechanism of aerial vehicles used in old ages in India.
225. धान्याद्वैर्विविधः प्राप्तिरासारस्तु सुहृद्बलम्।
विच्छिन्नविविधासारं बलं युद्धाय नेष्यते।। *Kāmandaka Nīti*, 14.87.
226. शोधनं कूपतीर्थानां मार्गाणां शिविरस्य च।
यवसादि च यत्किञ्चिद् विज्ञेयं विष्टिकर्म तत्।। Ibid., 20.7.; also *AS*, 10.4.17.
227. 'O Aśvins, with those aids wherewith ye guarded Kaṇva carefully, keep us, O Lords of Splendour. . . . O mighty ones, ye gave Sudās abundant food, brought on your treasure laden car.' *Ṛgveda*, 1.47.5-6.
228. A.C. Das, *Ṛgvedic Culture*, p. 341.
229. शकटापणवेशाश्च यानयुग्यं च सर्वशः।
कोशयन्त्रायुधं चैव ये च वैद्याश्चिकित्सकाः।। *MB*, Udyoga, 149.53.
230. *MB*, Karṇa, 15.28.
231. Ibid., 22.51.
232. *Rām*, Yuddha, 71.20-1; 69.22; 106.2.
233. *MB*, Udyoga, 149.75-82.
234. तत्रासञ्शिल्पिनः प्राज्ञाः शतशो दत्तवेतनाः।
सर्वोपकरणैर्युक्ता वैद्याश्च सुविशारदाः।।
ज्याधनुवर्मशस्त्राणां तथैव मधुसर्पिषोः।
ससर्जरसपांसूनां राशयः पर्वतोपमाः।।
बहूदकं सुयवसं तुषाङ्गारसमन्वितम्।
शिविरे शिविरे राजा सञ्चकार युधिष्ठिरः।। *MB*, Udyoga, 149.78-80.
235. Ibid.
236. अथ भूमिप्रदेशज्ञाः सूत्रकर्मविशारदाः।
स्वकर्माभिरताः शूराः खनकाः यन्त्रकास्तथा।।
कर्मान्तिकाः स्थपतयः पुरुषा यन्त्रकोविदाः।
तथा वर्धकयश्चैव मार्गिणो वृक्षतक्षकाः।।
सूपकाराः सुधाकारा वंशचर्मकृतस्तथा।

समर्था ये च द्रष्टारः पुरतश्च प्रतस्थिरे।। *Rām*, Ayodhyā, 80.1-3; also 83.12-16; *MB*, Udyoga, 149.76-80
This is put slightly differently in *Nītiprakāśikā* (6.33-5).
सैनिकान् परिधिस्थांश्च स्थापयित्वा नृपोत्तमः।
प्रस्थापयेनमार्गकरान् पुरस्ताच्छिल्पिनो बहून्।।
कमान्तिकान् यष्टिधरान् खनकान् तक्षकानपि।
सूत्रिणो रोपकांश्चैव सेतुबन्धकरानपि।।
तथा भूमिप्रदेशज्ञान् व्याधान् वनविशारदान्।

237. J.W. M'crindle, *Ancient India*, p. 88.
238. *AS*, 10.2.
239. Ibid., 10.2.1-3.
240. Ibid., 10.2.16.
241. शविरमार्गसेतुकूपतीर्थशोधनकर्म यंत्रायुधावरणोपकरणग्रासवहनमायोधनाञ्च प्रहरणावरणप्रतिविद्धापनयनमिति विष्टिकर्माणि। Ibid., 10.4.17.
242. Ibid., 10.1.9.
243. *Indian Antiquary*, vol. 7, p. 261.
244. *AS*, 10.2.5-7.
245. Ibid., 10.2.18-19.
246. Ibid., 12.4.9-12; in *Rāmāyaṇa* Rāma asked general Nīla to be extra vigilant so that Rākṣasas do not poison the foodstuff. *Rām*, Yuddha, 4.10-11; also *Manusmṛti*, 7.195-6.
247. Ibid., 13.4.7-9.
248. Ibid., 9.1.34-42.
249. Ibid., 13.4.9, etc.
250. G.C. Pandey, op. cit., p. 36.
251. *Harṣacarita*, pp. 199-201.
252. Ibid., p. 207.
253. Ibid., p. 190.
254. *Kāmandaka Nīti*, 19.45.
255. Ibid., 16.42.
256. Ibid., 14.87.
257. यावत्स एव समयः सममेव तावदव्याकुलाः पटमयान्यभितो वितत्य।
पर्यापतत्क्रयिकलोकमगण्यपण्यपूर्णापणं विपणिनो विपणिं विभेजुः।। *Śiśupālavadha*, 5.24.
258. *Śukranīti*, 4.7.226.
259. तृणान्नजलसम्भारा ये चान्ये शत्रुपोषकाः।
सम्यङ् निरुध्य तान् यत्नात् परितश्चिरमासनात्।। Ibid., 4.7.285-6.
260. गजोष्ट्रवृषभाश्वाः प्राक् श्रेष्ठाः सम्भारवाहने।।
सर्वेभ्यः शकटाः श्रेष्ठा वर्षाकालं विना स्मृताः।। Ibid., 4.7.176-7.
261. J.W. M'crindle, *Ancient India*, p. 88.

262. Ibid.
263. J.F. Fleet, op. cit., p. 214.
264. *Śukranīti*, 4.7.22-3.
265. S.D. Singh, *Ancient Indian Warfare*, p. 9.
266. Ibid.; also A.C. Das, *Ṛgvedic Culture*, p. 302.
267. विशंविशं युद्धाय सं शिशाधि। *Atharvaveda*, 4.31.4 ; also *Ṛgveda*, 10.84.4.
268. देवसेनानाम्। *Ṛgveda*, 10.103.8; मरुतामनीकम्। 6.47.28; महि वरूथम्। Ibid., 2.34.14; 8.18.20; 5.46.5; मरुतो वृद्धसेनाः। Ibid., 1.186.8.
269. Ibid., 2.34.12.
270. Ibid., 7.57.7.
271. Ibid., 1.168.2.
272. एको रथो गजश्चैको नराः पंच पदातयः।
त्रयश्च तुरगास्तज्ज्ञैः पत्तिरित्यभिधीयते।।
पत्तिं तु त्रिगुणामेतामाहुः सेनामुखं बुधाः।
त्रीणि सेनामुखान्येको गुल्म इत्यभिधीयते।।
त्रयो गुल्मा गणो नाम वाहिनी तु गणास्त्रयः।
स्मृतास्तिस्रस्तु वाहिन्यः पृतनेति विचक्षणैः।।
चमूस्तु पृतनास्तिस्रस्तिस्रश्चम्वस्त्वनीकिनी।
अनीकिनीं दशगुणां प्राहुरक्षौहिणीं बुधाः।। *MB*, Ādi, 2.15-18; These formations are also mentioned in the *Nītiprakāśikā* (7.3), a later work. Eighteen *akṣauhiṇīs* (army formations) are reported to have fought in the epic war.
273. E.C. Sachau, *Alberuni's India*, vol. I, pp. 407-8.
274. द्वात्रिंशत्त्वमनीकानि सर्वाण्येवाभिचोदय। *MB*, Bhīṣma, 95.5. It should be द्वाविंशित्वम् more appropriately.
275. For details see P.V. Kane, *History of Dharamaśāstra*, pp. 203-5.
276. रथस्यासन्दश गजा गजस्य दश वाजिनः।
नरा दश हयस्यासन्पादरक्षाः समन्ततः।।
रथस्य नागाः पंचाशन्नागस्यासञ्शतं हयाः।
हयस्य पुरुषाः सप्त भिन्नसंधानकारिणः।।
सेना पंचशतं नागा रथास्तावन्त एव च।
दश सेना च पृतना पृतना दश वाहिनी।।
वाहिनी पृतना सेना ध्वजिनी सादिनी चमूः।
अक्षौहिणीति पर्यायैर्निरुक्ताथ वरूथिनी।
एवं व्यूढान्यनीकानि कौरवेयेण धीमता।। *MB*, Udyoga, 152.19-22; also see *Amarakośa*, 2.8.80-1; *Garga Saṁhitā*, 7.7.34-8.
277. इयमक्षौहिणी सेना यस्याहं पत्तिरीश्वरः। *Ram*, Bāla, 20.3.
278. *Rām*, Ayodhyā, 83.3-5.
279. *Amarakośa*, 2.8.81.

280. *Garga Saṁhitā*, 7.8.34-8.
281. *Śāraṅgadharapaddhati*, Dhanurveda, 1915-21.
282. अक्षौहिण्यस्तु सप्तैव पाण्डवानामभूद्बलम्
अक्षौहिण्यो दशैका च कौरवाणामभूद्बलम्।। *MB*, Udyoga, 152.23.
283. *MB*, Āśvamedhika, 60.22-3 (*BE*).
284. दशायुतानामयुतं सहस्राणि च विंशतिः ।
कोट्यः षष्टिश्च षष्टैव येऽस्मिन्राजमृधे हताः ।।
अलक्ष्याणं तु वीराणां सहस्राणि चतुर्दश।
दश चान्यानि राजेन्द्र शतं षष्टिश्च पञ्च च ।। *MB*, Strī, 26.9-10; The army of Daśaratha comprised one अक्षौहिणी only. *Rām*, Bāla, 19.3.
285. गजानां दशसाहस्रं रथानामयुतं तथा।
हयानामयुते द्वे च साग्रकोटिश्च राक्षसाम्।। *Rām*, Yuddha, 37.16; also 93.31-3, 95.27-8.
286. Ibid., Yuddha, 30.27.
287. 'Army and Power in The Ancient World', paper by Romila Thapar appearing in *Angelos Chaniotis Pierre Ducrey*, 2002, pp. 30-1.
288. M.V. Creveld, *Command in War*, p. 24.
289. *AS*, 10.5.12-13.
290. Ibid.
291. Ibid., 10.5.14-15.
292. चतुर्गुणं हि पादातमश्वतो धारयेत् सदा।
पञ्चमांशांस्तु वृषभानष्टांशांश्च क्रमेलकान्।।
चतुर्थांशान् गजानुष्ट्रान गजार्धांश्च रथान् सदा।
रथात्तु द्विगुणं राजा बृहन्नालीकमेव च ।। *Śukranīti*, 4.7.19-20.
293. *MB*, Śānti, 84.
294. *AS*, 1.15.34-8.
295. Ibid., 1.15.1-6.
296. गिरिपृष्ठं समारुप्र प्रासादं वा रहोगतः।
अरण्ये निःशलाके वा मंत्रयेदविभाविताः।। *Manusmṛti*, 7.147.
297. *Rām*, Yuddha, 6.5-18; 12.7-11; 32.38-41.
298. मंत्रमूलं च विजयं प्रवदन्ति मनस्विनः। *Rām*, Yuddha, 6.5.
299. मौलाञ्छास्त्रविदः शूरांल्लब्धलक्षान्कुलोद्भवान्।
सचिवान्सप्त चाष्टौ वा प्रकुर्वीत परीक्षितान्।। *Manusmṛti*, 7.54.
300. Ibid., 7.45-7.
301. *Śukranīti*, 1.352-3.
302. अविज्ञातस्य विज्ञानं विज्ञातस्य च निश्चयः।
अर्थद्वैधस्य संदेहच्छेदनं शेषदर्शनम्।।
सहायाः साधनोपाया विभागो देशकालयोः।
विपत्तेश्च प्रतीकारः पञ्चाङ्गो मंत्र इष्यते।। *Agni Pu.*, 241.3-4.

303. *Ṛgveda*, 7.20.5, 9.96.1, 10.84.2; *Atharvaveda*, 3.6.
304. *Aitareya Brāhmaṇa*, 14.3.1.
305. *Yajurveda*, 7.38,40; 10.26.
306. Ibid., 20.40.
307. *Vedic Index*, vol. II, p. 472.
308. Ibid.
309. *MB*, Udyoga, 153.4-9.
310. एवं ये कुशलं शूरं हिते स्थितमकल्मषम्।
सेनापतिं प्रकुर्वन्ति ते जयन्ति रणे रिपून्।। *MB*, Udyoga, 153.10.
311. *Śiva Pu.*, 4.7.
312. *AS*, 10.3.45; also *Kāmandaka Nīti*, 20.17-21; *Agni Pu.*, 242.34-6.
313. यस्तु सेनापतिं हत्वा तद्यानमधिरोहति।
स विष्णुविक्रमक्रामी बृहस्पतिसमः क्रतुः।। *MB*, Śānti, 99.41.
314. S. Beal, *Life of Hiuen-tsang*, vol. IV, p. 147.
315. E.W. Hopkins, *Position of Ruling Caste in Ancient India*, p. 166; also p. 159.
316. S.D. Singh, *Ancient Indian Warfare*, p. 148.
317. सेनापत्ये तदा राजा गाङ्गेयमभिषिक्तवान्। *MB*, Udyoga, 153.31.
318. Ibid., 152.27.
319. Ibid., 154.11-13.
320. Ibid., Droṇa, 5.
321. *MB*, Karṇa, 6.35-46.
322. *MB*, Śalya, 6.
323. *Rām*, Uttara, 63.10-14.
324. *MB*, Udyoga, 149; also 153.
325. नमस्कृत्वा कुमाराय सेनान्ये शक्तिपाणये।
अहं सेनापतिस्तेऽद्य भविष्यामि न संशयः।।
सेनाकर्मण्यभिज्ञोऽस्मि व्यूहेषु विविधेषु च।
कर्म कारयितुं चैव भृतानप्यभृतांस्तथा।। Ibid., Udyoga, 162.7-8.
सोऽहं योत्स्यामि तत्त्वेन पालयंस्तव वाहिनीम्।
यथावच्छास्त्रतो राजन्व्येतु ते मानसो ज्वरः।। Ibid., 162.11;
326. *MB*, Karṇa, 6.11-17.
327. Ibid., 6.35-6.
328. Ibid., Udyoga, 152.28-9.
329. Ibid., 154.10.
330. Ibid., 149.5.
331. शूद्रा वा क्षत्रिया वैश्या म्लेच्छाः संकरसम्भवाः।
सेनाधिपाः सैनिकाश्च कार्या राज्ञा जयार्थिना।। *Śukranīti*, 2.139.
332. राज्ञा सेनापतिः कार्यो ब्राह्मणः क्षत्रियोऽथवा। *Matsya Pu.*, 215.10; also *Agni Pu.*, 220.1.

333. *Ṛgveda*, 7.20.5, 10.84.2.
334. S. Dey, *Indian Life in the Śukla-Yajurveda*, p. 88.
335. *Rām*, Yuddha, 12.2, 58.4, 12.1, 57.12, 58.35, 41.38, 70.30.
336. R.N. Mehta, *Pre-Buddhist India*, p. 166.
337. *AS*, 5.3.3.
338. *Epigraphia Indica*, vol. 16, p. 235.
339. J.F. Fleet, *CII*, vol. 3, nos. 23, 28, 43, 39, 55, 58; of these *mahābalādhikṛta* meaning a great officer placed at the head of the forces was a technical person, an officer superior to *balādhikṛtas. Mahābalādhyakṣa* was perhaps its synonym, p. 109 fn. 2.
340. Ibid., no. 39.
331. Ibid., nos. 55, 58.
342. *Epigraphica Carnatica*, vol. 10, p. 160.
343. V.R.R. Dikshitar, *The Gupta Polity*, pp. 218-19.
344. J. Marshall, *Archaelogical Survey of India, Annual Report, 1911-12*, p. 52.
345. *Bṛhatsamhitā*, 17.23, 5.29, 16.8, 68.47.
346. *AS*, 1.19.16.
347. *Rām*, Yuddha, 57.18-31.
348. *Harṣacarita*, p. 180.
349. *MB*, Udyoga, 149.
350. *Harṣacarita*, pp. 180-2.
351. Ibid.
352. कुलीन: शीलसम्पन्नो धनुर्वेदविशारद:।
    हस्तिशिक्षाश्वशिक्षासु कुशल: श्लक्ष्णभाषित:।
    निमित्ते शकुने ज्ञाते वेत्ता चैव चिकित्सिते।
    कृतज्ञ: कर्मणां शुरस्तथा क्लेशसहस्त्वृजु:।।
    व्यूहतत्त्वविधानज्ञ: फल्गुसारविशेषवित्। *Matsya Pu.*, 215.8-10.
353. *Kāmandaka Nīti*, 19.27-44.
354. *Śukranīti*, 2.138-40.
355. *Bṛhatsaṁhitā*, 73.4, 49.3-5.
356. Ibid., 49.3-5.
357. J.F. Fleet, op. cit., nos. 21, 38.
358. *Vedic Index*, vol. 1, p. 247, vol. 2, p. 341; S.D. Singh, *Ancient Indian Warfare*, p. 12; A.C. Das, *Ṛgvedic Culture*, pp. 119-22.
359. *Atharvaveda*, 7.62.1; *Yajurveda*, 16.19.
360. V.S. Agrawala, *India as Known to Pāṇini*, p. 420; also *Rām*, Yuddha, 4.109; 27.5, 9; 38.5; 15.1; 27.11, 35; 58.36, 45.
361. E.W. Hopkins, *The Social and Military Position of the Ruling Caste in Ancient India*, p. 148.
362. *MB*, Śānti, 101.28.

363. In the *Amarakośa* (2.8.61), the fighting soldiers are called *bhaṭa*, *yodhā* and *yuddhṛ*. The term *sainika* is not used for a fighting soldier but for watchman of the army. सेनारक्षस्तु सैनिकाः (*Amarakośa*, 2.8.61); at another place *sainika* is defined as सेनायां समवेता ये सैन्यास्ते सैनिकाश्च ते। *Amarakośa*, 2.8.61.
364. For details see *MB*, Udyoga, 166-69;
365. *MB*, Śānti, 100.3.
366. *MB*, Droṇa, 1.35-36.
367. *AS*, 2.18, 28-33.
368. अंगदशकस्यैकः पतिः पतिकः पतिकदशकस्यैकः सेनापतिः, तद्दशकस्यैको नायक इति। Ibid., 10.6.45.
369. For details see J.F. Fleet, *CII*, vol. 3; D.C. Sircar, *Indian Epigraphy*.
370. *Śukranīti*, 2.141-8.
371. Ibid., 2.144-5.
372. *Nītiprakāśikā*, 6.72-6.
373. यादृक्सैन्याधिपत्ये तु पूर्णं योऽधिकृतो भवेत्।
स ज्येष्ठभावे नियतस्तत्पाश्चात्यास्तु तद्वशे।।
पच्याद्यङ्गपतीनष्टावक्षौहिण्यधिपानुगान्।
कृत्वा ज्येष्ठानुसारेण नियम्यास्सर्वसैनिकाः।। Ibid., 6.79-80.
374. Ibid., 7.33-42.
375. A.C. Das, *Ṛgvedic Culture*, p. 340.
376. E.W. Hopkins, *The Social and Military Position of the Ruling Caste*, p. 134.
377. *Aitareya Brāhmaṇa*, 2.25.
378. वेतनादिभ्यो जीवति। *Aṣṭādhyāyī*, 4.4.12.
379. E.W. Hopkins, *The Social and Military Position of the Ruling Caste*, p. 134.
380. दत्तवेतनभक्तं च दत्तायुधपरिच्छदम्।
कृतापदानं च तदा बलमासीन्महाभुज।।
न कुप्यवेतनी कश्चिन्न चातिक्रान्तवेतनी।
नानुग्रहभृतः कश्चिन्न चादृष्टपराक्रमः।। *MB*, vana, 16.21-2.
381. Ibid., Sabhā, 5.49, 58.
382. E.B. Cowell, *The Jātaka*, vol. 2. pp. 60-1.
383. Ibid., vol. 5, p. 67.
384. *MB*, Sabhā, 5.38-9.
385. कच्चिद् बलस्य भक्तं च वेतनं च यथोचितम्।
सम्प्राप्तकालं दातव्यं ददासि न विलम्बसे।।
कालातिक्रमणे प्रेव भक्तवेतनयोर्भृताः।
भर्तुरप्यतिकुप्यन्ति सोऽनर्थः सुमहान् कृतः।। *Rām*, Ayodhyā, 100.32-3.

386. भृताश्च बहवो योधाः परीक्ष्यैव महारथाः।
वेतनेन यथायोग्यं प्रियवादेन चापरे।। *MB,* Droṇa, 89.21.
387. बलस्य परिमाणे च भक्तवेतनयोस्तथा।
नकुलं व्यादिशद् राजा कर्मिणामन्ववेक्षणे।। *MB*, Śānti, 41.11.
388. J.W. M'crindle, *Ancient India*, p. 211.
389. *AS*, 5.3.1-2; also see *Kāmandaka Nīti*, 13.13, 14.75.
390. Ibid., 2.15.43.
391. Ibid., 5.3.1-34.
392. Ibid., 5.3.3-9.
393. Ibid., 5.3.28.
394. J. Legge, *The Travels of Fa-hien*, p. 43.
395. R.C. Majumdar, *The Classical Age*, p. 346.
396. सैनिकाः शिक्षिता ये ये तेषु पूर्णा भृतिः स्मृता।।
व्यूहाभ्यासे नियुक्ता ये तेष्वर्धां भृतिमावहेत्। *Śukranīti*, 4.7.393-4.
397. याने सपादभृत्या तु स्वभृत्यान् वर्धयन्नृपः। Ibid., 4.7.354.
398. Ibid., 5.81-6.
399. Ibid., 1.183-6.
400. *Nītiprakāśikā*, 7.33-42.
401. *MB*, Sabhā, 5.44.
402. *Arthaśāstra*, 5.3.28-31; *MB*, Sabhā, 2.5.55.
403. *Nītiprakāśikā*, 6.106-8.
404. J. Marshall, *Mohenjo-daro and the Indus Civilization*, vol. I, pp. 35-6.
405. S. Piggot, *Pre-historic India*, p. 138.
406. *Yajurveda*, 30.7, 16.27, 46.
407. शरव्याया इषुकारं हेत्यै धनुष्कारं कर्मणे ज्याकारं दिष्टाय रज्जुसर्जम्। *Vājasaneyī Saṁhitā*, 30.7.
408. *Atharvaveda*, 11.10.22.
409. Ibid.
410. *Yajurveda*, 17.44.
411. *Ṛgveda*, 1.24.15; 1.25.21; 10.85.24; *Atharvaveda*, 4.16.6.
412. नमस्तक्षभ्यो, रथकारेभ्यश्च वो नमो नमः कुलालेभ्यः कमरिभ्यश्च वो नमो। *Yajurveda*, 16.27
इषुकृदभ्यो धनुषकृदभ्यश्च वो नमो। Ibid., 16.46.
413. *Aṣṭādhyāyī*, 6.2.63.
414. *Rām*, Bāla, 5.10.
415. *MB*, Sabhā, 5.60, 107-8.
416. गजानां पार्श्वचर्माणि गोवृषाजगराणि च।
शल्यकङ्कटलोहानि तनुत्राणि मतानि च।।
शितपीतानि शस्त्राणि संनाहा पीतलोहिताः।

नानारञ्जनरक्ताः स्युः पताकाःकेतवश्च ते।।
ऋष्टयस्तोमराः खड्गा निशिताश्च परश्वधाः।
फलकान्यथ चर्माणि प्रतिकल्प्यान्यनेकशः।। Ibid., Śānti, 101.6-8.

417. *Manusmṛti*, 4.220; also 4.215.
418. Ibid., 7.75.
419. Ibid., 7.222.
420. धनुःशराणां कर्त्ता। *Manusmṛti*, 3.160.
421. *AS*, 2.18.1-4.
422. Ibid., 2.4.12.
423. Ibid., 2.3.34-5; also 2.4.27.
424. Ibid., 2.18.5-18.
425. Ibid., 10.1.6.
426. *Agni Purāṇa*, 220.8-10.
427. M'crindle, *Ancient India*, pp. 42-3.
428. Ibid., p. 85.
429. Ibid., p. 211.
430. Ibid.
431. *Cambridge History of India*, vol. I, p. 205.
432. R.S. Sharma, 'Trends in the Economic History of India', p. 32 in *Mathurā the Cultural Heritage*, ed. D.M. Srinivasan.
433. वंशानामपि तच्छ्रेष्ठं यत्र गंगा महानदी।
सालानामपि तच्छ्रेष्ठं गोमती यत्र भार्गव।
वितस्ताकूलजं श्रेष्ठं वेतसीनां तथैव च।। *Viṣṇu Dh. Purāṇa*, 2.16.14-15.
434. शराः किरातजाः श्रेष्ठाः कांचीपुरसमीपतः।
तेभ्योऽपि ते श्रेष्ठतमाः स्कन्दजन्म महीभवाः।। Ibid., 2.16.20.
435. लोहं प्रधानं खड्गार्थे प्रशस्तं तद् विशेषतः।
कटीकदूरऋषिकं वङ्गेशूर्पारकेषु च।।
विदेहेषु तथाङ्गेषु मध्यमं ग्रामचेदिषु।
सहग्रामेषु नीपेषु तथा कलंजरेपि च।। Ibid., 2.17.21-2.
436. *Rām*, Yuddha, 127.49-52.
437. Ibid., Bāla, 47.21.
438. Ibid., Ayodhyā, 3.33.
439. Ibid., 4.10.
440. Ibid., Bāla, 11.22.
441. पुरः स्थितं शिरः कृपाणं बिभ्राणं बभाण युवानम्। *Harṣacarita*, p. 152.
442. *Ṛgveda*, 1.116.15, 118.8; also 1.112.10, 117.11.
443. *Ṛgveda*, 10.102; also A.C. Das, *Ṛgvedic Culture*, p. 329; also p. 249.
444. *Ṛgveda*, 5.30.9.
445. J.W. M'crindle, *The Invasion of India*, p. 270.

446. Ibid., *Ancient India*, pp. 72-3.
447. *AS*, 1.21.1.
448. J. Marshall and A. Foucher, *The Monuments of Sāñchī*, pls.
449. Debala Mitra, *Udayagiri and Khandagiri*, pl. 6a.
450. *MB*, Śalya, 46 (*BE*).
451. *Brahmāṇḍa Pu.*, pt. 4, 28.
452. मध्ये कलत्रं स्वामी च कोशः। *Kāmandaka Nīti*, 19.45.
453. कलत्रगर्भि चोन्नतिकलत्रं समरक्षयम्। Ibid., 14.80.

Chapter 3

Conduct of War

According to Śukrācārya, 'when two factions inimical to each other resort to weapons to protect their rival interests it is war'.[1] He refers to three kinds of war—*daivika* (godly), *āsura* (devilish) and *mānava* (human). The *daivika* war was fought by means of charms (*mantras*), *āsura* by means of mechanical devices (*yantras*) and *mānava* by means of weapons (*śastras*) and hands (*hastas*).[2] Śukra's definition of war broadly conforms with the view of L. Oppenheim that 'war is a contention between two or more states through their armed forces, for the purpose of overpowering each other and imposing such conditions of peace as the victor pleases'.[3] In the *Amarkośa* 31 synonyms of war (*yuddha*) are enumerated,[4] and to begin with each of these names may have denoted a particular type of war.

Kāmandaka has dealt with the causes of war (*vigraha*) in some detail. In his view 'possessed by the thoughts of revenge and with heart burning with anger caused by the infliction of mutual wrongs, people proceed to fight one another'.[5] According to him the causes of war include usurpation of kingdom, abduction of women, seizure of territory, carrying away of vehicles and treasures (*yāna, dhana*), arrogance (*mada*), morbid sense of humour, disorder in the kingdom, extinction of erudition, destruction of property, violation of laws, prostration of regal powers, influence of evil destiny, helping allies, disrespectful demeanour, destruction of friends, lack of compassion, disaffection of *prakṛti maṇḍala* and eagerness to possess a thing which others covet.[6] He has also described the measures to counter them.[7]

It appears that in the Vedic age lust for territory and greed for plunder were the two main causes of conflict among tribes and people. Vedas are replete with references to the loot of kine and destruction of forts by Indra. This in a way confirms definition of war as the display of bravery by the king in the *Śatapatha Brāhmaṇa.*[8]

Before launching a war a number of factors relevant to success were considered. These included time (*kāla*), place (*deśa*), own power (*svabala*), enemy power (*śatrubala*), four means (*upāyacatuṣṭaya*) and six measures (*ṣaḍguṇa*).[9] Some military thinkers believed that the factors of power (*śakti*), time (*kāla*), and place (*deśa*) each were important separately.[10] But Kauṭilya held the view that these factors were complementry to each other.[11] Kāmandaka, however, considered time and place as more important[12] and in this the *Matsya Purāṇa* also lends support to it.[13]

KĀLA (TIME) FACTOR

Indian military thinkers considered time (*kāla*) as a determining factor in the success or failure of a military venture. Kāmandaka explains this by illustrating that in an encounter during the night time an owl kills a crow but in an encounter during the day time a crow kills an owl. A king should, therefore, set out on an expedition after analysing the time or season factor, etc., for this is a key to success.[14] Tamil work *Tirukkural*, an earlier composition, also illustrates the time factor like Kāmandaka, and advises that a ruler should wait patiently till the proper time comes like a heron, which stands patiently for the prey with folded wings.[15]

Indian calendar divides the year into six seasons, viz., *Vasanta* (spring), *Śarada* (autumn), *Grīṣma* (summer), *Varṣā* (rainy season), *Hemanta* (mild winter) and *Śiśira* (winter). Of these, *Śarada* and *Hemanta* are considered ideal for mounting an invasion in the *Rāmāyaṇa.*[16] The *Manusmṛti*, however, considered the months of Mārgaśīrṣa, Phālguna and Caitra (November to April) as suitable for campaigning.[17] But the *Arthaśāstra* extends the period of campaigning from November to July (Mārgaśīrṣa to Āṣāḍha).[18] The *Śukranīti* considers *Śarada*, *Hemanta* and *Śiśira* as good for campaigning.[19]

The time factor also determined the choice of the army to be deployed in a war. The *Matsya Purāṇa* says that for campaigning during rains an army strong in infantry and elephants, for campaigning in the winters an army strong in chariots and cavalry and for campaigning in summers an army strong in camels and asses should be employed. But for campaigning during *Śarada* and *vasanta* all the four arms could be deployed profitably.[20]

In determining the time of invasion the duration of campaign was duly considered. In the event the duration of campaign was expected to be long the month of Mārgaśīrṣa or Pauṣa was considered the appropriate time. But for a campaign of medium or short duration any of the month of Caitra, Vaiśākha, Jyeṣṭha or Āṣāḍha was considered suitable.[21] Further, for waging war in a hot country the winter (Hemanta) months and for campaigning in a cold country summer (Grīṣma) months were considered ideal.[22] For campaigning in general, Śukrācārya considered the season of Śarada or Hemanta as ideal, Vasanta as medium, and Grīṣma as worst.[23] The *Mahābhārata* and the *Matsya Purāṇa* considered the full moon day (*pūrṇimā*) of Mārgaśīrṣa or Caitra as most auspicious for launching a victory campaign.[24]

DEŚA or *BHŪMI* (TERRAIN) FACTOR

The terrain was another important factor related to the conduct of war. According to Kāmandaka those incorrigible fools who without much deliberation, rashly enter into the enemy's territory which is long way off, soon feel the touch of the edge of the enemy's sword.[25] He illustrates the point by stating that a 'dog can overpower a crocodile when it is on land, and the crocodile can overpower the dog when it is in water'.[26]

The nature of the territory where the campaign is to be conducted also determined the choice of the army to be deployed against the enemy. The *Arthaśāstra* advises that in a land where rain is plentiful the attack should be mounted with elephants, but in dry lands horses, camels and asses can be used successfully. In a terrain which remained free of mud despite plentiful rains all the four arms could be deployed.[27] The terrain aspect is also dealt with in detail by Kāmandaka. He opines that operations should be conducted in even terrain with horses and in marshy lands and jungles with elephants. Desert tracks were to be attacked only when there is plently of rain and summer operations should be restricted to areas which abound in water.[28] Further, only those areas of the enemy territory were to be invaded where own troops could be supplied easily and friendly help could arrive conveniently.[29]

In certain situations both time and place factors had to be considered together. The *Matsya Purāṇa* says that the land (*deśa*) which received snowfall should be attacked in summer. It recommends Hemanta and Śiśira (winter months) ideal for campaigning as during these seasons fuel and fodder is available in abundance. For the same reason Śarada and Vasanta are considered tolerably good for campaigning.[30]

The Śukranīti has also dealt with terrain factor in some detail. It classifies the terrain in three categories, viz., *uttama*, *madhyama* and *adhama*. The terrain which provided adequate space to own troops for exercise but denied the same to enemy troops was considered the best. The terrain providing equal facility of exercise to both own and enemy troops was considered medium. The terrain providing better facility to the enemy troops to exercise, while denying the same to own troops was considered inferior.[31]

SVABALA (OWN ARMY) FACTOR

Army was another important factor which influenced the conduct of war. Some military thinkers believed that army was more important than time and place.[32] Kauṭilya, however, considered all the three factors equally important and also complementary to each other.[33] The *Manusmṛti* says that a ruler should venture out for invasion only after ensuring that his army is large and strong.[34] The *Matsya Purāṇa* also says that a ruler should march out with a large and strong army after ensuring proper protection of the fort.[35] He should also ensure that his army is loving, well fed, and satisfied.[36]

The *Matsya Purāṇa* speaks at length about the deployment of different arms (*caturaṅgiṇī*) in relation to terrain (*deśa*).[37] It says that a ruler strong in infantry could attack the enemy on an uneven ground. The enemy entrenched in wooded and marshy land could be attacked with elephants, whereas on even ground the chariots and horses were more useful in attack.

The Epic considered non-marshy, waterless and even-ground good for the deployment of horses. The chariots could be deployed in non-marshy, unpitted even ground. The elephants could operate effectively in wet and forest lands. The infantry could, however, operate in difficult, heavily wooded, and hilly areas.[38] Kāmandaka also expresses similar views on the suitability of various arms for fighting in various types of terrain.[39]

ŚATRUBALA (ENEMY ARMY) FACTOR

Śukrācārya considered a fair assessment of the enemy strength desirable before launching an attack.[40] Kauṭilya advises that it should be considered along with other aspects relevant to war.[41] The *Matsya Purāṇa* says that if an enemy was afflicted by divine, worldly or earthly calamities an invasion could be mounted against him.[42] Kauṭilya advises that a campaign could be launched against a ruler who is trapped in external and internal calamities.[43] Manu going a step further says that when a ruler is confident of his victory and at the same time finds his adversary afflicted by calamities, he should immediately launch an attack against him.[44]

MAṆḌALA FACTOR

The structure of Indian polity was based on *maṇḍala* (circle) theory.[45] It provided for four basic elements (*mūla-prakṛti*) of the *maṇḍala*, viz., *vijigīṣu*, *ari*, *madhyama* and *udāsīna*. *Vijigīṣu* (king desirous of victory) was central to the scheme of *maṇḍala* theory. *Ari* was the enemy king whom he targetted for conquest. In between the *vijigīṣu* and the *ari* there was the factor of *madhyama*, the king who was capable of conducting war or peace with either of the two. Further, besides *ari* and *madhyama* there was *udāsīna* or neutral king. He was considered most powerful of all and could take on all the three jointly or separately.

Besides these basic elements there were eight subsidiary elements relevant to the *maṇḍala* theory. These included *mitra*, *ari-mitra*, *mitra-mitra*, *ari-mitra-mitra*, *pārṣṇigraha*, *ākranda*, *pārṣṇigrahasāra* and *ākrandasāra*. *Mitra* was the friendly king. *Pārṣṇigraha* was the enemy king capable of attacking *vijigīṣu* from behind. *Ākranda* was the king who was a natural friend of *vijigīṣu* and therefore, a natural enemy of *pārṣṇigraha*. *Pārṣṇigrahasāra* king was a natural friend of *pārṣṇigraha* and therefore, natural enemy of *ākranda*. *Ākrandasāra* king, who had a common border with *pārṣṇigrahasāra*, was a natural friend of *ākranda* and a natural enemy of *pārṣṇigrahasāra*.

The aforesaid elements when combined variously formed as many as seventeen *maṇḍalas* such as *trikamaṇḍala* (*vijigīṣu*, *ari* and *madhyama*), *catuṣkamaṇḍala* (*vijigīṣu, ari, madhyama* and *udāsīna*), *ṣaṭkamaṇḍala*, *aṣṭakamaṇḍala*, *daśakamaṇḍala*, etc. The biggest *maṇḍala* comprised as many as 324 elements or kings (*caturviṁśatitriśatakamaṇḍala*).

Kāmandaka has stretched the *maṇḍala* theory too far and has in a way made its application universal. The basis of *maṇḍala* theory is, however, sound insofar as friends, enemies and neutrals are integral to every political system. The decision of a *vijigīṣu* king to wage war or to abstain from war was indeed dependent on his calculation of the elements which formed the *maṇḍala* around him.

UPĀYACATUṢṬAYA (FOUR MEANS)

Indian political thinkers considered *sāma*, *dāna*, *daṇḍa* and *bheda* (*upāyacatuṣṭaya*) as four important means of state policy. Sensible application of these means ensured success.[46] Kauṭilya has described these means and their application in some detail.[47] The *Kāmandaka Nīti*, however, speaks of seven means instead of four, the additional three being *māyā*, *upekṣā* and *indrajāla*.[48] Interestingly, these seven means are also referred to in the Purāṇas.[49]

Sāma (right conduct) is explained as the art of influencing a person by praising him. As a means of state policy it was applied against an adversary king to achieve an objective. The praise could be true (*tathya*) or false (*atathya*).[50] Kāmadaka refers to five subdivisions of *sāma*, viz., praising good deed, stressing strong relations, frank expressions, sweet language and self-surrender.[51] The application of praise whether true or false needed great discretion, or else it could lead to disastrous consequences.[52]

Dāna (gift) was considered a very effective means of influencing the adversary. Intelligent application of *dāna* could easily win over an enemy and disintegrate a rival confederacy.[53] *Dāna* could also help in gaining the favour of those kings who were loath to other temptations.[54] The *Agni Purāṇa* has referred to five sub-types of *dāna*.[55]

Bheda (discord) as a means of state policy was applied to create misunderstanding among the rival kings, who had joined hands.[56] Important state functionaries could be targetted by the spies (*cara*) with this intent.[57] Discord could be caused by three means, viz., encouraging disaffection, disobedience and terror.[58]

Daṇḍa (punishment) was applied to cause maximum harm to the enemy by way of killing him, by way of looting his wealth or by way of causing physical pain to him.[59] This could be done overtly or covertly.

Māyā (illusion) was considered an effective means of destroying the enemy. This could be done by changing appearance, showering stones, causing rains and merging in the darkness to confuse the enemy.[60]

Upekṣā (to ignore) was applied as a means of state policy in special circumstances. It demanded extreme tolerance in the face of injustice, vice and offensive by the enemy.[61]

Indrajāla (delusion) was used to scare away the enemy by causing before him the illusion of clouds, rains, fire and other terrorizing objects.[62] The use of charms and spells to conquer the enemy is first mentioned in the *Atharvaveda.* The following hymn amply proves this:

> Indra, confound the army of our enemies: with the blast of fire, of wind, make them disappear, scattering.
>
> Let Indra confound the army: let the Maruts slay with force: let Agni take away its eyes; let it go back conquered.
>
> Yonder army of our adversaries, O Maruts, that comes contending against us with force, pierce ye it with baffling darkness, that one of them may not know another.[63]

There is an interesting reference to the means of *indrajāla* (delusion), *māyā* (illusion) and *kuhakā* (jugglery) in the *Mahābhārata.* In an oblique reference to the act of *Viśvarūpadarśana* by Kṛṣṇa. Duryodhana in a message to Pāṇḍavas said that illusions like *indrajāla, māyā* and *kuhakā* only add to the fury of the warriors like him.[64] He also told Pāṇḍavas that Kauravas can also fly into the space (*antarikṣa*), enter into heaven (*Indrapurī*) and hell (*rasātala*) and assume different forms through *māyā* but added that such exhibitions neither help in attaining the desired objectives nor cause any fear to the enemy.[65] Obviously, these means of state policy were known in the epic times. In fact Ghaṭotkaca used the weapon of *māyā* on the eighth day of war and forced the Kaurava army to run away in terror.[66]

In the battle of Laṅkā Indrajit, the son of Rāvaṇa, also used *māyā* to tie-down Rāma and Lakṣmaṇa.[67] Rāvaṇa also played *māyā* to deceive Sītā that Rāma had been killed in a battle.[68]

DAṆḌA AS LAST OPTION

As a means of state policy the application of *daṇḍa* (war) is not advocated in the epics, Purāṇas and Nīti works. The *Mahābhārata* says that the victory earned by means of war was inferior (*jaghanya*).[69] The *Yājñavalkya Smṛti* says that the means of war should be resorted to only when all other options have been exhausted.[70] The *Manusmṛti* says that a king should try to achieve his political objectives by influencing or alluring the enemy king, his ministers, and commander-in-chief. Failing this, he should try to sow seeds of discord among ministers and other officials of the rival king and then taking advantage of the situation make him amenable to his demands.[71] Evidently, the *Manusmṛti* was in favour of avoiding the use of *daṇḍa* as far as possible.[72] Kāmandaka also reiterates this while recommending that *sāma*, *dāna* and *bheda* should be used consecutively and that when all these prove unsuccessful the means of *daṇḍa* should be applied for the security of the state.[73] According to the *Agni Purāṇa*, the option of *daṇḍa* could be applied against other countries, both openly and secretly.[74]

The application of four means in the inter-state relations is also referred to in the epics. Rāma, despite the great provocation caused by the abduction of his wife Sītā by Rāvaṇa first applied the means of *sāma* by sending Aṅgada on peace mission to Laṅkā. Despite his pleadings when Rāvaṇa refused to return Sītā, Rāma was left with no option other than using *daṇḍa* against him. On the eve of the epic war, Kṛṣṇa pleaded in favour of reconciliation and avoidance of war in the Pāṇḍava assembly. He even went to Kaurava court and pleaded against war. It was only after Duryodhana refused to return even five villages to Pāṇḍavas that Kṛṣṇa consented to the application of *daṇḍa* against the Kauravas.

ṢĀḌGUṆYA (SIX MEASURES)

The policy of the state was also governed by six measures (*ṣāḍguṇya*), viz., *sandhi* (treaty), *vigraha* (war), *yāna* (march), *āsana* (inaction), *saṁśraya* (shelter) and *dvaidhībhāva* (dual policy).[75] The application of these measures has been described in Smṛtis, Purāṇas and Nīti works.[76] Kauṭilya says that when weak, a ruler should conclude treaty with the enemy (*sandhi*) but when strong he should wage war against him (*vigraha*). If on equal footing with the adversary he should follow the policy of inactivity (*āsana*) but if on a strong footing he should march out to fight (*yāna*). When weak in strength he should seek shelter (*saṁśraya*) with a powerful king but in uncertain conditions he should follow dual policy (*dvaidhībhāva*) of no war no peace.[77] A resort to war was, however, advisable only when a ruler was financially sound and militarily strong. The *Manusmṛti* cautions that these measures should be applied after deep thought and hard deliberations.[78] This is also reiterated in the epics and the Purāṇas.[79] Each of these measures had various sub-types as follows:

Sandhi (Treaty)

In the *Mahābhārata* three types of treaties are mentioned as *vittasandhi*, *satkārasandhi* and *bhayasandhi*. The *vittasandhi* was concluded after exacting money from the vanquished king and was considered the best (*uttama*). The *satkārasandhi* was concluded after extending due hospitality to him and was considered the second best (*madhyama*). The *bhayasandhi* was concluded after terrorizing the defeated king and was considered inferior (*adhama*).[80]

In the *Arthaśāstra* three types of treaties are mentioned. These are called *daṇḍopanata*, *koṣopanata* and *deśopanata*. The first had three sub-types, viz., *āmiṣa*, *puruṣāntara* and *adṛṣṭapuruṣa*. The second included *parikraya*, *upagraha*, *atyaya* and *kapāla* sub-types. The third, i.e. *deśopanata* included *Adiṣṭa*, *ucchina*, *avakraya* and *paridūṣaṇa*.[81] These treaties entailed loss of power, wealth and territory to the defeated king and were considered inferior types by Kauṭilya.[82]

Kāmandaka, however, refers to sixteen forms of *sandhi* as follows:[83]

1. *Adṛṣṭanara* (अदृष्टनर) : The treaty between *vijigīṣu* and a weaker king with the stipulation that the latter would use his army for the benefit of the former.
2. *Ātmamiṣa* (आत्ममिष) : The treaty entered into by the king with his army.
3. *Adiṣṭa* (अदिष्ट) : Under this treaty the defeated king sought peace with the victor by surrendering territory.

4. *Acchinna* (अच्छिन्न) : Under this treaty the defeated king sought peace by surrendering fertile land to the victor.
5. *Upagraha* (उपग्रह) : The treaty involved surrender of all possessions in lieu of life.
6. *Upanyāsa* (उपन्यास) : This treaty was concluded with a view to some higher aims.
7. *Upahāra* (उपहार) : In this treaty the defeated king sought peace by offering valuable gifts to the victorious king.
8. *Kapāla* (कपाल) : It was a treaty concluded between kings of equal power.
9. *Parikraya* (परिक्रय) : This treaty was concluded to protect the subjects by offering part of the treasury or complete treasury to the conqueror. Kauṭilya, however, says that this treaty was entered into to seek the release of important state functionaries from enemy custody.
10. *Paradūṣaṇa* (परदूषण) : Under this treaty the weaker king promised to give the produce of his land to the stronger king.
11. *Puruṣāntara* (पुरुषान्तर) : Under this treaty two kings agreed that their principal warriors would endeavour to protect each other's interest.
12. *Pratikāra* (प्रतिकार) : This treaty was concluded by a king with a view to secure the help of the other king at an appropriate time.
13. *Saṅgata* (संगत) : It was the treaty of friendship concluded between two generous kings.
14. *Santāna* (संतान) : The treaty envisaged the offering of a daughter in marriage to another king. Kauṭilya has termed it as *suvarṇa-sandhi* (golden treaty).[84]
15. *Saṁyoga* (संयोग) : It was a treaty concluded between two rulers with a common objective.
16. *Skandhopaneya* (स्कन्धोपनेय) : Under this treaty the weaker king sent his servants, carrying the presents of fruits, etc., on their shoulders to the powerful king.

The *Manusmṛti* refers only to two types of *sandhis*, viz., *samānayānakarma* and *asamānayānakarma*[85] as against sixteen of the *Kāmandaka Nīti* and the *Agni Purāṇa*. The *Agni Purāṇa*, however, considered only four of them, viz., *upakāra*, *maitrī*, *sambandha* and *upahāra* as important.[86]

Vigraha (Waging of War)

According to the *Arthaśāstra* causing harm to someone is *vigraha.*[87] The *Manusmṛti* refers to two types of *vigraha:*[88]

1. To wage war to protect self-interest when the enemy was in distress.
2. To wage war in the defence of a friendly king.

Kāmandaka, however, refers to three objectives of war, viz., territory, wealth and friendship.[89] The *Agni Purāṇa* describes the types of *vigraha*, causes of *vigraha* and the circumstances under which *vigraha* should be avoided.[90]

Yāna (March or Campaign)

Marching against an enemy to conquer him was called *yāna.*[91] The *Manusmṛti* refers to two types of *yāna*:[92]

1. Marching against an enemy as a sudden move.
2. Marching against an enemy with the support of a friendly king.

Kāmandaka and Śukrācārya, however, refer to five sub-types of *yāna*, viz., *vigrahyayāna*, *sandhāyayāna*, *sambhūyayāna*, *prasaṅgayāna* and *upekṣāyāna.*[93]

Vigrahyayāna was marching out for waging war with the intent of destroying the ememy.[94] All forces of the state were involved in this war. Allies of *vijigīṣu* also fought with the allies of the targetted king.

Sandhāyayāna was a campaign launched against an enemy after securing own rear by concluding a treaty with the neighbouring king (*pārṣṇigraha*).[95]

In *sambhūyayāna* the king was accompanied by feudatories skilled in warfare. In it two or more kings joined hands to destroy the enemy and his elements (*prakṛti*).[96]

When a *vijigīṣu* incidentally attacked a king while proceeding to gain some other objective it was called *prasaṅgayāna.*[98]

When the *vijigīṣu* on victory campaign finds his adversary strong and beats a hasty retreat or invades some weaker king it was called *upekṣāyāna.*[97]

Briefly speaking, in the state of *vigrahya* the rival kings waited for an opportune time to attack each other.[99] In *sandhāya* the *vijigīṣu* and his adversary, weakened by the fatigue of war are reduced to a state of inactivity.[100] In *sambhūya* state the *vijigīṣu* joins hand with *madhyama* and *udāsīna* kings and lives peacefully.[101] In *prasaṅgayāna* the *vijigīṣu* after having obtained an unexpected victory settled in the conquered territory peacefully.[102] In *upekṣāyāna*, the *vijigīṣu* realizing that the adversary is more powerful, ignores him and stays quiet.[103]

Āsana (State of Inactivity)

The state of remaining inactive by a *vijigīṣu* king while awaiting the opportune time, was called *āsanayāna*.[104] Kauṭilya says that the state of *āsana* was to be resorted to only when a king is convinced that neither he nor his adversary was capable of harming each other.[105] The slumber was used to augment the capability to strike. Kauṭilya has described three states of *āsana* as *sthāna*, *āsana* and *upekṣaṇa*.[106] In the *sthāna* state the *vijigīṣu* remained quiet but kept on pondering over the measures to defeat the enemy. In the state of *āsana*, *vijigīṣu* made efforts to augment his power silently. *Upekṣaṇa* was the state of ignorance, where no measures were contemplated against the enemy.[107]

Manusmṛti has described two types of *āsanas*:

1. State of inactivity due to some misforture.
2. State of inactivity against a rival in the interest of a friendly king.[108]

Kāmandaka's concept of *āsana* is almost similar to Kauṭilya's, excepting that the former refers to five types of *āsanas* instead of three.[109]

Śukra interprets *āsana* as a situation where *vijigīṣu* lays a firm siege of the enemy.[110] But when both weakened by a prolonged war conclude a treaty and stay put in their territory it was called *sandhāyāsana*.[111]

Saṁśraya (Protection)

It was a state in which a weak ruler surrendered before a strong ruler with a view to seek his protection. *Manusmṛti*[112] and *Kāmandaka Nīti*[113] have referred to two types of *saṁśraya*:

1. *Saṁśraya* in the face of real enemy threat.
2. *Saṁśraya* in the face of possible enemy threat.

Dvaidhībhāva (Dual Policy)

It was a state where *vijigīṣu* outwardly maintained friendly relations with a ruler but inwardly considered him an enemy.[114] Kauṭilya says that when a *vijigīṣu* concludes treaty with one ruler and opens hostility against the other it is a state of *dvaidhībhāva.*[115] The king is advised to further his interests and destroy his enemies by following this policy.[116]

Kāmandaka has classified *dvaidhībhāva* in two categories, viz., *svatantra* and *paratantra.* When a ruler followed this policy independently it was called *svatantra-dvaidhībhāva* but when he followed it in subjection it is called *paratantra-dvaidhībhāva.*[117]

ŚAKTISTRIVIDHA (THREE CAPABILITIES)

With reference to Indian polity three capabilities of the state are generally referred to. These include *mantraśakti, prabhuśakti* and *utsāhaśakti.*[118] Kauṭilya explains that *jñānabala* or the power acquired through knowledge is *mantraśakti, kośabala* or the power acquired through treasury is *prabhuśakti* and *vikramabala* or the power acquired from valour is *utsāhaśakti.*[119] The ruler enjoying these three capabilities earned victories while others were weaklings.[120] The epic says that a wise ruler should evaluate his capabilities before launching an attack.[121]

Kāmandaka has given a slightly different interpretation of these capabilities stating that *prabhuśakti* emanated from the influence of the ruler, *mantraśakti* from consultations with advisers and *utsāhaśakti* from armies of the state.[122] In the *Mānasollāsa* these capabilities have been described in greater detail.[123]

RĀJADŪTA (ROYAL ENVOY)

In conducting the foreign policy of the state the rulers greatly depended on *dūta.* A person dauntless, accurate in memory, eloquent, accomplished in arms and letters and experienced in all kinds of works alone was considered qualified for appointment as the ambassador of the king.[124] *Sandhi* or *vigraha* depended on his threat perception and submission to his master. In the complicated *maṇḍala* system of the state nothing could have moved for the *vijigīṣu* without a competent posse of *dūtas.* In the *Arthaśāstra* the following three categories of *dūtas* are described:[125]

1. *Nisṛṣṭārtha*: This category of the envoys was authorized to conduct negotiations on war and peace on behalf of their master with the adversary kings. Such envoys were expected to possess all the qualities of a minister.
2. *Parimitārtha*: This category of envoys was authorized to conduct negotiations with an adversary king but could not conclude peace with him without prior approval of their master. Such envoys enjoyed the status of a minister and were expected to possess three-fourth of the qualities of a minister.
3. *Śāsanahara*: It was the third category of the envoys, who carried royal messages to other rulers. Such envoys were expected to possess half of the qualities of a minister.

The *Manusmṛti* says that a ruler should appoint an intelligent man of noble family, who is well versed in all the *śāstras* and is capable of interpreting other men's feelings from their means and demeanours, as a *dūta*. The person should also be skilful, pure-hearted, fearless, eloquent and capable of judging the spirit of the place and time.[126] Manu adds that *dūta* should be capable of making or breaking an alliance and handling the issues of war and peace.[127]

In the epics the role of a *dūta* in determining the state's policy on war is greatly stressed. During their stay with King Virāṭa Pāṇḍavas sent the royal priest as their envoy to Kauravas on a diplomatic mission. He pleaded for the return of Indraprastha kingdom to Pāṇḍavas peacefully as they did not want war.[128] Dhṛtarāṣṭra in return sent Sañjaya as his *dūta* to Pāṇḍavas.[129] He very tactfully pleaded with the Pāṇḍavas to eschew war in all circumstances even if Kauravas refused to return their kingdom, for life was momentary and it was better to live on alms than go to war for a kingdom.[130] Finally, Śrī-kṛṣṇa volunteered to go as a *dūta* to Kaurava court to plead in favour of peace.[131] He applied *sāma*, *dāna* and *bheda* in the Kaurava court to secure peace, but when unsuccessful finally decided upon *daṇḍa* (war). Pāṇḍavas indeed agreed to the assessment made by their *dūta*.[132] Rāvaṇa also sent Śuka as a *dūta* to Sugrīva to persuade him to dissociate from war as there was no cause of enemity between them.[133]

SAṄGRĀMA-SAJJĀ (BATTLE-DRESS)

Before marching out for the battefield the ruler held secret consultations on all aspects of war[134] and ordered soldiers to put on the battle-dress (*saṅgrāma-sajjā*).[135]

Little is known about the dress-material and dress-pattern of Indian soldiers in the Harappan age. Cotton was definitely known. According to Irfan Habib as the fibre obtained from the cultivated cotton bush or tree must have been small in quantity, we can, therefore, hardly imagine the ordinary Indus inhabitant to have worn more than very small bits of cotton clothing, and fuller clothing must have been a mark of some wealth.[136] Woollen clothing too could have been in use, specially in the harsh winters of the Punjab, since sheep had been long domesticated.[137] Presumably, they used turban to protect the head[138] and used a fillet to tie-up the hair.[139] The upper garment perhaps comprised a sheet of cloth like *uttarīya*[140] and the lower garment a lion cloth[141] or a kilt.[142] It is likely that soldiers also used some fabric armour.[143] No evidence is met on the use of footwear by the Indus valley people (Pl. 6).

Vedic Soldier

Perhaps, the Indians in the Vedic age dressed more lavishly than the Harappans. It is said that

> the Vedic Indians seem often to have worn three garments—an under-garment (cf. *Nīvi*), a garment, and an over-garment (cf. *Adhivāsa*) which was presumably a mantle, and for which the names *Atka* and *Drāpi* also seem to be used. This accords with the description of the sacrificial garments given in the *Śatapatha Brāhmaṇa* which comprise a *Tārpya*, perhaps a silken under-garment; secondly, a garment of undyed wool, and then a mantle, while the ends of the turban, after being tied behind the neck are brought forward and tucked away in front.[144]

The use of armour distinguished a soldier from a common man.

> The use of protective armour is evidenced in the *Ṛgveda* as well as the later texts. The common word denoting a coat of mail in the *Ṛgveda* is *varman*. There are references to the sewing of the armour though the material of which it was made has not been specified. It may have been in the form of a linen or leather corselet reinforced with metal. A passage of the *Ṛgveda* speaks of a mailed warrior falling before the arrows like bursting vessels. Whatever it was made of, leather, metal or both, the armour of the early Āryans must have afforded ample protection against the weapons of the day. A later passage mentions corselet of *ayas*, *loha* or *rajata*.[145]

Plate 6: Indus Valley Warrior (?)

In Vedic literature the terms *varman* and *kavaca* both are interpreted to convey the sense of armour but these were not one and the same thing. In the *Yajurveda*, Rudra is spoken of as wearing *kavaca* and *varman* both.[146] It was believed that armoured warriors could vanquish the unarmoured warriors easily and inflict serious injuries on them.[147]

Another important item of soldier's costume was *śipra* variously interpreted as turban, cap, or helmet.[148] Perhaps, it was a *pagree* like dress, worn to protect the head from a sword attack. The references to *ayas śipra*, *hiraṇya śipra* and *hari śipra* in the *Ṛgveda* suggest that it was made of metal.[149] The occurrence of the word *vatūriṇāpāda*[150] and *patasaṅgiṇī*[151] in Vedic literature suggests that men used some kind of shoe to protect their legs.

The Vedic soldier observed some kind of dress discipline. The *Maruts* (soldiers) bore an *añji*, carried a *rukma* on their chest and a *ṛṣṭi* on their shoulders.[152] It is believed that *añji* was an ornament or symbol which served as an identification mark, *rukma* was a shining ornament and *ṛṣṭi* was a weapon. These devices were of a similar make, and soldiers, bearing them looked like brothers.[153] In this connection it is notable that Vrātya people, who were natives, also observed some dress discipline.[154]

Epic Soldier

In the Epic age the costume of the soldiers was known as *saṅgrāmasajjā*.[155] State provided for the dress, weapons and accoutrements of the soldiers[156] in respect of some army formations as they looked alike in the battlefield.[157] In a particular context the commanders of Kaurava army are described as wearing *kavaca* and donning black deer skin.[158] Large stocks of military weapons and equipment including protective nets and armours were deposited at the gate of the fort for quick distribution to the soldiers.[159] *Kavaca* (armour), *śirastrāṇa* (helmet), *kaṇṭhatrāṇa* (neck-guard), *hastavāpa* (hand-guard) and *aṅgulitrāṇa* (finger-guard) had now become a part of the soldier's costume.[160] *Kavaca* was perhaps a heavy wear and, therefore, soldiers discarded it while fleeing from the battlefield.[161] Soldiers bore identification marks on their person for easy recognition.[162]

In the epics there is no reference to dress items like coat, trousers, cap or *dhotī*. People are occasionally referred to as wearing *uṣṇīṣa*, *antarīya*, *uttarīya*,[163] *vastra*,[164] *ambara*[165] and *vāsa*.[166] Of these *uṣṇīṣa* was the headdress, *antarīya* the lower garment and *uttarīya* the upper garment. But nothing specifically is said about the use of *vastra*, *ambara* and *vāsa*. Perhaps, *vastra* denoted an upper garment (unstitched) like *uttarīya*, as it was waived in the air by the warriors when there was occasion to rejoice at the battlefield. The *ambara* may have denoted the lower garment as there is no reference to its waiving in the air. *Vāsa* was probably a piece of cloth used to tie-up hair by the soldiers.[167]

It seems that in the Epic age no warrior of note joined the battle without putting on some kind of armour, i.e. *kavaca* or *varman*. While preparing to fight back the Kauravas King Virāṭa and his princes put on their armour. Virāṭa put on *abhedyakalpa kavaca* which could not be pierced by any weapon. It was decorated with motifs like sun, cakra, flowers, etc. His brother wore an armour made of steel. His son Śaṅkha put on an armour of white colour. Virāṭa provided armour to Pāṇḍava brothers also. His generals also wore armour commensurate to their status.[168]

It is significant that in the epic times soldiers carried an identification mark on their person while going to war. Yudhiṣṭhira provided his soldiers with such devices and ornaments on the eve of the war with a view to identify them at the battlefield.[169]

Maurya Soldier

In fourth century BC the Indians generally wore *adhovāsa* (*dhotī* like garment) *uttarīya* (mantle) and *uṣṇīṣa* (turban).[170] In this connection the observations made by Arrian are significant:

> The dress worn by Indians is made of cotton. . . . They wear an under-garment of cotton which reaches below the knee halfway down to the ankles, and also an upper garment which they throw partly over their shoulders and partly twist in fold round their head. The Indians wear also earrings of ivory, but only such of them do this as are very wealthy, for all Indians do not wear them. Their beards, Nearchos tells us, they dye of one hue and another, according to taste. . . . They wear shoes made of white leather and these are elaborately trimmed, while the soles are variegated and made of great thickness, to make the wearer seem so much taller.[171]

The account given by Curtius adds some more details to this:

They cover their person down to the feet with fine muslin, are shod with sandals, and coil round their heads cloths of linen (cotton). They hang precious stones as pendants from their ears, and persons of high social rank, or of great wealth, deck their wrist and upper arm with bracelets of gold. They frequently comb, but seldom cut, the hair of their head. The beard of the chin they never cut at all, but they shave off the hair from the rest of the face, so that it looks polished.[172]

Mauryan soldiers observed some dress discipline is evident from the account of Megasthenese. He says that among the Indians 'the fifth class consists of fighting men, who, when not engaged in active service pass their time in idleness and drinking. They are maintained at the king's expense and hence they are always ready, when the occasion calls, to take the field, for they carry nothing of their own with them but their own bodies'.[173] As these soldiers were maintained at state expense, it is likely that they dressed uniformally.

Foreign Influence

In the Bhārhut sculptures the dress of a soldier shows definite foreign influence.

His head is bare, and the short curly hair is bound with a broad band or ribbon, which is fastened at the back of the head in a bow, with its long ends streaming in the wind. His dress consists of tunic with long sleeves, and reaching nearly the mid thigh. It is tied in two places by cord. . . . The loins and thighs are covered with a dhoti which reaches below the knees with the ends hanging down to the ground in front. On the feet are boots which reach high up the legs. In his left hand the soldier carries a flower, and in his right a monstrously broad straight sword, sheathed in a scabbard, which is suspended from the left shoulder by a long flat belt.[174]

After the decline of the Mauryan empire the Bactrian Greeks, Pahlavas, Śakas and Kuṣāṇas invaded India one after another. The Śakas and Kuṣāṇas introduced notable changes in the costume of soldier. The Indian *uttarīya*, a loose upper garment, was replaced by close fitting *kūrpāsa* or *kañcuka*, as a result of the Śaka influence.[175] The trousers were also introduced by the Śakas.

By reason of their domestication of horse and horse-back riding the inhabitants of Central Asia were forced to discard the loose skirt-like costume and to develop that ingenious piece of clothing that we call trousers. With the popularity of horse-back riding it spread to other parts of globe.[176]

The use of top-boots was also introduced by the Central Asian invaders.[177]

This foreign influence is also perceptible in the dress of the soldiers represented in the art of Sāñcī. Marshall says that

it is tempting to see Yavana influence in the un-Indian attire of some of the figures in Pl. 36C1, comprising a tunic (Gr. Chiton) short cloaks (Gr. Chalmys) and fillet for the hair (Gr. Taenia); and even the pointed, Phrygian-looking caps worn by two of the figures in this relief would be appropriate to Yavanas hailing from the region of Bactria or thereabouts. But sleeved tunics, which these appear to be, leggings (patties) and pointed caps are still worn in the hills of western Nepal and Tibet, and it is reasonable to infer that in the first century BC they may have constituted the national costume of the Mallas, who came perhaps from the hill country.[178]

The foreign impact on Indian military costume is perceptible in the art of Bhārhut (Pl. 7) and Sāñcī (Pl. 8), and more particularly in the art of Gandhāra (Pl. 9) and Mathurā (Pl. 10).

While referring to two dress styles depicted in the art of Mathurā Richard Salomon says that

the Scythian men's costume was entirely different from that of the Indian. Not surprisingly it resembled quite closely the Scythian costume known from other regions and south and central Asia, and indeed is not unlike that which is still worn today in parts of the latter area. The basic garment was a close fitting tunic held at the waist by a belt and extending to the knees and below. . . . Over the tunic, many of the Scythian men had a heavy coat which was also joined by a belt or a clasp. The coat was usually longer than the tunic. In sharp contrast to the generally barefooted Indians the Scythians wore thick knee length central Asian boots with the straps around the ankle and under the sole.[179]

A unique feature of the soldier's costume represented in the art of Sāñcī is the waist-band. It was worn in a rope-like manner around the waist in strands, numbering from one to seven. Significantly, the number of strands in the case of swordsmen appears six or seven,[180] in the case of bowmen four or five[181] and in the case of standard-bearers and musicians two to four.[182] It is likely that larger number

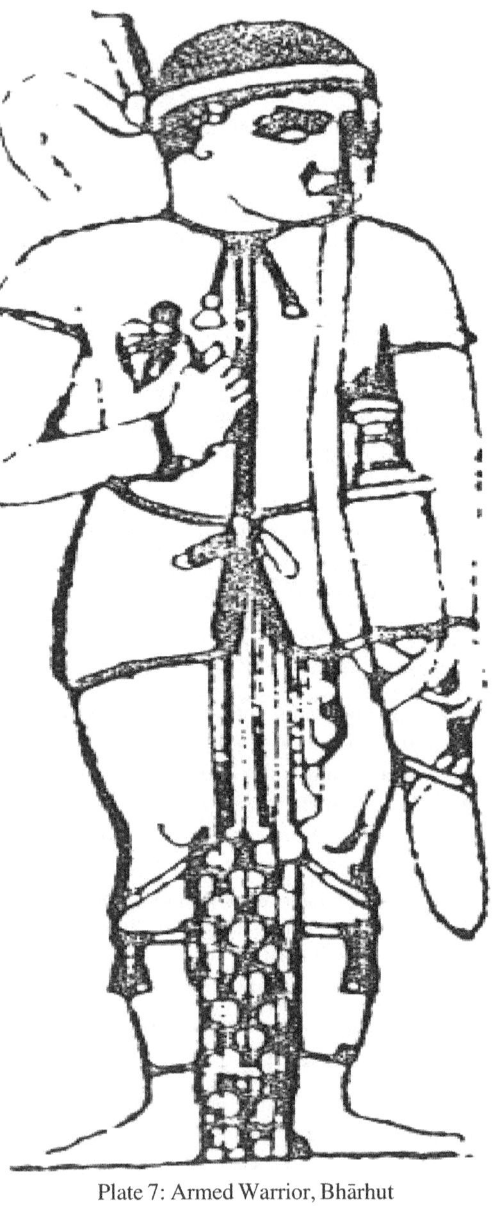

Plate 7: Armed Warrior, Bhārhut

Plate 8: Armed Soldiers, Sāñcī

Plate 9: Armed Soldiers, Gandhāra

Plate 10: Kaniṣka’s Statue, Mathurā

of strands indicated the higher status of the person in military hierarchy. It is also notable that such waist-bands are often worn by men dressed in tunic (short coat) and kilt (skirt), definitely a foreign dress style. Incidentally, the Greek historians who have described the costume of Indian soldiers in detail make no mention of the waistband. The archers wore their waistband in a cross-belt fashion to hang the quiver on their back.[183]

This incidence of two different dress styles is evident from the art of Bhārhut and Sāñcī. The idigenous type included a full-sleeved jacket, dhoti, sash with one or two broad bands, turban and sandals. The assimilated type comprised tunic, turban, kilt, waistband and the boots. The cross-belts were also peculiar to the later type. The art and numismatic evidence suggests that the foreign influence on military costume became more prominent in the Gupta period.

The Śakas and Kuṣāṇas continued with their heavy costume for some time as is evident from the art of Gandhāra (Pl. 9) and Mathurā (Pl. 10). But as the costume was most unsuited for Indian climate the invaders gradually discarded it and changed over to a dress style which was much lighter. It was a case of Indianizing the foreign dress style as is attested to by the Gupta coins and Ajantā frescoes.

The equipment of soldiers also underwent a change. But to say that 'helmets and plate armour for men, and horses and elephants were certainly foreign importations, as such defensive armour was quite unknown in early India'[184] is far from the truth. The evidence of Jātakas, Nikāyas and Greek historians is conclusive on the point that Indians used armour before fourth century BC.

During the Gupta and Vardhana rule the military costume appears an amalgam of traditional Indian and Śaka-Kuṣāṇa costume. On some coin types Gupta rulers are postrayed in helmet, coat and trausers, a dress style of Kuṣāṇa inspiration. The description of an infantry soldier in the *Harṣacarita* also confirms this

Before it (cavalry) ran an army of foot about a thousand strong, mostly young men, with clusters of crisp hanging hair upon their foreheads, and cheeks laughing with the bright gleans of their ear-ornaments; girt with scented jerkins spotted with a powder of black aloe wood paste; their upper garments formed into turbans; sparkling golden bracelets on their left forearms, daggers fastened in strong knots in their sashes of doubled cloth . . . clubs at their sides, swords in their hands.[185]

At another place describing the costume of a cavalry soldier *Harṣacarita* says:

Their shanks were covered with their proper covering of delicate tinted silk. Their copper-coloured legs were chequered with mud-stained wraps, and a whitened height was produced by contrast with trousers soft and dark as bees. They wore tunics darkened by black diamonds glistering on bright forms; Chinese cuirasses thrown over them, coats and doublets showing clusters of bright pearls, bodices speckled with a mixture of various colours, and shawls of the shade of parrot's tail. Fine wristbands were wound about flanks made thin by exercise.[186]

Preparing the vehicle before joining the battle was also a part of *Saṅgrāma-sajjā*. In the *Ṛgveda* there is reference to a chariot carrying weapons and armour for the destruction of enemy.[187] In the epics there are many references to well decorated chariots of war.[188] The war elephants and horses were also loaded with weapons and armour.[189]

Purāṇic Evidence

Purāṇas also yield some information on military costume. During a night battle in the Devāsura war, the army of Visaṅga (*Asura*) was dressed in dark-coloured turbans. The equipment of the soldiers was also made of dark colour so that it matched well with the surrounding darkness. Visaṅga himself put on the armour round his chest and his dress and accoutrement were fitted with the nocturnal battle.[190] This is a unique instance of camouflaging for the purpose of war in ancient India.

A general picture of military costume is also met in the *Bhāgavata Purāṇa:*

like two oceans swarming with sea monsters shone the two (warring) armies of Deva and Dānava warriors with their ranks of fighters distinguished by their flags of different colours, by their spotless white umbrellas . . . with their upper garments and turbans waved up by winds and with their burnished armour and ornaments glittering brightly and their sharp weapons sparkling in the rays of the sun.[191]

The *Matsya Purāṇa* describes the army of the demons as awfully striking like a sky covered with blue clouds and the army of the gods as dressed in black and white costume.[192]

In the *Kāmandaka Nīti* there are many references to the storage and supply of food and clothing to the army.[193] The *Śukranīti* says that the ruler paid a specified amount of money to soldiers as dress allowance.[194] These go to suggest that the state provided soldiers with clothing and these might have been of a uniform pattern.

MOUNTING OF *DHVAJA*

Before marching out for the battlefield a warrior circumambulated his chariot, worshipped it and raised his *dhvaja* on its top. Among the Pāṇḍava warriors, Arjuna displayed *kapi*, Yudhiṣṭhira a pair of *mṛdaṅgas*, Bhīma a *siṁha*, Nakula a *śarabha* and Sahadeva a *haṁsa* on his standard. Among the Kauravas Duryodhana displayed a serpent, Bhīṣma a *tāla* tree, and Karṇa an elephant-chain.[195]

When Porus marched to fight Alexander in the battle of Jhelum he was accompanied by a *dhvaja*. Gupta rulers used the *garuḍa-dhvaja*. They built *dhvaja-stambhas* and issued commemorative coins, with *garuḍa-dhvaja* marked on them.[196] As the most revered symbol of faith, *dhvaja* served the following objectives in a war:

1. A distinguishing mark of the leader.
2. A rallying point for the troops.
3. A motivating factor for keeping up the morale.
4. A signalling device to communicate the orders of the commander to the troops.

MILITARY RITUALS

Many rituals preceded the march of the army to the battlefield. In the Vedic age army march started after pouring oblations into the fire.[197] The Vedic Kalpasūtras describe these rituals in detail. To illustrate the point the *Āśvalāyana Gṛhyasūtra* lays down that with the recitation of appropriate *mantras* the *purohita* should make the king put on a coat of mail, hand over the bow and quiver to him, and tie a piece of leather on his arm as a protective device. *Purohita* did this to other warriors also.[198]

Before marching to the battlefield of Kurukṣetra, a *religious* fire-service (*havana*) was performed both by Pāṇḍavas and Kauravas.[199] In this ritual gods were invoked to destroy the foes of the sacrificer.[200]

It was believed that the *mantras* chanted by the priest during this ritual added to the strength of the soldiers.[201]

According to the *Arthaśāstra*, on the eve of the march the ruler should observe fast, sleep near his vehicle, and recite Vedic *mantras* for the destruction of his enemy.[202] Purāṇas also recommend many rituals for the occasion.[203] The *Kāmandaka Nīti* says that gods and Brāhmaṇas should be worshipped before launching a campaign.[204]

The *Harṣacarita* gives a graphic account of the rituals performed by king Harṣa before he moved out on a victory campaign.

> The king had bathed in golden and silver vessels, like autumn clouds which were skilled in pouring water; had with deep devotion offered worship to the adorable Nīlalohita; fed the up-flaming fire, whose masses of blaze formed a rightward whorl; bestowed upon Brāhmaṇas sesamum vessels of precious stones, silver and gold in thousand, myriads also of cows having hoofs and horn-tips adorned with creepers of gold-work.[205]

The army ready to move out was sprayed with sandal-dust and parched rice (*lāja*) on all sides.[206] Spinsters and Brāhmaṇas circumambulated the soldiers to wish them well.[207]

In the *Agni Purāṇa* a detailed description of war preparations (*raṇa-dīkṣā*) to be made by the king is given.[208] It included a seven-day long ritual to be performed by the king before setting out for war:

First day:	worship of Viṣṇu, Śiva and Gaṇeśa with *modakas.*
Second day:	worship of Dikpālas before going to bed.
Third day:	worship of Dikpālas and Rudras.
Fourth day:	worship of planets.
Fifth day:	worship of Aśvinikumāras and various gods and goddesses. Also sacrifices to gods
Sixth day:	*Vijaya-snāna* (victory bath).
Seventh day:	worhip of *trivikrama* (three steps of Viṣṇu), weapons and vehicles.[209] He then moved out with the chanting of victory *mantra* by the priets,[210] picked up his bow[211] and finally hit at the face of the image of the enemy king with his right foot.[212]

ARMY CAMP (*SKANDHĀVĀRA*)

Skandhāvāra generally denoted the royal camp or the army camp laid out in the vicinity of the territory to be attacked or invaded.

Kāmandaka has defined it in some detail, albeit in a different sense:

> The king is called the *skandha* inasmuch as he is said to be the root (of the prosperity) of the people. The functions of the ministers, the army and other members of a government are said to be *avara*. When for the advancement and prosperity of the people the *skandha* or the king is supported or helped forward by the great *avaras* or ministers, armies, etc. it is said to be *skandhāvāra*.[213]

This interpretation is also met in the *Mahābhārata*, where Duryodhana is described as moving out with his *skandhāvāra* to Kurukṣetra, where a *śivira* was laid subsequently.[214] In another context *skandhāvāra* is used in the sense of a military cantonment, adjacent to the capital.[215]

Śivira in Epic

In the *Mahābhārata* the term *śivira* has been used for army camp. Both Pāṇḍavas[216] and Kauravas[217] laid their camps at Kurukṣetra on an even ground. In the *Raghuvaṁśa* the term *senānīveśa* has been used for army camp.[218]

The *Mahābhārata* describes the Pāṇḍava and Kaurava army camps (*niveśa*) in some detail. Pāṇḍava camp was laid on a plain ground abounding in water, fuel and fodder, away from sacred spots, temples and hermitages. Separate tents (*śiviras*) were laid for kings and commanders. Expert artisans (*śilpīs*) and qualified doctors (*vaidyas*) were appointed to serve at the camps, well stocked with weapons, armour, food, fodder, fuel, water, etc.[219] Thousands of such tents were laid by Yudhiṣṭhira for his army outside the Sāmantapañcaka area on the river Hiraṇya.[220] After the battle for the day was over the troops returned to their tents, organized according to arms and units.[221] It was advisable to lay a camp adjacent to a forest as it could provide secrecy and security to troops and in the event of a military debacle they could seek shelter there.[222] Further, forest ensured abundant supply of fuel and fodder.

The camp of the Kaurava army, located on the western side of Kurukṣetra, looked like Hastināpura.[223] The tents of Duryodhana and his ally kings were well fortified. Soldiers were rested in groups of hundred, in the tents laid in lines beyond the battlefield. Food was provided to all combatants and non-combatants residing in the camp at state expense.[224]

ARTHAŚĀSTRA

According to the *Arthaśāstra*

on a site, approved by experts in the science of building, the commandant (*nāyaka*), carpenters (*vardhaki*) and astrologers (*muhūrtika*) should cause the camp to be set up, circular, rectangular or square or in conformity with the nature of the ground, with four gates, six roads and nine divisions, endowed with a moat, a rampart, a parapet, gates and towers, when there is danger and when the army has to halt.

In the ninth part to the north of the central (should be erected) quarters for the king, one hundred *dhanuṣes* in length and half that in width, (with) the royal residence in the western half of that. The palace guards should be stationed on the borders. In front (should be erected) the audience-hall, to the right the treasury and offices for issuing orders and carrying out works, to the left the place for elephants, horses and chariots intended for the king's use.

Beyond this at a distance of one hundred *dhanuṣes* from each other (there should be) four enclosures, with carts, stretches of thorny branches, pillars and the parapet. In the first (enclosure) in front, the councillor and the chaplain (should be encamped), to the right the magazine and the kitchen, to the left the store for forest produce and the armoury. In the second (there should be) quarters for hereditary and hired troops, for horses and chariots and for the commander-in-chief. In the third, elephants, banded troops and the camp superintendent (should be encamped). In the fourth, the labour-corps, the commandant and allied, alien and forest troops under the command of their own officers (should be encamped). Traders and courtesans (should be encamped) along the highways.[225]

KĀMANDAKA NĪTISĀRA

The *Kāmandaka Nīti* has also described the setting up of a *skandhāvāra*:

Having approached the vicinity of the enemy fort, after fully reconnoitering the locality and the ground by experienced scouts, military quarters should be pitched by persons who are adept in the art. The encampment should be quadrangular in shape, equipped with four gates, should have not very wide lanes but must possess large streets and massive walls with a girdle of a broad trench. The residence (encampments) may be shaped like a square, a semi-circle, a circle or a rectangle according to the nature of the locality. Special lodges should be systematically set up. In the center should be erected a royal palace charming to look at and treasury being located within the compound of royal mansions. In the vicinity and in all directions should be quartered in the order of the rank and position, the principal officers of the crown, the various trade guilds, the loyal citizens and the twelve divisions of forces experienced in forest fight. At the extremities should be in a circle the butchers, the fowlers and other classes of low, abject occupations whose fidelity has been bought off with ample remuneration.[226]

The routes through which the enemy could possibly make ingress were protected with covered walls concreted hollows and barbed wires. Rotating guards, organized in eighteen batches, protected the camp on all sides. Strict vigil was maintained in and around the camp all the twenty-four hours to prevent espionage. Desertion from the camp invited severe punishment.[227]

A detailed description of a royal camp is also met in the *Harṣacarita* in relation to the march of Harṣa against the king of Gauḍa.[228] Though many useful details of the camps are not clear, a picture of the royal camp can still be formed. It appears that Harṣa's military camp, was similar to the one described in the *Kāmandaka Nīti.*

Like the Indians ancient Romans also followed a procedure in laying the army camp.

At the end of each day's march the army constructed a temporary camp as if in enemy territory. The procedure was always the same. The units which had formed the vanguard for that day took up positions around the chosen composite and remained in formation and under arms to act as a covering force. Every other part of the army had its allotted task, marking out the camp with its tent lines and roads, or excavating the ditch and building the defensive rampart.[229]

OMEN (*ŚAKUNA*)

Indians were great believers in omens. On the eve of the Epic war Vyāsa spoke to Dhṛtarāṣṭra about many portents (*nimittas*) which indicated large-scale death and destruction (*mahān kṣayaḥ*) in the impending war.[230] Some of these portents were as follows:

1. Perching of birds like hawks, vultures, crows, etc., on tree tops in large numbers.
2. Clouds (*kabandha*) obscuring the sun at sunrise and sunset.
3. Sun, moon and stars appearing in flames (*jvalitaḥ*).
4. The moon appearing lustreless (*prabhayāhīnaḥ*) on the full moon day of Kārttika.
5. Icons of god appearing as trembling, laughing or vomiting blood (*vamantirudhiram*).
6. Drums emitting sound on their own (*anāhata*).
7. Sky roaring high without any clouds.
8. Vehicles weeping and shedding tears.

On the request of Dhṛtarāṣṭra Vyāsa also tells him about good omens which ensured victory to those who see them. These included:
1. Bright smokeless flames, rising above.
2. Burning oblations spreading fragrant smell all around.
3. Drums and conches emitting deep sound.
4. The rays of sun and moon shining brightly.
5. Birds like swans, peacocks, etc., encircling the soldiers.
6. Happy and courageous demeanour of soldiers.

There are many more references to omens in the *Mahābhārata*. On the ninth day of war many portents suggesting death and destruction are detailed.[231] On the tenth day of war when Bhīṣma was killed in the battlefield Droṇa spoke about some portents which didn't augur well for the Kauravas.[232]

So great was the faith of the people in planetary upheavals and supernatural happenings that rulers employed astrologers (*muhūrtika*), readers of omen (*naimitika*), soothsayers (*kārtāntika*) and intuitionists (*ikṣaṇika*) to explain the phenomenon.[233] They even accompanied armies to the battlefield.[234] It was the soothsayer who determined the time for army to march.[235] The *Bṛhatsaṁhitā* says that a ruler desirous of victory should worship the soothsayer (*daivajña*) and listen to his advice for even the might of one thousand elephants and four thousand horses cannot perform a task which a *daivajña* is capable of doing.[236]

The *Mānasollāsa* emphasizes that a ruler should march out with his army only after reading the omens.[237] In this regard the evidence furnished by the *Harṣacarita* is conclusive. 'Some days having passed on a day with care calculated and approved by a troupe of astronomers numbering hundred, was fixed an hour of marching suitable for the subjugation of all the four quarters.'[238] Even the commander-in-chief was expected to be well conversant in reading omens.[239]

It is notable that the soothsayers and astrologers were also engaged to boost up the morale of the troops. The *Arthaśāstra* says that 'the group of his astrologers and others should fill his own side with enthusiasm by proclaiming his omniscience and association with divine agencies and should fill the enemy's side with terror'.[240]

The most detailed description of omens (*śakunas*) is, however, met in the *Agni Purāṇa*.[241] It particularly interprets various sounds and movements of birds and animals in relation to army march or for that matter any human activity.[242]

Diviners and soothsayers also accompanied the Roman armies to the battlefield and this was often considered detrimental to their efficient functioning. A Roman general Scipio (185-129 BC) was so much disgusted with them that he ordered their expulsion from the army camp. Soothsayers also accompanied ancient Greek and German armies.[243]

ARMY ON THE MARCH

In the *Mahābhārata* the march of the Pāṇḍava and Kaurava armies to the battlefield of Kurukṣetra has been described in some detail. The Pāṇḍava army marched out in three formations or columns. The first column comprising Abhimanyu, Draupadeyas and Bṛhanta marched under the leadership of Dhṛṣṭadyumna. The second column was led by Bhīmasena, Yuyudhāna and Arjuna and the third by Yudhiṣṭhira, accompanied by Virāṭa and Drupada.[244] Yudhiṣṭhira reorganized his marching formations on the way as a military manoeuvre so as to deceive the Kauravas[245] about the deployment of his forces. After reorganization the leading column was placed under Bhīmasena, the central column under Arjuna and the rear column under Yudhiṣṭhira, who was accompanied by many great warriors.[246] The rear of the Pāṇḍava army was protected by two warriors named Kṣatradeva and Brahmadeva from behind.[247] The column led by Yudhiṣṭhira was also accompanied by carts laden with military provisions, shopkeepers, stores of weapons and uniforms, treasury, etc.[248] The noise caused by the men while loading the military supplies on the vehicles and in running around knew no bounds.[249]

The *Arthaśāstra* has devoted a full chapter to the subject of army march (*abhiyāsyatkarma*). It says that the king aspiring victory should march 'after ascertaining the (relative) strength or weakness of powers, place, time, seasons of marching, time for raising armies, revolts in the rear, losses, expenses, gains and troubles, of himself and of the enemy'.[250] He should proceed if superior in strength, otherwise stay quiet. Kauṭilya also discusses the relative merits of the factors like *utsāha* (courage), *prabhāva* (might), *mantraśakti* (counsel), *deśa* (place), *kāla* (time), *śakti* (army), etc., and tenders advice on their relative merits and application.[251] Elaborating on the time factor Kauṭilya says:

> He (*vijigīṣu*) should march against the enemy, whose old stocks of food are exhausted, who has not yet collected the new foodgrains and whose fort is unrepaired, on an expedition in Mārgaśirṣa, with a view to destroy his monsoon crops and winter sowings . . . in Caitra, with a view to destroy his winter crops and spring sowings . . . in Jyeṣṭha with a view to destroy his spring crops and monsoon sowings.[252] . . . He should march in winter against a country which is very hot or which has little fodder, fuel and water. He should march in summer against a country with showers of snow, or consisting mostly of deep water or with dense grass and trees. He should march when it is raining against a country suited to the operations of his own army and unsuited to those of the enemy.[253] . . . He should march on a expedition of long duration between the Mārgaśirṣa and the Pauṣa full-moon days, on one of medium duration between the Caitra and Vaiśākha full-moon days, on one of short duration between the Jyeṣṭha and Āṣāḍha full-moon days.[254]

In all situations the objective was to complete the operation before the onset of rains. Further, the use of four arms was also determined by the time factor.

> At a time when excessive heat is over, he should march with elephant divisions for the most part. . . . In the reverse case (he should march) with troops consisting mostly of donkeys, camels and horses, in a region with little rain and mud. In a region mostly desert, he should march with the fourfold army when it is raining.[255]

Kauṭilya has also discussed certain requirements related to the army march, such as supplies, time frame, deployment of troops, etc. He says that the king should start on an expedition from the camp after calculating the halts on the way in villages and in forests, in accordance with the supply of fodder, fuel and water, and (calculating) the time for camping, halting and marching. . . . He should cause food and equipment to be transported in double the quantity required to meet the case. Or, if unable to do so, he should assign it to the troops, or should store them at intervals on the route.[256]

It is notable that most of these aspects related to army march have also been described in the *Kāmandaka Nīti*, the *Agni Purāṇa* and the *Śukranīti*.

While marching out certain precautions were taken to obviate a surprise attack. The commander (*nāyaka*) took position in the forefront of the marching column while the king and the womenfolk followed. The flanks were protected by horses and the rear by elephants. The commander-in-chief (*senāpati*) marched with the rearguard. The army thus moved like a fort protected on all sides.[257]

The army was deployed keeping in view the possible threat perception. If an attack was anticipated on the front side the troops marched in *makara* (crocodile) array, if in the rear in the *śakaṭa* (cart) array, and if on the flanks in the *vajra* (thunderbolt) array. However, if there was a danger of attack on all sides the army marched in *sarvatobhadra* (good on all sides) array. Further, if the road was narrow, allowing the movement of only one person at a time, then the *sūcī* (needle) array was considered the best.[258] While negotiating rivers and forests the army had to be extra vigilant.[259]

Length of March

The length of the march on each day was determined, after considering the road conditions, the state of logistics, and of course the objective. The *Arthaśāstra* says that 1 *yojana* (15 km.) a day is the slowest rate of march, 1.5 *yojana* (22.5 km.) a day the medium rate of march and 2 *yojana* (30 km.) a day the fastest rate of march. The rate of march could, however, be slowed down in the following circumstances:[260]

1. When steps had to be taken to counteract the enemy-in-the rear, the enemy's rear ally, the middle king or the neutral king, any of whom may provide refuge to the enemy or use the opportunity to attack the rich lands of the conqueror.
2. When a difficult path had to be negotiated.
3. When the treasury, the army, allied, alien or forest troops, labourers or suitable season is awaited.

4. When a deterioration in the enemy's fortification, stores, precautionary measures or the moral of his mercenary or allied troops is expected.
5. When the secret agents have been slow in their task in sowing disaffection in the enemy's camp.
6. When the enemy was expected to commit some folly which could help the conqueror.

In the absence of these reasons the pace of march had to be speeded up.

Commenting on the length of 1 or 2 *yojana* march prescribed by the *Arthaśāstra* Basham says:

> The *yojana*, like the medieval English league, is an uncertain measure of distance, varying from four to ten miles; but internal evidence shows that the author of the *Arthaśāstra* had in mind a *yojana* of about five miles. Thus a march of ten miles per day was the most that could be expected even of a well-organised and efficient army. It is not surprising when we read of its complex and cumbrous organization.[261]

The army of King Harṣavardhana of Thānesar marched at the speed of 8 leagues (16 miles) a day. The number of leagues to be covered by the army on a particular day was announced in the early hour of the day. To quote *Harṣacarita*

> at the close of the third watch, when all creatures slept and all was still, the marching drum (*prayāṇa paṭaha*) was beaten with a boom deep as a gaping roar of the sky elephants. Then, after first a moment's pause, eight sharp strokes were distinctly given anew upon the drum, making up the number of the leagues in a day's march.[262]

The army marched in a prescribed formation, depending on the nature of road and the anticipated threat of the enemy. In the *Yajurveda* there are references to troops marching in a linear formation.[263] In the epics also the troops are described as marching in a specified order.[264] Indian military thinkers have actually prescribed the formations in which troops should march in the event of threat in the front, rear or wings.[265]

CHOICE OF BATTLEFIELD

As the layout of battlefield had a bearing on the result of the war, the rulers surveyed the likely site of battle before arraying the troops. In this exercise they also considered the nature of the ground, the available forces and the deployment of enemy. The *Arthaśāstra* says that a dog occupying an elevated position can drag an alligator while an alligator entrenched in a low wet land can drag a dog due to positional advantage.[266]

Kauṭilya classifies the battlefield in three categories, viz., *uttama* (best), *madhyama* (average) and *adhama* (below average). The battlefield which provided ample facility for the training of own troops but denied the same to the adversary was considered the best. The *madhyama* type provided similar facility to both sides while the *adhama* type provided no such facility to own troops.[267]

Elaborating on the choice of battlefield Kauṭilya says:

> Where a firm stand and speed in movements of the array have no favorable terrain there he would be conquered in either case, whether standing firm or moving quickly. In the reverse case, he wins in either case by standing firm or moving quickly.
>
> Ground being level, uneven or mixed, its nature in front, on the flanks and in the rear should be ascertained. On level ground (there should be) the staff and circle arrays, on uneven the snake and diffuse arrays, on mixed the mixed arrays.[268]

The Epic describes the terrain types suitable for conducting operations with different arms. For cavalry the terrain which was free of mud, water, dams and stones was considered suitable. For the operations of chariots the land free of mud and pits was considered good whereas elephants could operate better in land which was full of fodder, small trees and lakes. The infantry could operate in difficult mountainous terrain covered with grass, bamboo or cane.[269] The army with a large number of chariots and horses could operate better on dry days (*sudineṣu*) whereas the army with large infantry and elephant corps could fight better on rainy days.[270]

The *Manusmṛti*, describes the choice of battlefield in some detail. It says that an even or flat land was ideal for fighting with chariots and horses, the ground interspersed by water was good for fighting with elephants and naval forces while the ground full of trees and creepers but without thorns, was good for fighting with infantry.[271] The *Kāmandaka Nīti* and the *Agni Purāṇa* also hold similar views on the subject.[272]

The epic war was fought in the battlefield of Kurukṣetra, because it was a flat land, considered ideal for the deployment of chariots. Its circumference is said to have been 5 *yojanas* (45 miles).[273] At another place it is said to be many *yojana* long.[274]

In this context the views expressed in the *Tirukkural*, a Tamil work of first century AD, are significant:

> Do not begin any military operation till you have chosen the suitable place where you can offer battle to your enemy. Do not despise your foe. Even when you lead a powerful and efficient army to conquer your enemy, chosing a proper place for action will be of great advantage; Even with a small army you can stand at bay and defeat a large army if you choose a suitable place of action where you can defend yourself safely against the assault of the enemy.[275]

The *Kāmandaka Nīti* says that a king in an unfamiliar land is routed by a puny adversary in the same way as the king of elephants, who when in water, is overpowered even by a small shark.[276]

THE BATTLES

In the *Ṛgveda* there are many references to the battles fought by the Āryan tribes among themselves and also against the natives (*dasyus*). Among these the battle of Paruṣṇī (Ravi) fought by Sudās, chief of the Tṛtsu tribe, against a confederacy of ten kings, viz., Śimyus, Anus, Druhyus, Bharatas, Yadus, Turvaśas, Purus, Ajas, Śigrus and Yakṣus is described in some detail. Though the description of the battle is vague, still a story can be made out. Sudās, with the aid of Indra, crossed the deep Paruṣṇī River and put the Śimyus to flight. Some of the fugitives drowned in its waters. The confederates who were on the right or farther bank of Paruṣṇī, intending to attack Sudās and the Tṛtsus, appear to have attempted to make the river fordable by digging channels and so diverting the water, which it seems, rushed back into its natural bed and drowned the men who were crossing the stream. During this battle Indra destroyed the strongholds and seven castles of the foes. The Tṛtsus led by Sudās under the divine inspiration of Indra mounted such a furious attack that the confederates abandoned all their provisions and fled from the battlefield. In this battle five confederate leaders were drowned, 20 were slain and more than 66,000 warriors perished.[277]

A clear picture of the battles fought during the epic times emerges from the narrations made by Sañjaya for the benefit of Dhṛtarāṣṭra. The progress of the battle fought on the first day of war was narrated by him as follows:

> Desiring the fight with Bhīṣma, the Pāṇḍavas cheerfully advanced with Bhīmasena at their head. Thereupon lion-like roars, clamorous shouts, the noise of *krakacas*, the blare of cow-horn and the sound of drums, cymbals and tabors arose in both the armies. The soldiers of the enemy rushed upon us and we also rushed upon them with loud shouts . . . the great noise made by these troops . . . was like that of the ocean in a tempest. . . . Roaring like a deep mast of clouds and assuming a fearful appearance Bhīma filled your sons with great alarm. In the first encounter that resembled terrible twang of the bow and flapping of the leather feuces, none of your party or that of the enemy turned them back. The twang of the bow did not stop for a moment and the blazing arrows flashed through the air like meteors falling from the sky. The two armies of the Kurus and Pāṇḍavas, full of elephants, horses and chariots looked exceedingly beautiful on the field of battle like painted figures on canvas. . . . While fighting or retreating or rallying again neither the men of our side nor those of the enemy's could be distinguished.[278]

A pictorial representation of war in ancient India is met on the lower architrave of the southern gate of Sāñcī *stūpa*. In this representation called the 'War of Relics' on the right the Licchavis, Ajātaśatru, the Śākyas, the Bulis, the Koliyas, the Mallas of Pāvā and Brāhmaṇas are depicted advancing on Kuśinārā for capturing the relics of Buddha from the Mallas. In the middle, the siege of the town and on the left, the departure of the victors are illustrated.[279]

In the first scene the ruler bringing with him the relics of Buddha is depicted returning to his well fortified town triumphantly. The whole town is astir, the balconies are crowded, guards are keeping a vigil from the towers and riders are galloping through the streets.

The second scene depicts the siege of Kuśinārā and the assault on the fort by the seven claimants of the relics. In dense masses the military is approaching the vast body of an elephant towering mightily here and there. Cavalry and chariots full of soldiers can be seen. The vanguard is marshalled at the city gate, but hostilities have not yet begun. Posted upon towers and breathlessly awaiting, the defenders are not surprised. Heavy stones are hurled down and the assailants are met with long lances. The result of the battle is also narrated in this relief. The assailants have conquered and to the sound of military music they are shown carrying off the relics.

A war scene said to have been portrayed on a stone slab at Amarāvatī has been described as follows:

> on this stone is represented the escalade of a fort, a figure ascending a ladder, another from a turret on the walls shooting an arrow. Before the gate of the palace a figure with a round shield prostrating himself before a chief seated on an elephant, and followed by others on horses, bullocks, etc. The whole forms a group in a very different style from anything observed anywhere else in this country.[280]

Fergusson comments that 'the description read almost as if intended for Sāñcī, but the scaling ladder is an addition to the siege material there represented'.[281]

A Jātaka story called the 'Battle of Indra' has been portrayed in cave 17 at Ajantā.[282] The battle is depicted in four phases:[283]

1. The gods after losing the battle decide to retreat but Indra holds the ground and covers their retreat.
2. Indra (Śākyamuni incarnate) follows his retreating army.
3. Out of compassion for the *garuḍa* birds in their nest, threatened by his moving chariot, Indra decided to turn his chariot round. This sudden move put the Asuras to rout.
4. Gods pay homage to victorious Indra.

In accordance with these phases of action, the artist has arranged the painting as a composition with four scenes. The right section and even the lower part of the centre portrays Indra holding the enemy at bay with his chariot even when gods had run away before the fiery onslaught of the Asuras. In the foreground a number of horses are to be seen galloping towards the left. These horses are equipped with bridles, head-tufts, neck-collars and horse-rugs. The riders are wearing stockings, trousers, tunics and pointed caps, but wear no armour and bear no weapons.

In the very centre of the painting the retreating cavalry of the gods is overtaken by the Asura infantry, trying to cut off their retreat. The foot soldiers are lightly armed. The archers are arrayed behind the armoured soldiers equipped with curved swords and shields. The infantrymen are assailing the retreating cavalrymen who for their part are trying to ward off the attack. The foremost of the riders is just turning his horse round and is seizing with his hands the raised arm of one of the assailing infantrymen, who is brandishing a sword.

In the dramatic scene above, of which only dim outlines are traceable, the Asuras after having broken through the cavalry of the gods, are doing battle with Indra and trying to encircle his chariot. Indra facing the Asura forces on his right shoots arrows at them to cover the retreat of his cavalry.

This was the situation when Indra decided to turn around and follow his retreating army. The chariot drawn by three horses, is seen a second time, rushing towards the left. The silk cotton tree with *garuḍa* nest forms the turning point between the second and third scenes. In the next phase Indra's chariot has wheeled half round and is now facing towards the upper part of the centre, accompanied by infantrymen and followed by cavalrymen. The uppermost part of the painting may have depicted the flight of the Asuras and the triumph of Indra, but the details can no longer be discerned.

A relief in the art of Amarāvatī, now in Madras Museum, also depicts a battle between the four 'arms' of two armies. In the upper left of the surviving part of the picture a warrior, probably the god Indra, is standing on the battle-chariot. The chariot is facing left in the direction in which the army of gods is fleeing. Indra himself, however, has turned round, and to cover the retreat of his army, is shooting arrows at the pursuing enemy. Though the relief is badly damaged and not all the details of the story are discernible, it appears a prototype of the Ajantā story in relief.[284]

LAST RITES

The state performed the last rites of the soldiers who died in war. In the Vedic age the enemy soldiers were perhaps buried near the battle-field.[285] At the end of the Epic war King Dhṛtarāṣṭra expressed his anxiety about the disposal of the dead soldiers as the number of casualties was enormous.[286] Yudhiṣṭhira immediately asked important functionaries of the state like Vidura, Sañjaya, Dhaumya, etc., to conduct the last rites of all the dead so that not a single body was left to rot.[287]

On the orders of Yudhiṣṭhira pyres were raised by the officials. The dead bodies of the kings and commoners were consigned to the flames in a *śāstric* manner in accordance with their rank and status.[288] Even the bodies of the foreign soldiers scattered in the battlefield were collected, heaped in thousands and given a mass funeral.[289]

PRISONERS OF WAR

Some early references to prisoners of war are met in the *Atharvaveda*.[290] They were generally treated harshly and many of them were put to death. The *Aitareya Bhāhmaṇa* refers to 10,000 women prisoners,[291] hailing from respectable families, who were given away to Brāhmaṇas. King Ajātaśatru of Magadha is said to have been imprisoned by King Prasenjit of Kośala.[292] In the epics there are many references to prisoners of war. After defeating Kauravas, Gandharvas made them prisoners along with their women.[293] The Vṛṣṇi women were made prisoner and carried away by Ābhīra depredators, while Arjuna looked on helplessly. Rāvaṇa's seraglio included many women, whom he had made prisoner earlier.[294]

The Epic states that at the battlefield prisoners were made and that rules existed on the treatment to be extended to them. A soldier who was not wounded could be made a prisoner.[295] A wounded person, who was in distress due to the loss of his mount and weapon, if made captive, was to be provided with medical assistance or escorted back to his house.[296] A soldier whose armour has been broken, who has laid down his arms and has surrendered with folded hands could not be killed, even if made a captive.[297] A captive woman had to be freed if she refused to marry someone despite persuasion.[298]

In the later literature there are many references to prisoners, particularly women, being maltreated. The ruler of Mālwā after killing the Maukhari ruler Gṛhavarman harshly treated his wife Rājyaśrī and chained her legs in iron fetters.[299] It is said that King Yaśovarman after killing the ruler of Gauḍa enslaved the ladies of his seraglio and made them fly *cāmara* over his head.[300] There is ample inscriptional evidence to substantiate this practice in early medieval India.

SPIRITUOUS LIQUORS

Vedic Times

Soldiers joined battle after consuming invigorating drinks. The practice had started during the Vedic period. There are many references to *soma*, a spirituous drink, in the Vedas and it was respected as a deified juice or say divinity.[301] Indra, the Vedic god of war, was particularly fond of it.[302] In the *Ṛgveda* the following references suggest that it augmented the power of the warrior and inspired him to perform the deeds of bravery.

1. **Soma, let thou bestow upon us the glory of a hundred men, the greatest renown of mighty chiefs (I.43.7).**
2. **Indra, accordant with the branded Maruts drink *soma*, Hero, as wise Vṛtra-slayer (III.50.3).**
3. **Impetuous god (Indra) when thou hast drunk *soma*, enraptured send us cattle in abundance (III.50.3).**
4. **Flow onward with thy juice unto the banquet of the mighty gods. Flow hither for our strength and fame (IX.1.4).**

In the *Yajurveda, soma* is clearly said to be a spirituous drink related to war.[303] It also refers to another spirituous drink called *surā*, which was more invigorating than *soma*.[304] There are many more references to *surā* and *soma* in this Veda.[305]

Epic Times

By sixth century BC the intoxicating drinks had come into greater vogue. Pāṇini describes the wine types known during his times and also the production and trade of the commodity.[306] In the *Rāmāyaṇa* sage Bhāradvāja is reported to have entertained the army of Bharata with intoxicating drinks like *maireya* and *surā*.[307] The *Mahābhārata* refers to public drinking bouts among the Yādava and Madra people.[308] When the people of Dvārakā prepared to meet the invasion of Śālva, an announcement was made against the use of drinks by the soldiers. It was feared that Śālva knowing the proclivity of Vṛṣṇis and Andhakas for drinks could attack them when in an intoxicated frame.[309] However, no stigma was attached to the use of wines and great heroes like Rāma and Rāvaṇa are portrayed in the *Rāmāyaṇa* as enjoying drinks.[310] Before joining a battle with Kauravas Bhīma drank *kailātaka-madhu*, which made his eyes red and doubled his strength.[311] Sātyaki also drank *kailātaka* before marching out for the battlefield.[312] In fact, *kailātaka* was considered an essential item to be carried by the king, while marching out for a battle.[313] Even the horses were fed with intoxicating drinks before being yoked to chariots[314] to boost up their stamina.

In fourth century BC the soldiers of the elite army (*maula-bala*) were maintained by the state. Megasthenese says that when these soldiers were not engaged in war, they spent their time in idleness or drinking.[315] The armies of Alexander indulged in heavy drinking during their stay among the Nysaens, the inhabitants of the hill state of Nysa.[316]

Arthaśāstra, etc.

The *Arthaśāstra* has devoted a full chapter to the production, distribution and use of spirituous liquors.[317] *Surādhyakṣa* was the officer who regulated the matters relating to the liquors. 'The controller of spirituous liquors should cause trade in wines and ferments to be carried on in the forts, the country or the camp (*skandhāvāra*) through persons dealing in wines and ferments.'[318] The *Arthaśāstra* refers to six types of wines.[319] Liquors were widely used to conduct clandestine activities in the enemy camp.[320]

It seems that the foreign invaders popularized the use of alcoholic beverages in India. The Iranians, Greeks, Śakas and Kuṣāṇas were all fond of drinks. Around the beginning of the Christian era large quantities of wine were imported into India from Rome and Western Asia.[321] No doubt a major share of these imports was consumed by the soldiers. It seems that during the Gupta age the use of intoxicating drinks was not common as is evident from the observations made by Fa-hian, the Chinese traveller. 'Throughout the whole country people do not kill any living creature, nor drink intoxicating liquor, nor eat onions or garlic. . . . In the market there are no butcher shops and no dealers in inoxicating drink.'[322] But it is difficult to accept the statement of the traveller at face value.

The Chinese pilgrim Hiuen-tsang, however, refers to wide use of alcoholic drinks among soldiery. 'The state maintains a body of dauntless champions to the number of several hundreds. Each time they prepare for combat they drink wine to intoxicate themselves, and then one of these men with spear in hand, will defy thousands of enemies.'[323] At another place the pilgrim says that in the army of Pulakeśin the martial heroes who led the van of the army in battle went into conflict intoxicated, and their war elephants were also made drunk before the beginning of an engagement.[324] The *Śukranīti* says that troops should be fed with drinks (*mada*) to rouse their spirits before being inducted into battle.[325]

Victory was celebrated with a glass of wine (*madhu*). Kālidāsa says that the soldiers in the land surrounded by wine creepers, where they had spread deer-skins for sitting, removed their exhaustion involved in victory by drinking wine.[326] The *Amarakośa* says that drinks could be had before joining the war to boost up the spirits and after the end of war to sooth the nerves.[327]

Purāṇic Literature

There is an interesting reference to the use of beverages by the warriors in the Lalitā-māhātmya of *Brahmāṇḍa Purāṇa.*[328] During the battle with Dānavas when Śaktis (female warriors of the gods) became afflicted and overpowered by *tṛśastra* (missile of thrust) discharged by Vāsukī (Asura commander), they sought the help of *Madirāsindhu* (ocean of liquor) which alone could quench their thirst and enhance their strength. The *Madirāsindhu* showered those beverages by the mere fragrance of which even the dead might rise up perfectly well and the weak ones would become very strong. The beverages thus showered included *gauḍī* (distilled from molasses), *paiṣṭi* (from flour), *madhvī* (from honey), *kadambarī* (from *kadamba* flower), *haintali* (from palm tree) and *lāṅgala* (also from a palm tree). Each of the Śaktis joyously drank the torrent of liquor as big as the trunk of Airāvata elephant, uninterruptedly for one full *yāma* (3 hours). Due to inebriation, Śaktis were stumbling in their steps. Their eyes had become reddened. They were uttering heroic words though the syllables faltered now and then. They were proud of their ability to wage war.[329] In the *Mārkaṇḍeya Purāṇa* Caṇḍikā is said to have enjoyed drinks before joining the battle with Mahiṣāsura.[330] In the *Avantisundarī Kathā*, a work of eighth century, there are references to *pānagoṣṭhīs* (drinking sessions) in the army camps,[331] meant to boost up the spirit of the troops.

MILITARY INTELLIGENCE

Espionage was an important component of the military machine. The institution existed in the Vedic times and gods like Varuṇa, Agni, Soma, etc., were served by spies (*spaśaḥ*).[332] Spies are said to be the eyes of the kings[333] and in the epics there are numerous references to their use both by Pāṇḍavas and Kauravas, to know the secrets of the other camp.[334] It was considered necessary for a ruler to appoint three spies, not known to each other, to keep a watch on 18 high officials of the enemy kingdom and 15 high officials of his own kingdom.[335] Rāvaṇa appointed Śuka and Sarsana, his two ministers, to gather intelligence on the strength, leading warriors, layout of camp, weapons, etc., of Rāma's army incognito. They entered the camp of Rāma in the garb of monkeys.[336] On the other side Vibhīṣaṇa also appointed his four ministers to gather information on the deployment of Rāvaṇa's army. They assumed the garb of birds to enter the camp of Rāvaṇa.[337] It was believed that the enemy whose military secrets have been exposed can be conquered without much effort.[338] In the Smṛtis the ruler is enjoined to keep a close watch on enemy strength.[339]

In the *Mahābhārata* the institution of espionage has been described in detail. In fact, the Epic includes *cara* as one of the eight principal organs of the army (*aṣṭāṅgiṇī*).[340] The institution was considered so important that even the *nītiśāstra* (*trivarga*) compiled by Brahmā refers to various measures to be adopted by the spies (*caraśca vividhopāyaḥ*).[341] At another place the epic says that a ruler should appoint spies within his kingdom and also in the kingdom of his enemies. These spies should move around the gardens, temples, traverns, holy places, road crossings, crowded places, etc.[342] The spies detailed in the enemy country should move incognito or as mendicants.[343]

By fourth century BC an elaborate system of espionage had come to stay in India and the Greeks were greatly impressed by it. In fact, the number of spies employed by Indian rulers was so big that the Greeks mistook them as one of the seven constituent classes of the Indian society.

> The sixth caste consists of the inspectors. To them is entrusted the superintendence of all that goes on, and of making reports privately to the king. The city inspectors employ as their coadjutors the courtesans of the city, the inspectors of the camp and the courtesans who follow the army. The best and most trustworthy men are appointed to fill these offices.[344]

The *Arthaśāstra* gives a detailed account of espionage system encompassing all aspects of Indian polity.[345] The military espionage sought to collect information on the strength, plans, and movements of the enemy by infiltrating into his lines. 'Thus he should sow spies among the enemy, the ally, the middle king, the neutral king as well as among the eighteen high officers of (each of) those (kings).'[346] Spies marched alongside the troops, stayed in the camps and moved among the fighting troops. Those lodged in the opposite camp tried their best to harm the enemy and break his morale.[347]

Kauṭilya has classified spies into two categories: *saṁstha* (stationary) and *saṁcāra* (moving). The spies who kept on moving from one place to another in search of intelligence were called *saṁcāra* and those who gathered intelligence staying at one place were called *saṁstha*. The *saṁsthācara* category included *kāpaṭika* (sharp pupil), *udāsthita* (apostate mark), *grahapatika* (seeming householder), *vaidehaka* (seeming trader) and *tāpasa* (seeming ascetic). The *saṁcāracara* category included *sattri* (secret agent), *tīkṣṇa* (bravo), *rasada* (poison giver) and *bhikṣukī* (begging nun).[343] The secret agents who excelled in hatching conspiracies were known as *sastrapraṇidhi*, *agnipraṇidhi* and *rasapraṇidhi*. They used the means of weapon, fire and poison respectively to destroy the enemy.[349]

The *Arthaśātra* not only refers to a perfect system of intelligence gathering but also of communicating such intelligence to appropriate authority through secret channels.

> Assistants of the establishments should carryout the transmission of spied out news by means of sign-alphabets and neither the establishments nor these (assistants) should know each other.[350]

Kāmandaka has devoted a full chapter to the activities of spies. He says that 'spies are the eyes of the king; he should always look through them. He that does not look through them stumbles down, out of ignorance, even on level ground, for he is said to be blind'.[351] On the other hand 'a ruler who has spies for his eyes keeps awake even when he is asleep'.[352]

Though not many details of espionage system in the Gupta age are available, it seems that the system described in the *Arthaśāstra* continued to be in vogue during this period. The *Mudrārākṣasa* and *Mṛcchakaṭika* attest to this. Detailing the qualities of a spy the *Matsya Purāṇa* says:

A king's spy should be conscious enough to submit true and accurate reports, obedient to the king's injunctions, have a knowledge of dialects of many countries, viable to speak fluently and put up with rough life, of quiet disposition and capable of discharging his functions adequately according to the circumstances.[353]

In the *Agni Purāṇa* words *cara, spaśa* and *praṇidhi* have been used for a spy.[354]

In this context it is notable that rulers took special measures to prevent the breach of security. During the invasion of Dvārakā by Śālva nobody could enter the city or go out of the city without showing the required pass or *mudrā* issued to him for the purpose.[355] On the eve of the battle of Kurukṣetra Yudhiṣṭhira got necessary identity cards or symbols issued to his army for proper identification.[356] According to *Nītiprakāśikā* pass words (*saṁjñā*) were allotted to the army on day-to-day basis. Only commanders could know about it and soldiers and other people were not authorised to know it.[357] This was indeed a sure method to prevent enemy infiltration.

MEDICAL SERVICES

No army can fight without a proper system of medicine and surgery to attend to the casualties of war. 'In the *Ṛgveda* we find that legs were amputated and replaced by iron substitutes, injured eyes were plucked out and arrow shafts were extracted from limbs of Āryan warriors.'[358] Aśvins, the surgeons of gods, attended to the casualties suffered in the battlefield. Viśpalā, the queen of King Khela, who suffered a severed leg in an encounter was operated upon by them and provided with an iron leg.[359] In many Vedic *mantras* Rudra is beseeched to cure warriors with medicine and surgery.[360]

It is notable that the term *śalyam* is derived from the root *śal* or *śval* meaning arrow and hence the science which was related to extraction of arrows from the body, operation of the limb so wounded and the treatment of the wound thus caused, came to be known as *śalya-śāstra.* In course of time the term came to be applied to all kinds of surgeries. A good surgeon was expected to know all about the arrow shafts, flight of the arrows, symptoms of injury, etc., and then decide about the course of surgery applicable to the person concerned.[361]

The Epic warriors carried some kind of medicinal stuff in their vehicles.[362] Some highly effective medicines like *viśalyakarṇī* which could cure unconsciousness were known.[363] *Viśalya* was a herb which could prevent the flow of blood from an injured part of the body. In the *Rāmāyaṇa* there are references to herbs used in curing the war casualties. The army of Rāma was accompanied by Suṣena, a physician and surgeon, who knew all about the properties of herbs like *sañjīvakarṇī, viśalyakaraṇī, mṛtasañjīvanī, suvarṇakaraṇī* and *sandhānī*, which grew in the vicinity of Kailāsa mountain. When warriors were severely wounded and fell unconscious he administered these herbs to save their lives.[364] Some commanders of Laṅkan army are reported to have carried medicines with them while going to battlefield.[365]

Surgeons and physicians accompanied the Pāṇḍava army to the battlefield.[366] In a serious encounter with Karṇa, when Yudhiṣṭhira was gravely wounded he was immediately cured by the senior doctors (*Bhiṣajān Variṣṭhai*) by removing arrows from his body with the help of incantation (*mantra*) and medicines (*auṣadhi*).[367] In another context Bhīṣma recommends that a king must keep four kinds of physicians in his fort, and some of them must be specialists in handling the cases of poisoning and in the removal of arrow-heads from the body.[368] When Bhīṣma lay wounded in the battlefield surgeons expert in extracting splinters or arrow-heads from the body approached him to remove the darts.[369]

The *Arthaśāstra*, refers to adequate provision of medicines in the forts. When the army marched to the battlefield physicians with surgical instruments, apparatus, medicine, curative oils and bandages and women (nurses) in-charge of food and drinks accompanied it. They were, however, stationed in the rear to take care of the wounded.[370]

Physicians (*cikitsaka*) were entitled to a salary of 2,000 *paṇas* per annum.[371] The rulers also made land grants to them, perhaps as a token of honour.[372]

The *Arthaśāstra* also describes counter measures against injuries and afflictions caused by the enemy (*svabalopaghātaparatikāraḥ*).These included remedial measures against poisoning (*dūṣīviṣa*) and stupefaction (*madandoṣa*).[373]

The medical need of the animals were also taken care of. The superintendents in the departments of horses (*aśvādhyakṣa*) and elephants (*hastyadhyakṣa*) included veterinary practitioners in their staff to attend to matters relating to the health of the animals.[374] The *Arthaśāstra* specifies that 'physicians shall treat (elephants) afflicted by long journey, illness, work, rut or old age'.[375]

Surgeons had an important role to play when the king was on a military expedition. In the *Suśruta Saṁhitā* a separate chapter deals with the role of surgeons in a military camp. In times of war doctors had to protect the king and his army from all unhygienic articles. His tent was pitched next to that of the king and for easy identification a flag was hoisted over it.[376]

In the *Śiva Purāṇa* there is an interesting reference to medical care on the battlefield.[377] It is said that Bhārgava (Śukrācārya) resuscitated the Asuras killed in the battle with his *amṛtajīvanī-vidyā* and the drops of water sanctified by him with *mantras*. The sage Āṅgīrasa (Bṛhaspati) also revived the gods killed in the battle with the divine herbs brought from Droṇa mountain. When the Asura chief Jālandhara saw that all the gods killed by him came to life again and again he got livid with anger and asked his preceptor Bhārgava to explain the reason. Bhārgava told him that it was the herb brought from mountain Droṇa which was enlivening the gods and that if he was desirous of victory he should uproot that mountain and throw it into the sea. Asuras acted accordingly. Deprived of the life giving medicinal facility the gods were defeated in war and Jālandhara captured Amarāvatī, the city of gods.

The surgeons accompanied the army in military campaigns in seventh century AD. Prince Rājyavardhana, during his conquest of the Hūṇas, was accompanied by surgeons as is evident from the *Harṣacarita*. 'Long white bandages bound about arrow-wounds received in battle while conquering Hūṇas dotted his form like side-glances from his approaching royal glory.'[378] A.L. Basham says that 'Indian surgery remained ahead of European until the eighteenth century, when the surgeons of the East India Company were not ashamed to learn the art of rhinoplasty from the Indians.'[379]

A system of tending to casualties prevailed. It was primarily the responsibility of the foot-soldiers to remove the dead and wounded from the battlefield. The chariot warriors assisted in the evacuation of serious casualties.[380]

MILITARY ENGINEERS (*MĀRGADARŚAKA*)

Before marching out it was necessary to set the roads right for the movement of the troops. A team of officials led by Praśasta was dispatched to survey the roads, ensure their protection and make arrangements for water, etc. In the *Rāmāyaṇa* the men engaged in the task are called *mārgiṇaḥ*, i.e. repairer of roads, who could be equated with the military engineers of today. They marched in the forefront of the army and included specialists who knew about the nature of the land and could build sheds with ropes. Proficient diggers, tunnel makers, bridge builders, mechanics, carpenters and men of allied professions also formed a part of the team.[381] Manu refers to three kinds of roads, which passed through open country, marshy lands and forests.[382] Kauṭilya adds that the king should regulate the military campaign keeping in view the road conditions (even or uneven), the availability of water and the length of the march.[383]

The engineers duly considered the suitability of a road before launching an army. The *Mahābhārata* says that the road which did not have mud, water, bunds and clods was the best for a cavalry march. A road without pits or mud was suitable for chariots. A road which was marked by small trees and abundant grass was good for the movement of elephants. The infantry could, however, move on all kinds of roads.[384] Almost similar views regarding the battle zone or the area of operation are met in the *Arthaśāstra* and the *Agni Purāṇa*.[385]

MILITARY SIGNALS (*SAṄKETA*)

The early man may have communicated messages by facial expressions and body movements such as a smile, a shrug, a raised hand or a stretched hand. This was subsequently done by means of *kranda* (loud cries) as voice could be heard even when the person was at a distance and invisible. But over the years growing size of the armies rendered these mediums ineffective. The Vedic Indians, therefore, devised *dundubhi* (drum) to serve the purpose as is evident from the following hymn:

> Drive hither these, and these again bring hither: the war drum speaks aloud as battle's signal. Our heroes winged with horses, come together. Let our car warriors, Indra, he triumphant.[386]

Some kind of signal system had thus come to be associated with warfare during the Vedic times. It was fine tuned during the Epic times, when all situations of war could be indicated by playing different musical notes.[387] Senior commanders carried conches on their person to convey important messages.[388]

It is reported by the Greek historians that in India, in fourth century BC, the instructions regarding the formation of battle arrays were passed on to the soldiers by playing musical notes on *dundubhi* and *karatāla*.[389] Indians learnt the use of trumpet (*tūrya*) for signalling from the Greeks.[390] The *Arthaśāstra* says that the instructions of the commander were conveyed to the soldiers through the trumpet notes (*tūrya-ghoṣa*) as also with the help of *dhvajas* (standards) and *patākās* (flags).[391]

But the most detailed description of military signal system in ancient India is met in the *Śukranīti*.[392] A ruler was expected to deliberate over the signal system and fully educate his troops about the signals to be used in forming the battle arrays.[393] The army was to make various moves like assembling, spreading out, moving around, squeezing, marching slowly or speedily, withdrawing, etc., as per the signals. The troops were to form in a line like an eight petal lotus or in a circle like a *cakra* or in various battle arrays as signalled.[394] Even the use of weapons in the battlefield was directed by signals.[395] The Indians had thus perfected the science of military signalling at an early date.

CONCEPT OF *DHARMAYUDDHA*

In the *Mahābhārata* the wars are broadly classified in two categories, viz., *dharmayuddha* (just war) and *asurayuddha* (unjust war). The participation in *dharmayuddha* was considered praiseworthy and a matter of honour. The concept of just war which appears fully evolved in the Epic imposed certain restrictions on the combatants. The *Manusmṛti*[396] enumerates the rules which governed the conduct of just war as follows:

1. No use of treacherous weapons.
2. No use of barbed and poisoned arrows or arrows with points ablaze with fire.
3. No killing of a soldier who has lost his mount, or is approaching for surrender, or has fallen down, or has ceased to fight.
4. No killing of a soldier who has lost his armour or has fractured limbs or is unarmed.
5. No killing of a soldier who is scared, or is badly wounded, or is on the retreat.

On the eve of the *Mahābhārata* war the Pāṇḍavas, Kauravas and Somakas, jointly framed rules to regulate the conduct of soldiers in the *dharmayuddha*.[397] These rules generally follow the *Manusmṛti* but also add the following:

1. After the end of the battle at sunset the soldiers of opposite camps were to behave in a friendly manner with each other.
2. A chariot could fight a chariot and an elephant an elephant only. A mounted soldier could not take on an infantry soldier in battle.
3. Enemy could be attacked only after giving him proper warning.
4. Non-combatants such as keepers of chariots, carriers of load, players of martial music, etc., were not to be attacked.

These rules of just war are also repeated in the Śānti Parvan of the *Mahābhārata*.[398] It further adds that achieving victory in a just war by unfair means is self-destructive and that it is better to die fighting than to achieve a victory through unfair means.[399]

The ethics of war thus propounded by seers was, however, ignored by rival parties whenever it suited their convenience. The Kaurava warriors like Bhīṣma, Droṇa, Karṇa, Duryodhana, etc., were killed in an unfair manner. The massacre in the Pāṇḍava camp perpetrated by Aśvatthāman on the last night of the war was again against the ethics of war. Some fierce battles between Vānaras and Rākṣasas described in the *Rāmāyaṇa* also did not conform to the rules of just war.[400]

The *Arthaśāstra* refers to eight types of wars, viz., *nimna-yuddha* (naval war), *prakāśa-yuddha* (open war), *sthala-yuddha* (land war), *kūṭa-yuddha* (secret war), *khanaka-yuddha* (trench war), *ākāśa-yuddha* (sky war), *divā-yuddha* (day war), and *rātri-yuddha* (night war).[401] At another place the *Arthaśāstra* refers to three types of wars, viz., *prakāśa-yuddha* (open war), *tūṣṇīm-yuddha* (silent war) and *kūṭa-yuddha* (deceptive war).[402] Kāmandaka also follows this classification of the *Arthaśāstra*.[403] The *Śukranīti* refers to three kinds of war, viz., *daivika*, *asura* and *mānava*.[404] Not many of these types can be called just wars.

DHARMAVIJAYA

Related to *dharmayuddha* was the concept of *dharmavijaya* (righteous victory). The other two types of victories were known as *arthavijaya* (capture of wealth) and *asuravijaya* (taking of life).[405] In righteous victory the victor remained content with the acceptance of his suzerainty by the vanquished and did not deprive the latter of his territory, wealth or life.[406] Kauṭilya, however, disapproves even the exaction of tribute in *dharmavijaya.*[407] In the event the annexation of territory became unavoidable the subject people were to be treated very kindly.[408]

In this context the Buddhist concept of *Dharma* (Dhamma) *Vijaya* as preached and practised by Aśoka also needs mention. This kind of conquest demanded refrain from any kind of violence as its objective was material and spiritual betterment of the conquered. The conquest was pursued through the means of *dhamma-mahāmātras, dhamma-śrāvṇas, dhamma-yātras, dhamma-stambhas, dhamma-dāna,* etc.

The *purohita* or priest accompanied the army of the battlefield to ensure the victory of his master[409] (*RV*, 7.18.13). Priest Viśvāmitra offered prayers to rivers Vipāśā and Śatudri to enable the Bharata army to cross over[410] (*RV*, 3.33.3). In the *Atharvaveda* a priest is quoted as encouraging his men uttering the following hymn 'I perfect their kingdom, their might, their vigour, and their strength, with this oblation of cut-off the arms of their enemies. . . . Go forth, you men, and conquer; may your arms be terrible'[411] (*AV*, 3.19).

This ideal of just conquest was generally followed by Indian rulers. The Pāṇḍavas during their *Rājasūya* and *Aśvamedha* sacrifices did not annex territories of vanquished rulers but remained content with token submission and tribute. After defeating Rāvaṇa, Rāma consecrated his brother Vibhīṣaṇa and handed over the kingdom to him. Samudragupta defeated scores of rulers during his long campaign, but in most cases he did not annex their territories and made them just tributaries. The policy was followed by all great emperors of India.

In Indian warfare *digvijaya* or the conquest of four quarters was considered the highest achievement. It denoted complete sway over the land of Bhāratavarṣa from eastern to western Ocean. Raghu, the legendary king of Ayodhyā is said to have achieved this feat. Pāṇḍava brothers also conquered all the four quarters before undertaking the *Rājasūya* sacrifice.

The achiever of *digvijaya* was called a *cakravartin.* It is said that the wheel of a *cakravartin's* chariot rolled everywhere without obstruction. The term was also applied to the ruler of a *cakra* or country extending from sea to sea. In ancient literature 12 princes beginning with Bharat are described as *cakravartin.*

MORALE FACTOR

Man's most precious possession is his life and the war poses the gravest threat to it. To make a person overcome this fear and boost up his morale Indians observed some rituals before joining a battle as early as the Vedic age:

1. Prayers were offered to Indra, Varuṇa and other gods to seek protection and victory in war. One of these prayers was addressed to Indra-Varuṇa is follows:
   'O Indra-Varuṇa, the wickedness of foes and mine assailants' hatred sorely trouble me.
   Ye, Twain are Lords of riches both of earth and heaven: so grant to us your aid on the decisive day.' (*Ṛ V*, 7.83.5)
2. *Soma* sacrifice was performed at the battlefield and libations of drink were offered to Indra. The intent was to prop up the spirit of the combatants with the exhilarating drink. A related hymn runs as follows:
   'Yea, this is good to taste and full of sweetness, verily it is strong and rich in flavour.
   No one may conquer Indra in the battle when he hath drunken of the draught we offer.' (*Ṛ V*, 6.47.1)
3. Before joining the battle the combatants danced vigorously to the tune of war drums, seeking victory in war. A related hymn runs as follows:
   'Send forth thy voice aloud through earth and heaven and let the world in all its breadth regard thee;
   O Drum, accordant with the Gods and Indra, drive thou afar, yea, very far, our foemen.' (*Ṛ V*, 6.47.29)

The Buddhist *Nikāyas* advise that before the beginning of a war the priests accompanying the army, the commander or the king himself should deliver a passionate speech to encourage the soldiers to fight.[412] Before the commencement of the epic war Śrīkṛṣṇa exhorted Arjuna to fight fearlessly for in the event of victory he would enjoy glory of the earth and in the event of death attain the bliss of the heaven.[413] King Janaka also described vividly to his soldiers the glory of a martyr in the heaven and the ignominy of a coward in the hell to enthuse them on the eve of a war.[414] The *Manusmṛti* says that after arraying his troops the king should encourage (*praharṣayed*) them to fight fearlessly.[415] The *Raghuvaṁśa* endorses this while describing the ascent of fallen heroes to heaven in the company of nymphs.[416]

In the Bhīṣma Parvan the aspect of morale has been described in some detail. It emphasizes that the warriors whose hearts are full of joy (*harṣa*) and courage (*utsāha*) always earn victory.[417] Such determined men even if they are 50 or say five in number can force a large army to run away.[418] On the other hand, if one soldier lacking in courage flees from battlefield it may cause the rout of a big army. In that event even great warriors are compelled to flee and nothing can prevent the rout.[419] It was, therefore, necessary for wise rulers to keep up the morale of their fourfold army by all means.[420]

The profession of arms (*kṣātradharma*) has been greatly eulogized in ancient Indian literature. In the epic it is equated with the profession of the king (*rājadharma*). By observing the *kṣātradharma* Viṣṇu punished the demons and protected the gods and sages. Thus it was considered superior to all professions.[421] To keep up their morale warriors were given quick promotions and enhanced salaries. Distinguished soldiers were invited by the king to dine with him and sit on the throne with him.[422]

This aspect of war has been described in greater detail in the *Arthaśāstra.*

The following measures were taken to prop up the spirit of the warriors in the battlefield.[423]

1. It was impressed on the soldiers that the bliss of heaven was reserved for these who laid down their life in battle.
2. The king addressed the soldiers stating that 'I receive a wage like you; this kingdom is to be enjoyed together with you; the enemy should be attacked by you at my request.'
3. The minister and the chaplain encouraged warriors by impressing on them the excellence of their battle array.
4. Astrologers and others enthused men by proclaiming the omniscience and divine powers of their ruler and filled the enemy side with terror.

5. The commander announced awards for acts of bravery at the outset.
6. Physicians with surgical instruments, apparatus, medicines, oils and bandages, and women in charge of food and drinks and capable of filling men with enthusiasm were stationed in the rear.
7. Bards and panegyrists (*sūtamāgadhāḥ*) praised the caste, corporation, family deed and conduct of the warriors.
8. In later works it is said that *vīragoṣṭhīs* (talks of heroism) and *pānagoṣṭhīs* (drinking bouts) were organized in the army camps to boost up the morale of the soldiers.[424]
9. Kings narrated stories of brave deed to encourage the soldiers. Good music and dance performances entertained them. Further, the soldiers were not engaged in non-military activities.[425]

On the other hand, measures were taken to demoralize the enemy soldiers in the battlefield. The *Agni Purāṇa* enumerates some of these measures as follows:

1. Spread the rumour by shouting that the enemy army has been destroyed, its *nāyaka* and *senānī* have been killed and the king has fled from the battlefield. This indeed led to the rout of the enemy.[426]
2. Cause a kind of smoke in the battlefield to stupefy the enemy soldiers.[427]
3. Create scare among enemy troops by a grand display of flags, musical instruments and military supplies.[428]
4. Among the seven means of state policy (*saptāṅga*) mentioned by Kāmandaka *māyā* and *indrajāla* were definitely intended to exert psychological pressure on the enemy with a view to demoralize him.[429]

Related to the moral factor is the concept of war god in ancient India. In the Vedic times it was god Indra who was invoked to grant safety and victory to his followers. But over the centuries Indra faded out and a new war god called Skanda or Kārttikeya emerged around the beginning of Christian era.

Indians thus followed definite rules in conducting wars. The campaigning season was determined considering the climatic conditions obtaining in the country. Old roads were repaired and new ones laid out before marching out for war. Commanders mounted *dhvaja* on their chariots, and rituals were performed to gain victory. The warriors dressed in military costume. The timings of march were decided by the astrologer and the pace was determined in accordance with the developments on the war front. While making the choice of battlefield the availability of the forces and the nature of terrain were duly considered. The war effort was backed by an efficient intelligence set-up. Surgeons and nurses accompanied the army to provide immediate medical relief to the wounded. Soldiers drank wines to prop up their spirits. They tried to live up to the principles of *dharmayuddha* but in the heat of war these melted fast. Once in the battlefield various strategies and tactics were applied to defeat the enemy as detailed in the following chapters.

NOTES

1. आबिभ्रतोः शत्रुभावमुभयोः संयतात्मनोः।
   अस्त्राद्यैः स्वार्थसिद्ध्यर्थं व्यापारो युद्धमुच्यते।। *Śukraniti*, 4.7.220.
2. मन्त्रास्त्रैर्दैविकं युद्धं नालाद्यस्त्रैस्तथाऽऽसुरम्।
   शस्त्रबाहुसमुत्थं तु मानवं युद्धमीरितम्।। Ibid., 4.7.221.
3. L. Oppenheim, *International Law*, vol. 2, p. 202.
4. युद्ध, आयोधन, जन्य, प्रधन, प्रविदारण, मृघ, आस्कन्द, संख्य, समीक, सांपरायिक, समर, अनीक, रण, कलह, विग्रह, संप्रहार, अभिसंपात, कलि, संस्फोट, संयुग, अभ्यामर्द, समाघात, संग्राम, अभ्यागम, आहव, समुदाय, संयत्, समिति, आजि, समित्, युध्। *Amarakośa*, 2.8.103-5.
5. *Kāmandaka Nīti*, 10.1.
6. Ibid., 10.3-5.
7. Ibid., 10.6-18.
8. युद्धं वै राजनस्य वीर्यम्। *Śatapatha Brāhmaṇa*, 13.1.5.6.
9. कालं देशं शत्रुबलं दृष्ट्वा स्वीयबलं ततः।
   उपायान् षड्गुणं मन्त्रं भवेच्च युद्धकामुकः।। *Śukraniti*, 4.7.223.
10. 'शक्तिदेशकालानां तु शक्तिः श्रेयसी' इत्याचार्यः। *AS*, 9.1.26.
11. परस्परसाधका हि शक्तिदेशकालाः। Ibid., 9.1.33.
12. *Kāmandaka Nīti*, 16.37-8; also *Matsya Pu.*, 240.17.
13. एवं देशंच कालंच ज्ञात्वा यात्रां प्रयोजयेत्। *Matsya Pu.*, 240.19.
14. रात्रावुलूको विनिहन्ति काकान् काकोऽप्यलूकान् रजनीव्यपाये।
    इति स्म कालं समुदीक्ष्य यायात् काले फलन्तीह समीहितानि।। *Kāmandaka Nīti*, 16.37; also
    येनैव गच्छति पथा तेनैवाशु विनश्यति।
    अकालयुक्तसैन्यस्तु हन्यते कालयोधिना।। Ibid., 9.41.

15. *Tirukkural*, 481; also *AS*, 9.1.31.
16. *Rām*, Kiṣkindhā, 30.37.
17. मार्गशीर्षे शुभे मासि यायाद्यात्रां महीपतिः।
    फाल्गुनं वाऽथ चैत्रं वा मासौ प्रति यथाबलम्।। *Manusmṛti*, 7.182.
18. *AS*, 9.1.39-44.
19. शरद्धेमन्तशिशिरकालो युद्धेषु चोत्तमः।।
    वसन्तो मध्यमो ज्ञेयोऽधमो ग्रीष्मः स्मृतः सदा। *Śukranīti*, 4.7.223-4.
20. पदातिनागबहुलां सेनां प्रावृषि योजयेत्।
    हेमन्ते शिशिरे चैव रथवाजिसमाकुलाम्।।
    खरोष्ट्रबहुलां सेनां तथा ग्रीष्मे नराधिपः।
    चतुरंगबलोपेतां बसन्ते व शरद्यथ।। *Matsya Pu.*, 240.19-21; *Agni Pu.*, 228.6.7.
21. *AS*, 9.1.39-44.
22. Ibid., 9.1.40.
23. शरद्धेमन्तशिशिरकालो युद्धेषु चोत्तमः।
    वसन्तो मध्यमो ज्ञेयोऽधमो ग्रीष्मः स्मृतः सदा।।
    वर्षासु न प्रशंसन्ति युद्धं साम स्मृतं तदा। *Śukranīti*, 4.7.224-5.
24. *Matsya Pu.*, 240.5.
    चैत्रयां वा मार्गशीर्ष्यां वा सेनायोगः प्रशस्यते। *MB*, Śānti, 101.9.
25. ये दूरयात्रां सहसा विशन्ति मूढा रिपूणामविचार्य भूमिम्।
    ते यान्ति तेषामचिरेण खड्गधारापरिष्वङ्गमयत्नसाध्यम्।। *Kāmandaka Nīti*, 16.43.
26. श्वा नक्रमाकर्षति कूलसंस्थं श्वानं च नक्रः सलिलाभ्युपेतम्।
    व्यायच्छमानो ध्रुवमभ्युपैति देशस्थितः कर्मफलोपभोगम्।। Ibid., 16.38.
27. प्रभूतोदके देशे वर्षति च हस्थिबलप्रायो यायात्।
    विपर्यये खरोष्ट्राश्वबलप्रायो देशमल्पवर्षपंकम्।
    वर्षति मरुप्रायं चतुरंगबलो यायात्। *AS*, 9.1.48-50; also *Nītiprakāśikā*, 6.68-71.
28. *Kāmandaka Nīti*, 16.39-42; also *Manusmṛti*, 7.192.
29. Ibid.,16.42.
30. हिमपातयुते देशे स्थितं ग्रीष्मेऽभियोजयेत्।
    यवसेन्धनसंयुक्तः कालः पार्थिव हैमनः।
    शरद्वसन्तौ धर्म्मज्ञ कालौ साधारणौ स्मृतौ। *Matsya Pu.*, 240.25-6.
31. यस्मिन् देशे यथाकालं सैन्यव्यायामभूमयः।।
    परस्य विपरीताश्च स्मृतो देशः स उत्तमः।
    आत्मनश्च परेषां च तुल्यव्यायामभूमयः।।
    यत्र मध्यम उद्दिष्टो देशः शास्त्रविचिन्तकैः।।
    अरातिसैन्यव्यायामसुपर्य्याप्तमहीतलः।।
    आत्मनो विपरीतश्च स वै देशोर्धिमः स्मृतः। *Śukranīti*, 4.7.229-31.
32. 'शक्तिदेशकालानां तु शक्तिः श्रेयसी' इत्याचार्याः। *Arthaśāstra*, 9.1.26.

33. परस्परसाधका हि शक्तिदेशकालाः Ibid., 9.1.33.
34. यदा मन्येत भावेन हृष्टं पुष्टं बलं स्वकम्।
परस्य विपरीतं च तदा यायाद्रिपुं प्रति।। *Manusmṛti*, 7.171.
35. मूलरक्षासमर्थोऽस्मि तदा यात्रां प्रयोजयेत्।। *Matsya Pu.*, 240.3.
36. Ibid., 240.14.
37. Ibid., 240.20-7.
38. *Mahābhārata*, Śānti, 101.18-22.
39. *Kāmandaka Nīti*, 16.39.
40. *Śukranīti*, 4.7.222-3.
41. *AS*, 9.1.1.
42. दिव्यान्तरिक्षक्षितिजैरुत्पातैः पीडितं परम्।
षड्क्षपीडासन्तप्तं पीडितञ्च तथा ग्रहैः।। *Matsya Pu.*, 240.7.
43. *AS*, 9.1.42-45; also *Matsya Pu.*, 240.12.
44. *Manusmṛti*, 7.183.
45. मण्डलानि च बुध्येथाः परेषामात्मनस्तथा।
उदासीनगुणानां च मध्यमानां तथैव च।। *MB*, Āśrama, 11.1 *Kāmandaka Nīti*, 8; *AS*, 6.2; *Śukranīti*, 4.1.20-2; *Agni Pu.*, 233.13-16; *Viṣṇudharmottara Pu.*, 2.145; *Manusmṛti*, 7.156-9, 207.
46. *Kāmandaka Nīti*, 18; *Agni Pu.*, 241.46-62; also *Śukranīti*, 4.1.37.
47. उपायाः सामोपप्रदानभेददण्डाः। *AS*, 2.10.47; also, 2.10.48-56.
48. साम दानं च भेदश्च दण्डश्चेति चतुष्टयम्।
मायोपेक्षेन्द्रजालं च सप्तोपायाः प्रकीर्तिताः।। *Kāmandaka Nīti*, 18.3.
49. सामभेदस्तथा दानं दण्डश्च मनुजेश्वर।
उपेक्षा च तथा माया इन्द्रजालं च पार्थिव।। *Matsya Pu.*, 222.2; *Agni Pu.*, 241.46.
50. द्विविधं कथितं साम तथ्यं चातथ्यमेव च। *Matsya Pu.*, 222.3, *Agni Pu.*, 241.46; *Śukranīti*; 4.1.31.
51. परस्परोपकाराणां दर्शनं गुणकीर्तनम्।
सम्बन्धस्य समाख्यानमायतेः सम्प्रदर्शनम्।।
वाचा पेशलया साधु तवाहमीति चार्पणम्।
इति सामप्रभेदज्ञैः साम पंचविधं स्मृतम्।। *Kāmandaka Nīti*, 17.4-5.
Agni Pu. (241.47-8), however, refers to four types of *sāma*:
चतुर्विधं स्मृतं सामं उपकारानुकीर्तनात्।
मित्र सम्बन्धकथनं मृदुपूर्वं च भाषणम्।।
आयाते दर्शनं वाचा तवाहमिति चार्पणम्।
52. *Matsya Pu.*, 222.5-7.
53. दानवानेव शक्नोति संहतान्भेदितुं परान्। *Matsya Pu.*, 224.4; *Kāmandaka Nīti*, 17.6-7.
54. *Matsya Pu.*, 224.5-7.

55. यः सम्प्राप्तधनोत्सर्ग उत्तमाधममध्यमः।।
प्रतिदानं तदा तस्य गृहीतस्यानुमोदनम्।
द्रव्यदानमपूर्वं च स्वयंग्राहप्रवर्तनम्।।
देयश्च प्रतिमोक्षश्च दानं पञ्चविधिं स्मृतम्। *Agni Pu.*, 241.48-50.
56. संहता हि बिना भेदं शक्रेणापि सदुः सहाः। *Matsya Pu.*, 223.4.
57. *AS*, 9.6.2-7.
58. स्नेहरागापनयनं सङ्घर्षोत्पादनं तथा।
सन्तर्जनं च भेदज्ञैर्भेदस्तु त्रिविधः स्मृतः।। *Kāmandaka Nīti*, 18.8; also *Agni Pu.*, 241.50-1; *Matsya Pu.*, 223.4-10.
59. वधोऽर्थहरणं चैव परिक्लेशस्तथैव च।
इति दण्डविभागज्ञैर्दण्डस्तु त्रिविधः स्मृतः।। *Kāmandaka Nīti*, 18.9; *Agni Pu.*, 234.1-3.
60. देवताप्रतिमास्तम्भसुषिरान्तर्गता नराः।
पुमान स्त्रीवस्त्रसंवीतो निशि चाद्भुतदर्शनः।।
वेतलोल्कापिशाचानां शिलानां च सरूपता।
इत्यादिमाया विज्ञेया मानुषी मानुषेश्वरैः।।
कामतो रूपधारित्वं शस्त्रास्त्राश्माम्बुवर्षणम्।
तमोऽनिलोऽचलो मेघा इति माया ह्यमानुषी।। *Kāmandaka Nīti.*, 18.53-5; *Agni Pu.*, 234.8-13, 241.64-5.
61. *Kāmandaka Nīti.*, 18.57-9; *Agni Pu.*, 241.66.
62. मेघान्धकारवृष्ट्यग्निपर्वताद्भुतदर्शनम्।
दूरस्थानां च सैन्यानां दर्शनं ध्वजमालिनाम्।।
छिन्नपाटितभिन्नानां संस्रुतानां प्रदर्शनम्।
इतीन्द्रजालं द्विषतां भीत्यर्थमुपकल्पयेत्।। *Kāmandaka Nīti*, 18.60-1; also *Agni Pu.*, 241.67-8; 234.12-14.
इन्द्रजालं प्रवक्ष्यामि इन्द्रं कालेन दर्शयेत्।।
चतुरङ्गं बलं राजा सहायार्थं दिवौकसाम्।
बलं तु दर्शयेत्प्राप्तं रक्तवृष्टिं चरेद्रिपौ।।
छिन्नानि रिपुशीर्षाणि प्रसादाग्रेषु दर्शयेत्। *Agni Pu.*, 234.14-16; also 241.64; *AS*, 2.18.19; *Viṣṇudharmottara Pu.*, 3.149.
63. *Atharvaveda*, 3.2.6.
64. न माया हीन्द्रजालं वा कुहका वा विभीषणी।
आत्तशस्त्रस्य मे युद्धे वहन्ति प्रतिगर्जना: *MB*, Udyoga 158.35.
65. वयमप्युत्सहेम द्यां खं च गच्छेम मायया।
रसातलं विशामोऽपि ऐन्द्रं वा पुरमेव तु।।
दर्शयेम च रूपाणि स्वशरीरे बहून्यपि।
न तु पर्यायतः सिद्धिर्बुद्धिमाप्नोति मानुषीम्।। Ibid., 160.56-7 (BE).
66. प्रादुश्चक्रे महामायां घोररूपां सुदारुणाम्।।
मोहयन् समरे द्रौणिं मायावी राक्षसाधिपः। *MB*, Bhīṣma, 90.39.

67. प्रकाशरूपस्तु यदा न शक्तस्तौ बाधितुं राक्षसराजपुत्रः।
मायां प्रयोक्तुं समुपाजगाम बबन्ध तौ राजसुतौ दुरात्मा।। *Ram*, Yuddha, 44.39.
68. Ibid., 31.
69. उपायविजयं श्रेष्टमाहुर्भेदेन मध्यमम्।
जघन्य एष विजयो यो युद्धेन विशां पते।। *MB*, Bhīṣma, 4.32.
70. उपायाः साम दानं च भेदो दण्डस्तथैव च।
सम्यक्प्रयुक्ताः सिद्धेयुर्दण्ड स्त्वगतिका गतिः।। *Yājñavalkya Smṛti*, 1.346.
71. *Manusmṛti*, 7.197-200.
72. साम्ना दानेन भेदेन समस्तैरथवा पृथक्।
विजेतुः प्रयतेतारीन्न युद्धेन कदाचन।।
अनित्यो विजयो यस्माद् दृश्यते युध्यमानयोः।
पराजयश्च संग्रामे तस्माद् युद्धं विवर्जयेत्।। Ibid., 7.198-9.
73. सामादीनामुपायानां त्रयाणां विफले नये।
विनयेन्नयसम्पन्नो दण्डं दण्डेषु दण्डवित्।। *Kāmandaka Nīti*, 19.1.
74. दण्डः स्वदेशे कथितः परदेशे ब्रवीमि ते।
प्रकाशश्चाप्रकाशश्च द्विविधो दण्ड उच्यते।। *Agni Pu.*, 234.1-2.
75. संधिविग्रहासनयानसंश्रयद्वैधीभावाः षाडगुण्यम्। *AS*, 7.1.2; *MB*, Śānti, 69.67-8; Āśrama, 6.5-7.
76. *Manusmṛti*, 7.160-8; *AS*, 7.1; *Kāmandaka Nīti*, 9-11; *Śukranīti*, 4.7.232-61; *Matsya Pu.*, 215.16; *Agni Pu.*, 234; *Raghuvaṁśa*, 8.21.
77. परस्माद्धीयमानः संदधीत। अभ्युच्चीयमानो विगृह्णीयात्।
'न मां परो नाहं परमुपहन्तुं शक्तः' इत्यासीत्।
गुणातिशययुक्तो यायात्। शक्तिहीनः संश्रयेत।
सहायसाध्ये कार्ये द्वैधीभावं गच्छेत्। *AS*, 7.1.13-18.
78. *Manusmṛti*, 7.160-8; also *Yājñavalkya Smṛti*, 1.347.
79. षाड्गुण्यविधितत्त्वज्ञो देशभाषाविशारदः।
सान्धिविग्रहिकः कार्य्यो राज्ञा नयविशारदः।। *Matsya Pu.*, 215.16.
80. संधिश्च बिविधाभिख्यो हीनो मध्यस्तथोत्तमः।
भयसत्कारवित्ताख्यः कात्सर्न्येन परिवर्णितः।। *MB*, Śānti, 59.37.
81. *AS*, 7.3.22-36.
82. Ibid., 7.3.37.
83. *Kāmandaka Nīti*, 9.2-4; *Agni Pu.*, 240.5-8.
84. *AS*, 7.3.29.
85. *Manusmṛti*, 7.163.
86. परस्परोपकारश्च मैत्रः सम्बन्धकस्तथा।
उपहाराश्च चत्वारस्तेषु मुख्याश्च संधयः।। *Agni Pu.*, 240.9.
अपकारो विग्रहः। *AS*, 7.1.7
88. स्वयंकृतश्च कार्यार्थमकाले काल एव वा।
मित्रस्य चैवापकृते द्विविधो विग्रहः स्मृतः।। *Manusmṛti*, 7.164.

89. भूमिर्मित्रांहिरण्यञ्च विग्रहं च फलं त्रयम्।
यदैतन्नियतं भावि तदा विग्रहमाचरेत्।। *Kāmandaka Nīti*, 11.1.
90. *Agni Pu.*, 240.14-24.
91. उत्कृष्टबलवीर्यस्य विजिगीषोर्जयैषिणः।
गुणानुरक्तप्रकृतेयात्रा यानमिति स्मृतम्।। *Kāmandaka Nīti*, 11.1.
92. एकाकिनश्चात्ययिके कार्ये प्राप्ते यदृच्छया।
संहतस्य च मित्रेण द्विविधं यानमुच्यते।। *Manusmṛti*, 7.165.
93. विगृह्य सन्धाय तथा सम्भूयाथ प्रसंगतः।
उपेक्षा चेति निपुणैर्यानं पंचविधं स्मृतम्।। *Kāmandaka Nīti*, 11.2; also *Śukranīti*, 4.7.253-4, *AS*, 7.4; *Agni Pu.*, 240.
94. *Kāmandaka Nīti*, 11.3-4.
95. सन्धायान्यत्र यात्रायां पार्ष्णिग्राहेण शत्रुणा।
सन्धाय गमनं प्रोक्तं तज्जिगीषोः फलार्थिनः।। *Śukranīti*, 4.7.256-7; *Kāmandaka Nīti*, 11.5.
96. एको भूपो यदैकत्र सामन्तैः साम्परायिकैः।।
शक्तिशौर्ययुतैर्यानं सम्भूयगमनं हि तत्। *Śukranīti*, 4.7.257; *Kāmandaka Nīti*, 11.6-7.
97. अन्यत्र प्रस्थितः संगादन्यत्रैव च गच्छति।।
प्रसंगयानं तत् प्रोक्तं यानविद्भिश्च मन्त्रिभिः। *Śukranīti*, 4.7.258-9; *Kāmandaka Nīti*, 11.9.
98. रिपुं यातस्य बलिनः सम्प्राप्य विकृतं फलम्।
उपेक्ष्य तस्मिन् तद्यानमुपेक्षायानमुच्यते।। *Śukranīti*, 4.7.261; *Kāmandaka Nīti*, 11.10.
99. यदा दुर्गस्थितः शत्रुर्ग्रहीतुं न च शक्यते।
विगृह्यैनं तदासीत हत्वास्यासारवीवधौ।। *Kāmandaka Nīti*, 11.14.
100. Ibid., 11.16; also *Śukranīti*, 4.7.258.
101. उदासीने मध्यमे च समानप्रतिशङ्कया।
एकीभूय व्यवस्थानं सम्भूयासनमुच्यते।। *Kāmandaka Nīti*, 11.18.
102. Ibid., 11.20.
103. Ibid., 11.19, 11.21.
104. *AS*, 7.4.1; *Kāmandaka Nīti*, 11.22.
105. *AS*, 7.4.13-17.
106. स्थानमासनमुपेक्षणं चेत्यासनपर्यायाः। *AS*, 7.4.2.
107. उपायानामप्रयोग उपेक्षणम्। *AS*, 7.4.3.
108. क्षीणस्य चैव क्रमशो दैवात्पूर्वकृतेन वा।
मित्रस्य चानुरोधेन द्विविधं स्मृतमासनम्।। *Manusmṛti*, 7.166.
109. *Kāmandaka Nīti*, 11.14-23; also *Agni Pu.*, 240.27-8.
110. *Śukranīti*, 4.7.286-7.
111. अरेश्च विजिगीषोश्च विग्रहे हीयमानयोः।
सन्धाय यदवस्थानं सन्धायासनमुच्यते।। *Śukranīti*, 4.7.288; *Agni Pu.*, 234.9.

112. अर्थसम्पादनार्थं च पीड्यमानस्य शत्रुभिः।
साधुषु व्यपदेशार्थं द्विविधः संश्रयः स्मृतः।। *Manusmṛti*, 7.168.
113. *Kāmandaka Nīti*, 11.25.
114. बलिनोर्द्विषतोर्मध्ये वाचात्मानं समर्पयन्।
द्वैधीभावेन वर्त्तेत काकाक्षिवदलक्षितः।। *Kāmandaka Nīti*, 11.23; *Agni Pu.*, 240.28-9.
115. सधिविग्रहोपादानं द्वैधीभावः। *AS*, 7.1.11; *Agni Pu.*, however, explains it as marching on against the enemy with half the army. बलार्धेन प्रयाणं तु द्वैधीभावः स उच्यते। *Agni Pu.*, 234.19; *AS*, 7.1.11; also *Śukranīti*, 4.7.291.
116. *AS*, 7.1.37.
117. *Kāmandaka Nīti*, 11.26.
118. शक्तिस्त्रिविधा-ज्ञानबलं मंत्रशक्तिः, कोशदण्डबलं प्रभुशक्तिः, विक्रमबलमुत्साहशक्तिः।। *AS*, 6.2.33.
119. Ibid.
120. Ibid., 6.2.35.
121. प्रयास्यमानो नृपतिस्त्रिविधं परिचिन्तयेत्।
आत्मनश्चैव शत्रोश्च शक्तिं शास्त्रविशारदः।।
उत्साहप्रभुशक्तिभ्यां मन्त्रशक्त्या च भारत।
उपपन्नो नृपो यायाद्विरीतमतोऽन्यथा।। *MB*, Āśrama, 12.5-6.
122. मन्त्रस्य शक्तिं सुनयप्रचारं स्वकोशदण्डौ प्रभुशक्तिमाहुः।
उत्साहशक्तिं बलवद्विचेष्टां त्रिशक्तियुक्तो भवतीह जेता।। *Kāmandaka Nīti*, 16.32; also *Amarakośa*, 2.8.19.
123. *Mānasollāsa*, 2.8-9.
124. प्रगल्भः स्मृतिमान् वाग्मी शस्त्रे शास्त्रे च निष्ठितः।।
अभ्यस्तकर्मा नृपतेर्दूतो भवितुमर्हति। *Kāmandaka Nīti*, 13.2.
125. *Arthaśāstra*, 1.16; also *Kāmandaka Nīti*, 13.
126. दूतं चैव प्रकुर्वीत सर्वशास्त्रविशारदम्।
इङ्गिताकारचेष्टज्ञं शुचिं दक्षं कुलोद्भवम्।। *Manusmrti*, 7.63; also 7.64-88.
127. दूते संधि विपर्ययो, Ibid, 7.65.
128. न हि ते विग्रहं वीराः कुर्वन्ति कुरुभिः सह।
अविनाशेन लोकस्य काङ्क्षन्ते पाण्डवाः स्वकम्।। *MB*, Udyoga, 20.14.
129. Ibid., 22-32.
130. न चेद् भागं कुरवोऽन्यत्र युद्धात् प्रयच्छन्ते तुभ्यमजातशत्रो।
भैक्षचर्यामन्धकवृष्णिराज्ये श्रेयो मन्ये न तु युद्धेन राज्यम्। Ibid., 27.2.
131. Ibid., 68.148.
132. एवमुक्तस्तु दुष्टात्मा नैव भावं व्यमुञ्चत।
दण्डं चतुर्थं पश्यामि तेषु पापेषु नान्यथा।। Ibid., 148.17.
133. *Rām*, Yuddha, 20.
134. *Rām*, Ayodhyā, 100.15-16; *MB*, Virāṭa, 29.1-10.

135. संग्रामसज्जाः संहृष्टा धारयन् राक्षसास्तदा। *Rām*, Yuddha, 57.23; also 33.18-23.
136. Irfan Habib, *The Indus Civilization*, pp. 26-7.
137. Ibid., p. 27.
138. E.J.H. Mackay, *Further Excavations at Mohenjo-daro*, vol. II, pl. 76.16.
139. Ibid., pl. 72.8-10; 76.6.
140. Ibid., pl. 75.16.
141. Ibid., seals 222, 235, 420.
142. Ibid., seal 430; pl. 99A.
143. G.N. Pant, *Indian Arms and Armour*, p. 3.
144. *Vedic Index*, vol. II, p. 292.
145. S.D. Singh, *Ancient Indian Warfare*, p. 97.
146. नमो बिल्मिने च कवचिने च नमो वर्मिणे च। *Yajurveda*, 16.35.
147. *Ṛgveda*, 6.75.1.
148. शिप्राः शीर्षन् हिरण्ययीः शुभ्रा व्यञ्जत श्रिये। *Ṛgveda*, 8.7.25.
149. *Ṛgveda*, 4.37.4; 2.34.3; 10.96.4; also A.C. Das, *Ṛgvedic Culture*, p. 220.
150. *Ṛgveda*, 1.133.12.
151. *Atharvaveda*, 5.21.10.
152. चित्रैरञ्जिभिर्वपुषे व्यञ्जते वक्षःसु रुक्मां अधि येतिरे शुभे असेष्वेषां नि मिमृक्षुर्ऋष्टयः। *Ṛgveda*, 1.64.4.
153. यमाइव सुसदृशः। Ibid., 5.57.4; also 8.20.11.
154. Moti Chandra, *Prācīna Bhāratīya Veśa-bhūṣā*, p. 23.
155. संग्रामसज्जाः संहृष्टा धारयन् राक्षसास्तदाः। *Rām*, Yuddha, 57.23.
156. दत्तवेतनभक्तं च दत्तायुधपरिच्छदम्।
कृतापदानं च तदा बलमासीन्महाभुज।। *MB*, Vana, 16.21.
157. विचित्रकवचाः शूरा विचित्रध्वजकार्मुकाः।
विचित्राभरणाः सर्वे विचित्ररथवाहनाः।।
स्वदेशवेषाभरणा वीराः शतसहस्रशः।
तस्य सेनाप्रणेतारो बभूवुः क्षत्रियर्षभाः।। *MB*, Udyoga, 8.3-4.
रक्ताम्बरधराः सर्वे सर्वे रक्तविभूषणाः।
सर्वे रक्तपताकाश्च सर्वे वै हेममालिनः।। Droṇa, 33.14;
रक्तवर्मायुधध्वजाः। Droṇa, 9.52.
158. संनद्धाः समदृश्यन्त स्वेष्वनीकेष्ववस्थिताः।
बद्धकृष्णाजिनाः सर्वे ध्वजिनो मुञ्जमालिनः।। *MB*, Bhīṣma, 16.37.
159. While attacking the northern gate of Laṅkā, Rāma saw huge stock-pile of military stores there.
विन्यस्तानि च योधानां बहूनि विविधानि च।
ददर्शायुधजालानि तथैव कवचानि च।। *Rām*, Yuddha, 41.37-8.

160. E.W. Hopkins, *The Social and Military Position of the Ruling Caste*, pp. 248-51.
161. विमुच्य कवचानन्ये पाण्डुपुत्रस्य सैनिका:।
प्रकीर्य केशान्धावन्त: प्रत्यदृश्यन्त भारत।। *MB*, Bhīṣma, 102.28
162. अभिज्ञानानि सर्वेषां संज्ञाश्चाभरणानि च। *MB*, Bhīṣma, 1.12.
163. उष्णीषाणि नियच्छन्त: पुण्डरीकनिभै: करै:।
अन्तरीयोत्तरीयाणि भूषणानि च सर्वश:।। *MB*, Udyoga, 150.20.
164. वस्त्राणि दुधुवुश्च ह। *MB*, Droṇa, 20.8.
165. विशीर्णवर्माभरणाम्बरायुधै:। *MB*, Karṇa, 68.19.
166. शुक्लवासा: *MB*, Udyoga 179.14.
167. तत: समुद्ग्रथ्य सितेन वाससा। *MB*, Karṇa, 66.19.
168. *MB*, Virāṭa, 30.
169. अभिज्ञानानि सर्वेषां संज्ञाश्चाभरणानि च।
योजयामास कौरव्यौ युद्धकाल उपस्थिते।। Ibid., Bhīṣma, 1.12.
170. J.W. M'crindle, *Ancient India as Described by Megasthenese and Arrian*, p. 219.
171. Ibid., pp. 219-20.
172. Ibid., *The Invasion of India*, p. 188; also see p. 186 and fn.
173. Ibid., p. 85.
174. A. Cunningham, *The Stūpa of Bhārhut*, p. 32.
175. W.M. McGovern, *Early Empires of Central Asia*, pl. 1, etc.; Moti Chandra, *Prācīna Bhāratiya Veśa-bhūṣā*, p. 42.
176. McGovern, op. cit., p. 2.
177. J.M. Rosenfield, *The Dynastic Art of the Kuṣāṇs*, pls. 1, 2, 22, 24, 28, 29, etc.; The use of shoes had become common in India around the beginning of the Christian era is evident from the fact that there is a clear injunction in the *Manusmṛti* that it was sinful to take food with shoes on. *Manusmṛti*, 3.239; also 4.66.
178. J. Marshall and A. Foucher, *The Monuments of Sanchi*, p. 157; Fergusson has also dealt with the costume worn by these people, but has left the issue of their indentification unresolved. *Tree and Serpent Worship*, p. 122.
179. Richard Salomon, 'Daily life in Ancient Mathura', p. 40, in *Mathurā: The Cultural Heritage*, ed. D.M. Srinivasan; also see J.E. Van Lohuizen-de-Leeuw, *Foreign Elements in Indian Culture*, Ibid., p. 75.
180. Marshall and Foucher, op. cit., pl. 15.
181. Ibid.
182. Ibid., pl. 29, 61, 64.
183. Ibid., pl. 65.
184. J. Marshall, *Taxilā*, pp. 208, 549.

185. *Harṣacarita*, p. 16.
186. Ibid., p. 202.
187. *Ṛgveda*, 6.75.8.
188. किङ्किणीशतनिर्घोषं वैयाघ्रपरिवारणम्। *MB*, Udyoga, 138.21; Vana 18.1-2.
189. आयुधं सर्वमादाय ततः प्रायाद्धनंजयः। *MB*, Virāṭa, 41.1; Bhīṣma, 50.53-6.
रुक्मच्छन्नैरुरच्छदैः। Bhīṣma, 92.70.
गजाः कङ्कटसंनाहा लोहवर्मोत्तरच्छदाः। Ibid., Udyoga, 149.82.
तस्य सर्वानुपासङ्गान्सर्वोपकरणानि च।
रथे प्रास्थापयद्राजा शस्त्राणि विविधानि च।। Ibid., Droṇa, 87.53.
190. *Brahmāṇḍa Pu.*, 25.42-50.
191. *Bhāgavata Pu.*, 8.10.13-15.
192. *Matsya Pu.*, 176.
193. *Kāmandaka Nīti*, 14.87, 17.39.
194. प्रतिवर्षं स्ववेशार्थं सैनिकेभ्यो धनं हरेत्। *Śukranīti*, 4.7.30.
195. For details on *dhvaja* see Chap. 9.
196. Ibid.
197. *Atharvaveda*, 11.9.6.
198. Ram Gopal, *India in Vedic Kalpasūtras*, p. 185.
199. *MB*, Udyoga, 193, 197; *Raghuvaṁśa*, 4.25.
200. *MB*, ibid.
201. Ibid.
202. *AS*, 10.3.34-7.
203. *Agni Pu.*, 236; *Matsya Pu.*, 240; *Viṣṇudharmottara Pu.*, 2.176.
204. देवानभ्यर्च्य विप्रांश्च प्रशास्तग्रहतारकाः।
षड्विधं तु बलं व्यूह्य द्विषतोऽभिमुखं ब्रजेत्।। *Kāmandaka Nīti*, 19.2.
205. *Harṣacarita*, p. 197; *Mānasollāsa*, 2.20.1151-4.
206. ततश्चन्दनचूर्णैश्च लाजैश्चापि समन्ततः।
निर्ययौ महाबाहुः कार्यमाणो जनार्दनः।। *Harivaṁśa Pu., Viṣṇu*, 109.77; *MB*, Droṇa, 87.60-3; *Raghuvaṁśa*, 4.27.
207. *MB*, Droṇa, 87.63.
208. *Agni Pu.*, 236.
209. यात्रादिने सप्तमे च पूज्ययेच्च त्रिविक्रमम्।।
नीराजनोक्तमन्त्रैश्च प्रायुधं वाहनं यजेत्। *Agni Pu.*, 236.15-16.
210. दिव्यान्तरिक्षभूमिष्ठाः सन्त्वायुर्दाः सुराश्च ते।
देवसिद्धिं प्राप्नुहि त्वं देवयात्राऽस्तु सा तव।। Ibid., 236.17.
211. गृहीत्वा सशरं चापं धनुर्नागेतिमन्त्रतः। Ibid., 236.18.
212. रिपुमुखे पदम्। Ibid., 236.19.
213. तन्मूलत्वात् प्रजानां तु राजा स्कन्ध उदाहृतः।
आवारोऽमात्यदण्डादिर्वृतिरावार उच्यते।।
भूतानां भूतिनिष्पत्तेवारेण महीयसा।
आवृतस्तु यतः स्कन्धः स्कन्धावारस्ततः स्मृतः।। *Kāmandaka Nīti*, 17.38-9.

214. आपगेयं पुरस्कृत्य भ्रातृभिः सहितस्तदा।
स्कन्धावारेण महता कुरुक्षेत्रं जगाम ह।। *MB*, Udyoga, 153.33.
215. ते तु दृष्ट्वा पुरं तच्च स्कन्धावारं च पाण्डवाः। *MB*, Ādi, 184.6 (*BE*).
216. शिविरं मापयामास धृष्टद्युम्नश्च पार्षतः।
सात्यकिश्च रथोदारो युयुधानः प्रतापवान्।। Ibid., Udyoga, 149.72.
217. पारक्रम्य कुरुक्षेत्रं कर्णेन सह कौरवः।
शिविरं मापयामास समे देशे नराधिपः।। Ibid., 153.34; also Karṇa, 95.
218. *Raghuvaṁśa*, 7.2.
219. Ibid., Udyoga, 149.75-82; also Udyoga 196; Bhīṣma, 1.10-11.
220. शिविराणि सहस्रशः। *MB*, Bhīṣma, 1.6; also Udyoga, 149.
221. ते सेने शिविरं गत्वा न्यविशेतां विशाम्पते।
यथाभागं यथान्यायं यथागुल्मं च सर्वशः।। *MB*, Droṇa, 16.1.
222. आवासस्तोयवान्दुर्गः पर्याकाशः प्रशस्यते।
परेषामुपसर्पाणां प्रतिषेधस्तथा भवेत्।।
आकाशं तु वनाभ्याशे मन्यन्ते गुणवत्तरम्।
बहुभिः गुणजातैस्तु ये युद्धकुशला जनाः।।
उपन्यासोऽपसर्पाणां पदातीनां च गूहनम्।
अथ शत्रुप्रतीघातमापदर्थं परायणम्।। Ibid., Śānti, 101.13-15.
223. *MB*, Udyoga, 150.14-16.
224. Ibid., 196.11-19.
225. *AS*, 10.1.1-10.
226. *Kāmandaka Nīti*, 17.
227. *AS*, 10.1.16.
228. *Harṣacarita*, pp. 207-10; also pp. 48-56.
229. A. Goldsworthy, *In the Name of Rome*, p. 122; also see pp. 234-6.
230. *MB*, Bhīṣma, 1.2-3; also Udyoga, 141.
231. Ibid., 99.21-30.
232. Ibid., 112.5-15.
233. कार्तान्तिकनैमित्तिकमौहूर्तिकपौराणिकेक्षणिकगूढपुरुषाः। *AS*, 13.1.7.
234. Ibid.
235. Ibid.
236. *Bṛhatsaṁhitā*, 2.36-7.
237. शरत्काले वसन्ते वा रिपोर्नाशमुपस्थिते।
निमित्तं शकुनं लब्ध्वा यात्रा कुर्वीत भूपतिः।। *Mānasollāsa*, 2.12.745.
238. *Harṣacarita*, p. 197.
239. *Kāmandaka Nīti*, 9.37-8; The omens are described in detail in the book. Ibid., 17.23-41.
240. कर्तान्तिकादिश्चास्य वर्गः सर्वज्ञदैवतसंयोगख्यापनाभ्यां स्वपक्षमुद्धर्षयेत्, परपक्षं चोद्वेजयेत्। *AS*, 10.3.33, 13.1.7; also *MB*, Udyoga, 141; *Rām*, Yuddha, 40.6-8, 46-53; 41.25-6; 57.34-6; 65.47-52.

241. *Agni Pu.*, 229-32.
242. Ibid.
243. J.W. M'crindle, *The Invasion of India*, p. 236; A. Goldsworthy, *In the Name of Rome*, pp. 120, 217.
244. *MB*, Udyoga, 196.8-10 (*BE*).
245. ततः पुनरनीकानि न्ययोजयत बुद्धिमान्।
मोहयन् धृतराष्ट्रस्य पुत्राणां बुद्धिनिश्चयम्।। Ibid., 196.13 (*BE*).
246. Ibid., 196.14-18 (*BE*).
247. Ibid., 196.25 (*BE*).
248. Ibid., 196.26-7 (*BE*).
249. भाण्डं समरोपयतां चरतां सम्प्रधावताम्।
हृष्टानां तत्र योधानां शब्दो दिवमिवास्पृशत्।। Ibid., 196.10 (*BE*).
250. *AS*, 9.1.1.
251. Ibid., 9.1.2-33.
252. Ibid., 9.1.34-6.
253. Ibid., 9.1.37-9.
254. Ibid., 9.1.40.
255. Ibid., 9.1.45, 49.
256. Ibid., 10.2.1-3.
257. *AS*, 10.2.4; also *Kāmandaka Nīti*, 19.45-7.
258. पुरस्तादभ्याघाते मकरेण यायात्, पश्चाच्छकटेन, पार्श्वयोर्वज्रेण, समन्ततः सर्वतोभद्रेण, एकायने सूच्या। Ibid., 10.2.9; also *Kāmandaka Nīti*, 19.48-9.
259. Ibid., 10.2.14.
260. Ibid., 10.2.12-13.
261. A.L. Basham, *The Wonder that was India*, p. 135.
262. *Harṣacarita*, p. 199.
263. *Yajurveda*, 18.24.
234. *MB*, Udyoga, 149.56-63; Karṇa, 7.13-21; *Rām*, Yuddha, 4.9-35.
265. For details see section on *Vyūhas.*
266. 'स्थलगतो हि श्वा नक्रं विकर्षति, निम्नगतो नक्रः श्वानम्'। *AS*, 9.1.29.
267. *AS*, 9.1.21.
268. Ibid., 10.3.50-4.
269. अकर्दमामनुदकाममर्यादामलोष्टकाम्।
अश्वभूमिं प्रशंसन्ति ये युद्धकुशला जनाः।।
समा निरुदकाकाशा रथभूमिः प्रशस्यते।
नीचद्रुमा महाकक्षा सोदका हस्तियोधिनाम्।।
बहुदुर्गा महावृक्षा वेत्रवेणुभिरास्तृता।
पदातीनां क्षमा भूमिः पर्वतोपवनानि च।। *MB*, Śānti, 101.18-20; also *Agni Pu.*, 242.28-31.
270. रथाश्वबहुला सेना सुदिनेषु प्रशस्यते।।
पदातिनागबहुला प्रावृट्काले प्रशस्यते। Ibid., 101.21-2; also *Kāmandaka Nīti*, 20.10-14.

271. स्यन्दनाश्वैः समे युद्धयेदनूपे नौद्विपैस्तथा।
वृक्षगुल्मावृते चापैरसिचर्मायुधैः स्थले।। *Manusmṛti*, 7.192.
272. *Kāmandaka Nīti*, 15.7-12; also see *Mānasollāsa*, 1168-78.
273. पञ्चयोजनमुत्सृज्य मण्डलं तद्रणाजिरम्।
सेनानिवेशास्ते राजन्नाविशञ्शतसंघशः।। *MB*, Udyoga, 196.15.
274. मंडलं बहुयोजनम्। Ibid., Bhīṣma, 1.9.
275. *Tirukkural*, 491-3.
276. *Kāmandaka Nīti*, 19.
277. *Ṛgveda*, 7.18; for details see A.C. Das, *Rgvedic Culture*, pp. 352-67.
278. *MB*, Bhīṣma, 44.3-30 (Datt's trans).
279. L. Bachhofer, *Early Indian Sculpture*, pp. 33-4; also see A. Cunningham, *Bhilsa Topes*, p. 138; J. Fergusson, *Tree and Serpent Worship*, pl. 38, pp. 141-2.
280. J. Fergusson, op. cit., p. 152.
281. Ibid.
282. G. Yazdani, *Ajantā*, pt. 4, pl. 270C (2-4) pl. 28 (1).
283. D. Schlingloff, *Studies in the Ajantā Paintings*, pp. 13-16. According to Yazdani this painting forms a part of the story of *Sutasoma Jātaka, Ajantā*, text, p. 64.
284. Ibid., pp. 115-16.
285. *Ṛgveda*, 1.133.1.
286. *MB*, Stri, 26.21-3.
287. भवन्तः कारयन्त्वेषां प्रेतकार्याणि सर्वशः।
यथा चानाथवत् किंचिच्छरीरं न विनश्यति।। Ibid., 26.26.
288. चिताः कृत्वा प्रयत्नेन यथामुख्यान् नराधिपान्।
दाहयामासुरव्यग्रा विधिदृष्टेन कर्मणा।। Ibid., 26.30.
289. Ibid., 26.42-3.
290. *Atharvaveda*, 6.103-4; 8.8.16; 5.20.4.
291. *Aitareya Brāhmaṇa*, 8.22.
292. *Saṁyutta Nikāya*, 1.83-4.
293. *MB*, Vana, 231.12.
294. *Rām*, Sundara, 9.6, 69.
295. *MB*, Śānti, 96.13.
296. Ibid.
297. Ibid., 97.3.
298. Ibid., 97.5.
299. *HC*, p. 153.
300. *Gauḍavāho*, p. 191.
301. Soma drops: 'Libations of the juice of the *Soma*, or Moon plant, said to be the Acid Asclepias or Sarcostema, Viminalis. The plant

was gathered by moonlight on certain mountains stripped of its leaves, and then carried to the place of sacrifice; the stalks having been there crushed by the priests were sprinkled with water and placed on a sieve or stainer, whence, after further pressure, the acid juice trickled into a vessel called *Droṇa*; after which it was mixed with flour, etc., made to ferment, and then offered in libations to the Gods or drunk by the Brāhmanas, by both of whom its exhilarating qualities were supposed to be highly prized.' Ralph T.H. Griffith, *The Hymns of the Ṛgveda*, p. 1.

302. अस्य पीत्वा शतक्रतो घनो वृत्राणामभवः। *Ṛgveda*, 1.4.8.
303. मरुत्वान् इन्द्र वृषभो रणाय पिबा सोममनुष्वधं मदाय। *Yajurveda*, 7.38.
304. सुरा त्वमसि शुष्मिणी सोम एष मा मा हिंसीः। Ibid., 19.7.
305. Ibid., 19.13-14, 21.59-60; *Sāmaveda*, 4.410; also *Śatapatha Brāhmaṇa*, 12.8.1.6.
306. V.S. Agrawala, *India as Known to Pāṇini*, pp. 114-19.
307. अन्याः स्रवन्तु मैरेयं सुरामन्याः सुनिष्ठिताम्। *Rām*, Ayodhyā, 91.15; also see Yuddha, 63.58; 75.15.
308. *MB*, Mausala, 4; Karṇa, 30.14-15.
309. Ibid., Vana, 16.12-13.
310. *Rām*, Uttara, 42.18; Sundara, 9.34, 41; Yuddha, 75.15, 60.91-3.
311. आलभ्य मङ्गलान्यष्टौ पीत्वा कैरातकं मधु।
द्विगुणद्रविणो वीरो मदरक्तान्तलोचनाः।। *MB*, Droṇa, 127.14 (*BE*).
312. ततः स मधुपर्काहः पीत्वा कैलावतं मधु।
लोहिताक्षो बभौ तत्र मदविोललोचनः।। Ibid., 87.61.
313. *Nītiprakāśikā*, 6.51.
314. रसवत् पाययामासुः पानं मदसमीरणम्। *MB*, Droṇa, 87.54.
315. J.W. M'crindle, *Ancient India*, p. 85; also p. 211.
316. R.S. Tripathi, *History of Ancient India*, p. 119.
317. *AS*, 2.25.
318. Ibid., 2.25.1.
319. मेदकप्रसन्नासवारिष्टमैरेयमधूनाम्। Ibid., 2.25.16.
320. Ibid., 12.4.4-6.
321. U.P. Thapliyal, *Foreign Elements in Ancient Indian Society*, pp. 85-9.
322. J. Legge, *The Travels of Fa-hian*, p. 43.
323. S. Beal, *Travels of Hiuen-tsang*, p. 82.
324. T. Watters, *Travels*, vol. II, p. 239; R.S. Shukla, *India as known to Haribhadra Sūrī*, p. 47.
325. पाययित्वा मदं सम्यक् सैनिकान शौर्यवर्द्धनम्।
उत्तेजितांश्च निर्द्वैधान् वीरान् युद्धे नियोजयेत।। *Śukranīti*, 4.7.355.

326. विनयन्ते स्म तद्यौधा मधुभिर्विजयश्रमम्। *Raghuvaṁśa*, 4.65; also 4-42; *Rām*, Sundara, 62.
327. वीरपाणं तु यत्पानं वृत्ते श्राविनि वारणे। *Amarakośa*, 2.8.103.
328. *Brahmāṇḍa Pu.*, part 4, 28.57-76.
329. Ibid., 28.95-7.
330. *Mārkaṇḍeya Mahāpurāṇa*, 80.34-7.
331. D.K. Gupta, *Society and Culture in the Time of Daṇḍin*, p.186; but *Kāmandaka Nīti* (17.15) says that drinks were not allowed in the *Skandhāvāra* (पानाच्च वारित:).
332. *Ṛgveda*, 1.25.13; 7.87.3, etc.
333. चारै: पश्यन्ति राजान:। *MB*, Udyoga, 34.32.
चारेण तस्मादुच्यन्ते राजानो दीर्घचक्षुष:। *Rām*, Araṇya, 33.10.
334. *MB*, Droṇa, 52.1, Udyoga, 195.2.
335. कच्चिदष्टादशान्येषु स्वपक्षे दश पञ्च च।
त्रिभिस्त्रिभिरविज्ञातैर्वेत्सि तीर्थानि चारकै:।। *Rām*, Ayodhyā, 100.36; *MB*, Śānti, 69.8-13.
336. भवन्तौ वानरं सैन्यं प्रविश्यानुपलक्षितौ।
परिमाणं च वीर्यं च ये च मुख्या: प्लवंगमा:।। *Rām*, Yuddha, 25.4.
332. भूत्वा शकुनय: सर्वे प्रविष्टाश्च रिपोर्बलम्।
विधानं विहितं यच्च तद दृष्ट्वा समुपस्थिता:।। *Rām*, Yuddha, 37.8.
338. चारेण विदित: शत्रु: पण्डितैर्वसुधाधिपै:।
युद्धे स्वल्पेन यत्नेन समासाद्य निरस्यते।। *Rām*, Yuddha, 29.21; also see Bāla, 7.9; Yuddha, 25.13-18, 30.1-35.
339. चारणोत्साहयोगेन क्रिययैव च कर्मणाम्।
स्वशक्तिं परशक्तिं च नित्यं विद्यान्महीपति:।। *Manusmṛti*, 9.298; also *Viṣṇu Smṛti*, 3.35.
340. *MB*, Śānti, 59.41.
341. Ibid., Śānti, 59.34-5.
342. Ibid., Ādi, 139.63-5 (*BE*).
343. पाषण्डास्तापसादींश्च परराष्ट्रेषु योजयेत्। Ibid., 139.63 (*BE*).
344. J.W. M'crindle, *Ancient India*, p. 58.
345. *AS*, 1.11-12; 1.13; 1.16.
346. Ibid., 1.12.20.
347. Ibid., 1.12.4.
348. Ibid., 1.11-12.
349. Ibid., 12.4.
350. Ibid., 1.12.11-12.
351. चरचक्षुर्नरेन्द्रस्तु सम्प्लवेत् तेन भूयसा।
अनेनासम्पतन् मार्गात् पतत्यन्ध: समेऽपि हि।। *Kāmandaka Nīti*, 13.31.
352. स्वपन्नपि हि जागर्ति चारचक्षुर्महीपति:। Ibid., 13.29.

353. *Matsya Pu.*, 215.12-13.
354. *Agni Pu.*, 366.6.
355. न चामुद्रोऽभिनिर्याति न चामुद्रः प्रवेश्यते। *MB*, Vana, 16.19.
356. संज्ञाश्च विविधास्तास्तास्तेषां चक्रे युधिष्ठिरः।
एवंवादी वेदितव्यः पाण्डवेयोऽयमित्युत।।
अभिज्ञानानि सर्वेषां संज्ञाश्चाभरणानि च।
योजयामास कौरव्यो युद्धकाल उपस्थिते।। Ibid., Bhīṣma, 6.1.12-3.
357. दिवसे दिवसे संज्ञाः पृथककार्यास्स्वके बले।
ता जानीयुस्सैन्यपाला न भटा नेतरे जनाः।। *Nītiprakāśikā*, 6.77.
358. Satya Prakash, *Founders of Science in Ancient India,* p. 239.
359. सद्यो जङ्घामायसीं विश्पलायै। *Ṛgveda*, 1.116.15; also see 1.117.17, 10.39.8-10.
360. उन्नो वीरां अर्पय भेषजेभिर्भिषक्तमं त्वा भिषजां शृणोमि। *Ṛgveda*, 2.33.4.
इदमिद्वा उ भेषजमिदं रुद्रस्य भेषजम्।
येनेषुमेकतेजनां शतशल्यामपब्रवत्।। *Atharvaveda*, 6.57.1.
361. *Suśruta Saṁhitā*, Sūtrasthāna, 26.
362. शकटापणवेशाश्च यानयुग्यं च सर्वशः।
कोशयन्त्रायुधं चैव ये च वैद्याश्चिकित्सकाः।। *MB*, Udyoga, 149.53.
सर्वोपकरणैर्युक्ता वैद्याश्च सुविशारदाः। Ibid., 149.78.
363. एवमुक्त्वा ददौ चास्मै विशल्यकरणीं शुभाम्।
ओषधीं वीर्यसम्पन्नां विशल्यश्चाभवत्तदा।। *MB*, Bhīṣma, 77.10.
364. मृतसंजीवनीं चैव विशल्यकरणीमपि।
सुवर्णकरणीं चैव संधानीं च महौषधीम्।। *Rām*, Yuddha, 74.33; also 50.26-33; 91.20-7.
365. सर्वौषधीभिर्गन्धैश्च समालभ्य महाबलाः। *Rām*, Yuddha, 69.18.
366. कोश्यन्त्रायुधं चैव ये च वैद्याश्चिकित्सकाः। *MB*, Udyoga, 149.53
सर्वोपकरणैर्युक्ता वैद्याश्चः सुविशारदाः।। Ibid., 149.78.
367. अथोपयातस्त्वरितो दिदृक्षु
र्मन्त्रोषधीभिर्निरुजो विशल्यः। *MB*, Karṇa, 89.70 (*BE*).
368. औषधानि च सर्वाणि मूलानि च फलानि च।
चतुर्विधांश्च वैद्यान्वै संगृह्णीयाद्विशेषतः।। Ibid., Śānti, 69.57
369. उपातिष्ठन्नथो वैद्याः शल्योद्धरणकोविदाः।
सर्वोपकरणैर्युक्ताः कुशलास्ते सुशिक्षिताः। *MB*, Bhīṣma, 115.51.
370. चिकित्सकाः शस्त्रयन्त्रागदस्नेहवस्त्रहस्ताः स्त्रियश्चान्नपानरक्षिण्यः पुरुषाणामुद्धर्षणीयाः पृष्ठतस्तिष्ठेयुः। *AS*, 10.3.47.
371. Ibid., 5.3.12.
372. Ibid., 2.1.7.
373. Ibid., 14.4.1-3.
374. Ibid., 2.30.26, 42; 2.31.1, etc.

375. Ibid., 2.32.18.
376. *Suśruta Saṁhitā.*
377. *Śiva Pu.*, 5.15.47-61.
378. *Harṣacarita*, p. 165.
379. A.L. Basham, *The Wonder That Was India*, p. 500.
380. *Agni Pu.*, 236.44-8.
381. *Rām*, Ayodhyā, 80; also *AS*, 10.1.17.
382. संशोध्य त्रिविधं मार्ग *Manusmṛti*, 7.185; *Kāmandaka Nīti*, 16.6.
383. *AS*, 9.1.51.
384. *MB*, Śānti, 101.18-20.
385. *AS*, 10.4.1-10, *Agni Pu.*, 236.49-50; 242.28-31.
386. *Ṛgveda*, 6.47.31.
387. *MB*, Udyoga, 153.27; *Rām*, Yuddha, 32.43, etc.
388. *MB*, Bhīṣma, 23.15-16.
389. J.W. M'crindle, *The Invasion of India*, p. 206.
390. Ibid., p. 340; also p. 208.
391. स तूर्यघोषध्वजपताकाभिर्व्यूहाङ्गानां संज्ञा: स्थापयेदङ्गविभागे संघाते स्थाने गमने व्यावर्तने प्रहरणे च। *AS*, 10.6.46.
392. *Śukranīti*, 4.7.266-76.
393. सदैव व्यूहसङ्केतवाद्यशब्दान्तवर्तिन:।
संचरेयु: सैनिकाश्च राजराष्ट्रहितैषिण:।। Ibid., 4.7.364-5.
394. Ibid., 4.7.270-1.
395. Ibid., 4.7.272-3.
396. *Manusmṛti*, 7.90-2; almost similar restrictions are imposed in *Yājñavalkya Smṛti* (1.326), and *Gautama Dharmasūtram* (10.17).
397. *MB*, Bhīṣma, 1.26-32.
398. *MB*, Śānti, 96-7.
399. धर्मेण निधनं श्रेयो न जय: पापकर्मणा। *MB*, Śānti, 96.16; for details see P.V. Kane, *History of Dharmaśāstra*, vol. III, pp. 209-11.
400. *Rām*, Yuddha, 44.75.
401. *AS*, 2.33.8.
402. Ibid., 7.6.40-1.
403. विशिष्टो देशकालाभ्यां भिन्नारिप्रकृतिर्वली।
कुर्यात प्रकाशयुद्धं हि कूटयुद्धं विपर्यये।। *Kāmandaka Nīti*, 19.54.
404. दैव्यासुरी मानवी च पूर्वपूर्वा बलाधिका। *Śukranīti*, 4.7.2.
405. *MB*, Śānti, 59.38-9.
406. गृहीतप्रतिमुक्तस्य स धर्मविजयी नृप:।
श्रियं महेन्द्रनाथस्य जहार न तु मेदनीम्।। *Raghuvaṁśa*, 4.43.
407. तेषामभ्यवपत्या धर्मविजयी तुष्यति ... भूमिद्रव्यहरणेन लोभविजयी तुष्यति ... भूमिद्रव्य पुत्रदारप्राणहरणेनासुरविजयी। *AS*, 12.1.11-15; in the *Aitareya Brāhmaṇa* (8.37.5) four types of victories, viz., *jiti*, *abhijiti*, *vijiti* and *saṁjiti* are mentioned.

408. स्थापयेत्तत्र तद्वंश्यं कुर्याच्च समयक्रियाम्। *Manusmṛti*, 7.202; also *Śukranīti*, 4.7.376-7, 400-4.
409. *Ṛgveda*, 7.8.13.
410. Ibid., 3.33.3.
411. *Atharvaveda*, 3.19.
412. D.K. Barua, *An Analytical Study of Four Nikāyas*, p. 215.
413. हतो वा प्राप्स्यसि स्वर्गं जित्वा वा भोक्ष्यसे महीम्। *MB*, Bhīṣma, 24.37.
414. Ibid., Śānti, 99.4-6; also Sabhā, 12.21; Stri, 26.12-17.
415. *Manusmṛti*, 7.194.
416. *Raghuvaṁśa*, 7.51-3; also *Yājñavalkya Smṛti*, 1.324; *Manusmṛti*, 7.89.
417. हर्षो योधगणस्यैकं जयलक्षणमुच्यते।। *MB*, Bhīṣma, 4.26.
418. Ibid., 4.33.
419. एको दीर्णो दारयति सेनां सुमहतीमपि। Ibid., 4.27.
420. Ibid., 4.27-29.
421. सर्वधर्मपरं क्षत्रं लोकज्येष्ठं सनातनम्।
शश्वदक्षरपर्यन्तमक्षरं सर्वतोमुखम्।। Ibid., Śānti, 64.29, etc.
422. For details see Chap. 2.
423. *AS*, 10.3.30-47; *Agni Pu.*, 234; *MB*, Udyoga, 196.18.
424. D.K. Gupta, *Society and Culture in the Time of Daṇḍin*, p. 186.
425. श्रावयेत् सैनिकान्नित्यं धर्मं शौर्य्यविवर्धनम्।
सुवाद्यनृत्यगीतानि शौर्य्यवृद्धिकराण्यपि।।
युद्धक्रियां बिना सैन्यं योजयेन्नान्यकर्मणि। *Śukranīti*, 5.92-3.
426. *Agni Pu.*, 236.59-60.
427. धूपाश्च देया धर्मज्ञ तथा च परमोहनाः। Ibid., 236.61.
428. पताकाश्चैव संभारो वादित्राणां भयावहः। Ibid., 236.62.
429. *Kāmandaka Nīti*, 18.53-61.

Chapter 4

Strategical and Tactical Concepts: Vedas, Epics and Smṛtis

MEANING OF *VYŪHA*

The term *vyūha* (array) literally means an assemblage, a multitude or a collection.[1] But in the military context it denotes the deployment of troops in formations.[2] Therefore, marshalling or arraying of troops in the battlefield in a specified manner, was called *vyūha*.[3] It was imperative for *senāpati* to array his army and assign his commanders specific positions in a *vyūha* before joining a battle.[4] Indian military thinkers, laid stress on the science of *vyūha* because in a tactically favourable situation even a weak army could defeat a much stronger and larger army.[5] Thus, victory or defeat in a battle largely depended on *vyūha* or the deployment of troops.

In the deployment of forces or their tactical positioning the arms (cavalry, infantry, etc.) and weapons (bow, sword, etc.) may have played a crucial role. To illustrate the point an army strong in cavalry arm may have required a different kind of deployment in the field than an army strong in infantry. Similarly, an archer and sword-bearer could not have been deployed in the same manner. Thus the war tactics of a people were to a great extent determined by the weapons of war known to them.

VEDIC AGE

The science of arraying troops in battle formations was known to the Vedic Indians though the term *vyūha* as such had not then come into use. A war hymn in the *Ṛgveda* says that the *maruts* (soldiers) moved in linear formations like birds.[6] Another hymn says that soldiers (*maruts*) assumed the shape of man, horse or pigeon at different times.[7] Evidently, soldiers formed in different arrays symbolic of a man, animal or bird before joining a battle, the choice of formation of course depending on the situation of war. Another war hymn of the *Ṛgveda* runs as follows: 'Indra guide these: Bṛhaspati precede them, the guerdon, and the sacrifice, and Soma; and let the banded Maruts march in forefront of heavenly hosts that conquer and demolish. Ours be the potent host of mighty Indra, king Varuṇa, and Maruts, and Ādityas.'[8] The Vedic gods thus arrayed their troops in a specified manner, under the leadership of Indra, before joining the battle (Fig. 1). The men formed in 21 (thrice seven) units are actually referred to in the *Ṛgveda*.[9] There are also references to Maruts arrayed in a formation of 49 (seven times seven)[10] and 180 (three times sixty)[11] in the *Ṛgveda*.

In the war of ten kings, described in the *Ṛgveda*, Tṛtsus and the Bharatas both engineered to cross the rivers Bias (Vipāśā) and Sutlej (Śutudrī) to launch a surprise attack on each other. Finally, the Tṛtsus caught the Bharatas unprepared and wiped them out completely.[12] Thus surprise and deception had also become a part of the war strategy in the Vedic period.

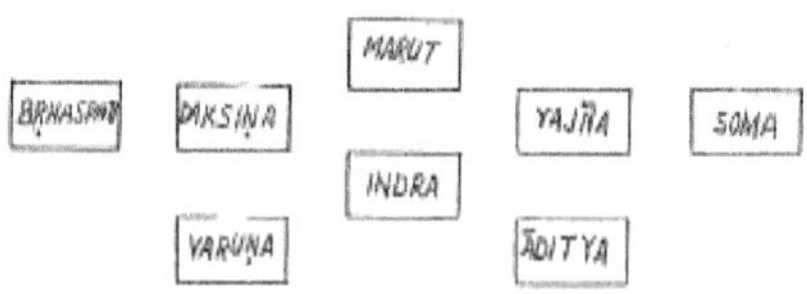

Fig. 1: Vedic Array (*Ṛgveda* 10.103.9-10)

The term *yukteṣu* in the *Sāmaveda* seems to denote a kind of military formation.[13] In the *Yajurveda* there are references to sacrificial formulations of possible military bearing, such as a linear formation (Fig. 2). In a particular formation of this kind the men could be deployed in lines in uneven numbers such as one in the first line, three in the second line, five in the third line, etc. (Fig. 3).[14] In another formation, the number of

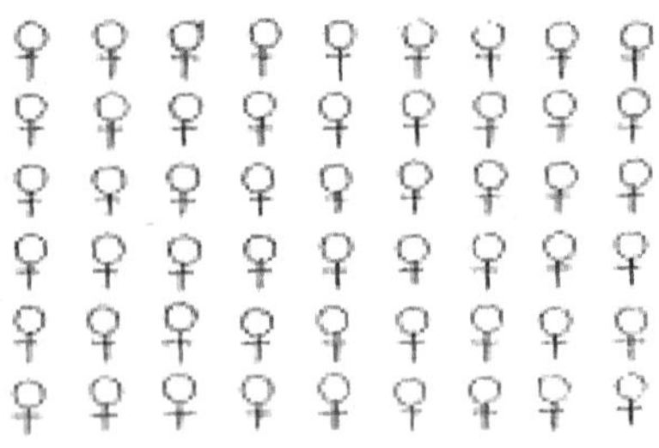

Fig. 2: Vedic Linear Array (1)
(*Ṛgveda* 8.96.8; *Śatapatha Brāhmaṇa* 5.4.3.17, 9.31.15)

troops could be increased by four in each subsequent line, such as 4 in the first line, 8 in the second, 12 in the third, etc. (Fig. 4).[15] Still in another formation the number of troops in each following line could be increased by 10 such as 10 in the first line, 20 in the second, 30 in the third, etc. (Fig. 5).[16] There is an indirect reference to *vyūha* in the *Atharvaveda* also. The concerned hymn as translated by Whitney runs as follows: 'Stand thou up; O! god-folk, Arbudi, with the Army; breaking (*bhanj*) the army of our enemies, envelop in with (thy) coils (*bhoga*).'[17] In

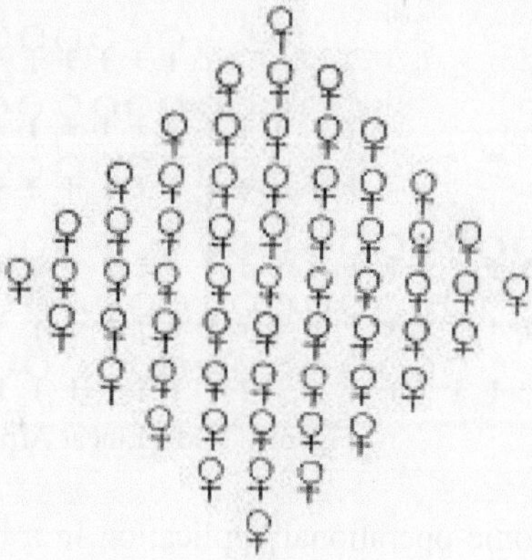

Figure 3: Vedic Linear Array (2)
(*Yajurveda* 18.24)

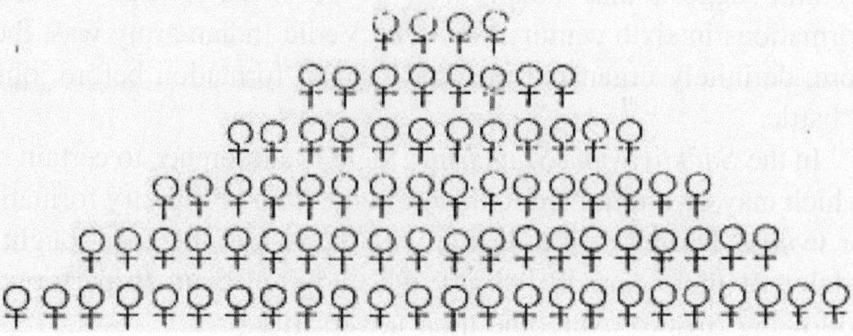

Figure 4: Vedic Linear Array (3)
(*Yajurveda* 18.24)

this hymn the reference to enveloping the enemy with coils certainly refers to some kind of military formation or array in which the enemy was trapped. In this context it is noteworthy that in the *Arthaśāstra* a particular type of formation was called *bhoga-vyūha* (serpent array).[18]

It may be added here that many terms of military significance such as इषुमद्‌भ्यः, धन्वायिभ्यः, विसृजद्‌भ्यः, विध्यद्‌भ्यः, प्रतिधानभ्यः, जाग्रद्‌भ्यः, आसीनेभ्यः, तिष्ठद्‌भ्यः, and धावद्‌भ्यः used in the *Yajurveda* may have had

Figure 5: Vedic Linear Array (4) (*Yajurveda* 18.33)

some operational application in a battle.[19] In the *Taittirīya Saṁhitā* the Maruts, the divine soldiers, are described as organized in seven units.[20] In the *Aitareya Brāhmaṇa* it is said that god Agni while fighting the demons organized his army in three rows and each row was placed under the charge of a commander.[21] Pāṇini has not used the terms *vyūha* in the *Aṣṭādhyāyī* but the use of the terms like *abhiṣeṇayati* (attack), *pariṣeṇayati* (encircle) and *pradrava* (withdraw) by him suggests that Indians were aware of the science of military formations in sixth century BC.[22] The Vedic Indian army was, therefore, definitely organized in some kind of formation before joining a battle.

In the *Sāṅkhyāyana Śrautasūtra* there is a reference to certain rites which may be interpreted to denote some kind of military formations or *vyūhas*. During their long war with the Asuras the gods sought the advice of their *guru*, Bṛhaspati, who advised them to perform the following rites to overcome their adversaries:[23]

1. *Durasa* (difficult to reach) (14.32.1)
2. *Vinutti* (repell) (14.38.1)
3. *Abhibhūti* (overcoming) (14.38.11)
4. *Sarvajit* (all-conquering) (14.48.2)
5. *Nṛjit* (conquered) (14.43.1)
6. *Pratanaja* (battle winning) (14.44.1)
7. *Abhijit* (conquering) (14.42.15)
8. *Viśvajit* (world conquering) (14.42.16)

It seems that these rites were actually the battle formations, which Bṛhaspati advised his followers to adopt in different situations of war.

VYŪHA IN EPICS

The *vyūhas*, appear in a developed form in the epics. The *Mahābhārata* ascribes the concept of *vyūha* to Śukrācārya and Bṛhaspati. It also refers to four kinds of *vyūhas*, viz., *mānuṣa*, *daiva*, *gāndharva* and *āsura*.[24] Of these *āsura* and *daiva* are associated with Śukra and Bṛhaspati respectively. In the Epic war, lasting for eighteen days, the following *vyūhas* were formed by the Pāṇḍavas and Kauravas:

Day	Pāṇḍavas	Kauravas
1.	*Vajra-vyūha*	*Sarvatobhadra-vyūha*
2.	*Krauñcāruṇa-vyūha*	*Mahā-vyūha*
3.	*Ardhacandra-vyūha*	*Garuḍa-vyūha*
4.	*Vajra-vyūha*	*Vyāla-vyūha*
5.	*Śyena-vyūha*	*Makara-vyūha*
6.	*Makara-vyūha*	*Krauñca-vyūha*
7.	*Vajra-vyūha*	*Maṇḍala-vyūha*
8.	*Śṛṅgāṭaka-vyūha*	*Mahā-vyūha*
9.	*Mahā-vyūha*	*Sarvatobhadra-vyūha*
10.	Not specified	Not specified
11.	*Krauñca-vyūha*	*Śakaṭa-vyūha*
12.	*Maṇḍalārdha-vyūha*	*Garuḍa-vyūha* *Candrākāra-vyūha*
13.	Not specified	*Cakra-vyūha*
14.	-do-	*Cakra-*, *Śakaṭa-*, *Padma-*, and *Sūcī-vyūha*
15.	-do-	Not specified
16.	*Ardhacandra-vyūha*	*Makara-vyūha*
17.	*Durjaya-vyūha*	*Mahā-vyūha*
18.	Not specified	*Sarvatobhadra-vyūha*

It follows that Pāṇḍavas formed *ardhacandra-vyūha* on two days and *vajra-vyūha* on three days. Kauravas formed *makara-vyūha* and *mahā-vyūha* on two days and *sarvatobhadra-vyūha* on three days. *Sūcī-vyūha, krauñca-vyūha* and *garuḍa-vyūha* were formed by both sides on one day each. *Śyena-*, *krauñcāruṇa* and *śṛṅgāṭaka-vyūhas* were formed by the Pāṇḍavas only whereas *vyāla*, *maṇḍala* and *śakaṭa* were formed by Kauravas only. *Krauñcāruṇa-vyūha* and *sṛṅgāṭaka-vyūha* formed by the Pāṇḍavas on third and eighth day of war and *cakra-vyūha* and *cakra-śakaṭa-vyūha* formed by the Kauravas on the thirteenth and fourteenth day of war were complicated formations.

In grave situations the commanders formed mixed arrays. Droṇācārya deployed Kaurava forces in a mixed array, a combination of *cakra-*, *śakaṭa-*, *padma-* and *sūcī-vyūhas*, to protect Jayadratha from the reach of Arjuna.[25]

If for some reason the battlefield was divided into two sectors or battle was waged on two fronts, separate arrays were formed in each sector. On the twelfth day of war when Kauravas and Pāṇḍavas were fighting, arrayed in *garuḍa-* and *maṇḍalārdha-vyūha* respectively, the Saṁsaptakas engaged Arjuna arrayed in *candrākāra-vyūha.*[26]

CHOICE OF ARRAY

The choice of array was made after considerable deliberations among the senior commanders and the ruler.[27] Only commanders, well versed in the principles of war, as enunciated by great strategicians like Śukra and Bṛhaspati participated in these deliberations. On the Pāṇḍava side Yudhiṣṭhira (the king), Dhṛṣṭadyumna (the commander-in-chief) and front ranking warriors like Arjuna and Śikhaṇḍin and on the Kaurava side veterans like Bhīṣma, Droṇa, Kṛpācārya, Karṇa, Śalya and Duryodhana were involved in the selection of the battle array.

Occasionally, serious differences arose between commanders on the issue. On the first day of the Mahābhārata war Yudhiṣṭhira, favoured the deployment of his army in *sūcīmukha-vyūha* in view of the numerical superiority enjoyed by the Kauravas (Kaurava and Pāṇḍava forces numbered eleven and seven *akṣauhiṇīs* respectively). He quoted Bṛhaspati in support of his view and asked Arjuna to array the troops accordingly.[28] Arjuna, however, differed with the king in his appreciation and pleaded in favour of *vajra-vyūha.* In support of his contention he quoted the view of Indra that the forces deployed in *vajra-vyūha*, sweep away the enemy by sheer speed like a hurricane.[29] Arjuna's view prevailed and the Pāṇḍava army was arrayed in *vajra-vyūha.*

Though *sūcīmukha* and *vajra* both were offensive arrays, perhaps the latter was considered more effective because it could pierce the enemy array at three points, whereas the former could pierce it only at one point. But in the case of *vajra-vyūha* the offensive power was dissipated.

In the epics the science of *vyūhas* is generally associated with Śukra and Bṛhaspati, the master strategicians. The two *vyūhas*, viz., *sūcīmukha* and *krauñcāruṇa* were designed by Bṛhaspati,[30] whereas three, viz., *śakaṭa*, *padma* and *vajra* were created by Śukra.[31] *Vajra* is also associated with Indra.[32]

During the epic war, which lasted for eighteen days, more than thirty-six *vyūhas* were formed by both sides. A brief description of these *vyūhas* may be helpful in understanding the strategical and tactical concepts of warfare in ancient India.

Vajra-vyūha (Fig. 6)
Śukrācārya had devised this *vyūha* with a view to confront a numerically superior enemy. Arjuna argued in its favour on the first day of war so that the large Kaurava army could be defeated.[33] The army was arrayed in *vajra-vyūha* by Dhṛṣṭadyumna, the Pāṇḍava commander-in-chief.[34] Bhīma led the *vyūha*. Nakula and Sahadeva protected the front wheels of his chariot whereas Abhimanyu and Draupadeyas protected the rear wheels. Arjuna supported Bhīma from behind and was in turn shielded by Śikhaṇḍin. Yudhāmanyu and Uttamaujas protected the front wheels of Arjuna whereas Sātyaki supported him from behind. Yudhiṣṭhira took his position in the middle of the array and behind him came Virāṭa and Drupada, one after another, forming the tail of the *vyūha*. Dhṛṣṭadyumna, supported the array from the front but when he found that the middle of the array, held by Yudhiṣṭhira, was threatened he shifted to that positon.[35] Pāṇḍavas formed this *vyūha* again on the fourth[36] and the seventh day of war.[37]

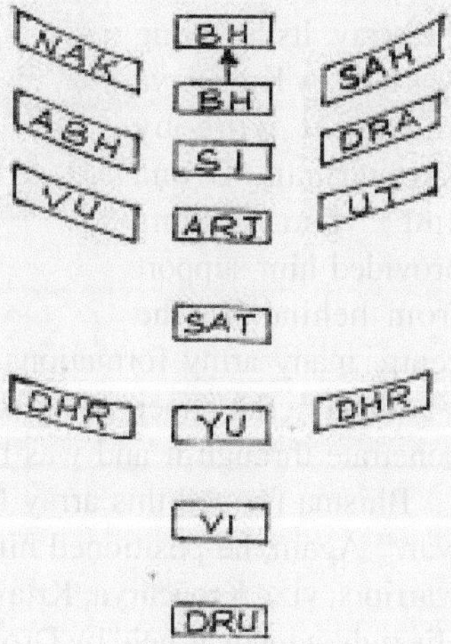

Fig. 6: *Vajra* (Thunderbolt) Array

The general description of *vajra-vyūha* suggests that it was an offensive array. Its objective was to pierce through the powerful enemy array with a killing instinct. It could perhaps beat a large army, but not a large and strong army deployed in a defensive manner in *sarvatobhadra-vyūha.* The array provided for a strong centre but it was weak in flanks and wings and was thus exposed to the danger of encirclement.

Sarvatobhadra-vyūha (Fig. 7)

It provided for heavy deployment of forces on all sides and this enabled it to defeat attack from any direction. Kaurava army was deployed in this array on the first,[38] ninth,[39] and eighteenth day of war.[40] On the opening day of war, Bhīṣma, the Kaurava *senāpati*, held long parleys on its efficacy and usefulness with strategicians like Droṇa, Aśvatthāman, Śalya and Kṛpācārya.[41] Bhīṣma himself led the array. Its left wing was held by Kṛpācārya and right wing by Kṛtavarman. Droṇa and Duryodhana provided him support from behind. In the centre many army formations were deployed. It looked awful and Yudhiṣṭhira felt unnerved by it.[42] The Pāṇḍava *vajra-vyūha* could not penetrate through it and was blunted.[43]

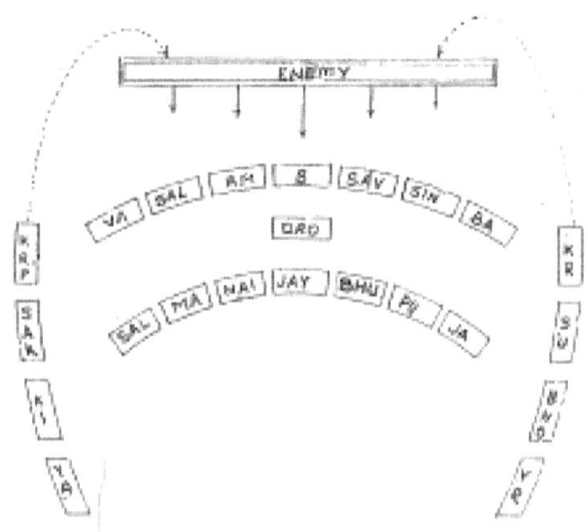

Fig. 7: Sarvatobhadra Array

Bhīṣma formed this array for a second time on the ninth day of war.[44] Again, he positioned himself in the vanguard along with five warriors, viz., Kṛpācārya, Kṛtavarmā, Śaibya, Śakuni and Jayadratha. His right wing was held by Droṇa, Bhūriśravas, Śalya and Bhagadatta and left wing by Aśvatthāman, Somadatta and Avantikumāra. Duryodhana held the middle and Alambuṣa and Śrutāyu the rear of the *vyūha.*[45] Śalya also formed this *vyūha* on eighteenth day of war.[46]

Sarvatobhadra was basically a defensive battle array. Its objective was to blunt the fiercest offensive of the enemy. A very strong centre adequately supported from behind and powerful wings made an ingress by the enemy almost impossible. Two very strong lines of defence interspersed by a no less strong middle, and the whole ensemble well protected by the wings in depth, made it invincible. The positioning of the commander-in-chief at the centre of the vanguard was considered crucial.

Krauñcāruṇa-vyūha (Fig. 8)

This powerful array was originally conceived by Bṛhaspati. Indra is said to have formed it during *Devāsura-saṅgrāma* (war between Devas and Asuras).[47] As Pāṇḍavas had suffered defeat on the first day of war, Yudhiṣṭhira asked Dhṛṣṭadyumna, to form this powerful array on the second day.[48]

Dhṛṣṭadyumna formed it before the sunrise in accordance with the instructions of Bṛhaspati. Arjuna was placed in the vanguard to lead

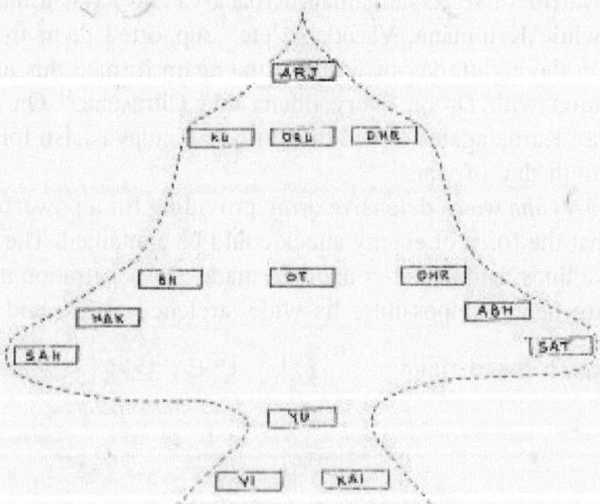

Fig. 8: *Krauñcāruṇa* Array

the array. Dhṛṣṭadyumna and Bhīmasena occupied the wings. Abhimanyu and Sātyaki were placed in support of the right wing and Nakula and Sahadeva in support of the left wing. Drupada formed the head, Kuntībhoja and Dhṛṣṭaketu the eyes and tribesmen the neck of the array. Yudhiṣṭhira formed the back of the array. The waist-line (*jaghana*) was protected by Virāṭa and Kaikeya princes whereas Kāśīrāja and Śaibya supported the whole ensemble from behind.

Krauñcāruṇa was an offensive array intended to be strong and penetrating. The wide spread wings were provided to sweep the enemy completely.

MAHĀ-VYŪHA (Fig.9)

Mahā-vyūha literally means a great array. Perhaps, it stretched over a large area and involved a large number of troops. Kauravas formed it on the second day of war to counter the Pāṇḍava *krauñcāruṇa* array.[49] It was led by Bhīṣma in the vanguard. Bhūriśravas, Śalya and Bhagadatta protected his left wing and Bhūri, Sudakṣiṇa, Suśarman and Śrutāyu the right wing. Behind Bhīṣma came Droṇācārya with Śakuni and Kaurava brothers in support. The array was protected by mighty warriors like Aśvatthāman, Kṛpācārya and Kṛtavarman from behind while Ketumāna, Vasūdana, etc., supported them from behind.[50] On the eighth day of war Bhīṣma again formed this array in consultation with Droṇa, Duryodhana and Citrasena.[51] On seventeenth day Karṇa again formed this array.[52] Pāṇḍavas also formed it on the ninth day of war.[53]

Mahā-vyūha was a defensive array providing for a powerful centre, so that the force of enemy attack could be contained. The strong defensive lines, laid one after another, made any penetration through the centre nearly impossible. Its wide stretched flanks and wings

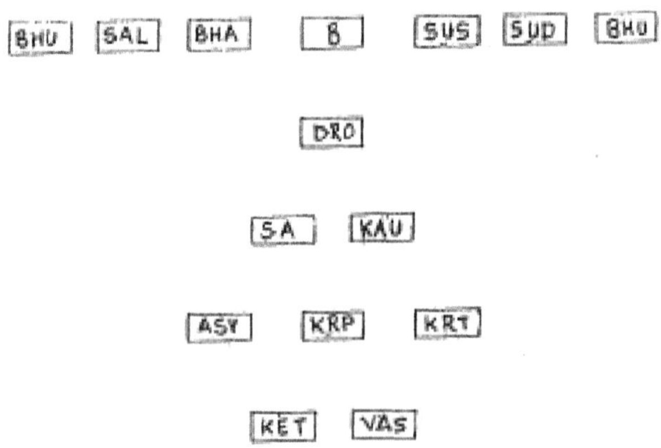

Fig. 9: *Mahā* Array

could thwart any outflanking move of the enemy. In an offensive role the outstretched wings of *mahā-vyūha* could easily outflank the enemy and encircle him.

GARUḌA-VYŪHA (Fig. 10)

Garuḍa-vyūha was formed on two days during the war by the Kauravas. On the third day the array was formed by placing Bhīṣma at the beak, Droṇa and Kṛtavarman at the eyes, Aśvatthāman and Kṛpācārya at the head, Jayadratha, Śalya and Bhagadatta at the neck, Duryodhana at the back and tribesmen like Śakas and Kāmbojas at the tail. The right wing was occupied by the Kaliṅgas and Māgadhas whereas the left wing was held by Bṛhadbala.[54] On the twelfth day of war Droṇa led this array positioning himself at the beak.[55]

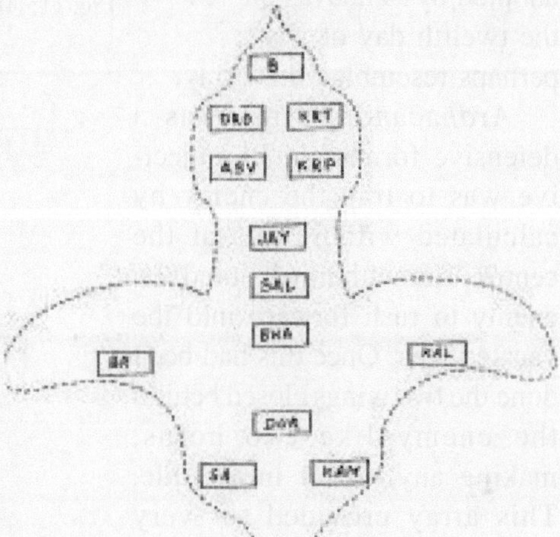

Fig. 10: *Garuḍa* Array

Garuḍa-vyūha was basically an offensive array intended to pierce through the enemy formation with speed and strength. Wide stretched wings and strong tail provided it stability and therefore, the enemy could not imbalance it easily. The array negated any enemy attempt at outflanking or encirclement. The positioning of the commander at the vanguard was crucial in this array.

ARDHACANDRA-VYŪHA (Fig. 11)

Pāṇḍavas formed this *vyūha* on the third and the sixteenth day of war.[56] Arjuna considered it very effective against *garuḍa-vyūha.* On the third day the right and left horns of the *ardhacandra-vyūha* were held by Bhīmasena and Arjuna respectively. The right horn was supported by Virāṭa and Drupada from behind and they in turn were followed by Nīla and Dhṛṣṭaketu. The centre was held by Dhṛṣṭadyumna, Śikhaṇḍin and Yudhiṣṭhira and was strengthened by Sātyaki, Abhimanyu, Irāvān, Ghaṭotkaca and Kaikeya. The left horn was held by Arjuna alone.[57] *Maṇḍalārdha-vyūha* adopted by Pāṇḍavas on the twelfth day of war[58] perhaps resembled this array.

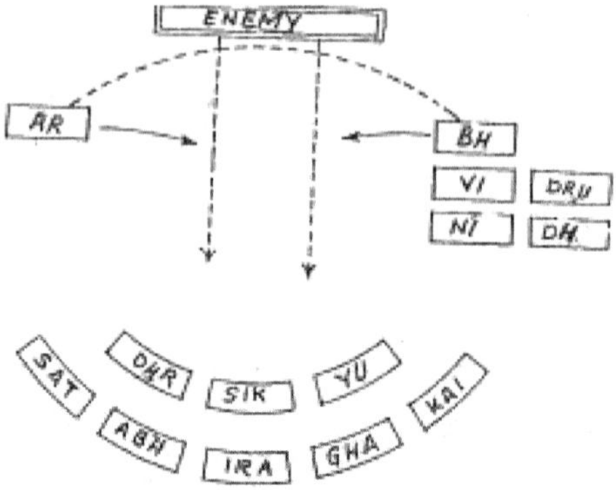

Fig. 11: *Ardhacandra* Array

Ardhacandra array was a defensive formation. Its objective was to trap the enemy by calculated withdrawals at the centre. The withdrawls lured the enemy to rush forward into the vacated area. Once this had been done the two wings closed behind the enemy like two horns, making any retreat impossible. This array provided for very powerful wings indeed. This type of *vyūha* was successfully used by the Carthaginian general Hannibal in the battle of Canae in 217 BC. The result was total massacre of the Romans.

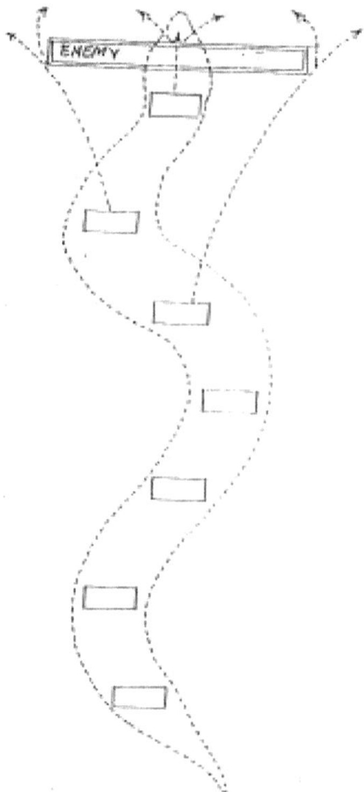

Fig. 12: *Vyāla* Array

VYĀLA-VYŪHA (Fig. 12)

Kauravas adopted *vyāla-vyūha* on the fourth day of war.[59] The Epic provides no details about the make and shape of this array and therefore, it is difficult to sketch it accurately. But it might have looked like a snake. Pāṇḍava army formed in *ardhacandra-vyūha* contained it successfully.[60]

It was perhaps an offensive array, intended to squeeze the rival army in folds, like a snake, after penetrating through the gaps in his formation. The attack was launched on a limited front with a view to confuse the enemy. Though powerful in attack the array was weak in base and was always exposed to the danger of encirclement.

MAKARA-VYŪHA (Fig. 13)

Makara-vyūha was formed three times during the Epic war, on the fifth[61] and the sixteenth day[62] by the Kauravas, and on the sixth day by the Pāṇḍavas.[63] Dhṛṣṭadyumna formed it by positioning Bhīmasena at the mouth, Arjuna and Virāṭa at the head and Nakula and Sahadeva at the eyes of the array. Abhimanyu, Draupadeyas, Ghaṭotkaca, Sātyaki and Yudhiṣṭhira stood at the neck and Dhṛṣṭadyumna took position in the rear of the array. The left wing was formed by Kaikeya princes and the right wing by Dhṛṣṭaketu and Cekitāna. At the leg stood Kuntībhoja and Satānīka and the tail was formed by Śikhaṇḍin and Irāvān. The details of Kaurava *makara-vyūha* formed on fifth day of the war, are not given but it might have been formed by Droṇa in a similar manner. In this array chariots, infantry, elephants and cavalry marched one after another giving the formation an appearance of snake. On the seventeenth day of war, Karṇa also formed it.[64]

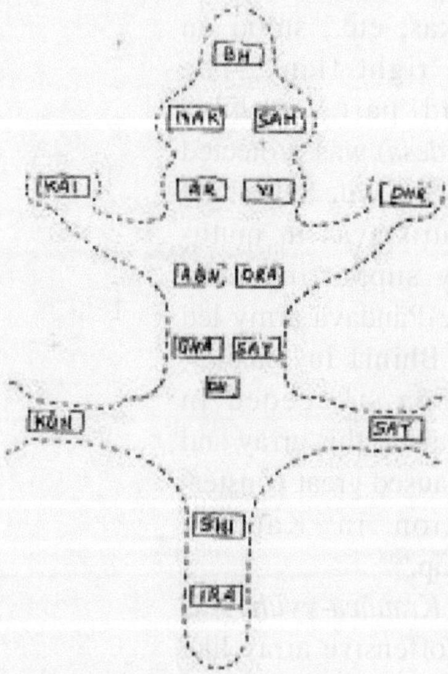

Fig. 13: *Makara* Array

Makara-vyūha was an offensive array imbued with great destructive power. It provided for a powerful centre so that repeated attacks could be mounted on the enemy. The wings, though not very strong, were meant to foil enemy attempt at outflanking and encirclement. It was somewhat like *vajra-vyūha*, though far more stronger at the centre.

Krauñca-vyūha (Fig. 14)

Kauravas formed *krauñca-vyūha*[65] on the sixth day of war to counter the Pāṇḍava *makara-vyūha*. Droṇa positioned himself at the beak to lead the array. Aśvatthāman and Kṛpācārya stood at the eyes and Kṛtavarman at the head of the array. The neck was protected by Śūrasena and Duryodhana and the chest by Bhagadatta. Suśarman took the position on the left flank whereas Tuṣāras, Yavanas, Śakas, etc., stood on the right flank. The hind part (*jaghana pradeśa*) was protected by Śrutāyu, Śalya and Bhūriśravas in mutually supporting role. The Pāṇḍava army led by Bhīma in *makara-vyūha* succeeded in breaking this array and it caused great consternation in Kaurava camp.[66]

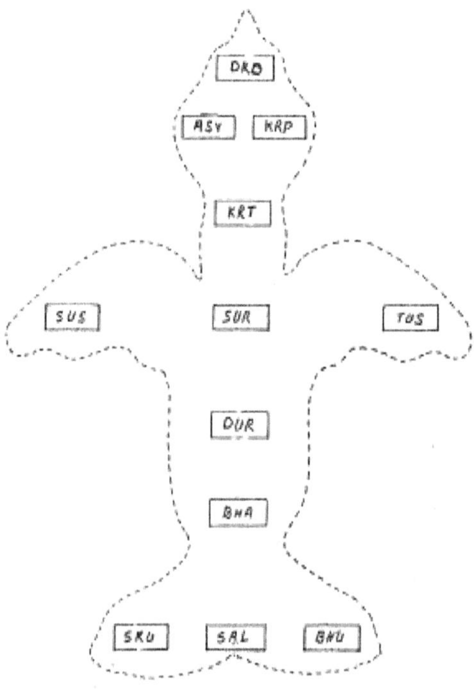

Fig. 14: *Krauñca* Array

Krauñca-vyūha was an offensive array like *garuḍa-vyūha*, but it was comparatively weak as its vanguard lacked the power to blunt a sustained attack. This perhaps explains for the success of the Pāṇḍava *makara-vyūha* against the Kaurava *krauñca-vyūha*.

Śyena-vyūha (Fig. 15)

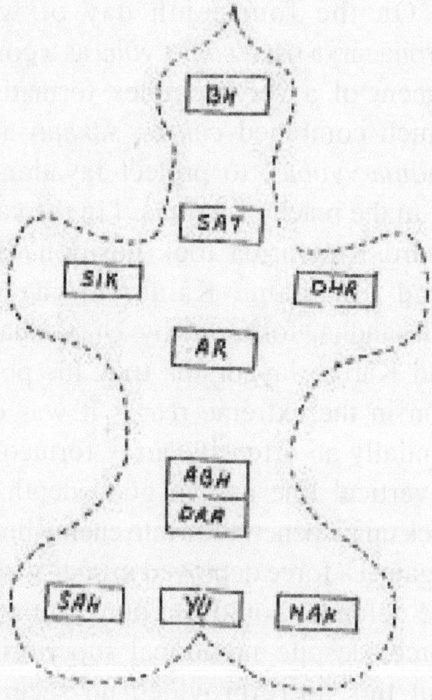

Fig. 15: *Śyena* Array

Śyena-vyūha was an intricate array. Dhaumya, the family priest of the Pāṇḍavas, was the only person, who could form it, owing to his knowledge of sacrificial matters.[67] It may be mentioned that in the *Śatapatha Brāhmaṇa* a particular type of sacrificial altar is called *śyena-citi* and archaeological remains of this alter have been discovered from Kauśāmbī, near Allahabad[68] and more recently from Purola, Garhwal, in Uttarākhaṇḍa. Obviously, *śyena-vyūha* had some relationship with *śyena-citi.* It is notable that this relationship of priests with warfare is as old as the Vedas.[69]

Yudhiṣṭhira formed this array on the fifth day of war, under the instructions of Dhaumya. Bhīma formed the beak, Śikhaṇḍin and Dhṛṣṭadyumna the eyes, Sātyaki the head and Arjuna the neck of the array. Abhimanyu and Draupadeyas stood at the back whereas Yudhiṣṭhira with Nakula and Sahadeva positioned in the rear.[70] *Śyena-vyūha* was an offensive array intended to penetrate deep into enemy lines with speed so as to tear them apart. The lack of depth and weight was the weakness of this array.

Sūcīmukha-vyūha (Fig. 16)

Bṛhaspati, the divine priest, was the innovator of this *vyūha.* It was considered effective against a numerically superior enemy. Yudhiṣṭhira unsuccessfully pleaded in favour of this array, on the first day of the Epic war, against the numerically superior Kaurava army.[71] On the sixth day of war it was formed by the Pāṇḍavas to achieve a break-through when Bhīmasena and Dhṛṣṭadyumna got entrapped in the enemy array.[72]

On the fourteenth day of war Droṇācārya used *sūcī-vyūha* as a component of a very complex formation which combined *cakra-*, *śakaṭa-* and *padma-vyūhas*, to protect Jayadratha from the reach of Arjuna.[73] In the vanguard Kṛtavarmā took position. Behind him came Kāmbojarāja and Jalasandha, followed by Duryodhana and Karṇa. Jayadratha took his position in the extreme rear.[74] It was essentially an offensive array formed in a vertical line and in good depth to seek quick penetration into enemy lines. Against a force deployed in *sūcī-vyūha* the defender could use only a limited force, despite numerical superiority. But this array provided no security against the danger of encirclement.

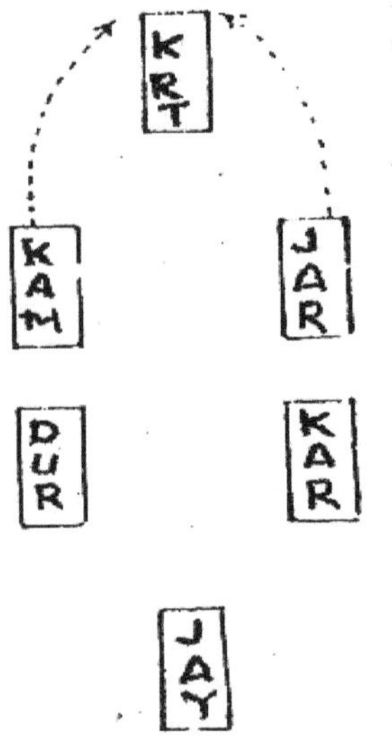

Fig. 16: *Sūcīmukha* Array

MAṆḌALA-VYŪHA (Fig. 17)

Bhīṣma formed his army in *maṇḍala-vyūha* on the seventh day of war. It was protected by chariots on all sides. The troops were deployed in such a manner that each elephant was accompanied by seven chariots, each chariot by seven horses, each horse by ten archers and each archer by ten swordsmen. The array was supervised on all sides by Bhīṣma.[75] Pāṇḍavas countered it with a *vajra-vyūha*.[76]

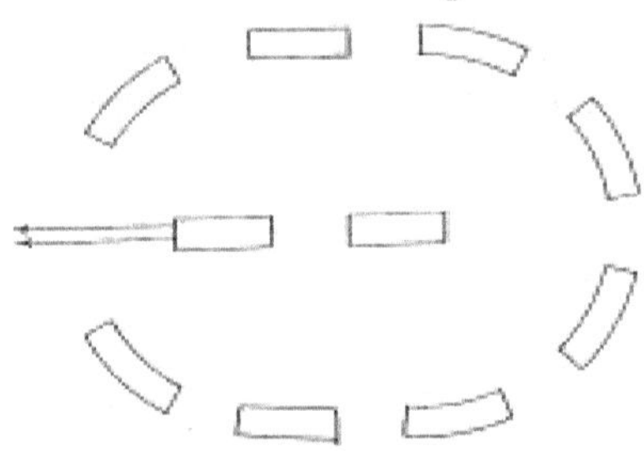
Fig. 17: *Maṇḍala* Array

Maṇḍala-vyūha was considered useful both in offence and defence. Impregnable and imbued with great destructive power it was formed west-oriented (*paścimāvimukha*). Once trapped in this *vyūha* there was no escape from sure destruction.

Śṛṅgāṭaka-vyūha (Fig. 18)

It was formed by the Pāṇḍavas on the eighth day of war to counter the Kaurava *mahā-vyūha.*[77] Bhīmasena and Sātyaki formed the horns of this array. Between them in the vanguard Arjuna took up his position. Behind him Yudhiṣṭhira, Nakula, and Sahadeva were positioned in the middle. Abhimanyu, Virāṭa, Ghaṭotkaca, and Draupadeyas occupied the rear of the array.[78]

Śṛṅgāṭaka-vyūha was a powerful offensive array. Its centre was formed in depth and the whole formation was well supported from behind. The wings (horns) of the array could endanger the enemy on the flanks and even encircle him.

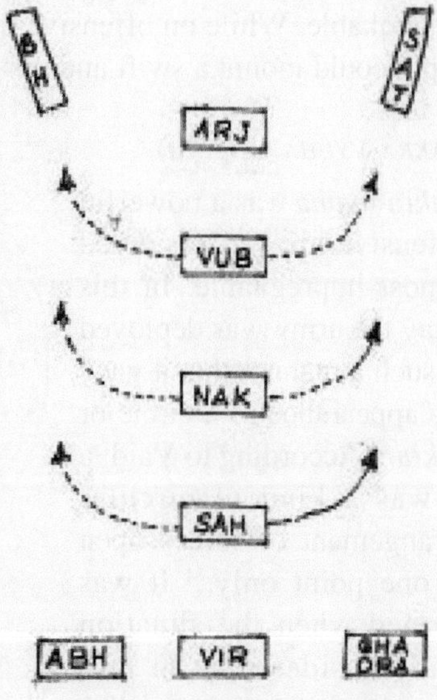

Fig. 18: *Śṛṅgāṭaka* Array

Śakaṭa-vyūha (Fig. 19)

Śakaṭa-vyūha was a solid formation, strong on the wings and the rear. Droṇa formed this array on the eleventh day of war.[79] He positioned Karṇa in the vanguard, Jayadratha on his right wing and Kṛpācārya on his left wing. Śakuni supported the right and Sudakṣiṇa the left wing. Duryodhana supported Karṇa from behind.[80] The formation gave the look of a cart indeed.[81] To counter the challenge of Kaurava *śakaṭa-vyūha* Pāṇḍavas formed *krauñca-vyūha.*[82]

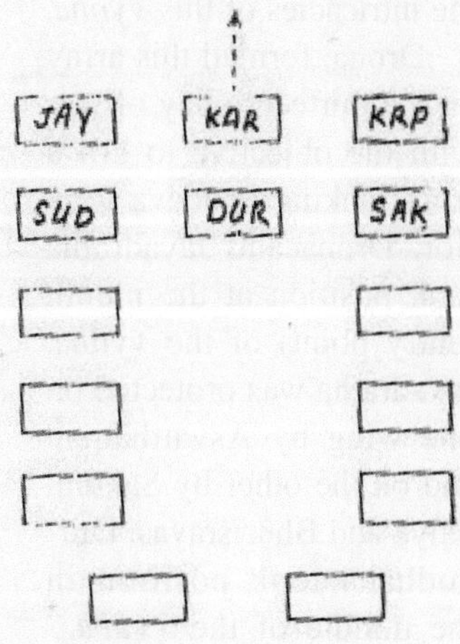

Fig. 19: *Śakaṭa* Array

Śakaṭa-vyūha was both an offensive and defensive array. Its wings were formed like strong pillars. In a defensive role it was almost unbreakable. While on offensive the wings taking advantage of their depth could mount a swift and powerful attack to destroy the enemy.

CAKRA-VYŪHA (Fig. 20)

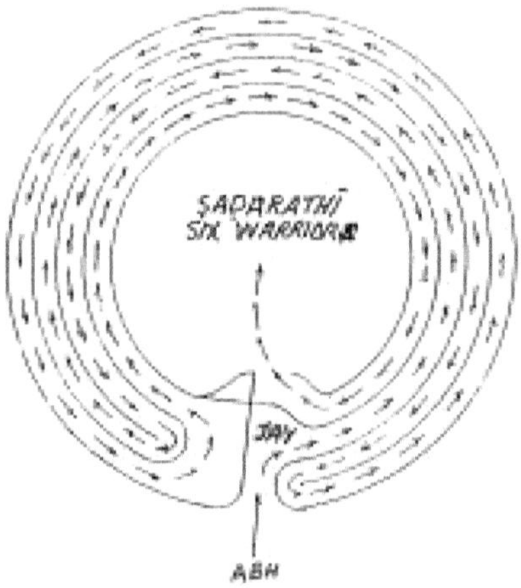

Fig. 20: *Cakra* Array (Imaginary)

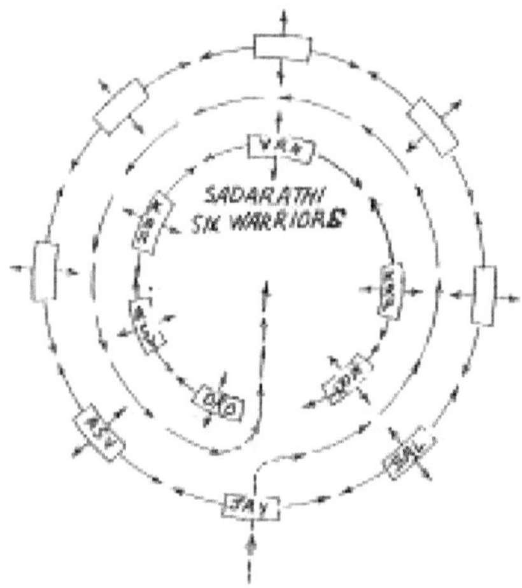

Fig. 20A: *Cakra* Array (Possible)

Cakra-vyūha was a powerful defensive array, considered almost impregnable. In this array the army was deployed in such a manner that it gave the appearance of a circle or *cakra.*[83] According to Vaidya it was a kind of circular arrangement of forces open at one point only.[84] It was formed when the situation was considered grim and demanded drastic remedial measures. Among the Epic warriors only Droṇa, Kṛṣṇa, Pradyumna and Arjuna knew the intricacies of this *vyūha.*

Droṇa, formed this array on the thirteenth day of war with the objective to kill a front ranking Pāṇḍava warrior. Droṇa and Jayadratha took position at the mouth (entry point) of the *vyūha.* Jayadratha was protected on one wing by Aśvatthāman and on the other by Śakuni, Śalya and Bhūriśravas. Duryodhana took position in the middle of the *vyūha.*[85] Abhimanyu who led the Pāṇḍava attack on this *vyūha* was killed.[86]

Cakra-vyūha was a complex military formation in which troops were spread over a large area in large numbers. The objective was to trap the enemy and force him into the premeditated killing ground. As the enemy pushed forward the exit routes closed behind him. Defeat was inevitable in this situation.

Cakra-Śakaṭa-Padma-Sūcī-vyūha (Fig. 21)

This complex *vyūha* was formed by Droṇa on the fourteenth day of the war to protect Jayadratha, whom Arjuna had vowed to kill by the last light of the day. The outer ring of this mixed *vyūha* was formed in *cakra-vyūha. Śakaṭa-vyūha* gave it the support from behind. Inside the *śakaṭa-vyūha* a *padma-vyūha* and in the centre of the *padma-vyūha* a *sūcī-vyūha* was formed.[87] In spite of his best efforts Arjuna could not penetrate this array to reach Jayadratha. Ultimately, it was the strategy of deception (*māyā*) applied by Kṛṣṇa which enabled Arjuna to kill Jayadratha.[88]

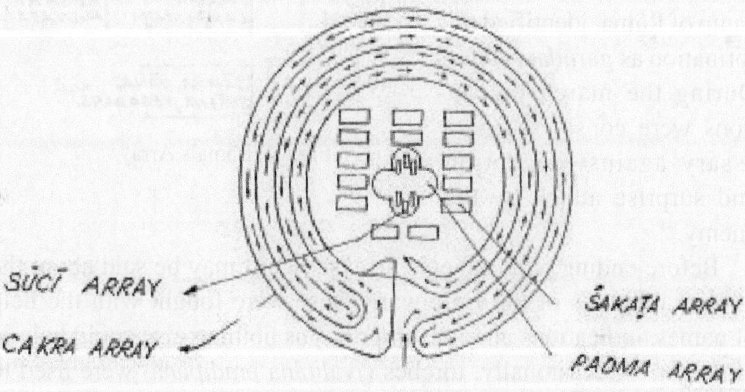

Fig. 21: *Sūcī-Padma-Śakaṭa-Cakra* Array

It was a complex defensive formation comprising four *vyūhas*. It required the attacking force to conquer them, one after another, and not at one go, to reach the objective. This *vyūha* was formed to ensure protection to vital military objectives.

There are also references to some other types of *vyūhas* in the Epic, though these have not been described in detail. Bhīṣma is said to have excelled in the use of *daiva*, *gandharva* and *mānuṣa* type of *vyūhas*.[89] Elsewhere, there is also a reference to *asura, piśāca* and *rākṣasa vyūhas.*[90]

VYŪHA IN *RĀMĀYAṆA* (Fig.22)

Some of the *vyūhas* mentioned in the *Mahābhārata* also figure in the *Rāmāyaṇa*. While marching against Laṅkā Rāma ordered his army to proceed in an array, which appears to have been a *garuḍa-vyūha*. While positioning himself with Lakṣmaṇa in the centre he placed Gavākṣa in the vanguard (*ura*), Ṛṣabha on the right wing (*pakṣa*) and Gandhamādana on the left wing. Further, Keśari and Panāsa supported the right wing and Gaja and Arka the left wing. The back (*kukṣī*) of the array was defended by Jāmbavān, Suṣeṇa and Vegadarśī. Nīla, the commander, controlled the whole ensemble.[91]

While launching attack on Laṅkā Rāma formed his army in *mahā-vyūha* in a prescribed (*śāstric*) manner.[92] Śārdūla, a spy of Rāvaṇa, who came to gather the intelligence in the camp of Rāma, identified this formation as *garuḍa-vyūha*.[93] During the march precautions were considered necessary against deception and surprise attack by the enemy.[94]

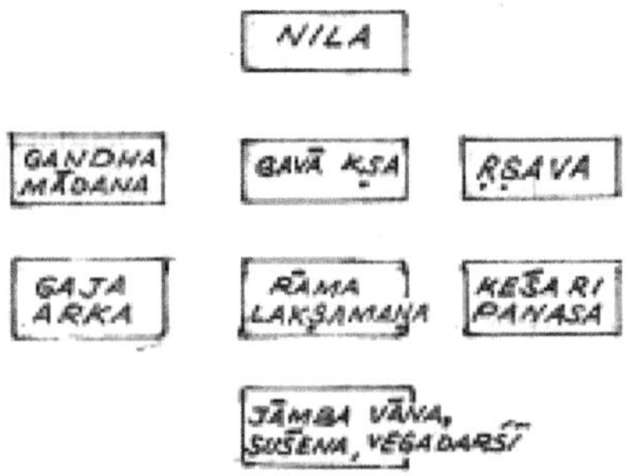

Fig. 22: Rāma's Array

Before ending with the epic arrays a word may be said about the nocturnal battles of the Epic war. These were fought with the help of names, indications and presumptions as nothing else could help in the night.[95] Occasionally, torches (*jvalitāna pradīpāna*) were used to lit the battleground. In the Kaurava army each war-chariot was accompained by five torch-bearers, each elephant by three torch-bearers and each horse by one torch-bearer.[96] But in the Pāṇḍava army each war chariot was accompained by ten torch-bearers, each elephant by seven torch-bearers and each horse by two torch-bearers.[97] The torch-bearers were the infantry soldiers. In the *Rāmāyaṇa* also there are references to nocturnal battles.[98] In one such battle monkeys attacked Laṅkā with burning torches (*ulkā*) in hand.[99] Purāṇas also refer to such battles.[100]

In the *Mahābhārata* there is a reference to a military move called *apasavya*, intended to outflank the enemy on his right. It was considered a unique move to put the enemy in an indefensible situation. Outflanking by an adversary was indeed a challenge to a commander and he made every effort to undo it.[101]

On the fifteenth day of war a similar strategy was applied by the Pāṇḍavas led by Arjuna on the advice of Kṛṣṇa. Droṇācārya had divided his army into two separate formations to attack the Pāṇḍavas, Somakas and Pañcālas. This arrangement resulted in a gap between the two formations. Kṛṣṇa sensing an opportunity here advised Arjuna to push through the gap keeping Droṇa on his right, and ignoring the other formation on his left. It was indeed an outflanking move from the left side, aimed at the encirclement of Kaurava forces.[102]

VYŪHA IN *JĀTAKAS*

The Buddhist *Jātakas* refer to *padma*, *cakra* and *śakaṭa vyūhas.* A story in *Vaddhakī-Śukra Jātaka*[103] relates that when King Pasendi of Kośala suffered repeated defeat at the hands of Ajātaśatru he became very worried. He convened a conference of his courtiers to find an answer to this. The courtiers advised him to send couriers to Jetavana monastery to listen to the conversation of the brothers (Buddhist monks) so as to find an answer to this. Consequently, a courier was despatched to the monastery and he heard Tissa stating the following in reply to Utta's query as to how Pasendi could defeat Ajātaśatru. 'War Sir' said he, 'consists of three kinds: the lotus array, the wheel array and the wagon array. Of those who wish to capture Ajātaśatru will post garrisons in two hill forts right away in the hills and pretend that they are weak, and watch till they get him among the hills and bar his passage, leap out from the two forts and take him in front and the rear, and shout aloud, they will quickly have him like a landed fish, like a frog in the fist; and so they will be able to secure him.' When these contents were brought to the notice of Kośalan king he deployed his army in *śakaṭa-vyūha*, thwarted the attack of Ajātaśatru and captured him.

The references to *vyūhas* in the *Jātakas* suggest that the science of battle arrays had developed in India before the invasion of Alexander. Surprisingly, even the Buddhist monks were conversant with the tactics of war and the Buddhist religious centres entertained discussions on issues of military importance.

VYŪHA IN SMṚTIS

The *Manusmṛti* refers to some most widely known arrays of the Epic times, viz., *śakaṭa, makara, sūcī, vajra* and *garuḍa.* It also refers to *daṇḍa* and *varāha* arrays which do not figure in the Epic.[104] Buhler likens *daṇḍa* as an oblong, *śakaṭa* as a wedge, *varāha* as a rhombus, such as a long line, *makara* as two triangles with apices joined and *garuḍa* as a rhomboid with far extended wings.[105] According to Hopkins

> The formal account of possible military manoeuvre given in the Monavic code is as compared with the Epic, both redundant and deficient. Enough remains of exact similarity to show that the code speaks of movements well authorised by traditions as by precepts. Probably both the Monavic law and the Epic are indebted for their full facts to the military codes published by the two greatest authorities on such matters, Bṛhaspati and Ucanas. That is to say, the completing Epic supplied itself with descriptions from the usually recognised possibilities of warfare, and the Monavic code copied the current military rules (*yuddha-dharma*) ascribed to these men, and which may well have been existent in some form or other (as a manual) before our present Manu was composed.[106]

BATTLE ARRAY OF PORUS (Figs.23,24)

The art of warfare as practised by Indians in fourth century BC finds mention in the Greek accounts. But it is the battle of Hydaspes,

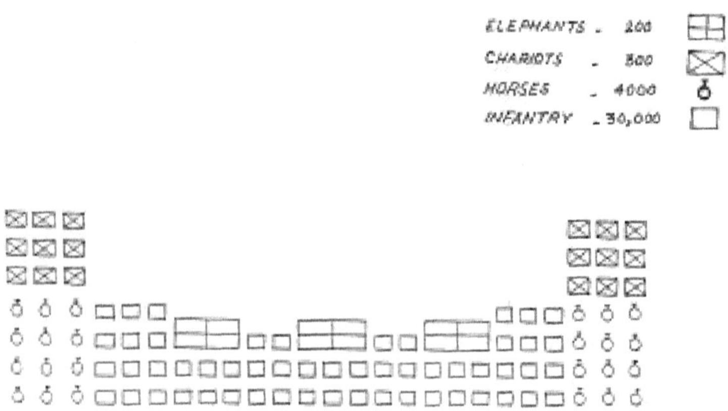

Fig. 23: Battle of Jhelum (Array of Porus)

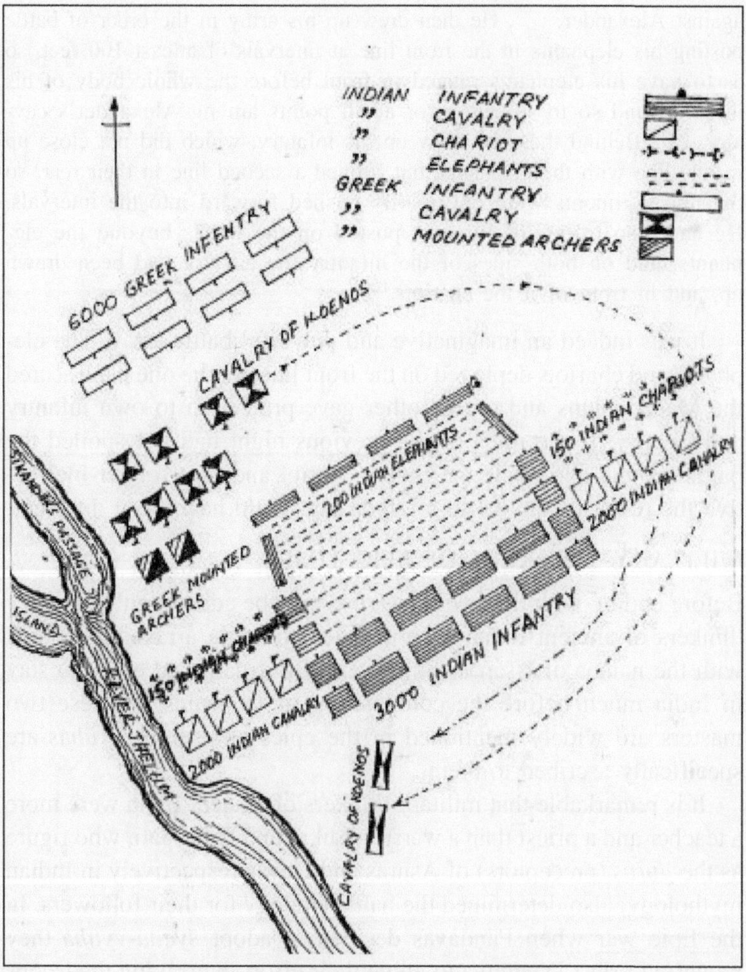

Fig. 24: Battle of Jhelum (after Smith)

fought between Porus and Alexander, which is most graphically described in them. According to Diodotus Porus had an army of more than 50,000 foot, 3,000 horses, 1,000 chariots and 130 elephants.[107] Arrian describes the strength and deployment of his forces as follows:

> He then took all his cavalry 4,000 strong, all his chariots, 300 in number, 200 of his elephants and 30,000 efficient infantry, and marched

against Alexander. . . . He then drew up his army in the order of battle posting his elephants in the front line at intervals of atleast 100 feet, so as to have his elephants ranged in front before the whole body of his infantry, and so to spread terror at all points among Alexander's cavalry. . . . Behind these he drew up his infantry, which did not close up in one line with the elephants, but formed a second line in their rear, so that the regiments were only partly pushed forward into the intervals. He had also troops of infantry posted on the wings beyond the elephants, and on both sides of the infantry the cavalry had been drawn up, and in front of it the chariots.[108]

It was indeed an imaginative and powerful battle array. The elephants and chariots deployed on the front line, on the one hand scared the Macedonians and on the other gave protection to own infantry and cavalry. If the rains of the previous night had not spoiled the battle ground and made the Indian chariot and foot-soldier ineffective the result of the battle of Hydaspes could have been different.

MILITARY THINKERS OF EPIC TIMES

Before ending with the *vyūhas* a word may be added on the military thinkers of ancient India. Two theories on battle arrays, associated with the names of Uśanas (Śukra) and Bṛhaspati, had come to stay in India much before the composition of the epics.[109] These two masters are widely mentioned in the epics and many *vyūhas* are specifically ascribed to them.

It is remarkable that military thinkers of ancient India were more a teacher and a priest than a warrior. Śukra and Bṛhaspati, who figure as the *gurus* (preceptors) of Asuras and Devas respectively in Indian mythology, also determined the battle strategy for their followers. In the Epic war when Pāṇḍavas decided to adopt *śyena-vyūha* they requested priest Dhaumya to guide their effort in arraying the troops as he was an expert in it, owing to his knowledge of sacrificial rituals.[110]

Śukrācārya

In the Epic the three *vyūhas,* viz., *śakaṭa*, *padma* and *vajra* are stated to be the creation of Śukra.[111] Rāvaṇa was well versed in the war doctrines of Śukra and he formed the *vyūhas* propounded by the latter in his war with Rāma.[112] Perhaps, the *asura*, *rākṣasa* and *piśāca vyūhas* formed by Bhīṣma on the tenth day of the Epic war[113] were also a product of Śukra's mind. The *Arthaśāstra* also refers to the military code of Uśanā, which provided for three divisions of a *vyūha,* viz., *ura* (centre), *pakṣa* (wings) and *pratigraha* (reserve).[114]

Bṛhaspati

Bṛhaspati was another great military thinker. He was known as an expert military strategician as early as the Vedic times. This is borne out by many war hymns in the *Ṛgveda.*[115] In the Epic *sūcīmukha-vyūha* and *krauñcāruṇa-vyūha* are said to be the creations of Bṛhaspati.[116] All military commanders of the epic fame were well-versed in the military code of Bṛhaspati.[117] Rāma is said to have followed Bṛhaspati's code of war in his battle against Rāvaṇa.[118] The *Arthaśāstra* refers to the military code of Bṛhaspati, which provided for four divisions of a *vyūha,* viz., *ura*, *pakṣa*, *kakṣa* (flanks) and *pratigraha.*[119]

Yudhiṣṭhira

In the epic besides Śukrācārya and Bṛhaspati, some other master strategicians also figure on the Pāṇḍava and Kaurava sides. King Yudhiṣṭhira, reputed for his truthfulness, was also a military strategician. Generally, he determined the choice of *vyūha* for his army. In arriving at a decision he took into account deployment of enemy forces and strength of his own forces and also used his intimate knowledge of the military arrays as propounded by Śukra and Bṛhaspati. On the opening day of war he favoured *sūcī-vyūha* because according to Bṛhaspati's code a numerically inferior army if formed in this array could take on a numerically superior army.[120] On the second day of war he suggested the deployment of army in *krauñcāruṇa* array, a contribution of Bṛhaspati.[121] On the seventeenth day of war he advised Arjuna to array the troops in such a manner that the enemy may not overwhelm them.[122] It is notable that leading generals debated over the issue before making the final choice of an array.[123]

Dhṛṣṭadyumna

Dhṛṣṭadyumna was another strategician on the Pāṇḍava side. His elevation to the rank of commander-in-chief of the Pāṇḍava army was indeed a tribute to his mastery in military matters.[124] He actively participated in the deliberations on the choice of array and the actual formation of array on the battlefield was also his responsibility. Yudhiṣṭhira greatly depended on him.[125] On the third day of war Arjuna chose *ardhacandra-vyūha* in consultation with him.[126] On the eighth day of war he decided upon *śṛṅgāṭaka-vyūha* to defeat the Kaurava *mahā-vyūha.*[127]

Arjuna

Arjuna was a great warrior as well as a strategician. On the first day of the war he strongly and successfully pleaded in favour of *vajra-vyūha* against *sūcī-vyūha* suggested by Yudhiṣṭhira.[128] On the third day Arjuna advised the adoption of *ardhacandra-vyūha* to meet the challenge of Kaurava *garuḍa-vyūha.*[129] Thus, Arjuna was one of the key figures who determined the Pāṇḍava strategy of war.

Śikhaṇḍin

Śikhaṇḍin was another expert in the science of arrays. On the tenth day of war, when Bhīṣma the greatest of the Kaurava warriors was killed, it was Śikhaṇḍin who had planned the array.[130] In this successful encounter he led the Pāṇḍava forces, staying in the van.

Bhīṣma

On the Kaurava side Bhīṣma was the master strategician. He had studied the codes of Bṛhaspati and Śukra thoroughly in texts as well as in commentaries.[131] The arrays formed by Bhīṣma during the Epic war included *garuḍa*, *makara*, *krauñca*, *sarvatobhadra* and *mahā.*[132] He, however, made a choice only after consultations with other strategicians, viz., Droṇa, Aśvatthāman, Kṛpācārya, Duryodhana and Śalya.[133] Such was his mastery in matters of war that as long as he lived Pāṇḍavas could make little impression in the battlefield.[134]

Droṇācārya

Droṇa was another military genius and strategician. Bhīṣma appointed him as *ācārya* to train the princes of his family in matters of war.[135] In the mastery of weapons he was unparalleled[136] and in thoughts on war he was equal to Śukra and Bṛhaspati.[137] Bhīṣma, while commanding the Kaurava forces, always made his choice of *vyūha* in consultation with Droṇa.

Droṇa commanded the Kaurava army for five days. He used *śakaṭa, garuḍa, cakra, cakraśakaṭa, padma,* and *sūcī vyūhas* on various days of war.[138] The *cakra-vyūha* formed by him on the thirteenth day of war, in which the Pāṇḍava warrior Abhimanyu was killed, was a masterly work.[139] On the fourteenth day of war he formed an intricate array, combining *cakra, śakaṭa, padma* and *sūcī vyūhas* to protect Jayadratha[140] from the reach of Arjuna. But for the deception played by Kṛṣṇa, Arjuna could have never reached Jayadratha.

Karṇa

Karṇa was another strategician on the Kaurava side. He was well-versed in the military code of Bṛhaspati.[141] On the seventeenth day of war he formed a *vyūha* in conformity with the instructions of Bṛhaspati.[142] Śalya was also a great strategician, comparable to Bhīṣma and Droṇa.[143] Kṛpācārya and Aśvatthāman were also important strategicians on the Kaurava side.

Rāma

Rāma was also a military strategist. While planning the invasion of Laṅkā he first acquired all details about its defences from Hanumān, who had been there earlier.[144] While mounting the actual attack he enquired about the defence system of Laṅkā from Vibhīṣaṇa and then appointed commanders to launch attack on different gates of the city.[145] Before marching out on invasion he asked commander Nīla to lead troops through a route which provided for abundant supply of fruits and roots, cold water, and honey.[146] He also alerted his army against poisoned wells and fruits and surprise attacks.[147]

Rāma always sought the advice of his commanders in matters military, notwithstanding the fact that he was well-versed in Bṛhaspati's code of war. He applied this knowledge in his war against Rāvaṇa successfully.[148] He held the status of *atirathī.*[149] In the battle of Laṅkā he organized his army in *garuḍa-vyūha.*[150]

Rāvaṇa

Rāvaṇa, a military strategist of repute, was well-versed in Śukra's code.[151] However, when the security of the state was threatened he sought the advice of his ministers on the course of action to be adopted.[152] Even when he was faced with reverses he consulted his *senāpati.*[153] After the death of his son Indrajita he again consulted his ministers and decided upon a new strategy. It was intended to mount a concentrated attack on Rāma with a view to eliminate him.[154] Though in the battle of Laṅkā Rāvaṇa was finally defeated, his bravery evoked the praise of his principal adversary more than once.

The military thinkers of ancient India had thus developed a pattern of military formations to meet varying situations of war. These thinkers were highly respected people and the rulers were always guided by the norms established by them. It is rather surprising that Brāhmaṇa priests and Buddhist monks were considered equally proficient in their knowledge of battle arrays. A more detailed account of the *vyūhas,* as met in the *Arthaśāstra* of Kauṭilya and the Nīti works, is given in the following chapter.

NOTES

***Following abbreviations are used in the Figs 1-65:**

ABH	Abhimanyu	INF	Infantry	RCE	Rear Centre
AMB	Ambaṣṭha	IRA	Irāvan	RE	Reserve
ARJ	Arjuna	JA	Jaya	SA	Śaka
ARC	Archers	JAR	Jarāsandha	SAH	Sahadeva
ARMD	Armoured	JAY	Jayadratha	SAK	Śakuni
AS	*Arthaśāstra*	KAI	Kaikeyas	SAL	Śalya
B	Bhīṣma	KAL	Kaliṅgas	SAT	Sātyaki
BAH	Bāhlikas	KAM	Kambojas	SAU	Sauvīra
BH	Bhīma	KAR	Karṇa	SIK	Śikhaṇḍin
BHA	Bhāgadatta	KAS	Kāśirāja	SIN	Sindhu
BHO	Bhoja	KAV	Kauravas	SRU	Śrutāyu
BHU	Bhūriśravas	KAT	Ketumāna	SUD	Sudakṣiṇa
BR	Bṛhadbala	KI	Kirātas	SUR	Śūrasena
CE	Centre	KRP	Kṛpācārya	SUS	Suśarman
CH	Chariot	KRT	Kṛtavarman	TUS	Tuṣāras
DH	Dhṛṣṭaketu	KUN	Kuntibhoja	UT	Uttamaujas
DHR	Dhṛṣṭadyumna	MA	Matsya	VA	Vāsudeva
DRA	Draupadeyas	*MB*	*Mahābhārata*	VIR	Virāṭa
DRO	Droṇācārya	NAK	Nakula	VR	Vṛṣṇis
DRU	Drupada	NL	Nīla	W	Wing
EL	Elephant	OT	Others	YAV	Yavanas
F	Flank	OW	Outer wing	YU	Yudhāmanyu
FS	Foot Soldier	*PU*	*Purāṇa*	YUD	Yudhiṣṭhira
GHA	Ghaṭotkaca	PUR	Purumitra		
HO	Horse	*RAM*	*Rāmāyaṇa*		

1. समूहोनिवहोव्यूहसंदोहविसरव्रजा:। *Amarakośa*, 2.5.39.
2. व्यूहस्तु बलविन्यासो। Ibid., 2.8.79.
3. युद्धर्थं सैन्यस्य देशविशेषे विभज्य दुर्लध्यत्वनिमितं स्थापनं व्यूह:। *Śabdakalpadruma*, p. 553.
4. सेनां सेनापतिनायकौ व्यूहेयाताम्। *AS*, 10.5.2.
5. Ibid., 9.1.30.
6. वयो न ये श्रेणी: पप्तु। *Ṛgveda*, 5.59.7; हंसा इव श्रेणिशो यतन्ते यदाक्षिषुर्दिव्य-मज्ममश्वा:। *Yajurveda*, 29.21.
7. अधा नरो न्योहतेऽधा नियुत ओहते।
   अधा पारावता इति चित्रा रूपाणि दर्श्या।। Ibid., 5.52.11.
8. Ibid., 10.103.8.
9. Ibid., 1.133.6.
10. Ibid., 5.52.17.
11. Ibid., 8.85.8.
12. Ibid., 7.33.
13. यं युक्तेषु तुरयन्तो। *Sāmaveda*, 3.337.
14. *Yajurveda*, 18.24.
15. Ibid., 18.25.
16. Ibid., 27.33.
17. उत्तिष्ठ त्वं देवजनार्बुदे सेनया सह।
   भञ्जन्नमित्राणां सेनां भोगेभि: परि वारय।। *Atharvaveda*, 11.9.5; there is a reference to *Bhoga-vyūha* in the *Arthaśāstra.*
18. *AS*, 10.6.24-5.
19. *Yajurveda*, 16.22-3.
20. *Taittirīya Saṁhitā*, 5.4.7.36.
21. *Aitareya Brāhmaṇa*, 3.14.1.
22. V.S. Agrawala, *India as Known to Pāṇini*, p. 423.
23. *Saṅkhyāyana Śrautasūtra*, 14.
24. अव्यूहन् मानुषं व्यूहं दैवं गान्धर्वमासुरम्।
   दिवसे दिवसे प्राप्ते भीष्म: शान्तनवोऽग्रणी:।। *MB*, Bhīṣma, 20.18; also 19.2;
   व्यूहानपि महारम्भान्दैवगान्धर्वमानुषान्।
   तैरहं मोहयिष्यामि पाण्डवान्व्येतु ते ज्वर:।। Udyoga, 162.10.
25. Ibid., Droṇa, 53.26-7, 63.21-8.
26. Ibid., 17.1.
27. Ibid., Bhīṣma, 19.1-17.
28. Yudhiṣṭhira and Arjuna differed on the choice of array on the first day of war. Yudhiṣṭhira recommended *sūcī-vyūha* whereas Arjuna favoured *vajra-vyūha. MB*, Bhīṣma, 19.5-7; also Śānti, 101.44.
29. य: स वात इवोद्धत: समरे दु:सह: परै:। Ibid., Bhiṣma, 19.8.

30. Ibid., Bhīṣma, 19.4-5; Karṇa, 31.26.
31. अथोपपत्त्या शकटं पद्मं वज्रं च भारत।
उशना वेद यच्छास्त्रं तत्रैतद् विहितं विभौ।। Ibid., Āśrama, 12.15.
32. Ibid., Bhīṣma, 19.7.
33. Ibid., 19.7-8.
34. पश्यैतां पाण्डुपुत्राणामाचार्य महतीं चमूम्।
व्यूढां द्रुपदपुत्रेण तव शिष्येण धीमता।। Ibid., 23.3.
35. Ibid., 19.18.
36. यथा हि पूर्वेऽहनि धर्मराज्ञा
व्यूहः कृतः कौरवनन्दनेन। Ibid., 56.11.
37. Ibid., 77.21.
38. Ibid., 17.38; Hopkins is inclined to call it 'Circle' array, op. cit., p.150.
39. Ibid., 95.26.
40. Ibid., Śalya, 7.19.
41. द्रोणेन विहितोराजन् राज्ञा शान्तनवेन च।
तथैवाचार्यपुत्रेण बाह्लीकेन कृपेण च।। Ibid., Bhīṣma, 17.39.
42. Ibid., 21.1-6; it has been described as *abhedya* and *akṣobhya*. Ibid., 21.2-4.
43. Ibid., 45.59-63; according to the *Śukranīti* it had eight faces on all sides.
चतुर्दिक्ष्वष्टपरिधिः सर्वतोभद्रसंज्ञकः।।
अमार्गश्चाष्टवलयी गोलकः सर्वतोमुखः। *Śukranīti*, 4.7.282-3.
44. ततः शान्तनवो भीष्मो निर्ययौ सेनया सह।
व्यूहं चाव्यूहत महत्सर्वतोभद्रमाहवे।। Ibid., 95.26.
45. Ibid., 95.27-35.
46. व्यूह्य व्यूहं महाराज सर्वतोभद्रमृद्धिमत्। Ibid., Śalya, 7.19.
47. व्यूहः क्रौंचारुणो नाम सर्व शत्रुनिबर्हणः।।
यं वृहस्पतिरिन्द्राय तदा दैवासुरेऽब्रवीत्। Ibid., Bhīṣma, 46.39.
48. Ibid., 46.36-9; according to *Śukranīti* (4.7.278-9) it was formed like the line of pigeons flying in the sky. The neck of this array was thin, tail medium and wings thick.
49. ततो द्रोणश्च भीष्मश्च तव पुत्रश्च मारिष।
अव्यूहन्त महाव्यूहं पाण्डूनां प्रतिबाधने।। Ibid., 47.10.
50. Ibid., 47.11-20.
51. भीष्मः कृत्वा महाव्यूहं पिता तव विशाम्पते। Ibid., 83.5.
52. पश्यार्जुन महाव्यूहं कर्णेन विहितं रणे। Ibid., Karṇa, 31.29; also 31.26. *Mahā-vyūha* was formed by Karṇa to beat back the *durjaya-vyūha* formed by Yudhiṣṭhira.
तेऽपश्यन्विहितं व्यूहं धर्मराजेन दुर्जयम्।
प्रयत्नात्कुरुमुख्येन बृहस्पत्युशनोमतात्।। *MB*, Karṇa, 22.11.

53. एवं तेऽपि महाव्यूहं प्रतिव्यूह्य सुदुर्जयम्। Ibid., Bhīṣma, 95.38.
54. गारुडं च महाव्यूहं चक्रे शान्तनवस्तदा। Ibid., 52.2.
55. Ibid., Droṇa, 19.4-5.
56. अर्धचन्द्रेण व्यूहेन व्यूहं तमतिदारुणम्। Ibid., Bhīṣma, 52.10; Karṇa, 7.27.
57. Ibid., 52.11-18.
58. व्यूहं दृष्ट्वा सुपर्णं तु भारद्वाजकृतं तदा।
    व्यूहेन मण्डलार्धेन प्रतिव्यूहद् युधिष्ठिरः।। Ibid., Droṇa, 19.4.
59. तं व्यालनानाविधगूढसारं गजाश्वपादातरथौघपक्षम्। Ibid., Bhīṣma, 56.7.
60. यथा हि पूर्वेहिनि धर्मराज्ञा व्यूहः कृतः कौरवनन्दनेन। Ibid., 56.11.
61. अरक्षन्मकरव्यूहं भीष्मो राजन्समन्ततः। Ibid., Bhīṣma, 65.4.
62. Ibid., Karṇa, 7.14.
63. व्यूहं व्यूह महाबाहो मकरं शत्रुतापनम्। Ibid., Bhīṣma, 71.4; according to the *Śukranīti* (4.7.280) this array had four legs, long and thick mouth and two lips.
64. Ibid., Karṇa, 7.14.
65. व्यूहं दृष्ट्वा तु तत्सैन्यं पिता देवव्रतस्तव।
    क्रौञ्चेन महता राजन्प्रतिव्यूहत वाहिनीम्।। Ibid., Bhīṣma, 71.14.
66. Ibid., 76.5-6.
67. श्येनवद् व्यूह्य तं व्यूहं धौम्यस्य वचनात् स्वयम्। Ibid., 69.5 (*BE*).
68. G.R. Sharma, *Excavations at Kauśāmbī*, p. 87.
69. संशितं न इदं ब्रह्म संशितं वीर्यं बलम्।
    संशितं क्षत्रमजरमस्तु जिष्णुर्येषामस्मि पुरोहितः।। *Atharvaveda*, 3.19.1, 2-8.
70. *MB*, Bhīṣma, 65.7-12; according to the *Śukranīti* (4.7.280) this array had large wings, medium throat and tail and small mouth.
71. *MB*, Bhīṣma, 19.3-5; according to *Śukranīti* (4.7.281) this array had narrow face and long *daṇḍa* and there was a gap at its end.
72. Ibid., 73.54-6.
73. Ibid., Droṇa, 63.23.
74. Ibid., 63.27.
75. Ibid., Bhīṣma, 77.12-16.
76. Ibid., 77.21-4.
77. शृङ्गाटकं महाराज परव्यूहविनाशनम्। Ibid., 83.17.
78. Ibid., 83.18-22.
79. अस्माकं शकटव्यूहो द्रोणेन विहितोऽभवत्।
    परेषां क्रौंच एवासीद्व्यूहो राजन्महात्मनाम्। Ibid., Droṇa, 6.15.
80. Ibid., 6.1-8.
81. *Śukranīti* says that *śakaṭa-vyūha* was shaped like a cart शकट शकटाकारो (4.7.283).
82. *MB*, *Droṇa*, 6.15.

83. In *Śabdakalpadruma* (p. 410) *cakra-vyūha* is described as follows:
अष्टारं वर्तुलाकारं व्यूहचक्रं त्रिनाडिकम्।
दण्डचतुष्टयं वाह्ये कर्तव्यत्रच चतुर्द्दिशम्।।
पूर्वदण्डाग्रतो अन्यस्य दिनभाद्यं भूमण्डलम्।
प्रवेशे निर्गमे चैव त्रीणि त्रीणि प्रदक्षिणे।।
शंशिसंज्ञाष्टकं मध्ये तद्वाह्ये भानुसंज्ञकम्।
तृतीयं राहुसंज्ञच केतुदण्डचतुष्टये।।
चन्द्रर्क्षे विजयो लाभः सूर्यर्क्षे मध्यमं फलम्।
राहुधिष्णाष्टके विघ्नं मृत्युः केतुचतुष्टये।।
एवमुक्तं चतुःस्थाने यद्दिने यस्य नामभम।
तद्दिने तत् फलं तस्य सर्वकार्येषु सर्वदा।।
At another place (p. 414) *cakra-vyūha* is defined as चक्रवत मण्डलाकारेण रचितो व्यूहः रचनयाधिष्ठापितःसेनासमूह इति यावत्।
84. C.N. Vaidya, *Epic India*, p. 260.
85. चक्रव्यूहो महाराज आचार्येणाभिकल्पितः
तत्र शक्रोपमाः सर्वे राजानो विनिवेशिताः। *MB*, Droṇa, 33.12; according to the *Śukranīti* the *cakra* array had one passage and eight concentric rings. चक्रव्यूहश्चैकमार्गो ह्यष्टधा कुण्डलीकृतः। *Śukranīti*, 4.7.281.
86. *MB*, Droṇa, 32.18-20.
87. व्यूहः स चक्रशकटो भारद्वाजेन निर्मितः।। Ibid., 63.21.
पश्चार्धे तस्य पद्मस्तु गर्भव्यूहः सुदुर्भिदः।
सूची पद्मस्य मध्यस्थो गूढो व्यूहः पुनः कृतः।। Ibid., 63.23; for a detailed explanation of this *vyūha* see E.W. Hopkins, op. cit., p. 157.
88. Ibid., 121.15-6.
89. व्यूहानपि महारभ्मान् दैवगन्धर्वमानुषान्।
तैरहं मोहयिष्मामि पाण्डवान् व्येतु ते ज्वरः।। *MB*, Udyoga, 162.10.
90. दिवसे दिवसे प्राप्ते भीष्मः शान्तनवो युधि।
आसुरानकरोद् व्यूहान् पैशाचानथ राक्षसान्।। *MB*, Bhīṣma, 104.16.
91. *Rām*, Yuddha, 4.9.
92. Ibid., 24.13-19.
93. गरुडव्यूहमास्थाय सर्वतो हरिभिर्वृतः।
मां विसृज्य महातेजा लङ्कामेवातिवर्तते।। Ibid., 30.12; also 41.11.
94. Ibid., 4.12.
95. नापश्यन्त रणे योधाः परस्परमवस्थिताः।
अनुमानेन संज्ञाभिर्युद्धं तद्व्रवृते महत्। *MB*, Droṇa, 138.2.
96. Ibid., 163.16-17 (*BE*); in critical edition the number of lamps is not given.
97. Ibid., 138.25-7.
98. सम्प्रवृत्तं निशायुद्धं तदा वानरराक्षसाम्। *Rām*, Yuddha, 44.2.

99. Ibid., Yuddha, 75.3-6; the term *ulkā* also appears in *MB* in the same sense. उल्काशतैः प्रज्वलितै रणभूमिर्व्यराजत। *MB*, Droṇa, 139.4.
100. *Brahmāṇḍa Pu.*, 25.42-50.
101. सोऽपसव्यां चमूं तस्य शाल्वस्य भरतर्षभ।
चकार नातियत्नेन तद्भुतमिवाभवत्।।
अमृस्यमाणोऽपसव्यं प्रद्युम्नेन च सौभराट्।
यन्तारमस्य सहसा त्रिभिर्बाणैः समर्पयत्।। *MB*, Vana, 20.11-12.
102. *MB*, Droṇa, 186.5-12.
103. E.B. Cowell, *The Jātaka* (No. 283), vol. II, p. 275.
104. दण्डव्यूहेन तन्मार्गं यायात्तु शकटेन वा।
वाराहमकराभ्यां वा सूच्या वा गरुड़ेन वा।।
यतश्च भयामाशङ्केत्ततो विस्तारयेद् बलम्।
पद्मेन चैव व्यूहेन निविशेत सदा स्वयम्।। *Manusmṛti*, 7.187-8; also 7.191.
105. G. Buhlar, *Manusmṛti*, p. 246.
106. E.W. Hopkins, op. cit., p. 135.
107. J.W. M'crindle, *Invasion of India*, p. 102.
108. Ibid.
109. *MB*, Bhīṣma, 19.3-6; Karṇa, 31.26.
110. Ibid., Bhīṣma, 69.5 (*BE*).
111. अथोपपत्त्या शकटं पद्मं वज्रं च भारत।
उशना वेद यच्छास्त्रं तत्रैतद् विहितं विभो।। Ibid., Āśrama, 12.15.
112. आमृष्यमाणः सबलो रावणोनिर्ययावथ।
व्यूह्य चौशनसं व्यूहं हरीन्सर्वानहारयत्।। Ibid., Vana, 269.5.
113. आसुरानकरोद्व्यूहान्पैशाचानथ राक्षसान्। Ibid., Bhīṣma, 104.16.
114. *Arthaśāstra*, 10.6.1.
115. *Ṛgveda*, 6.73; 10.103.8, etc.; *Atharvaveda*, 11.10.9-13; *Yajurveda*, 17.36, 9.11-13.
116. *MB*, Bhīṣma, 19.3-6; 46.40; Karṇa, 31.26.
117. Bhīṣma, Droṇa, Karṇa, Yudhiṣṭhira, Arjuna, Dhṛṣṭdyumna, etc., were well versed in Bṛhaspati's code.
118. राघवस्त्वभिनिर्याय व्यूढानीकं दशाननम्।
बार्हस्पत्यं विधिं कृत्वा प्रत्यव्यूहन्निशाचरम्।। *MB*, Vana, 269.6.
119. *AS*, 10.6.2.
120. *MB*, Bhīṣma, 19.3-6.
121. Ibid., 46.39-40.
122. *MB*, Karṇa, 31.28-30.
123. On the first day of war, the Pāṇḍavas decided upon *vajra-vyūha* after a long debate between Yudhiṣṭhira and Arjuna. Dhṛṣṭadyumna also participated (*MB*, Bhīṣma, 19). Bhīṣma choose *sarvatobhadra-vyūha* in consultation with Droṇa, Aśvatthāmā, Śalya and Kṛpācārya

(Bhīṣma, 17.39). On the third day Arjuna decided in favour of *ardhacandra-vyūha* in consultation with Dhṛṣṭadyumna (Bhīṣma, 56.10). On the fifth day Yudhiṣṭhira choose *śyena-vyūha* in consultation with Dhaumya, the Pāṇḍava priest (Bhīṣma 65.12). On the eighth day Bhīṣma, formed *mahā-vyūha* in consultation with Droṇa, Duryodhana Citrasena and Vivinśata (Bhīṣma, 83.3).

124. *MB*, Udyoga, 149.19-28.
125. Ibid., Bhīṣma, 46.32-7.
126. Ibid., 52.10.
127. Ibid., 83.17.
128. Ibid., 19.7-8.
129. Ibid., 52.10.
130. Ibid., 104.4-9.
131. उशना वेद यच्छास्त्रं देवासुरगुरुर्द्विजः।
    तच्च सर्वं सवैयाख्यं प्राप्तवान् कुरुसत्तमः।। Ibid., Śānti, 38.10.
132. Ibid., Bhīṣma, 47.10 (*mahā*), 52.2 (*garuḍa*), 65.4 (*makara*) 71.14 (*krauñca*), 95.26 (*sarvatobhadra*).
133. Ibid., Bhīṣma, 47.10, 83.3-4.
134. धनुर्वेदविदो मुख्या अजेयाः शत्रुभिर्युधि। Ibid., 57.13.
135. Ibid., Ādi, 121.
136. युक्तः सेनापतिः कर्तुं द्रोणः शस्त्रभृतां वरः। Ibid., Droṇa, 5.16.
137. Ibid., 5.17.
138. Ibid., 6.15 (*śakaṭa*); 19.4 (*garuḍa*); 33.12 (*cakra*); 63.23-28 (*cakra, śakaṭa, padma, sūcī*).
139. Ibid., 33.12.
140. Ibid., 63.23-8.
141. Ibid., Karṇa, 31.26.
142. Ibid.
143. Ibid., Śalya, 6.26.
144. कति दुर्गाणि दुर्गाया लङ्कायास्तद् ब्रवीष्व मे।
    ज्ञातुमिच्छामि तत् सर्वं दर्शनादिव वानर।। *Rām*, Yuddha, 3.3.
145. Ibid., 37.
146. Ibid., 4.10-12.
147. Ibid., 4.12.
148. *MB*, Araṇya, 269.6.
149. *Rām*, Yuddha, 28.18.
150. गरुडव्यूहमास्थाय सर्वतो हरिभिर्वृतः। Ibid., 30.12.
151. *MB*, Araṇya, 269.5.
152. *Rām*, Yuddha, 6.8-12.
153. Ibid., 57.1-2.
154. Ibid., 94.3-5.

Chapter 5

Strategical and Tactical Concepts: *Arthaśāstra* and *Nīti* Works

The *Arthaśāstra*, a treatise composed some time after the beginning of the Christian era, describes the application of *daṇḍa* (war or military option) in some detail. It also elucidates three other measures of diplomacy, viz., *sāma, dāna* and *bheda* which determined the application of *daṇḍa* as an instrument of state policy.

FOUR MEANS (*UPĀYACATUṢṬAYA*)

Kauṭilya held the view that the option of war (*daṇḍa*) could be exercised by the aspirant of victory (*vijigīṣu*) to subjugate the enemy. However, it was to be resorted to only when the other three means of state policy, viz., conciliation (*sāma*), gift (*dāna*) and dissension (*bheda*), had failed to yield the desired result.[1] The choice of either of these four means depended on the military capability of the adversary. To illustrate the point, a weak king could be bought over by means of conciliation or gift but a strong king could be contained only by means of dissension or war. Application of means also depended on the disposition (*prakṛti*)—friendly (*mitra*) or unfriendly (*śatru*)—of the ruler who was the target of the state policy. Therefore, great care had to be taken in deciding the application of one or more means against a given adversary. Application of one of the four means against the targetted king was called *niyoga.* When the choice was made between two of the four means, it was called *vikalpa* and when more than one of the four means were applied simultaneously, it was called *samuccaya.*[2]

Daṇḍa as a means of state policy could be applied against an adversary by way of open war (*prakāśa-yuddha*), secret war (*kūṭa-*

yuddha) or silent war (*tūṣṇī-yuddha*).[3] In an open war, the enemy was defeated in the battlefield, but in other two cases he was eliminated through dubious means.[4] The aspirant of victory (*vijigīṣu*) was to seek the option of open war only in favourable circumstances, such as convenient terrain, suitable season and adequate supplies. It was an added advantage if the enemy lacked the protection of a fort and the support of a faithful ally.[5]

In an open war, if the enemy was routed by a frontal attack, his retreat could be blocked by attacking him with elephants and horses in the rear so as to annihilate him. But if the enemy was scattered by a rear attack or was retreating in the reverse direction, then he should be destroyed frontally by the brave troops. In the event the enemy was attacked from either flank he was to be contained in the same very manner as in the frontal or rear attack.[6] In an open war, the terrain factor generally determined the direction of attack (frontal, rear or flank) but in special circumstances, the attack could by mounted on the side, held by the weakest troops (*dusyafālgubalam*)[7] of the enemy. *Prakāśa-yuddha* was also called *dharma-yuddha* (just war) as it was fought according to established norms of war.[8]

In a secret war (*kūṭa-yuddha*), all means, fair or foul, could be applied to defeat the enemy. Unfair means included surprise attack, harassment of troops, killing by betrayal, etc.[9] Prudent use was to be made of *deśa* and *kāla* factors. The *deśa* stood for advantage of place such as forest land, marshy land, dry land, etc., in conducting military operations. The *kāla* meant the advantage of season and time, for attacking the enemy when he was least prepared.[10]

DEPLOYMENT OF FORCES

The army was to be deployed keeping in view the terrain of the battlefield, the forces available to self and the likely build up of the rival army. In a close order formation the foot-soldiers were positioned at a distance of about 26.5 cm (14 *aṅgulas*) from each other, the horses at a distance of 79.5 cm (42 *aṅgulas*) and chariots at a distance of 127.5 cm (70 *aṅgulas*). This distance could, however, be increased according to the nature of the terrain. A good elbow space between the troops was considered convenient.[11]

The foot-archers were deployed at a distance of 2.25 m (5 hands) from each other. The archers mounted on horses stood at a distance of 6.75 m (15 hands) and those mounted on chariots or elephants at a distance of 11.25 m (25 hands). The distance between the troops positioned at the centre, flanks and wings was kept at 11.25 m (25 hands).[12]

BATTLE FORMATIONS

In the *Arthaśāstra* battle formations have been described with their divisions and sub-divisions.[13] Detailed classification of *vyūhas* in the *Arthaśāstra* suggests that the system of warfare had undergone considerable change since the epic times. The nomenclature of the *vyūhas* and their classification given in it is entirely different from the one met in the Epic. The *Arthaśāstra* describes the battle arrays as *sama* (even), *viṣama* (uneven), *miśra* (mixed) and *śuddha* (pure).

SAMA-VYŪHA (Fig. 25)

In *sama-vyūha* (even formation) each of the five constituents of the *vyūha,* viz., centre (*ura*), two flanks (*kakṣa*), and two wings (*pakṣa*) was provided with equal number of units. A unit for that purpose was based on a chariot or elephant and included five horsemen, fifteen soldiers in the front and fifteen guards in the rear. Thus a formation of three chariot unit (*trika*) in three rows comprised 45 chariots, 225 horses, 675 foot-soldiers and the same number of foot-guards. The three chariot unit could be enlarged by adding two chariot units at a time, thereby raising the strength to a twenty-one chariot-unit. In this manner a *sama-vyūha* could be formed with 3, 5, 7, 9, 11, 13, 15, 17, 19 or 21 chariot units.[14]

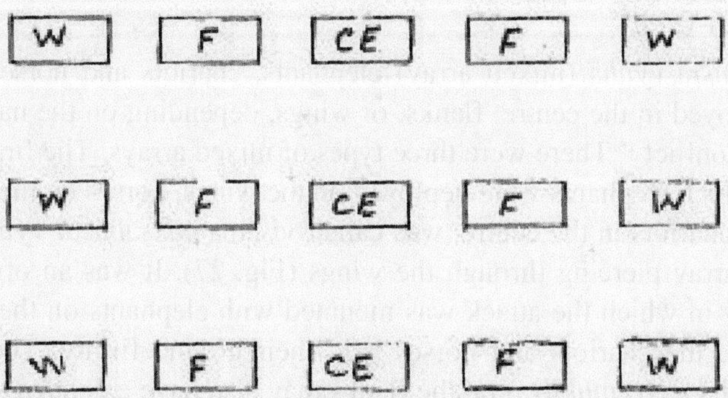

Fig. 25: *Sama* Array

Sama-vyūha was defensive in nature. It was formed in such a manner that the enemy could find no chinks to penetrate through it. A balanced combination of chariots, horses and foot-soldiers made it impregnable indeed.

VIṢAMA-VYŪHA (Fig. 26)

In *viṣama-vyūha* (uneven array) the number of units deployed in the wings, flanks and centre was not uniform. The numbers could be increased or decreased according to the exigencies of the battle. The surplus troops, left over after the formation of *vyūha*, could be adjusted keeping in view the enemy deployment.[15] It was perhaps an offensive formation, in which the number of units in the centre, flanks and wings could be increased or reduced in accordance with the developments on the battle front.

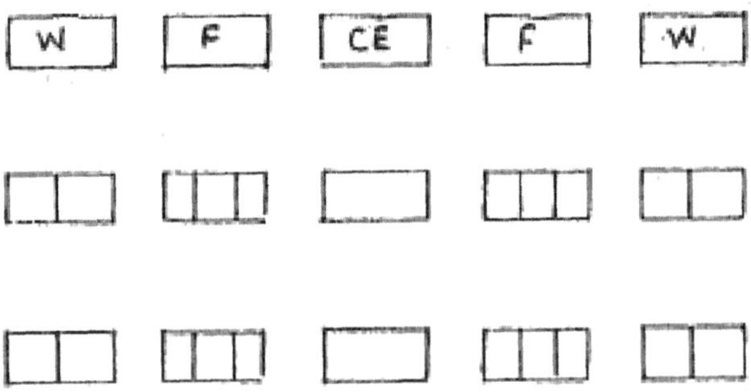

Fig. 26: *Viṣama* Array

MIŚRA-VYŪHA

In *miśra-vyūha* (mixed array) elephants, chariots and horses were deployed in the centre, flanks, or wings, depending on the nature of the conflict.[16] There were three types of mixed arrays. The first type, in which elephants were deployed on the wings, horses on the flanks and chariots in the centre, was called *viṣama pakṣabhedī vyūha*, i.e. the array piercing through the wings (Fig. 27). It was an offensive array in which the attack was mounted with elephants on the wings while the chariots and horses held their ground firmly. The main cavalry (*aśvamukhya*) on the flanks may also have extended support to the attacking elephants.

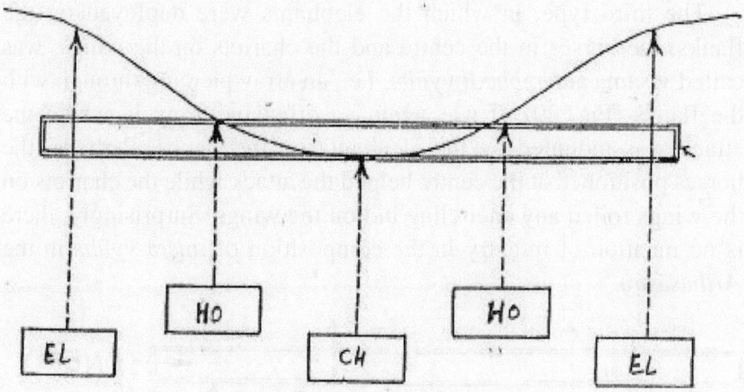

Fig. 27: *Viṣama Pakṣabhedī* Array

The second type, in which the elephants were deployed in the centre, the chariots on the flanks and the horses on the wings, was called *viṣama madhyabhedī vyūha*, i.e. the array piercing through the centre (Fig. 28). This was again an offensive array in which the elephants broke through the enemy defences in the centre supported by the chariots on the flanks. The horses on the wings could have made an encircling move by breaking through the enemy flanks.

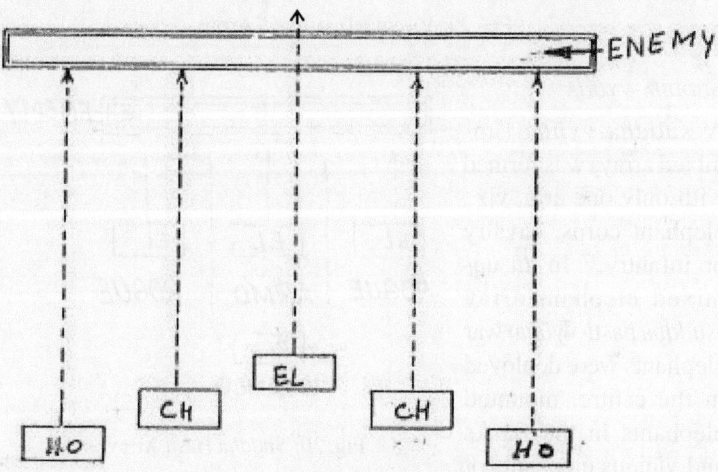

Fig. 28: *Viṣama Madhyabhedī* Array

The third type, in which the elephants were deployed on the flanks, the horses in the centre and the chariots on the wings, was called *viṣama antarabhedī vyūha*, i.e., an array piercing through with the flanks (Fig. 29). It was again an offensive array in which the attack was mounted by the elephants on the flanks. Perhaps, the horses positioned at the centre helped the attack while the chariots on the wings foiled any encircling bid on the wings. Surprisingly, there is no mention of infantry in the composition of *miśra-vyūha* in the *Arthaśāstra*.

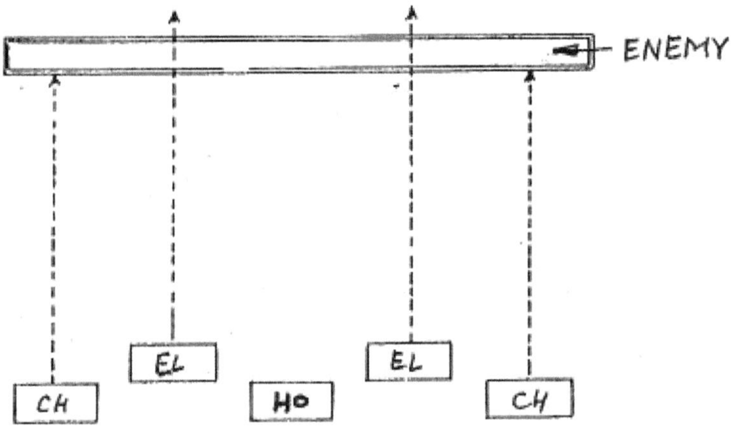

Fig. 29: *Viṣama Antarbhedī* Array

Śuddha-vyūha

A *śuddha-vyūha* (unmixed array) was formed with only one arm, viz., elephant corps, cavalry or infantry.[17] In an unmixed elephant array (*śuddha hasti-vyūha*) war elephants were deployed in the centre, mounted elephants in the flanks and vicious elephants on the wings (Fig. 30). It was an offensive formation in which the war

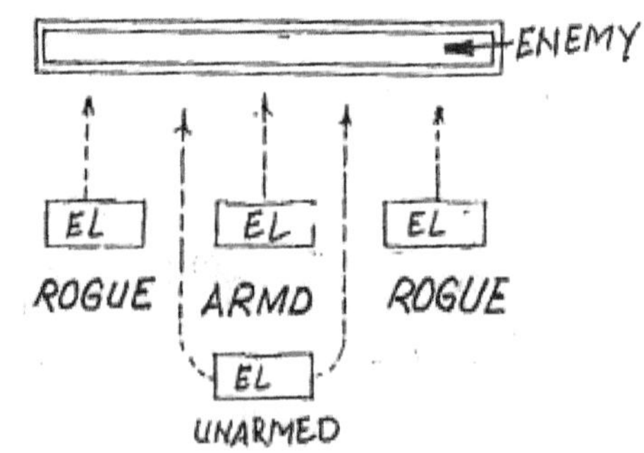

Fig. 30: *Śuddha Hasti* Array

elephants deployed in the centre advanced to breakthrough the enemy defensive lines. The mounted elephants assisted them in the attack from behind. The vicious elephants deployed on the wings precluded any danger of encirclement by the enemy.

In an unmixed horse array (*śuddha aśva-vyūha*) the armoured horses were deployed in the centre and unarmoured horses in the flanks and wings (Fig. 31). It was an offensive array in which the armoured horses made a direct attack on the frontline of the enemy to secure a breakthrough. It appears that in this attack the unarmoured horses in the flanks supported the centre and those in the wings prevented enemy attempt at encirclement.

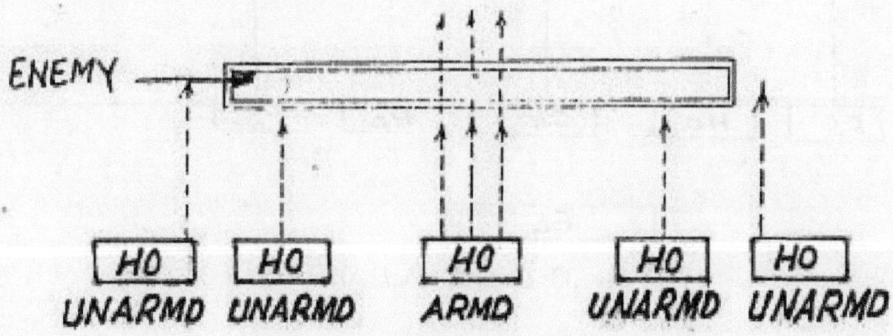

Fig. 31: *Śuddha Aśva* Array

In an unmixed infantry array (*śuddha patti-vyūha*) the armoured soldiers were deployed in the vanguard, and the archers took position behind them (Fig. 32). It was perhaps a defensive array in which the archers protected by armoured soldiers on the front harassed the enemy by shooting arrows. The armoured soldiers prevented the enemy from seeking a breakthrough. There is no mention of a *śuddha* chariot array in the *Arthaśāstra.*

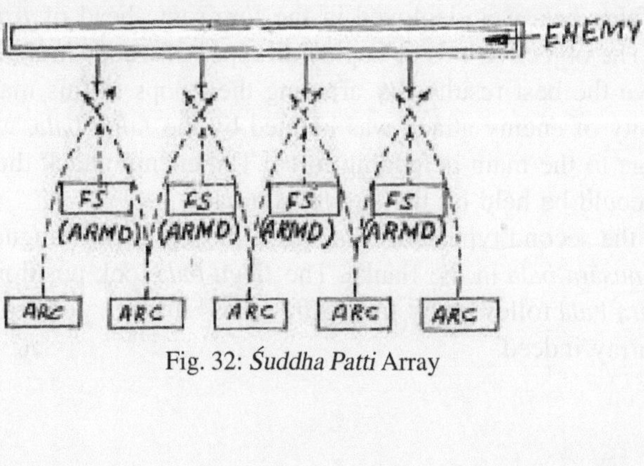

Fig. 32: *Śuddha Patti* Array

The *Arthaśāstra* also refers to a mixed array of a slightly different type called *caturaṅgabala vibhāga*. In this *vyūha* chariots were deployed in the vanguard, horses in the flanks, foot-soldier on the wings and elephants in the rear (Fig. 33).[18] Perhaps it was an offensive formation, with chariots in a leading role. The horses positioned on the flanks extended support to the chariots on both sides. Elephants in the rear provided a firm base to the array.

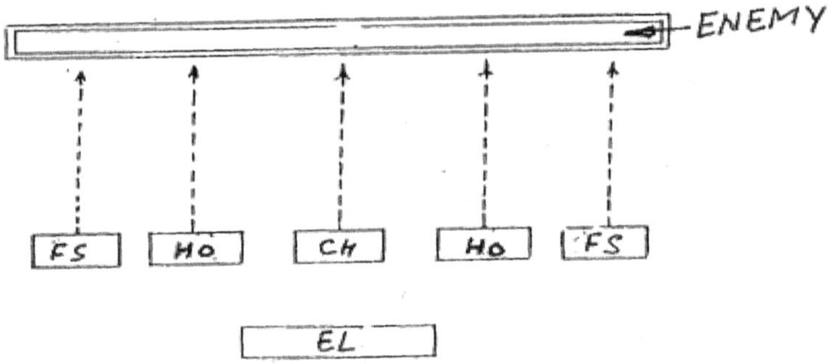

Fig. 33: *Caturaṅgabala* Array

BALA (ARMY) FACTOR

In forming an array, the quality of the troops available for deployment was a major consideration. Quality-wise the troops were classified into four groups, viz., the best called *sāra-bala*, the second best called *anusāra-bala*, the third best called *tṛtīya sāra-bala*, and the last called *falgu-bala*. These *balas* could be formed into two types of arrays. In the first type *sāra-bala* (from four arms) was evenly distributed in the centre, flanks and wings. *Anusāra-bala* was placed behind the *sāra-bala* and the *tṛtīya sāra-bala* ahead of the *sāra-bala*.[19] The *falgu-bala* was deployed in the forefront ahead of *tṛtīya sāra-bala*. The objective was to deploy all types of troops in the battle to achieve the best results. By arraying the troops in this manner the intensity of enemy attack was blunted by the *falgu-bala*, with little damage to the main defending force. The enemy attack thus weakened could be held by the strong *sāra-bala*.

In the second type *sāra-bala* was deployed in the vanguard (*ura*) and *anusāra-bala* in the flanks. The *falgu-bala* took position behind the *sāra-bala* followed by *tṛtīya sāra-bala*.[20] It was a powerful defensive array indeed.

PRAKṚTI (BASIC) *VYŪHAS*

The above classification of *vyūhas* by Kauṭilya is related to the deployment of various arms and types of armies. But his most significant contribution relates to the tactical deployment of units in a war. In this context he has referred to two military codes, one known after Uśanas (Śukrācārya) and the other after Bṛhaspati. The code of Uśanas provided for three components of *vyūha*, viz., *ura* (centre), *pakṣa* (wings) and *pratigraha* (reserve).[21] Bṛhaspati added a fourth component, viz., *kakṣa* (flanks) to this code.[22] Following the code of Bṛhaspati, Kauṭilya has classified military formations into four basic arrays (*prakṛti-vyūhas*) as follows.[23]

1. *Daṇḍa-vyūha* (staff array)
2. *Bhoga-vyūha* (snake array)
3. *Maṇḍala-vyūha* (circle array)
4. *Asaṁhata-vyūha* (diffuse array)

1. *DAṆḌA*- (STAFF) *VYŪHA* (Fig.34)

In *daṇḍa-vyūha* the centre flanks and wings operated in a straight line.[24] It could be formed in seventeen ways, depending on the exigencies of war, as follows:

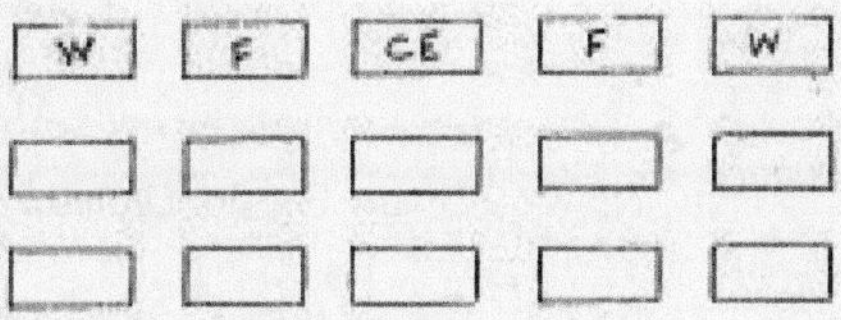

Fig. 34: *Daṇḍa* Array

PRADARA- (SPLITTER) *VYŪHA* (Fig.35)

When the army formed in a straight line like a *daṇḍa* surged ahead or advanced with the flanks, the formation was called *pradara-vyūha*. The wings and centre did not move out and remained firm in their position.[25] It was an offensive array, in which the flanks were used effectively to pierce through the enemy lines at two

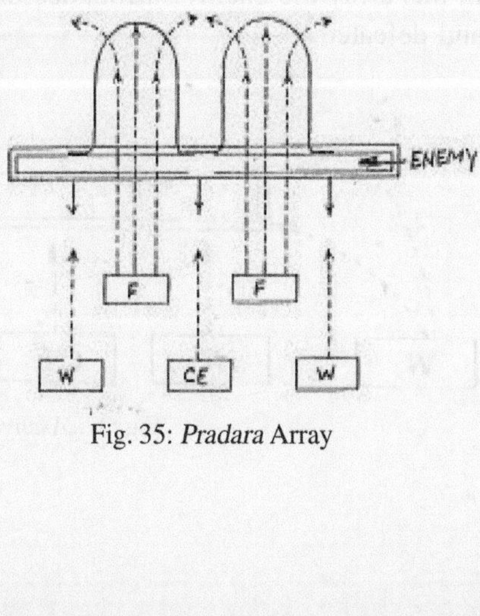

Fig. 35: *Pradara* Array

vital points. While the centre supported the attack from behind, the wings threatened the enemy with outflanking moves.

DṚḌHAKA- (STRENGTHENER) *VYŪHA* (Fig. 36)

In *Dṛḍhaka* array the army fell back with flanks and wings.[26] It was a defensive array, intended to contain the enemy attack. The flanks and wings were tactically withdrawn so as to support the centre from behind. The enemy was allowed to advance on both sides of the centre so that it could be simultaneously attacked by own centre, flanks and wings and also the reserve.

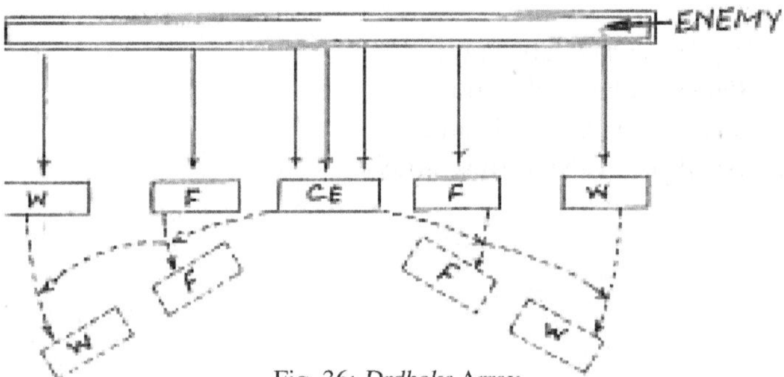

Fig. 36: *Dṛḍhaka* Array

ASAHYA- (UNBEARABLE) *VYŪHA* (Fig. 37)

When the army marched out with the wings leaving behind the centre and the flanks the formation was called *asahya.*[27] It was an offensive array in which powerful wings attacked the enemy and encircled it. In this array the enemy surrounded on all sides was outmanoeuvred and defeated.

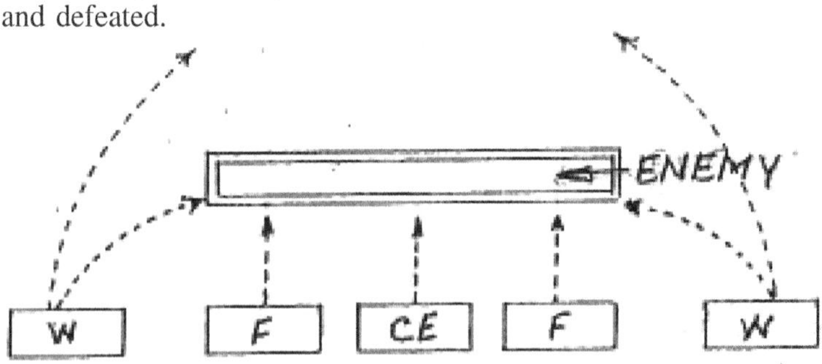

Fig. 37: *Asahya* Array

Śyena- (Falcon) vyūha (Fig. 38)

When the army marched out with the centre leaving behind the flanks and wings the formation was called *śyena.*[28] It was a swift and powerful offensive formation in which the centre broke through the enemy defence line with speed. Thus bisected, the enemy was attacked by the flanks and wings together and destroyed.

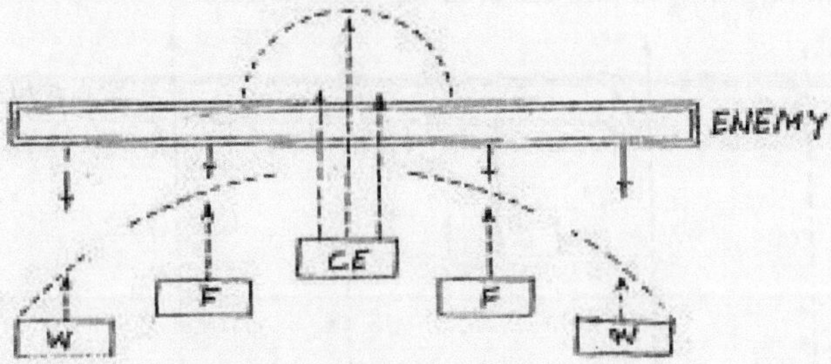

Fig. 38: *Śyena* Array

Cāpa- (Bow) vyūha (Fig. 39)

Pradara-vyūha in reverse, i.e. army falling back with the flanks while allowing the centre and the wings to hold on to their position, was called *cāpa-vyūha.*[29] It was a defensive array in which flanks were withdrawn with the objective to lure the enemy into the vacant space between the centre and the wings. Once the enemy entered the bow (*cāpa*) he was attacked by the centre, the wings and the flanks on all sides. Encircled inside the *cāpa* the enemy might have suffered total destruction.

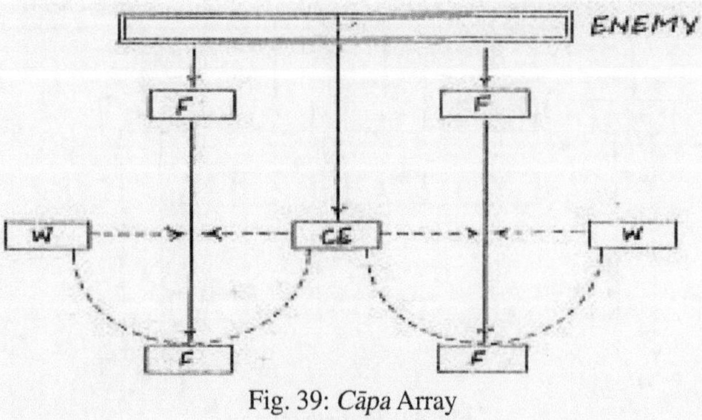

Fig. 39: *Cāpa* Array

Cāpakukṣi- (Bow's Belly) *Vyūha* (Fig.40)

Dṛḍhaka array in reverse, i.e. breaking out with flanks and wings while centre remaining firm was called *chāpakukṣi-vyūha.*[30] It was an offensive formation intended to attack the enemy with flanks and wings. The centre provided a firm base and prevented the enemy from securing a breakthrough. The wings threatened the enemy by outflanking moves and ensured his destruction.

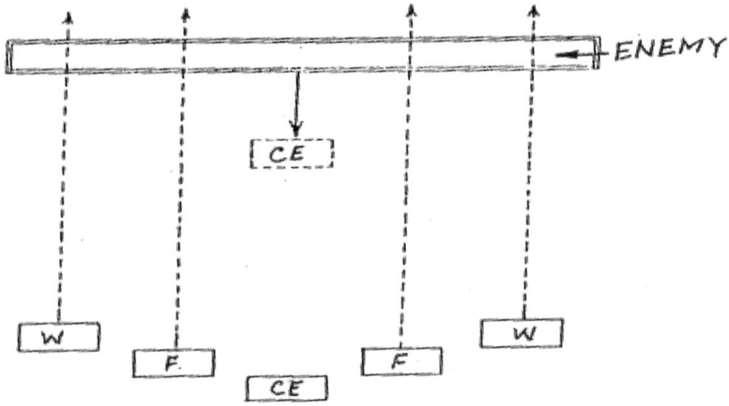

Fig. 40: *Cāpakukṣi* Array

Pratiṣṭha- (Established) *vyūha* (Fig.41)

Asahya array in reverse, i.e. falling back with the wings while centre and flanks holding on to their position, was called *pratiṣṭha-vyūha.*[31] It was a defensive formation. When the enemy mounted the attack the

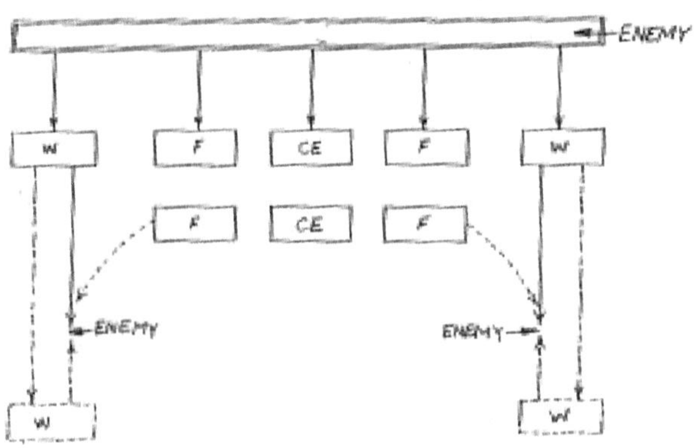

Fig. 41: *Pratiṣṭha* Array

wings carried an withdrawal so as to entice the enemy to attempt an outflanking move. Once the enemy broke through the wings he was attacked by the retreating wings and flanks. Sandwitched between the flanks and wings the enemy was destroyed.

SUPRATIṢṬHA- (FIRMLY ESTABLISHED) *VYŪHA* (Fig. 42)

Śyena array in reverse, i.e. falling back with the centre, while flanks and wings held on to their position, was called *supratiṣṭha-vyūha.*[32]

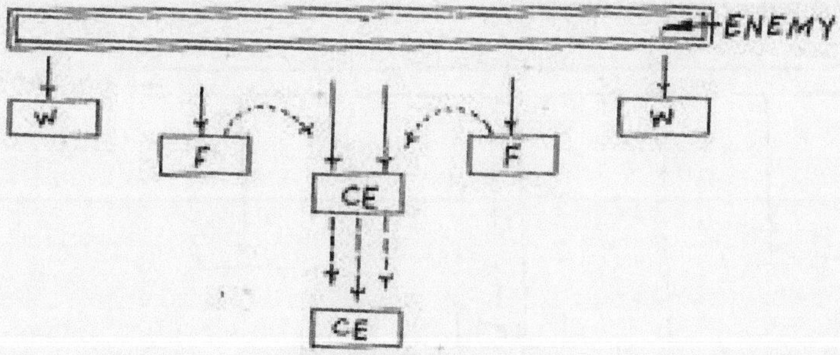

Fig. 42: *Supratiṣṭha* Array

It was a defensive formation. When the enemy mounted the attack the centre pulled back to allow the enemy ingress. Once he entered the vacated area, the flanks turned inwards to attack him from the sides and behind. The enemy was thus completely encircled making any escape for him impossible.

SAÑJAYA- (CONQUEROR) *VYŪHA* (Fig. 43)

In *sañjaya* array the wings were formed like a bow.[33] It was a defensive array in which the wings were intended to play an aggressive

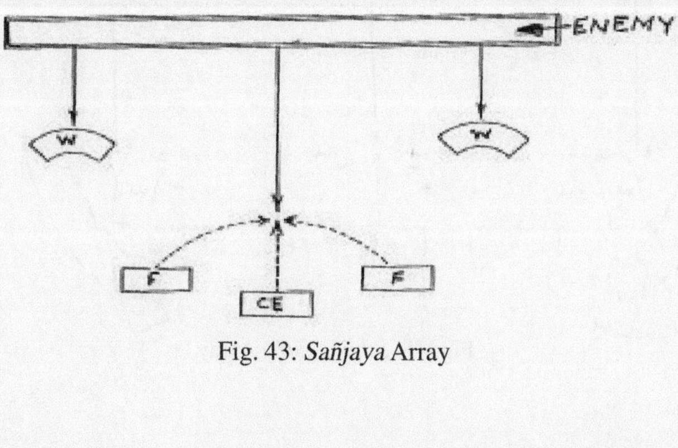

Fig. 43: *Sañjaya* Array

role. In fact, the wings served as a shield for the entire *vyūha* and could thwart any outflanking move by the enemy.

VIJAYA- (VICTORY) VYŪHA (Fig. 44)

When the army formed in *sañjaya-vyūha* marched out with the centre the formation was called *vijaya-vyūha*.[34] It was an offensive array in which the centre mounted the attack, with flanks in strong support. The wings prevented any outflanking move by the enemy. The *vyūha* ensured certain victory.

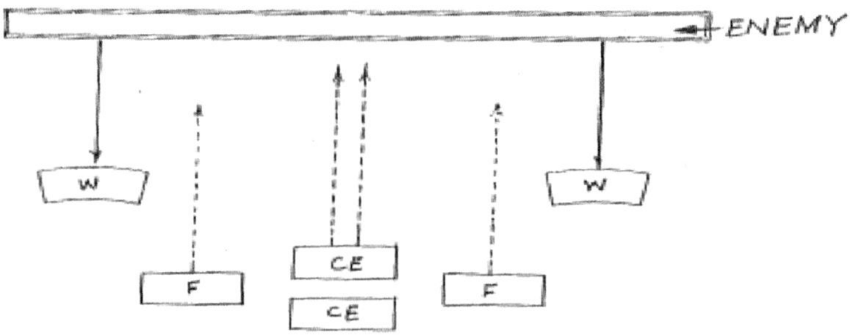

Fig. 44: *Vijaya* Array

STHŪNAKARṆA- (LARGE-EARED) VYŪHA (Fig. 45)

In this sub-type of *daṇḍa-vyūha* the wings were shaped like big ears.[35] It was a defensive formation in which the strong wings could foil any outflanking move and also lend support to the flanks and the centre. Perhaps this *vyūha* was formed when the enemy attack was expected on a wider front.

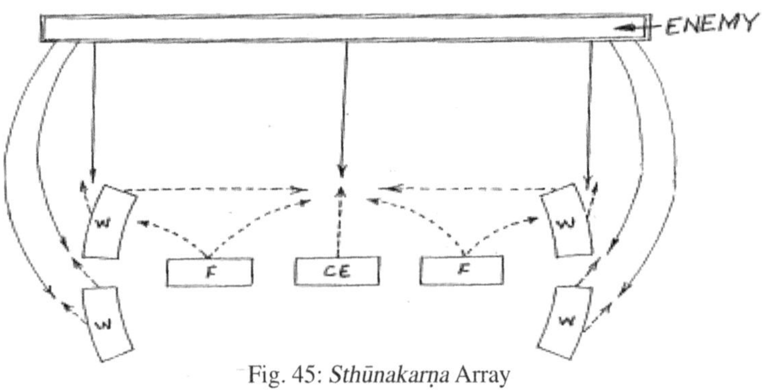

Fig. 45: *Sthūnakarṇa* Array

VIŚĀLA-VIJAYA- (EXTENSIVE VICTORY) VYŪHA (Fig.46)

In this formation the wings were made two times stronger than in *sthūnakarṇa* and looked like twain pillars.[36] It was an offensive formation with strong wings intended to mount an outflanking attack on the enemy. The strong wings could easily outflank the enemy thus leaving no escape route to him. The *vyūha* might have resulted in a comprehensive victory.

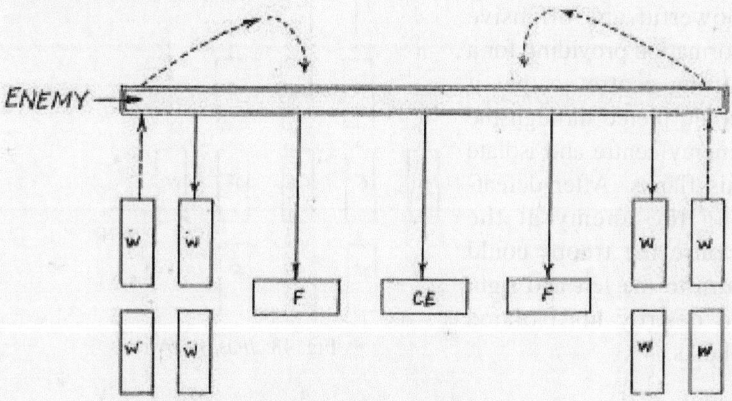

Fig. 46: *Viśālavijaya* Array

CAMŪMUKHA- (ARMY-FACED) VYŪHA (Fig.47)

In this array the number of troops deployed on the wings was three times more than that at the centre and the flanks.[37] This array could be used both for offensive and defensive purposes. It could contain the enemy and also mount a powerful attack on him.

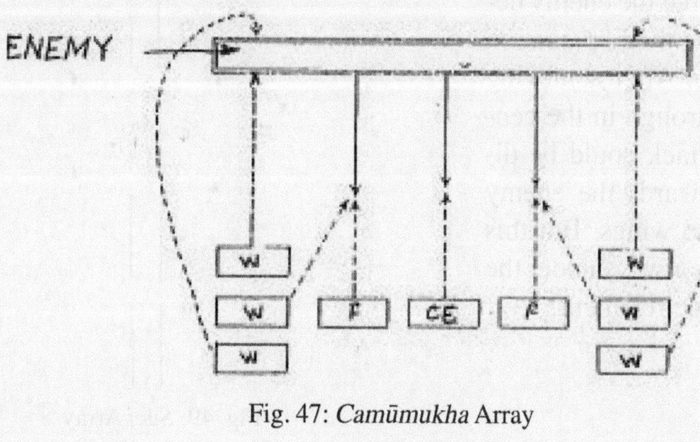

Fig. 47: *Camūmukha* Array

JHAṢĀSYA- (FISH-MOUTHED) *VYŪHA* (Fig. 48)

Camūmukha in reverse, i.e. keeping the strength of the centre three times more than that of the wings was called *jhaṣāsya* array.[38] It was an uneven, powerful and offensive formation providing for a strong centre so that it could pierce through the enemy centre and isolate his flanks. After defeating the enemy at the centre the troops could turn to the left and right to destroy his isolated flanks.

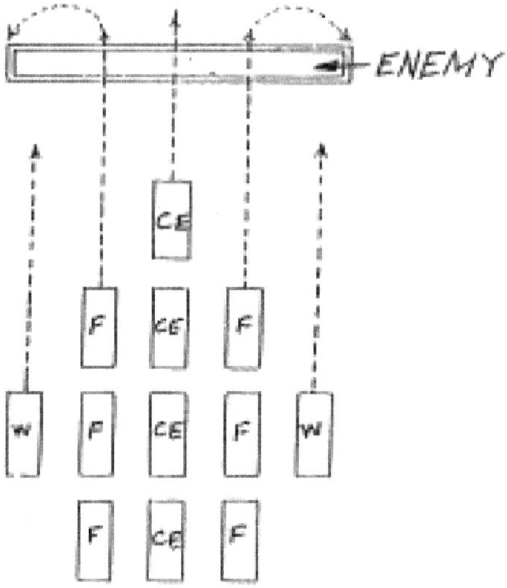

Fig. 48: *Jhaṣāsya* Array

SŪCĪ- (NEEDLE) *VYŪHA* (Fig. 49)

In *sūcī* array the troops were arrayed in a single column with centre, flanks and wings moving one behind the other.[39] It was a powerful offensive array which could pierce the enemy defence line with precision and force. After achieving a breakthrough in the centre the attack could be directed towards the enemy flanks and wings. But this array was always under the risk of encirclement.

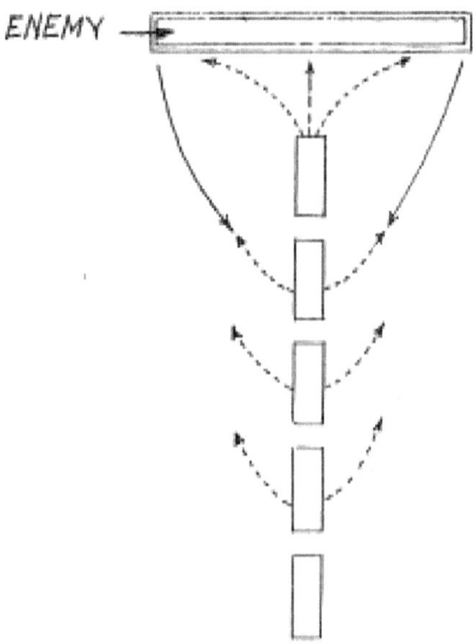

Fig. 49: *Sūcī* Array

VALAYA- (GARLAND) VYŪHA (Fig. 50)

In *valaya* the army units were arrayed in two straight columns like a garland.[40] It was an offensive formation like *sūcī-vyūha* but was double in strength. It could pierce the enemy defences at two points simultaneously and thus destroy the enemy forces convincingly.

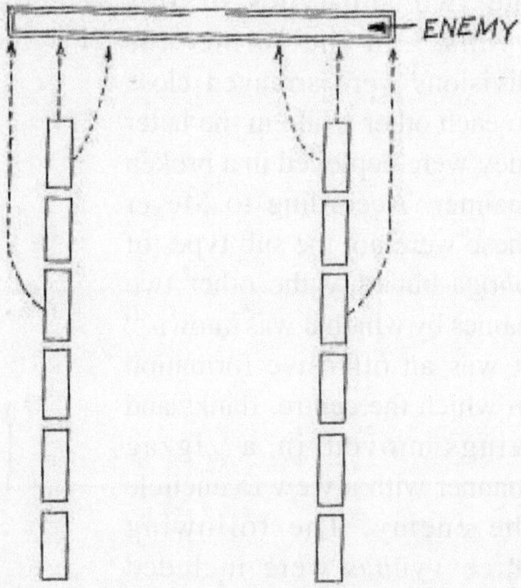

Fig. 50: *Valaya* Array

DURJAYA- (INVINCIBLE) VYŪHA (Fig. 51)

In *durjaya* array the army was deployed in four columns as against one in *sūcī* and two in *valaya.*[41] It was both an offensive and defensive array and was four times stronger than *sūcī-vyūha* and two times stronger than *valaya-vyūha.* It could pierce through the enemy defences at four points and thus create havoc in his ranks.

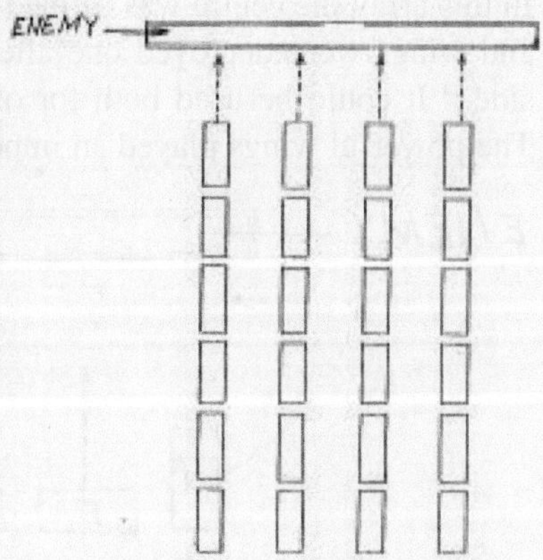

Fig. 51: *Durjaya* Array

2. *BHOGA*- (SERPENT) *VYŪHA* (Fig. 52)

In this array the army moved unevenly, i.e. in a zigzag way. *Sarpasāri* (similar to the movement of snake) and *gomūtrikā* (similar to the course of cow's urine) were the two sub-types of this *vyūha*.[42] In the former the divisions were arranged close to each other while in the latter they were deployed in a broken manner. According to Meyer these were not the sub-types of *bhoga* but only the other two names by which it was known.[43] It was an offensive formation in which the centre, flanks and wings moved in a zigzag manner with a view to encircle the enemy. The following three *vyūhas* were included in the category of basic *bhoga* array.

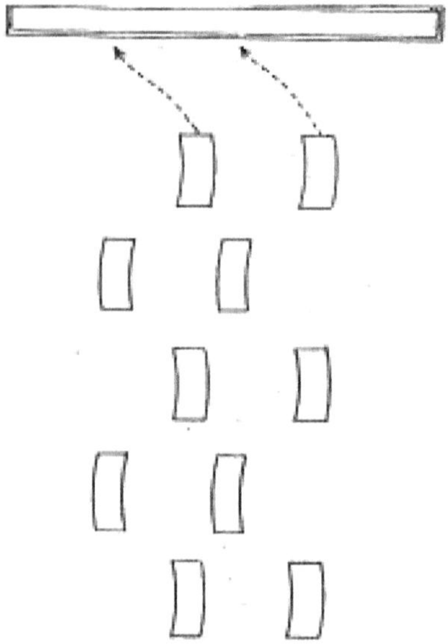

Fig. 52: *Bhoga* Array

Śakaṭa- (Cart) vyūha (Fig. 53)

In this array the centre was formed in double strength and the flanks and wings were deployed one after another like a *daṇḍa* on either side.[44] It could be used both for offensive and defensive purposes. The powerful wings played an important part as they could outflank

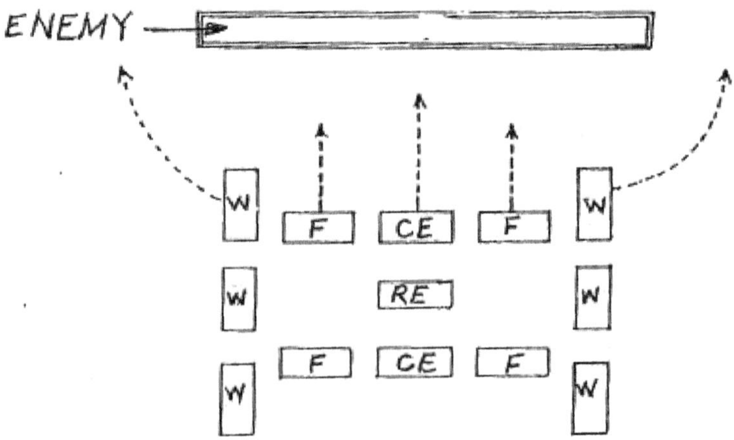

Fig. 53: *Śakaṭa* Array

the attacking enemy while the strong centre could prevent any ingress. The array was well defended on all sides.

MAKARA- (CROCODILE) *VYŪHA* (Fig.54)

Śakaṭa-vyūha in reverse was called *makara-vyūha.*[45] It implies that the centre was formed like a *daṇḍa* by placing the troops one after another while the wings and flanks were made twice strong. It was an offensive formation in which the centre sought penetration through the enemy defences. The breakthrough thus achieved by the centre could then be exploited by the wings.

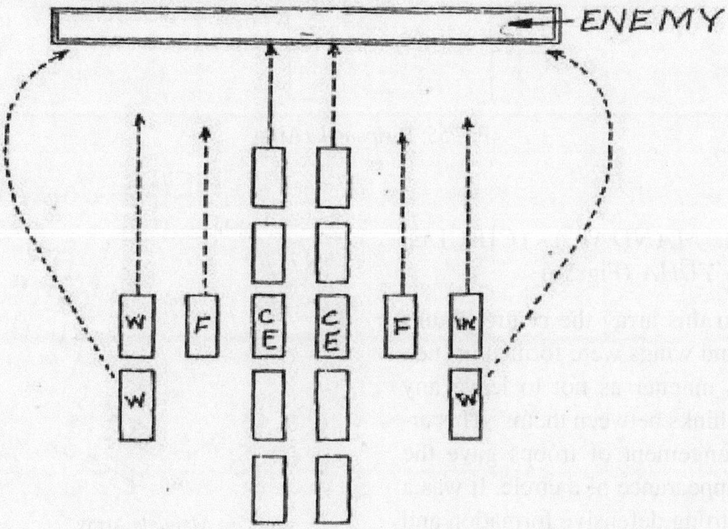

Fig. 54: *Makara* Array

PARIPANTAKA- (FLYING ABOUT) *VYŪHA* (Fig.55)

The *śakaṭa-vyūha* when well provided with chariots, elephants and horses was called *paripantaka-vyūha.*[46] It was a powerful offensive formation in which the centre, flanks and wings were held by the chariots, elephants and horses respectively. The positioning of horses on the wings provided the array an advantage in manoeuvring and outflanking. With the chariots strongly holding the centre no breakthrough was possible for the enemy.

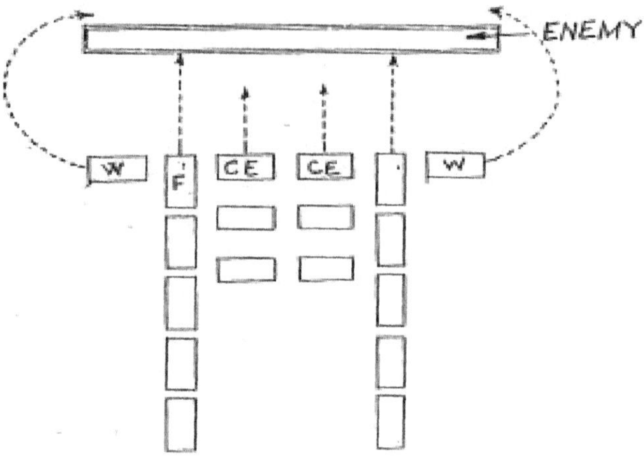

Fig. 55: *Paripantaka* Array

3. *MAṆḌALA*- (CIRCLE) *VYŪHA* (Fig.56)

In this array the centre, flanks and wings were formed in such a manner as not to leave any chinks between them.[47] This arrangement of troops gave the appearance of a circle. It was a strong defensive formation and comprised two sub-types.

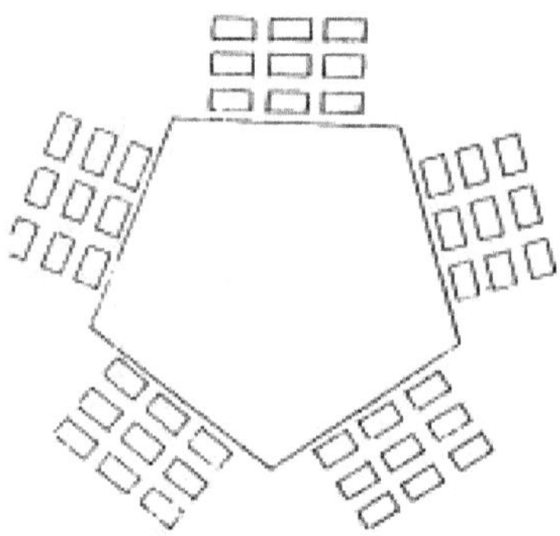

Fig. 56: *Maṇḍala* Array

SARVATOBHADRA- (GOOD ON ALL SIDES) *VYŪHA* (Fig.57)

It was a circular array with faces on all sides.[48] As a defensive array, it had the potential to beat back the enemy attack from whichever side it came. Further, it negated any enemy attempt at encirclement.

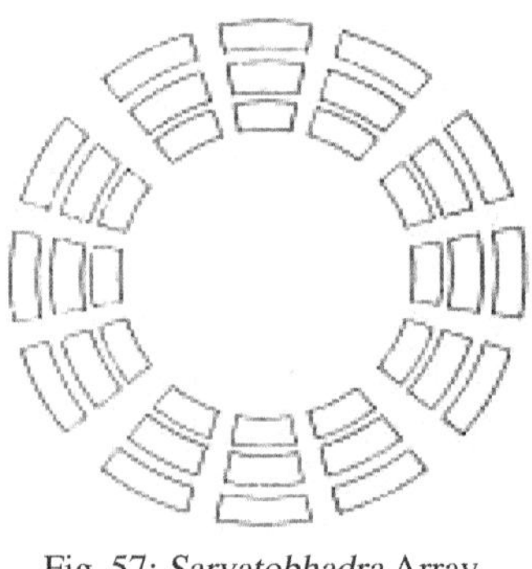

Fig. 57: *Sarvatobhadra* Array

DURJAYA- (INVINCIBLE) VYŪHA (Fig. 58)

In this array eight divisions of the army were deployed[49] two in the centre, two in the flanks and four in the wings. The four divisions could have been placed in the flanks as well.[50] It was an invincible defensive array. A type of *daṇḍa-vyūha* was also known as *durjaya-vyūha.*

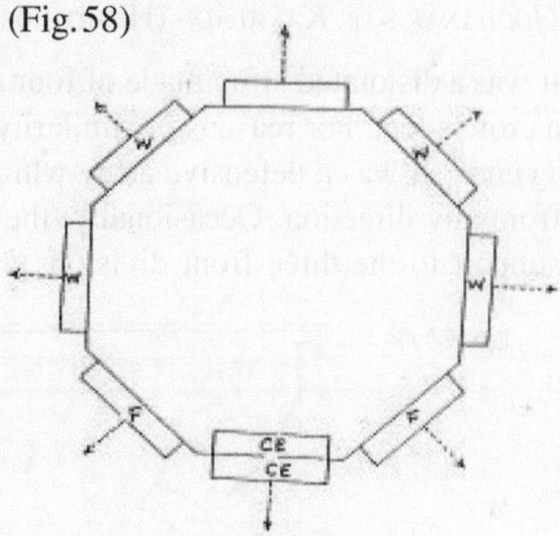

Fig. 58: *Durjaya* Array

4. *ASAṀHATA*- (DIFFUSE) *VYŪHA*

In this array wings, flanks and centre were formed independent of each other.[51] The following three sub-types were included in the basic *asaṁhata* array.

VAJRA- OR GODHĀ- (THUNDERBOLT OR LIZARD) VYŪHA (Fig. 59)

It was a disjointed array made with five divisions (*anīkas*) in the *vajra* pattern. For reasons of appearance it was called *godhā-vyūha* also.[52] It was a powerful offensive array in which a strong centre supported by wings penetrated through the enemy defences at three points with devastating effect. The supporting divisions did the mopping up from behind. While on defensive it could have been difficult to seek a breakthrough against this *vyūha* on account of its strong centre.

Fig. 59: *Vajra* Array

UDDHĀNAKA- OR *KĀKAPADĪ*- (HEARTH OR CROW'S FEET) *VYŪHA* (Fig. 60).

It was a disjointed array made of four army divisions and shaped like a crow's feet. For reasons of similarity it was also called *uddhānaka-vyūha.*[53] It was a defensive array which could face the enemy attack from any direction. Occasionally, the reserve division could extend support to the three front divisions.

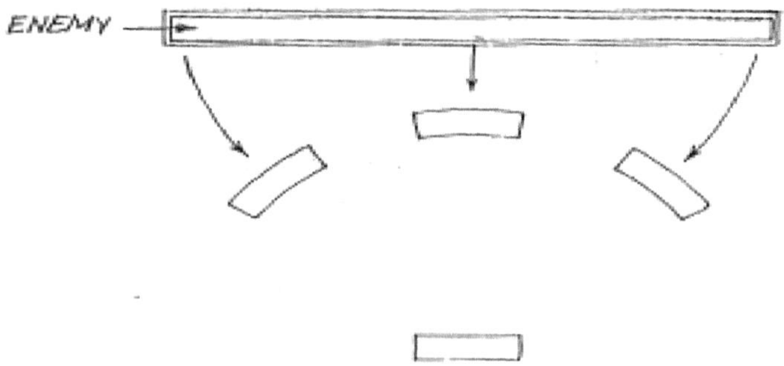

Fig. 60: *Kākapadī* Array

ARDHACANDRA- OR *KARKAṬAKAŚṚṄGĪ*-
(CRESCENT OR PRONE-HORN) *VYŪHA* (Fig. 61)

It was again a disjointed array, made with three army divisions.[54] For reasons of resemblance it was called *karkaṭakaśṛṅgī* also. It was a defensive array in which divisions fought independently, without any support or reserve. Though comparatively a weak array, it was capable of effecting an encircling move to trap the enemy.

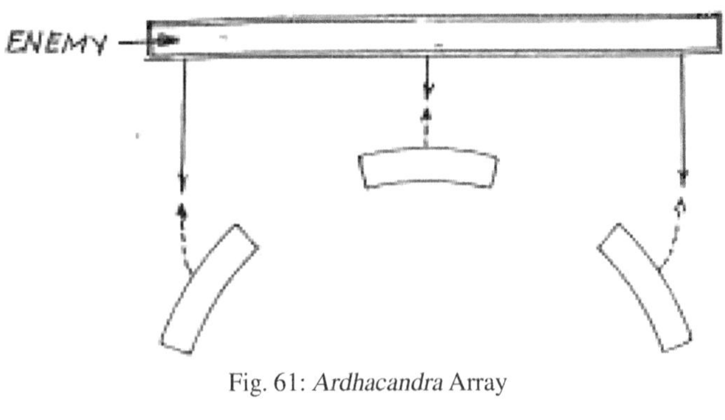

Fig. 61: *Ardhacandra* Array

5. MISCELLANEOUS ARRAYS

Besides the four basic arrays described above some other types were also known. These included the following:

ARIṢṬA- (UNHARMED) *VYŪHA* (Fig.62)

In this array the chariots, elephants and horses were deployed in the centre, flanks and rear respectively.[55] The foot-soldiers though not mentioned by Kauṭilya might have been placed in the wings. It was a defensive formation in which an attack was contained with chariots and elephants. The enemy bypassing the main defences could be taken care of by the infantry on the wings. The cavalry provided support to the whole ensemble from behind.

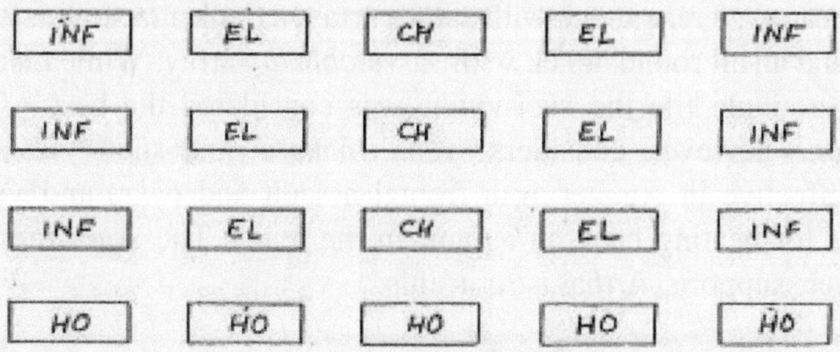

Fig. 62: *Ariṣṭa* Array

ACALA- (IMMOVABLE) *VYŪHA* (Fig.63)

In this array the foot-soldiers, horses, chariots and elephants were deployed one behind another.[56] As the name suggests it was a powerful defensive array which could not be pierced by the enemy.

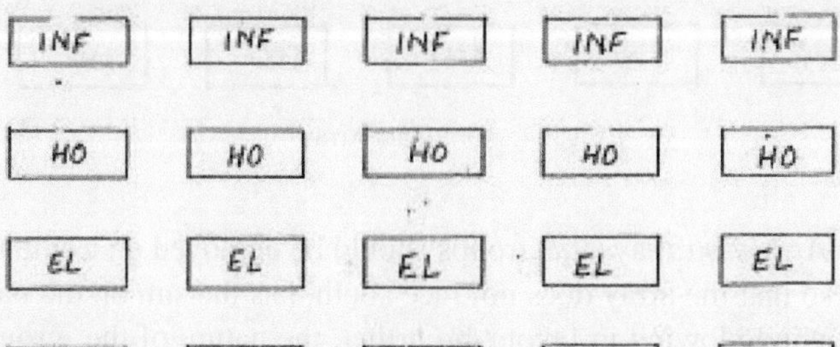

Fig. 63: *Acala* Array

Apratihata- (Unrepulsed) *vyūha* (Fig.64)

In this array elephants, horses, chariots, and foot-soldiers were deployed one behind the other.[57] It was a powerful offensive array in which the attack was led by elephants.

Kauṭilya also mentions antidotes to these *vyūhas* stating that *pradara* (splitter) could be contained with *dṛḍhaka* (strengthener), *dṛḍhaka* with *asahya* (unbearable), *śyena* (falcon) with *cāpa* (bow), *pratiṣṭha* (established) with *supratiṣṭha* (well established), *sañjaya* (conqueror) with *vijaya* (victory), *sthūnakarṇa* (pillar-eared) with *viśālavijaya* (extensive victory) and *paripantaka* (flying about) with *sarvatobhadra* (good on all sides). *Durjaya* (invincible) could take on any array.[58]

The *Arthaśāstra* advises that a frontal attack could be faced with *makara* array, a rear attack with *śakaṭa* array, a flank attack with *vajra* array and an all round attack with *sarvatobhadra* array. While marching in a single file the *sūcī-vyūha* was considered the best.[59] The *Śukranīti*, however, considers *śyena, makara* and *sūcī-vyūhas* as most effective in countering a frontal assault and *cakra* and *vyāla vyūhas* for beating back an assault in the rear.[60] The *Agni Purāṇa,* however, supports *Arthaśāstra* in this.[61]

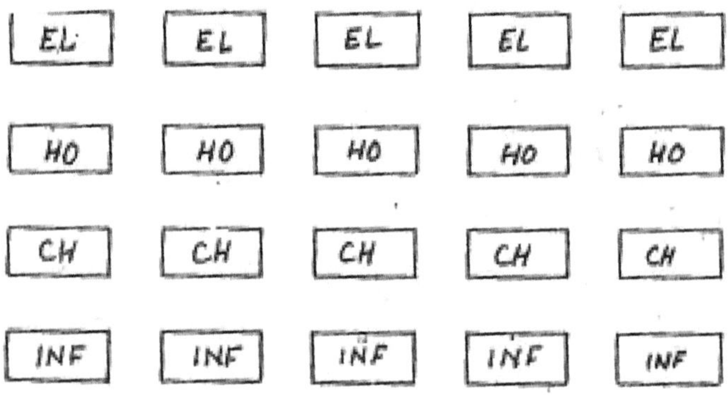

Fig. 64: *Apratihata* Array

The *Arthaśāstra* says that troops should be deployed on a suitable ground so that the array does not face south, has the sun on the back and the wind blowing in favour.[62] Further, the nature of the ground being level, uneven or mixed in front, on the flanks and in the rear should also be ascertained, before laying an array. On the level ground staff (*daṇḍa*) or circle (*maṇḍala*) arrays, on uneven ground snake (*bhoga*) and diffuse (*asaṁhata*) arrays and on mixed ground uneven (*biṣama*) arrays should be formed.[63]

In ancient India the battle-arrays were formed to the tune of the war music. The commander passed on instructions regarding the formation of an array to his subordinate commanders with the sound of *mṛdaṅga* (a musical instrument).[64] Formation of *vyūha* as per the signals of *mṛdaṅga* was considered an art, which finds mention in the *Dhanurveda.*[65] An army which was ignorant of this art was considered as untrained.[66]

KĀMANDAKA NĪTI ON *VYŪHA*

Though the *Kāmandaka Nīti* follows the *Arthaśāstra* in classifying the arrays into four basic categories, i.e. *daṇḍa, bhoga, maṇḍala,* and *asaṁhata,*[67] it represents another stage in the evolution of *vyūha.* It refers to seven components of *vyūha*, viz., *ura* (chest), *kakṣa* (flanks), *pakṣa* (wings), *madhya* (centre), *pṛṣṭha* (back), *pratigraha* (reserve) and *koṭi* (outer flanks)[68] against three of Śukra (*ura, pakṣa* and *pratigraha*) and four of *Bṛhaspati* (*ura, kakṣa, pakṣa* and *pratigraha*). Quite indeed the middle (*madhya*), back (*pṛṣṭha*) and outer flanks (*koṭi*). were new innovations in Kāmandakīya concept of *vyūha* (Fig. 65).

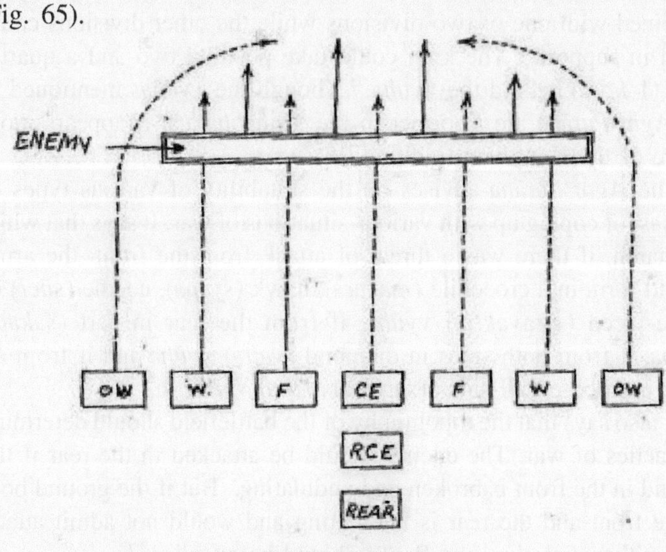

Fig. 65: *Kāmandaka's* Array

The inclusion of *koṭi* as a component of *vyūha* by Kāmandaka may have revolutionized the whole system of warfare. The *Arthaśāstra*, had laid down that after arraying the army on the battle-field an attack could be made with one or two troops from the wings, flanks and the centre while rest could support the attack.[69] But *Kāmandaka Nīti* says that the enemy should be attacked first on the wings and then the rest of the army was to be engaged. When a break through had been affected on the wings the *koṭis* could encircle the enemy. After securing own wings and reserves, the enemy *koṭis* could be outflanked and his rear (*jaghana*) hammered with own *koṭis*. Finally, the centre (*ura*) could chastise him.[70]

AGNI PURĀṆA ON *VYŪHA*

There are many references to *vyūhas* in the Purāṇic literature. The description given in the *Agni Purāṇa* is, however, most informative. It classifies *vyūhas* in two categories, viz., *prāṇyāṅgarūpa* (limb like) and *dravyarūpa* (object like), and adds that an army could be arrayed in 10 ways like animals or objects such as *garuḍa*, *makara*, *cakra*, *maṇḍala*, *śeyna*, *ardhacandra*, *vajra*, *śakaṭa*, *sarvatobhadra* and *sūcī*.[71] These *vyūhas* could comprise five divisions—two in the wings (*pakṣa*), two in the flanks (*kakṣa*) and one in the centre.[72] The battle could be joined with one or two divisions while the other divisions could stand in support.[73] The king could take position two and a quarter mile (1 *kośa*) behind the *vyūha*.[74] Though the *vyūhas* mentioned in the *Agni Purāṇa* are also met in the *Mahābhārata*, it appears more aware of the Kauṭilyan tradition.[75]

The *Agni Purāṇa* advises on the suitability of various types of *vyūhas* for coping up with various situations of war. It says that while on march, if there was a threat of attack from the front, the army should form in a crocodile (*makara*), hawk (*śyena*), needle (*sūcī*) or brave-faced (*vīravaktra*) *vyūha*, if from the rear in cart (*śakaṭa*) *vyūha*, if from both sides in diamond (*vajra*) *vyūha* and if from all sides in good-on-all-sides (*sarvatobhadra*) *vyūha*.[76]

It also says that the topography of the battlefield should determine the tactics of war. The enemy should be attacked in the rear if the ground in the front is broken and undulating. But if the ground both in the front and the rear is undulating and would not admit attack from either direction, the flanks should be attacked.[77]

In its definition of *vyūha* the *Agni Purāṇa* follows the *Arthaśāstra* and the *Kāmandaka Nīti.*[78] Like the former it refers to the doctrines of *vyūha* as enunciated by Śukra and Bṛhaspati. But going further it refers to seven constituents (*saptāṅga*) of the *vyūha* as enumerated by Kāmandaka, indicating that many advances had been made in the field after Kauṭilya.

The *Mānasollāsa* seems to represent the last stage in the development of the *vyūhas* in ancient India. It describes nine components of a *vyūha*, viz., vanguard (*mukha*), centre (*ura*), rear centre (*praurasya*), reserve (*pratigraha*), flanks (*kakṣa*), outer flanks (*prakakṣa*), wings (*pakṣa*), outer wings (*prapakṣa*) and march-out position (*prasthāna*).[79]

ŚUKRANĪTI ON *VYŪHA*

The *Śukranīti* generally refers to the *vyūhas* mentioned in the *Mahābhārata,* viz., *makara*, *śyena*, *sūcīmukha*, *śakaṭa*, *vajra*, *sarvatobhadra*, *cakra*, *vyāla*, *ardhacandra* and *krauñca.* It not only refers to *vyūhas* but also explains their characteristics[80] and these have already been mentioned in Chapter 4.

The *Śukranīti* particularly mentions the importance of instructions passed on to the army through musical notes regarding the formation of *vyūhas*, stating that nobody other than own troops should know these indications (*saṅketas*).[81] In this manner the wise commanders proceeded to form the *vyūha.*[82] The troops were to act according to the indications to form up, spread out, move around, squeeze in, slow march, quick march, retreat, stand up, lie down, line up like a eight-petal lotus, stand in a circle like a *cakra,* etc.[83] In fact, all moves and formations in the battlefield were governed by these indications.[84] Even the king was expected to practice the formation of battle-arrays with his troops every day.[85] An officer named Śatānīka imparted instructions to soldiers on the formation of *vyūhas.*[86] The *Śukranīti* also refers to *saṅkara vyūha* (mixed array), formed in special circumstances.[87]

The description of *vyūhas* furnished by the military thinkers of ancient India suggests four stages of evolution:

1. The first stage is represented by the code of Uśanas. It says that an array should consist of three components, viz., vanguard (*ura*), wings (*pakṣa*) and reserve or rear-guard (*pratigraha*).

2. The second stage is represented by the code of Bṛhaspati. It says that an array should consist of four components, viz., vanguard (*ura*), wings (*pakṣa*), flanks (*kakṣa*) and reserve (*pratigraha*).
3. The third stage is represented by the code of Kāmandaka. It says that a *vyūha* should consist of seven components viz., centre (*ura*), flanks (*kakṣa*), wings (*pakṣa*), middle (*madhya*), rear centre (*pṛṣṭha*), rear guard (*pratigraha*), and outer flanks (*koṭi*).
4. The fourth and the last stage is represented in the *Mānasollāsa*. It refers to nine components of *vyūha*, viz., vanguard (*mukha*), centre (*ura*), rear centre (*praurasya*), rear-guard (*pratigraha*), flanks (*kakṣa*), outer-flanks (*prakakṣa*), wings (*pakṣa*), outer wings (*prapakṣa*) and march-out position (*prasthāna*).

GUERRILLA WARFARE

Besides the *vyūhas* conceived by the military thinkers of India, there were other formulations of war which were guerrilla in nature. Such formulations were known even in the Vedic times.[88] During the *Mahābhārata* war, the fierce battle waged by the Kauravas during the night after the fourteenth day of war[89] and the great massacre carried by Aśvatthāman in the night after the eighteenth day of war[90] were indeed guerrilla in nature. The *Rāmāyaṇa* also refers to a nocturnal battle between Vānaras and Rākṣasas.[91] The *Agni Purāṇa*, deals with the guerrilla warfare extensively and a quote from the text would be revealing:

> An enemy should be openly encountered only at places where the nature of the ground as well as the feeling of their inhabitants and the time of engagement would ensure a decisive victory, or otherwise a general should take resort to guerrilla warfare. A general leading an army in his own country should hang on to the rear of a hostile army, cut all means of supplies and fastly retreating from its own jurisdiction, order the forester border-men owning allegiance to his sovereign to intercept the flight and cut it off with all its baggage and transport. In the alternative he should order a column of picked men to obstruct the vanguard of a retreating army, demoralised by fright and dissension, and command a swift moving column of picked soldiers to overtake and attack the rear by forced marches. On the contrary, the rear should be obstructed and columns of picked men should be despatched to

attack it in the front. The two sorts of tactics described above together with those of side attacks should be adopted in a guerrilla war.[92]

The *Brahmāṇḍa Purāṇa*, a composition of fourth century AD, also gives a vivid description of guerrilla warfare. When Visaṅga, the Daitya general, mounted a guerrilla attack on Lalitā, the commander of the army of gods, no *dundubhi* was sounded. The roaring rambling sound of *mṛdala* was not heard. The sound of *paṇavas*, *ānakas* and *bherīs* did not rise up. Enveloped in darkness, they proceeded ahead with concealed movements that could not be seen by the enemies. They had taken their swords out of scabbards.[93] Through the northern path they surrounded the army of Lalitā that was proceeding to the west. They then resorted to the eastern part. They proceeded ahead slowly and cautiously at every step without making any noise even in breathing. Taking their steps very slowly, they went back once again in the direction of the city. There they pointed out the army of Lalitā to their own people who asked about it. For the purpose of attacking the rear, Dānavas returned quietly with armours covering their bodies. The troops of Lalitā were caught in a difficult situation. Their vulnerable points were wounded when the armours were hit and split by the arrows of the Dānavas whose forms were hidden by darkness and whose weapons and coats of mail were invisible.[94]

Indians had also perfected the scorched earth strategy of war. It was adopted as a defensive measure to deny the invader the facilities available in the conquered land. This aspect of war is graphically described in the Epic.

> He (the defending king) should retire to his chief fortress and remove his cattle from the jungle and keep them on the highways. He should lay his own country waste and remove all the villagers to the important towns. Rich men should be removed to fortified places which should have garrisons from the army. What cannot be removed should be burned including grass. Bridges and passages of rivers should be let loose and such as cannot be let loose should be vitiated by poison.[95]

The *Manusmṛti* says that the invader should lay waste the kingdom of the rival king and destroy his resources of food, fodder, water and fuel. The lakes, forts and trenches in the enemy kingdom should also be ravaged.[96] The *Arthaśāstra* and later Nīti works also refer to this strategy of war.

LATER DEVELOPMENTS

The *Mānasollāsa* appears to be the last work to describe the *vyūha* system in some detail. This suggests that innovative thinking on the science of warfare ceased after its composition. Alternately, in view of standard works like the *Arthaśāstra* and the *Kāmandaka Nīti* no further effort was considered necessary in this regard. The political fragmentation of the country after the Guptas and subsequent Turk invasions, lend support to the earlier conjecture.

The Indians, however, continued to be guided in warfare by the doctrines propounded by ancient military thinkers. In the *Śiśupālavadha*, a work of tenth century, *vyūhas* like *makara*, *viṣama*, *sarvatobhadra*, *cakra* and *gomūtrikā* are referred to.[97] The *Pṛthvīrāja Rāso* of poet Canda says that in his first encounter with Mohammad Ghori, Pṛthvīrāja Chauhan and Rāval Samara Vikrama arrayed their troops in *candra-vyūha* and succeeded in arresting the invader.[98] In the final war against Ghori, Rāval formed his army in *gṛddha-vyūha*.[99] On one wing he placed Balibhadra Kachvāhā and on another Jamarāya Yādava. On the beak and shoulders, in front of the Shahi forces, he posted Pāvas Puṇḍīra, on legs and calf (*piṇḍa*) a Nāda king took position and the tail was occupied by Maṇi Mahā. Pṛthvīrāja occupied the left of the array. To counter this Rajput formation the Turks formed in the *ardhacandra* array.[100]

FOREIGN INFLUENCE

Indian history has been a witness to continual foreign invasions and immigrations. The Achaemenids invaded India and occupied some of its territory in sixth century BC. They were followed by Macedonians. After the Maurya interlude invasions became more frequent. The Greeks, the Parthians, the Scythians, the Kuṣāṇas, and after some time the Sassanids and the Hūṇas occupied large Indian territories and exercised considerable political influence in the country.

These invaders owed their success in India to their military might, a combination of superior weapons, strategy and tactics. Even after settling in India they might have continued with their mode of fighting and thus may have introduced revolutionary changes in the Indian warfare. The fact that the invaders introduced new innovations in fortification, armour, weapons and costume suggests that 'the Central

Asian nomads brought in India some battle tactics and weapons which had originated in Eurasean steppes including those of north Central Asian tribes'.[101]

In this connection the Scythian mode of warfare as described by Bachhofer is very instructive.

> Scyths were famous for their horsemanship and archery. These achievements were the basis of their tactics. Riding in widely spaced extended order they rushed upon the enemy, shot the arrows, threw their javelins, turned shot again while apparently flying to return when the close units of their foes had been thrown into disorder. It was only then that they dismounted and mopped up their adversaries with akinakes, the battle-axe, and the dagger. Militarily they relied exclusively on mobility which was extraordinarily high and upon long range weapons. The Parthians had adopted the same costume, the same weapons and the same tactics.[102]

In this context the observations made by Sulimirski are also significant.

> The Sarmatians' manner of waging war was much the same as that of the Scythians and other steppe peoples. In the early periods, they attacked the enemy with large groups of mounted bowmen, consumate horsemen who had perfected the art of shooting while at full gallop. In the second century BC the armament of some Sarmatian tribes changed radically, especially that of Roxolani, who became the leading Sarmatian people of the North Pontic steppes. Their principal weapons were heavy, long iron-headed lances and long swords with a wooden grip. . . . Bows and arrows then played a secondary role. They were clad in armour made either of small iron plates on leather, or of thick hide, and the horses were protected in the same manner; helmets too were made mostly of hide. At first this armour was worn only by the chiefs.[103]

This long quotation is intended to highlight the two systems of warfare that evolved in the steppes, the second superceding the first around 200 BC. In the earlier system the soldiers clad in helmets and corselets of raw ox hide, carried lighter arms like reflex bow and akinakes. In the later system soldiers donned armour made either of small iron plates sewn on leather or of thick hide and carried heavy swords and lances.

Both these systems of Sarmatian or Scythian origins entered India.

> The coin portraits of Maues and Azes show the princes heavily armoured in the manner of Persian cataphracti. . . . The Persian riders wore helmets and both they and their horses were protected with chain mail or with body plates of metal or leather. A long spear and a long sword were the basic offensive weapons. According to historical records this armament was used by the aristocracy among the Sarmatians of south Russia and the Parthians of Iran, whereas their retainers were armed with bows and arrows and comprised the light cavalry. Indo-Śaka princes are shown in much the same guise on their coins, except that their horses appear not to have had that same degree of protection. Some sculptures from Mathurā actually show some Kuṣāṇa worshippers in armour. The coins of Vāsudeva I and his successors also represent king in a mailed tunic or cuirass with round disks on the upper part.[104]

The discovery of heavy armour at Taxilā as also the appearance of heavy swords and lances in the art of Kuṣāṇa period indicates the influx of the latter. This has led R.S. Sharma to conclude that 'apparantly the Śakas spread over western India, in regions around Mathurā and in the Punjab and North-Western Frontier on account of their skill in the use of heavy armed cavalry, and the same factor explains the success and the long rule of the Kuṣāṇas in North India'.[105]

Despite the presence of heavy body-armour and spear in Indian art Rosenfield holds that there is very little evidence to support the idea that the Kuṣāṇas employed heavy cavalry so fundamental to the military tactics of the other contemporary nations of former Central Asians. Perhaps, the system of warfare based on heavy armour and arms could not take root in India and in the Gupta age a clear preference for lighter weapons and armour is perceptible.[106] Maybe this again was a Śaka influence.

It may be added here that the foreign invaders introduced a new concept of war, what may be called the strategy of annihilation. This was quite natural as the foreigners had to be ruthless in asserting their authority. Literature of the age describes the depredation of invaders and its ruinous consequences for the established social order.[107] A

Kuṣāṇa *kṣatrapa* of Banaras is said to have been ruthless in his dealings with the Brāhmaṇas.[108] Śākala, identified with modern Sialkot in Punjab, was depleted of Brāhmaṇas, Śramaṇas and the intellectuals for years.[109] Needless to say that Śākala remained under the occupation of foreign invaders for centuries.

In this context the archaeological evidence on the Indo-Greek invasion in the Gaṅgā valley is immensely valuable. It suggests an extensive conflagration and massive destruction of the entire township of Kauśāmbī around the first quarter of second century BC. Even the Buddhist monastery of Ghoṣitārāma was not spared. The palace was destroyed and the defences of the town demolished. These invaders were indeed the Indo-Greeks as is evidenced by the recovery of a large number of double-tanged arrow-heads of Greek origins from various sites there.[110]

A large number of Hūṇas came to settle in India in fifth century AD. They fought some battles and ruled some territories as well. The military tactics they applied in India may not have been dissimilar to those used by them against the Romans in AD 390.

> They enter the battle in tactical formation, while their medley of voices makes a savage noise. And as they are lightly equipped for swift motion, and unexpected in action, they purposely divide suddenly in scattered bands, and attack, rushing about in disorder here and there, dealing terrific slaughter. . . . And on this account you would not hesitate to call them the most terrible of all warriors, because they fight from a distance with missiles having sharp bone, instead of their usual points, joined to the shafts with wonderful skill; then they gallop over the intervening spaces and fight hand to hand with sword regardless of their own lives; and while the enemy are guarding against wounds from sword-thrusts, they throw strip of cloth plaited into nooses over their opponents and so entangle them that they fetter their limbs and take from them the power of riding or walking.[111]

To what extent these Hūṇas influenced the Indian military system is difficult to say in the present state of our knowledge.

The foregoing description of *vyūhas* suggests that in ancient India there were two schools of thought on *vyūhas*, one represented by the epics and Purāṇas and the other by the Nīti works. Significantly, both schools considered Śukra and Bṛhaspati as the pioneer thinkers on the subject. Of the two the one represented by Nīti works seems more practical. The extent to which ancient Indian armies implemented these theories in the battlefield is difficult to say. But these *vyūhas* undoubtedly failed before the marching columns of foreign invaders. In the following chapter the weapons and armour used by the armies in ancient India are described.

NOTES

1. सामदानाभ्यां दुर्बलानुपनमयेत् भेददण्डाभ्यां बलवतः। *AS*, 7.16.3; four means of state policy and six measures have been described in Chapter 2 in detail.
2. नियोगविकल्पसमुच्चयैश्चोपायानामनन्तरैकान्तराः प्रकृतीः साधयेत्। Ibid., 7.16.4.
3. पूर्वे च प्रहरणकालाः कूटयुद्धहेतवः। संग्रामस्तु निर्दिष्टदेशकालो धर्मिष्ठः। Ibid., 10.3.25-6.
4. योगगूढोपजापार्थं तूष्णींयुद्धस्य लक्षणम्। Ibid., 7.6.41.
5. अदुर्गापसारः शत्रुरपार्ष्णिरनासारश्च, ततो यायात्। Ibid., 7.16.1, 10.3.1-3.
6. Ibid., 10.3.7.
7. Ibid., 10.3.11-18.
8. संग्रामस्तु निर्दिष्टदेशकालो धर्मिष्ठः। Ibid., 10.3.26.
9. Ibid., 7.6.40-1.
10. Ibid., 9.1.17-33.
11. Ibid., 10.5.3-5; *Agni Pu.*, 236.35.
12. Ibid., 10.5.6-8.
13. Ibid., 10.5-6.
14. Ibid., 10.5.9-14.
15. Ibid., 10.5.17-23.
16. Ibid., 10.5.31-3.
17. Ibid., 10.5.34-7.
18. Ibid., 10.5.38-40.
19. Ibid., 10.5.43-4.
20. Ibid., 10.5.46-7.
21. पक्षावुरस्यं प्रतिग्रह इत्यौशनसो व्यूहविभागः। Ibid., 10.6.1, Śukra does not provide for flanks; also see *Kāmandaka Nīti*, 20.31; *Agni Pu.*, 242.42-3.
22. पक्षौ कक्षावुरस्यं प्रतिग्रह इति बार्हस्पत्यः। Ibid., 10.6.2.
23. दण्डभोगमंडलासंहताः प्रकृतिव्यूहाः। Ibid., 10.6.3; also *Nītiprakāśikā*, 6.3.

24. पक्षकक्षोरस्यैः समं वर्तमानो दण्डः। Ibid., 10.6.8.
25. स कक्षातिक्रान्तः प्रदरः। Ibid., 10.6.9.
26. स एव पक्षकक्षाभ्यां प्रतिकान्तो दृढकः। Ibid., 10.6.10.
27. स एवातिक्रान्तः पक्षाभ्यामसप्रः। Ibid., 10.6.11.
28. पक्षाववस्थाप्योरस्यातिक्रान्तः श्येनः। Ibid., 10.6.12.
    According to *Śukranīti* (4.7.280) in *śyena* array wings are large, the throat and tail medium and the mouth small.
29. विपर्यये चापं चापकुक्षिः प्रतिष्ठः सुप्रतिष्ठश्च। Ibid., 10.6.13.
30. Ibid.
31. Ibid.
32. Ibid.
33. चापपक्षः संजयः। Ibid., 10.6.14.
34. स एवोरस्यातिक्रान्तो विजयः। Ibid., 10.6.15.
35. स्थूलकर्णपक्षः स्थूणाकर्णः।
    Ibid., 10.6.16; according to Kāmandaka (20.47) each of the wings has two *anīkas* instead of one.
36. द्विगुणपक्षस्थूणो विशालविजयः। Ibid., 10.6.17; Kangle has interpreted it to mean that the size of the *pakṣa* is twice that of the *sthūnakarṇa*, i.e. four *anīkas* in each.
37. त्र्यभिक्रान्तपक्षश्चमूमुखः। Ibid., 10.6.18.
38. विपर्यये झषास्यः Ibid., 10.6.19.
39. उर्ध्वराजिर्दण्डः सूची। Ibid., 10.6.20; according to *Śukranīti* (4.7.281) it has a narrow mouth and long staff. At the end of the staff there was a hole.
40. द्वौ दण्डो बलयः। Ibid., 10.6.21.
41. चत्वारो दुर्जयः। Ibid., 10.6.22.
42. पक्षकक्षोरस्यैर्विषमं वर्तमानो भोगः। स सर्पसारी गोमूत्रिका वा। *AS*, 10.6.24-5; according to *Śukranīti* (4.7.283) *vyāla-vyūha* resembled a snake in shape.
43. R.P. Kangle, *The Kauṭilīya Arthaśāstra*, vol. II, p. 451.
44. स युग्मोरस्यो दण्डपक्षः शकटः। Ibid., 10.6.26; according to *Śukranīti* (4.7.283) it resembled a cart.
45. विपर्यये मकरः। Ibid., 10.6.27; according to *Śukranīti* (4.7.280) *makara* array had four legs, long and thick mouth and two lips.
46. हस्त्यश्वरथैर्व्यतिकीर्णः शकटः पारिपन्तकः। Ibid., 10.6.28; *Arthaśāstra*, includes four *vyūhas* in this category. But Kāmandaka substitutes *sañcārī* for *sarpasārī* and considers it a separate array.
47. पक्षकक्षोरस्यानामेकीभावे मण्डलः। Ibid., 10.6.30.

48. स सर्वतोमुखः सर्वतोभद्रः। Ibid., 10.6.31; according to *Śukranīti* (4.7.282) it has eight sides covering all directions.
49. अष्टानीको दुर्जयः। Ibid., 10.6.32.
50. R.P. Kangle, *The Kauṭilīya Arthaśāstra*, p. 451.
51. पक्षकक्षोरस्यानामसंहतादसंहतः। *AS*., 10.6.34.
52. स पंचानीकानामाकृतिस्थापनाद्वज्रो गोधा वा। Ibid., 10.6.35.
53. चतुर्णामुद्धानकः काकपदी वा। Ibid., 10.6.36.
54. त्रयाणामर्धचन्द्रकः कर्कटकशृङ्गी वा। Ibid., 10.6.37; *Kāmandaka Nīti* includes the following *vyūhas* in this category.
    अर्धचन्द्रक उद्धानो वज्रो भेदास्त्वसंहते।
    तथा कर्कटशृङ्गी च काकपादी च गोधिका।। *Kāmandaka Nīti*, 20.51.
55. रथोरस्यो हस्तिकक्षोऽश्वपृष्टो अरिष्टः। *AS*, 10.6.39.
56. पत्तयोऽश्वा रथा हस्तिनश्चानुपृष्टमचलः। Ibid., 10.6.40.
57. हस्तिनोऽश्वाः रथाः पत्तयश्चानुपृष्टमप्रतिहतः। Ibid., 10.6.41.
58. Ibid., 10.6.42-3; according to the *Arthaśāstra* elephants were very useful in breaking arrays.
59. Ibid., 10.2.9.
60. *Śukranīti*, 4.7.264-5.
61. यायाद्व्यूहेन महता मकरेण पुरो भये।
    श्येनेनोद्धृतपक्षेण सूच्या वा वीरवक्त्रया।।
    पश्चाद्भये तु शकटं पार्श्वयोर्वज्रसंज्ञितम्।
    सर्वतः सर्वतोभद्रं भये व्यूहं प्रकल्पयेत्।। *Agni Pu.*, 242.7-8; also *Kāmandaka Nīti*, 19.48-9.
62. *AS*, 10.3.48.
63. Ibid., 10.3.52-3.
64. *AS*, 10.6.46.
65. यथादेशं कल्पयेद्वा शत्रुसेनाविभेदकम्।
    व्यूहरचनसङ्केतान् वाद्यभाषासमीरितान्।।
    स्वसैनिकैर्विना कोऽपि न जानाति तथाविधान्।
    नियोजयेच्च मतिमान् व्यूहान्नानाविधान् सदा।। *Śukranīti*, 4.7.266-7, 368.
66. शिक्षितं व्यूहकुशलं विपरीतमशिक्षितम्। Ibid., 4.7.12.
67. तिर्यग्वृत्तिस्तु दण्डः स्याद् भोगोऽन्वावृत्तिरेव च।
    मंडलः सर्वतोवृत्तिः पर्थगवृत्तिरसंहतः।। *Kāmandaka Nīti*, 20.42; *Agni Pu.*, 242.49-50.
68. उरः कक्षो च पक्षो च मध्यः पृष्ठं प्रतिग्रहः।
    कोटी च व्यूहशास्त्रज्ञैः सप्तांगो व्यूह इष्यते।। Ibid., 20.30; also *Agni Pu.*, 242.41-2.
69. व्यूहं च स्थापयित्वा पक्षकक्षोरस्यानामेकेन द्वाभ्यां वा प्रहरेत, शेषैः प्रतिगृह्णीयात्। *AS*, 10.5.48.

70. पक्षादीनामथैकेन हत्वा शेषैः परिक्षिपेत्। उरसा वा समाहत्य कोटिभ्यां परिवेष्टयेत्।
परकोटीसमाक्रम्य पक्षाभ्यांसप्रतिग्रहः।
कोटिभ्यां जघनं हन्यादुरसा च प्रपीडयेत्। *Kāmandaka Nīti*, 19.55-6.
71. देशे त्वदृश्यः शत्रूणां कुर्यात्प्रकृतिकल्पनाम्।
संहतान्योधयेदल्पान्कामं विस्तारयेद् बहून्।।
सूचिमुखमनीकं स्यादल्पानां बहुभिः सह।
व्यूहाः प्राण्यङ्गरूपाश्च द्रव्यरूपाश्च कीर्तिताः।
गरुडो मकरव्यूहश्चक्रः श्येनस्तथैव च।
अर्धचन्द्रश्च वज्रश्च शकटव्यूह एवं च।।
मण्डलः सर्वतोभद्रः सूचीव्यूहश्च ते नव। *Agni Pu.*, 236.28-30.
72. व्यूहानामथ सर्वेषां पञ्चधा सैन्यकल्पना।।
द्वौ पक्षावनुपक्षौ द्वाववश्यं पञ्चम भवेत्। Ibid., 236.30-1.
73. एकेन यदि वा द्वाभ्यां भागाभ्यां युद्धमाचरेत्। Ibid., 236.31.
74. सैन्यस्य पश्चात्तिष्ठेत्तु क्रोशमात्रे महीपतिः। *Agni Pu.*, 236.33.
75. Ibid., 242.7-8, 49-59.
76. Ibid., 242.7-8; in the *Devī Purāṇa* (43.23-9) 43 kinds of *vyūhas* are referred to. Of these *kakṣa, pakṣa, abhoga, maṇḍala* and *saṁghāta* are stated to be *prakṛta.* Others like *pradara, dṛḍha, kośaḍya*, etc., were not considered truly *prakṛta.*
77. Ibid., 242.17-18.
78. उरस्य कक्षपक्षांस्तु कल्प्यानेतान्प्रचक्षते।
उरः कक्षौ च पक्षौ च मध्यं पृष्ठं प्रतिग्रहः।।
कोटी च व्यूहशास्त्रज्ञैः सप्ताङ्गो व्यूह उच्यते।
उरस्यकक्षपक्षास्तु व्यूहोऽयं सप्रतिग्रहः।।
गुरोरेष च शुक्रस्य कक्षाभ्यां परिवर्जितः। *Agni Pu.*, 242.41-3; also *Nītiprakāśikā*, 6.11.
79. सर्वलक्षणसम्पूर्णे भूभागे रिपुमर्दनः।
रचयेदुत्तमं व्यूहं परव्यूहविभेदकम्।।
मुखं पूर्वविभागः स्यादुरश्च तदनन्तरम्।
उरसः पश्चिमे भागे प्रौरस्यं परिकीर्तितम्।।
प्रौररस्य तथा पृष्टे प्रतिग्रह इतीरितः।
कक्षौ प्रकक्षौ पक्षौ च प्रपक्षौ पार्श्वयोः क्रमात्।
प्रतिग्रहपरो भागः पृष्ठमित्यभिधीयते।
एवं व्यूहविभागांश्च विज्ञाय नृपतिस्ततः।। *Mānasollāsa*, 2.20.1178-81; it is significant that *pakṣa* and *prapakṣa* are mentioned in the *Mahābhārata* as well. *MB*, Karṇa, 50.3.
80. *Śukranīti*, 4.7.264-83.
81. व्यूहरचनसङ्केतान् वाद्यभाषासमीरितान्
स्वसैनिकैर्विना कोऽपि न जानाति तथाविधाम्।। Ibid., 4.7.267.

82. Ibid.
83. Ibid., 4.7.270-1.
84. Ibid., 4.7.272-7.
85. Ibid., 4.7.390; also 4.7.368.
86. व्यूहाभ्यासं शिक्षयेद्यः सायं प्रातश्च सैनिकान्।
जानाति स शतानीकः सुयोद्धुं युद्धभूमिकाम्।। Ibid., 2.143-4.
87. सैन्यमल्पं बृहद्वापि दृष्ट्वा मार्गं रणस्थलम्।।
व्यूहैर्व्यूहेन व्यूहाभ्यां सङ्करेणापि कल्पयेत्। Ibid., 4.7.284.
88. *Ṛgveda*, 10.103.9.
89. *MB*, Droṇa, 138.
90. Ibid., Sauptika, 8.
91. *Rām*, yuddha, 44 & 75; *Kāmandaka Nīti*, 19.65-6.
92. *Agni Pu.*, 242.13-17; also *Kāmandaka Nīti*, 18.60-8.
93. *Brahmāṇḍa Pu.*, 25.49-50.
94. Ibid., 25.50-65.
95. C.V. Vaidya, *Epic India*, vol. I, p. 262; for details see *MB*, Śānti, 69.
96. *Manusmṛti*, 7.195-6.
97. विषमं सर्वतोभद्रचक्रगोमूत्रिकादिभिः। *Śiśupālavadha*, 19.41; also 16.67.
98. चन्द्रव्यूहअंकुरिय राज दुअ इहां एकत्रे। *Pṛthvīrāja Rāso*, Samaya, 25.45; in the *Rāso* there are references to battle arrays lilke *śakaṭa*, *sarpa*, *mayūra*, *gaja*, *garuḍa*, etc.
99. Ibid., Samaya, 61.265.
100. अर्धचन्द्र तात्तार खानि रणि खानि सुरेसी। Ibid., Samaya, 61.266.
101. G.M. Bongard Levin, in *Kuṣāṇa Studies in USSR*, p. 48.
102. Bachhofer, *Journal of the American Oriental Studies*, vol. 61, pp. 247-8.
103. T. Sulimirski, *The Sarmatians*, pp. 28-30.
104. John M. Resenfield, *The Dynastic Art of the Kushāṇs*, p. 55.
105. R.S. Sharma, 'Central Asia and Early Indian Cavalry (*c.* 200 BC-AD 1200)', a paper included in *Central Asia*, ed. A. Guha, p. 175; in this connection it is notable that many persons in the art of Gandhāra are represented in exactly the same armour as seen in bas-reliefs of Galerius Arch in Thessaloniki. T. Sulimirski, *The Sarmatians*, Fig. 6.
106. John M. Rosenfield, op. cit., p. 55.
107. चतुर्भागं तु शस्त्रेण नाशयिष्यन्ति प्राणिनाम्।
शकाः शेषां हरिष्यन्ति चतुर्भागस्वकं पुरम्।। *GS*, *Yuga Pu.*, 56-7, in *JBORS*, vol. 16.
तत्र वर्णास्तु चतुरः स नृपो नाशयिष्यति।
वर्णधोवस्थितान् सर्वान कृत्वा पूर्यामवस्थितान्।। Ibid., 63-4.

108. K.P. Jayaswal, *An Imperial History of India*, pp. 41-4.
109. *Milindapañho*, 1.1.4.
110. G.R. Sharma, *Reh Inscription of Menander and the Indo-Greek Invasion of the Ganga Valley*, pp. 12-15.
111. Marcellinus as quoted by J. Otto Maenchen-Helfen in *The World of The Huns*, pp. 201-2.

Chapter 6

Weapons and Armour

Indians used chopper tools and hand-axes during the Stone Age. Some pre-historic cave paintings from central India, dated around 7000 BC, depict hunters carrying long spears and arrows tipped with sharp-edged stones. These figures are related to late Stone Age or Mesolithic people. Subsequently, the horns and bones were also used for making arrow heads and javelin points.

CHALCOLITHIC AGE

The people of Indus Valley knew metallurgy and made weapons of bronze and copper. Occasionally, copper was hardened by alloying it with other metals, like tin, arsenic, nickel, or lead. Their weapons included bow and arrow, spear, knife, axe and mace and also a kind of missile. According to B.B. Lal spear was the principal weapon of the Harappans.

> While thinking in terms of possible weapons with which the Harappans could have fought a war, it is these long spears that may have to be considered besides probably the above mentioned arrowheads, though the latter are rather small. That is about all. And then there is no evidence of any shields, body armour or helmets, items met with in Egyptian and Mesopotamian contexts. It would thus appear that the Harappans were ill-equipped for major warfare.[1]

But the fact that the Indus empire had been created and that it survived for many centuries suggests that 'the original Indus state needed to have armed means to both conquer and keep in subjugation a large population'.[2]

Regarding the production of weapons by the Indus valley people the observations made by Bridget and Raymond Allchin are significant.

Nearly all the basic tool types—flat axes, chisels, knives, spearheads and arrowheads, small saws, etc.—could have been made by simple casting, and/or chiselling and hammering. Daggers, knives or dirks with mid ribs and flat tangs begin to appear in the upper levels at Mohenjo-daro. Although they may show foreign influence, we concur with Child's remark that they are 'technically very Indian'.[3]

VEDIC AGE

The inhabitants of the Indus valley were presumably conquered by the Āryans, who may have introduced a new system of weapons and warfare in India. Some people relate the swords, spears and axes associated with the Copper Hoard Culture of India (1800-1000 BC) with the Āryans. In the *Ṛgveda* there are references to weapons like axes (*svadhiti*), shining spears (*ṛṣṭih*) and arrows (*iṣu*) made of copper or brass.[4] The developments in mineralogy may also have led to some refinement in the production of weapons.[4]

Bow was the most popular weapon among the Vedic Āryans and hymns were composed in its honour. The arrows, about a yard in length, were provided with feathers to balance the flight. These were carried in a quiver (*iṣudhi*). Spear was widely used and the terms *rambhiṇī* and *śakti* were applied to it. Āryans also used the sword. The other weapons of the Vedic age included axe and mace. Āryans also knew the use of armour (*varman*), head-gear (*śirastrāṇa*) and hand-guard (*hastaghna*).[5]

By the later Vedic age, say about 1000 BC, the metallurgy had made considerable progress. People could now differentiate iron and copper and make use of lead, and tin. The discovery of iron called black metal (*śyāma ayas*)[6] added a new dimension to the science of weaponry. The weapons were now manufactured by professionals like bow-makers (*dhanuṣkāra*), arrow-makers (*iṣukāra*) and thread-makers (*jyākāra*).[7]

USE OF IRON

The discovery of iron is intimately related to the development of weapons. But it is still an unsettled issue as to when iron was introduced in India. According to R.E.M. Wheeler it was introduced in sixth century BC by the Achaemenians. M.N. Banerjee and P. Niyogi believe that it was introduced in India by the Vedic Āryans.

R.G. Forbes associates iron with the earliest Āryan settlers in India. Lallanji Gopal holds that it was introduced in the later Vedic period. N.R. Banerjee believes that iron was introduced by the Āryans around 1000 BC.[8] However, R.S. Sharma appears much nearer to truth while concluding that painted grey ware phase marked by the use of iron in the upper Gangetic plains and Indo-Gangetic divide can be reasonably dated between 1000-500 BC.[9] More recently T.N. Roy has said that 'iron age in India would begin at about 800 BC from its first emergence in the form of "working tools" in the Gaṅgā plains, but its full impact leading to urbanization was felt in the whole of sub-continent only from the late phase of NBPW period, about 400-300 BC onward'.[10] D.H. Gordon also confirms this stating that

> There is no archaeological find to support the use of iron in India before 400 BC. Herodotus and Ktesias were the earliest to refer to iron in india. Herodotus has reported that iron-tipped arrows were carried by Indian contingent of Xerxes army. On the other hand Ktesias refers to two fine swords of Indian steel presented to Artaxerxes Mnemon.[11]

Aṣṭādhyāyī, a work composed in sixth century BC, refers to weapons like sword, arrow, spear, axe and javelin and these could have been made of iron.[12] On the basis of some recent excavations in UP Rakesh Tiwari pushes back the antiquity of iron in India to second millennium BC.

In this connection, it is notable that iron implements and weapons have been found at excavated sites at Atranjikhera, Jakhera and adjoining region in western UP and their date is placed in the time bracket of the later Vedic period. South Indian megalithic tombs have also yielded a large number of iron weapons. Significantly, the number of iron weapons discovered here is more than that of agricultural tools and implements. Evidently, iron was more widely used for weapons than other purposes in early India. This might have added a new dimension to the system of warfare as iron weapons were more solid and lethal than bronze and copper weapons. This might have also necessitated readjustments in the existing strategy and tactics of war.

CLASSIFICATION OF WEAPONS

In the Epic age the growing number of weapons necessitated some kind of classification. The *Mahābhārata* refers to four types of weapons, but does not mention them.[13] These were indeed *mukta*, *amukta*, *muktāmukta* and *mantramukta*, as described in the *Nītiprakāśikā*.[14] The *mukta* type were long range weapons like spears and arrows which were hurled. The *amukta* type were used by holding them in hand such as sword. *Muktāmukta* type could be used both ways, by hurling or by holding, such as javelin. *Mantramukta* were used with the power of *mantras* and these included *brahmāstra*, *āgneyāstra*, etc. The Epic also classifies weapons as divine and man-made.[15] The former could be used sparingly and that also under divine dispensation.

ARTHAŚĀSTRA

The *Arthaśāstra* gives an entirely different classification of weapons as follows:[16]

1. Fixed machines (स्थितयन्त्राणि)
2. Mobile machines (चलयन्त्राणि)
3. Weapons with piercing points (हुलमुखानि)
4. Arrows (इषवः)
5. Swords (खड्ग)
6. Razor type weapons (क्षुरकल्पाः)
7. Stone weapons (अश्मायुधानि)
8. Defensive weapons (वर्माणि)

The fixed machines included weapons such as *sarvatobhadra*, *jāmadagnya*, etc. These were operated from fixed positions. The second category, i.e. mobile machines included fifteen types of weapons intended to be hurled down from the ramparts of a fort. The third category included more than eleven weapons such as *śakti*, *prāsa*, *kunta*, *śūla*, etc. These were all javelin types with minor variations. Arrows with tips of iron, bone, or wood performed triple functions of cutting, piercing and striking. Swords were used for slashing and cutting. The razor types included seven varieties like *paraśu*, *kuṭhāra*, *paṭṭasa*, etc. Stones were also used as weapons. These were hurled with the help of machines, slings and even hands. The defensive weapons included coat of mail, armour of fabrics, helmet, shield, etc. The weapons were manufactured under the supervision of *āyudhāgārādhyakṣa*.[17]

AGNI PURĀṆA

The *Agni Purāṇa* classifies weapons into five categories, viz., *yantramukta* (discharged by machine), *pāṇimukta* (discharged by hand), *mukta-sandhārita* (discharged and held), *amukta* (not discharged) and *bāhu* (arms).[18] The *Matsya Purāṇa* gives a slightly different classification, viz., *yantramukta*, *pāṇimukta*, *vimukta* and *muktadhārita*.[19]

DHANURVEDA

The *Dhanurveda* refers to seven kinds of weapons including bow (*dhanu*), quoit (*cakra*), spear (*kunta*), sword (*khaḍga*), dagger (*churikā*), mace (*gadā*) and arms (*bāhu*). A person who had mastered the use of all these weapons was called *ācārya*. A soldier was expected to be proficient in the use of any two of these weapons.[20]

ŚIŚUPĀLAVADHA

Śiśupālavadha classifies the weapons into four categories, viz., *astra*, *apastra*, *vyāstra* and *mahāstra*. *Astra* category included bow, etc., *apastra* noose, etc., *vyāstra* club, etc., and *mahāstra*, fire arms, etc.[21]

P.C. Chakravarty has classified weapons into two categories, viz., offensive and defensive.[22] The category of offensive weapons included bow, sword and spear, while the defensive weapons included shield, armour and helmet. All the other weapons could be included in either category. Some important weapons of war in ancient India are described below:

BOW (*DHANUṢ*)

Bow was the most ancient weapon of the Indians. The people of Indus Valley used it as early as 2500 BC is evident from the discovery of copper and brass arrow-heads.[23] It was also the chief weapon of the Vedic Āryans.[24] Hymns were composed in its honour. 'with Bow let us win kine, with Bow the battle, with Bow be victors in our hot encounters. The Bow brings grief and sorrow to the foeman: armed with the Bow may we subdue all regions'.[25] The dominance of bow in the Indian battlefield was total and the Indians applied the term *dhanurveda* not only to the science of weapons but also to the art of warfare. Expertise in bowmanship was the touch-stone of bravery.

According to the *Śukranīti* the *Dhanurveda* was a subsidiary of *Yajurveda* and its knowledge enabled a person to battle, to wield weapons and to form battle arrays.[26]

The Vedic bow was made of a stout staff bent into a curved shape (*vakra*), and a bowstring (*jyā*) made of cow-hide, which joined the ends of the staff. The tips of the bow, when fastened with string were called *ārtni*. It was strung up only when required for shooting.[27] No warrior ever went out without his bow and parted company with it only when dead. In fact the last act of the funeral rite of an Āryan included the removal of the bow from the right hand of the dead.[28] The Āryan reverence to bow is echoed in many hymns:[29]

Bow figures as the most important weapon in the epics. It is variously called, *dhanuṣa*, *cāpa*, *śarāsana*, *kārmuka* and *śāraṅga*. The bows of reputed warriors were worked with gold and inlaid with animal figures and geometrical patterns.[30] The Gāṇḍīva *dhanuṣ* wielded by Arjuna was the most powerful weapon of the Epic war. His main adversary Karṇa carried Vijaya *dhanuṣ*.

The *Arthaśāstra* refers to bows made of *cāpa* (bamboo), *dāru* (wood), *tāla* (wood of *tāla* tree) and *śṛṅga* (horn) and these were called *kodaṇḍa*, *drauma*, *kārmuka* and *dhanu* respectively.[31] Of these the bows made of bamboo and horn were used more widely.

Little is known about the shape or size of the bow, used by the Harappans and the Vedic Āryans. But the bow carried by the soldiers of Porus in the fourth century BC is described by Greek historians in detail. According to Arrian the Indian foot soldiers carried a bow made of equal length with the man who bore it.

> This they rest upon the ground, and pressing against it their left foot thus discharge the arrow, having drawn the string far backwards; for the shaft they use is little short of being three yards long, and there is nothing which can resist an Indian archers shot, neither shield, nor breastplate, nor any stronger defence if such there be.[32]

Interestingly, the length of Arjuna's bow is said to be 4 cubits (80 inches) in the epic.[33]

It seems that after the battle of Jhelum the Indians discarded this big bow. The Śaka-Kuṣāṇa mounted archers also did not find it useful.[34] The frequent representation of smaller bows in the art of Sāñcī[35] indicates this change, though the big bow was not altogether abandoned.

The *Agni Purāṇa* says that the bow could be made of iron, horn or wood with a string of bamboo fibre or hide[36] and that a quality bow could be four cubits long.[37] It adds that

> the tip of the bow made of horn or iron (should be having) minute edge (covered) by hides. The edge (should be) like the creeper, (like) the eyebrow of a beautiful damsel and should be fastened well. . . . One should make the bow separately of the horn or iron or (the two) mixed. A good bow should suitably be decorated with particles of gold. A bow (made of) sandal, cane, *sāla, dhavala* and *kakubha* (trees) (is good). The most excellent bow is that made of bamboo, cut and collected in the autumn.[38]

It seems that the use of horn for making bows came into vogue in India around the beginning of the Christian era. Indians either learnt its use from the nomadic invaders or the changing mode of warfare led to its invention. In this connection the observation of P.C. Chakravarty is notable.

> It is quite probable that originally wooden and bamboo bows were alone used, and horn bows were later inventions. In search after materials to improve the casting power of the bow, man would naturally be struck by the elastic properties of the horns of animals. The combined testimony of the Jātakas, the epics and the *Arthaśāstra* of Kauṭilya proves that horn bows had come into use in India before the beginning of the Christian era.[39]

Perhaps, the bow of horn intervened between the wooden bow and the composite bow.

The composite bow has been described as 'a bow whose stave embodies a laminated construction involving more than one type of material, such as wood, sinew, and horn; as a rule the wooden core is backed by sinew and bellied by horn'.[40] The composite bow began as five pieces of plain or laminated wood—a central grip, two arms and two tips. Once glued together, this timber 'skeleton' was then steamed into a curve, opposite to that it would assume when strung, and steamed strips of horn were glued to the 'belly'. It was then bent into a complete circle again against its strung shape and fenders were glued to its 'back'. It was then left to 'cure' and only when all its elements had indissolubly married was it untied and strung for the first time. Stringing a composite bow, against its natural relaxed shape, required both great strength and dexterity.[41]

The composite bow may have served the mounted archer exceedingly well. It may have been contributed to the Indian weaponry by the Śaka-Kuṣāṇas who had learnt its use from the Sarmatians and the Hūṇas, their one time neighbours in Central Asia. Such bows are widely met in the Gupta gold coins.

Comparing the long and composite bow J. Keegan remarks that

> The disadvantage of the long bow, however, was precisely its length; it could only be used by an archer on foot. The composite bow was short, reaching only from the top of a man's head to his waist when strung, and therefore suiting itself perfectly to use from a chariot or horse. It shot a lighter arrow—the best weight was about an ounce—than the long bow would, but could still carry to 300 yards with great accuracy . . . and penetrate armour at a hundred yards.[42]

Elsewhere, it is said that the range of a composite bow was quite accurate upto 50 to 60 metres and its effective range extended at least 160 to 175 metres but not as far as 350 to 450 metres.[43]

ARROW (*VĀṆA*)

The earliest evidence of arrow-heads in India comes from the microlithic sites in Baluchistan, Rajasthan and Gujarat. The excavations at Mohenjo-daro have yielded a large number of arrow-heads suggesting that it was a popular weapon. These arrow-heads are thin flat pieces of copper with barbs and no tang. These might have been inserted into a shaft of bamboo or wood.

In the Vedic age the arrow comprised a shaft, a pointed-head and feathers. A Vedic hymn imploring the arrow says: 'Now to the Shaft with venom smeared, tipped with deer-horn, with iron mouth, Celestial, of Parjanya's seed, be this great adoration paid. Loosed from the bowstring fly away, thou Arrow, sharpened by our prayer. Go to the foemen, strike them home, and let not one be left alive.'[44] In the *Aitareya Brāhmaṇa* the four vital parts of the arrow are called *anīka* (head-piece), *śalya* (sharp blade), *tejana* (tip of the blade) and *parṇa* (the feather).[45] The shaft was generally made of reed, though metal, wood and bamboo were also used. It seems that the warriors of repute engraved their names on their arrow shaft.[46] The feathers which balanced the arrow during the flight, were gathered from birds like goose, peacock, osprey, vulture, wild-cock, etc.[47] The arrow-head was generally made of wood, bone or metal so as to pierce, rend or cut.[48] In the epic the arrow-heads made of monkey-bone, elephant-bone, cow-bone, etc., are mentioned.[49] Poisoned arrow-tips were also used.[50] Arrows were washed in oil to make them more effective.[51] An expert bowman was supposed to know the twelve methods of shooting.[52] In ancient India Kirāta and Kāñcīpura regions were famous for producing fine arrows.[53]

It appears that the type of the arrows used by the Indians in fourth century BC were not considered superior by the Greeks. According to Curtius 'The arrows which are two cubits long, are discharged with more effort than effect, for though the force of these missiles depends on their lightness they are loaded with an obnoxious weight.'[54]

The shape and size of the bow underwent a change around the beginning of the Christian era as a result of foreign invasions. This entailed a change in the cast of the arrows as is evident from the findings at Taxilā.

> Without exception all the arrow-heads found at Taxilā were intended for shafts made of reeds not of solid wood, and were provided accordingly with long tangs instead of hollow sockets. Since the reed arrow was in general use among the Iranian and Central Asian as well as Indian peoples, it is reasonable to infer that these 'double tanged' heads, as we may call them, were an adoption of Western socketed type rather than an Eastern one, and, this being so, it seems not improbable that they were introduced at Taxilā by the Bactrian Greeks.[55]

Around the beginning of the Christian era two new types of arrows, viz., conical and three-bladed, also made appearance. The latter seems to have been specially favoured by the Śakas. This type has been found along with a four-bladed type at many sites in Taxilā, which was destroyed by the Hūṇas in fifth century AD.

In the excavations at Kauśāmbī, near Allahabad, double-tanged arrow-heads and three-bladed types have been discovered. These are different from other types discovered at the site and, therefore, indicate their foreign association. Incidentally, prior to Kauśāmbī no such arrow-heads have been discovered from any site in the Gangetic Valley. Their different make and resemblance with the types met at Taxilā suggests that these were brought to Kauśāmbī by foreign invaders from the north-west. It is notable that the Greeks, Śakas and Hūṇas, who have been associated by Marshall with the aforesaid arrow-head types at Taxilā, were also associated with Kauśāmbī, politically.[56]

On the length of arrows no specified standard seems to have been followed. Perhaps, these were made in accordance with the size of the bow in various periods of history. In fourth century BC the arrows were made about 3 cubits (4' 6") long.[57] In the Sāñcī reliefs the length of arrows ranges between 3 to 5 feet.

About the capability of the arrow-shot such as its range, speed and effectiveness hardly any information is available. The casual reference in the *Mahābhārata* that the flight of Arjuna's arrow could cover a distance of 1 *kroṣa* (2 miles), is just unrealistic.[58] The *Vaśiṣṭha Dhanurveda*, however, furnishes some reliable information on the range of arrow while stating that 'the target placed at a distance of 60 *dhanuṣ* (240 cubits) from the bowman is the best, that placed at a distance of 40 *dhanuṣ* (160 cubits) is medium while that located at a distance of 20 *dhanuṣ* (80 cubits) is inferior'.[59] This implies that an arrow-shot could be effective up to a distance of 120 yards (240 cubits).

QUIVER (*TUṆĪRA*)

In the Vedic times the quiver (*iṣudhi* or *niṣaṅga*) was slung by a bowman on his back to carry the arrows.[60] It was revered like a weapon and *hymns* were composed in its honour. 'Slung on the back pouring his brood, the Quiver vanquishes all opposing bands and armies.'[61] The Epic warriors carried two large quivers fastened together on the right back.[62] In the considered opinion of Hopkins a quiver carried ten to twenty arrows.[63] Various types of quivers are represented in the art of Sāñcī and Ajantā. In the *Amarakośa* the person who carried arrows, perhaps alongside the bowman, was called *Kāṇḍavat* or *Kaṇḍīra*.[64] This suggests that renowned bowmen were accompanied by quiver-bearers.

MOUNTED ARCHER (*SĀDIN*)

Before ending with the bow a word may be said about the archer who fought mounted on the horseback. Though cavalry as an arm was known to Indians since Vedic times the earliest references to mounted-archer are met in the *Mahābhārata*.[65] The antiquity of these references is, however, suspect as 'the reference to mounted archery appearing in the text of the *Mahābhārata* has been inserted at a time, when Indians came to know it as a result of their contact with Scythians or Śakas, who invaded India about 150-140 BC'.[66]

But the horse-archer had been introduced in the Indian battlefield by the Macedonians much before the Śakas. Alexander soon after crossing the Hydaspes, deployed his horse archers in front of the cavalry to face the Indians.[67] It were these horse-archers who routed the advance guard led by the son of Porus.[68] During the battle main with Porus Alexander deployed 1,000 horse-archers against the Indian left wing.[69] He also used horse-archers effectively during his encounters with Indian tribes called Glausai and Kathians.[70]

That the Śaka-Kuṣāṇas popularized horse-archer in the Indian battlefield is also confirmed by the art evidence discovered at Harwan in Kashmir. Some brick tiles, dated prior to third centruy AD, depict horsemen in armour, drawing bows. On the right side a quiver is attached to the saddle.[71] The weapons and accoutrement of the archers definitely suggest a Central Asian connection. Significantly, the earliest evidence of mounted archer in India is traceable to the coins of Pahlava rulers of north-west India.[72]

In the Śaka-Kuṣāṇa system of warfare the mounted bowman played an all important role. The Gupta rulers, following the Śaka-Kuṣāṇas, also patronized this arm[73] but it soon faded out from the Indian battlefield. According to Chakravarty 'the art of mounted archery did not strike deep roots in the Indian soil. Introduced by the Parthians and continuing for a time as a sickly exotic, it withered away shortly after the Gupta period. This is the impression that one gathers from a study of the records of post-Gupta India.'[74] Indians had to pay dearly for neglecting this arm during the Turk invasions.

STIRRUP (*PĀDAPHALIKĀ*)

With the horse-mounted archer accoutrements like the stirrup, bit and saddle also came into vogue. But the most important equipment which provided him a definite advantage over his adversaries was the stirrup. It gave stability to the archer while manoeuvring the mount and shooting the arrow.

It is generally believed that the use of stirrup started in India around the beginning of the Christian era. In this connection the observations made by Sir Mortimer Wheeler are significant:

It occurs quite early, however, in Central Asia and in China where it is found in the Han and Tang periods. The Sarmatians also used it in the first century BC-AD. I have not yet investigated the earliest occurrence in India but I expect it reached India from the Sarmatians very likely via the great track route of north-west India through the Hindukush.[75]

Lohuizen-de Leeuw also holds similar views on the appearance of stirrup in India.

An object which was certainly introduced by the nomadic invaders is the stirrup, the earliest representation of which can be found at Bhaja, where it occurs twice . . . , Mathurā . . . and Sāñchī, where there are four examples in all on the railings of stūpa-II. . . . It does not, however, occur at Bhārhut which probably implies that it begain to be used in India only in the first century BC, when the foreign invasions had started. Being a piece of equestrian equipment, it seems quite reasonable to assume that the stirrup was brought along by the nomads entering the subcontinent around this time.[76]

A Kuṣāṇa seal portraying an equestrian depicts a look like foot support, something like a stirrup on his saddle.[77]

Moti Chandra after analysing the art evidence on stirrup says that

as far as my knowledge goes there is no representation of the stirrup in the bas-reliefs of Bhārhut and Sāñcī. However, a kind of stirrup made by looping rope appears in the lowest beam of a *toraṇa* (archway) in the railing round a *stūpa* which was recovered at Kankalitila, Mathurā. There is, however, no sign of iron stirrup as we find in Mughal paintings. The sculptural evidence, therefore, proves that such kind of footrest was known in India in the first century BC, but before that it was unknown. We can, therefore, put a suggestion that probably it was an innovation introduced by the Śakas in the first century BC.[77]

Herman Goetz while subscribing to the theory of foreign origin of stirrup finds a different source of its introduction.

As far as I remember the stirrups are clearly connected with the problem of heavily armed cavalry. A rider in a heavy armour was not so easily able to maintain his seat on horseback and, when slipping more helpless, because the weight of the armour would drag him down as soon as he lost his balance. Stirrups were thus a necessity. Now heavily armed cavalry was used especially by the Parthians and Sassanians. Thus the introduction of stirrups in India must coincide with their rule over northwestern India.[79]

An early evidence of stirrup in India is met in the art of Sāñcī.[80] According to Marshall this is the earliest example by some five centuries of the use of stirrups in any part of the world.[81] On the other hand, a Mathurā sculpture of first century BC represents a woman putting her legs in stirrup. According to Coomaraswamy this use of stirrup in India was the earliest in the world.[82]

The literary evidence also suggests the foreign origin theory of the stirrup. According to P.K. Gode 'The words *padādhāra* and *ārohiṇī* used for stirrup are no Sanskrit words suggesting that the contrivance was adopted by the Indians from foreigners'.[83] In the *Harṣacarita* the term *pādafalikā* has been used for stirrup.[84] Surprisingly, in the art of Ajantā no stirrups are represented.

The early stirrups met at Sāñcī and other sites, were, however, just loose rope loops. The real metal stirrup seems to have come into vogue some time after ninth century AD, but much before the Turkish horseman made his appearance on the Indian battlefield.[85] A true replica of stirrup in India is met in a sculpture from Amarakaṇṭaka.[86]

In the context of stirrup the following extract from *Encyclopaedia Britannica* may be found informative.

> The first stirrups appeared as big toe stirrups in India in the (last) 2nd century BC. These were diffused widely in the warm regions, where horsemen were bare-foot, from Timor and southern Philippines on the east to Ethiopia on the west. The wave of Indian culture that took Buddhism to China likewise carried the idea of stirrup which the booted Chinese, in their chillier climate, expanded into foot stirrup by the 5th century AD. The foot stirrup reached Korea in the 5th century and Japan and some of the central Asian countries in 6th century. In AD 694 Muslim armies in northern Persia received the stirrup from Turkistan. Before the support of the stirrup supplemented that of pommel and cantle, a mounted warrior could thrust his spear only with the strength of his own arm. With stirrups he could lay the spear at rest under upper arm while his hand guided the blow that was now delivered by the force of his charging horse. The increase of violence was immense. Since it made possible mounted shock combat, the stirrup is the most significant invention in the history of warfare prior to the gun powder.[87]

BRIDLE (*RAŚMI*)

The domestication of horse implies the use of some kind of bridle to control the animal. In the Vedic literature the word *raśmi* and *rasana* signify the reins fastened to the bit in the horse's mouth.[88] In fourth century BC the Indians knew bit but no curb bit, and they directed the horse by a spike outside, that is behind the jaw. To quote Indica,

It is a practice with them (Indians) to control their horse with bit and bridle, and to make them move at a measured pace and in a straight course. They neither, however, gall their tongue by the use of spiked muzzles nor torture the roof of their mouth.[89]

Arrian explaining it in greater detail says that

nor do they (Indians) curb them (horses) with bits like the bits in use among the Greeks or the Kelts, but (they) fit on round the extremity of the horse's mouth a circular piece of stitched raw ox-hide studded with pricks of iron or brass pointing inwards, but not very sharp: if a man is rich he used pricks made of ivory. Within horse's mouth is put an iron prong like a skewer, to which the reins are attached. When the rider, then, pulls the reins, the prong controls the horse and pricks which are attached to their prong goad the mouth, so that it cannot but obey the reins.[90]

In the *Mahābhārata* there is no reference to the bit.[91]

Fergusson doubts the presence of bit in the Sāñcī sculptures stating that sculptures still leave it uncertain whether the horse was controlled by a bit in his month or by pressure on front of his face above his nostrils.[92] But P.C. Chakravarty states that

a closer examination of the Sāñcī sculptures will reveal the presence of both bitted and unbitted horses. The former are specially noticeable in the South and West *toraṇas*, the latter in the North. Where bits are used, the horses have but two bands in their head-stall. But when the spike (behind the jaw) is intended, the head-stall has three bands, one passing over the nostrils, another beneath and a third above the eyes.[93]

In this connection it is remarkable that snuffle bits have been discovered at Taxilā. These are joined in the middle with cheek rings made in one piece with each section of the bar; the cheek bars of bone and horn are also noticed. The cheek bars of the horse bridle are either 'S' shaped with two holes for rein strap or having slight curves.[94] In the art of Ajantā the horses are represented with bits and without bits both.[95]

There is an interesting reference to thorny bit called *Kharkhalīna* in the *Harṣacarita*.[96] It is believed that the term *Khalīna* was borrowed in Sanskrit from Greek language.[97] If this is true then the thorny bit came into vogue in India as a result of Greek influence some time before the beginning of the Christian era.

SADDLE (*PĪṬHAKA*)

The Indian cavalry was not equipped with saddle in fourth century BC.[98] However, some kind of covering for the horse called *pīṭhaka*, *paristoma*, *rāṅkava*, etc., was known to the Epic warrior. It seems to have consisted of only blankets (*kambala*).[99] Perhaps, a proper saddle became necessary when cavalry gained in importance as a result of foreign invasions around the beginning of the Christian era. This seems to explain the appearance of saddle in the art of Sāñcī and Bhārhut.[100] *Aśvamedha* type coins of Kumāragupta furnish the best specimen of saddle in ancient India.[101] Some horses are also represented with saddle in the Ajantā art.[102] Perhaps, the use of proper saddle was restricted to aristocracy as people in general could not afford it.[103]

SWORD (*ASI*)

The authors of Indus Valley civilization did not use a sword.[104] In the Vedas *asi* usually denotes the sacrificial knife, but occasionally it might have been used as weapon.[105] As an effective weapon it came into greater vogue during the Epic times.[106] Indians had started exporting swords to West Asian countries as early as the fifth century BC, and two Indian swords were reportedly seen by Ktesias in the court of an Achaemenid emperor.[107]

In fourth century BC the Greeks had seen Indian soldiers wielding a heavy sword. According to Arrian 'all (soldiers) bear a sword, which is broad in the blade, but not longer than three cubits; and this, when they engage in close fight (which they do with reluctance) they wield with both hands, to fetch down a lustier blow'.[108]

Some Indian adversaries of Alexander also used poisoned swords. According to Curtius in one case Alexander won a convincing victory against the barbarians.

> But this victory did not end so happily as at first sight it promised to do, for the barbarians had used poisoned swords, and the wounded soon after died; while the surgeons were at a loss to discover why a

slight wound should be incurable, and followed by so violent a death. . . . Ptolemy was wounded on the left shoulder, slightly indeed, but yet dangerously on account of the poison, and his case caused the king especial anxiety.[109]

The earliest representation of sword in Indian sculptures is met at Bhārhut, and it is dated around first century BC. It is being carried by a soldier sculptured on the gateway. The weapon is shown scabbarded and suspended on the left side by a strap. The blade is invisible in the scabbard but appears to be very broad, probably about 4 inches and about 2.5 feet long. It is straight and seems to be double-edged since there is nothing on the hilt to indicate that it is not reversible. The scabbard is formed as a simple sheath, probably of leather. A scabbarded sword exactly similar to that worn by the Bhārhut soldier, save some variation in the hilt, is also worn by a soldier represented in a Sāñcī gateway.[110] This was perhaps the same type as used by Indians in fourth century BC.

The *Arthaśāstra* refers to three types of sword, viz., *nistriṁśa* (with curved point), *asiyaṣṭi* (rod-shaped) and *maṇḍalāgra* (with rounded point).[111] This suggests the growing popularity of the weapon. Meanwhile, the Śaka-Kuṣāṇa invaders introduced some new types. On the coins of Scythian kings both straight and curved swords are represented. The Kuṣāṇas introduced a new type of sword, which was broad in shape, heavy in weight and long in measurement.[112]

It appears that the long and broad sword of the Kuṣāṇas did not last long in India. The *Bṛhatsaṁhitā*[113] and the *Agni Purāṇa*[114] consider the length of a good sword as 50 *aṅgulas,* of a medium type between 25 and 50 *aṅgulas* and of an inferior type as 25 *aṅgulas.* Among the swords represented in the art of Ajantā no Kuṣāṇa type of sword is met.[115] In ancient India the territories of Vaṅga, Surpāraka, Videha, Aṅga Ṛṣika, etc., were famous for producing fine steel for making swords.[116]

Vātsya, a writer of antiquity, is said to have compiled a treatise on swords made from different metals. Śārṅgadhara, another author, is credited to have compiled two works called *Lauhārṇava* and *Lauhapradīpa.* It is said that various types of weapons made of iron and steel had been described in detail in these works. These works are not traceable now and in later works only references to them are available.[117]

Hilt was an integral part of the sword. It could be made of the horn of buffalo or rhinoceros, the tusk of an elephant, wood or bamboo root.[118] With the passage of time it became a fashion to decorate the hilt with carvings, etc.

SHEATH (*KOŚA*)

The excavations at Sinauli, Baghpat have yielded the earliest evidence of a sheath in India. It is made of copper for a short antene sword with midrib and is dated in second millennium BC.[119] In the later Vedic age the sword was carried in a sheath (*vavrī*) to which a belt (*vāla*) was attached.[120] In the *Vājasaneyī Saṁhitā* a female scabbard maker (*kośakārin*) is referred to.[121] During the Epic times it was made of the skin of cow, tiger or goat.[122] Rosenfield has suggested that scabbard slide originated among the nomads of Central Asia and was carried in all directions by Yueh-chi.[123] If true, the Kuṣāṇas may have introduced a new type of sheath in India. Swordman type coins of Kumāragupta seem to represent this type.[124] Before the beginning of Christian era the sword was carried hanging down from the shoulder with the help of a belt,[125] because it was heavy in weight. In the Kuṣāṇa period a heavy sword was carried on the left side, tied to a waist-belt.[126]

Indians had attained excellence in the production of swords before the invasion of Alexander. The Greeks were greatly impressed by the big Indian sword.[127] In the *Mahābhārata* the kingdoms of Niṣāda and Aparānta are admired as the producers of quality swords.[128] The *Agni Purāṇa* is very discerning when it says that the swords manufactured in Khaṭī and Khaṭṭara country are worthy of being seen. Those of the region called Ṛṣika were noted for their cutting edge, those of Surpāraka for their strength, those of Aṅga for their sharpness, and those of Vaṅga for their sharpness and capability to cut.[129] With the popularity of sword as an effective weapon various methods of wielding it also came into vogue and in the *Agni Purāṇa* thirty-two such methods are mentioned.[130]

SPEAR (*ŚŪLA*)

The spear, known both to Harappans[131] and Vedic Āryans[132] was widely used by the Epic soldiers.[133] In fourth century BC Greeks had seen Indians fighting with spears.[134] In the *Arthaśāstra* many weapons with a piercing point, such as *śakti, prāsa, kunta, hāṭaka, bhiṇḍipāla, śūla, tomara, varāhakarṇa, karpaṇa, kaṇaya, trāsika*, etc., have been included in this category.[135]

Spear gained in popularity around the beginning of the Christian era and it was widely patronised by the Indo-Greeks and the Śaka-Kuṣāṇas.[136] In this connection it is notable that a heavy spear type discovered at Taxilā is stated to be a foreign type, which was introduced in India either by the Bactrian Greeks or by the Śakas or the Parthians.[137] According to Rosenfield 'a giant spear as a war implement was, however, a prominent part of the armament and symbolism of the Indo-Śakas. This in itself involves basic issues of military tactics and larger cultural orientation'.[138] It gained further popularity during the Gupta age.[139] The *Agni Purāṇa* mentions six functions of *śūla* as *asfoṭa, kṣedana, bheda, trāṣana, āndolita* and *āghāta.*[140]

MACE (*GADĀ*)

The antiquity of mace is traceable to proto-historic times.[141] It was used in the Epic times and warriors like Balarāma, Bhīma, Duryodhana and Śalya excelled in its use. In the *Arthaśāstra*, the terms *mausala, yaṣṭi* and *gadā* have been used for the mace.[142]

In fourth century BC Indian soldiers fought with mace and Alexander is said to have suffered a blow of mace on his neck while fighting the army of Malloi.[143] A real representation of mace is met in the Kaniṣka statue at Mathurā Museum. It is also represented in the art of Sāñcī.[144] In the *Mahābhārata* four types of manoeuvres, viz., *prakṣepa, vikṣepa, parikṣepa* and *abhikṣepa* related to the use of mace are mentioned.[145] In another context 20 such manoeuvres are referred to.[146] The *Agni Purāṇa* refers to 12 manoeuvres and various methods related to the use of mace.[147]

NOOSE (*PĀŚA*)

The *Pāśa* as a weapon was known to Vedic Āryans. Though in the *Ṛgveda* it is occasionally associated with gods like Indra, Agni, Mitra, Rudra, etc., it was mainly a weapon of Varuṇa.[148] *Pāśa* was a rope like device used to tie or bind the enemy.[149] In the *Atharvaveda* it is described as made of seven or three strands.[150] Various types of nooses such is *jyā-pāśa,*[151] *kavaca-pāśa,*[152] *apvā-pāśa,*[153] *varuṇa-pāśa,*[154] etc., were known. The *Mahābhārata* says that *pāśa* was hurled at the enemy with raised hand[155] with the objective of capturing him or rendering him immobile.[156]

The *Agni Purāṇa* describes the weapon in some detail.

> A noose should be ten cubits long, round, and such as to be held in hand. The thread of the noose should be made either of cotton or *munja* (grass), tendon, *arka* (plant) or hide. It can be made of any other strong material well twined with thirty pieces. A wise man should make the noose well rounded. . . . After having made the noose into a loop it should be whirled round the head and thrown quickly on a person covered by armour and quiver. One that is well trained should be employed after having made him proficient to use the noose on the horsemen galloping, capering, and running away.[157]

The noose could be used in eleven ways to achieve the objective.[158]

In this context it may be mentioned that the use of noose as a weapon of war was not confined to Indians. It was known to Scythians, Sarmatians, Sargatians, Parthians, Sassanians, etc. It was particularly popular with the Hūṇas, 'while the enemy are guarding against wounds from the sword-thrusts, the Huns throw strips of cloth plaited into nooses over their opponents and so entangle them that they fetter their limbs and take from them the power of riding or walking'.[159]

BATTLE-AXE (*PARAŚU*)

The antiquity of *paraśu* is traceable to palaeolithic times. In the *Ṛgveda* it is mentioned as a weapon of war wielded by Maruts, the divine warriors.[160] In a particular context soldiers armed with broad-axes (*pṛthu parśavāḥ*) are described as proceeding to battle.[161] Pāṇini has described a particular tribe as Paraśugaṇa suggesting that this particular tribe used battle-axe as a weapon.[162] It was an important weapon in the Epic times and was variously called *paraśu*, *kuṭhāra*, *kuliśa* and *paraśvadha*.[163] It was a favourite weapon of Paraśurāma, a saint and warrior.

The *Arthaśāstra* includes battle-axe in the list of weapons, but it makes a distinction between *paraśu* and *kuṭhāra*.[164] It was particularly popular with the infantry.[165] The *Agni Purāṇa* enumerates six uses of battle-axe, viz., *karāla*, *avaghāta*, *daṁsopapluta*, *kṣiptahasta*, *sthita* and *śūnya*[166] but the connotation of these terms is incomprehensible.

Battle-axe occupied a place of honour among the weapons in ancient India as is evident from the fact that it is represented on the coins of many rulers. Samudragupta in particular issued a series of coins representing the weapon on the obverse.[167] It is also represented in the art of Sāñcī.[168]

THUNDERBOLT (*VAJRA*)

The *vajra* was considered a very powerful weapon by the Āryans. There are more than one hundred and fifty references to it in the *Ṛgveda* alone. It is particularly mentioned in relation to Indra, the commander-in-chief of the Āryans. It was generally made of *ayas* (copper or iron)[169] and occasionally of *hiraṇya* (gold)[170] and bone.[171] In the Vedas various types of *vajra* such as *asramukhī*,[172] *dhūmākṣī*,[173] *dhūmaśikhā*,[174] *agnijihvā*,[175] and *ayomukha*[176] are mentioned.

In the Vedic age *vajra* was made in various shapes and sizes. Indra is reported to have used four-cornered *vajra* during the battle of Paruṣṇi River,[177] but while fighting against the Asuras he wielded a round-shaped *vajra* (*cakrākāra vajra*).[178] In the *Ṛgveda* there is also a reference to arrow-shaped *vajra.*[179] In Brāhmaṇic literature, particularly the *Śatapatha Brāhmaṇa*, *vajras* of various shapes are mentioned.[180] In the *Agni Purāṇa* four functions of *vajra* are mentioned as *antya, madhya, parāvṛtta* and *nideśānta.*[181]

It seems that this Vedic weapon gradually faded out and was replaced by some more effective weapon like *śūla* or *triśūla.*

MACHINES (*YANTRAS*)

The earliest evidence about the use of some kind of machines in ancient India is met in Indus Valley Civilization. In the excavations at Mohenjo-daro a large number of earthen balls have been found near the ramparts of the fort and these were perhaps hurled by the defenders on the attackers. These balls weighing 150 to 300 grams could have been hurled with the help of some contrivance made of bamboo and ropes or a sling.[182]

The term *yantra* is variously used in the epics and it could be explained as a contrivance of almost any kind. 'It is a restrainer or protector, and serves as armour or holder of a fastening, as the rope of the holder of a banner; it is even a drumstick; . . . it is part of the trappings of a war car, the bands of the chariot.' It is used to sail a boat with and for hoisting heavy things with.[183] But generally speaking the *yantra* is a defence in a fort over the gates of towns[184] and could be equated with modern artillery. In the *Rāmāyaṇa* it is said that *yantras* were used to shoot arrows and stones to prevent the enemy from effecting a break through at the gate.[185] In the *Agni Purāṇa*, the functions of a *yantra* are described as *trāṣaṇa*, *rakṣaṇa*, *ghāta*, *baloddharaṇa*, *āyata*, *kṣepaṇa*.[186]

The *yantras* as weapons of defence are described in some detail in the *Arthaśāstra*.[187] It classifies *yantras* into two categories—the immobile (*sthita*) and mobile (*cala*). The immobile category comprised the following machines of war: *sarvatobhadra*, *jāmadagnya*, *bahumukha*, *viśvāsaghātin*, *saṁghāti*, *yānaka*, *parjanyaka*, *bāhū*, *ūrdhvabāhu* and *ardhabāhu*. *Sarvatobhadra* was of the size of a cart wheel with a sharp rim and was capable of discharging stones or arrows in all directions, when turned around. *Jāmadagnya* could discharge big arrows through a hole in the centre. *Bahumukha* was a tower on the top of the fort provided with a leather cover. *Viśvāsaghātin* was a beam outside the city wall placed crosswise, to be released on the unsuspecting enemy, while approaching the city. *Saṁghāti* was a long pole used to set fire to turrets (*aṭṭālaka*). *Yānaka* was a pole or rod carried on wheels for discharge against the enemies. *Parjanyaka* was a machine by which two 25-cubit high pillars, facing each other, were released to crush the enemy. By *ūrdhvabāhu* a 50-cubit high single pillar and by *ardhabāhu* a 12-cubit high pillar was released.[188]

Among the mobile machines the *Arthaśāstra* includes the following: *pāñcālika*, *devadaṇḍa*, *sūkarikā*, *mausalayaṣṭi*, *hastivāraka*, *tālavṛnta*, *mudgara*, *gadā*, *spṛktalā*, *āsphāṭima*, *utpāṭima*, *uddhāṭima*, *śataghnī*, *triśūla* and *cakra*.[189] *Pāñcālikā* was a wooden plank thickly studded with iron nails, placed in the moat to obstruct the enemy advance. *Devadaṇḍa* was a big beam, placed on the fort wall for hurling down. *Sūkarikā* was a leather bag stuffed with cotton for protecting turrets from stone hits, etc. *Mausalayaṣṭi* was a pike made of *khadira* wood. *Hastivāraka* was a bar for striking down elephants. *Tālavṛnta* was a machine which produced strong wind and raised dust. *Mudgara* and *gadā* were hurled with the help of machines. *Spṛktalā* was a mace with sharp nails. *Asphāṭima* was a sort of catapult with four leather covered pillars. *Utpāṭima* was a kind of wrench for pulling down pillars. *Uddhāṭima* was a *mudgara*-shaped machine.

Śataghnī was a big pillar studded with nails, intended to be hurled down.[190] The evidence of *Mahābhārata*, however, suggests that *śataghnī* was discharged with force by hands, moved on wheels and had round balls or stones in it.[191] Literally meaning killer of hundred people, *śataghnī* is frequently mentioned in the *Rāmāyaṇa* and the *Mahābhārata* in relation to the defence of forts. The gates of the fort of Laṅkā were defended by hundreds of iron *śataghnīs*.[192] According to Kane it looks probable that in *śataghnīs* resinous powder was used in some cylindrical contrivance (or rockets) mounted on wheels to hurl stones.[193] But the *Rāmāyaṇa* describes it as a weapon, which was manipulated with the help of ropes.[194] Occasionally, soldiers carried a mini *śataghnī* to battlefield for use like any other weapon.[195]

In the *Mahābhārata* besides the widely mentioned *śataghnī* some other machines are also referred to. While referring to the war preparations of the Kaurava army the following machines have been enumerated alongside some weapons and equipment:[196]

1. *Parichada:*	A hidden machine
2. *Kacagrahavikṣepa:*	A machine to hold the enemy by hair and hurl him away
3. *Tailaguḍavālūka:*	A machine which hurled boiling oil, jaggery and hot sand on enemy.
4. *Āśīviṣaghaṭa:*	Round pitcher full of poison, to be hurled on the enemy.
5. *Sarjarasapāṅsava:*	Vessels full of imflammable material.
6. *Ayogudajalopata:*	Liquid waste jaggery to be hurled on enemy
7. *Ghaṇṭaphalaka*	
8. *Śālabhiṇḍipāla*	
9. *Madhūcchiṣṭamudgara*	: The meaning and use not known.
10. *Kāṇḍadaṇḍaka*	
11. *Śūrpapiṭaka*	

Some more defensive *yantras* are mentioned in the context of the battle of Dvārakā. These include *huḍā*, *cakra*, *upaśalyapratolikā*, *cakragrahaṇī*, *ulkātatāvapothikā*, *aśmaguḍakā*, *guḍaśṛṅgikā*.[197] The meaning and application of these devices is not known for certain, but all were intended to prevent the enemy engress into the fort or the down.

According to Basham

> Indians possessed the ancient world's equipment of artillery-balistas (not known before Mauryan times), battering rams and other siege engines. The inspiration for the wonderful weapons of the poets may have come from the incendiary missiles, fireballs, fire-arrows and the like, which were a special feature of Indian military equipment, though disapproved of as unfair by the *Smṛti* writers. It gives brief formulae for the composition of inflammable material, which are clear enough to show that this was not gunpowder.[198]

The *yantras* played an important part in Indian warfare is evident from the epics[199] and this earned them the status of a separate arm in the sixfold division of the army.[200]

Occasionally, new types of weapons were devised keeping in view the nature of impending war. King Ajātaśatru of Magadha, who ruled in fifth century BC, got some new types of weapons manufactured before attacking Vaiśālī, the capital of Vrijjis. These included *mahāśailakaṇṭaka* and *rathamauśala*. The former was a massive catapult to hurl rock missiles at the fort and latter a chariot provided with heavy rollers which could mow down the enemy when rushed into his formations.

Some means, other than weapons, were also adopted to scare away or beat back the enemy. In the *Atharvaveda* there are many hymns which refer to charms (*mohana*) or stupefying tactics, which could bewilder the enemy.[201] Perhaps, some kind of chemical or mixture was burnt in the fire, the smell of which stupefied the enemy as in some hymns Agni is clearly mentioned as a medium of such charms.[202] Later, in the *Agni Purāṇa* it is advised that incense should be burnt to stupefy the enemy.[203] These could be considered as the precursors of modern poisonous gases, occasionally used in war. In the *Arthaśāstra* there are references to many kinds of mixtures and the methods of preparing them. These mixtures when burnt produced a smoke which could blind or stupefy the enemy.[204] Ancient Indians also believed in the efficacy of incantations (*mantras*), medicines (*bhiṣaj*) and illusions (*māyā*), as weapons of both destruction and protection.[205]

SHIELD (*CARMAN*)

Shield was an important weapon of defence for swordsmen. In fourth century BC an Indian soldier carried a buckler of undressed ox-hide in his left hand, which was not as broad as the soldier who carried it, but was about as long. Bucklers used by cavalry were somewhat shorter than those of the infantry.[206] In the *Mahābhārata* the shields made of the ox-hide[207] and tiger-skin[208] are frequently mentioned. *Saravara*[209] and *phalaka*[210] were the other two shield types known to epic India. These were generally decorated with the symbols of moon and stars.

The *Arthaśāstra* mentions as many as eight shield types, viz., *carman, hastikarṇa, tālamūla, dhamanikā, kapāṭa, kiṭikā, apratihata* and *balāhakānta.*[211] *Carman* was made of skin. *Hastikarṇa* is said to have been like a board but it could more appropriately be explained as a shield type which was shaped like the ear of an elephant. Such types are actually represented in the art of Sāñcī. *Tālamūla* was perhaps made of the roots of the *tāla* tree. *Kapāṭa* was door-shaped and *kiṭikā* was made of cane and leather. *Apratihata* was a strong shield which could even ward off elephants. *Balāhakānta* was like *apratihata* but was provided with iron stripes at the ends.[212]

Some early representations of shield are met in the art of Sāñcī. These are rectangular with a rounded top, like those of ancient Egypt, and decorated with a double cross. Cavalry shields are small and bell-shaped, with a broad rounded base. About the material used in making them nothing can be said with certainty but wood faced with leather seems to be the most likely construction. These types continued to be in use for about another three hundred years[213] and were often embossed with geometrical patterns and moon and star symbols.[214] Some of the shield types suggest foreign connection and these may have been introduced by Śaka-Kuṣāṇas. This could be said with greater certainty about the round shields represented in the Gandhāra art dated around second century AD.

A.L. Srivastava in his study on Sāñcī refers to four kinds of shield.

> The first is oblong with a rounded top. It is met in both large and small size. The second variety is triangular in shape. It also had a rounded top. The third variety is round in shape like a basket and the fourth was rectangular with three projections at the top. The large-sized shields of

the first variety are illustrated in the war scene on the southern gateway. . . . Small-sized shields of the same variety and these of the second are found in a scene representing an army on the march. The third variety is visible in the scene of the fleeing army of the demons and the fourth in some decorative panels.[215]

Codrington has classified the shields represented in Ajantā art in three types—parrying, round and curved oblong. The first was made of metal, the second of hide and the third of black and white bamboo basket work.[216] It seems that after the beginning of the Christian era smaller shields became more common because of the mounting popularity of cavalry arm in the wake of foreign invasions.

In the *Harṣacarita* there is an interesting reference to *kārdaraṅga* shields of various colours carried by the chieftains of Harṣa's army.[217] Incidentally, such shields were also presented to King Harṣa by the ruler of Assam in a large quantity.[218] *Kārdaraṅga* is stated to be an island kingdom in South-East Asia and Indians perhaps imported some quality shields from this island.[219]

ARMOUR (*KAVACA*)

The wide use of the term *varman* in the *Ṛgveda* suggests that body armour was known to Indians in the Vedic age. In this context the following references are notable:

1. Varuṇa, wearing golden mail, hath clad him in a shining robe (1.25.13).
2. (Agni) like well sewn armour thou guardest on every side (1.31.15).
3. A warrior's look is like a thunderous rain-cloud's, when armed with mail, he seeks the lap of battle. Be thou victorious with unwounded body: so let the thickness (strength) of thy mail protect thee (6.75.1).[220]

The *Vedic Index* explains that '*Varman* denotes "body armour", "coat of mail", "corselet", in the *Ṛgveda* and later. Of what material it was made is uncertain; there are references to sewing (*syūta*) which may be reckoned in favour of the use of linen corselets. . . .'[221] A *mantra* in the *Yajurveda* also denotes this: 'Homage to him (Rudra) who wears a helmet (*vilmin*) and to him who bears a cuirass (*kavacin*), salutation to him who wears mail and defensive armour (*varmin*).'[222]

It also refers to hundred royal princes clad in armour.[223] The word *kavaca* came in vogue for corselet in the later Vedic period.[224]

In fourth century BC Porus went to fight Alexander clad in a body-armour which was shot-proof and remarkable for its strength and the closeness with which it fitted, his person. In the battle he was wounded in the right shoulder, which was unprotected by mail.[225] The armour was ornamented with gold and silver and looked majestic.[226] It seems that the use of armour was then restricted to rulers and nobles as the soldiers are not reported to have donned it.

The repeated mention of *kavaca* and *varman* in the *Mahābhārata* attests to their importance in Indian warfare. Before joining a battle soldiers necessarily dressed in *kavaca*[227] made of iron, copper, brass, silver, gold, wood or hide.[228] When made of a metal other than gold it was gilded with gold.[229] *Jāla*, a kind of netted armour was also in vogue.[230] Armour was generally decorated with symbols of sun, moon and stars.[231] But *kavaca* could not provide complete protection as the Yavana warriors, who were known for their strong iron and brass breast plates were routed when arrows pierced their armour.[232] The *Amarakośa* refers to seven kinds of armour.[233]

Giving a detailed description of armour (*varman*) the *Arthaśāstra* refers to the following types: *loha-jālikā, paṭṭa, kavaca, sūtrakaṅkaṭa, carmakhūra, kañcuka, varavāṇa, paṭṭa* and *nāgodarikā*.[234] Commentators have explained *lohajāla* as the helmet for the head, *jālikā* as headless armour, *paṭṭa* as armour, *kavaca* as armour with many flaps or folds, *sūtrakaṅkaṭa* as made of cotton cloth with stuffings inside and *carmakhūra* as the entire skin with hooves, horns, etc. *Kūrpāsa* was half-sleeved. *Kañcuka* came down to the knees. *Varavāṇa* ended at the ankles and *paṭṭa* was a sleeveless coat of cotton. *Nāgodarikā* was a thigh-guard.[235] The *Arthaśāstra*, further states that armour was made either of metal rings or metal plates, fabrics and skins.[236] In course of time armour made of cotton and tree-barks also came into vogue.[237]

Whatever the material and shape of the armour it was considered a vital component of soldier's costume even in Vedic times. Hymns were composed in its honour. 'The warrior's look is like a thunderous rain-cloud's, when, armed with mail, he seeks the lap of battle. Be thou victorious with unwounded body: so let the thickness of thy mail protect thee.'[238] The *Agni Purāṇa*, though a later work, also conveys similar sentiment 'O armour: you cause (the enemy forces) to feel ashamed in battle. I will have fame in the army today. O sinless one, protect me, worthy of being protected by you! Obeisance to you.'[239]

FOREIGN IMPACT

It is widely believed that the use of armour in India was the result of foreign impact. According to Robinson 'as far as we can judge the Indians were without defence armour except for the shield which for centuries is the only protection shown in Hindu sculptures'.[240] Marshall says that the helmets and plate armour for men and horses, and elephants were certainly foreign importations, as such defensive armour was quite unknown in early India.[241] In his study Basham has also opined that 'the warriors depicted in early sculpture are only lightly defended with armour, but the use of the armour of metal or leather developed as a result of the influx of invaders from the North-West and in the middle ages coats of mail became more usual, together with armour for horses and elephants'.[242] Surprisingly, the use of armour in Indian art is generally met in association with the soldiers, who look certainly un-Indian.

Sarmatians, a people inhabiting Central Asia, were famous for their heavy armour. 'They were clad in armour made either of small iron plates sewn on leather, or of thick hide, and the horses were protected in the same manner; helmets too were made mostly of hide. At first this armour was worn only by the chiefs.'[243] The Śakas and Kuṣāṇas, who had lived in their proximity earlier, perhaps learnt the use of heavy armour from them. It is, therefore, likely that the heavy armour of the type discovered by archaeologists from Taxilā was introduced in India by them. In this context, it is remarkable that in the *Mahābhārata*, the armour is particularly related to the foreigners like Śakas and Kambojas.[244]

In contrast, there is ample evidence to negate the theory of foreign origin. The repeated references to *kavaca* and *varman* in relation to soldiers as well as war horses and elephants both in the *Rāmāyaṇa*, and the *Mahābhārata* suggest that Indians were familiar with these protective devices earlier to foreign invasions.[245] In the *Arthaśāstra* it is stated that during a silent attack in the night elephants were provided with leather cases on their feet, so that no noise was created.[246] In fact, the antiquity of armour in India is traceable to Vedic times.

In the epic age a helmet (*śirastrāṇa*), made of metal, was worn by the soldiers to protect their head.[247] The *Arthaśāstra* refers to *śirastrāṇa* as an *āvaraṇa* or covering like *kūrpāsa, kaṇṭhatrāṇa,* etc.[248] In the Gupta coins the rulers are widely represented with a helmet.[249] The neck-guard (*kaṇṭhatrāṇa*),[250] hand-guard (*talatraih*)[251] and finger-guard (*aṅgulitraiḥ*)[252] were also worn as protective measures. The *Amara-kośa* refers to three types of *śirastrāṇas.*[253] In view of the above it is difficult to agree with Basham that 'helmets are not often depicted until the middle ages, and it would seem that the Indian soldier relied mainly on the thick fold of his turban to protect his head'.[254]

The *Arthaśāstra* also includes some accoutrements (*upakaraṇas*) in the category of weapons (*āyudhas*). These included objects used in giving training to elephants, chariots and horses, in decorating them, and in equipping them for battle.[255] These objects were maintained in the state armoury like other war machines, weapons, etc.[256]

DIVINE WEAPONS

An interesting aspect of the Indian weapon system is that some sort of divinity has always been attached to them. The *Rāmāyaṇa* says that arrows and other weapons were devised by Jayā and Suprabhā, two daughters of Dakṣa Prajāpati.[257] Elsewhere, the gods are credited to have created the arrow—Agni providing for arrow-head, Soma for socket, Viṣṇu for shaft and Varuṇa for feathers.[258]

In the Vedas, epics and Purāṇas every weapon is associated with one or the other god. *Cakra* was the weapon of Viṣṇu, which was also wielded by Śrīkṛṣṇa. *Śūla* was the weapon of Śiva, who is also known as Śūlapāṇi. Indra was called Vajrapāṇi after his weapon *vajra. Paraśu* was the weapon of Paraśurāma. *Khaḍga* (sword) was born from the sacrificial altar of Brahmā, the creator. The supernatural weapons *brahmāstra, āgneyāstra, nārāyaṇāstra, pāśupatāstra* and *vāyavyāstra* were associated with gods Brahmā, Agni, Viṣṇu, Śiva and Vāyu respectively. *Pāśa* was the weapon of Yama and Varuṇa. *Śakti* was wielded by Goddess Durgā and Kārttikeya. Other supernatural weapons included *varuṇāstra, garuḍāstra, vaiṣṇavāstra, raudrāstra, aindrāstra, ādityāstra, asurāstra,* etc. In short there was no weapon used in Indian warfare which was not related to some god. This also explains for the wide display of weapons in Indian temples.[259]

Indians greatly revered their weapons and even worshipped them as these were generally known as *divyāstras.* Some scholars in their zeal to trace the ancient origin of gun and gun-powder in India have added to the confusion created by this supernatural syndrome. Some even believe in the efficacy of Arjuna's arrow to throw a whole army in delusion and pierce the core of the earth to release a river. But Sankalia rightly holds that weapons like *āgneyāstra* and *vāyavyāstra* were 'imaginary', because 'had the use of *astras* been common we would not have been worsted in any war against a foreign invader. Therefore, it is my considered view that *astras* are mythical.'[260]

This enigma of *divyāstras* perhaps needs a palatable explanation. The *divyāstras* mentioned in the epics include *pāśupatāstra, aindrāstra, sammohanāstra, parjanyāstra, jaladāstra, vaiṣṇavāstra, nārāyaṇāstra, sudarśana cakra, brahamāstra,* etc. Briefly speaking, *pāśupatāstra* could create a situation of deluge in the battlefield. *Aindrāstra* could send the enemy into faintness whereas *sammohanāstra* could send him into delusion. *Prajanyāstra* could pierce the earth to release water. *Jaladāstra* could cause rains whereas *ādityāstra* could stop rains. *Vaiṣṇavāstra* could chase and kill a person after whom it was shot. *Nārāyaṇāstra* could destroy all other weapons and the only safety against it was to cast away own weapon. *Sudarśana cakra* was a lethal weapon which could be retrieved after use. *Brahmāstra* could destroy the whole universe.

The capability of these weapons is highly exaggerated, but the epic poet might have had some basis to say so. It would be a reasonable surmise that Indians in the epic times had visualised the capability of missile weapons such as arrow to create deluge, fire, rain, delusion, etc. In fact, most of these *divya* weapons may have been simply arrows, with incendiary heads.[261] Various allusions to arrows such as *dīpta, mahājvālā, pradīpta, jvalita, agniśikhākara* and *agniśaṅkāśa* in the *Mahābhārata*[262] seem to support this. It is likely that Indians knew of some chemicals which could cause fire or emanate some smell to cause delusion. Further the widely used word *nālikā* for some kind of weapon need not be interpreted as gun. It was perhaps a contrivance used to discharge missiles like stones or rubble against the enemy.

FIRE ARMS (*ĀGNEYĀSTRAS*)

A word may be added here on the use of firearms in ancient India. While describing the method of laying siege of the fort and storming it, Kauṭilya furnishes some clinching evidence on the advances made by Indians in the sphere of fire-power and firearms. The evidence is quoted verbatim:[263]

1. Getting hawks, crows, pheasants, kites, parrots, *sārikās*, owls, and pigeons, with nests in the fort, caught, he should release them in the enemy's fort with fire mixtures (*agniyogayuktān*) tied to the tails.
2. Or, from the camp stationed at a distance (from the fort) he should set fire to the enemy's fort with human fire (*manuṣenāgninā paradurgamādīpayet*).
3. Secret agents serving as guards inside the fort, should place a fire mixture in the tail of monkeys, cats and dogs, and let them loose in stores of reeds, fortifications and houses (*puccheṣ-vāgniyogamādhāya visṛjeyuḥ*).
4. Placing fire in the interior of dried fish or in dried meat, they should have carried it through birds by offering it to crows. (*śuṣkamatsyānamudareṣvagnimādhāya*).

Kauṭilya also describes three recipes of fire-powder, viz., *agni-dhāraṇa*, *agni-yoga* and *viśvāsaghātī*. Different ingredients went to make each one of them. Balls of *sarala*, *devadāru*, 'stinking grass', bedellium, pine-resin, *śāla* resin and lac and the dung of donkeys, camels, goats and sheep are (good) retainers of fire (*agni-dhāraṇa*). The powder of *priyāla*, the soot of *avalguja*, wax and the dung of horses, donkeys, camels and bullocks make a fire mixture which can be thrown (*kṣepyoganiyogaḥ*). The powder of all metals of the colour of fire, or the powder of *kumbhī*, lead or tin, mixed with the flowers of *paribhadraka* and *palāśa*, the soot of *keśa*, oil, wax and pine-resin makes a fire-mixture, one that kills the trusting (*agniyogo viśvā-saghātī*). An arrow smeared with it (and) covered with hemp and the bark of *trapusa*, is a (means of) causing fire.

The destructive potentiality of these fire causing means was immense and was called divine calamity (*daivapīḍanam*). Thus the Indians had made considerable advances in developing some inflammable and mixtures and their use for the purpose of war. The *Arthaśāstra* has not, however, mentioned any *nālikā* or gun-like contrivance to launch fire-causing devices. Men, animals, birds and indeed the arrows were used as fire carriers.

It would thus appear that Indians had perfected a dependable weapon system by fourth century BC. The Macedonians found no deficiency in Indian weapons of the day. In fact they had invented a large variety of weapons for use in different situations of war. Bow, sword, javelin and mace were the principal weapons and these were produced in various shapes and sizes. The defensive weapons meant to protect the forts received special attention. Of these the mobile types could be carried to any part of the fort which was under threat, whereas the immobile types were tactically deployed over the ramparts and gates to foil any scaling or breaching attempt of the enemy.

NOTES

1. B.B. Lal, *The Earliest Civilization of South Asia*, pp. 165-6.
2. Irfan Habib, *The Indus Civilization*, p. 61.
3. Bridget and Raymond Allchin, *The Rise of Civilization in India and Pakistan*, p. 193; also see E.J.H. Mackay, *Early Indus Civilization*, pp. 96-9.
4. *Ṛgveda*, 5.57.2; For details on Vedic weapons see A.C. Das, *Ṛgvedic Culture*, pp. 331-7; S.D. Singh, *Ancient Indian Warfare*, pp. 86-95.
5. G.C. Pandey, *Dimensions of Ancient Indian Social History*, vol. 2, p. 100.
6. श्याम अयस। *Atharvaveda*, 11.3.7.
7. G.C. Pandey, op. cit., p. 100.
8. N.R. Banerjee, *The Iron Age in India*, p. 233; Vibha Tripathi has dealt with the issue in greater detail. See *The Painted Grey Ware: An Iron Age Culture of Northern India*, p. 272.
9. R.S. Sharma, *Material Culture and Social Formations in Ancient India*, p. 58.
10. T.N. Roy, 'The Ushering of Iron Age in Indian Context', *South Asian Archeology*, 1987, pt. 1, p. 580; also see Bridget and Allchin, *The Rise of Civilization in India and Pakistan*, p. 309.
11. D.H. Gordon, *The Pre-historic Background of Indian Culture*, p. 155.
12. V.S. Agrawala, *India as Known to Pāṇini*, p. 420; some scholars hold that the term *ayas* used in the Vedas should be taken as copper or bronze as iron technology developed in later Vedic times.
13. यस्मिन्महास्त्राणि समर्पितानि चित्राणि शुभ्राणि चतुर्विधानि। *MB*, Karṇa, 4.90.
14. मुक्तञ्चैव ह्यमुक्तञ्च मुक्तामुक्तमतः परम्।
मन्त्रमुक्तञ्च चत्वारि धनुर्वेदपदानि वै।।

मुक्तं वाणादि विज्ञेयं खड्गादिकममुक्तकम्।
सोपसंहारमस्त्रं तु मुक्तामुक्तमुदाहृतम्।।
उपसंहाररहितं मन्त्रमुक्तमिहोच्यते। *Nītiprakāśikā*, 2.11-13; a similar classification is given in *Mānasollāsa.*
यंत्रमुक्तायुधाः केचित् केचिन्मुक्तायुधास्तथा।
अमुक्तायुधहस्ताश्च मुक्तायुधकरास्तथा।। *Mānasollāsa*, 2.6.683.
Some scholars consider मुक्तामुक्त as the correct reading.

15. अस्त्राणि पश्याद्य ममोत्तमानि ब्राह्माणि दिव्यान्यथ मानुषाणि। *MB*, Karṇa, 29.26.
16. *Arthaśāstra*, 2.18.
17. Ibid.
18. यन्त्रमुक्तं पाणिमुक्तं मुक्तसंधारितं तथा।
अमुक्तं बाहुयुद्धं च पञ्चधा तत्प्रकीर्तितम्।। *Agni Pu.*, 249.2.
19. *Matsya Pu.*, 215.39.
20. धनुश्चक्रं च कुन्तं च खड्गं च च्छुरिका गदा।
सप्तमं बाहुयुद्धं स्यादेवं युद्धानि सप्तधा।।
आचार्यः सप्तयुद्धः स्याच्चतुर्युद्धस्तु भार्गवः।
द्वाभ्यां चैव भवेद्योध एकेन गणको भवेत्।। *Dhanurveda* (*Śārṅgadhara-paddhati*) 1721-2; for a detailed description of weapons see *Nītiprakāśikā*, Chaps. 2-5.
21. चातुर्विध्यमस्त्रादिभेदात्। *Śiśupālavadha*, 18.11.
22. P.C. Chakravarty, *The Art of War in Ancient India*, p. 151.
23. J. Marshall, *Mohenjo-daro and the Indus Civilization*, p. 499; it is believed that bow and arrow came into vogue in the barbaric age but after the spear. It was perhaps a chance discovery. The Polynesians and Austrasians had no knowledge of this weapon. This proves that man had advanced ahead of the early barbaric stage when he first used the bow.
24. Macdonell and Keith, *Vedic Index*, vol.1, p. 388.
25. *Ṛgveda*, 6.75.2.
26. युद्धशस्त्रास्त्रकुशलो रचनाकुशलो भवेत्।
यजुर्वेदोपवेदोऽयं धनुर्वेदस्तु येन सः।। *Śukranīti*, 4.3.38.
27. *Vedic Index*, vol. I, pp. 388-9.
28. *Ṛgveda*, 10.18.9.
29. Ibid., 6.75.2-3.
30. *MB*, Virāṭa, 38.20, 56.4.
31. तालचापदारवंशाङ्गाणि कार्मुककोदण्डद्रूणाधनूंषि। *AS*, 2.18.8.
32. J.W. M'crindle, *Ancient India*, pp. 220-1; also *The Invasion of India*, p. 210.
33. जानामि ते गाण्डिवं तालमात्रम्। *MB*, Udyoga, 158.25.
34. It did not suit their mode of fighting.

35. J. Marshall, *A Guide to Sāñchī*, pls. 4, 5.
36. *Agni Pu.*, 245.4-5.
37. चतुर्हस्तं धनुः श्रेष्ठं त्रयः सार्धं तु मध्यमम्।
कनीयस्तु त्रयः प्रोक्तं नित्यमेव पदातिनः।। Ibid., 249.37.
38. Ibid., 245.7-11.
39. P.C. Chakravarty, op. cit., p. 154; the *Dhanurveda* associates the horn bow with Viṣṇu and considers it more useful for elephant and horse riders.
प्रायो योग्यं धनुः शार्ङ्गं गजारोहाश्वसादिनाम्।
रथिनां च पदातीनां वांशं चापि प्रकीर्तितम्।। *Dhanurveda*, 1760.
40. J. Otto, Maenchen-Helfen, *The World of the Huns*, p. 223.
41. J. Keegan, *A History of Warfare*, pp. 162-3.
42. Ibid., p. 163.
43. Mcleod quoted by Maenchen-Helfen in *The World of the Huns*, p. 327. For more details on Scythian bow, Sassanian bow and Hunic bow see ibid., pp. 221-32.
44. *Ṛgveda*, 6.75.15-16.
45. *Aitareya Brāhmaṇa*, 1.4.8.
46. वाणाक्षरैरेव परस्परस्य नामोर्जितं चापभृतः शशंसुः। *Raghuvaṁśa*, VII.38.
47. कङ्कहंसशशादीनां मत्स्यादंक्रौञ्चकेकिनाम्।
गृध्राणां कुक्कुटानां च पक्षा एतेषु शोभनाः।। *Dhanurveda*, 1771; *Mahābhārata* also refers to it.
48. *AS*, 2.18.11; also *Agni Pu.*, 245.12-13.
49. E.W. Hopkins, *Social & Military Position of the Ruling Caste*, p. 224.
Various types of arrows mentioned in the *Rāmāyaṇa* include—अंजलिक, अर्धचन्द्र, अर्धनाराच, भल्ल, चन्द्रवक्त्र, धूमकेतुमुख, ग्रहवक्त्र, गृद्धमुख, ईहामृगमुख, इषु, काकमुख, कङ्कमुख, कर्णी, खरमुख, क्षुर, क्षुरप्र, कुक्कुटवक्त्र, मकरानन, नक्षत्रवक्त्र, नालिका, पंचास्य, प्रसन्नाग्र, शल्य, शिलीमुख, सिंहमुख, शृगालवदन, वराहमुख, सूर्यमुख, श्वानमुख, श्येनमुख, सर, सिंहदमस्त्र, सायक, उल्कामुख, शल्य, शिलीमुख, श्वानवक्त्र, वत्सदन्त, विपाट, वाण, व्यादितास्य, व्याध्रमुख, विकर्णी, आशीविषानन, अधोगति, अग्निदीप, आशुग, उल्कामुख, कंकपत्रिन्, नाराच, नागमय। See P.C. Dharma, *Rāmāyaṇa Polity*, pp. 84, 85.
In the *Mahābhārata* the following types are met:
क्षुरप्र, अर्धचन्द्र, वत्सदन्त, विपाट, अंजलिक, वैतस्तिक, सूक्ष्मकर्णी, क्षुद्रक, वराहकर्ण, विकर्ण, तीक्ष्णकर्णी, स्थूलकर्णी
Arrow was the most widely used weapon in the Epic war. It is referred to 1150 times in the Droṇa Parvan, whereas spear the next most important weapon is mentioned only 276 times.

50. लिप्तो। *MB, Droṇa,* 189. 11; Poisoned arrows were used by Indians against the Macedonians in fourth century BC. There is a reference to poisoned arrows in the *Ṛgveda* (6.75.15), *Majjhima Nikāya* also refers to such arrows (2.216).
51. तैलधौता व्यराजन्त। *MB*, Bhīṣma, 92.48; *Agni Pu.*, 245.13.
52. E.B. Cowell, *The Jātaka*, vol. 5, p. 68.
53. शरा: किरातजा: श्रेष्ठा: कांचीपुरसमपिता:।
तेभ्योऽपि ते श्रेष्ठतमा: स्कन्दजन्म सहीभवा:।। *Vis. Dh. Pu.*, 2.16.20-1.
54. J.W. M'crindle, *The Invasion of India*, p. 189.
55. J. Marshall, *Taxilā*, p. 547.
56. G.R. Sharma, *Excavations at Kauśambi*, p. 46.
57. J.W. M'crindle, *Ancient India*, pp. 220-1.
58. रथस्थित: क्रोशमात्रे यानस्यत्यर्जुन: शरान्।
रथे क्रोशमतिक्रान्ते तस्य ते घ्नन्ति शात्रवान्।। *MB*, Drona, 74.9.
59. *Vaśiṣṭha Dhanurveda*, 5-7.
60. इषुधि: सङ्का पृतनाश्च सर्वा: पृष्ठे निनद्धो जयति प्रसूत:। *Yajurveda*, 29.42; also *Rgveda* 10.103.3.
61. *Ṛgveda*, 6.75.5.
62. *MB*, Ādi, 55.37, Udyoga, 59.12; Śalya, 61.9.
63. E.W. Hopkins, op. cit., p. 218. According to *Dhanurveda* an archar was supposed to carry two quivers (*iṣudhi* and *tūṇa*), each containing 60 arrows. In special circumstances even 40 arrows could be carried in each quiver but in the event this number was reduced to 20 after use, replenishment was necessary. In the ease of *nārācas* (iron arrows) 40 or even 30 could suffice in each quiver. G.N. Pant, *Indian Archery*, pp. 202-3; S.D. Singh hold that the two quivers could not have carried more than 20 or 25 arrows. *Ancient India Warfare*, p. 107.
64. *Amarakośa*, 2.8.69; it refers to six names of quiver तूण, उपासंग, तूणीर, निषंग, इषुधि तूणी। *Amarakośa*, 2.8.88.
65. ते स्म लक्ष्याणि विविधुर्बाणैर्नामाङ्कशोभितै:।
विविधैर्लाघवोत्सृष्टै रुपन्तो वाजिभिर्द्रुतम्।। *MB*, Ādi, 124.24.
कृत्वा धनुषि ते मार्गान् रथचर्यासु चासकृत्।
गजपृष्ठेऽश्वपृष्ठे च नियुद्धे च महाबला:।। *MB*, Ādi, 124.27.
66. P.K. Gode, *Studies in Indian Cultural History*, vol. 2, p. 66.
67. J.W. M'crindle, *The Invasion of India*, p. 100.
68. Ibid., p. 101.
69. Ibid., p. 104.
70. Ibid., pp. 111, 116.
71. R.C. Kak, *Ancient Monuments of Kashmir*, pls. 23.3, 28.14.

72. V. Smith, *Catalogue of the Coins in the Indian Museum Calcutta*, p. 43, pl. 9.
73. A.S. Altekar, *The Coinage of the Gupta Empire*, pls. 8.1-5, 10.11-15, 15.14-15.
74. P.C. Chakravarty, op. cit., p. 42.
75. M. Wheeler, Quoted by P.K. Gode, *Studies in Indian Cultural History*, vol. 2, p. 74; Riasanovsky, a well-known Russian historian also associates it with Sarmatians, who ruled over southern Russia from third century BC to third century AD. *A History of Russia*, p. 14.
76. J.E. Van Lohuizen-de Leeuw, 'Foreign Elements in Indian Culture, introduced during the Scythian period with special reference to Mathurā', a paper appearing in *Mathurā: The Cultural Heritage*, ed. D.M. Srinivasan, p. 77.
77. John M. Rosenfield, *The Dynastic Art of the Kushāṇs*, p. 102; also *American Historical Review*, 1960, p. 516.
78. Moti Chandra, op. cit., pp. 74-5.
79. H. Goetz, op. cit., pp. 76-7; the Hūṇas are said to have used leather or wooden stirrups. For details see Maenchen-Helfen, *The World of the Huns*, pp. 206-7.
80. F.C. Maisey, *Sāñchī and its Remains*, pls. 6.2, 9.2, 20.27; also S. Piggot, *Pre-historic India*, p. 268.
81. J. Marshall, *A Guide to Sāñchī*, p. 152, n. 3; also see Bachhofer, *Early Indian Sculpture*, vol. 2, pl. 72; *Ancient India*, no. 35. The Rock cut Caves of Pitalkhora, pl. 55B; A.L. Basham, *The Wonder That was India*, p. 374, fig. 23.
82. *Bullletin of Boston Museum*, 1944, fig. 3.
83. P.K. Gode, *Studies in Indian Cultural History*, vol. 2, p. 72.
84. प्रचलपादफलिका। *Harṣacarita* (Śaṅkara), p. 206.
85. S.D. Singh, *Ancient Indian Warfare*, p. 63.
86. *MASI*, no. 23, 1931, pl. 51B, p. 118.
87. *Encyclopaedia Britannica*, 1975, p. 657.
88. *Vedic Index*, vol. 2, p. 223; S.D. Singh, op. cit., p. 28 fn. 5.
89. M'crindle, *Ancient India*, p. 89.
90. Ibid., p. 221.
91. E.W. Hopkins, op. cit., p. 208.
92. J. Fergusson, *Tree and Serpent Worship*, p. 134.
93. P.C. Chakravarty, *The Art of War in Ancient India*, p. 38.
94. J. Marshall, *Taxilā*, vol. 2, pp. 550-1, vol. 3, pl. 165.96-98.100.
95. Ibid., p. 39; also see *Agni Pu.*, 288.30-3.
96. खणखणायमानस्खलत्खलीनक्षतनिजतुरगमुखक्षिप्तेन क्षतजेनेव। *HC*, p. 18.
97. V.S. Agrawala, *Harṣacarita Eka Sāṁskṛtika Adhyayana*, pp. 21-2.
98. J.W. M'crindle, *Ancient India*, p. 221.

99. E.W. Hopkins, op. cit, p. 209.
100. F.C. Maisey, *Sāñchī and its Remains*, pl. 6, fig. 2; pl 9., fig. 2; pl. 15; fig. 20; also A. Cunningham, *The Stūpa of Bhārhut*, p. 42, pl. 32; for wooden saddle among Eurasian nomads see Maenchen-Helfen's book *The World of the Huns*, pp. 208-9.
101. A.S. Altekar, *The Coinage of the Gupta Empire*, pls.
102. J. Griffiths, *The Paintings in the Buddhist Cave Temples of Ajantā*, pls.
103. E.C. Sachau, *Alberuni's India*, vol. 1, p. 181.
104. J. Marshall, *Mohenjo-daro and the Indus Civilization*, pp. 35, 494-9.
105. *Vedic Index*, vol. I, p. 47.
106. धनु: प्रहरणं श्रेष्ठमिति वाद: पितामह।
मतस्तु मम धर्मज्ञ खङ्ग एव सुसंशित:।। *MB*, Śānti, 160.2.
शरासनधरांश्चैव गदाशक्तिधरांस्तथा।
एक खड्गधरोवीर: समर्थ: प्रतिबाधितुम्।। Ibid., Śānti, 160.4.
107. D.H. Gordon, *The Pre-historic Background of Indian Culture*, p. 155; also see J.W. M'crindle, *The Invasion of India*, p. 252, fn. 1.
108. J.W. M'crindle, *Ancient India as described by Megasthenese and Arrian*, p. 221.
109. J.W. M'crindle, *The Invasion of India*, p. 255.
110. A. Cunningham, *The Stūpa of Bhārhut*, pls. 32.4; also P.S. Rawson, *The Indian Sword*, p. 16.
111. *AS*, 2.18.12.
112. J.M. Rosenfield, *The Dynastic Art of the Kushāņs*, pls. 2.2A; for details on Kuṣāṇa sword see P.S. Rawson, *The Indian Sword*, pp. 17-19.
113. *Bṛhatsaṁhitā*, 50.1.
114. शतार्धमङ्गुलानां च श्रेष्ठं खड्गं प्रकीर्तितम्।
तदर्धं मध्यमं ज्ञेयं ततो हीनं न धारयेत्।। *Agni Pu.*, 245.23.
115. M.K. Dhavalikar, *Ajantā*, pl. 27.
116. लोहं प्रधानं खड्गार्थे प्रशस्तं तद विशेषत:।
कटीकदूरऋषिकं वङ्गे शूर्पारकेषु च।।
विदेहेषु तथाङ्गेषु मध्यमं ग्रामचेदिषु।
सहग्रामेषु नीपेषु तथा कलंजरे पि च।। *Viṣṇudharmottara Pu.*, 2.17.21-3; also *Agni Pu.*, 245.21-2.
117. D.K. Kanjilal, *Vimāna in Ancient India*, p. 53.
118. *AS*, 2.18.12; नागदन्तकृतत्सरु:। *MB*, Sānti, 99.19.
119. I am indented to Shri R.S. Bisht for this information.
120. *Vedic Index*, vol. I, p. 47.
121. S.D. Singh, op. cit., p. 109.

122. E.W. Hopkins, op. cit., p. 230; *Amarakośa* (3.3.221) uses the term *Khaḍgapidhāna* for it.
123. J.M. Rosenfield, op. cit., p. 179.
124. J. Allan, *Catalogue of the Coins of the Gupta Dynasties*, pl. 12; कट्यां बद्ध्वा ततः खड्गं वामपार्श्वविलम्बितम्। *Agni Pu.*, 251.7.
125. A. Cunningham, op. cit., pl. 32.4; F.C. Maisey, *Sāñchī and Its Remains*, pl. 35.26-8.
126. J.M. Rosenfield, op. cit., pl. 2.
127. J.W. M'crindle, *Ancient India*, p. 221.
128. *MB*, Sabhā, 47.24.
129. खटीखट्टरजाता ये दर्शनीयास्तु ते स्मृताः।
कायच्छिदस्त्वार्षिकाः स्युर्दृढाः सुर्पारकोद्भवाः।
तीक्ष्णाश्छेदसहा वङ्गास्तीक्ष्णाः स्युश्चाङ्गदेशजाः।। *Agni Pu.*, 245.21-2.
130. भ्रांत, उद्भ्रांत, आबिद्ध, आप्लुत, विप्लुत, प्लुत, सम्पात, समुदीश, श्येनपात, आकुल, उद्धूत, अवधूत, सव्य, दक्षिण, अनालक्षित, विस्फोट, कराल, इन्द्रमहासखा, विकराल, निपात, विभीषण, भयानक, समग्र, अर्ध, त्रतीयांश, पाद, पादार्ध, वारिज, प्रत्यालीढ, आलीढ, वराह, लुलित। *Agni Pu.*, 252.1-4; also *Nītiprakāśikā*, 3.25-8.
131. J. Marshall, *Mohenjo-daro and the Indus Civilization*, vol. I, pp. 35, 497-8.
132. *Ṛgveda*, 1.37.1, 5.52.6, 8.20.11.
133. शक्तीश्च विविधास्तीक्ष्णाः। *MB*, Ādi. 26.44.
134. J.W. M'crindle, *Ancient India*, p. 221.
135. *AS*, 2.18.7.
136. J.M. Rosenfield, op. cit., pls 40b, 49, 62.
137. J. Marshall, *Taxilā*, p. 546.
138. J.M. Rosenfield, op. cit., p. 55; also see T. Sulimirski, *The Sarmatians*, p. 29.
139. N.K. Dhavalikar, *Ajantā*, pl. 28.
140. *Agni Pu.*, 252.9.
141. J. Marshall, *Mohenjo-daro and the Indus Civilization*, p. 35.
142. *AS*, 2.18.6.
143. J.W. M'crindle, *The Invasion of India*, p. 312.
144. F.C. Maisey, op. cit., pl. 35.
145. *MB*, Ādi, 68.13 (*BE*).
146. *MB*, Śalya, 57.19-22.
147. आहतं विप्र गोमूत्रप्रभूतं कमलासनं।
ततोर्ध्वगात्रं नमितं वामदक्षिणमेव च।।
आवृत्तं च परावृत्तं पादोद्धूतमवप्लुतं।
हंसमर्दं विमर्दं च गदाकर्म प्रकीर्तितम्।। *Agni Pu.*, 252.11-12; also 19-24.
148. *Ṛgveda*, 10.85.24, 6.74.4, 7.65.3.

149. प्र त्वा मुञ्चामि वरुणस्य पाशाद्। *Ṛgveda*, 10.85.24.
150. ये ते पाशा वरुण सप्तसप्त त्रेधा तिष्ठन्ति विषिता रुशन्तः। *Atharvaveda*, 4.16.6.
151. *Atharvaveda*, 11.10.22.
152. Ibid.
153. *Yajurveda*, 17.44.
154. *Ṛgveda*, 1.24.15, 1.25.21, 6.74.4, etc.
155. *MB*, Śalya, 44.103.
156. Ibid.
157. *Agni Pu.*, 251.2-6.
158. परावृत्तमपावृत्तं गृहीतं लधुसंज्ञितं।
ऊर्ध्वक्षिप्तमघःक्षिप्तं सन्धारितविधारितम्।।
श्येनपातं गजपातं ग्राह्यग्राह्यं तथैव च।
एवमेकादश विधा ज्ञेयाः पाशविधारणे।। Ibid., 252.5-6.
159. Ammianus quoted by Maenchen-Helfen in *The World of the Huns*, pp. 239-40.
160. A.C. Das, *Ṛgvedic Culture*, p. 335.
161. *Ṛgveda*, 7.83.1.
162. *Aṣṭādhyāyī*, 5.3.117.
163. E.W. Hopkins, op. cit., p. 235; *Amarakośa*, 2.8.92.
164. *AS*, 2.18.14.
165. S. Beal, *Buddhist Records*, vol. I, p. 73.
166. *Agni Pu.*, 252.12.
167. A.S. Altekar, *The Coinage of the Gupta Empire*, pls.
168. F.C. Maisey, op. cit., pls. 35-7.
169. *Ṛgveda*, 1.52.8; 1.56.3; 8.90.3; 10.48.3, etc.
170. Ibid., 1.85.9, 1.57.2, etc.
171. इन्द्रो दधीचो अस्थिभिः वृत्राण्यप्रतिष्कुतः। *Ṛgveda*, 1.84.13.
172. *Yajurveda*, 10.4.
173. *Atharvaveda*, 11.10.7.
174. Ibid., 11.9.19.
175. Ibid.
176. Ibid., 11.10.3.
177. चतुरश्रिमस्यन्। *Ṛgveda*, 4.22.2.
178. Ibid., 3.96.9.
179. Ibid., 1.32.3, 1.84.11.
180. *Śatapatha Br.*, 2.1.2.16; 3.9.4.3; 11.5.9.7, etc.
181. *Agni Pu.*, 252.16.
182. J. Marshall, op. cit., pt. 2, pp. 465-7. M. Wheeler, *Cambridge History of India* (Supplementary Volume), pt. I, pp. 76-9.
183. E.W. Hopkins, op. cit., p. 245.

184. Ibid., p. 246.
185. तत्रेषूपलयन्त्राणि बलवन्ति महान्ति च।
आगतं प्रतिसैन्यं तैस्तत्र प्रतिनिवार्यते।। *Rām*, Yuddha, 3.12.
Ancient cities of Indraprastha, Dvārakā and Ayodhyā vere well protected by *yantras*, *MB*, Ādi, 199.33; Vana 16.5; *Rām*, Bāla, 5.10.
186. त्रासनं रक्षणं घातो बलोद्धरणमायतं।
क्षेपणीकर्म निर्दिष्टं यंत्रकर्मैतदेव तु।। *Agni Pu.*, 252.18.
187. *AS*, 2.18.5-6.
188. R.P. Kangle, *The Kauṭilīya Arthaśāstra*, vol. II, pp. 131-2.
189. *AS*, 2.18.6; On *yantras* we have followed the interpretation given by Kangle. But the subject needs further study.
190. R.P. Kangle, op. cit., p. 132; in *Nītiprakāśikā Śataghnī* is described as follows:
शतघ्नी कण्टकयुता कालायसमयी दृढा।
मुद्गरामा चतुर्हस्ता बर्तुला त्सरुणा युता।। *Nītiprakāśikā*, 5.48.
शतघ्नी च चतुर्हस्ता लोहकण्टकिनीगदा। *Vaijayantī*
191. परिगृप्र शतघ्नीश्च सचक्रा: सहुडोपला:।
चिक्षिपुर्भुजवेगेन लङ्कामध्ये महाबला:।। *MB*, Vana, 268.30.
192. द्वारेषु संस्कृता भीमा: कालायसमया: शिता:।
शतशो रचिता वीरै: शतघ्न्यो राक्षसां गणै:।। *Rām*, Yuddha, 3.13.
193. P.V. Kane, *History of Darmaśāstra*, vol. III, p. 214; for details see P.C. Chakravarty, *The Art of War in Ancient India*, pp. 172-4.
194. रज्जुबन्धनबद्धाभि: शतघ्नीभिश्च सर्वत:। *Rām*, Yuddha, 60.54.
195. *MB*, Karṇa, 6.22; Bhīṣma, 114.2, etc.
196. *MB*, Udyoga, 152.5-17; also see 155 (*BE*).
197. Ibid., Vana, 16.6-8.
198. A.L. Basham, *The Wonder That Was India*, p. 133.
199. तत्रेषूपलयन्त्राणि बलवन्ति महान्ति च।
आगतं प्रतिसैन्यं तैस्तत्र प्रतिनिवार्यते।। *Rām*, Yuddha, 3.12.
200. *MB*, Śānti,104.39.
201. इन्द्र सेनां मोहयामित्राणाम्। *Atharvaveda*, 3.1.5.
इन्द्र सेनां मोहयतु।। Ibid., 3.1.6.
202. अग्निर्नो दूत: प्रत्येतु विद्वान्प्रतिदहन्नभिशस्तिमरातिम्।
स चित्तानि मोहयतु परेषां निर्हस्तांश्च कृणवज्जातवेदा:।। Ibid., 3.2.1.
अयमग्निरमूमुहद्यानि चित्तानि वो हृदि। Ibid., 3.2.2.
203. धूपाश्च देया धर्मज्ञ तथा च परमोहना:।। *Agni Pu.*, 236.61.
204. *AS*, 14.1.
205. मंत्रभैषज्यपसंयुक्ता योगा मायाकृताश्च ये।
उपहन्यादमित्रांस्तै: स्वजनं चाभिपालयेत्।। *AS*, 14.3.88

206. J.W. M'crindle, *Ancient India*, p. 221.
207. आर्षभे चर्मणी चित्रे शतचन्द्रपरिष्कृते।
तारकाशतचित्रौ च निस्त्रिंशौ सुमहाप्रभौ।। *MB*, Bhīṣma, 112.19; also 67.28.
208. द्वीपिचर्मावनद्धैश्च व्याघ्रचर्मशयैरपि। Ibid., 44.32.
209. सुवर्णतारागणभूषितानि, शरावराणि प्रहितानि वीरैः।
Ibid., 56.17, 86.36.
210. *MB*, Sauptika, 8.55, Śānti, 101.8.
211. *AS*, 2.18.17.
212. R.P. Kangle, op. cit., p. 133.
213. H.R. Robinson, *Oriental Armour*, p. 92.
214. F.C. Maisey, *Sāñcī and its Remains*, pls. 20, 27, 35.
215. A.L. Srivastava, *Life in Sāñchī Sculptures*, p. 105.
216. K. De. B. Codrington, *Indian Antiquary*, vol. 59, 1930, p. 170, M.K. Dhavalikar, *Ajantā: A Cultural Study*, pp. 111-13, pl. 28; for weapon types in Ajantā see J. Griffiths, *The Paintings in the Buddhist Cave Temples of Ajantā*, vol. 1, figs. 33, 35, 36, 37, 39, 40.
217. क्रिमिरकार्दरङ्गचर्ममंडल। *Harṣacarita*, p. 207.
218. *Harṣacarita* (Cowell), p. 214.
219. V.S. Agrawal, *Harṣacarita: Eka Sāṁskṛtika, Adhyayana*, p. 156.
220. जीमूतस्येव भवति प्रतीकं यद वर्मी याति समदामुपस्थे।
अनाविद्धया तन्वा जय त्वं स त्वा वर्मिणो महिमा पिपर्तु।। *Rgveda*, 6.75.1; also *Atharvaveda*, 3.13.1. for detailed information on armour in India the reader is advised to consult G.N. Pant's *Indian Arms and Armour* (in 3 vols.).
221. *Vedic Index*, vol. II, pp. 271-2; ibid., vol. 1, p. 383; but there is an indication in the *Ṛgveda* (10.16.7) that it was made of cow hide (*gocarma*).
222. नमो विल्मिने च कवचिने च नमो वर्मिणे च। *Yajurveda*, 16.35.
मर्माणि ते वर्माणि छादयामि। Ibid., 17.49; also 29.45; also see S. Dey, *Indian Life in the Śukla-Yajurveda*, p. 88; it appears that *kavaca* and *varma* though protective in nature were two separate kinds of armour to begin with.
223. S. Dey, ibid.
224. *Atharvaveda*, 11.10.22.
225. J.W. M'crindle, *The Invasion of India*, p. 108.
226. Ibid., p. 204.
227. ततस्तव सुतो राजन्वर्म जग्राह कांचनम्।
विचित्रं च शिरस्त्राणं जम्बूनदपरिष्कृतम्।।
सोऽवबद्धशिरस्त्राण: शुभकांचनवर्मभृत्।
रराज राजनपुत्रस्ते कांचन: शैलराडिव।। *MB*, Śalya, 31.54-5; Virāṭa, 30.12-24.
वर्माणि चापविद्धानि रुक्मपृष्ठानि भारत। Karṇa, 14.31.

228. E.W. Hopkins, op. cit., p. 248.
229. कंचनवर्मभृत्। *MB*, Śalya, 31.55, Ādi, 26.31; Droṇa, 102.54-5.
230. शूरा हेममयैर्जालैर्दीप्यमाना इवाचला: *MB*, Bhīṣma, 19.30.
231. शतसूर्यं शतावर्तं शतबिन्दु शताक्षिमत् *MB*, Virāṭa, 30.12.
232. Ibid., Droṇa, 95.34-5.
233. तनुत्र, वर्म, दंशन, उरच्छद, कंकटक, जगर, कवच, *Amarakośa*, 2.8.64; the person equipped with armour was called सन्नध, वर्मित, सज्ज, दंशित, or व्यूहकङ्कट
234. *AS*, 2.18.16-17; also 2.23.17.
235. R.P. Kangle, op. cit., p. 133.
236. *AS*, 2.18.16.
237. लोहचर्मविनिर्माणा: कार्पासरचिता अपि।
शल्कैश्च घटिता: कार्या: सन्नाहा: सुदृढ़ा: सदा।। *Mānasollāsa*, 2.6.562.
238. *Ṛgveda*, 6.75.1.
239. शर्मप्रदस्त्वं समरे वर्म सैन्ये यशोऽद्य मे।
रक्ष मां रक्षणीयोऽहं तवानघ नमोऽस्तु ते।। *Agni Pu.*, 269.34.
240. H.R. Robinson, *Oriental Armour*, p. 89.
241. J. Marshall, *Taxilā*, p. 208; also p. 549; the earliest specimen of armour in Indian art is met at Bhārhut. A. Cunningham, op. cit., pl. 32.4.
242. A.L. Basham, *The Wonder That Was India*, p. 133.
243. T. Sulmirski, *The Sarmatians*, pp. 31-2.
244. *MB*, Droṇa, 95.34-8.
245. तनुत्राणि च योधानां हस्त्यश्वानां च वर्म च। *Rām*, Yuddha, 75.11.
गजानां पार्श्वचर्माणि गोवृषाजगराणि च।
शल्यकङ्कटलोहानि तनुत्राणि मतानि च।। *MB*, Śānti, 101.6.
प्रथक काञ्चनसंनाहान् रथेष्वश्वानयोजयन्। *MB*, Virāṭa, 30.16
दंशितैर्हरिभिर्युक्तं रथमास्थाय काञ्चनम्। Ibid., Vana 18.1.
246. सपादचर्मकोशैर्वा हस्तिभि: सौप्तिकं दद्यात्। *AS*, 10.3.20.
247. जातरूपशिरस्त्राण स्त्रासयन्निव मे मना:। *MB*, Virāṭa, 50.20, Śalya, 31.54.
248. *AS*, 2.18.17.
249. A.S. Altekar, *The Coinage of the Gupta Empire*, pls.
250. E.W. Hopkins, op. cit., pp. 248-51.
251. *MB*, Karṇa, 16.21; Bhīṣma, 43.4.
252. तलत्रैरङ्गुलित्रैश्च। *MB*, Bhīṣma, 102.22. Droṇa, 40.16; *Rām*, Yuddha, 19.12.
253. *Śīrṣaka, śirṣaṇya* and *śirāstra, Amarakośa*, 2.8.63.
254. A.L. Basham, *The Wonder That Was India*, p. 133.
255. हस्तिरथवाजिनां योग्याभाण्डमालंकारिकं संनाहकल्पनाश्चोपकरणानि। *AS*, 2.18.18.
256. Ibid.

257. जया च सुप्रभा चैव दक्षकन्ये सुमध्यमे।
ते सूतेऽस्त्राणि शस्त्राणि शतं परमभास्वरम्।। *Rām*, Bāla, 21.15; also *Nītiprakāśikā*, 1.45-6.
258. V.R.R. Dikshitar, *War in Ancient India*, p. 94.
259. For details see Gopinath Rao's *Hindu Iconography*, pls.
260. H.D. Sankalia, *Rāmāyaṇa Myth and Reality*, pp. 15-16, 60.
261. J.C. Roy, *IHQ*, vol. 6.
262. *MB*, Droṇa, 15.3, 79.30, 92.37, 98.31, 143.21-2.
263. *AS*, 13.4.14-22.

Chapter 7

Fortification and Siege-craft

For reasons of safety the early man lived in caves. Subsequently, he built houses and then came up the villages and towns. In his hunt for better security he went about raising walls around the villages and towns. Ancient Egyptians are said to have raised these protective walls to a height of 120 feet. A wide ditch made an approach to the fort difficult. The great China Wall built in third century BC is 1,400 miles long, 17 feet thick and 25 feet high.

The rampart was the most important component of the fort complex. The other components such as the moat and the towers were added to strengthen it. The moat prevented easy access to wall and also denied a platform to the assailants closer to the wall. It also added height to the rampart so that it may not be scaled with ladders, ordinarily. The towers on top of wall enabled the defenders to keep a watch on the assailants and foil any attempt at scaling by hurling stones or shooting arrows. In course of time guard-rooms were provided at the gates to prevent entry into the fort. Weapons and machines were stored at the gates to beat back any assault. This system of fortification was followed all over the ancient world.

IMPORTANCE OF FORT

In ancient Indian literature terms like *durga*, *pur*, *nagaram*, *paṭṭanam*, *kaṭakam*, *nigama*, etc., are used in the sense of the fort.[1] Of these, *pur* had come into vogue in the Vedic age.[2] *Durga* has been explained as denotative of a place which was 'difficult to reach' or 'difficult to negotiate' in Sanskrit lexicons.[3] It has been used in this sense in the *Ṛgveda*.[4] In the *Mahābhārata*, the king has been advised to seek shelter in the fort, when threatened by a powerful enemy.[5]

The role of fort in the security of the state has been extensively debated by the military thinkers of India. According to Parāśara calamity to a fortified town was far more serious than to the countryside (territory lying outside the fort) because the treasury and army both were located inside the fort. Further, the people residing inside the fort were more faithful to the ruler.[6] Kauṭilya, however, considered the calamity to the countryside more serious because the fort, treasury and the army depended on the countryside for sustenance.[7] The school of Piśuna, on the other hand, believed that calamity to the treasury was more serious than to the fort because the building, maintenance and repair of fort depended on treasury. Kauṭilya, however, disagreed with Piśuna stating that calamity to fort was more serious as in the absence of fort the treasury falls into the hands of enemy.[8]

The *Manusmṛti* says that an archer lodged inside the fort could fight one hundred adversaries and one hundred such archers could beat back ten thousand adversaries.[9] It adds that just as animals like deer need not fear the hunter in the shelter of dense jungle, similarly a king protected by a fort need not be afraid of an invader.[10] Śukra also follows Manu in emphasizing the importance of fort.[11] Kauṭilya considered fort a vital limb of the state as the ruler could stay safe inside it.[12] Kāmandaka considered a ruler without fort as weak as a cloud before the wind.[13] The *Yuktikalpataru* says that the power of a ruler is enshrined in his fort.[14] The military thinkers have also debated the merits and demerits of various types of forts. Manu believed that *giridurga* was the best of all forts,[15] but Bhīṣma considered *naradurga* as the most secure.[16]

HISTORY

The history of fortification in India can be traced back to chalcolithic age. At Kot-Diji, near Mohenjo-daro, a pre-historic strongly walled citadel, protected with rectangular towers of stones and mud bricks, has been discovered.[17] The remains of pre-Harappan Amri (on the Indus) and Kulli (in south Afghanistan) cultures also attest to the existence of forts.[18] Irfan Habib has rightly said that 'the rulers of the area would find it convenient to live in citadels or forts in or near the towns for safety'.[19] He adds that 'defensive walls which are most likely to have been the work of the rulers are found at Kot-Diji,

Kalibangan, Kohtras Buthi (West Sindh) and Rehman Deheri. But the impression one gets is of small principalities rather than large powerful states.'[20]

The excavations at Harappa and Mohenjo-daro suggest that the cities were protected either by walling or by fortification.[21] That there existed lofty citadels as in other large cities of ancient times, seems more than probable. A large number of round balls of baked clay or roughly chipped stone have been found in various parts of Mohenjo-daro. Their shape, material, and finding spots lead us to regard them as weapons of offence or, rather, defence. This is also true of the sling balls. The vary presence of these balls suggests the existance of raised walls or ramparts from where these were hurled on the approaching enemy.[22] The excavations at the Harappan site of Kalibangan in Rajasthan, have also revealed the existence of a citadel.[23] Contradicting the view that this citadel could have been raised as an anti-flood measure B.B. Lal says that

> Since at Kalibangan no evidence of flood has been encountered, the theory that fortification walls were erected as measures against flood does not seem to hold good. On balance it would appear that Kalibangan fortifications were a response to the general concept of defence.[24]

Some more archaeological evidence is forthcoming on this point.

> At some of the Harappan sites, small rooms adjacent to bigger structures have been called guard-rooms. Barrack like structures have been identified at Lothal, Mohenjo-daro and Harappa. Moreover, if the Harappans were indeed imperialists who, as Sankalia (1973) maintains, colonized the peripheral area outside the Indus Valley proper; we cannot but think of a series of garrisoned and fortified outposts to hold the colonies under control.[25]

Further, acording to J.P. Joshi (1979) Surkotada in Kutch was a 'defence complex' guarding a vital route of communication between Saurashtra and Sind.

A complete configuration of a full-fledged Harappan city has been discovered at Dhaulavira in Gujarat. It is an intricately fortified settlement consisting of castle, bailey, middle town, lower town, stadium, etc., all surrounded by a series of reservoirs on all sides and enclosed by extensive fortification. The massive defensive walls are duly provided with gateways, salients or corner towers.[26]

The proliferation of forts during the Harappan age is suggestive of some major threat to the security of the people. The Harappans may have reacted to this threat by way of building forts for safety against raid and plunder. Charioteers are said to have been the first great aggressors in human history. Going by the evidence furnished by the *Ṛgveda*, it appears that the Āryan charioteers were also raiders and destroyers of forts. Interpretation of these facts of history from the military angle suggests that the threat perceived by the Harappans was none other than the Āryan.

Vedic and Post-Vedic Period

It is almost certain that the Vedic references to forts (*pur*) which the Āryans destroyed during their march through India belonged to Harappans or the natives, called Dāsas or Dasyus. Indra and Agni are credited to have destroyed many of their forts in the *Ṛgveda*:

1. Indra broke through Ilībiśa's strong castles (1.33.12).
2. Indra broke down Pipru's fort (1.51.5).
3. Indra demolished 99 castles of Sambara (1.54.6; also 4.26.3; 5.29.6; 6.47.2).
4. Fighting on the side of Purukutsa Indra destroyed seven castles (1.63.7; also 7.18.13).
5. Indra wandered shattering the forts of Dāsas (1.15.10).
6. To assist Puru Indra shattered 90 forts (1.30.7).

For his capabilities in destroying the forts Indra also came to he known as Purandara, i.e. shatterer of forts.[27] Subsequently, Āryans also started living in the forts and there is a reference to their hundred forts in the *Ṛgveda*.[28]

In his connection the following obseravations in the *Vedic Index* are significant:

> *Pura* is a word of frequent occurrence in the *Rigveda* and later, meaning 'rampart', 'fort' or 'stronghold'. Such fortifications must have been occasionally of considerable size, as one is called broad (*pṛthvī*) and wide (*urvī*). Elsewhere, a fort made of stone (*aṣmamayī*) is mentioned. Sometimes strongholds of iron (*āyasī*) are referred to but these are probably only metaphorical. . . . It would probably be a mistake to regard these forts as permanently occupied fortified places like the fortresses of the

medieval barony. They were probably merely places of refuge against attack, ramparts of hardened earth with palisades and a ditch (cf. Dehī).[29]

A.B. Keith interprets *pur* in a slightly different way.

The *pura*, which is often referred to and which in later days denotes 'a town', was, as we have seen, probably no more than a mere earthwork fortification which may in some cases at least have been part of the village. In certain passages these *puras* are called autumnal, and by far the most probable explanation of this epithet is that it refers to the flooding of the plains by the rising rivers in the autumn, when the cultivators and herdsmen had to take refuse within the earthworks which at other times served as defence againts human foes.[30]

Das holds that forts were meant for permanent occupation.

As the Ṛgvedic times were full of unrest and wars were constantly going on among all the tribes, Vedic and non-Vedic, forts or fortfied towns would be permanently occupied by Kings and Nobles for safety and protection, and defended against attacks and raids. . . . The mention of stone-walls and stone-forts undoubtedly points to the fact that they were intended for permanent occupation.[31]

In the *Ṛgveda* there are repeated prayers to Agni to preserve the faithful with forts of *ayas*.[32] The guardian of the fort was called *purpati*.[33] Gradually, the fort was integrated in the military system of the Āryans.[34]

It is likely that the fort unearthed at Kauśāmbī pertains to the later Vedic age.

The mounds of the ancient rampart together with surrounding moat form a semi-circle, with the Yamuna as the base (Pl.V). The ramparts have a peripheral circuit of more than 21,000 ft. or approximately four miles. The average height of the rampart is about 35 ft., the individual towers being as high as 70 to 75 feet. . . . The three sides, eastern, northern and western of the rampart, marked by a series of salients and towers at regular intervals (pls. 6-10) are pierced by 12 gateways, 5 of which were principal ones.[35]

While some scholars suspect the antiquity of Kauśāmbī fort, Coan in MP has certainly yielded evidence of a Chalcolithic fort. The fortified settlement of Balathal in Rajasthan is also assigned the same date.

MAHĀJANAPADA AGE

The *Aṣṭādhyāyī* of Pāṇini refers to fort and its components like ramparts, moats, gates, and watch-towers.[36] The Buddhist *Nikāyas* suggest that

> forts and fortification around the capital city or important seats of governments, sometimes also around smaller cities, seemed to have been very familiar. There are frequent references in the early Buddhist texts to *prākāra* and *toraṇa* or wall or ramparts and towers or gates in connection with cities. Stone and iron ramparts are also mentioned, though not very frequently. The fact that hills or raised mounds of considerable proportion at any rate, were relatively the most suitable sites for fortified cities was amply proved by what the spade of the archaeologist had unearthed.[37]

In the *Jātakas* there are many references to forts. The *Mahāummaga Jātaka* refers to a big fort, which was provided with watch towers and surrounded by moats—a water-moat, a mud-moat and a dry-moat.[38] A fine specimen of such an elaborately laid out citadel has been discovered at Sanghol in Punjab.

Remains of a fort dated around sixth century BC have been unearthed from Rajgir or Girivraja. Though the town was protected by a cluster of hills it was further defended by artificial fortifications. There were two lines of walls around the city, the length of the inner wall being four and a quarter mile.

> The faces of the walls are built of massive undressed stones between three to five feet in length, carefully fitted and bounded together, while the core between them is composed of small blocks less carefully cut and laid with chips or fragments of stone, packing the interstices between them. No mortar or cement is visible anywhere in the stone work. . . . From the fact that whenever the height of between eleven and twelve feet is reached the walls are invariably finished off with a course of small stones, and that there are no fallen blocks of stone lying near, we may assume that this was the original height of the massive masonry described above. Above this substructure, there was no doubt a superstructure composed either of small stonework or of bricks baked or unbaked, or possibly of wood and stone or brick combined.[39]

The bastions (towers) were attached to the outer side of the walls wherever special strength was required and sixteen such structures have been discovered. Further the outer wall was provided with stairs or ramps, built in the thickness of the wall along its inner face in order to give access to the top. The defences were further supplemented by watch towers erected at important points on the hills. The thickness of the wall ranged between fourteen to seventeen and a half feet.[40] The specimen of contemporary fortification have also been discovered from Unchdih,[41] Bhita, and Ahicchatra.[42]

Maurya Period

The Greek sources furnish detailed information about the system of fortification in India in fourth century BC. In this connection the fortification of the city of Massaga, as described by Arrian, is illuminating:

> An army of 38,000 infantry defended the city which was strongly fortified both by nature and art. For on the east, an impetuous mountain-stream with steep banks on both sides barred approach to the city, while to the south and west nature, as if designing to form a rampart, had piled up gigantic rocks at the base of which lay sloughs and yawning chasms hallowed in the course of ages to vast depths, while a ditch of mighty labour drawn from their extremity continued the line of defence. The city was besides surrounded with a wall of 35 stadia in circumference which had a basis of stonework supporting a super-structure of unburnt sun-dried bricks. The brickwork was bound into a solid fabric by means of stones so interposed that the more brittle material rested upon the harder, while moist clay had been used for mortar. Lest, however, the structure should all at once sink, strong beams had been laid upon these supporting wooden floors which covered the walls and afforded a passage along them.[43]

The Greeks have referred to many more hill forts of India in their accounts.[44]

The towns located in the plains were protected by defensive works. According to Arrian, Sangala, the capital of Cathaeans, was strongly fortified by brick walls.[45] About the capital of Malloi he says that it was very well defended by walls and within that there was a citadel with gates, towers and parapet.[46] But the most important fort referred to by the Greeks was that of Pāṭaliputra, the capital of Magadha kingdom, situated at the junction of rivers Sone and Gaṅgā. It was a long narrow parallelogram in shape, measuring about nine and one fifth miles in length (eighty stadia) and one and a half miles (fifteen stadia) in breadth. It was defended by a massive wooden palisade, pierced by sixty-four gates and crowned by five hundred seventy towers. The palisade had loopholes for the archers to shoot through, and outside there was a ditch, 30 cubits deep and 400 cubits broad. The ditch was filled from the waters of Sone.[47]

In this connection the distinction between the Harappan forts and the Mauryan forts brought out by L. Woolly is significant.

> The burnt-brick and bitumen construction which was the most striking feature of the Mohenjo-daro architecture is a long-forgotten art in the earlier post-Harappan buildings of which we have any knowledge. Those at Hastināpura, 80 miles north-east of Delhi, wood is the basic material, and the Mauryan palace at Pāṭaliputra is also of timber. It would seem that when the Āryans began to build for themselves they made a fresh start; the monuments which they set up were certainly not inspired by any memories of Mohenjo-daro.[48]

Perhaps, the use of wood as a building material at Hastināpur and Pāṭaliputra is related to easy and abundant availability of wood in the Gangetic plains rather than a case of breaking with the past.

Arthaśāstra on Fort

The most detailed information on the forts in ancient India is met in the *Arthaśāstra.* Advising the ruler it says that

> in all four quarters, on the frontiers of the country, he should cause a nature-made fortress, equipped for fight, to be made: a water fort (either) on island in the midst of water or high land shut in by water, or a mountain fort (either) consisting of rocks or a cave, (or) a desert fort (either) one without water and shrubs or a salty region, or a jungle fort (either) a marshy track with water or a thicket of shrubs. Among them a river fort and the mountain fort are places for the protectors of the country, a desert fort and jungle fort are places for foresters or places of retreat in times of calamity.[49]

But Kauṭilya's main concern was the defence of the capital city, located at the confluence of the rivers or on the bank of a lake. He says that three moats shall be dug around it, at a distance of one *daṇḍa* (6 feet) from each other, fourteen, twelve and ten *daṇḍas* broad, three-quarters and a half of the breadth deep, with arrangements for filling and draining out water and stocked with lotuses and crocodiles. At a distance of four *daṇḍas* from the moat (innermost) a rampart shall be built from the earth dug out from the moats. The outer side of the rampart shall be planted with thorny bushes and poisonous creepers. The top of the rampart shall be covered with rounded stones with chariot tracks made of trunks of palm trees.

A parapet of height between 18 and 36 feet (12 and 24 *hastas*) and breadth half its height, shall be built on top of the rampart with stone or bricks. Along this rampart there shall be turrets, and between every two turrets, a square tower. Between each tower and turret, a high wooden board with holes and caves shall be erected big enough for three archers (to defend the ramparts using the board as protection). In between these structures there shall be strong wooden planks projecting outwards (to make boarding difficult). Passages (for soldiers to go out on attack), an escape door and an exit door, shall also be built in an unassailable part of the rampart.

Kauṭilya adds that defensive structures shall be made outside the ramparts to obstruct the enemy advance. These included a covered road strewn with knee-breakers, a mass of pikes, pits, concealed traps, barbed wires, serpent backs, palm leaves, etc. A gateway shall be built with a tower consisting of a hall, a wall and a border post (in the ground floor), an upper chamber and a turret. The gateway shall have a main door and a side door and defences against ramming by elephants. The bridges over the moat in front of the gate shall be removable.[50]

For use in emergency the fort was provided with twelve gateways, with passages, both open and secret, passing through land and water. These passages opened in nearby forests or countryside, etc., of course for reasons of security.[51]

The details furnished by Kauṭilya highlight the following features of Indian system of fortification:

1. Ramparts made of stone, mud or timber.
2. Ditches (3 in number) spiked and filled with mud, sand or flowing water.
3. Ramparts planted with poisonous bushes and crowned with several ring walls of brick.
4. Ring walls with roofed walks, wide enough to accommodate patrols in both directions and square towers.
5. Gates of the fort approachable only through a drawbridge spanning the ditches.

6. The invaders had to overcome numerous obstructions before approaching the rampart.
7. Forts were protected by a large number of mobile and stationary machines.
8. Forts were provided with chambers along the ramparts so as to store various kinds of weapons.

This goes to prove that

> apart from their fundamental grasp of all the advantages to be drawn from naturally defensible sites it is clear from Kauṭilya that the ancient soldiers were familiar with the two basic methods of augmenting them: walls covered by flanking fire from regularly spaced towers; defence in depth privided by concentric rings of walls and moats with advanced outworks controlling the approach.[52]

Epic and Purāṇic View

There are many references to forts in the epics. The *Rāmāyaṇa* refers to four types of forts, viz., *nādeya* (river), *pārvata* (mountain), *vānya* (forest) and *kṛtrima* (artificial).[53] Ayodhyā was a well-fortified city provided with strong gates, massive walls, various *yantras* and *śataghnīs.* A fathomless moat encircled the ramparts of the fort.[54] Laṅkā was equally well fortified. The city was surrounded by a massive rampart (*prākāra*) difficult to scale or assult. Many wide and deep moats (*parikhā*) of cold water, full of crocodiles and large fish, a sure death trap for the enemy, encircled the ramparts. Four large and wide gates (*dvāras*) with strong doors (*kapāṭanī*) provided entry to the city. Big towers (*saṁkrāmāḥ*) surmounting the gates were provided with machines (*yantraiḥ*) to prevent any ingress through the moats to the gate. Of the four towers, the one built over the main gate was the most beautiful, strongest and unassailable. Hundreds of *śataghnīs* were stocked above the gates for hurling down on the assaulting troops.[54] Thus machines, moats, and *śataghnīs* ensured safety of Laṅkā.[55] All the four gates were strongly defended but the maximum concentration was made on the northern gate,[57] which was perhaps the most vulnerable.

The *Mahābhārata* elaborating on forts refers to six types, viz., *dhanva-durga, mahī-durga, giri-durga, manuṣya-durga, ab-durga,* and *vana-durga.*[56] The town of Indraprastha was surrounded by a wide moat, lofty walls and numerous gates. An abundant stock of weapons promised a stout defence; the battlements bristled with sharp hooks and *śataghnīs* and also machines (*yantras*) of war and the walls were manned along their length.[59] The rulers were advised to protect the gate (*dvāra*) with heavy machines and *śataghnīs*.[60]

> On the forts *Pragaṇḍis* and *Ākāśajanis* should be constructed while the moats should be filled up and provided with concealed spikes and crocodiles. There should be secret gates for egress from the town to be used in case of necessity. At the fort gates engines should be constructed and *śataghnīs* placed upon them and kept in hand.[61]

Indians do not appear to have known any engine of destruction, like catapults, previous to the invasion of Alexander. The Greek accounts mention that Alexander succeeded in storming and capturing Indian forts and cities mainly on account of his engines. The Indians could not understand such contrivances and were often overawed by them. It appears that subsequently these instruments of war were borrowed by Indians from the Greeks.[62]

The *Manusmṛti* gives a similar classification of forts, excepting that it uses the term *nṛdurga* for *manuṣya-durga* and *vārakṣa-durga* for *vana-durga*.[63] Manu, however, considered *giri-durga* as the best.[64] The *Mahābhārata* on the other hand considered *nara-durga* as the best of all.[65] The epics seem to represent a stage when the evolution of big armies had revolutionized the system of warfare. The *Agni Purāṇa* also repeats the said sixfold classification of forts but it lays special emphasis on designing the facade and its proper maintenance.[66] The *Matsya Purāṇa*,[67] which generally follows the *Agni Purāṇa* in the classification of forts, recommends the following:

1. Main entrance of the fort should be big so as to allow a comfortable passage to king even when mounted on an elephant.
2. Rampart and ditch which are important components of a fort, should be given special attention.
3. The fort should be guarded by various kinds of machines, because weapons that can kill thousands alone can protect the king.
4. The secret doors and other passages within the fort should be protected by *śataghnīs* or by skilled archers or soldiers.

The *Devī Purāṇa* does not include *mahī-durga* and *nara-durga* in its list of forts and suggests a height of 9 cubits for fort walls.[68] But

Brahmavaivartta Purāṇa[69] recommends a height of 12 cubits, which could be raised to a maximum of 20 cubits. Raising the height of the fort could be related to the threat perception of the day.

The *Śukranīti* mentions nine fort types, viz., *airiṇa-durga*, *pārikha-durga* (surrounded by ditches), *pāridha-durga* (surrounded by walls), *vana-durga, dhanva-durga, jala-durga, giri-durga, sainya-durga* and *sahāya-durga* (fort of the ally). It considered *sainya-durga* as the best of all fortresses.[70]

The *Kāmandaka Nīti* refers to the calamities to the fort. It says that a ruler well settled in a fort is respected by both his supporters and his adversaries but in the event calamity strikes the fort (*durgavyasana*) everything goes wrong.[71] It enumerates the calamities to the fort as follows:[72]

1. Decaying ramparts
2. Silting of ditches
3. Worn out machines
4. Neglect of arsenal
5. Shortage of food and fodder, etc.

Greek and Kuṣāṇa Innovations

After the disintegration of Maurya empire India suffered repeated foreign invasions. Consequently, many parts of the country came to be ruled by Greeks, Śakas, Pahlavas and Kuṣāṇas. These foreign invaders may have introduced an alien system of fortification in India. To illustrate the point, Alexander founded some towns in north-west India,[73] and many more may have come up during the rule of Bactrian Greeks.

> There is every reason to believe that Demetrius, like Alexander, must have settled Greek garrisons in particular localities to protect his flank and rear during this Indian advance, and these became the nuclei of several later settlements of the Bactrian Greeks, when their rule was confined to their Indian territories only.[74]

Sirkap (Taxilā), built during early second century BC, was a Greek settlement.[75] Its earthen wall has been assigned to Greeks while the later stone wall to Śakas, who ousted them and occupied the city. The wall was nearly 3½ mile in length, 15 to 21 feet in thickness and 20 to 30 feet in height. The core of the entire wall was made of random rubble in mud while the facing revealed the construction of coarsed rubble. On the north side of the city the wall was buttressed on the outside by a raised berm about 25 feet in width, and a number of rectangular bastions built at irregular intervals along its face. The berm which was made to protect the foundations of the wall from possible undermining was composed of rubble and mud. The bastions were made two or three storied high, hollow and loop holed, for the use of the defenders. However, only the upper portions of bastions at Sirkap were loop-holed. The fort was perhaps provided with four gates, though only the remains of northern gate have been discovered. It was so designed as to give protection to the city from a direct attack, by screening the city streets.

There is an interesting reference of the city of Taxilā in the biography of Appolonius of Tyana. It was 'a city about the size of Nineveh, walled like a Greek town, and the residence of a sovereign'. Phrotes, the ruler spoke Greek.[76] The city fortified in the Greek style was perhaps ruled by a Indo-Greek ruler.

The *Milindapañho*, a Buddhist work, describes the Greek settlement of Śākala as 'brave is its defence, with many and various strong towers and ramparts, with super gates and entrance archways, and with the royal citadel in its midst, white walled and deeply moated'.[77] During their long rule in north-western and western India the Greeks must have influenced the Indian system of fortification.

The remains of Kuṣāṇa fortification have been discovered at Sirsukh, again a Taxilā site. The walls were made of rough rubble and were overlaid with lime stone masonry of heavy diaper type. The thickness of walls was 15 feet 6 inch. Its base is supported on the outer face with a heavy roll plinth which was added after the wall itself had been completed with a view to strengthen the foundations and prevent undermining.[78] This unusual feature is not noticed at Sirkap or any other contemporary Indian site. Perhaps, this method of strengthening the fortification was a feature of Central Asian forts, the homeland of Kuṣāṇas. According to Marshall the fortification at Sirsukh were built by Wema Kadphises who may have adopted the idea of rectangular planning from Central Asia.[79]

A comparison between the Sirkap fortification of the Greeks and Sirsukh fortification of the Kuṣāṇas reveals certain similarities. At both sites the upper storeyes were generally much hollow and walls were loopholed and invariably provided with beams or galleries for stationing armed guards on the upper floors. The upper floors had open terraces and battlements.[80]

But the differences between the two are more marked. The walls at Sirkap betray Greek and Śaka influence as these were built of coarse rubble masonry whereas the walls at Sirsukh were made of heavy diaper masonry, a characteristic of Parthian and early Kuṣāṇa period. Secondly, at Sirkap only the upper portions of the bastion were loopholed whereas at Sirsukh both lower and upper portions are loopholed. Thirdly, the bastions at Sirkap were rectangular in plan but those at Sirsukh were semi-circular.[81] Further, in the fortification at Sirsukh the place of a flat beam is taken by a heavy roll footing.[82]

The traces of Kuṣāṇa fortification are also seen at Kauśāmbī. The entire fortification measured about 4 miles. The height of the ramparts was between 30 and 40 feet. The rampart was characterized by a series of salients or bastions, the space in between filled with rammed mud. Gates were provided invariably between the centre of two salients. Traces of a deep moat surrounding the entire rampart could also be seen. Besides, at a distance of nearly a mile from the ramparts the existence of some mounds suggest that they formed the outermost line of the defence system at Kauśāmbī.[83] This twofold defence system as met in Kauśāmbī has not been found anywhere else in India, suggesting that it was a foreign, perhaps Kuṣāṇa, contribution.

In Gandhāra art city walls and geteways are widely represented.[84] These may be considered as true representation of the fortification at Sirsukh. Mathurā, which served as the chief metropolis of the Kuṣāṇa empire in the east for a considerable period, may have also been fortified in a similar manner.

There is also some archaeological evidence on Mathurā. It is said that during the Kuṣāṇa phase the Mathurā fortifications were revived, enlarged and repaired. Further, an inner fort of mud was also built inside the walled town. This inner fortification possibly had semi-circular bastions and a moat on at least its western and north-western side. This was indeed meant to provide additional security to the rulers of the day. Carvings on stone slabs, pillars and architraves discovered at Mathurā, datable around the same time, also represent gates and gate-towers.[85]

Another well planned citadel of the Kuṣāṇa period has been discovered at Sanghol in Punjab.[86] Three of its arms which are discernible and partly invested show that the eastern and western ones run parallel to each other. The citadel was secured by four lines of defence, three of which were moats. The water-moat complement is a 28 metre broad ditch, now filled up with water-borne deposits. The second line of defence comprised the earthen rampart, which was as broad as the moat. The third moat measured 14 metres at the top. Then there is a provision of a raised walkway measuring 7.5 metres across.

The provision of three moats in this citadel is in tune with the prescription of the *Arthaśāstra* and the *Mahāummaga Jātaka* in respect of moats. Inside the enclosed area palaces of Kuṣāṇa and Gupta age have been unearthed. Perhaps, this fort was devastated by the Hūṇa invaders.

SĀÑCĪ EVIDENCE

As the forts depicted in Gandhāra art represent the Kuṣāṇa style, so the forts sketched in Sāñcī art represent the conventional Indian style. In the *Arthaśāstra* moats (*parikhā*), printh (*vapra*), parapet (*prākāra*), tower (*aṭṭālaka*), gateways (*dvāra*), gatehouses (*pratolī*), etc., are considered essential ingredients of a fort.[87] In the Sāñcī art most of these ingredients are depicted, within the limitations of space indeed. In this connection the depiction of the town in the 'War of Relics' scene (southern gateway) is illuminating.

> The town itself he (artist) places boldly, against all precedent, in the centre of the composition. Space demands that his sketch of it shall be but the barest summary; yet he manages to give us a remarkably clear idea of how an ancient Indian town looked, with its battlemented walls of stone or brick, its storied towers and bastions, its plastered gateways, its timbered super-structures, pillared balconies and vaulted roofs. And the siege he depicts is very real siege. . . . Some of the assailants are struggling across the moat and scaling the wall beyond; others are hammering away at the gates; others shooting into the upper stories; while the defenders with every sort of weapon, including stones torn from the battlements, seek to repel the attack.[88]

This provides a vivid picture of an Indian fort around the beginning of the Christian era.

Among the most curious to be learnt from the picture of a besieged town, we may point out; as regards the town itself the line of lotuses in the middle of the foreground marking the ditch in which some of the fighters are standing; the walls made of big bricks or stones, the indication of which is perhaps meant to show by contrast that the two gates and the tower at the left, with their smooth surface, were coated with stucco; the battlements and merions, the loopholes with or without a dripstone, the loggias with balconies etc.[89]

A comparison of literary and art evidence indicates some marked similarities.[90]

1. In Sāñcī reliefs a single moat is shown though the *Arthaśāstra* and some Buddhist works provide for three moats. Perhaps, for space constraint the artist could depict only one moat.
2. The Sāñcī reliefs represent the city protected by a wall as described in literature. The ramparts were built either of bricks or dressed stones or mud. The boundary wall on the upper architrave, furnished with battlements, appears smooth, as if plastered.
3. A small part of brick rampart finished with capping and provided with regular and internal turnings is seen on the right side of the city gate of Kuśinārā in the 'War of Relics' scene. On the other side of the gate there appears a brick boundary-wall topped by staircase-like formation. The presence of fighters behind these parapets indicates that defensive positions were provided inside the wall. Battlement brick boundary can be seen in many scenes. The battlements surrounding these defence walls are in some cases triangular and in others conical in shape. Ramparts without battlements were also constructed. All this is in tune with the description of fort in the *Arthaśāstra*.
4. As prescribed in literature high towers (*aṭṭālaka*) at regular intervals were added internally to the rampart wall, so as to keep a watch on the enemy and if necessary fight him from a secured place. Such defensive towers are represented in the lower architrave of southern gateway at Sāñcī.
5. In Sāñcī reliefs gate-houses (*pratoli*) are widely represented. Normally, a gate-house comprised a closed room at the top, a pillared accommodation at the centre and two bastions projecting from the rampart wall on the ground. The bastions were either made of

> brick or mud. But due to their straight and smooth linings, the bastions at Sāñcī appear to have been constructed with brick and then plastered. The bastions have a regular window opening in the upper part with or without a dripstone on each outer side. From these openings the defenders could watch the movement of the enemy outside and could also shoot arrows and hurl missiles on him.

The construction of forts continued during the Gupta period. *Durgapāla* or *koṭapāla* was the officer responsible for the protection of fort. In the *Raghuvaṁśa* there are references to the fortification of capital and border areas. Rulers ensured proper defence of their fort before marching out on a victory campaign.[91] The Chinese traveller Hiuen-tsang who visited India in seventh century AD found villages and towns well fortified. The thick and high ramparts were built with bricks or tiles. When the Arabs invaded Sindh in seventh century they also found Indian cities to be well fortified.

Forts of South India

Forts were built for the protection of the cities and towns in south India as well. Ancient Madurā was protected by a rampart, built of undressed stones. It had four entry gates. The rampart was encircled by a deep ditch and surrounded by a dense forest of thorny trees. The roads leading to the entry gates were so broad that many elephants could walk abreast. On both sides of the entry gate, above the walls, weapons and missiles were stored for use against the enemy.[92] In an inscription Kāñcī has been described as 'the mighty abode of enmity that was hard to be surmounted and difficult to be borne, which was girt about by a moat that was very deep and difficult to be crossed'.[93] Many such fortified cities existed in south India.

In the great forts of Madurā, Karūra, and Kāñcī many curious engines were mounted on the battlements to shoot arrows or fling stones on the besiegers. There were machines like the fishing rod and angle to catch and drag up those who approached the wall and like iron fingers to siege and tear them to pieces. There were besides furnaces from which hot oil and molten metal might be poured on those who attempted to scale the wall and iron spokes and spears to shove down those that might succeed in mounting the ramparts.[94]

The above review of forts in ancient India indicates that these were generally built on the river banks or on the hills. A ditch or a moat full of water surrounded the fort. Next to the moat, after some spacing, stood the rampart. The space in between the moat and the rampart was covered with thorny and poisonous bushes. A bridge connected the moat with the gates of the fort. The parapets built over the ramparts provided protection to the defenders from the arrow shots of the enemy. In between the parapets there were towers, which were occupied by the guards of the fort. In between the towers, *machans* were provided to facilitate the shooting of the assulting troops.

FORT TYPES

The *Mahābhārata* refers to six types of forts, viz., *dhanva, mahī, giri, manuṣya, mṛda* and *vana.*[95] The *Rāmāyaṇa, Manusmṛti, Agni Purāṇa, Matsya Purāṇa*, etc., also refer to some of these types.[96] The *Arthaśāstra* refers to four types of forts, viz., *pārvata, odaka, dhānvan* and *vana.*[97] The *Śukranīti*, however, refers to nine fort types, viz., *airiṇa pārikha, pāridha, vana, jala, giri, dhanva, sainya* and *sahāya.*[98] The literature on forts continued to be produced and *Mānasollāsa, Samarāṅgaṇa sūtradhāra*, etc., furnish detailed information on fortification in India. A brief description of principal fort types of ancient India is given below:

GIRI-DURGA

Giri-durga located at a height, was provided with adequate water supply, and was considered impregnable.[99] It was a popular type of fort and in later literature its three sub-types, viz., *prāntara durga, giri pārśvaka* and *giri upatyoka* are mentioned. Perhaps, *prāntara* was located on the border of the mountain, *pārśvaka* at close proximity of the mountain and *upatyoka* at the foot of the mountain.[100]

JALA-DURGA

Jala or *audaka durga* was encircled by water. It was of two types—*antardvīpa* and *sthaladvīpa.*[101] The earlier was like an island encircled by water on all sides whereas the latter, though encircled by water, was built at a height. It could be negotiated only with boats.[102]

Dhanva-durga

This fort type was surrounded by sand on all sides.[103] Its two sub-types were *nirudaka* and *iriṇa.* The earlier was located at the centre of a big waterless desert whereas the latter was surrounded by land, laid barren by saline water.

Vana-durga

It was surrounded by thorny bushes and dense forests.[104] According to the *Arthaśāstra* it was either surrounded by marshy land or by thorny bushes. In the first case it was called *khañjanodaka* and in the latter case *stambagahana.*[105]

Mahī-durga

It was built of stone and earth.[106] The *Arthaśāstra* calls it *mṛda-durga.*[107]

Manuṣya-durga

In this type of fort the soldiers were arrayed in a defensive posture, making any enemy ingress difficult.[108] In the *Śukranīti* it is called *sainya-durga.*[109]

In ancient Indian literature many more types of forts are mentioned such as *deva-durga, parikhā-durga, sahāya-durga,* etc., but these could be covered by one of the principal types detailed above.

SECURITY OF FORT

As fort was the best insurance for the security of the state, all possible measures were taken to protect it from siege, assault, scaling, mining, sabotage, etc. The *Mahābhārata* mentions some of these measures as follows:[110]

1. To keep the fort well stocked with food grains and weapons and provide tunnels for secret movement to and from the fort.
2. To stop entertaining activity inside the fort when the security of the state was threatened. This included prohibition on music and dance concerts and eviction of such performers from the fort.
3. To destroy the bridges and dry out the wells on the approach road of the enemy.
4. To stop the movement of boats, lay thorns in the ditches and spread poisonous nails on the road, as far as possible.

5. To take special measures against fire hazards, such as plastering of thatched roofs.
6. To prevent ingress.

The *Mahābhārata* refers to many types of weapons stored in a fort to fight back the invaders. Those, particularly useful in defeating the besiegers, included *taṅgalā* (pole-like device), *śataghnī* (killer beam), *cakragrahaṇī* (a *cakra*-like device), *bhuśuṇḍi* (a kind of weapon), *aśmalaguḍkā* (stone pieces), *avapothika* (defence against hurled objects), *agni saguṣasṛṅgikā* (a fire weapon), etc.[111]

The *Arthaśāstra* recommends some aggressive measures including scorch earth policy, mining, destruction of supplies, and attack in the rear[112] for defeating the enemy siege. In fact, the director of weapons produced machines which could defeat the enemy assault on the fort. There were ten types of fixed machines, which were exclusively meant for the defence of the fort. Sixteen mobile machines were also used to protect the fort from enemy assault.[113] Stone was always a handly weapon for defeating siege.[114] In fourth century BC an Indian ruler used stones to defeat the siege laid by Alexander.[115] The *Mahābhārata* refers to measures such as plastering of thatched roofs, to prevent the occurrence of fire inside the fort.[116]

SIEGE-CRAFT

There could be no final victory without reducing the fort of the adversary. The Vedic Āryans had perfected this art some 3500 years ago. They applied the method of siege (*upasada*) or assault through the breached walls (*pravidha*) to capture a fort. The *pura-cariṣṇu*, a device mentioned in the *Ṛgveda* (*Vedic Index* II, p. 417) may have been some kind of battering ram used for assaulting a fort. Agni is often described as destroyer of forts. The *Taittirīya Saṁhitā* speaks of three citadels of the Asuras cleft by a shaft, whose point was Agni.[117]

Subsequently, many methods were devised to reduce an enemy fort. One of the methods was to lay siege of the fort, prevent supplies or help from reaching it and thus forcing it to capitulate. This method of reducing a fort was called *aparodha.*[118] In the *Mahāummagga Jātaka* there is a reference to the siege of Videha by King Brahmadatta and its ultimate surrender.[119] Kauṭilya, however, refers to various means of reducing a fort as *durgalambhopāyaḥ.*[120] It mentions five means, viz., instigation to sedition (*upajāpa*), drawing out the enemy by means of strategem (*yogavamana*), employment of secret agents (*apasarpa*), laying a siege (*paryupāsana*) and storming (*avamarda*).[121] The *Mahābhārata* also mentions many methods by which the capitulation of fort could be achieved.[122]

But before choosing harder options like siege or assault the invader could try other means like psychological war to frighten those inside the fort. This could be done by subverting the enemy officials and devastating his territory. The second option was to draw the enemy out of the protection of fort clandestinely and kill him. The third option was to infiltrate trusted men into the fort, who after gaining the confidence of the besieged could bretray him and thus weaken him from inside. The means of laying siege and assaulting the fort were to be adopted only as a last resort. An assault on fort involved cleaning of the surroundings, undermining of the ramparts, breaching of the walls and setting the fort afire.

In the *Mahābhārata* elephant has been called the breaker of forts.[123] A *Jātaka* story refers to the destruction of a fort by an elephant.[124] The *Arthaśāstra* also refers to this method.[125] Another method of destroying a fort was by mining. By making a passage under the fort the ramparts and towns could be demolished.[126] A fort could also be destroyed by setting it afire. The *Arthaśāstra* has described in detail the use of birds and animals for this purpose, but it also cautions about the risks involved in using the means of fire.[127]

Some special weapons were also used to break open the gates of enemy forts. One such weapon called *parigha*, which had the capacity to destroy the city gates, is mentioned in the *Rāmāyaṇa*. It was hard like *vajra* and had iron nails on all sides.[128]

In the Sāñcī art there is a real portrayal of a siege of a town in the 'War of Relics' scene. It is best put in the words of Fergusson

> in the centre the siege is carried on vigorously. Two men on the right with a kilt and a breast plate like a Roman soldier, are acting as slingers. A body of archers and spearmen are assaulting a low outwork in the centre, and bowmen and spearmen are storming the gateway, at which two of the assailants seem to have effected an entrance.
>
> The besieged defend themselves with arrows and spears, and throw down large masses of stone on the heads of their assailants; but what seems strange, no engines of war are used—neither ladders nor batter-

ing rams nor is any attempt made to set fire to the place. In all these respects the Hindus seem to have been very much behind the stage we know from Nineveh sculptures that the Assyrians reached at a much earlier age.[129]

In this context a reference to Alexander's attack on a Malloi stronghold, situated somewhere in modern Montgomery district, as detailed in Greek accounts would be found instructive.

> There was a city in India into which many had fled for refuge—one that was of immense size and of impregnable strength. Alexander, when in the act of besieging it called for ladders of unusual length, such as were in proportion to the height of the wall; and when the defenders were breaking these when brought up by hurling great pieces of rock down upon them, that ladder alone escaped destruction by which the king with two attendants had succeeded in gaining the top, even though many from above, each to the best of his power, were trying to thrust him down. Then though he had seen all the ladders of his men shattered to pieces . . . he nevertheless flung himself alone.
>
> So then, seconded by his attendants, he all day long did the fighting of an entire army, and would have held on, were it not that he was wounded in the side. . . . The Macedonians who were fighting outside (knowing) that all the people within the walls were to a man engaged in attacking the king, while no one was posted on the ramparts to prevent any one forcing his way inside, stormed the gates and brought succour to the king.[130]

In this context it is notable that the Macedonians frequently used ladders to scale the fort walls. Alexander used them during an assault on Aspasian city[131] and a Malloi stronghold.[132] Indians do not appear to have used this device for scaling the forts. The *Arthaśāstra* which deals with the siege-craft in some detail makes no mention of the ladders. The 'battle of relics' scene portrayed in Sāñcī reliefs also does not depict any ladders.

Thus, the fort was an integral part of Indian defence system from the earliest times. The Dāsas and Dasyus, the original inhabitants of India lived in the forts. These, however, proved of little use before the invaders, as Indra, the leader of the Āryans, destroyed their forts without encountering much resistance. In the fourth century BC, north-west India was heavily fortifed. Each state, small or big, had built forts as a protective measure. However, these forts failed before the assault of Alexander's army. Subsequently, the Bactrian Greeks, the Pahlavas, the Śakas and the Kuṣāṇas also built forts but they also lost their kingdoms sooner or later. In short the system of fortification perfected by ancient Indians proved ineffective when threatened by invaders.

In conclusion, it seems that in ancient India fort did not form a part of overall military strategy. It was never intended to be used for offensive purpose. When an invasion came people sought shelter in it and invader laid siege. The besieged made no effort at break through or take on besieging troops from behind. The *koṭapālas* and *durgapālas* who were posted to defend the borders perhaps watched the invader from the safety of the ramparts, at best hoping for their withdrawal.

NOTES

1. *Śabdakalpadruma, Vācaspatyam,* see *durga.*
2. *Ṛgveda,* 1.53.7, 58.8; 3.15.4; 4.27.1.
3. *Vācaspatyam,* see *durga.*
4. परिणो वृणजन्नघा दुर्गाणि रथ्यो यथा। *Ṛgveda,* 8.47.5.
5. *MB,* Śānti, 69.32-43; also *Kāmandaka Nīti,* 4.59.
6. *AS,* 8.1.24-7.
7. Ibid., 8.1.28-32.
8. Ibid., 8.1.33-40.
9. एकः शतं योधयति प्राकारस्थो धनुर्धरः।
   शतं दशसहस्राणि तस्माद् दुर्गं विधीयते।। *Manusmṛti,* 7.74.
10. Ibid., 7.73.
11. *Śukranīti,* 4.6.1-14; also 1.238-41.
12. *AS,* 6.1.1; 7.15.9-13.
13. दुर्गहीनो नरपतिर्वाताभ्रामयवैः समः। *Kāmandaka Nīti,* 4.56.
14. *Yuktikalpataru,* p. 17.
15. सर्वेण तु प्रयत्नेन गिरिदुर्गं समाश्रयेत्।
    एषां हि बाहुगुण्येन गिरिदुर्गं विशिष्यते।। *Manusmṛti,* 7.71.
16. दुर्गेषु च महाराज षट्सु ये शास्त्रनिश्चिताः।
    सर्वेषु तेषु मन्यन्ते नरदुर्गं सुदुस्तरम्।। *MB,* Śānti, 56.35.
17. R.E.M. Wheeler, *Early India and Pakistan,* p. 106.
18. S. Piggot, *Pre-historic India,* pp. 115-16.
19. Irfan Habib, *The Indus Civilization,* p. 2.
20. Ibid., p. 12.
21. J. Marshall, *Mohenjo-daro and the Indus Civilization,* p. 282.

22. Ibid., pp. 465-6.
23. *Indian Archaeology, 1960-61*, pp. 31-2.
24. B.B Lal, *Kalibangan and the Indus Civilization and Essays in Indian Proto History*, p. 65.
25. Y.M. Chitalwala, Paper in the *Frontiers of the Indus Valley Civilization* (ed. B.B. Lal and P.S. Gupta), pp. 212-13.
26. I am grateful to R.S. Bisht of ASI for this information.
27. *Ṛgveda*, 2.20.7, 8.1.8.
28. शतं मा पुर आयसीररक्ष। *Ṛgveda*, 4.27.1.
29. *Vedic Index*, vol. I, pp. 538-9.
30. A.B. Keith, *The Cambridge History of India*, vol. I, p. 88.
31. A.C. Das, *Ṛgvedic Culture*, p. 187.
32. *Ṛgveda*, 1.58.8; some Scholars have taken the *ayas* to mean iron. But there are grave doubts on this.
33. Ibid., 1.173.10.
34. S.D. Singh, op. cit., pp. 126-8.
35. G.R. Sharma, *The Excavations at Kauśāmbī*, p. 24.
36. V.S. Agrawala, *India as Known to Pāṇini*, pp. 137-40.
37. D.K. Barua, *An Analytical Study of four Nikāyas*, p. 215.
38. E.B. Cowell, *The Jātaka*, vol. 6, p. 197.
39. *ASI Report*, 1905-6, pp. 88-9.
40. Ibid.
41. *Indian Archaeology, 1959-60*, p. 46.
42. M. Wheeler, op. cit., pp. 131-2.
43. J.W. M'crindle, *The Invasion of India*, pp. 194-5.
44. Ibid., pp. 69-71, etc.
45. Ibid., pp. 117-18.
46. Ibid., p. 142.
47. Ibid., *Ancient India*, p. 205.
48. L. Woolley, *History of Mankind; Culture and Scientific Development*, vol. 1., pt. 2, p. 258, quoted by D. Chattopadhyaya, *History of Science and Technology in Ancient India*, p. 372.
49. *AS*, 2.3.1-2.
50. Ibid., 2.3.
51. Ibid., 2.4.1-4.
52. C. Tedgell, *History of Architecture in India*, p. 8.
53. लङ्का पुनर्निरालम्बा देवदुर्गा भयावहा।
    नादेयं पार्वतं वान्यं कृत्रिमं च चतुर्विधम्।। *Rām*, Yuddha, 3.20.
54. *Ram*, Bāla, 5.10-13.
55. तत्रेषूपलयन्त्राणि बलवन्ति महान्ति च।
    आगतं प्रतिसैन्यं तैस्तत्र प्रतिनिवार्यते।।

द्वारेषु संस्कृता भीमाः कालायसमयाः शिताः।
शतशो रचिता वीरैः शतघ्न्यो राक्षसां गणैः। *Rām*, Yuddha, 3.12-13

56. परिखाश्च शतघ्न्यश्च यन्त्राणि विविधानि च।
शोभयन्ति पुरीं लकां रावणस्य दुरात्मनः।। Ibid., 3.23.

57. Ibid., 3.27.

58. धन्वदुर्गं महीदुर्गं गिरिदुर्गं तथैव च।
मनुष्यदुर्गमब्दुर्गं वनदुर्गं च तानि षट्।। *MB*, Śānti, 87.5.

59. सागरप्रतिरूपाभिः परिखाभिरलंकृतम्।
प्राकारेण च संपन्नं दिवमावृत्य तिष्ठता।।
द्विपक्षगरुडप्रख्यैद्वरैर्घोरप्रदर्शनैः।
गुप्तमभ्रचयप्रख्यैर्गोपुरैर्मन्दरोपमैः।।
विविधैरतिनिर्विद्धैः शस्त्रोपेतैः सुसंवृतैः।
शक्तिभिश्चावृतं तद्धि द्विजौरिव पन्नगैः।
तल्पैश्चाभ्यासिकैर्युक्तं शुशुभे योधरक्षितम्।।
तीक्ष्णाङ्कुशशतघ्नीभिर्यन्त्रजालैश्च शोभितम्।
आयसैश्च महाचक्रैः शुशुभे तत्पुरोत्तमम्।। *MB*, Ādi, 199.29-33.

60. पुरं च ते सुगुप्तं स्याद् दृढप्राकारतोरणम्।
अट्टाट्टालकसम्बाधं षट्पथं सर्वतोदिशम्।।
तस्य द्वाराणि कार्याणि पर्याप्तानि बृहन्ति च।
सर्वतः सुविभक्तानि यन्त्रैरारक्षितानि च।। Ibid., Āśrama, 9.16-17.

61. C.V. Vaidya, *Epic India*, vol. I, p. 263; also see T. Bhattacharya, *The Canons of Indian Art*, pp. 53-4; the actual reference in the epic runs as follows:
प्रकण्ठीः कारयेत्सम्यगाकाशजनीस्तथा।
आपूरयेच्च परिखाः स्थाणुनक्रझषाकुलाः।। *MB*, Śānti, 69.41.
द्वारेषु च गुरूण्येव यंत्राणि स्थापयेत्सदा।
आरोपयेच्छतघ्नीश्च स्वाधीनानि च कारयेत्।। Ibid., 69.43.
Prakaṇṭhīs have been explained as the defensive posts on the ramparts of the fort and *ākāśajanīs* as the small openings in the wall, through which enemy could be seen and shot at.

62. C.V. Vaidya, Ibid., p. 201.

63. धन्वदुर्गं महीदुर्गमब्दुर्गं वार्क्षमेव वा।
नृदुर्गं गिरिदुर्गं वा समाश्रित्य वसेत्पुरम्।।
सर्वेण तु प्रयत्नेन गिरिदुर्गं समाश्रयेत्।
एषां हि बाहुगुण्येन गिरिदुर्गं विशिष्यते।। *Manusmṛti*, 7.70-71; also *Mānasollāsa*, 2.4.541-42; *Kāmandaka Nīti*, 4.57.

64. Ibid., 7.71.

65. दुर्गेषु च महाराज षट्सु ये शास्त्रनिश्चिताः।
सर्वेषु तेषु मन्यन्ते नरदुर्गं सदुस्तरम्।। *MB*, Śānti, 56.35.

66. पृथुसीमं महाखातमुच्चप्राकारतोरणम्।
पुरं समावसेच्छैलसरिन्मरुवनाश्रयं।।
जलबद्धान्यधनवद्दुर्गं कालसहं महत्।
औदकं पार्वतं वार्क्षमैरिणं धन्विनं च षद्।। *Agni Pu.*, 239.28-9; also 222.3-5.
67. *Matsya Pu.*, 217.8-13.
68. *Devī Pu.*, 72.
69. *Brahmavaivartta Pu.*, 103.
70. *Śukranīti.*, 4.6.9; for details see 4.6.1-14.
71. स्वपक्षै परपक्षैश्च दुर्गस्थ: पूज्यते नृप:।
एतद्धि दुर्गव्यसनात् सर्वमेव विपद्यते।। *Kāmandaka Nīti*, 14.30.
72. विशीर्णयन्त्रप्राकारपरिखात्वमशस्त्रता।
क्षीणद्यासन्धनान्नत्वाद् दुर्गव्यसनमुच्यते।। Ibid., 14.65; *Agni Pu.*, 241.28.
73. G. Woodcock, *The Greeks in India*, pp. 110-11.
74. J.N. Banerjee, *Comprehensive History of India*, vol. II, p. 152.
75. J. Marshall, *Taxilā*, pp. 113-14.
76. J.W. M'crindle, *Ancient India as Described in Classical Literature*, p. 192.
77. *Milindapañho*, p. 2.
78. J. Marshall, *Taxilā*, pp. 217-18.
79. Ibid., p. 218.
80. Ibid.
81. Ibid.
82. Ibid.
83. G.R. Sharma, *Excavations at Kauśāmbī*, 1945-50, *Memoirs ASI*, no.74, pp. 1-3.
84. H. Ingholt, *Gandhāra Art in Pakistan*, pls. 48, 91, 103, 151, 152, 464; also W. Zwalf, *A Catalogue of the Gandhara Sculptures in the British Museum*, vol. 2, pls. 155, 161, 163-4, 176, 205, 214, 218, 323-4.
85. M.C. Joshi, *Journal of the Indian Society of Oriental Art*, vol. 8, p. 17; also B.N. Mukherjee, 'Growth of Mathurā and its Society', in *Mathurā: The Cultural Heritage*, pp. 63-4.
86. I am indebted to Shri R.S. Bisht, Archaeologist, for this information.
87. *AS*, 2.3.
88. J. Marshall and A. Foucher, *The Monuments of Sāñchī*, vol. 1, p. 118, pl. 15.
89. Ibid.
90. A.L. Srivastava, *Life in Sāñchī Sculptures*, pp. 50-2.
91. *Raghuvaṁśa*, 4.26.

92. V. Kanakasabhai, *The Tamils Eighteen Hundred Years Ago*, p. 12; also pp. 15, 24, 86, 100.
93. J.F. Fleet, *Indian Antiquary*, vol. 6, p. 78.
94. Ibid., p. 130.
95. *MB*, Śānti, 87.5.
96. *Rām*, Yuddha, 3.20-2; *Manusmṛti*, 7.70; *Agni Pu.*, 222.4-5; *Matsya Pu.*, 217.6-7; *Samarāṅgaṇasūtradhāra*, 45.39-40; *Kāmandaka Nīti*, 4.57.
97. अन्तर्द्वीपं स्थलं वा निम्नावरुद्धमौदकं, प्रास्तरं गुहां वा पार्वतं, निरुदकस्तम्बमिरिणं वा धान्वनं खंजनोदकं स्तम्बगहनं वा वनदुर्गम्। *AS*, 2.3.1.
98. *Śukranīti*, 4.6.1-9.
99. Ibid., 4.6.4,6.
100. Ibid., 4.6.8, 12.
101. *AS*, 2.3.1; *Devī Pu.*, 72.
102. अग्निना तामसं दुर्गं नौभिराप्यं च गम्यते।
राजदुर्गावितरणे नोपायं पण्डिता विदुः।। *MB*, Śānti, 83.40.
103. *AS*, 2.3.1.
104. *Śukranīti*, 4.6.3.
105. *AS*, 2.3.1, also *Devī Pu.*, 72.
106. *Manusmṛti*, 7.70; *Śukranīti*, (4.6.2) calls it *pāridha*.
107. *AS*, 2.3.5.
108. सुदुस्तरम्। *MB*, Śānti, 56.35.
109. *Śukranīti*, 4.6.9, 11.
110. *MB*, Vana, 16.
111. Ibid., Śānti, 69.43-45; Vana, 15.6-8.
112. *AS.*, 12.5.
113. Ibid., 2.18.1.
114. यंत्रगोष्पणमुष्टिपाषाणरोचनीदृषदश्चाश्मायुधानि। *AS*, 2.18.15.
115. J.W. M'crindle, *The Invasion of India*, p. 199.
116. तृणच्छन्नानि वेश्मानि पङ्केनापि प्रलेपयेत्।
निर्हरेच्च तृणं मासे चैत्रे वह्निभयात्पुरः।। *MB*, Śānti, 69.45.
117. S.D. Singh, op. cit., p. 126.
118. *Śabdakalpadruma*, see *aparodha*; also *Harivaṁśa*, Viṣṇu, 118.81-5.
119. E.B. Cowell, *The Jātaka*, vol. 6, p. 156.
120. *AS*, 13.1-5.
121. Ibid.
122. *MB*, Vana, 268.
123. पुरः भेत्तारो। *MB*, Sabhā, 54.10.
124. E.B. Cowell, *The Jātaka*, vol. 2, pp. 64-5.

125. दारं च गुडेन। *AS*, 13.4.9.
126. सुरुङ्गाबलकुटिकाभ्यां वप्रप्राकारौ हारयेत्। Ibid., 13.4.9; Kauṭilya has also described in detail the measures which could be adopted to defeat a mining attempt.
127. Ibid., 13.4.14-22.
128. वज्राशनिसमस्पर्शं परगोपुरदारणम्। *Rām*, Araṇya, 26.11.
129. J. Fergusson, *Tree and Serpent Worship*, p. 141, pl. XXXVIII.
130. J.W. M'crindle, *Ancient India as described in Classical Literature*, p. 155; also p. 206.
131. J.W. M'crindle, *The Invasion of India*, p. 62.
132. Ibid., pp. 146, 148; also pp. 237, 288, 311.

Chapter 8

Education and Training

The inhabitants of Indus Valley who lived in forts and used weapons may also have devised some system of training soldiers in offensive and defensive skills. The Vedic Āryans may also have followed some system of military training. According to Das,

> we shall not, therefore, be wrong in inferring that every village had some kind of organization for training men in the use of arms, the art of riding, physical culture, skilful driving of chariots, and the rudimentary arts of warfare. Horse-racing and chariot-racing were indulged in probably not so much for amusement, as for the necessity of developing and promoting a skill in horse-riding and chariot-driving. It appears that *grāmaṇi* who was both the civil and military leader of the village took a lead in the matter and organized his village contingent not only for the defence of the village, but also for taking an active part in any war that the king might wage against a powerful enemy.[1]

The term *śrutasenāya*[2] perhaps denoted a well trained army.

DHANURVEDA

As the *dhanuṣ* (bow) dominated the Indian weapon system from the earliest times, the *Dhanurveda* or the science of archery came to denote the knowledge of all weapons and warfare (*yuddha-vidyā*).[3] In the *Mahābhārata* it has been defined as four-legged and ten-limbed[4] suggesting its wide application. It specifies that the knowledge of wielding sword, shield and mace as also the art of handling elephants was a part of it.[5] The *Rāmāyaṇa* includes not only physical exercise, hunting and art of warfare within the ambit of *Dhanurveda*,[6] but also the art of mounting horse, elephant and chariot.[7] In fact, it considers all knowladge of warfare as part of *Dhanurveda*.[8] Among the epic warriors Gautama, Bhīṣma, Droṇa, Kṛpācārya, Karṇa and Arjuna are stated to have mastered *Dhanurveda.*[9] The *Agni Purāṇa* says that *Dhanurveda* included the knowledge of all the four arms, all kinds of weapons, personal combat, etc.[10] According to the *Śukranīti, as* an *upaveda* of *Yajurveda*, it encompassed the knowledge of war, weapons and battle arrays.[11] Elsewhere, it says that the five military activities, viz., hurling of weapon at the objective, formation of *vyūha* in accord with musical notes and deployment of horse, elephant and chariot formed a part of *Dhanurveda.*[12]

IMPORTANCE OF TRAINING

There is an interesting reference to military training in *Saṁyutta Nikāya*, an early Buddhist work. Once Buddha enquired of King Prasenajit whether he would like to keep a Brāhmaṇa, Kṣatriya, Vaiśya or Śilpakāra, who is uneducated, untrained, inexperienced, undisciplined and lacked courage in his service, to which the king replied in negative. But when asked whether he would keep an educated, capable, trained, experienced, disciplined and fearless person, unmindful of caste distinction in his service the king replied in the affirmative.[13] The *Mahābhārata* says that a smaller army, if well-trained, was preferable to a large army which was untrained.[14] The *Arthaśāstra* also supports this while stating that a well-trained Kṣatriya army is far more useful than a large but untrained Brāhmaṇa, Vaiśya or Śūdra army.[15]

In the Kauṭilyan concept of warfare there was no place for an untrained soldier. The commander-in-chief conveyed his instructions regarding the formation of battle-arrays by means of signals passed through trumpets, standards and flags.[16] It implies that the troops had to be educated and trained in all military moves and all kinds of signals. He adds that footmen, horses, chariots and elephants shall be given necessary training in the art of war at sunrise on all days but those of conjunction (of planets); on these occasions of training, the king shall ever be present and witness the exercise.[17]

The *Kāmandaka Nīti* emphasizes the need of regular practice for soldiers to achieve excellence in fighting. 'By constant practice one becomes an adept in fighting from chariots, horses, elephants and boats, and a past-master in archery; by constant and regular practice an intelligent man can perform the difficult feats.'[18] The *Śukranīti* also adds that an intelligent person can achieve anything by regular practice.[19] The *Saṅgam* literature also refers to the practice of horsemanship and target shooting by the soldiers.[20]

The *Śukranīti* compares an untrained army with a heap of cotton.[21] As a trained army, led by a warrior could easily face the enemy, it was incumbent on the ruler to attack the enemy only with a trained army.[22] Further, as the orders regarding the formation of battle arrays, etc., were passed on to the troops by means of trumpet, a thorough training was necessary to understand the signals.[23] The training process continued even when the army was camping for the battle and the commander while making a choice of battlefield, ensured that it provided for adequate space for the exercise and parade of the troops. According to Kāmandaka while in camp, the drilling of the soldiers should be conducted with various appliances on the ground cleared of trees, shrubs, stones, mounds, etc., on a regular basis.[24] The defeat of an untrained and unskilled army was considered a certainty.[25]

SYSTEM OF EDUCATION

The basic military education was imparted to children within the house. The Kaurava princes, Dhṛtarāṣṭra, Pāṇḍu and Vidura received their military training under the tutelage of Bhīṣma. This included the use of mace, sword, shield, and bow and also the skill of controlling elephants.[26] Subsequently, Bhīṣma organized the military training of Kaurava and Pāṇḍava princes in the palace under the tutelage of Kṛpācārya. Later on, Droṇācārya took over this responsibility.[27] Rāma and Lakṣmaṇa received their basic military training from Ācārya Sudhanvan, who had mastered the weapon systems.[28]

Āśramas

After learning the basics in the house the boys were sent to some *āśrama*, run by a Brāhmaṇa, who was highly proficient in *Dhanurveda*. Rāma and Lakṣmaṇa received their early education and training in weapons in an *āśrama* located in Ayodhyā, not far from the palace. They kept their prized weapons in the custody of the teacher.[29] Subsequently, they learnt *Dhanurveda* in the *āśrama* of Viśvāmitra.[30] The sage blessed them with two disciplines of knowledge called *balā* and *atibalā*[31] and also taught them weapon systems including the use of divine weapons (*divyāstra*).[32] The great warriors like Bhīṣma and Karṇa received their lessons in the *āśrama* of Paraśurāma. *Ācārya* Śukra and Bṛhaspati, two great military thinkers of India, might have run *āśramas* for the benefit of their respective proteges, i.e. Asuras and Devas. It is notable that all wars fought between the Devas and Asuras were monitored by their respective *gurus*. Surprisingly, despite the total monopoly of Brāhmaṇas in the teaching of *Dhanurveda* the *Manusmṛti* speaks lowly of the profession of *yuddhācārya* (master of warfare).[33]

Pupils desirous of learning *Dhanurveda* flocked to reputed *āśramas* from distant lands. In the *āśrama* of Kṛpācārya,many princes besides the Pāṇḍavas and Kauravas received instructions in the art of war.[34] So was the case in the *āśrama* of Droṇa.[35] Occasionally, instructors were appointed to train the princes within the state capital, but still the students had to lead a regimented life in an *āśrama* like atmosphere. This was how the Pāṇḍava and Kaurava brothers received their military training. In the epics there are references to many *āśramas,* viz., Ṛṣyasṛṅga Āśrama, Viśvāmitra Āśrama, Gautama Āśrama, Vaśiṣṭha Āśrama, Jamdagni Āśrama, Jarāsandha Āśrama, Kṛpa Āśrama, Droṇa Āśrama, Baladeva Āśrama, Agastya Āśrama, Bhārgava Āśrama, Sandīpa Āśrama, Bhāradvāja Āśrama, Vālmīki Āśrama, etc., which imparted education and training in various disciplines, including *Dhanurveda.*

There was a tradition of offering presents (*gurudakṣiṇā*) to the master by the pupils on completion of their training. Eklavya gladly offered his severed thumb as *gurudakṣiṇā* to Droṇācārya, when asked to do so. Pāṇḍava brothers conquered Pañcāla and imprisoned King Drupada to make an oppropriate present to *guru* Droṇa.[36]

Taxilā Centre

Taxilā was a great centre of military education and training in ancient times. Many *āśramas* run by military experts were located in this city. In a particular *āśrama* at Taxilā as many as 300 pupils belonging to various kingdoms of India received military training.[37] The training included various disciplines of warfare such as art of mounting the horse, elephant and chariot and the handling of various types of weapons. Some institutions provided for special training in bowmanship.[38] One Brāhmaṇa boy Jotipāla was sent to Taxilā by the ruler of Vārāṇasī, at state expense, to master the art of bowmanship. The teacher was so impressed by his excellence that he offered him the chair of *ācārya.*[39] The *Mahābhāṣya*, while referring to the schools which imparted instructions in military matters (*kṣātravidyā*) and sword fights (*asibhiryuddham*) and cavalry encounters (*aśvair-yuddham*)[40] was perhaps speaking of these institutions. It is not known whether these institutions were funded by the state or were run privately. Presumably, these were run on the line of *āśramas* with some aid from the state.

Village Centres

The village seems to have served as the basic training centre for aspiring soldiers in Vedic times.[41] In the *Arthaśāstra* there is a reference that some villages sent military assistance to the state in times of need and in return were allowed relief in land tax.[42] Such voluntary armies might have been trained in the village itself. The militias encountered by Alexander during his Indian campaign[43] might have been similar armies.

State Centres

The Mauryan army was organized as a regular force, educated, trained and equipped at the state expense. It seems that with the state taking over the responsibility the *āśramas* gradually ceased to serve as centres of military education and training. The silence of Greek historians, *Arthaśāstra*, and Nīti works about such centres also confirms this. The *Kādambarī*, a work of seventh century AD, refers to an institution where the princes and high-ups of the state received military education. It was a huge complex surrounded by high walls and provided with big and strong gates. Additional protection was ensured by constructing a moat around it. There was only one passage to enter it. Within the boundary wall a big stable was located on one side and a gymnasium on the other. Teachers accomplished in various disciplines of learning were appointed in the academy after a rigorous selection process.[44]

Vihāras

Like the Brāhmaṇic *āśramas*, Buddhist *vihāras* also served as the centres of military education and training.[45] When King Prasenajit was repeatedly defeated by Ajātaśatru he called an assembly to analyse the cause of his defeat. The members debated the issue and concluded that an answer to this could be obtained by dispatching a messenger to a Buddhist *vihāra.* Evidently, Buddhist *vihāras* served as educational centres where military matters were also taught and debated. Monks were supposed to be fully conversant with issues related to military strategy and tactics. Perhaps, Brāhmaṇic temples, which served as educational centres, taught *Dhanurveda* as well.

Guru Tradition

In ancient India the knowledge passed on from master to pupil. Ācārya Bṛhaspati had mastered *āgneyāstra* (weapon that caused fire) and from him the knowledge passed on to Bhāradvāja, Agniveśa, Droṇācārya and Arjuna respectively.[46] Warriors introduced themselves by citing the name of their *guru.* Introducing himself to Bhīṣma, Droṇācārya proudly said that he had learnt *Dhanurvidyā* from his *guru* Agniveśa.[47] Drupada, Droṇa, and Karṇa were the disciples of Paraśurāma. Bhīmasena and Duryodhana had learnt the use of mace (*gadā*) from Balarāma.

Before imparting the knowledge of weapons to a person the *guru* first considered his eligibility. When Karṇa requested Droṇācārya to bless him with the knowledge of *brahmāstra,* the latter regretted his inability to do so as only Brāhmaṇas and pious Kṣatriyas were entitled to it.[48] Droṇa even refused to accept low-born Ekalavya as his disciple.[49] Paraśurāma admitted Karṇa as his disciple and taught him the use of *brahmāstra* only after the latter convinced him of his Brāhmaṇa pedigree. This false statement proved very costly for Karṇa ultimately.

Ācārya Droṇa treated all his students as equal but Arjuna being most hardworking and sincere was his favourite. Droṇa taught him to fight on foot as also mounted on chariot, elephant and horse. He also taught him the art of fighting with weapons like mace, bow, sword, spear, etc., as also the strategy of encountering a numerically superior enemy. But he excelled in bowmanship.[50] Among the other disciples of Droṇa, Bhīma and Duryodhana specialized in mace, Nakula and Sahadeva in sword, and Yudhiṣṭhira in spear. During the training, tests were conducted to assess the capability of students.[51]

After the completion of training a show was organized to enable the students to display their skills in weaponry.[52] Droṇācārya sought the permission of King Dhṛtarāṣṭra to conduct such a show. All members of the royal family including women attended the great show. Before the beginning of the show auspicious *mantras* were recited and the *gurus* were honoured with costly gifts. The participant princes entered the arena (*raṅgabhūmi*) dressed in military attire.[53] After seeking the blessings of the teachers they went about showing their skills in bowmanship, art of fighting mounted on chariot, horse and elephant, swordsmanship, wrestling, etc. Bhīma and Duryodhana displayed their skills in fighting with mace. When the supporters of the two princes started getting restive and the duel assumed dangerous overtones Droṇācārya ordered them to stop the fight. Arjuna captivated the hearts of the onlookers by displaying unbelievable feats in bowmanship.

SCOPE OF TRAINING

In Vedic India military training may have included the use of very few weapons. However, in fifth century BC, mock fights, roll calls, parade of troops, marching of troops through the streets and manoeuvres had come to form a part of military training as is evident from Buddhist *Nikāyas.*[54] The *Mahābhāṣya* refers to some professional schools which imparted instructions on military subjects (*kṣātra vidyā*)[55] such as sword fights and cavalry encounters.[56] However, during the Epic times military training came to include almost all aspects of warfare. The trainee was now expected to learn the tackling of mounts, use of military machines and recognition of magical weapons besides *Dhanurveda.*[57] Rāma was taught *Dhanurveda* and also *balā* and *atibalā*, two related subjects, by *guru* Viśvāmitra.[58]

In the *Arthaśāstra* the importance of military training is repeatedly emphasized. Regular training sessions were held for all soldiers during the morning hours, under the supervision of *patyādhyakṣa, aśvādhyakṣa, hastyadhyakṣa* and *rathādhyakṣa.*[59] The commander-in-chief carried overall supervision,[60] though the king also attended these training sessions. The curriculum included the mounting of chariot, elephant, and horse and practice of various weapons.[61] Hunting was also a part of military training.[62]

The *Śukranīti*, which describes the system of military training in detail, includes close combat, wrestling, exercise, and nursing food in the training programme.[63] King seated on a raised platform witnesses the training, while his aides kept a close watch on the practice and exercises. The training was conducted in accordance with the signals passed on through the trumpet.[64] King himself practised with various mounts, and exchanged his knowledge of the *vyūhas* with his men during the training sessions.[65] He augmented his stamina by practising weapons with warriors and hunting tigers.[66] It is notable that the king spent two hours and fifteen minutes of his daytime in military training and some forty-five minutes in practicing with soldiers.[67] Hunting took another forty-five minutes.[68] Horse riding, chariot-racing, etc., consumed forty-five minutes.[69] Thus military matters alone took some five hours of the king's time everyday. The officers who organized military training were called Śatānīka and Anuśātika.[70] Details on military training are also met in later works like the *Nītiprakāśikā*, the *Dhanurveda* and the *Mānasollāsa*.

The royal academy, described in the *Kādambarī*, which imparted education in various disciplines also provided for military training. Prince Candrāpīḍa received special training in wrestling, use of weapons like bow, sword, shield, spear, axe and mace, tunnelling, climbing, swimming, *āyurveda*, veterinary science, etc., at the academy. Exercise was an integral part of curriculum. The blow of his sword could cut down palm trees at one stroke and the power of his shaft could destroy the loftiest peaks.[71] The sons of ministers and high-ups of the state also received similar training.

Hunting

Hunting was an integral part of military training. Kauṭilya considered it necessary for a ruler[72] because 'in hunting, there is exercise, getting rid of phlegm, bile, fat and (a tendency to) perspiration, practice in hitting the targets of moving and stationary bodies, knowledge of the minds of animals in anger, fear and condition of ease, and (only) occasional marching'.[73] The forests were reserved for royal hunting.[74] According to Daṇḍin there is nothing so beneficial as hunting.

It gives the leg magnificent exercise; and long-winded speed might prove handy after a defeat. It dries up the phlegmatic humor, thus promoting digestion, the safe foundation of health. By reducing fat it makes the body vigorous, sinewy, and agile. It gives power to endure cold, heat, wind, rain, hunger, thirst. . . . It wins the confidence of jungle tribes. It fosters energy, thus impressing hostile armies.[75]

Hunting was both an exercise and entertainment for the rulers. Kings entered dense forests full of ferocious animals for hunting, accompanied by their army,[76] though occasionally, they moved into the forest alone. King Daśaratha, killed Śravaṇakumāra during one such hunting jaunt.[77] Rāma also used to go for hunting near the banks of Sarayū.[78] Mahārāja Pāṇḍu killed a pair of deers by mistake and paid for it with his life.[79] Rainy season was considered ideal for hunting.[80]

In fourth century BC hunting was considered as the main exercise for rulers.[81] The ruler of Saubhūti maintained a good number of hunting dogs that were amazingly courageous. He presented 1500 such dogs to Alexander.[82] When the Maurya emperor left for hunting he proceeded in bacchanalian fashion,

crowds of women surrounded him and outside of this circle spearmen are ranged. The road is marked off with ropes, and it is death, for men and women alike to pass within the ropes. Men with drums and gongs lead the procession. The king hunts in enclosures and shoots arrows from a platform. At his side stand two or three women. If he hunts in the open ground he shoots from the back of the elephant. Of the women some are on chariots, some on horses and some even on elephants, and they are equipped with weapons of every kind as if they were going on a campaign.[83]

The art of Bhārhut and Sāñcī also represents some hunting scenes.

The Gupta rulers were very fond of hunting as is evident from their coins.[84] On his gold issues Samudragupta is shown as aiming his weapon at a lion. Candragupta II in one of his rare issues is depicted as attacking a lion with a sword. Kumāragupta was also fond of hunting as his coins are replete with hunting scenes. According to Rosenfield hunting was an Iranian theme, which the Guptas borrowed from their coins.[85] This appears probable because hunting themes are exclusive to Gupta coins in India.

Hunting was a popular sport for the rulers is also evident from the literature. King Duṣyanta met Śakuntalā at Kaṇvāśrama while on a hunting jaunt in the forest.[86] Prince Harṣavardhana, while accompanying his brother on an expedition, spent many days outside the camp hunting lions, tigers, etc.[87] Prince Candrāpīḍa was also very fond of hunting and during one such jaunt he killed a large number of lions, bears, and antilopes.[88]

The way the rulers went about hunting is described in the *Kāmandaka Nīti*:

Desirous of hunting, a light-handed monarch, in order that his aim might not fail, should enter, being followed by a well disciplined and well accoutred army, a wood, the access to which is easy, the outskirts of which have been reconnoitred and are guarded by soldiers, and which abound in game and is (therefore) a suitable place (to hunt in).[89]

The *Śukranīti* advises kings to sport with tigers, peacocks, etc., and kill the dangerous animals.[90] It adds that hunting improved the aiming of the target, sharpened the skill in weaponry and generated a feeling of fearlessness.[91] Some hunting scenes are also represented in the art of Ajantā. 'A chief on a white horse, an umbrella being held over him, goes a-hunting, accompanied by two companions on horse-back, followed by two elephants, and attended by foot-soldiers and a number of servants, who lead dogs in leashes. In front of them is an antelope in a handsome cast.'[92] Hunting continued to be a favourite sport of rulers in medieval India.

TRAINING IN WEAPONS

Learning the use of various weapons was an important aspect of *Dhanurveda*. Among the weapons known to Indians, bow, sword, mace, spear and shield were most widely used. They had also evolved a separate system of training for each of these weapons. The training included complete knowledge of the weapon, its application in offence and defence, and the actual use.

Bow (*Dhanuṣ*)

Bow was the most ancient and popular weapon of India. To learn its use the trainee had to pass through four basic stages called *atama*, *prati*, *ayam* and *asa*.[93] In the first stage (*atama*) the trainee learnt the technique of holding the bow, in the second stage (*prati*) fixing of the arrow on the bow, in the third stage (*ayam*) aiming of the target and in the fourth stage (*asa*) release of the arrow. After this basic education the trainee learnt the skills and postures related to bowmanship (*kodaṇḍacāturī*).[94] Hitting a target, while mounting a chariot, elephant or horse, may have required special training and practice. Hunting was considered useful for mastering this art.

In the *Dhanurveda* it is advised that an archer should shoot 400 arrows everyday, 200 in the morning and 200 in the evening. The period from October to April was considered most suitable for the practice of archery. In six months one could learn all the basics of archery whereas in one year one could become an expert archer.[95]

The *Mahābhārata* refers to ten methods or ways (*gatis*) of shooting arrows.[96] Nīlakaṇṭha in his commentary describes these as *unmukhī, abhimukhī, tiryaka, mandā, gomūtrikā, dhruvā, skhalitā, yamakākrāntā, kruṣṭā* and *atikruṣṭā*. He further explains that *unmukhī-gati* targetted the head, *abhimukhī* the chest and *tiryaka* the body sides. *Mandā* cut through the skin, *gomūtrikā* pierced the armour, *dhruvā* was a sure destroyer, *skhalitā* was a failed shot, *yamakākrāntā* pierced through the body, *kruṣṭā* severed a limb and *atikruṣṭā* cut the head of the enemy. The bowmen may have been taught all these *gatis* (moves) of the arrow by masters like Droṇācārya and Kṛpācārya.

Sword (*Khaḍga*)

Indians had devised a procedure for training in swordsmanship. In the *Mahābhārata* 21 techniques of wielding sword have been mentioned. These included *bhrānta, āviddha, udbhrānta, āpluta, prasrata, srata, parivṛtta, nivṛtta, sampāta, samudīrṇa, bhārata, kauśika, sāttvata*, etc.[97] In the *Agni Purāṇa* 32 techniques are mentioned.[98] Soldiers also learnt the art of fighting with sword while mounted on horse-back.[99]

Mace (*Gadā*)

In the *Mahābhārata* many manoeuvres related to the use of mace are mentioned. These include *maṇḍala, gomūtrika, gata, pratyāgata, parimokṣa, praharaṇa, varjana, paridharaṇa*, etc.[100] The *Agni Purāṇa* also refers to these manoeuvres.[101] A mace wielder was supposed to know all about them.

Short Sword (*Kaṭāra*)

Kaṭāra served the dual purpose of cutting and thrusting. Its wielder had to be well-versed in all the postures related to its use. The *Mānasollāsa* refers to twelve such postures.[102]

Shield (*Carman*)

The safety of a warrior depended on his skill to hold the shield. In the *Mānasollāsa* five ways of holding a shield are mentioned, viz., *kapolaka, śrīvatsa, bhūmaṇḍala, tikacakra* and *dalaga.*[103]

Noose (*Pāśa*)

Noose, made of rope, was used to catch hold of an enemy. In Vedic period it served as the weapon of Varuṇa, the lord of the seas. In the Epic war it figures as an important weapon. Ten methods of using a noose are mentioned in the *Agni Purāṇa.*[104] In the *gurukulas* the trainees perfected this art by flinging noose on the fakes covered with skins.[105]

Movements

Besides learning the art of wielding weapons the soldiers, particularly the foot-men, also acquired skills in various movements. Some of these movements are referred to in the *Avantisundarīkathā.* To illustrate *caturāstra* was a quadrangular movement, *vaiśākhāgati* was moving like a churning stick, *sadhvālīḍagati* was moving straight like *ālīḍa* (right knee being advanced and the left leg retracted), *vallinartan* was moving like a creeper, *bāhyāvarta* was moving zigzag, *bhadragati* was moving gently or leisurely, *anukākṣaṇa* was moving constantly, *śyenapata* was moving like a falcon, *svastikākriyā* was moving like a *svastika* symbol.[106]

TRAINING OF ANIMALS

Man has been using animals in war from the earliest times. Indians had devised a system of training elephants, horses, camels, oxen and dogs for the purpose. There existed institutions which specialized in imparting such training and in the Epic times Bhāradvāja *āśrama* might have been one of them.[107]

Elephants

The archaeological remains indicate that Indians had domesticated elephant some 2500 years before the beginning of the Christian era. The Vedic Āryans also used elephants. In the Epic war elephants were used and an officer designated *granthika* looked after their training,[108] though occasionally mahout could also do it.[109] In sixth century BC there existed institutions which specialized in training elephants for war purposes.[110] It was believed that trained elephant remained firm in the battlefield whereas an untrained elephant sulked under pressure.[111]

The training of elephants was called *sannāhya karma*[112] and Kauṭilya believed that it augmented the valour, speed, and spirit of the beast.[113] An official called *anīkastha* supervised the training.[114] Elephants were trained in seven kinds of activities called *upasthāna, saṁvartana, samayāna, vadhāvadha, hasti-yuddha, nāgarāyaṇa* and *sāṅgrāmika.*[115] In *upasthāna* the elephant was trained to raise or squeese body organs and crossover the hurdles like standards, bamboo poles, etc. In *saṁvartana* it learnt to lie down, sit on the earth and jump over the ditches. In *samayāna* it was trained to move in straight, bent, or zigzag way. In *vadhāvadha* the elephant learnt to kill men or horses by means of the trunk, body or tusk. In *hasti-yuddha* the animal was trained to fight with elephants of greater power, equal power, or lesser power. In *nāgarāyaṇa* elephant was taught to break open the doors, walls, and chains. In *saṅgrāmika* elephant was trained to fight. In the *Harṣacarita* it is said that the *mahāmātras* trained the elephants with the help of a dummy created after filling the skin of a dead elephant.[116] The *Śukranīti* also refers to the training of elephants.[117]

HORSES

In the *Ṛgveda* there is a reference to one thousand well-trained, swift-going horses.[118] The horse was thus introduced in the Indian battlefield by the Āryans and this could not have been possible without proper training. The Buddhist *Nikāyas* refer to the taming and training of the horse and the institution of horse trainers (*aśvadamaka*). The *Bhaḍḍalisutta* describes the training of the horse in bearing the bit and harness, going straight, running in a circle, walking on the hoofs silently, galloping and neighing to command, performing royal acrobatic feat, high speed and manners.[119] In the Epic age the horse-trainer was called *granthika* or *aśvabandha.*[120] In the *Arthaśāstra* there is a detailed description of horse training which generally related to movements such as *valgana, nicairagata, laṅghaṇa, ghoraṇa* and *nirostra.*[121] These meant moving at a gallop, moving at a centre, leaping, moving at a trot and responding to signals respectively. Each of these five moves comprised many sub-moves in which the horse was trained.[122] In the *Śukranīti* 11 movements of the horse are mentioned. These included *cakrita, recita, valgitaka, dhaurita, āpluta, tura, maṇḍa, kuṭila, sarpaṇa, parivartana* and *askandita.* A person well-versed in all these movements could alone be made a horse trainer.[123]

There is an interesting reference to Indian way of horse training in the Greek accounts.

It is a practice with them (Indians) to control their horses with bit and bridle, and to make them move at a measured pace and in a straight course. They neither, however, gall their tongue by the use of spiked muzzles, nor torture the roof of their mouth. The professional trainer breaks them in by forcing them to gallop round and round in a ring, specially when they see them refractory. Such an undertaking demanded a strong hand as well as a thorough knowledge of horse on the part of trainer. The greatest proficients tested their skill by driving a chariot round and round in a ring; and in truth it would be no trifling feat to control with ease a team of four high-mettled steeds when whirling round in a circle.[124]

Among the later works the *Agni Purāṇa* has devoted a full chapter to the training of horse.[125] In the *Śukranīti*[126] and the *Mānasollāsa*[127] also the training of horse is described in detail.

Camels, Etc.

The ass was used to pull the chariot in the Vedic times.[128] The *Arthaśāstra* recommends that during the campaign in semi-arid zones ass and camel could be pressed into service.[129] Further, when there was a shortage of horses, bullocks could also be yoked to chariots. Similarly, when not enough elephants were available for war, the carts driven by donkeys and camels could form the centre of the battle array.[130] The *Harṣacarita* specifically mentions *uṣṭrabala.*[131] But above all, these animals were required to carry military supplies. The *Śukranīti* enumerates methods by which these animals could be kept under control.[132]

Dogs

Dogs were also used in war. In fifth century BC a large number of dogs, imported from India, accompanied the army of Xerxes, the

Achaemenid king, during his campaign in Greece.[133] During his invasion of India, Alexander saw a large number of ferocious dogs with the king of Saubhūti in north-west India.[134] There is no doubt that all these dogs were highly trained.

Indians had thus perfected a system of military education and training much before the beginning of the Christian era. The basic military education was imparted at the village level under the tutelage of village headman. Higher education was, however, imparted at bigger centres like Taxilā, where students from all parts of the country came to specialize in different disciplines of military education from teachers of great eminence. *Gurukulas* or *āśramas* run by great masters of military science (*dhanurveda*) attracted students of elite class including royal princes. They mastered the art of wielding all kinds of weapons, mounting all kinds of vehicles and understanding all kinds of battle arrays as propounded by Śukrācārya and Bṛhaspati. But despite the great advances made by the Indians in the field of military science, it is rather sad that when it came to fighting in the battlefield they suffered defeat like the cursed Karṇa, who forgot all his lessons at the crucial juncture.

NOTES

1. A.C. Das, *Ṛgvedic Culture*, p. 330.
2. *Yajurveda*, 16.35.
3. पाणिलाघवम्। *MB*, Bhīṣma, 70.9, 78.34, 86.38; Droṇa, 117.36-9, 169.1.
4. चतुष्पादं दशविधं धनुर्वेदमरिंदमः। *MB*, Ādi, 213.65; these four legs were as follows:

   मंत्रमुक्तं पाणिमुक्तं मुक्तामुक्तं तथैव च।
   अमुक्तं च धनुर्वेदे चतुष्पाच्छस्त्रमीरितम्।।

   Ten divisions of *Dhanurveda* included the following:

   आदानमथ संधानं मोक्षणं विनिवर्तनम्।
   स्थानं मुष्ठिः प्रयोगश्च प्रायाश्चित्तानि मण्डलम्।।
   रहस्यं चेति दशधा धनुर्वेदाङ्गमिष्यते।

   But Nīlakaṇṭha in his commentary has explained the four legs of *Dhanurveda* as *dīkṣā* (initiation), *śikṣā* (education), *ātmarakṣā* (self-defence) and *sādhana* (means). The ten organs have been stated to be *vṛta, prāpti, kṛti, puṣṭi, smṛti, kṣepa, aribhedana, cikitsā, uddīpana,* and *kṛṣṭi.*

5. धनुर्वेदेअश्वपृष्ठे च गदायुद्धेऽसिचर्मणि।
तथैव गजशिक्षायां नीतिशास्त्रे च पारगाः।। *MB*, Ādi, 102.17;
शिष्यः कृत्स्नं धनुर्वेदं चतुष्पादमवाप्तवान्। Udyoga, 155.3.
6. *Rām*, Bāla, 18.27-28, 36; also *MB*, Ādi, 123.15.
7. *Rām*, Ibid.
8. Ibid.
9. Sage Gautama, the father of Kṛpācārya was well-versed in *Dhanurveda.*
न तस्य वेदाध्ययने तथा बुद्धिरजायत।
यथास्य बुद्धिरभवद्धनुर्वेदे परंतप।। *MB*, Ādi, 120.3.
He taught his son Kṛpācārya complete *Dhanurveda.*
चतुर्विधं धनुर्वेदमस्त्राणि विविधानि च।
निखिलेनास्य तत्सर्वं गुह्याख्यातवांस्तदा।। Ibid., 120.20.
सरहस्यव्रतं चैव धनुर्वेदमशेषतः। Ibid., 121.22.
Arjuna also imparted the knowledge of *Dhanurveda* to his son Abhimanyu.
चतुष्पादं दशविधं धनुर्वेदमरिंदम। Ibid., 213.65.
In their childhood Dhṛtarāṣṭra and Pāṇḍu had also learnt *Dhanurveda.* Ibid., 102.17. Pāṇḍavas and Kauravas both learnt *Dhanurveda* from Droṇācārya.
10. चतुष्पादं धनुर्वेदं वदे पञ्चविधं द्विज।
रथनागाश्वपत्तीनां योधांश्चाऽऽश्रित्य कीर्तितम्।।
यन्त्रमुक्तं पाणिमुक्तं मुक्तसंधारितं तथा।
अमुक्तं बाहुयुद्धं च पञ्चधा तत्प्रकीर्तितम्।। *Agni Pu.*, 249.1-2.
11. युद्धशस्त्रास्त्रकुशलो रचनाकुशलो भवेत्।
यजुर्वेदोपवेदोऽयं धनुर्वेदस्तु येन सः।। *Śukranīti*, 4.3.38.
12. कलाऽभिलक्षिते देशे यन्त्राद्यस्त्रनिपातनम्।
वाद्यसङ्केततो व्यूहरचनादि कला स्मृता।।
गजाश्वरथगत्या तु युद्धसंयोजनं कला।
कलापञ्चकमेतद्धि धनुर्वेदागये स्थितम्।। *Vis. Dh. Pu.*, 2.180.
13. *Saṁyukta Nikāya*, vol. I, pp. 123-4.
14. *MB*, Bhīṣma, 4.26-28; Śānti, 103.20-1.
15. प्रहरणविद्याविनीतं तु क्षत्रियबलं श्रेयः। *AS*, 9.2.24.
16. तूर्यध्वजपताकाभिर्व्यूहसंज्ञाः प्रकल्पयेत्।
स्थाने याने प्रहरणे सैन्यानां विनये रतः।। Ibid., 2.33.11.
17. Ibid., 5.3.35-6.
18. रथाश्वनौकुञ्जरयानयोग्यो नित्यक्रियः स्याद्धनुषि प्रगल्भः।
सुमेघसां कर्मणि दुष्करेऽपि नित्यक्रियाकौशलमादधाति।। *Kāmandaka Nīti*, 16.50.
19. *Śukranīti*, 4.7.362-4.
20. N. Subrahmanian, *Saṅgam Polity*, pp. 143-4.

21. अशिक्षितमसारं च साद्यस्कं तूलवच्च तत्। *Śukranīti*, 4.7.180.
22. सुसिद्धाल्पबलः शूरो विजेतुं क्षमते रिपुम्। Ibid., 4.7.181.
23. Ibid., 4.7.266-76; also *AS*, 2.33.11.
24. *Kāmandaka Nīti*, 17.18-19.
25. *Śukranīti*, 4.7.178.
26. *MB*, Ādi, 102.17; the Pāṇḍava brothers had earlier received military training in the *āśrama* of saint-king (*rājarṣī*) Śuka, located at Śataśṛṅga Parvata near Haridwar. Ibid., 123.
27. Ibid., 122.
28. *Rām*, Ayodhyā, 100.14.
29. सत्कृत्य निहितं सर्वमेतदाचार्यसद्मनि।
 सर्वमायुधमादाय क्षिप्रमाव्रज लक्ष्मण।। Ibid., Ayodhyā, 31.31.
30. Ibid., Bāla, 27, 28, 29.
31. Ibid., 22.15.
32. Ibid., 27,28; these included *daṇḍacakra, dharmacakra, kālacakra, viṣṇucakra, aindracakra, vajrāstra, triśūla, brahmāstra, pināka, nārāyaṇāstra, mānavāstra, mahānāstra*, etc.
33. *Manusmṛti*, 3.162.
34. ततोऽधिजग्मुः सर्वे ते धनुर्वेदं महारथाः।
 धृतराष्ट्रात्मजाश्चैव पांडवाश्च महाबलाः।।
 वृष्णयश्च नृपाश्चान्ये नानादेशसमागताः।। *MB*, Ādi, 120.21.
35. राजपुत्रास्तथैवान्ये समेत्य भरतर्षभ।
 अभिजग्मुस्ततो द्रोणमस्त्रार्थे द्विजसत्तमम्।
 वृष्णयश्चान्धकाश्चैव नानादेश्याश्च पार्थिवाः।। Ibid., 122.46.
 सूतपुत्रश्च राधेयो गुरुं द्रोणमियात्तदा। Ibid., 122.47.
 तस्य तत् कौशलं दृष्ट्वा धनुर्वेदजिघृक्षवः।
 राजानो राजपुत्राश्च समाजग्मुः सहस्रशः।। Ibid., 123.9.
36. *MB*, Ādi. 128; 123.33-7.
37. E.B. Cowell, *The Jātaka*, vol. 5, p. 66.
38. Ibid., vol. 2, p. 60.
39. Ibid., vol. 5, pp. 66-9.
40. *Mahābhāṣya*, 4.2.60, 5.1.59.
41. A.C. Das, *Ṛgvedic Culture*, p. 330.
42. *AS*, 2.35.1.
43. J.W. M'crindle, *The Invasion of India*, p. 115.
44. *Kādambarī*, p. 58.
45. E.B. Cowell, *The Jātaka*, vol. 2, p. 275.
46. *MB*, Ādi, 158.26-7.
47. महर्षेरग्निवेश्यस्य सकाशमहमच्युत।
 अस्त्रार्थमगमं पूर्वं धनुर्वेदजिघृक्षया।। *MB*, Ādi, 122.24.

48. ब्रह्मास्त्रं ब्राह्मणो विद्याद्यथावच्चरितव्रतः।
क्षत्रियो वा तपस्वी यो नान्यो विद्यात्कथंचन।। *MB*, Śānti, 2.13.
49. *MB*, Ādi, 123.
50. तदभ्यासकृतं मत्वा रात्रावभ्यस्तपाण्डवः।।
तस्य ज्यातलनिर्धोषं द्रोणः शुश्राव भारत।
उपेत्य चैनमुत्थाय परिष्वज्येदमब्रवीत्।।
प्रयतिष्ये तथा कर्तुं यथा नान्यो धनुर्धरः।
त्वत्समो भविता लोके सत्यमेतद् ब्रवीमि ते।।
ततो द्रोणोऽर्जुनं भूयो रथेषु च गजेषु च।
अश्वेषु भूमावपि रणशिक्षामशिक्षयत्।।
गदायुद्धेऽसिचर्यायां तोमरप्रासशक्तिषु।
द्रोणः संकीर्णयुद्धेषु शिक्षयामास पांडवम्।। *MB*, Ādi, 123. 4-8.
51. Ibid., 123.45-73.
52. Ibid., 124-6; in the *Sarabhaṅga Jātaka* (vol. 5, p. 67) a competition of bowmen is described. Four bowmen fighting jointly could not injure Jotipāla whereas he alone injured all of them. Pāṇini (4.2.57) has termed such competitions as प्रहरणक्रीड़ा।
53. ततो बद्धतनुत्राणा बद्धकक्ष्या महाबलाः।
बद्धतूणाः सधनुषो विविशुर्भरतर्षभाः।। *MB*, Ādi, 124.21.
54. B.C. Law, *Indological Studies*, vol. 4, p. 356.
55. असिभिरयुद्धम्। *Mahābhāṣya*, 4.2.60.
56. अश्वैरयुद्धम्। Ibid., 5.1.59.
57. कच्चित्सूत्राणि सर्वाणि गृह्णासि भरतर्षभ।
हस्तिसूत्राश्वसूत्राणि रथसूत्राणि चाभिभो।।
कच्चिदभ्यस्यते शश्वद्गृहे ते भरतर्षभ।
धनुर्वेदस्य सूत्रं च यंत्रसूत्रं च नागरम्।। *MB*, Sabhā, 5.109-10.
ततो द्रोणोऽर्जुनं भूयो रथेषु च गजेषु च।
अश्वेषु भूमावपि च रणशिक्षामशिक्षयत्।। *MB*, Ādi, 123.7; also *Rām*, Bāla, 18.27-8; *MB*, Ādi, 122-3.
58. बलामतिबलां चैव पठतस्तात राघव।। *Rām*, Bāla, 22.15.
59. *AS*, 5.3.35.
60. Ibid., 2.33.9-11.
61. पूर्वमहर्भागं हस्त्यश्वरथप्रहरणविद्यासु विनयं गच्छेत्। *AS*, 1.5.12.
62. चललक्ष्यपरिचयार्थं मृगारण्यं गच्छेत्। *AS*, 1.21.23
63. *Śukranīti*, 4.7.16-18.
64. Ibid., 4.7.266.
65. Ibid., 4.7.390.
66. Ibid., 1.283.
67. Ibid., One *muhūrta* lasted for 45 minutes.

68. Ibid.
69. गजाश्वरथयानं तु प्रातः सायं सदाभ्यसेत्।
व्यूहाभ्यासं सैनिकानां स्वयं शिक्षेच्च शिक्षयेत्।। Ibid., 1.331; also see
धनुर्वेदे च वेदे च यत्नः कार्यो नराधिप।।
हस्तिपृष्ठेऽश्वपृष्ठे च रथचर्यासु चैव ह।
यत्नवान्भव राजेन्द्र यत्नवान्सुखमेधते।। *MB*, Anuśāsana, 107.138.
70. Ibid., 2.143-4.
71. *Kādambarī*, pp. 60-1.
72. चललक्ष्यपरिचयार्थं मृगारण्यं गच्छेत्। *AS*, 1.21.23.
73. मृगयायां तु व्यायामः श्लेष्मपित्तमेदः स्वेदनाशश्चले स्थिते च काये लक्ष्यपरिचयः। Ibid., 8.3.46; *Kāmandaka Nīti*, 15.25-8.
74. मृगवनं विहारार्थं राज्ञः कारयेत्। *AS*, 2.2.3; also *Kāmandaka Nīti*, 7.36, 15.29-42.
75. *Daśakumāracarita*, p. 209.
76. *MB*, Ādi, 63; also Vana, 229.1-11.
77. *Rām*, Ayodhyā, 63.20-3.
78. Ibid., 49.15-6.
79. *MB*, Ādi, 109.5-6.
80. *Rām*, Ayodhyā, 63.14-20.
81. J.W. M'crindle, *The Invasion of India*, pp. 189, 280-1.
82. Ibid., pp. 280-1.
83. Ibid., pp. 72-3.
84. A.S. Altekar, *The Coinage of the Gupta Empire*, pls.
85. J.M. Rosenfield, *Dynastic Art of the Kushāṇs*, p. 182.
86. *Śākuntalam*, Act 2; also *Raghuvaṁśa*, 9.48-50.
87. *Harṣacarita*, p. 132.
88. *Kādambarī*, p. 73.
89. *Kāmandaka Nīti*, 7.36.
90. व्याघ्रादिभिर्वनचरैर्मयूराद्यैश्च पक्षिभिः।
क्रीडयेत् मृगयां कुर्याद् दुष्टसत्त्वान्निपातयन्।। *Śukranīti*, 1.332.
91. शौर्यं प्रवर्द्धते नित्यं लक्ष्यसन्धानसाधनम्।
अकातरत्वं शस्त्रास्त्रशीघ्रपातनकारिता।। Ibid., 1.333.
92. J. Griffiths, *The Paintings in the Buddhist Cave Temples of Ajantā*, vol. I, p. 39, pl. 83.
93. *Śuklayajurveda Saṁhitā*, 16.22; *Agni Pu.*, 249-50.
94. For details see *Agni Pu.*, 249-50.
95. *Dhanurveda*, op. cit.
96. *MB*, Karṇa, 15.21-2.
97. भ्रान्तमुद्भ्रान्तमाविद्धमाप्लुतं प्रसृतं सृतम्।
संपातं समुदीर्यं च दर्शयामास पाण्डवः।। *MB*, Bhīṣma, 50.45; also Droṇa, 13.51-2.

98. *Agni Pu.*, 252.1-4.
99. *MB*, Ādi, 63.16.
100. अचरद्भीमसेनस्तु मार्गान्बहुविधांस्तथा।
मण्डलानि विचित्राणि स्थानानि विविधानि च।।
गोमूत्रिकाणि चित्राणि गतप्रत्यागतानि च।
परिमोक्षं प्रहाराणां वर्जनं परिधावनम्।।
अभिद्रवणमाक्षेपमवस्थानं सविग्रहम्।
परावर्तनसंवर्तमवप्लुतमथाप्लुतम्।
उपन्यस्तमपन्यस्तं गदायुद्धविशारदौ।। *MB*, Śalya, 56.17-19.
101. आहतं विप्र गोमूत्रप्रभूतं कमलासनम्।
ततोर्ध्वगात्रं निमितं वामदक्षिणमेव च।।
आवृत्तं च परावृत्तं पादोद्धूतमवप्लुतम्।
हंसमर्दं विमर्दं च गदाकर्म प्रकीर्तितम्।। *Agni Pu.*, 252.11-12, also 19-30.
102. *Mānasollāsa*, 4.1.20-35; *MB*, Droṇa, 120.34.
103. Ibid., 4.1.14-20.
104. परावृतम्, अपावृतम्, गृहीतम्, लघु, उर्ध्वक्षिप्तम् अधःक्षिप्तम्, सन्धारितम्, विधारितम्, श्येनपातम्, गजपातम्, ग्राह्यग्राह्यम्। *Agni Pu.*, 252.5-6.
105. Ibid.
106. *Avantisundarīkathā*, pp. 97-8.
107. *Rām*, Ayodhyā, 92.55-7.
108. आरालिको गोविकर्ता सूपकर्ता नियोधकः। *MB*, Virāṭa, 2.7.
109. Ibid., Karṇa, 27.9.
110. E.B. Cowell, *The Jātaka*, vol. 2, pp. 31-4.
111. Ibid., vol. 5, p. 162; also vol. 2, pp. 64, 155, 280.
112. *AS*, 7.12.8-12.
113. सर्वेषां कर्मणा वीर्यं जवस्तेजश्च वर्धते। Ibid., 2.2.16.
114. Ibid., 2.32.16.
115. Ibid., 2.32.4; also 2.31.4-6.
116. महामात्रपेटकैश्च प्रकटितकरिकर्मचर्मपुटैः। *HC*, p. 196.
117. *Śukranīti*, 2.128-9; also 4.7.34-42.
118. सहस्रं व्यतीनां युक्तानामिन्द्रमीमहे। *Ṛgveda*, 4.32.17.
119. *Majjhima Nikāya*, 1.446; also *Saṁyutta Nikāya*, 4.310.
120. अश्वबन्धो भविष्यामि विराटनृपतेरहम्।
ग्रन्थिको नाम नाम्नाहं कर्मैतत्सुप्रियं मम।।
कुशलोऽस्म्यश्वशिक्षायां तथैवाश्वचिकित्सिते।
प्रियाश्च सततं मेऽश्वाः कुरुराज यथा तव।। *MB*, Virāṭa, 3.2-3.
121. *AS*, 2.30.32.
122. Ibid., 2.30.33-41.
123. *Śukranīti*, 2.135-6.
124. J.W. M'crindle, *Ancient India*, pp. 89-90.

125. *Agni Pu.*, 288.
126. *Śukranīti*, 2.131-37, 4.7.122-49.
127 *Mānasollāsa*, 4.4.43.
128. *Ṛgveda*, 8.74.7.
129. *AS*, 9.1.49.
130. Ibid., 10.4.18.
131. *Harṣacarita*, pp. 46-7.
132. *Śukranīti*, 4.7.170-4.
133. E.J. Rapson, *Cambridge History of India*, vol. I, p. 305, fn.
134. J.W. M'crindle, *The Invasion of India*, pp. 280-1.

Chapter 9

Military Symbols and Ceremonials

Some kind of symbolism has always been associated with warfare. Symbols like *dhvaja* (standard), *patākā* (flag) and *dundubhi* (drum) and ceremonies like *aśvamedha* (horse sacrifice) and *dhvajārohaṇa* (mounting of *dhvaja*) were integral to the faith of the people and their conduct of warfare. So was the institution of honours and awards.

DHVAJA

In its early form *dhvaja* was a totem, a protective symbol, carried by man on hunting or fighting missions. It was made of clay, wood or stone. Subsequently, when organized armies came into play the totem was carried on a pole for a better view. Still later a piece of cloth was attached to the pole-top for a much wider view.

Symbol of Faith

The *dhvaja* as a symbol of faith was considered a harbinger of victory. The *Viṣṇudharmottara Purāṇa* relates the story that when Devas could not match the might of the Asuras they went to Nārāyaṇa for help. Nārāyaṇa blessed them with a *dhvaja* and the Devas fighting under its protection defeated the Asuras.[1] Another story says that Devas, protected by a *dhvaja*, marked by divine weapons, defeated Dānavas.[2] A third story says that Devas realizing that their position was vulnerable to Daitya onslaught went to Brahmā for guidance. He advised them to acquire an invincible *dhvaja* from Viṣṇu, which would scare away the Daityas.[3]

The *dhvaja* has always been an object of faith.[4] A seal from Mohenjo-daro representing four men in file, each carrying a standard, illustrates the point.[5] This old association of *dhvaja* with religion subsequently led to the erection of *dhvaja-stambhas* at temple premises. The act of installing *dhvaja* in the honour of a deity was called *dhvaja-dāna*.[6] In 140 BC one Bhāgavata Heliodora, an inhabitant of Taxilā and an ambassador of Greek King Antialkidas, came to King Kāśīputra Bhāgabhadra of Vidiśā and erected a *garuḍa-stambha* at Besnagar.[7]

EARLY DHVAJAS

The earliest traces of *dhvaja* in ancient India pertain to proto-historic (pre-Harappan) period. On a Kulli ware a bull tied to a pillar with a rope is represented. The pillar comprises a shaft, a bulbous pot and a circular object with twelve spokes, placed one above the other. The whole ensemble is surmounted by a four-cornered rectangular frame.[8] This device can be called Kulli standard as it bears a marked resemblance with the Harappan standards. On a seal discovered at Chanhudaro two nude women are represented carrying a standard each.[9] But the most definite evidence on standard comes from a Mohenjo-daro seal, which represents four persons carrying a standard each.[10] The motifs borne on the first two standards are not clear but the third and fourth standards certainly bear an unicorn and an incense-burner respectively (Pl. 11). The *dhvaja* bearers are either leading a procession or a march to the battlefield. In this connection it may be mentioned that the early Egyptians also carried standards to the battlefield.

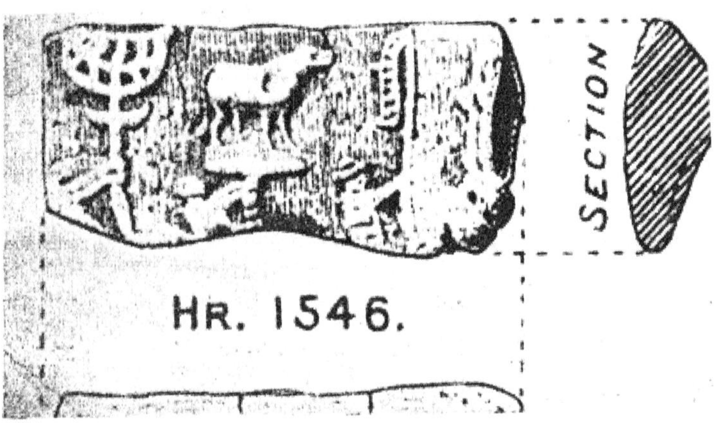

Plate 11: Standard-bearers, Mohenjo-daro

Vedic Age

Dhvaja played an important role in the Vedic warfare.[11] It was perhaps a symbol of Indra, the Āryan god of war, as suggested by a hymn in the *Ṛgveda*: 'when the standards meet together (or when the battle starts) at that time Indra may be our defender'.[12] At another place there is a reference to targetting the enemy standard.[13] In the Vedic age soldiers joined war with a *dhvaja* and those who did not possess one borrowed it for the purpose.[14]

About the shape of Vedic *dhvaja* nothing can be said precisely. However, the following hymn indicates the make of the then *dhvaja:* 'The chanters hymn thee, they who say the word of praise magnify thee. The priests have raised thee up on high, O Śatakratu (Indra), like a pole.'[15] This symbol of Indra which accompanied the army of gods was perhaps a Sūrya (sun).[16]

Epic Times

Warriors of repute joined the battle only after mounting their *dhvaja* on the chariot. Arjuna while using the chariot of Uttara, the son of Virāṭa, in a battle mounted his *Kapi-dhvaja* on it.[17] Guru Droṇa could confirm the presence of Arjuna from a distance by looking at his *dhvaja.*[18] Lakṣmaṇa could recognize the raised *kovidāra-dhvaja* of Bharata from a long distance.[19]

Dhvaja had assumed a definite shape and meaning during the Epic age. In this connection the following observations of Hopkins are significant:

> We have next to distinguish between ensign (*dhvaja*) and banner (*patākā*). At the back of the car, perhaps on one side, rises a staff, straight up high from the floor. The main staff, I incline to think, was in the back middle of the car while the little flags were on the side. This staff bore the ensign or signum at its top, and apparently below this top floated the flag. The flag pole was often the first objective point of the foe's arrows, which seem aimed not so much at the symbol as at the pole itself, doubtless because the former was of metal and the latter of bamboo; though of course the ultimate purpose was to disgrace the knight by bringing down his symbol. When the symbol falls, the whole party falls into dismay and disorder. On the top of the staff was placed the *dhvaja* or *Ketu,* the former meaning sometimes the whole arrangement, staff and image or banner; the latter the symbol or banner alone.[20]

It seems that the concept of state *dhvaja* or the royal *dhvaja* did not exist in the Epic age. Each commander displayed his own *dhvaja* on the chariot.[21] This was perhaps in tune with the Vedic tradition which allowed all the tribal leaders, who by and large were independent of each other, to carry their personal standards in war. It seems that in the epic wars *atirathīs* and *mahārathīs* carried their personal standards whereas their followers bore a miniature of it or even went without it.

Among the Pāṇḍava warriors, Arjuna displayed a *vānara*,[22] Yudhiṣṭhira a pair of *mṛdaṅgas*,[23] Bhīma a *siṁha*,[24] Nakula a *śarabha*[25] and Sahadeva a *haṁsa*[26] symbol on their standards. Abhimanyu chose the bird *śāraṅga*,[27] five sons of Draupadi the images of Dharma, Vāyu, Indra and Aśvinīkumāras,[28] Dhṛṣṭadyumna a *kovidāra*[29] and Ghaṭotkaca a *gṛddhra*[30] as *dhvaja* symbols.

Among the Kaurava heroes, Duryodhana displayed on his standard a serpent,[31] Bhīṣma a *tāla* tree,[32] Droṇa an altar covered with deer skin and a water-jar,[33] Karṇa an elephant chain,[34] Kṛpācārya a bull,[35] and Aśvatthāman a lion-tail.[36] Jayadratha had a bear on his *dhvaja*,[37] Somadatta a *yūpa*,[38] Śalya a plough line,[39] Bhoja an elephant,[40] Alāyudha a band of jackals,[41] Vṛṣasena a peacock,[42] Bhūriśravas a sacrificial post,[43] Bṛhadbala a lion,[44] Kaliṅgarāja a flame,[45] Pradyumna a crocodile[46] and Uttara a lion.[47]

In the Epic there are references to the standards of Devas and Asuras also. Skanda, the commander of the gods displayed a peacock on his *dhvaja*,[48] Śiva a bull,[49] Kṛṣṇa a *garuḍa*,[50] Indra a garland,[51] Durgā[52] a *śikhi* bird and Balarāma a *tāla* tree.[53] Rāvaṇa displayed a human-head,[54] Meghanāda a lion,[55] Atikāya a Rāhu image,[56] Prahasta a snake,[57] Khara a vulture,[58] and Sambha a Śeśanāga[59] on their *dhvajas*.

Nanda-Maurya Age

Pāṇini refers to *lakṣaṇa* (symbol) and *aṅka* (mark) as distinguishing features of *saṁghas* or federations in sixth century BC.[60] Perhaps, these symbols were borne on their *dhvajas* as well.[61] In fourth century BC the *dhvaja* accompanied the armies to the battlefield. The marching army of Porus was led by a standard-bearer:

> An image of Heracles was borne in front of the line of infantry, and this acted as the strongest of all incentives to make the soldiers fight well. To desert the bearers of this image was reckoned as a disgraceful mili-

tary offence, and they had even ordained death as a penalty for those who failed to bring it back from the battlefield, for the dread which the Indians had conceived for the god when he was their enemy had been toned down to a feeling of religious awe and veneration.[62]

The Aśokan pillars provide a clue to the shape of the *dhvaja* carried by the army of Porus. It was perhaps made of wood like a miniature Aśoka pillar.[63] The *Arthaśāstra* also says that in military expeditions soldiers carried portable standards[64] and these were displayed at the military camps.[65] The most authentic representation of the *dhvaja* in ancient India is met in the art of Bhārhut[66] (Pl. 12). In Sāñcī art *triratna-dhvaja* and some other *dhvaja* types are widely represented.[67] In ancient Rome all legions and their sub-units carried eagle standard to the battlefield.

On some tribal coins dated around the beginning of Christian era *dhvajas* are depicted.[68] Among these *matsya-dhvaja* (fish-standand) and *kukkuṭa-dhvaja* (cock-standard) are more widely represented. Some Kuṣāṇa coins also depict Kārttikeya with a cock-standard.[69] Significantly, during this period a piece of drapery had also come to be associated with the *dhvaja*.[70]

Gupta Age

The *dhvaja* continued to enjoy the same inportance in Gupta period. The Gupta rulers, owing to their Brāhmanic leanings, adopted *garuḍa*, the vehicle of Viṣṇu, as their *dhvaja* motif. It is widely represented on the coins of Samudragupta and his successors.[71] Some Gupta rulers also displayed *ardhacandra-dhvaja* (crescent-standard) and *cakra-dhvaja*.[72] The Hūṇa kings Toramāṇa and Mihirakula displayed sun and bull standards respectively.[73] On a Gupta coin a horse-standard is also portrayed.[74]

A unique fifth-century terracotta plaque from Ahicchatra represents two standards—a *varāha-dhvaja* (boar-standard) and a *candra-dhvaja* (crescent-standard).[75] These are displayed alongside two warriors, identified as Jayadratha and Yudhiṣṭhira, engaged in battle. In both cases the *dhvaja-daṇḍa* is decorated with ribbons flying on either side, just below the *dhvaja* motif.

In the Ajantā art *dhvajas* are displayed in abundance. In this connection the observations of Griffith are significant:

Plate 12: Mounted Standard-bearer, Bhārhut

Banners and ensigns, although painted in somewhat sombre colours—green, brown and grey-were important part of military pomp. At the top of a slender staff, about 8 or 9 feet long, is a bordered disc, probably of metal, with three yak or horse tail tassels on the top and sides. Below this hangs a short horizontal bar, from which floats a longitudinally striped swallow-tailed banner about 6 or 8 feet long (Pl. 69). In some cases the head of the flag staff is an ornamental spear with turned mouldings (Pl. 80). Sometimes a narrow scarf is tied to a staff bearing but a single horse tail, the two ends enriched by cross stripes, hanging in fluttering folds (Pl. 83).[76]

It is notable that these *dhvajas* are far more ornamental than those at Sāñcī. The *patākās* (banners) are long and colourful, but no motifs are represented on them (Pl. 13).

Post-Gupta Period

A significant change in the shape of *dhvaja* appeared when the crowning motif came to be represented on the *dhvaja-paṭṭa* or flag. This probably happened in the post-Gupta period. The *Agni Purāṇa* attests to this while stating that the flag should be impressed in the middle within the mark of a circle, the figure of the celestial bird (*garuḍa*) or that of the man-lion (*narasiṁha*) manifestation of Viṣṇu being marked on the space within the aforesaid circle.[77] Inscriptional evidence confirms this while stating that 'the crest or the symbol were drawn on cloth and fixed to a rod and were carried either by hand or attached to the chariot or howdah'.[78] The *Naiṣadhacarita* also refers to flags bearing the figure of horse, elephant or tiger.[79]

The *dhvaja* underwent some changes in its shape and make over the years. The following five stages are clearly discernible:

1. The first stage when the symbol or motif was made of clay, wood or stone and was carried in hand.
2. The second stage when the motif was carried on a pole for better display.
3. The third stage when a flag (cloth) was added to the pole for still better display and also for decoration.
4. The fourth stage when the motif displayed on the top of the staff also came to be painted on the flag.
5. The final stage when the display of the motif on the top of the staff discontinued and it was just represented on the flag.

Plate 13: *Dhvaja-patākās*, Ajantā

PATĀKĀ

Though *dhvaja* and *patākā* became synonymous at a later date, in the beginning there was fundamental difference in the meaning, shape, display and the use of the two. *Patākā* was a simple piece of cloth used for decorative purpose and no symbolism was attached to it. In the *Arthaśāstra dhvaja* and *patākā* are intended to serve different purposes.[80] In the *Mahābhārata, patākās* (flags) appear in two forms, viz., *dhvaja-patākā* and *patākā.* The former was carried on the *dhvaja-yaṣṭi* while the latter was used for decorative purpose.

RELATED CUSTOMS

In ancient India rulers issued coins, portraying their *dhvaja*, to commemorate victories. On many Gupta coins *dhvaja* appears alongside the king. On the standard type coins of Samudragupta

> the depiction of a *Garuḍa* standard or *Garuḍa* pillar as a part of the obverse device which is a scene of worshipping Agni as a mark of the celebration of victory in battles, is purely an art motif that was introduced with a purpose. The representation of that mythical bird as perching on a pillar, is nothing but a suggestion by means of a suitable symbol, viz., the supremacy of Samudragupta over all human beings like that of a *Garuḍa* over all birds and snakes.

The accompanying motto 'the conqueror of hundred wars' also confirms this.[81] The Hūṇa ruler Mihirakula displayed *vṛṣabha-dhvaja* on his coins along with the legend 'may the bull be victorious'.[82]

Occasionally, inscriptions were issued by the rulers in the honour of their *dhvaja.* An inscription of king Yaśodharman sings the glory of his *dhvaja* as follows:

> May that very long banner of (the god) Śūlapāṇi destroy the glory of your enemies: that (banner), which bears (a representation of) the bull (Nandi), marked by the five fingers (dipped in some dye and then) placed on him by (*Pārvatī*) the daughter of the mountain (*Himālaya*), who causes the distant regions, in which the demons are driven wild with fear by (his) terrible bellowings, to shape; (and) who makes the glens of (the mountain) Sumeru to have their rocks split open by the blows of his horns.[83]

The *dhvaja* commanded respect and was treated as a sacred object. The rulers worshipped it, along with parasol (*chatra*) and weapons (*āyudhas*), after a holy bath (*puṇya-snāna*).[84]

The victory in war was also commemorated by erecting *dhvaja-stambhas*. The Mehrauli inscription of Candragupta II and Bhitari inscription of Skandagupta attest to this. In the *Raghuvaṁśa* there is a reference to the erection of *jaya-stambha* by Raghu at the end of his victory campaign.[85] The practice continued even afterwards.

It was a matter of pride to capture or destroy the enemy *dhvaja*. In the Vedic age the enemy's *dhvaja* was targetted,[86] with a view to deprive him of the divine protection. Arjuna in his encounter with Karṇa, first destroyed the latter's *dhvaja* and then killed him.[87] In the epic war warriors are often described as targetting the standards of their adversaries.

Dhvaja-Mahotsava

The rulers performed the ceremony of *dhvaja-mahotsava*, or *indra-dhvaja-mahotsava*, after Indra, the Vedic god of war. Earlier it was performed by the rulers before launching a military campaign[88] but later it assumed the form of a ritual. This custom of honouring *dhvaja* finds mention even in the *Ṛgveda*: 'The chanters hymn thee, they who say the word of praise magnify thee. The priests have raised thee up on high, O! Śatakratu, like a pole.'[89] The *Rāmāyaṇa* says that *indra-dhvaja* was held aloft on a pole with the help of a cord at the time of *mahotsava*.[90] The custom continued till much later period.[91]

WAR-GOD

Indians have been worshipping some kind of war-god since the earliest times. The Indus Valley people perhaps patronized a war god, and the symbols like unicorn and incense-burner, carried by them on their standards, may have been his manifestations.

In the *Ṛgveda* Indra appears as the war god and commander-in-chief of the Āryans. The devotees offered prayers to him to grant victories, and perhaps carried some symbol related to him on their *dhvajas*, while joining a battle.

In the later Vedic age Rudra emerges as another god of war. In the *Śukla Yajurveda*[92] he is variously addressed as *senānī, senāpati, pattīnām pati, āśu senah* and *āśu rathāh*. He is also described as the bearer of thousand weapons, including *pināka, vajra, dhanu, khaḍga*, etc. A hymn dedicated to him reads:

Homage to him (Rudra) who wears a helmet and to him who bears a cuirass; salutation to him who wears a mail and defensive armour and to him who possesses strong hold on elephant back to fight therefrom; homage to the far famed one whose army is renowned.

As Rudra is not related to war in the Vedas it seems that the concept of Rudra as a war god was a later development. It is likely that he was the war god of the natives, called Dāsas and Dasyus in the *Ṛgveda,* and was incorporated in the Brāhmaṇic pantheon later.

Around the beginning of the Christian era another war-god called Skanda or Kārttikeya appeared. This new deity was perhaps related to the foreign invaders like the Śakas and the Kuṣāṇas. The former worshipped a god of war ever since they lived in Central Asia and it is likely that they continued with it even after settling in India. Significantly, the earliest images of Kārttikeya in India are met at Taxilā and Mathurā, the main centres of Śaka-Kuṣāṇa power. Further, these images were produced during the Kuṣāṇa times. Kuṣāṇas also portrayed the image of Kārttikeya on their coins. Incidentally, some attributes of Kārttikeya like the cock-standard and Śaka-Kuṣāṇa dress style also suggest foreign connection of the deity.[93]

About the same time or perhaps a little later, a goddess of war called Devī or Kālī also makes her appearance in India. The extreme violence associated with this goddess, however, suggests some nomadic linkage or Śaka-Kuṣāṇa connection. According to R.C. Hazra

the conception of Devī as a war goddess is not met in the Vedic *Saṁhitās* and *Brāhmaṇas.* It seems that the concept was borrowed by Āryans from the aboriginal tribes much after when the assimilation of the two people started. But by the epic times it had come into full play as Durgā is called *siddhasenānī* and *raṇapriyā* in the *Mahābhārata* (6.23.4-8).[94]

MILITARY CEREMONIALS

Besides the *dhvaja-mahotsava* ancient Indians performed many more ceremonies of military significance. These included *vājapeya, rājasūya, aśvamedha* and *nīrājana* ceremonies, briefly described below:

VĀJAPEYA

The *vājapeya* is a combination of words *vāja* and *peya* meaning food and drink respectively.[95] It is interpreted to mean the drink of strength. The performance of this sacrifice earned emperorhood (*samrāṭ*) to a ruler.[96] Though this sacrifice was a prerogative of the Brāhmaṇas, Kṣatriyas could also perform it. Indra and Bṛhaspati are said to have performed it.

The ceremony lasting for 17 days comprised three main rites: chariot race, mounting of sacrificial post and besprinkling of the sacrificer. The initial rites included offering of 17 animals, 17 objects and 17 vessels of *surā* to Prajāpati. In the chariot race the sacrificer emerged victorious in a contest with 17 others. It was symbolic of the pre-eminence of the sacrificer. The objective of the sacrifice was to ensure sovereignty, prosperity and domination.[97]

Rājasūya

It was a consecration ceremony to which only the kings were entitled. The main objective of this sacrifice was the attainment of *śraiṣṭhya*, *svarājya* and *ādhipatya* over the heaven, sky and earth.[98] The ritual took more than two years to complete. It commenced on the first day of the month of *Phālguna* but the actual consecration (*abhiṣecanīya*) was performed after 13 months in *caitra*. The king was anointed with holy waters collected from 17 sources by the priests and representatives of the people.

In the end the king drove in a chariot, drawn by four horses, to the north where more than 100 cows belonging to his kinsmen were assembled. There he made a sham plunder of these cows. Elsewhere, it is stated that after anointment ceremony the king mounted a chariot looking at the sun and the subjects, symbolizing his assumption of universal sovereignty.[99]

Aśvamedha

The *aśvamedha* or horse sacrifice was performed by a monarch desirous of gaining everlasting sovereignty and unchallenged supremacy. The Vedic Āryans performed this ceremony as is evident from the *Ṛgveda*.[100] It is mentioned as an important military ceremonial by the *Śatapatha Brāhmaṇa:*

> One who performed the *aśvamedha* conquers all quarters, conquers the world, the priest makes him a ruler and upholder.[101]

> He acquires all kingdoms, all people, all the Vedas, all the gods and all created beings.[102]

The sacrifice commenced on eighth or ninth day of the bright fortnight of *Phālguna* or *Āṣāḍha* with offerings of gold and cows to Brāhmaṇas. The following morning the horse selected for the sacrifice was bound before the sacrificial fire and besprinkled by the priest with water. The horse was then freed to wander, the *aśvapālas* (cavalry) accompanying it as protectors. Any ruler who stopped this horse had to be defeated by the army of the performing ruler. Failure to get the horse released implied defeat and abandonment of the sacrifice. However, if the horse returned safely it was anointed by the queens. Finally, it was tied to the sacrificial post and killed along with many other animals.[103]

The highest ambition of a ruler in ancient India was to perform horse sacrifice. Pāṇḍavas performed this sacrifice after their victory in Kurukṣetra war. Rāma performed it after consolidating his empire of Ayodhyā. Puṣyamitra Śuṅga performed it after usurping the Maurya throne to establish his hegemony. Samudragupta performed it to celebrate his conquests, and to commemorate the event he issued *aśvamedha* type of gold coins. The Bayana hoard has yielded twenty such coins. Altekar has described one of these coins as follows:[104]

Obverse: Uncaparisoned horse, in some cases with a strap on the neck to left before the sacrificial post (*yūpa*) adorned with a pedestal; pennon flies over the horse from the top of the post. The name of the horse is sometimes plaited, and there is a string of beads and a crescent above the back in some cases. Beneath the horse is the letter सी, and below also a pedestal in some rare cases circular legend राजाधिराजः पृथिवीम् विजित्य दिवं जयत्याहृत-वाजिमेधः meaning the king of kings who had performed the *Vājimedha* sacrifice wins heaven after protecting the earth.

Reverse: The crowned queen standing to left on a pearl bordered circular mat, dressed in a *sārī* and bodice, earrings, necklace, armlets and anklets on her person; she holds a chouri over her right shoulder in the right hand hanging by her side. In her front is an ornamental *sūcī* bound with fillet. Legend अश्वमेधपराक्रमः.

The queen was represented on the reverse of the coin because she played an important role in the ritual of *aśvamedha*. Many more

Indian rulers, some of them of a modest standing, are reported to have performed *aśvamedha.* Epigraphic evidence is abounding on this.

The diplomatic and military consequences of the sacrifice could have been devastating when 'a special horse was permitted to wander at will, the king claiming the territory over which it wandered . . . an illustration of non-territoriality, arbitrariness, shifting frontiers determined by grazing impulses of horse freed from its stable and keepers'.[105] The myth of *aśvamedha* as related in the epics and Purāṇas was perhaps diluted when it came to real application to suit the interest of performing king, and the horse may not have had a free run as it is made out to be.

Nīrājana (Lustration Rite)

It was a ritual of military significance performed by kings and generals. In this ceremony royal emblems, horses, elephants, soldiers and weapons were touched with sacred water (*nīra* + *ajana*), perhaps for better performance in war.

The *Bṛhatsaṁhitā* says that the ceremony should be performed when god Viṣṇu wakes up from his sleep on eighth, twelfth or fifteenth day of the bright half of *Aśvayuja* or *Kārttika.*[106] The *Arthaśāstra,* however, says that it should be performed on the ninth day of *Aśvayuja,* at the beginning or the end of an expedition.[107] At another place the *Arthaśāstra* says that three lustration rites should be performed in the four monthly junctures of the seasons, i.e. the full moon day of *Kārttika, Phālguna* and *Āṣāḍha.* It further adds that offerings on the junctures of dark halves should be made to the spirits and on the junctures of bright halves to Senāni (Kārttikeya).[108]

In the *Agni Purāṇa*[109] there is a detailed description of *nīrājana.* A chamber was built for the purpose in which various gods and eight elephants were worshipped. Then followed the bath of five elephants and horses of the state and the worship of the royal insignia and god Varuṇa. Spirits were made offerings during the night.

Finally, when the sun had entered *Viśākhā* (a heavenly body), various insignias of royalty, viz., chariot, elephant, horse, umbrella, sword, bow, war-drum, flagstaff and flag were consecrated by the astrologer. In the end the king riding the royal horse and elephant, one after another, circumambulated the city thrice. The *Agni Purāṇa* concludes that the rite of *nīrājana* led the ruler to prosperity and destroyed his enemies.

The *Bṛhatsaṁhitā* says that the ceremony concluded after a mock military march by the king in the north-eastern direction. The march started with the chanting of magic hymns of the *Atharvaveda*, and piercing the heart of the clay figure supposed to be the enemy, by the royal priest. The priest then reined the horse and the ruler mounting it marched out, as if on a victory campaign.[110] The *Kālikā Purāṇa* describes *bala-nīrājana* and says that at the end of the ceremony symbolic *śatru-bali* was performed.[111]

Kane has interpreted *nīrājanavidhi* as a ritual in which light was waved before horses, elephants, banners, armies, etc.[112] This, however, looks unconvincing as *nīrājana* is generally described as a justification rite performed at the beginning of a military campaign. The evidence of the *Arthaśāstra*,[113] *Raghuvaṁśa*[114] and *Kāmandaka Nīti*[115] clearly says so. Occasionally, *nīrājana* was performed at the end of a victory campaign. When Tāraka was defeated and slain the gods celebrated the event by performing the rite of *nīrājana*.[116]

Śatru-bali

Śatru-bali, a malevolent rite, perhaps came into vogue in India some time before the beginning of the Christian era, as a result of tribal influence. It is also likely that foreign invaders like Śakas and Kuṣāṇas introduced this ceremony in India.

The *Bṛhatsaṁhitā* refers to *śatru-bali* as a pacificatory rite performed by the royal priest for the benefit of his patron.[117] The ceremony as described in the Purāṇas, however, appears symbolic and may not have involved the actual killing of the enemy. The *Devī Purāṇa* describes the ritual in which the king first took his bath, then destroyed the effigy of the enemy made of powdered rice and finally offered it to Skanda, the god of war.[118] This association of *śatru-bali* with Durgā, the goddess of war, is significant as she is also called Mahiṣāsuramardinī (the killer of demon Mahiṣa). Her worship involves the sacrifice of a buffalow even today. It is notable that Devī worship is performed in October, the month considered ideal for the launching of military campaigns in ancient India.

HONOURS AND AWARDS

Indra, the Vedic god of war is said to have showered favours upon Maruts, the soldiers who assisted him in his war against Vṛtra.[119] The Epic says that a king should reward his army.[120] Thus it was customary to reward soldiers who staked their life in the service of the state.[121] It was believed that the army of a king who rewarded his soldiers well always remained faithful to him.[122] The rulers made gifts of land and money to soldiers and honoured them with sweet words, decorations and titles,[123] so that they did not desert him, and earned him victories.[124]

The institution of honours and awards underwent change from time to time. To begin with, it was the spoils of war or the lure of the heaven which prompted a warrior to lay down his life in the battlefield. Subsequently, the cash awards, land grants, promotions, decorations, state honours, etc., also motivated them to fight resolutely. Exceptional performance in the battlefield, entitled the warriors to the following honours and awards:

Spoils of War

In the Vedic age the soldiers were entitled to a share in the spoils of war, proportionate to their contribution. That they looked forward to the spoils is evident from the following hymn: 'Of wealth and homes of men thou art the ruler, and opener of the stable of the cattle. Helper of men, winner of spoil in combats, thou leadest to an ample heap of riches.'[125] The king shared spoils with his men and it was perhaps this share in loot which prompted them to join him in forays.[126] The charioteers, as members of a superior arm, were entitled to one-fourth of the booty.[127] In the Purāṇas rulers have been advised to distribute the spoils of war among soldiers in an equitable manner.[128] The *Manusmṛti* lays down that the booty such as chariots, elephants, parasols, animals, women, and vessels should go to the brave who captured them, whereas the booty obtained as a result of collective action should be justly distributed by the ruler among his soldiers.[129] The *Nītiprakāśikā* says that the king should divide the booty captured from the enemy country. Half of it should be given to the soldiers and the other half should be kept by the king. Further, a soldier who captured a horse or a chariot with its appurtenances, should, being praised by the king, obtain the fourth part of its value.[130]

The king also compensated the soldiers, who suffered loss of weapons, etc., in war.[131] Thus the lure of booty has been a motivating factor for soldiers through the ages.

Heavenly Bliss

In the Vedic age death in battlefield was considered glorious. The *Ṛgveda* says that a martyr earned the same merit as the donor of one thousand cows.[132] The epics lay greater emphasis on the heavenly rewards. Martyrdom in the defence of *dharma* was considered as the easiest way to heaven. On the eve of an impending battle, King Janaka revealed to his soldiers, through his yogic powers, the glory of a martyr in heaven and the ignominy of a coward in hell. He addressed them,

> Behold! these are the regions endowed with great splendour for those that fight fearlessly; Full of Gandharva girls, those regions are eternal and capable of granting every wish. There on the other side are regions of hell intended for those that fly away from battle. They would have to rot there for eternity in everlasting ingloriousness. Resolved upon casting away your lives, do you conquer your foes. Do not fall into inglorious hell. The laying down of life (in battle) contributes in respect of heroes, their happy door of heaven.[133]

In another context the epic says that the palace of Indra is reserved for those who seek death in battle. In fact, any kind of death in the battlefield was considered glorious.

> They that die slaughtered by chance go to world of gods and kings; they that die with the thought 'I will die' join the angels; they that hold out against all odds go to the house of Brahmā; while even those that have begged for mercy, if they still die with their faces to the foe, go to the Guhyaka world; moreover, those that die anyhow on the field of battle, even if killed by accident, go to the Kurus of the north after death.[134]

This concept of martyrdom also finds echo in subsequent literature. The *Arthaśāstra* states that the heroes who die fighting a *dharmayuddha* (just war) attain those *lokas* (worlds) which the Brāhmaṇas, aspiring for heaven, attain after performing many sacrifices, penances and donations.[135] The *Raghuvaṁśa*, a composition of Gupta period, describes the ascent of fallen heroes to heaven accompanied by nymphs.[136] The *Śukranīti* says that the dead heroes should not be grieved for they ascend to heaven, freed from all sins and purified.[137] Thus the attainment of *svarga* (heaven) was considered the highest award for a warrior.[138]

Memorials

The concept of martyrdom met in the literature, later found expression in the institution of *Vīrakkalas* (memorials of the gallant) widely found in southern India. That such memorials had come into vogue around the beginning of the Christian era is evident from the *Saṅgam* literature. When a warrior fell fighting in the battlefield his companions marked the spot by raising a stone bearing his name and fame. The raising of hero-stones became so common at one stage that a procedure had to be laid down for the occasion.[139] These stones, which often depicted the dead hero ascending to heaven in the company of a nymph, soon became the object of worship.[140] In the *Saṅgam* age, the death on the battlefield commanded so much respect that even when a king died on his bed, his body was laid postmortem on a bed of green grass and cut in twain with a spear. This seemed to give that dead person a passport to *turakkam* and status equal to that of a hero in the eyes of the world.[141] The popularity of this belief is confirmed by the discovery of hero-stones in many parts of the country. The largest number of hero-stones have been discovered from Karnataka, followed by Tamil Nadu.[142]

Cash Awards

The attraction of cash award also motivated soldiers to fight. The *Mahābhārata* says that a warrior who broke through the enemy array or prevented the collapse of his own array was entitled to royal treatment, promotion in rank and doubled emoluments.[143] *Jātakas* say that the braves were honoured with royal treatment.[144] After the victory in Laṅkā Rāma advised Vibhīṣaṇa to honour all Vānaras and Rākṣasas who had displayed bravery in the battlefield by presenting them with jewels and other gifts.[145] The *Arthaśāstra* gives an elaborate account of the gallantry awards. It even specifies the quantum of award for various types of gallant acts:

> One hundred thousand (*paṇas*) for slaying the king (enemy); fifty thousand for slaying the commander-in-chief or the heir apparent, ten thou-

sand for slaying the chief of the braves, five thousand for destroying an elephant or a chariot; a thousand for killing a horse; a hundred for slaying the chief of the infantry; twenty for bringing a head; and twice the pay in addition to whatever is seized.[146]

The *Agni purāṇa* gives almost a similar account of awards.

On gaining a battle a king should give ample rewards to his soldiers and generals. Hundred thousand precious articles should be given by a king as reward to the general of his victorious army on the death of his royal adversary; half of that on the fall of his son in the field of battle; a quarter of that on the death of commander-in-chief of the enemy forces and a half of the latter on the destruction of the war elephants of the adversary.[147]

The *Kāmandaka Nīti* says that a king should remunerate the warriors liberally. He should cheerfully give 10 million *varvas* to the slayer of his royal antagonist; half the amount should be given while the latter's son or his general is slain; when a chief of a brave detachment of heroes is slain, 10,000 *varvas* should be given; when an elephant or a car is destroyed half of this amount should be given; and a 1,000 *varvas* should be given when an archer or a foremost foot soldier is slain. A score of cows or any other object of enjoyment or gold or any other base metal belong to them who conquer them. The king should cheerfully remunerate the soldiers according to the things they bring.[148]

The *Nītiprakāśikā* says that if an extraordinary deed has been performed the king should admire and honour the performer and present him with a vessel full of money.[149] It also describes the cash awards admissible to a warrior for slaying the following adversaries:[150]

King	-	1,00,000 *varvas*
Crown prince or Commander-in-Chief	-	50,000 "
Akṣauhiṇi-pati	-	25,000 "
Anīkinī-pati	-	12,500 "
Camū-pati	-	6,250 "
Pṛtanā-pati	-	3,125 "
Mahārathī	-	2,000 "
Vāhinī-pati	-	1,560 "

Cavalier or Commander of infantry	-	1,000	*varvas*
Gaṇa-pati	-	760	”
Gulma-pati	-	390	”
Senāmukha-pati	-	195	”
Patti-pati	-	100	”

A warrior who captured an elephant or chariot of the enemy was awarded 500 *varvas*. One who captured an armed enemy was awarded 5 *varvas*. For capturing a deserter from own camp a warrior was given 3 *varvas*.[151]

It seems that the said list of the commanders was picked up by *Nītiprakāśikā* from the *Mahābhārata*. But *varvas*, the currency used for rewarding the warrior, did not exist in the Epic times and may have been borrowed from Kauṭilya or Kāmandaka.

Land Grants

Exceptional military service was honoured with land grants and relief in taxation. The *Arthaśāstra* refers to a village which was granted immunity from land revenue for the contribution made by its inhabitants to the state's war effort.[152] The Sātavāhana ruler Pulamāvi granted large fiefs to his military officers.[153] In *Saṅgam* literature there are references to tax-free grants made to soldiers.[154] King Harṣa of Thānesar honoured his officers by making land grants to them.[155] The tradition continued in post-Harṣa period. The epithet *caturāṣṭika*, i.e. the holder of eighty-four villages, met in the later epigraphs, was indeed related to it.

Fillet of Honour

The rulers also honoured the braves with *prasāda-paṭṭa* (a band or fillet), worn around the head. It was an inch broad plain strap made of gold[156] or quality cloth. In the *Harṣacarita* a category of royal servants is called *karpaṭī* or the recipient of *karpaṭa*. *Karpaṭa* denoted a piece of cloth (*cīrikā*), which was bestowed by the rulers on distinguished servants.[157] The king could also withdraw the honour in the event he got displeased with a recipient.[158] In the art of Ajantā many men-in-arms are shown as wearing fillet.[159] In the *Harṣacarita* two important servants of the state, a messenger and a bodyguard, are described as wearing a *cīra*, with loose ends waving in the air around their head.[160] The *Avantisundarīkathā*, an eighth century work, also refers to *paṭṭas* worn on the forehead by *sāmantas*.[161] The fact that the use of *paṭṭa* is met with exclusively in association with soldiers and guards suggests that it was a royal honour. The custom continued and the Cālukya King Tailapadeva is reported to have conferred a *paṭṭa* or the golden band, on his victorious general Ereyama in AD 1096.[162] The *vibhūti-paṭṭa*, often referred to in the Hoysala records,[163] though not directly mentioned in relation to brave, had probably the same significance. *Prasāda-patra*, or document of appreciation, was also an award, which entitled the recipient to certain facilities.[164]

Enhanced Pay and Promotions

The *Mahābhārata* says that the pay of a warrior should be doubled for exceptional bravery.[165] Promotion in service was another way of rewarding a soldier. For brave acts a leader of 10 soldiers was promoted as the leader of 100 soldiers and that of 100 soldiers as a leader of 1000 soldiers.[166] According to the *Śukranīti* a soldier who displayed extraordinary bravery should be rewarded with wealth and power.[167] It adds that the salary of the soldiers should be enhanced when a military expedition is launched.[168] According to the *Nītiprakāśikā* the person who brought the secret plans of the enemy to the notice of the king was entitled to doubled wages. The braves, who sowed dissension in the hostile army, scaled the enemy forts and gained territory for the king were assigned a large amount of money.[169] In the Hoysala kingdom brave soldiers were promoted as *muruṇḍa* or royal guard.

Royal Emblems and Titles

The acts of gallantry and distinguished service were also honoured by conferring the emblems of royalty such as palanquin, throne, *pañcamahāśabda*, etc. The growth of chivalric titles was, however, a special feature of early medieval India. *Sahasrabhaṭṭa* was the hero who could fight 1000 adversaries single-handed. *Śatayodhas* possessed the power of 100 warriors. The other titles met in the contemporary literature include *sahasrānika, sahasrayodhi, bhīmabhaṭṭa*, etc.

The title *marayan* was conferred for bravery in the battlefield among the Colas.[170] Colas also observed the custom of honouring the captains of the army with the title *enadi* at a formal investiture ceremony.[171] Among the Hoysalas the skilled bowmen were honoured with the title *subhaṭṭa.*[172] An eleventh-century Cālukyan epigraph refers to a title *rājya samudharaṇam* (supporter of the kingdom) conferred on a renowned *senāpati*, in gold.[173] The rulers also honoured their commanders with rings or other insignias.[174]

In the Hoysala kingdom the warriors, promoted as guards of the king, were conferred with a *todar*, a medal of gold inscribed with symbolic figures, to be worn on the left foot.[175] Brave soldiers were also honoured with *ganda pendara*, a *nūpura*-like ornament, worn on the right foot.[176] It was a very old custom dating back to first century BC, as it finds mention in *Tirukkural.*[177] The warriors also wore an anklet called *virakkala*, on which their heroic exploits were engraved.[178] A *senāpati* honoured by the king received a medal, an ornament for the trunk of his elephant and some land.[179] The soldiers who staked their life in the service of the state were offered *tāmbūla* (betel) by the king.[180] Royal insignia and robe were also presented as a token of regard.[181] If the king was displeased with an awardee he could deprive him of the honour.[182]

MARTIAL MUSIC (*YUDDHA GĀNDHARVA*)[183]

The ability to shout or roar was used by the early man to scare away his enemies, animals or humans. In the Vedic age soldiers made loud shouts (*krandana*) while attacking the enemy.[184] Indra, the commander of the gods, was famous for his battle-cry (*kranda*).[185] Maruts, the Vedic warriors, were born with a battle-cry, and not many could keep composure before their terrible roar in the battlefield.[186] Soldiers joined the battle making loud and terrible noise to scare away the enemy.[187] *Helayo helayah* was the battle cry of the Asuras and Patañjali refers to it as an example of barbarous speech.[188] In the *Amarakośa* the word *yodhasaṁrāva* and *krandana*, have been used for battle-cry.[189] Subsequently, *kṣveḍā* and *siṁhanāda* also came to denote it.[190] Even today the soldiers charge the enemy shouting a battle cry.

VEDIC AGE

As warfare became a big and organised affair *kranda* lost some of its usefulness. The man then searched for some medium more powerful than *kranda,* and *dundubhi* (war drum) was the answer. It sounded loud and rhythmic and like *kranda* could enthuse the soldiers and terrorise the enemy. In the Vedas there are many hymns imploring *dundubhi* to scare away the enemies. It was regarded as a sacred object and seers composed hymns in its honour:[191]

Send forth thy voice aloud through earth and heaven, and let the world in all its breadth regard thee; O drum, accordant with the Gods and Indra, drive thou afar, yea, very far, our foemen.

Thunder out strength and fill us full of vigour; yea, thunder forth and drive away all dangers. Drive hence, O War drum, drive away misfortune: thou art the fist of Indra: show thy firmness.

Drive hither these, and these again bring hither: the War drum speaks aloud as battle's signal. Our heroes, winged with horses, come together. Let our car warriors, Indra, be triumphant.[192]

The enemies running away from the battlefield were chased by shooting arrows and beating of drums.[193] In the *Atharvaveda* many hymns are dedicated to *dundubhi.*[194]

Similar sentiments have been expressed in the honour of *dundubhi* in The *Agni Purāṇa*, a much later work:

O war drum! you cause the hearts of the enemies to tremble by your sound. You beat in such a way that you may achieve victory for the king's army. . . . Just as the rumbling clouds cause fright in women so also let our enemies get frightened by your sound in the battle.[195]

Another important musical instrument of the Vedic age was *bakura* which was played by the Aśvins to enthuse soldiers, while attacking the Dasyus.[196] Conch seems to have come into vogue in the later Vedic age.[197]

The martial music had thus come to be associated with warfare in the Vedic age. In the *Kauśika Sūtra* it is said that before the commencement of war all musical instruments should be washed, besmeared with fragrant substances and handed over to the musicians by the *purohita* with the recitation of *mantras.*[198] Evidently, the players of martial music accompanied the army to the battlefield along with their instruments.

Epic Times

In the Epic times the system of martial music grew more elaborate. All situations of a war could now be indicated by the musical instruments.[199] Soldiers prepared for war after the orders were conveyed to them through the musical notes.[200] The consecration of *senāpati* was communicated to the army by playing *bheri* and *śaṁkha.*[201] Playing of war music indicated a state of war.[202] Soldiers marched to battlefield to the tune of *dundubhi* and *bheri,* and war commenced with the blowing of conches.[203] Martial music was played even when the forces were locked in bitter fighting.[204] When an enemy warrior was killed victory-music was played as a mark of joy.[205] The camp of the army which was mourning its dead, did not play music.[206] Important commanders carried conches on their person. In the epic war Śrī Kṛṣṇa and the five Pāṇḍava brothers carried the conches named *pāñcajanya, anantavijaya, pauṇḍra, devadatta, sughoṣa* and *maṇipuṣpaka* respectively.[207]

Maurya Period and After

Early Buddhist literature also refers to the use of musical instruments in war.[208] In fourth century BC the instructions regarding the formation of battle arrays were conveyed to the soldiers by playing *dundubhi* and *kartāla.*[209] In the battlefield the players of war music positioned themselves behind the elephants among foot-soldiers and archers. Greek soldiers of Alexander were very much surprised to see that the din caused by the Indian instrument players did not disturb their war elephants.[210] The trumpet (*turahī*), a speciality of the Greeks, was not then known to Indians.[211] However, it was soon incorporated in the Indian system and the *Arthaśāstra* refers to the instructions of the commander being conveyed to the soldiers through the trumpet (*tūrya-ghoṣa*).[212] The playing of *bheri* indicated a state of war.[213]

A glimpse of martial music around the beginning of the Christian era is met in the art of Bhārhut and Sāñcī. In a Sāñcī relief a band of musicians playing drum, flute and conch is depicted walking behind some standard-bearers.[214] At another place the musicians are depicted walking before a prince.[215] In another relief a soldier equipped with sword and bow, is depicted marching to the tune of *mṛdaṅga* and flute.[216] The art of Bhārhut and Sāñcī is replete with such reliefs.

In the Gupta age the martial music continued to inspire the troops.[217] The battle started with the blowing of trumpet[218] and the conch.[219] The victory in war was also announced by blowing a conch.[220] Even when a fierce battle was raging the soldiers were enthused by the sound of the trumpet.[221] The *śṛṅga*, *ḍamarū*, *śahanāyī* and *ḍamāon* were some important musical instruments of the period.[222]

Purāṇic Evidence

The *Brahmāṇḍa Purāṇa* gives a vivid account of the martial music played in a war between the Devas and the Daityas. When the army of the gods marched against the Daitya Bhaṇḍāsura under the leadership of goddess Śrīlalitā 'the sounds of the drums of march of victory of Śrīdevī who was rushing on as the soldiers passed over, were heard by the leading Daityas. They caused excessive earache for them'.[223]

> The sound of *dundubhi* (war drum) of the leading Asuras that rose up then, became a proud response of sound to that produced by the war drums of the army of Śrīlalitā. The three worlds shook and trembled on account of that sound that deafened the world, suppressed the cardinal points, and stirred up the bowels of the ocean.[224]

Similar account of war music is also met in the *Bhāgavata Purāṇa* and *Śiva Mahāpurāṇa.*[225]

Seventh Century and After

The *Harṣacarita* provides a detailed account of war music while describing the march of Harṣa's army:

> At the close of the third watch, when all creatures slept and all was still, the marching drum was beaten with a boom deep as the gaping roar of the sky elephants. Then, after first a moment's pause, eight sharp strokes were distinctly given anew upon the drum, making up the number of the leagues in a day's march . . . straightaway the drums rattled, the *nāndīs* rang out joyously, the trumpets brayed, the *kāhalas* hummed, the horns blared; the noise of the camp gradually increased. Officers occupied themselves in arousing the courtiers. The heavens were confounded by a confused noise of drumsticks added to a rapid tapping of mallets.[226]

> When the adorable sun arose, the signal conch rang out repeatedly, announcing the moment of king's arraying the army.[227]

The king having started, the echo of musical instruments spread loudly hither and thither about the four quarters of heaven, like the snorting of sky elephants affrighted at the tumult.[228]

The martial music continued to be played in the succeeding centuries though *mṛdaṅga* and *turahī* now came to dominate the battlefield.[229]

Martial music was also played in peninsular wars as is evident from *Kaliṅgaṭṭu Parāṇi*, 'The conch shells sounded, the big drums thundered, and the reeds and pipes squeaked till the ears of the elephants, which guard the eight points, were deafened.'[230] Pallava inscriptions refer to two musical instruments, viz., *kaṭumukhavaditra* and *samudraghoṣa* and these have been identified as trumpet and drum.[231] The drums (*nagāḍās*) were carried to the battlefield mounted on elephants.[232]

Some omens and wonders were also associated with martial music. If a *bheri* emitted sound, on its own, without human effort, it was considered a good omen. On the other hand, it was bad omen if despite all efforts it did not sound well.[233] Musical instruments were always revered as sacred objects.

The martial music of India may have received some foreign influence as well. The Śakas, Pahlavas and Kuṣāṇas, the foreign invaders, might have introduced their own system of martial music in India. The art of Sāñcī also suggests this. Here double *veṇu* replaces the old Indian flute, *mṛdaṅga* is made differently and *tūrya* appears in a form met nowhere else in sculptures.[234] Trumpet was undoubtedly introduced in India by the Greeks in fourth century BC.[235] It is said that some musical instruments depicted in the art of Amarāvatī bear resemblance to those depicted in the art of Egypt and Assyria.[236]

It appears that besides enthusing soldiers in the battlefield, *yuddha-gandharva* was also used to pass on military instructions to the soldiers.[237] After the Greek contact Indians learnt the use of trumpet for passing on specific battle-related instructions to the soldiers as is evident from the *Arthaśāstra.*[238] Subsequently, the formation of battle arrays came to be intimately related to *yuddha-gandharva.* The *Śukranīti.* advises the ruler to keep such instrument players in his service who could pass on military instructions to the troops.[239] It further says that the secret of these instructions should be known only to own troops and none else.[240] In fact, only those soldiers were considered trained and entitled to full salary who were well coversant with the formation of *vyūhas,*[241] of course in accondance with the notes of the martial music.

Bardic Tradition

In the Vedic age seers composed hymns and recited them to enthuse warriors to perform heroic deeds. Inspired by the praise, thus showered on him, Indra could kill numerous enemies. 'Alone, when Indra Maghavan is lauded, he slayeth many ne'er-resisted Vṛtras. . . . Now Indra! lauded, glorified with praises, let power swell high like rivers for the singer. For thee a new hymn, Lord of Bays! is fashioned. May we, car-borne, through song be victors ever.'[242] This is more clearly bought out in the following hymn: 'And lauds which strengthen thee for great bounty and valour, and exalt Indra who doeth glorious deeds, And songs to thee who lovest song, and all those hymns addressed to thee. These evermore confirm thy might.'[243] The roots of the later bardic tradition could perhaps be traced to these Vedic hymns.

SOME MUSICAL INSTRUMENTS

In ancient India many types of musical instruments were used—some in ceremonials, some in wars and some both in ceremonials and wars.[244] The instruments used in war were again of two types, viz., soft and harsh. The former type was played in military camps while the latter type was played in the battlefield.[245]

Dundubhi

Dundubhi, as an instrument of war, was known in the Vedic period.[246] According to the *Atharvaveda* it was made of wood and covered with cow-hide.[247] Occasionally, deer-skin was also used for the coverings.[248] When sounded at a high pitch it scared the enemy and even compelled him to run away from the battlefield.[249] It also finds mention in the Brāhmaṇas.[250]

In the Epic age many instruments such as *paṇava*, *mahānaka*, *bheri*, *jharjhara*, *pesi* and *puṣkara*, in the category of *dundubhi*, were used in war.[251] In the *Amarakośa bheri*, *ānaka*, and *dundubhi* have been treated as identical instruments.[252] *Paṭaha* was another name of *dundubhi*.[253] *Jharjhara* and *paṇava* are also stated to be *dundubhi* types.[254] *Mṛdaṅga* was also included in this category.

In the art of Sāñcī many types of drums, large and small, are represented. The large drums were occasionally hanged with some support and played with drum-sticks (*koṇa*),[255] as it was not possible to carry them. Occasionally, large drums suspended from a pole were carried by two drum beaters.[256] Small drums were played with sticks either suspended from the neck or placed on the lap.[257]

Śaṁkha

Śaṁkha had come into vogue as an important musical instrument related to war in the Vedic times. In the *Atharvaveda* it is described as bright and shining like a jewel, carried by warriors in their *tuṇīra*, while going to war.[258] It has devoted a complete *sūkta* to describe the qualities of *śaṁkha*.[259] In the Epic times warriors of repute carried a conch with them.[260] In the Gupta age the king or his commander signalled the cessation of hostilities by blowing conch.[261] The professionals who blew the conch were called *śaṁkhadhamakāḥ*.[262]

In the art of Sāñcī two types of *śaṁkhas* have been represented. The common type was blown by placing the perforated end of the shell on the lip.[263] But in the uncommon type a pipe was attached to the perforated end so that the conch could be blown easily and effectively.[264]

Tūrya

The trumpet was included in the Indian martial music sometime after the fourth century BC as a result of Greek contact. Earlier Indians arrayed their armies to the tune of *mṛdaṅga*.[265] By the Epic times the use of trumpet had become common.[266] In the Buddhist *Nikāyas* and *Jātakas* trumpet is widely mentioned.[267] According to the *Arthaśāstra* the instructions of the commander were conveyed to the army by means of a trumpet.[268] In the art of Sāñcī two types of trumpets are represented. One has a straight tube with a broad opening at the end. The other is horn-shaped with the opening patterned like the mouth of an animal.[269] It was perhaps the same as *gomukha* of the *Mahābhārata*.[270] It appears that the importance of trumpet in the Indian battlefield continued in the Gupta age. According to the *Raghuvaṁśa* the trumpets were blown at a very high pitch to enthuse the soldiers and nothing could be heard in the din.[271] In the *Mahābhārata* there is a reference to an instrument called *goviṣāṇa*,[272] a trumpet like instrument. In ancient Rome trumpeters accompanied the armies and blowing of a trumpet was a signal for advancing against the enemy.[273]

It thus follows that standards and flags, ceremonials, honours and awards and martial music played an important role in ancient Indian warfare. The basic purpose of these appendages in warfare was to boost up the morale of the troops. The rulers conferred honours and awards on their soldiers so that they remained a contented lot and did not desert. The music, besides enthusing the soldiers, also served the additional purpose of communicating messages in the battlefield, such as to form up in a particular array or disperse. The ceremonials, besides being a show of military might, were also intended to propitiate gods and beseech them to grant victories.

NOTES

1. ध्वजमेतं प्रदास्यामि भवतामरिनाशनम्।
   दृष्टमात्रेण येनेह विद्राविष्यन्ति दानवाः।। *Viṣṇudharmottara Pu.*, 2.154.12; also 2.154.57.
2. ध्वजं कृत्वा सुरैर्दैत्या जिताः शस्त्रादिचिह्नितम्। *Agni Pu.*, 61.28.
3. देवानुवाच भगवान् क्षीरोदे केशवः स वः केतुम्।
   यं दास्यति तं दृष्ट्वा नाजौ स्थास्यन्ति वो दैत्याः।। *Bṛhatsaṁhitā*, 43.2.
4. For details see U.P. Thapliyal, *The Dhvaja*, pp. 11-19.
5. J. Marshall, *Mohenjo-daro and the Indus Civilization*, p. 69.
6. *Devī Pu.*, 35.24; *Agni Pu.*, 61.50; for details see U.P. Thapliyal, op. cit., pp. 13-19.
7. J.N. Banerjee, *Development of Hindu Iconography*, p. 92.
8. S. Piggot, *Pre-historic India*, fig. 7, facing p. 104.
9. E.J.H. Mackay, *Chanhu-daro Excavations*, pl. I.36, pp. 149-50.
10. J. Marshall, *Mohenjo-daro and the Indus Civilization*, p. 384, 395, pls. 116.5, 8; 118.9.
11. *Ṛgveda*, 7.85.2, 10.103.11; *Atharvaveda*, 5.21.12.
12. अस्माकमिन्द्रः समृतेषु ध्वजेष्वस्माकं या इषवस्ता जयन्तु। *Ṛgveda*, 10.103.11; also *Yajurveda*, 17.43.
13. स्पर्धन्ते वा उ देवहूये अत्र येषु ध्वजेषु दिद्यवः पतन्ति। *Ṛgveda*, 7.85.2.
14. A.C. Das, *Ṛgvedic Culture*, p. 143.
15. *Ṛgveda*, 1.10.1; later in the *Rāmāyaṇa* it is stated that *indradhvaja* was raised on top of a pole with the help of a rope. *Rām*, Kiṣkindhā, 16.37.
16. एता देवसेनाः सूर्यकेतवः सचेतसः। *Atharvaveda*, 5.21.12.
17. *MB*, Virāṭa, 41.3-4.
18. एतद्ध्वजाग्रं पार्थस्य दूरतः सम्प्रकाशते।
    एष घोषः सजलदो रोरवीति च वानरः।। *MB*, Virāṭa, 48.4.

चिह्नमात्रेण भीष्मं तु प्रजज्ञुस्तत्र कौरवाः।
तथा पांडुसुताः पार्थ चिह्नमात्रेण जज्ञिरे।। *MB*, Bhīṣma, 48.58.

19. कोविदारध्वजो रथे। *Rām*, Ayodhyā, 96.18.
20. E.W. Hopkins, *The Social and Military Position of the Ruling Caste in Ancient India*, pp. 187-8; in the epic *patākā* has been referred to in two ways—*patākā* as an integral part of *dhvaja* and *patākā* as Independent of *dhvaja*.
21. सूर्यचन्द्रप्रतीकाशो रथे दिव्ये हिरण्मयः।
महानुभावो मत्स्यस्य ध्वज उच्छिश्रिये तदा।।
अथान्यान्विविधाकारान्ध्वजान्हेमविभूषितान्।
यथास्वं क्षत्रियाः शूरा रथेषु समयोजयन्।। *MB*, Virāṭa, 30.17-18; 41.6.
22. जयध्वजो दृश्यते पांडवस्य, समुच्छ्रितो वानरराज उग्रः। *MB*, Udyoga, 140.3; Bhīṣma, 67.3.
23. ध्वजं तु कुरुराजस्य पांडवस्य महौजसः।
दृष्टवानस्मि सौवर्णं सोमं ग्रहगणान्वितम्।।
मृदङ्गौ चात्र विपुलौ दिव्यौ नन्दोपनन्दकौ।
यन्त्रेणाहन्यमानौ च सुस्वनौ हर्षवर्धनौ।। *MB*, Droṇa, 23.84-85 (*BE*).
This suggests that the *dhvaja* of Yudhiṣṭhira displayed *mṛdaṅgas* and moon and star symbols were borne on the flag of the *dhvaja*. The symbols of star and moon symbolized everlasting glory. The *dhvaja* of Arjuna also bore these symbols. These are also represented on the coins of Śaka *kṣatrapas* of western India and the Sātavāhanas. In the *dhvaja-patākās* represented in the art of Bhārhut, these symbols have been widely used.
24. ध्वजं तु भीमसेनस्य वैदूर्यमणिलोचनम्।
भ्राजमानं महासिंहं राजन्तं दृष्टवानहम्।। *MB*, Droṇa, 23.83 (*BE*).
जम्बूनदमयः केतुः केसरी नरसत्तम।
पपात भीमसेनस्य भीष्मेण मथितो रथात्।। Ibid., Bhīṣma, 45.33.
25. शरभं पृष्ठसौवर्णं नकुलस्य महाध्वजम्। Ibid., Droṇa, 23.86 (*BE*).
26. हंसस्तु राजतः श्रीमान् ध्वजे घंटापताकवान्। Ibid., Droṇa, 23.87 (*BE*).
27. अभिमन्योः कुमारस्य शार्ङ्गपक्षी हिरण्मयः। Ibid., Droṇa, 23.89 (*BE*).
28. धर्ममारुतशक्राणामश्विनोः प्रतिमास्तथा। Ibid., Droṇa, 39.16.
29. कोविदारध्वजम्। Ibid., Bhīṣma, 50.89.
30. घटोत्कचस्य राजेन्द्र ध्वजे गृध्रो व्यरोचत। Ibid., Droṇa, 23.90 (*BE*).
Elsewhere he is described as रथचक्रध्वजं वीरम्। Ibid., Droṇa, 22.60.
31. यस्य नागो ध्वजाग्रे वै हेमकेतनसंश्रितः। Ibid., Virāṭa, 50.12; also Bhīṣma, 17.25.
32. हेमतालध्वजं भीष्मं राजते स्यन्दने स्थितम्। Ibid., Bhīṣma, 16.41.
यस्तु नीलानुसारेण पञ्चतारेण केतुना। Ibid., Virāṭa, 50.17.

यस्य तारार्कचित्रोऽसौ रथे ध्वजवरः स्थितः। Ibid., 50.18.
This suggests that Bhīṣma bore *tāla* tree on his *dhvaja* and its flag represented moon and stars.

33. यत्रैषा कांचनी वेदी प्रदीप्ताग्निशिखोपमा।
उच्छ्रिता कांचने दण्डे पताकाभिरलंकृता।। *MB*, Virāṭa, 53.1,
34. नागकक्ष्या तु रुचिरा ध्वजाग्रे यस्य तिष्ठति। Ibid., 50.15.
35. स्यन्दनेन महार्हेण केतुना वृषभेण च। Ibid., Bhīṣma, 17.27; Droṇa, 80.14.
36. धनुर्ध्वजाग्रे यस्य दृश्यते। Ibid., Virāṭa, 50.9.
अश्वत्थामा ययौ यत्तः सिंहलांगूलकेतनः। Ibid., Bhīṣma, 17.21.
सिंहलांगूललक्ष्माणम्। Ibid., Droṇa, 24.30; also 80.10.
Perhaps, the bow was his *dhvaja* symbol and lion's tail was represented on his *dhvaja-patākā*.
37. वराहः सिन्धुराजस्य। Ibid., Droṇa, 80.20.
38. सोमदत्तेः पुनर्यूपो। Ibid., Droṇa, 80.22; *Yūpa* was also carried on the *dhvaja* of Bhūriśravas. Ibid., 24.53.
39. मद्रराजस्य शल्यस्य ध्वजाग्रे अग्निशिखामिव।
सौवर्णी प्रतिपश्याम सीतामप्रतिमां शुभाम्।। Ibid., 80.18.
शल्यस्य तु महाराज राजतो द्विरदो महान्।
केतुः कांचनचित्रांगैर्मयूरैरुपशोभितः।। Ibid., 80.24.
This suggests that Śalya displayed two *dhvaja* motifs, viz., elephant and *sītā*. Perhaps, elephant was his *dhvaja* motif and *sītā* (plough line) was borne on his *dhvaja-patākā*.
40. मार्तिकावतकं भोजं ततः कुंजरकेतनम्। Ibid., Droṇa, 47.8.
41. तस्यापि गोमायुबडाभिगुप्तो। Ibid., 151.18.
42. मयूरो वृषसेनस्य। Ibid., 80.16.
43. यूपकेतुं महारणे। Ibid., Bhīṣma, 70.12.
44. सिंह केतुः। Ibid., 111.31.
45. शुशुभे केतुमुख्येन पादपेन कलिंगपः। Ibid., 17.34.
46. उच्छ्रित्य मकरं केतुम्। Ibid., Vana, 18.2.
47. ध्वजं च सिंहम्। Ibid., Virāṭa, 33.17.
48. तेन तस्य रथो भाति मयूरेण महात्मनः।
यथा स्कन्दस्य राजेन्द्र मयूरेण विराजता।। Ibid., Drona, 80.17.
49. त्रिपुरघ्नरथो यद्वद् गोवृषेण विराजते। Ibid., Drona, 80.15.
50. Kṛṣṇa was the incarnation of Viṣṇu and, therefore, he was called *Garuḍa-dhvaja*.
51. वैजयन्तम्। *MB*, Vana, 43.8.
52. शिखिपिच्छध्वजंधरे। Ibid., Bhīṣma, 23.6 (*BE*).
53. तालकेतुः। Ibid., Śalya, 40.35.
54. ध्वजं मनुष्यशीर्षम्। *Ram*, Yuddha, 100.14.

55. मृगराजकेतुः। Ibid., 59.15.
56. ध्वजशृंगप्रतिष्ठेन राहुणाभिविराजते। Ibid., 71.17.
57. उरगध्वज। Ibid., 57.26.
58. *Rām*, Araṇya, 23.4.
59. पन्नगराजकेतुः। Ibid., 59.20.
60. *Aṣṭādhyāyī*, 4.3.126.
61. For details on *lakṣaṇa* and *aṅka* which have been interpreted to mean the state symbol and personal symbol respectively, see V.S. Agrawal, *India as Known to Pāṇini*, p. 433; U.P. Thapliyal, *The Dhvaja*, p. 35.
62. J.W. M'crindle, *The Invasion of India*, pp. 208-9; the Greek historians have not correctly identified this symbol. Coomaraswamy calls it the icon of Śiva or Yakṣa (*History of Indian and Indonesian Art*, p. 42 fn. 5). J.N. Banerjee identifies it as Kṛṣṇa (*Comprehensive History of India*. vol. II, p. 283). M.A. Sastri calls it a Lokapāla (*Journal of Indian History*, vol. 42, p. 125).
    Persian armies were also accompanied by the royal standard. In the battle of Gaugamela, Alexander at the head of the companion cavalry played havoc with the troops which guarded the royal standard. J.W. M'crindle, op. cit., p. 30.
63. John Irwin, *Warlington Magazine*, vol. 116, December 1974, p. 715.
64. तूर्यध्वजपताकाभिर्व्यूहसंज्ञाः प्रकल्पयेत्।
    स्थाने याने प्रहरणे सैन्यानां विनये रतः।। *AS*, 2.33.11; also 10.6.46.
    Arthaśāstra, relates *dhvaja* to the temple (देवध्वजप्रतिमाभिर्वा। *AS*, pp. 13.3.45), Kangle (*AS*, vol. II, pp. 181, 452) and Sham Shastri (*AS*, p. 157) have translated ध्वजपताकाभिः as banners and flags. Kangle's explanation that *dhvaja* was a big banner whereas *patākā* was a smaller banner does not appear convincing.
    As a state symbol *dhvaja* was displayed at the main gate (*Mahādvāra*) of the city (*AS*, 2.21.1). Traders had to declare the quantity and the price of the goods they intended to carry to the city at this *dhvaja* point (*dhvajamūla*). Carrying goods beyond this point without proper declaration invited heavy penalty (*AS*, 2.21.7,16).
65. स्कन्धावारादुच्छ्रितध्वजघन्वारक्षो। *AS*, 13.4.15.
66. A. Cunningham, *The Stūpa of Bhārhut*, pls. 12, 32.
67. F.C. Maisey, *Sāñchī and its Remains*, pl. 17; also pl. 27. It appears that this belonged to some foreign royal house.
68. J. Allan, *Catalogue of the Coins of Ancient India*, pp. 135-9, 229; pls. 17-18.
69. P. Gardner, *The Coins of Greek and Scythian Kings of Bactria and India*, pl. 27.16, p. 138; pl. 28.22-3, p. 149.

70. L. Bachhofer, *Early Indian Sculpture*, vol. II, pl. 131; H. Zimmer, *The Art of Indian Asia*, vol. 2, pl. 42; it is notable that in other countries of the world, *patākā* came to be associated with *dhvaja* in the same manner.
71. *Garuḍa-dhvaja* is represented on the coins of Gupta rulers like Samudragupta, Skandagupta, Ghaṭotkacagupta, Narasiṁhagupta, Buddhagupta, Viṣṇugupta, Vainyagupta, etc., A.S. Altekar, *Catalogue of the Gupta Gold Coins in the Bayana Hoard*, pls. 2 & 3.
72. Ibid., pls. 6.11-15, 7.1-10.
73. V.A. Smith, *Coins of Ancient India*, vol. I, pp. 235-6, pl. 25.
74. A.S. Altekar, *Catalogue of the Gupta Gold Coins in the Bayana Hoard*, p. 314, pl. 32.14.
75. For details, see *Ancient India*, no. 4, p. 171.
76. J. Griffith, *The Paintings in the Buddhist Cave Temples of Ajantā*, p. 15.
77. अण्डोर्ध्वं कलशं न्यस्य तदूर्ध्वं विन्यसेद् ध्वजम्। *Agni Pu.*, 61.29-30.
78. L. Rice, *Mysore Inscriptions*, p. 33.
79. *Naiṣadhacarita*, 16.6.
80. ध्वजपताकाभिः। *AS*, 2.33.11.
81. C.D. Chatterjee, *Journal of the U.P. Historical Society*, 1947, p. 45.
82. V.A. Smith, *Coins of Ancient India*, vol. I, p. 236, pl. 25.5.
83. J.F. Fleet, *CII*, vol. 3, p. 147.
84. *Bṛhatsaṁhitā*, 48.73.
85. *Raghuvaṁśa*, 4.36.
86. स्पर्धन्ते वा उ देवहूये अत्र येषु ध्वजेषु दिद्यवः पतन्ति। *Ṛgveda*, 7.85.2.
87. *MB*, Karṇa, 54.10.
88. For details see *Agni Purāṇa*, chaps. 268-9; *Viṣṇudharmottara Pu.*, 2.154-6.
89. गायन्ति त्वा गायत्रिणोऽर्चन्त्यर्कमर्किणः।
ब्रह्माणस्त्वा शतक्रत उद् वंशमिव येमिरे।। *Ṛgveda*, 1.10.1.
90. *Rām*, Kiṣkindhā, 16.37; also *MB*, Ādi, 57.17-27.
91. *Kālikā Pu.*, 87; *Bṛhatsaṁhitā*, 43; also *Samarāṅgaṇa Sūtradhāra*, 17.
92. S. Dey, *Indian Life in The Śukla-Yajurveda*, pp. 88-9.
93. U.P. Thapliyal, *Foreign Elements in Ancient Indian Society*, pp. 144-6.
94. R.C. Hazra, *Studies in the Upapurāṇas*, vol. I, p. 21.
95. *Sāṅkhyāyana Śrauta Sūtra*, 15.1.4-6.
96. राजा वै राजसूयेनेष्ट्वा भवति, सम्राट् वाजपेयेन अवरम् हि राज्यं परं साम्राज्यम्। *Śatapatha Brāhmaṇa*, 5.1.1.13.
97. This was true of all sacrifices.

98. *Sāṅkhyāyana Śrauta-Sūtra*, 15.12.1.
99. *Brāhmaṇas* and *Śrauta-Sūtras* contain detailed description of this sacrifice.
100. *Ṛgveda*, 1.162-163; also 5.27.5-6.
101. अश्वमेधयाजी सर्वा दिशोऽभिजयति ˙ ˙ भुवनं तज्जयतित ˙ ˙ यन्तारमेवैनन् धर्तारं करोति। *Śatapatha Brāhmaṇa*, 13.1.2.3.
102. सर्वाणि राज्यान्याचष्टे सर्वा विशः सर्वान् वेदान् सर्वान् देवान् सर्वाणि भूतानि अश्नुते। Ibid., 13.4.3.15; in the *Rāmāyaṇa* a story relates that Indra was relieved of the sin of *Brahmahatyā* by performing *Aśvamedha* (Uttara, 86). King Ela was restored to manhood by god Śiva when pleased with *Aśvamedha* (Uttara, 90).
103. Details of *Aśvamedha* are given in *Śukla Yajurveda Saṁhitā*, *Śatapatha Brāhmaṇa*, *Sāṅkhyāyana Śrauta-Sūtra*, etc.
104. A.S. Altekar, *Catalogue of the Gupta Gold Coins in the Bayana Hoard*, pls. 4, 5.
105. Romila Thapar, *A History of India*, vol. I, p. 54.
106. भगवति जलधरपक्ष्मक्षपाकरार्केक्षणे कमलनाभे।
उन्मीलयति तुरङ्गमकरिनरनीराजनं कुर्यात्।।
द्वादश्यामष्टम्यां कार्तिकशुक्लस्य पञ्चदश्यां वा।
आश्वयुजे वा कुर्यान्नीराजनसञ्ज्ञितां शान्तिम्।। *Bṛhatsaṁhitā*, 44.1-2.
107. नीराजनामाश्वयुजे कारयेन्नवमेऽहनि।
यात्रादाववसाने वा व्याधो वा शान्तिके रतः।। *Arthaśāstra*, 2.30.51.
108. तिस्रो नीराजनाः कुर्याश्चातुर्मास्यर्तुसंधिषु।
भूतानां कृष्णसंधीज्याः सेनान्यः शुक्लसंधिषु।। Ibid., 2.32.21.
109. *Agni Pu.*, 268.16-30; *Kāmandaka* also states that horses and elephants were purified at *nīrājana* ceremony.
110. *Bṛhatsaṁhitā*, 43.21-28; *Viṣṇudharmottara Pu.*, 2.159.
111. मृन्मय शात्रवं कृत्वा चाभिचारिकमंत्रकैः।
प्रदि शूलेन विध्वा तं शिरं खड्गेन छेदयेत्।। *Kālikā Pu.*, 85.61; also 85.18-60; *Devī Pu.*, 22.16.
112. P.V. Kane, *History of Dharmaśāstra*, vol. III, pp. 230-1.
113. *AS*, 2.30.51; 2.32.21.
114. *Raghuvaṁśa*, 4.25.
115. *Kāmandaka Nīti* (4.64); *Bṛhatsaṁhitā* and *Yukti Kalpataru* (p. 178). describe the ceremony in greater detail.
116. *Śiva Pu.*, 4.10.49.
117. शान्ति राष्ट्रवृद्धये कृत्वा भूयोऽमिचारकैर्मन्त्रैः।
मृण्मयमरिं विभिन्द्याच्छूलेनोरः स्थले विप्रः।। *Bṛhatsaṁhitā*, 44.21; *Kālikā Pu.*, 85.61.
118. *Devī Pu.*, 22-16; also see R.C. Hazra, *Studies in the Upapurāṇas*, pp. 80-5.

119. *Aitareya Brāhmaṇa*, 3.12.9.
120. बलं प्रसादयेद् राजा। *MB*, Āśrama, 7.17.
121. *Kāmandaka Nīti*, 20.17-21.
122. *Śukranīti*, 4.7.354, 369-70.
123. Ibid., 2.419, also 421-5
124. Ibid., 4.7.354; also 231-2.
125. *Ṛgveda*, 4.20.8.
126. Ibid., 10.142.4.
127. *Aitareya Brāhmaṇa*, 2.25.
128. *Agni Pu.*, 236.65-6; also *Śukranīti*, 4.7.375.
129. रथाश्वं हस्तिनं छत्रं धनं धान्यं पशून्स्त्रियः। सर्वद्रव्याणि कुप्यं च यो यज्जयति तस्य तत्।। *Manusmṛti*, 7.96, 7.97; also *Bṛhaspati Smṛti*, 12.31-2 (*SBE*, 33).
130. परराष्ट्रार्जितं द्रव्यमर्धं राजा विभज्य तु।
योधेभ्योऽर्धं प्रदेयं स्यादर्धं च स्वयमाहरेत्।।
हयं वा शकटीं वापि हरेत् सोपस्कृतां भटः
तदर्धतुर्यमंशं तु स लभेद्राजसत्कृतः।। *Nītiprakāśikā*, 6.103-4.
131. Ibid., 6.105.
132. ये युध्यन्ते प्रधनेषु शूरासो ये तनूत्यजः। ये वा सहस्रदक्षिणास्तांश्चिदेवापि गच्छतात्। *Ṛgveda*, 10.154.3; *Atharvaveda*, 18.2.17.
133. *MB*, Śānti, 100. 4-7.
134. Ibid., Stri, 26.12-17.
135. यान यज्ञसंघैस्तपसा च विप्राः स्वर्गैषिणः पात्रचयैश्च यान्ति।
क्षणेन तानप्यतियान्ति शूराः प्राणान् सुयुद्धेषु परित्यजन्तः।। *AS*, 10.3.30.
136. *Raghuvaṁśa*, 7.51-53; *Agni Pu.*, 236.54.
137. *Śukranīti*, 4.7.310-14.
138. For details see *Memorial Stones*, ed. S. Settar and Günther D.-Sontheimer.
139. K.A. Nilakanta Sastri, *The Colas*, p. 73.
140. Ibid.
141. N. Subrahmanian, *Saṅgam Polity*, pp. 127-8; अधर्मः क्षत्रियस्यैष यच्छय्यामरणं भवेत्। *MB*, Śānti, 98.23.
142. For details see *Memorial Stones*, op. cit.
143. अनीकं ये प्रभिन्दन्ति भिन्नं ये स्थगयन्ति च।
समानाशनपानास्ते कार्या द्विगुणवेतनाः।।
दशाधिपतयः कार्याः शताधिपतयस्तथा।
तेषां सहस्राधिपतिं कुर्याच्छूरमतन्द्रितम्।। *MB*, Śānti, 101.27-8.
144. E.B. Cowell, *The Jātaka*, vol. 6, p. 142.
145. *Rām*, Yuddha, 122.4-9, *MB*, Sabhā, 5.44-9.
146. *AS*, 10.3.45.
147. *Agni Pu.*, 242.34-6.

148. *Kāmandaka Nīti*, 20.17-21; *Mānasollāsa*, 2.20, 1163-7.
149. प्रत्यग्रे कर्मणि कृते श्लाघमानः कृतादरः।
योधेभ्यः पूर्णपात्रं हि दद्याद्राजा विशेषतः।। *Nītiprakāśikā*, 6.88.
150. Ibid., 6.89-98.
151. Ibid., 6.96, 99.
152. आयुधीयम्। *AS*, 2.35.1; in the *Mahābhārata* such villages have been called *'Parihāra'*. *MB*, Āśrama, 16.15.
153. *Epigraphia Indica*, vol. 14, p. 155.
154. N. Subrahmanian, *Saṅgam Polity*, p. 164.
155. T. Watters, *Travels*, vol. 2, p. 176.
156. *Bṛhatsaṁhitā*, 49.3; it did not carry any crest (प्रसादपट्टो विना शिखया) Ibid., 49.
157. प्रभुप्रसादीकृतपाटितपटच्चरचलच्चोलकधारिभिश्च। *Harṣacarita*, p. 213.
158. क्लिष्टकार्पटिककुलपुत्रलोकमोचितैः प्रसाददानैः। Ibid., p. 202.
159. J. Griffith, *The Paintings in the Buddhist Cave Temples of Ajantā*, vol. I, pls. 70-7.
160. *Harṣacarita* , pp. 58-9; *Paṭṭikā* was used in ancient Persia. P. Sykes, *History of Persia*, pt. 1, p. 368.
161. D.K. Gupta, *Society and Culture in the time of Daṇḍin*, p. 147.
162. *Epigraphica Carnatica*, vol. 8, no. 80; an eighth-century epigraph refers to an honour called *śrīpaṭṭa*, which was granted by rulers as a token of appreciation. *Epigraphia Indica*, vol. 2, p. 344.
163. *Epigraphica Carnatica*, vol. 11, no. 105.
164. देशादिकं यस्य राजा लिखितेन प्रयच्छति।
सेवाशौर्यादिभिस्तुष्टः प्रसादलिखितं हि तत्।। *Śukranīti*, 2.303.
165. अनीकं ये प्रभिन्दन्ति भिन्नं ये स्थगयन्ति च।
समानाशनपानास्ते कार्या द्विगुणवेतनाः।। Ibid., Śānti, 101.27.
166. दशाधिपतयः कार्याः शताधिपतयस्तथा।
तेषां सहस्राधिपतिः कुर्याच्छूरमतिन्द्रितम्।। *MB*, Śānti, 101.28
167. प्रत्यग्रे कर्मणि कृते यौधैर्दद्याद्धनं च तान्।
परितोष्यं चाधिकारं, क्रमतोऽर्हं नृपः सदा।। *Śukranīti*, 4.7.369-70.
168. Ibid., 4.7.354.
169. *Nītiprakāśikā*, 6.109-10.
170. K.A. Nilakanta Sastri, *The Colas*, p. 462.
171. Ibid., p. 72.
172. *Epigraphica Carnatica*, vol. 5, no. 108.
173. Ibid., vol. 8, no. 80.
174. K.A. Nilakanta Sastri, op. cit., p. 72.
175. *Epigraphica Carnatica*, vol. 5, no. 112. In *Pṛthvirāja Rāso* a general of Kanauj army has also been described as wearing a *toḍara* on his left leg.

176. Ibid.
177. *Tirukkural*, 777.
178. N. Subrahmanian, *Saṅgam Polity*, p. 44.
179. *Epigraphica Carnatica*, vol. 6, KD 34.
180. L. Rice. *Mysore and Coorg*, p. 171.
181. *Śukranīti*, 2.245.
182. Ibid., 5.7.
183. The term युद्धगान्धर्व is used in the *Rāmāyaṇa. Rām*, Yuddha, 52.24; युद्धगान्धर्वसेवी। *MB*, Sabhā, 5.9 (*BE*).
184. यं क्रन्दसी संयती वियेते परेऽवर उभया अमित्राः।
 समानं चिद् रथमातस्थिवांसा नाना हवेते स जनास इन्द्रः। *Rgveda*, 2.12.8.
185. Ibid.
186. In the *Yajurveda* there are many references to *jaya-ghoṣa*: उच्चैर्घोषायाक्रन्दयते। 16.19
 घोषो देवानां जयतामुदस्थात्। 17.41
 रथानां जयतां यन्तु धोषाः। 17.42.
187. शब्दवन्तोऽनुधावेयुः कुर्वन्तो भैरवं रवम्। *MB*, Śānti, 101.46; *Rām*, Yuddha, 57.9.
188. D.D. Kosambi, *Origin of Brāhman Gotras*, p. 31.
189. क्रन्दनं योधसंरावा। *Amarakośa*, 2.8.107.
190. क्ष्वेडा तु सिंहनाद स्यात्। Ibid., *Siṁhanāda* was made by soldiers to scare away the enemy even in tenth century AD. सिंहनादैर्भटानां तु त्रासयेद् रिपु-सैनिकान्। *Mānasollāsa*, 2.20.1151.
191. दमयन्तसपत्नानिंत्सह इव जेष्यन्नभि तंस्तनीहि। *Atharvaveda*, 5.20.1.
 अभि क्रन्द स्तनयोत्पिपानः श्लोककृन्मित्रतूर्यायस्वर्धी। Ibid., 5.20.7.
192. *Ṛgveda*, 6.47.29-31.
193. ज्याधोषा दुन्दुभयोऽभि क्रोशन्तु या दिशः।
 सेनाः पराजिता यतीरमित्राणामनीकशः।। *Atharvaveda*, 5.21.9.
194. उच्चैर्घोषो दुन्दुभिः। Ibid., 5.20.1.
 देवी वाचं दुन्दभ। Ibid., 5.20.4
 विहृदयं वैमनस्यं वदामित्रेषु दुन्दुभे। Ibid., 5.21.1.
 नमो दुन्दुभ्याय चाहनन्याय च। *Yajurveda*, 16.35.
195. दुन्दभे त्वं सपत्नानां घोषाद्हृदयकम्पनः।
 भव भूमिपसैन्यानां यथा विजयवर्धनः।। *Agni Pu.*, 269.35.
 यथा जीमूतशब्देन स्त्रीणां त्रासोऽभिजायते।
 तथा तु तव शब्देन त्रस्यन्त्वस्मद्द्विषो रणे।। Ibid., 269.37; also
 पताकाश्चैव संभारो वादित्राणां भयावहः। Ibid., 236.61.
196. अभि दस्युं बकुरेणा धमन्तोरु ज्योतिश्चक्रथुरार्याय। *Ṛgveda*, 1.117.21.
197. *Bṛhadāraṇyaka Up*, 2.4.6.

198. *Kauśika Sūtra*, 14.22-3.
199. धनुर्ज्यातन्त्रिमधुरं हिक्कातालसमन्वितम्।
मन्दस्तनितगीतं तद् युद्धगान्धर्वमाबभौ।। *Rām*, Yuddha, 52.24; 32.43, 33.19-21; also E.W. Hopkins, op. cit., pp. 262-6.
200. ततो भेरीश्च शंखाश्च शतशश्चैव पुष्करान्।
वादयामासुरव्यग्राः पुरुषा राजशासनात्।। *MB*, Uddyoga, 153.27; *Rām*, Yuddha, 32.43.
201. शंखदुन्दुभिनिर्घोषस्तुमुलः सर्वतोऽभवत। Ibid., 149.48; also *Rām*, Yuddha, 35.1, 42.39, 50.62.
202. ततस्तूर्यनिनादैश्च भेरीणां च महास्वनैः।
तावकानामनीकानि परेषां चापि निर्ययुः।। *MB*, Droṇa, 1.19.
शंखदुन्दुभिनिर्घोषः सिंहनादस्तरस्विनाम्।
पृथिवीं चान्तरिक्षं च सागरं चाभ्यनादयत्।। *Rām*, Yuddha, 42.39.
203. ततः शंखाश्च भेर्यश्च पणवानकगोमुखाः।
सहसैवाभ्यहन्यन्त स शब्दस्तुमुलोऽभवत्।। *MB*, Bhīṣma, 23.13;
क्षणेन भेरीपणवप्रणादानन्तर्दधुः शंखमहास्वनाश्च। *MB*, Bhīṣma, 56.13.
204. क्ष्वेडाः किलकिलाः शंखाः क्रकचा गोविषाणिकान्।
भेरीमृदंगपणवान्नादयेयुश्च कुंजरान्।। *MB*, Śānti, 101.47; Bhīṣma, 42.4-6.
205. On the death of Jayadratha the Pāṇḍava camp enjoyed joyous music.
सिंहनादेन महता पूरयामास रोदसी।।
तं श्रुत्वा तु महानादं धर्मपुत्रो युधिष्ठिरः।
सैन्धवं निहतं मेने फल्गुनेन महात्मना।।
ततो वादित्रघोषेण स्वान्योधानभिहर्षयन्। *MB*, Droṇa, 121.42-4.
206. On the death of Abhimanyu no music was played in the Pāṇḍava camp. *MB*, Droṇa, 50.11-12.
207. पांचजन्यं हृषीकेशो देवदत्तं धनंजयः।
पौण्ड्रं दध्मौ महाशंखं भीमकर्मा वृकोदरः।।
अनन्तविजयं राजा कुन्तीपुत्रो युधिष्ठिरः।
नकुलः सहदेवश्च सुघोषमणिपुष्पकौ।। *MB*, Bhīṣma, 23.15-16.
208. *Aṅguttara Nikāya*, vol. 3, pp. 120-2; E.B. Cowell, *The Jātaka*, vol. 5, p. 170; vol. 6, p. 14; The *Jātakas* mention musical instruments like *śaṁkha*, *jhanjhā*, *ghaḍiyāl*, *turahī*, etc. *Milindapraśna* also refers to these instruments.
209. J.W. M'crindle, *The Invasion of India*, p. 208.
210. Ibid.
211. Ibid., p. 340; Curtius has said that Indians used drum instead of trumpet in war. Ibid., p. 208.
212. *AS*, 10.6.46; it appears that in this respect Indians learnt something from the Macedonians.

213. Rock Edict, 6.
214. J. Ferguson, *Tree and Serpent Worship*, pl. 34.
215. Ibid., pl. 36.2.
216. Ibid., pl. 38.1; here the drum is of a smaller size and is hung on the shoulder. Perhaps, in their nomadic life the Śaka-Kuṣāṇas used this type of drum for the sake of convenience.
217. M.K. Dhavalikar, *Ajantā: A Cultural Study*, 115-22; pl. 29.
218. नदत्सु तूर्येष्वविभाव्यवाचो नोदीरयन्ति स्म कुलोपदेशान्। *Raghuvaṁśa*, 7.38.
219. Ibid., 7.63.
220. Ibid., 7.64.
221. Ibid., 7.38.
222. R.D. Banerjee, *The Shiva Temple at Bhumara*, pl. 10; *Amarakośa* refers to many musical instruments like *kāñsyathāla*, *ghaṅṭā*, *mṛdaṅga, nagādā, bheri, ṣamaru, maḍu, ḍugḍugi, jhanjhā, mardala, ḍhola,* etc. *Mṛdaṅga* and *murāja* were the same. *Mṛdaṅga* had three varieties, viz., *ankaya*, *alingaya* and *urdhvaka*. *Nagāḍā* was also known as *yasa, paṭaha* and *ḍhakka. Bherī* was also known as *anala* and *dundubhi*.
223. *Brahmāṇḍa Pu.*, 21.101.
224. Ibid., 22.1-2; also 16.1-2.
225. *Bhāgavata Pu.*, 1.10.15; 10.50.38.
226. *Harṣacarita*, p. 199; also. p. 203; *Paumcariyam* (57.72-74) mentions the following instruments; *paṭa-paṭaha-bheri-jhalari, kahālā-huḍuka-pakya-kāñsyathālikā. Yaśastilaka Campū* refers to the following instruments: *śaṁkha, kahālā, dundubhi, puṣkara, ḍhakka, ānaka, bhambha, karata, trivila, ḍamru, runja, jayaghanṭā, veṇu, vinā and jhaleri.* V. Raghavan, *Gleanings from Yaśastilaka Campū*, p. 379.
227. *Harṣacarita*, p. 203.
228. Ibid., p. 205.
229. *Śiśupālavadha*, 15.72-4; *Avantisundarī Kathā* mentions *dundubhi, paṭaha, tūrya, śaṁkha, kahālā, mardala, kāñsyathāla, viṣāṇa, ānaka, piñcola* and *gomukha.* See D.K. Gupta, *Society and Culture in the Time of Daṇḍin*, p. 379.
230. *The Kalingaṭṭuparāṇi, Indian Antiquary*, vol. 19, p. 334; also V.R.R. Dikshitar, *War in Ancient India*, pp. 381-2.
231. C. Minakshi, *Administration and Social Life under Pallavas*, p. 67.
232. *Indian Antiquary*, vol. 18, p. 262.
233. धृतराष्ट्रस्य सैन्येषु भेरीणां नास्ति निस्वनः।
अनाहताः पाण्डवानां नदन्ति पटहाः किल।। *MB*, Udyoga, 141.19.
234. C.R. Dey, *The Music and Musical Instruments of Southern India and Deccan*, pp. 99-100.

235. J.W. M'crindle, *The Invasion of India*, p. 340.
236. C.R. Dey, op. cit., pp. 99-100.
237. J.W. M'crindle, *The Invasion of India*, p. 208.
238. *AS*, 10.6.46.
239. भेरीपटहगोपुच्छ-शंखवेण्वादिनिः स्वनैः।।
ये व्यूहरचका यानव्यपयानादिबोधकाः।। *Śukranīti*, 2.200.
240. व्यूहरचनसङ्केतान् वाद्यभाषासमीरितान्।।
स्वसैनिकैर्विना कोऽपि न जानीयात् तथाविधान्। Ibid., 4.7.267.
241. Ibid., 4.7.393.
242. *Ṛgveda*, 4.17.19-21; also 7.33.4.
243. Ibid., 8.2.29-30.
244. V.R.R. Dikshitar, op. cit., p. 379.
245. Ibid., p. 381.
246. *Ṛgveda*, 1.28.5; 6.47.29; *Atharvaveda*, 5.20.1, 5.21.7, 6.38.4.
247. संभृत उस्त्रियाभिः। *Atharvaveda*, 5.20.1, 5.21.3.
248. दुन्दुभिना हरिणस्याजिनेन च। Ibid., 5.21.7.
249. Ibid., 5.20.3; 5.21.9; in the *Atharvaveda* one *sūkta* (5.20) is devoted to *dundubhi* only.
250. *Śatapatha Brāhmaṇa*, 5.1.5.6.
251. E.W. Hopkins, op. cit., p. 263.
252. *Amarakośa*, 1.7.6.
253. Ibid.
254. Ibid., 1.7.8.
255. J. Marshall, *Sāñchī*, pl. 34c.
256. C. Sivaramamurti, *Amarāvatī Sculptures in Madras Museum*, pl. 13, fig. 13.
257. F.C. Maisey, *Sāñchī and its Remains*, pl. 35, figs. 5, 8.10, etc.; B.M. Barua, *Bhārhut*, fig. 34.
258. *Atharvaveda*, 4.10.6.
259. Ibid., 4.10.
260. *MB*, Bhīṣma, 23.15-16.
261. *Raghuvaṁśa*, 7.63-4.
262. E.B. Cowell, *The Jātaka*, vol. I, 283-84, vol. VI, p. 7.
263. F.C. Maisey, op. cit., pl. 35, figs. 15-16.
264. B.M. Barua, *Bhārhut*, fig. 148c; also C. Sivaramamurti, *Amarāvatī*, pl. 13, fig. 5.
265. J.W. M'crindle, *Invasion of India*, p. 340.
266. ततस्तूर्यनिनादैश्च भेरीणां च महास्वनैः। *MB*, Droṇa, 1.19.
267. *Aṅguttara Nikāya*, vol. III, pp. 120, 122; E.B. Cowell, *The Jātaka*, vol. V, p. 170; vol. VI, p. 14.
268. *AS*, 10.6.46; also Śukranīti, 4.7.266-7.

269. F.C. Maisey, op. cit., pl. 35, figs. 21-2.
270. *MB*, Bhīṣma, 23.13.
271. *Raghuvaṁśa*, 7.38.
272. *MB*, Śānti, 101.47.
273. A. Goldsworthy, *In the Name of Rome*, pp. 194, 258.

Chapter 10

Conclusion

'War is father of all things' said Heraclitus, an ancient Greek philosopher. And truly so, as to a large extent the human progress has been inspired or promoted by war. In ancient India the need for better agricultural implements and weapons led to the development of metallurgy. Some communities such as *rathakāras* (chariot-makers), *iṣukāras* (arrow-makers), *dhanuṣkāras* (bow-makers), *jyākāras* (string-makers), etc., were engaged in manufacturing weapons. The need for the fortification of cities encouraged the growth of military engineering. The necessity to provide for the care of war casualties led to the growth of the science of surgery and medicine. Wars were even central to the theme of great literary works like the *Ṛgveda*, the *Rāmāyaṇa* and the *Mahābhārata*.

SOCIAL FRAMEWORK

The very social set-up in ancient India was attuned to the needs of war. A major segment of the society called Kṣatriya was primarily devoted to warfare though the other segments, viz., Brāhmaṇas, Vaiśyas and Śūdras also contributed to it in some measure. The Brāhmaṇas like Bṛhaspati, Śukra, Paraśurāma, Kṛpācārya, Droṇācārya, etc., generally imparted military training and determined the strategy and tactics of war. Vaiśyas contributed soldiers and also produced food for the armies engaged in war. Śūdras were engaged in the production of weapons and also supply of food and fodder to the army, building of roads, digging of wells, etc. Thus, in a way, the whole social setup was oriented to meet the military needs of the state.

POLITICAL BEARINGS

The evolution of the state and its institutions had definite military orientation. The origin of kingship is traceable in the military needs of the society. It appears that the early king was primarily a *senāpati*, who led his followers to war. Subsequently, due to increase in the responsibilities of the king, a separate office of *senāpati* came into being to share his military duties. The *amātya* determined the policy on war and peace and implemented the four means of state policy, viz., *sāma*, *dāna*, *daṇḍa* and *bheda*.

The military machine, which was originally created to meet the defence related needs was subsequently used in aggressive pursuits also. Large armies were raised by the rulers to conquer territories. Resources generated from agriculture, commerce and industry were marshalled for maintaining these armies. To assert their military prowess rulers assumed titles like *ekarāṭ*, *samrāṭ*, *mahārājādhirāja*, etc.

The foreign policy of the state always had a military orientation. The *vijigīṣu* (king aspiring victory) framed his policy on war and peace with a view to the friendly, unfriendly or neutral disposition of the constituent kings of the *maṇḍala* in terms of their military potential and the capability for military intervention.

Despite loud talks of just war (*dharma-yuddha*) in the epics and Smṛtis, no effort, fair or foul, was spared to crush or kill the enemy. The tactics of surprise and deception were often applied in the battlefield. Poisonous weapons were used. The tactics of *indrajāla* and *māyājāla* were played to deceive the enemy. Occasionally, the battles were waged during the night.

UNENDING WARS

The military orientation of the state apparatus was conducive for waging war. In the *Ṛgveda* there are numerous references to battles between the Āryan tribes and also between the Āryans and the natives, whom they called *dāsas* and *dasyus.* The large size of the country and the existence of many kingdoms and tribal states contributed to the frequency of wars. Big kingdoms fought wars to augment their trritory and influence while small ones tried to defend themselves by any means, including surrender.

The emergence of powerful kingdoms like Maurya, Kuṣāṇa and Gupta expanded the area of warfare. Mauryas conquered the whole of India except some peninsular states in the extreme south. Samudragupta, after consolidating his power in the north, led a campaign to subjugate the peninsular kingdoms. His son Candragupta, despite having inherited a powerful empire, also waged a long war against the Śakas in western India.

To this plethora of wars a substantial contribution was made by foreign invaders. They waged wars to extend their political power as also to secure a status in the society. The series of invasions, started by the Persian monarch Cyrus, was continued by Alexander, Bactrian Greeks, Śakas, Pahlavas, Kuṣāṇas, Hūṇas and finally the Turks. It is notable that most of these invaders settled in India and contributed to the making of Indian culture in no small measure.

ORGANIZATIONAL SET-UP

A proper military organization is necessary to wage war. Indian armies (*balas*) were classified as *maula, bhṛtya, śreṇi, mitra, dviṣada* and *aṭavī* types keeping in view their composition and capability to fight. The *maulabala* or the standing army was the kernel of the military organization. The other armies like *bhṛtyabala* comprised second grade troops somewhat like the present day para-military forces. *Aṭavībala,* composed of forest dwellers, was used by kings in negotiating forest areas and harassing the enemy troops. It is notable that in ancient times large tracks of north Indian plains were covered by dense forests and inhabited by forest tribes. *Aṭavībala,* therefore, came to play a major role in Indian warfare.

The armies, particularly the standing army, was organized in four arms, viz., infantry, cavalry, elephant corps and chariot corps (*caturaṅgiṇī*). These arms evolved over a period of time, of course depending upon the military needs of the people. Chariot corps occupied a superior position among the arms during the Vedic and Epic times, but its utility was limited to even or plain battle grounds. As chariot could not cope up with the complex strategies and tactics and rapid manoeuvres introduced by foreign invaders like the Greeks, the Śakas and the Kuṣāṇas, it appears to be losing ground to elephant and horse around the beginning of the Christian era. The decline of the chariot was also inevitable, because the Scytho-Kuṣāṇa rulers who dominated the Indian battlefield during this period patronized cavalry as their principal arm. The Guptas and their successor Puṣyabhūti rulers also appear to have neglected chariot as it hardly finds any representation in the art of Ajantā or on the Gupta coins.

Consequent upon the foreign invasions the cavalry gained importance in Indian warfare. The mounted cavalry was the principal arm of the Scytho-Kuṣāṇas and its component force of mounted archers was particularly very effective in war. The use of stirrup made the mounted arches more effective as he could now use both his hands freely. Guptas, following Śaka-Kuṣāṇas, maintained substantial cavalry as is evident from art and coin portrayals. The cavalry of Harṣavardhana of Thānesar comprised 1,00,000 horses.

The elephant corps, however, maintained its superiority in the Indian battlefield through the ages. Even the defeat in the battle of Jhelum (326 BC) did not sully its reputation. In fact, the decline of chariot augmented its stature as a superior arm. The army of Candragupta Maurya included 36,000 elephants as against 20,000 chariots. Some one thousand years later the army of Harṣavardhana included 60,000 elephants. In the art of Sāñcī and Ajantā the elephants are widely represented in a military role.

EXAGGERATED NUMBERS

For better command and control the armies were constituted in units or formations. In the *Mahābhārata* the smallest unit is called *patti* and it included elements from all the four arms (1 chariot, 1 elephant, 3 horses, 5 foot). *Akṣauhiṇī* was the largest formation comprising 21,870 chariots, 21,870 elephants, 65,610 horses and 1,09,350 foot-soldiers, all totalling to 2,18,700. Occasionally, these figures add to crores.

It is surprising that the figures pertaining to the size of armies of India given in the Vedas, epics and the Purāṇas are highly exaggerated. Even the figures given by the Greek historians who have based their accounts on the *Indica* of Megasthenese are unbelievable. To illustrate the point the army of Candragupta Maurya is said to have comprised 7,00,000 men including all arms. Conceding that Candragupta was a mighty ruler, could he have afforded such a large army with the resources available to him. The figures given in respect of the armies of tiny states of north-west India by the Greek writers are equally suspect. Perhaps they exaggerated the numbers of Indian troops, they fought against, with a view to convey that Greeks earned victories in India in the face of a formidable opposition.

Even the account of Hiuen-tsang, which otherwise depicts a true picture of the life and times of Harṣavardhana, errs while enumerating the strength of his army. He says that Harṣa's army comprised 60,000 elephants, 1,00,000 horses, and a large infantry. Harṣa was certainly far less capable of maintaining such a large army than Candragupta Maurya.

In the military organization *senāpati* stood at the top. He was expected to lead the army to success. In the Epic war the 18 *akṣauhiṇīs* were led by a *senāpati* each. Bhīṣma and Dhṛṣṭadyumna served as the chief *senāpatis* of Kaurava and Pāṇḍava forces respectively. *Senāpati* was consecrated before assuming his office. Under the guidance of *senāpati* a large number of officers looked after various departments of the army in peace time.

SALARIED SOLDIERS

Indians followed the system of salaried soldiers as early as sixth century BC. Earlier to that in the Vedic times, greed for the spoils of war was the prime motivating factor. It seems that the payment of salaries (*vetana*) to the soldiers started with the creation of standing armies by the monarchs. In the epics rulers are advised to take special care to distribute salaries among soldiers on time to keep them contented. In fact, Indian soldiers were paid handsome salaries in fourth century BC to enable them to live lavishly.

The *Arthaśāstra* refers to a definite system of salaries payable to military functionaries. The highest salary of 48,000 *paṇas* was paid to the commander-in-chief while a trained soldier received 500 *paṇas* per annum. Salaries were paid to the soldiers during the Gupta times as well.

PURSUIT OF WAR

The pursuit of war demanded adherence to certain established principles. In this context four means (*upāyacatuṣṭaya*) and six measures (*ṣāḍguṇya*) are particularly notable. Of the four means, viz., *sāma, dāna, daṇḍa* and *bheda,* a resort to *daṇḍa* (war) was made only when the application of the other three failed to secure the objective. In a war like situation either of the six measures, viz., *sandhi, vigraha, āsana, yāna, saṁśraya* and *dvaidhībhāva* could be adopted. It is notable that *vigraha* was one of the six measures and not the only measure open to a king.

Before opting for a war certain factors like the time (*kāla*), terrain (*bhūmi*), state of own army, state of enemy army, disposition of *maṇḍala* kings, state of the roads, etc., had to be considered. Once a decision had been taken to commence the war soldiers were asked to get ready in battle-dress (*saṅgrāma-sajjā*).

After performing certain rituals the army marched out for *skandhāvāra* (camp) laid near the battlefield. The selection of battleground was made after due thought as the victory to a large extent depended on the right choice. Military spies, engineers, signallers and doctors assisted the army in fighting the war efficiently. Spirituous drinks were provided to the soldiers to boost up their spirits. Every effort was made to keep up the morale of the troops engaged in war.

STRATEGY AND TACTICS

Once in the battlefield armies were deployed in various formations (*vyūhas*). The earliest references to army formations are met in Vedic literature. Subsequently, two great military thinkers, viz., Śukrācārya and Bṛhaspati perfected the science of *vyūhas*. In the Epic war which lasted for eighteen days more than thirty *vyūhas* were formed by the Pāṇḍava and Kaurava armies.

The war strategy to be adopted or the *vyūha* to be formed on a particular day of war was decided by the king and his commanders after considerable debate. On the first day of the Epic war Pāṇḍavas adopted *vajra-vyūha* to fight the large Kaurava army after a long discussion. On the Kaurava side Bhīṣma decided the strategy of war in consultation with senior commanders like Droṇa, Kṛpācārya, etc.

It is notable that the classification of *vyūhas* met in the epics also appears in Purāṇas and Smṛtis. The *Arthaśāstra*, however, treads an entirely different line. It describes *vyūhas* as *sama, viṣama, miśra, śuddha*, etc., based on the deployment of different arms in different formations. The most significant reference in the *Arthaśāstra*, however, pertains to the tactical deployment of units in four basic arrays, viz., *daṇḍa, bhoga, maṇḍala* and *asaṁhata* denoting their functional role. In this, the *Arthaśāstra* generally follows the principles laid down by military strategists like Śukrācārya and Bṛhaspati. The *Kāmandaka Nīti, Agni Purāṇa* and *Mānasollāsa* further improved upon the principles laid down by Kauṭilya.

Indians had also learnt about the 'guerrilla tactics' of war and 'scorched earth' policy of defence. These appear to be fresh innovations in Indian warfare. Perhaps, foreign invaders like the Śakas and Kuṣāṇas had perfected these tactics and introduced them in India.

IMPLEMENTS OF WAR

Weapons of bronze and copper had come into vogue in India during the Harappan age. The production of weapons was refined during the Vedic age and it is believed that swords, spears and axes related to Copper Hoard Culture of the Gangetic valley were Āryan weapons. The bow was the most popular weapon of the Āryans.

The production of strong weapons is directly related to the discovery of iron. Scholars have placed the antiquity of iron in India anywhere between 1000 to 300 BC. But the references to iron-tipped arrowheads and steel swords of India by Herodotus and Ktesias respectively certainly push back the antiquity of iron to sixth century BC. Recently, Rakesh Tiwari on the basis of his excavations in Uttar Pradesh has claimed that iron was known to Indians in second millennium BC.

In India there has always been a class of professionals who were engaged in the production of weapons such as bow, arrow, sword, javelin, etc. They were settled in the capital and paid well. In the situation of war even new weapons were manufactured. King Ajātaśatru, during his long war with the Vajjis, introduced *mahāśailakaṇṭaka* and *ratha mauśala*, two new weapon types.

Some scholars hold that Indians did not use armour earlier than their contact with the foreign invaders. But the references to *varman* and *kavaca* in Vedic literature negate this theory. In fourth century BC Porus joined the battle with Alexander dressed in a *kavaca*.

As for the enigma of divine (*divya*) weapons like *brahmāstra, garuḍāstra, rudrāstra, ādityāstra*, etc., widely referred to in the epics and Purāṇas there is no definite explanation. These might have been various types of arrows with incendiary heads of some potential. No fire arms seem to have been known to ancient Indians but fire as a destructive medium was definitely known to them.

A revolutionary change appeared in Indian weapon system around the beginning of the Christian era with the introduction of horn-bow and composite-bow by the foreign invaders. These new bow-types though smaller in size, were more effective than the earlier Indian bow. But more than the bow it was the new arrow-head which proved lethal. It is said that double tanged arrow-heads and three bladed types were brought in by the Greeks and Scytho-Kuṣāṇas to India around the beginning of the Christian era. They also contributed a heavy javelin, a large sword and a mace to the Indian weapon system.

DEFENSIVE MENTALITY

Insecurity breeds defensive mentality. Indians, like other people of the world, raised walls around their settlements as a protective measure. It was believed that an archer protected by the fort could fight 100 adversaries and 100 archers could beat back 10,000 adversaries. The fortifications at Mohenjo-daro and Harappa and the Vedic references to a large number of forts destroyed by Indra confirm that early Indians looked to fort for security.

Ajātaśatru, the ruler of Magadha, is said to have built a fort at the confluence of Soṇa and Gaṅgā, to meet the threat posed by Pradyota, the ruler of Avanti. Later his son Udāyin built the city of Pāṭaliputra here. Megasthenese has described the fortification of this city in great detail.

The Indian forts, built as a measure of protection from internal and external foes, generally failed in their objective and succumbed under the pressure of the invaders. Various *yantras* (machines), mobile and immobile, intended to protect the forts just proved ineffective in beating back the invaders.

The Greeks and Scytho-Kuṣāṇas may have introduced a new system of fortification in India. They planned their fortifications at Sirkap and Sirsukh respectively in an un-Indian style for obvious reasons. They may have built many more forts in the like manner.

EDUCATION AND TRAINING

Some kind of military training was imparted to soldiers during the Vedic times. In the Epics military education and training is called *dhanurveda,* and included physical exercise, hunting and practice of weapons. In sixth century BC Taxilā had emerged as a great centre of military education and training. People from all over the country flocked to Taxilā to seek specialization in military matters. It is said that Cāṇakya and Candragupta Maurya learnt their military lessons here.

Buddhist *vihāras* and Brāhmaṇic *āśramas* also provided for military education. The *āśramas* of Droṇa, Kṛpācārya, Paraśurāma, Bhāradvāja, Agniveśa, Viśvāmitra, etc., were famous centres of such education where princes from various parts of the country were enrolled. There were also state academies, where select teachers taught various subjects including the art of fighting. The *Kādambarī*, a composition of seventh century AD, refers to one such academy. The epics, the *Arthaśāstra* and the Nīti works suggest that Indian soldiers and their mounts were well-trained in the art of war.

CEREMONIALS

Indians observed many rituals and ceremonials to augment their military might and earn victories. These included *dhvajārohaṇa, nīrājana, aśvamedha,* etc. Soldiers were bestowed with honours and awards to encourage them. Martial music was played to prop up their spirits in the battlefield. Around the beginning of the Christian era the concept of war god Kārttikeya had evolved, perhaps as a result of foreign inspiration.

REVOLUTIONARY CHANGES

The art of warfare in ancient India might have undergone changes from time to time, as a result of the shift in political scenario. The rise and fall of the Indus Valley Civilization, the Āryan immigration and evolution of Brāhmaṇic order and finally foreign invasions and the assimilation of foreigners were the three major events of this period. Each of these major events might have left its imprint on the then existing system of warfare.

To illustrate the point, fort was central to the military system of the Harappans and the fact is clearly borne out by the archaeological discoveries. The Ṛgvedic references to forts also allude to this. It seems that life was insecure during these times and people sought refuge in the forts when threatened. Forts are also reflective of the defensive mentality of the people, who built them.

In the Vedic and epic times chariot came to dominate the Indian battlefield as it was central to the Āryan system of warfare. Āryans being immigrants were aggressive in nature and therefore, depended on their fast moving chariots and strong weapons. The natives called *dāsas* and *dasyus* in the *Ṛgveda* could not withstand the chariot mounted bowmen and their forts crumbled before powerful Āryan assaults.

In the third phase of history, marked by invasions carried by Iranians, Greeks, Parthians, Śakas, Kuṣāṇas and Hūṇas, the Cavalry, and particularly the bow wielding cavalry, became central to Indian warfare. The Indians depending on their chariots and elephants could not cope up with rapid manoeuvres of the foreign invaders. By virtue of their military superiority the foreigners came to dominate large areas of Indian territory and this domination lasted for some 500 years. Gradually, they were completely assimilated in the Indian social system.

FOREIGN IMPACT

During her long history India witnessed large scale invasions and immigrations leading to foreign occupation of northern India and parts of the Deccan. The story of invasions in ancient India which started with Cyrus, the Achaemenid emperor, in sixth century BC ended with the Hūṇa invasion in sixth century AD. In between came the powerful invaders like the Yavanas (Greeks), the Pahlavas, the Śakas, the Kuṣāṇas, and perhaps many more. Most of these invaders settled in India and some of them established powerful kingdoms.

The invaders must have greatly influenced the system of warfare in India, particularly because they ruled over large territories. Briefly speaking, they must have brought in new strategy and tactics of war, new weapons, new organizational set-up, new fortification system, etc. Cavalry, though known to Indians earlier, now became the principal arm. The Scytho-Kuṣāṇa bow-men mounting well-equipped horses defeated their Indian adversaries who fought mounted on elephants and chariots. These invaders also popularized a new battle dress comprising coats, trousers and armour among soldiery, for convenience and safety. The Gupta rulers adopted the new system of warfare to an extent as can be discerned from contemporary art and coins.

The eclipse of the chariot from the Indian battlefield could perhaps be related to foreign invasions. It failed to cope up with the pressure mounted by the agile cavalry of the Greeks and the Scytho-Kuṣāṇas, and was forced out of the battlefield. Consequently, chariot is rarely seen in the Indian art after the beginning of the Christian era.

The Scytho-Kuṣāṇas also brought in the concept of a war god, which subsequently got amalgamated with the Indian cult of Skanda-Kārttikeya.

SOCIAL CONSEQUENCES

Violence in any form is anathema to peaceful social order. Around 1500 BC the Āryans defeated the native Indians called Dāsas and Dasyus, who were dark-complexioned, snub-nosed and phallus worshippers. Led by Indra and Agni Āryans destroyed their forts, looted their cattle and forced them to migrate to safer locations (*Ṛgveda*, 7.5.3, 1.133.3; *Taittirīya Br.* 2.4.6,8). The resultant social upheaval perhaps needs to be studied in greater depth.

Many more invasions took place between sixth century BC and second century AD and consequently, foreigners like Yavanas, Śakas and Kuṣāṇas came to rule over large parts of northern India and Deccan. As a result considerable foreign population also came to settle in India. This might have created a crisis situation for the Brāhmaṇic social order, which was based on *varṇāśramadharma*. The *Mahābhārata* and the Purāṇas say that in the *Kali* age the world deprived of sacrificial activities would be reduced to *mleccha* state. The *Matsya Purāṇa* states that in the *Kali* age almost all kings would be of Śūdra origin. The *Gārgī Saṁhitā* names a Scythian king Amlāṭa who destroyed the four-fold Brāhmaṇic social order. The Śaka depredations continued to haunt the minds of Indians for centuries. Alberuni, who visited India in tenth century records that a Śaka king 'interdicted Hindus from considering and representing themselves as anything but Śakas'.

It seems that harsh measures were adopted by the foreign rulers to break the Brāhmaṇic resistance to their assimilation. The might of the sword prevailed and ultimately the Brāhmaṇic and Buddhist orders opened to their entry. The foreigners also calmed the native opposition by making large donations to religious establishments and Brāhmaṇas.

The social unrest gradually subsided and the invaders secured appropriate place in the Indian social order. There is reason to believe that by third century AD the crisis situation as described in the Purāṇas, etc., had calmed down, for short of that the all-round progress witnessed in the Gupta age would not have been possible.

DISMAL SHOWING

Despite having developed sound basics of warfare Indians suffered defeat at the hands of foreign invaders, repeatedly. The internecine wars and the resultant political instability left the territories in the north-west unguarded and uncared for. Even when the conditions were somewhat stable the supreme power if any, was seated far in the east to protect the far north-west.

Earlier to the invasion of Alexander north-west India and Punjab was ruled by many tiny kingdoms and tribal states, generally at war with each other. Their armies may not have been sufficiently strong to challenge an invader leading a disciplined army. The victories of invaders like Cyrus, Darius, Alexander, etc., could possibly be ascribed to this weakness.

Subsequent to the end of Mauryan hegemony of say 150 years the north-west India again disintegrated into tiny tribal states. The gateway of India again lay open to foreign invaders like the Bactrian Greeks, the Pahlavas, the Śakas and the Kuṣāṇas. Absence of a powerful opposition facilitated their march to the east.

It is notable that when a powerful dynasty, like the Maurya or the Gupta, ruled over India no foreign invasion succeeded. The armies of Candragupta Maurya defeated the Greek invaders Seleukos. Candragupta II led a successful military campaign against the Śakas who were ruling in western India. One of his successors Skandagupta defeated the Hūṇa invaders and forced them to retreat, albeit temporarily.

Indians refused to learn anything from their failures in the battlefield and therefore, had to suffer defeat again and again. They had developed a sound military system but they did not modify or update it in the light of experience and clung to their traditional mode of warfare unmindful of the ground realities. Though chariot had been discredited in the battle of Jhelum and elsewhere it took Indians centuries to discard it as an instrument of war. On the other hand, despite the established superiority of mounted archer of the Śaka-Kuṣāṇa army, they refused to incorporate this novelty into their system of warfare. Ironically, soon after settling in India, the invaders also became enamoured of the Indian system and discarded the advantage of mobility in war associated with the use of horse.

Later, when it came to fighting with the Arabs and Turks, the Indians suffered badly as they could not muster a strong cavalry. In this connection, the following account of Marco Polo, though specific to a southern state, may hold true for all states of India.

> The King (of Thana) does this (procures horses) because he had no horse of his own, whilst many are shipped from abroad towards India. The number of horses exported from (the Arab cities of the Red Sea) to India yearly is something astonishing. One reason is that no horses are bred there, and another that they die as soon as they get there, through ignorant handling; for people there do not know how to take care of these. (Marco Polo quoted by D.D. Kosambi, *An Introduction to the Study of Indian History*, p. 329)

Obviously, Indian ecology was detrimental to the breeding and maintenance of quality horses.

As for the elephant, it generally failed to stand before the rapid moving cavalry of the invaders. Still, Indian rulers continued to repose trust on elephants over the centuries.

Again for climatic reasons Indians could not develop a heavy infantry arm. The foot-soldier could neither wear nor bear heavy armour under a scorching sun. The scantily clad Indian soldier just failed to stand before the onslaught of the invading cavalries.

In conclusion, it appears that the system of warfare in ancient India, though conceptually sound, proved a failure when it came to application, as it could not adjust to the changing times and situations.

Chronology of Important Events

2800 BC-2000 BC	Age of Indus Valley Civilization
1500 BC	Āryan conquests and immigration
1500 BC-1000 BC	Early Vedic age
1400 BC	Battle of Puruṣṇi between Sudās and ten kings.
1400 BC-1000 BC	Wars among the Āryan tribes
1000 BC-500 BC	Later Vedic age
600 BC-500 BC	Age of sixteen *Mahājanapadas*
600 BC-AD 200	Age of *Sūtras*
566 BC-AD 486	Age of Buddha
550 BC	Cyrus Invades Gandhāra
519 BC	Darius invades Sind and Punjab
516 BC-489 BC	Reign of Ajātaśatru
400 BC-200 BC	Date of *Rāmāyaṇa*
400 BC-AD 400	Date of *Mahābhārata*
380 BC	Mahāpadma Nanda usurps the throne of Magadha
327 BC-326 BC	Alexander invades India
325 BC	Alexander leaves India
321 BC	Candragupta Maurya defeats Nandas and ascends the throne
305 BC	Indian invasion of Seleukos and his defeat by Candragupta Maurya
300 BC-AD 1279	Colas of Colamaṇḍalam (Coromandal Coast)
273 BC-232 BC	Reign of Aśoka
260 BC	Battle of Kaliṅga
206 BC	Antiochus III (Seleucid ling) invades Gandhāra
185 BC	Puṣyamitra Śuṅga usurps the throne of Magadha
190 BC	Demetrius (223 BC-187 BC), Greek ruler of Bactria, invades India and occupies Sind and eastern Punjab
165 BC-160 BC	Eukratides, invades India and establishes a kingdom in Gandhāra and western Punjab

90 BC-AD 388	The Śaka rule in Taxilā, Mathurā, Ujjain and western India
60 BC-AD 225	Sātavāhana rule in the Deccan
AD 10-AD 45	Parthian invasion of north-west India
AD 300-AD 1310	Pāṇḍyan Dynasty of Madurā
AD 48	Kuṣāṇa invasion of India
AD 78	Kaniṣka ascends the throne
AD 85	Kaniṣka's expedition across the Pamirs
AD 128-AD 150	Reign of Śaka *kṣatrapa* Rudradāman
AD 225-AD 550	Vākāṭaka rule in Deccan
AD 275-AD 510	Gupta Period of Indian history
AD 320-AD 335	Reign of Candragupta I
AD 335-AD 375	Reign of Samudragupta
AD 350-AD 890	Pallava dynasty of Kāñcī
AD 375-AD 413	Reign of Candragupta II, Vikramāditya
AD 399-AD 414	Fa-hian's Itinerary
AD 484	Hūṇa invasion
AD 480-AD 770	Valabhī rule in Saurāṣṭra
AD 550-AD 700	Later Gupta rulers of Magadha
AD 554-AD 606	Maukhari rule in Kanauj
AD 500-AD 648	Vardhana rule in Thānesar
AD 712	Arab conquest of Sind

Bibliography

ORIGINAL SOURCES

Agni Purāṇa, ed. and tr. (Hindi) Tarinish Jha and Ghanshyam Tripathi, Hindi Sahitya Sammelan, Prayag, 1988.

———, English tr. J.L. Sastri, Motilal Banarsidass, Delhi, 1984.

Aitareya Brāhmaṇa, English tr. M. Haug, Bharatiya Publishing Home, Delhi, 1976.

Amarakośa, ed. Hargovind Sastri, Chaukhamba Sanskrit Series, Varanasi, 1970.

Aṅgutara Nikāya, English tr. E.M. Hare, Pali Text Society, London, 1935.

Arthaśāstra, ed. and tr. R.P. Kangle, University of Bombay, Bombay, 1965-72.

Aṣṭādhyāyī, ed. and tr. S.C. Basu, Motilal Banarsidass, Delhi, 1962.

Atharvaveda Saṁhitā, ibid., 1985; English tr. W.T. Whitney, Motilal Banarsidass, Delhi, 1962.

Baudhāyana Dharmasūtra, Hindi tr. N.K. Acharya, Delhi, 1999.

Bhāgavata Purāṇa (tr.), ibid., 1987.

Brahma Purāṇa (tr.), ibid., 1985.

Brahmāṇḍa Purāṇa (tr.), ibid., 1984.

Bṛhatsaṁhitā, ed. and tr. A. Jha, Chaukhamba Vidya Bhavan, Varanasi, 1969.

Brahmavaivartta Purāṇa, Sri Vainkateswara Press edn., Bombay, 1988 Vikrami.

Bṛhad Vimānaśāstra of Bhāradvāja, Sarvadesika Arya Pratinidhi Sabha, New Delhi, 1959.

Daśakumāracarita, ed. N.R. Acharya, Munshiram Manoharlal, New Delhi, 1983.

Devī Purāṇa, ed. P.K. Sharma, Lal Bahadur Shastri Kendriya Vidyapitha, New Delhi, 1976.

Dhanurveda, Reproduced in Śārṅgadhara Paddhati, ed. Peter Peterson, Chaukhamba Sanskrit Pratisthan, Delhi, 1987.

Gautama Dharmasūtra, ed. Ved Mitra, Ved Mitra and Sons, New Delhi, 1969.

Harṣacarita (with Sankara's commentary), Nirnaya Sagar Press, Bombay, 1834 Saka.

———, English tr. E.B. Cowell and F.W. Thomas, Motilal Banarsidass, Delhi, 1968.

Harivaṁśa Purāṇa, ed. P.L. Vaidya, BORI, Poona, 1969.

Jātakas, English tr. E.B. Cowell, Motilal Banarsidass, Delhi, 1973.

Kādambarī, English tr. C.M. Ridding, Oriental Book Reprint Corporation, New Delhi, 1974.

Kālikā Purāṇa, ed. Visvanarayana Sastri, Chaukhamba Sanskrit Series, Varanasi, 1972.

Kāmandakīya Nītisāra, English tr. M.L. Dutt, Chaukhamba Sanskrit Series, Varanasi, 1979.

———, ed. T. Ganapati Sastri, Trivandrum, 1912.

Kātyāyana Śrautasūtra, ed. H.G. Ranade, Ministry of Education and Social Welfare, Pune, 1978.

Mahābhārata, ibid.

———, BORI, Poona, 1933-68.

Mālavikāgnimitram, ibid., Kalidasa-Gvanthavali.

Mānasollāsa, ed. G.K. Shrigondekar, Oriental Institute, Baroda, 1967.

Manusmṛti, ed. Rajvira Shastri, Arsh Sahitya Prachara Trust, Delhi, 1985.

———, ed. and tr. G. Buhler, Motilal Banarsidass, Varanasi, 1975.

Matsya Purāṇa, ed. and tr. H.H. Wilson, Nag Publishers, Delhi, 1997.

Milindapañho, English tr. T.W. Rhys Davids, SBE, Oxford, 1890.

Naiṣadhīya Caritam, ed. N.R. Acharya, N.S. Press, Bombay, 1962.

Nītiprakāśikā, ed. T. Chandrasekharan, Govt. of Madras, 1953.

Raghuvaṁśa, (*Kālidāsa-Granthāvali*), ed. and tr. S. Chaturvedi, Bharat Prakasan Mandir, Aligarh, 2019 Vikrami.

Rāmāyaṇa, Geeta Press, Gorakhpur, Sam. 2053.

Ṛgveda Saṁhitā, ed. and tr. S.D. Satvalekar, Swadhyaya Mandal, Paradi, 1978; English tr. Ralph T.H. Griffith, Motilal Banarsidass, Delhi, 1973.

Sāmaveda Saṁhitā, ed. and tr. S.D. Satvalekar, Swadhyaya Mandal, Paradi, 1958.

Sāma Vidhāna Brāhmaṇa, ed. B.R. Sharma, Kendriya Sanskrit Vidyapitha, Tirupati, 1964.

Saṁyutta Nikāya, English tr. Woodword, Pali Text Society, London, 1924.

Sāṅkhyāyana Śrauta-Sūtra, English tr. W. Caland, Motilal Banarsidass, Delhi, 1980.

Śatapatha Brāhmaṇa, ed. C.D. Sharma, Achutagranthamalakaryalaya, Kashi, Sam. 1994-7.

Śiśupālavadha, tr. Hargovind Sastri, Chaukhamba Vidya Bhavan, Varanasi, 1955.

Śiva Purāṇa (tr.), ibid., 1970.

———, Chaukhamba Sanskrit Pratishthan, Delhi, 2049 Vikrami.

Śukla Yajurveda Saṁhitā, ed. V.L. Pansikar, Nirnaya Sagar Press, Bombay, 1912.

Śukranīti, ed. J. Mishra, Chaukhambha Surbharti Prakashan, Varanasi, 1998.

Suśruta Saṁhitā, ed. Ambikadatta Shastri, Chaukhamba, Varanasi, 1959.

Taittirīya Saṁhitā, ed. T.N. Dharmadhikari, Vaidika Samsodhana Mandal, Poona, 1981.

Tirukkural, English tr. A. Chakravorti, Diocesan Press, Madras, 1953.

Vaśiṣṭha Dhanurveda, ed. Purnima Roy, Meharchand Lachhmandass, Delhi, 1991.

Viṣṇudharmottara Purāṇa, ed. Ksemraja Srikrsnadasa, Naga Publishers, Delhi, 1985.

———, Priyabala Shah, Parimal Publications, Delhi, 2002.

Viṣṇu Smṛti, English tr. Julius Jolly, Motilal Banarsidass, Delhi, 1965.

Yājñavalkya Smṛti, ed. U. Pandey, Chaukhamba, Varanasi, 1967.

Yajurveda Saṁhitā, ibid., 1985.

Yuga Purāṇa, JUPHS, vol. 20.

OTHER ORIGINAL WORKS

Allan, J., *Catalogue of the Coins of the Gupta Dynasties and Sasanka King of Gauda*, British Museum, London, 1914.

———, *Catalogue of the Coins of Ancient India*, British Museum, London, 1936.

Altekar, A.S., *The Coinage of the Gupta Empire*, Numismatic Society of India, Varansi, 1957.

———, *Catalogue of the Gupta Gold Coins in the Bayana Hoard*, Numismatic Society of India, Bombay, 1954.

Fleet, J.F., *Corpus Inscriptionum Indicarum*, vol. 3, Indological Book House, Varanasi, 1963.

Foucher, A. and J., Marshall, *Momuments of Sanchi*, Archaeological Survey of India, Calcutta.

Gardner, Percy, *The Coins of Greek and Scythian Kings of Bactria and India in the British Museum*, Sagar Publication, New Delhi, 1971.

Marshall, J., *Taxila*, University Press Cambridge, London, 1951.

———, *Mohenjo-daro and the Indus Civilization*, Indological Book House, Delhi, 1973.

M'crindle, J.W., *Ancient India as Described by Megasthenese and Arrian*, Today and Tomorrow Printers and Publishers, New Delhi, 1972.

———, *Ancient India as Described in Classical Literature*, Oriental Book Reprint Corporation, New Delhi, 1979.

Sachau, E.C., *Alberuni's India*, London, 1914.

Sharma, G.R., *Excavations of Kausambi*, Allahabad University, Allahabad, 1960.

Smith, V.A., *Catalogue of the Coins in Indian Museum Calcutta*, Clarendon Press, Oxford, 1968.

Vats, M.S., *Excavations at Harappa*, Manager of Publications, Delhi, 1984.

Watters, T., *On Yuan Chwang's Travels in India*, Munshiram Manoharlal, Delhi, 1973.

Zwalf, W., *A Catalogue of Gandhara Sculptures in the British Museum*, British Museum, London, 1996.

SECONDARY SOURCES

Agrawala, V.S., *Harṣacarita Eka Sāṁskṛtika Adhyayana*, Bihar Rashtrabhasa Parishad, Patna, 1953.

———, *India as Known to Pāṇini*, University of Lucknow, Lucknow, 1953.

Altekar, A.S., *State and Government in Ancient India*, Motilal Banarsidass, Delhi, 1958.

Bachhofer, L., *Early Indian Sculpture*, Munshiram Manoharlal, New Delhi, 1973.

Bakshi, G.D., *Mahabharata: A Military Analysis*, Lancer International, New Delhi, 1990.

Banerjea, J.N., *Development of Hindu Iconography*, University of Calcutta, Calcutta, 1956.

Banerji, G.N., *Hellenism in Ancient India*, Butterworth, Calcutta, 1919.

Banerjee, N.R., *The Iron Age in India*, Munshiram Manoharlal, New Delhi, 1965.

Barua, B.M., *Bhārhut*, Indological Book Corporation, Patna, 1979.

Barua, D.K., *An Analytical Study of Four Nikāyas*, Rabindra Bharati University, Calcutta, 1971.

Basham, A.L., *The Wonder that was India*, Sidgwick & Jackson, London, 1954.

Basu, J., *India of the Age of Brāhmaṇas*, Sanskrit Pustak Bhandar, Calcutta, 1969.

Begde, Prabhakar V., *Forts and Palaces of India*, Sagar Publications, New Delhi, 1982.

Beni Prasad, *Theory of Government in Ancient India*, Central Book Depot, Allahabad, 1968.

Biswas, Atreyi, *The Political History of the Hūṇas in India*, Munshiram Manoharlal, Delhi, 1973.

Bongrad Levin, G.M., *Studies in Ancient India and Central Asia*, Indian Studies, Calcutta, 1971.

Bridget & Raymond Allchin, *The Rise of Civilization in India and Pakistan*, Cambridge University Press, New Delhi, 2008.

Chakravarty, P.C., *The Art of War in Ancient India*, Karan Publications, Delhi, 1987.

Chattopadhyaya, B., *The Age of the Kuṣāṇas—A Numismatic Study*, Punthi Pustak, Calcutta, 1967.

Chattopadhyaya, D., *History of Science & Technology in Ancient India—The Beginnings*, Firma KLM, Calcutta, 1986.

Coomaraswamy, A.K., *History of Indian and Indonesian Art*, Munshiram Manoharlal, New Delhi, 1972.

Cunningham, A., *The Stūpa of Bhārhut*, Indological Book House, Varanasi, 1962.

———, *Bhilsa Topes*, Indological Book House, Varanasi, 1966.

Creveld, M.V., *Command in War*, Harvard University Press, Cambridge, 1985.

Das, A.C., *Ṛgvedic Culture*, Bharatiya Publishing House, Delhi, 1979.

Date, G.T., *The Art of War in Ancient India*, Calcutta, 1943.

Dey, S.N., *Indian Life in the Śukla Yajurveda*, Firma KLM, Calcutta, 1985.

Dhavalikar, M.K., *Ajantā—A Cultural Study*, University of Poona, Poona, 1973.

Dikshitar, V.R.R., *War in Ancient India*, Motilal Banarsidass, Delhi, 1987.

———, *The Gupta Polity*, University of Madras, Madras, 1962.

Dutt, R.C., *History of Civilization in Ancient India, based on Sanskrit Literature*, Vishal Publishers, Delhi, 1972.

Ferguson, J., *Tree & Serpent Worship*, Indological Book House, Delhi, 1971.

Foucher, A., *L'Art Greco Bouddique Du Gandhāra*, vols. 1 & 2, Imprimerie National Paris, Paris, 1914, 1918.

Frye, R.N., *The Heritage of Persia*, Weidenfeld and Nicolson, London, 1962.

Gardner, Percy, *The Coins of Greek and Scythian Kings of Bactria and India in the British Museum*, Sagar Publications, New Delhi, 1971.

Ghoshal, U.N., *A History of Indian Political Ideas*, Oxford University Press, London, 1959.

———, *A History of Indian Public Life*, vol. II, Bombay, 1966.

Gode, P.K., *Studies in Indian Cultural History*, vol. 1, Vishveshvaranand Vedic Research Institute, Hoshiarpur, 1961.

———, *Studies in Indian Cultural History*, vol. 2, P.K. Gode Collected Works Publications Committee, Poona, 1960.

Goldsworthy, A., *In the Name of Rome,* Phoenix, London, 2004.

Gordon, D.H., *The Pre-historic Background of Indian Culture*, Bhulabhai Memorial Institute, Bombay, 1958.

Griffith, J., *The Paintings in the Buddhist Cave Temples of Ajantā*, Secretary of State for India in Council, London, 1896.

Gupta, D.K., *Society and Culture in the Time of Daṇḍin*, Meharchand Lachhmandass, Delhi, 1972.

Gupta, S.P. and K.S. Ramachandran, *Mahabharata—Myth and Reality*, Agam Prakashan, Delhi, 1976.

Habib, Irfan, *The Indus Civilization*, Tulika Books, New Delhi, 2002.

Hallade, M., *The Gandhāra Style and the Evolution of Buddhist Art*, Thames and Hudson, London, 1968.

Hazra, R.C., *Studies in the Upapurāṇas*, 2 vols., Sanskrit College, Calcutta, 1958, 1963.

Hopkins, E.W., *The Social and Military Position of the Ruling Caste in Ancient India*, Bharat Bharti, Varanasi, 1972.

Ingholt, H., *Gandhāra Art in Pakistan*, Lyons Islay, New York, 1957.

Joshi, J. and R.S. Bisht, *India and the Indus Civilization,* National Museum Institute, New Delhi, 1994.

Kak, R.C., *Ancient Monuments of Kashmir*, The Indian Society, London, 1933.

Kanakasabhai, V., *The Tamils Eighteen Hundred Years Ago*, Asian Educational Services, New Delhi, 1979.

Kane, P.V., *History of Dharmaśāstra* (5 vols.), BORI, Poona, 1968-75.

Keegan, John, *A History of Warfare*, Hutchinson, London, 1993.

Kosambi, D.D., *An Introduction to the Study of Indian History*, Popular Book Depot, Bombay, 1956.

Lal, B.B., *The Earliest Civilization of South Asia*, Aryan Book International, New Delhi, 1997.

Law, B.C., *Indological Studies*, vol. IV, G.N. Jha Research Institute, Allahabad, 1962.

Macdonell, A.A. and A.B. Keith, *Vedic Index of Names and Subjects*, Motilal Banarsidass, Varanasi, 1958.

Mackay, E.J.H., *Further Excavations at Mohenjo-daro*, Indological Book Corporation, New Delhi, 1976.

———, *Early Indus Civilization*, New Delhi, 1976.

Maenchen-Helfen, J. Otto, *The World of the Huns*, University of California Press, Los Angeles, 1973.

Maisey, F.C., *Sāñchī and its Rmains*, Indological Book House, Delhi, 1972.

Majumdar, B.K., *Military System in Ancient India*, World Press Ltd., Calcutta, 1955.

Majumdar, R.C. (ed.), *The Vedic Age*, Bharatiya Vidya Bhavan, Bombay, 1965.

———, *The Age of Imperial Unity*, Bharatiya Vidya Bhawan, Bombay, 1960.

———, *The Classical Age*, Bharatiya Vidya Bhawan, Bombay, 1962.

Majumdar, R.C. and A.S. Altekar, *The Vākāṭaka Gupta Age*, Motilal Banarsidass, Delhi, 1960.

Mani, B.R., *The Kuṣāṇa Civilization*, B.R. Publishing Corporation, Delhi, 1987.

Marshall., J., *Taxilā*, University Press Cambridge, London, 1951.

———, *Mohenjo-daro and the Indus Civilization*, Indological Book House, Delhi, 1973.

———, *A Guide to Sāñchī*, Manager of Publication, Delhi, 1936.

McGovern, W.M., *Early Empires of Central Asia*, University of North Carolina Press, Chapel Hill, 1939.

M'crindle, J.W., *The Invasion of India by Alexander the Great*, Today and Tomorrow's Printers and Publishers, New Delhi, 1974.

———, *Ancient India as Described in Classical Literature*, Oriental Book Reprint Corporation, New Delhi, 1979.

Mehta, R.N., *Pre-Buddhist India*, University of Bombay, Bombay, 1939.

Minakshi, C., *Administration and Social Life under the Pallavas*, Madras University, Madras, 1938.

Mookerji, R.K., *Indian Slipping*, Orient Longmans, Calcutta, 1957.

Moti Chandra, *Prācīna Bhāratīya Veśa-bhūṣā*, Bharat Bhandar, Prayag, 2007.

Narain, A.K., *The Indo-Greeks*, Oxford University Press, London, 1957.

Oppert, Gustav, *On the Weapons, Army Organization and Political Maxims of the Ancient Hindus*, New Order Book, Ahmedabad, 1967.

Pandey, G.C., *Dimensions of Ancient Indian Social History*, vol. II, Books and Books, Delhi, 1985.

Pandey, R., *Prācīna Bhārata Kī Saṅgrāmiktā*, Bihar Rashtrabhasha Parishad, Patna, 1957.

Pant, G.N., *Studies in Indian Weapons and Warfare*, Army Educational Stores, New Delhi, 1970.

———, *Indian Archery*, Agam Kala Prakashan, Delhi, 1978.

———, *Indian Arms and Armour* (3 vols.), Army Educational Stores, New Delhi, 1978-83.

Piggot, S., *Pre-historic India*, Cassell and Company Ltd., London, 1950.

Priyavrata, Vedavacaspati, *Prācīna Bhārata Men Pratirakṣā Vyavasthā*, Meenakshi Prakashan, Meerut, 1984.

Rama, K., *Buddhist Art of Nāgārjunikoṇḍa*, Sandeep Prakashan, Delhi, 1995.

Ram Gopal, *India in Vedic Kalpasūtras*, Delhi, 1959.

Rangarajan, L.N., *The Arthaśāstra*, Penguin Book India, New Delhi, 1992.

Rao, Manjushree, *Sāñchī Sculptures*, Akay Book Corporation, Delhi, 1994.

Rapson, E.J., *Cambridge History of India*, vol. 1, S. Chand and Co., Delhi, 1955.

Rawson, P.S., *The Indian Sword*, Herbert Jenkins, Copenhagen, 1968.

Ray, H.C., *Dynastic History of Northern India* (Early Mediaeval Period), Munshiram Manoharlal, New Delhi, 1973.

Raychaudhuri, H.C., *Political History of Ancient India*, University of Calcutta, Calcutta, 1953.

Rhys Davids, T.W., *Buddhist India*, Indological Book House, Delhi, 1970.

Riasanovsky, Nicholas V., *A History of Russia*, Oxford University Press, Oxford, 2000.

Rice, T.T., *The Scythians*, Thames and Hudson, London, 1957.

Robinson, H. Russel, *Oriental Armour*, London, 1967.

Ropen, Stephen Peter, *Societies and Military Power—India and its Armies*, Oxford University Press, New Delhi, 1996.

Rosenfield, J.M., *The Dynastic Art of the Kushāṇs*, University of California Press, Berkeley, 1967.

Sankalia, H.D., *Prehistory of India*, Munshiram Manoharlal, New Delhi, 1977.

Sastri, A.M., *India as seen in the Bṛhatsaṁhitā of Varāhamihira*, Motilal Banarsidass, Delhi, 1969.

Sastri, K.A. Nilakanta (ed.), *Comprehensive History of India*, vol. 2, Orient Longman, Bombay, 1957.

———, *A History of South India*, Oxford University Press, London, 1966.

———, *The Colas*, University of Madras, Madras, 1975.

———, *The Age of Nandas and Mauryas*, Motilal Banarsidass, Varaṇasi, 1952.

Satya Prakash, *Founders of Science in Ancient India*, The Research Institute of Ancient Scientific Studies, New Delhi, 1965.

Sensarma, P., *Kurukshetra War: A Military Study*, Noya Prokash, Calcutta, 1982.

Settar, S. and Günther D. Sontheimer, *Memorial Stones*, Institute of Indian Art History, Karnataka University, Dharvad, 1982.

Sharma, G.R., *Excavations at Kauśāmbī*, Allahabad University, Allahabad, 1960.

———, *Reh Inscription of Menander and the Indo-Greek Invasion of Ganga Valley*, Abinash Prakashan, Allahabad, 1980.

Sharma, R.N., *Culture and Civilization as Revealed in Śrautasūtras*, Nag Publishers, Delhi, 1977.

Sharma, R.S., *New Light on Ancient Indian Society and Economy*, Manaktalas, Bombay, 1966.

Shukla, R.S., *India as known to Haribhadra Sūrī*, Kusumanjali Prakashan, Meerut, 1989.

Singh, Sabhapati, *Prācīna Bhārata Mein Sainya Vyavasthā*, Durga Publications, Delhi, 1990.

Singh, S.D., *Ancient Indian Warfare with Special Reference to Vedic Period*, E.J. Brill, Leiden, 1965.

Sinha, G.N., *Post-Gupta Polity*, Punthi Pustak, Calcutta, 1972.

Sircar, D.C., *Select Inscriptions*, Vol. I, University of Calcutta, Calcutta, 1965.

———, *Indian Epigraphy*, Motilal Banarsidass, Delhi, 1965.

Smith V.A., *The Early History of India*, Oxford University Press, London, 1957.

Sridharan, K., *A Maritime History of India*, Publication Division, New Delhi, 1982.

Srinivasan, D.M. (ed.), *Mathurā—The Cultural Heritage*, Manohar, New Delhi, 1989.

Srivastava, A.L., *Life in Sāñchī Sculptures*, Abhinava Publications, New Delhi, 1983.

Subrahmanian, N., *Saṅgam Polity*, Asia Publishing House, New Delhi, 1966.

Sulimirski, T., *The Sarmatians*, Thames and Hudson, London, 1970.

Sykes, P., *History of Persia*, Macmillan and Co., London, 1921.

Tadgell, C., *History of Architecture in India*, Viking, New Delhi, 1990.

Thapar, Romila, *Early India*, Penguin Books, New Delhi, 2002.

———, *Interpreting Early India*, Oxford University Press, New Delhi, 1992.

Thapliyal, K.K., *Inscriptions of the Maukharis, Later Guptas, Puṣpabhūtis and Yaśovarman of Kannauj*, New Delhi, 1984.

Thapliyal, U.P., *Foreign Elements in Ancient Indian Society*, Munshiram Manoharlal, New Delhi, 1979.

———, *The Dhvaja*, B.R. Publishing Corporation, Delhi, 1983.

———, *Military Costumes of India*, Ministry of Defence, Delhi, 1991.

———, *Pracina Bharatiya Yuddha-paddhati*, Meharchand Lachhamandass Publications, New Delhi, 1992.

———, *Prācīna Bhāratīya Vyūha-Vijñāna*, Montu Publishing House, New Delhi, 1997.

Trautmann, Thomas R., *Kauṭilya and the Arthaśāstra*, E.J. Brill, Leiden, 1971.

Tripathi, R.S., *History of Ancient India*, Motilal Banarsidass, Delhi, 1981.

Tripathi, Vibha, *Archaeometallurgy in India*, Sharda Publishing House, Delhi, 1998.

Vaidya, C.V., *Epic India*, vol. I, Cosmo Publications, Delhi, 1984.

Vyas, S.N., *India in the Rāmāyaṇa Age*, Atma Ram and Sons, Delhi, 1967.

Watson, G.R., *The Roman Soldier*, London, 1969.

Wheeler, R.E.M., *Early India and Pakistan*, Thames and Hudson, London, 1959.

Woodcock, G., *The Greeks in India*, Faber and Faber, London, 1966.

Yazdani, G., *Ajantā*, Oxford University Press, London, 1930.

Zimmer. H., *The Art of Indian Asia*, Pantheon Books, New York, 1955.

Index

Printed and bound by CPI Group (UK) Ltd, Croydon, CR0 4YY

19/07/2026

14923662-0001